The Union Cavalry and the
Chickamauga Campaign

ALSO BY DENNIS W. BELCHER
AND FROM McFARLAND

The Cavalries at Stones River: An Analytical History (2017)

The Cavalry of the Army of the Cumberland (2016)

*General David S. Stanley, USA:
A Civil War Biography* (2014)

*"This Terrible Struggle for Life":
The Civil War Letters of a Union Regimental Surgeon
by Thomas S. Hawley, M.D., edited by Dennis W. Belcher* (2012)

*The 11th Missouri Volunteer Infantry in the Civil War:
A History and Roster* (2011)

*The 10th Kentucky Volunteer Infantry in the Civil War:
A History and Roster* (2009)

The Union Cavalry and the Chickamauga Campaign

Dennis W. Belcher

Foreword by Eric J. Wittenberg

McFarland & Company, Inc., Publishers
Jefferson, North Carolina

ISBN (print) 978-1-4766-7082-9
ISBN (ebook) 978-1-4766-3357-2

Library of Congress cataloguing data are available

British Library cataloguing data are available

© 2018 Dennis W. Belcher. All rights reserved

No part of this book may be reproduced or transmitted in any form or by any means, electronic or mechanical, including photocopying or recording, or by any information storage and retrieval system, without permission in writing from the publisher.

Front cover image of *The Charge*, oil painting, artist W. T. Trego, 1887 (accession # H.531.1, scan # 10032890 History Colorado)

Printed in the United States of America

McFarland & Company, Inc., Publishers
Box 611, Jefferson, North Carolina 28640
www.mcfarlandpub.com

To the National Parks Service,
and especially to all the rangers, historians, volunteers
and other employees who work every day to protect
our national heritage.
In particular, I want to thank those employees who work
at the Civil War parks who help keep history alive.

Table of Contents

Acknowledgments	1
Foreword by Eric J. Wittenberg	3
Preface	5

Part 1—Prelude

ONE. The Cavalry of the Army of the Cumberland (July 1863)	9
TWO. The Campaign So Far	32
THREE. The Confederate Cavalry—Worthy Adversaries	49

Part 2—The Advance on Chattanooga

FOUR. The Two Armies Prepare for the Campaign (July 5–August 15)	62
FIVE. The Advance to the Tennessee River (August 16–September 1)	86
SIX. Bragg at Bay (September 1–8)	115
SEVEN. Bragg Gains the Initiative (September 9–17)	142

Part 3—Battle of Chickamauga

EIGHT. The Battle Begins—Reed's Bridge (September 18)	179
NINE. September 19–20 and the Battle at Glass Mill	195
TEN. Retreat to Chattanooga (September 21)—Watkins at Cooper's Gap	224
ELEVEN. Wheeler's Tennessee Raid (September 30–October 9)	238
TWELVE. The Aftermath—Conclusion	260
Appendix I: Organization of the Army of the Cumberland—September 19–20	267
Appendix II: Organization of the Army of Tennessee—September 19–20	270
Chapter Notes	273
Bibliography	300
Index	309

No more shall the war cry sever,
Or the winding rivers be red;
They banish our anger forever
When they laurel the graves of our dead!
Under the sod and the dew,
Waiting the judgment day,
Love and tears for the Blue,
Tears and love for the Gray.

—Francis Miles Finch,
"The Blue and the Gray" (1867)

Acknowledgments

I have long wanted to write a detailed history of the Union cavalry during the Chickamauga Campaign and this is a topic that has been long neglected. This work could not have been accomplished without the efforts of many people. First of all, I would offer my gratitude to Darla Brock, archivist at the Tennessee State Library and Archives, for her assistance with the important material in that collection. In addition, Brooke Guthrie, Research Services Coordinator at the David M. Rubenstein Rare Book & Manuscript Library, is a wonder at her position. Both of these archivists have been ever helpful and their efforts are greatly appreciated.

In addition, there are many helpful experts from various institutions who contributed to completion of this project. Debbie May, Special Collections Librarian, Nashville Public Library; Daisy Rearick, Research & Instruction Librarian at Pickler Library, Truman State University; Jessica Vest, Archivist, B. D. Owens Library at Northwest Missouri State Library; Mazie Bowen, Public Service Coordinator, at the Hargett Rare Book and Manuscript Library at the University of Georgia; Brigid Shields, Reference Librarian, at the Minnesota Historical Society; Kendall Newton, Reference Librarian, The Dolph Briscoe Center for American History, University of Texas at Austin; Elizabeth E. Engel, Senior Archivist, Research Center–Columbia at The State Historical Society of Missouri; Allison DeArcangelis, Special Collections Library, Newberry Library, Chicago; Kathy Shoemaker, Research Services, Stuart A. Rose Manuscript, Archives, & Rare Book Library, Emory University; Alinda Borell, Archivist, The Gilder Lehrman Collection; Diana Bachman, Reference Librarian, and Cinda Nofziger, Archivist, at the Bentley Historical Library, University of Michigan; Eric Honneffer, Document Conservator/Manuscript Specialist at Bowling Green State University; Stephanie Prochaska, archivist at the Colorado Springs Pioneers Museum; Peggy Dillard, Special Collections Manager, at the Rosenberg Library in Galveston; Nancy Dupree, Research Archivist, Alabama Department of History and Archives; Tutti Jackson, Research Services Department, Ohio Historical Society; Kaitlyn Pettengill, Archivist at the Pennsylvania Historical Society; Marlea D. Leljedal, U.S. Army Heritage and Education Center; James Pritchard, Manuscript Cataloger of the Filson Historical Society; Amy S. Wong and Simon Elliott, Library Special Collections, UCLA; Kyle Hovis, University of Tennessee Special Collections; Krista L. Gray, Archival Operations and Reference Specialist, Illinois History and Lincoln Collections, University of Illinois at Urbana-Champaign Library; Matt Holdzkom, Reference Services, Indiana Historical Society; Barbara A. McClurkin, Archivist, Western History Collections, University of Oklahoma Libraries; Emma Parker, Louis Round Wilson Special Collections Library at the University of North Carolina; Anne Causey at the Albert and Shirley Small, Special Collections Library at the University of Virginia; and finally, Melody Klaas, Librarian, Missouri River Regional Library, have all been instrumental in the collection of the materials used in this book.

There a few people who deserve special attention. Jonathan Webb Deiss provided invaluable assistance with the material at the National Archives. This is inglorious duty, but the collection of this material resulted in much-needed details about the cavalry battles. Deiss is professional, efficient, and dedicated to his tasks. Likewise, Martin Schipper provided the support in obtaining material from the regimental collections at the National Archives. Martin provided a wealth of information and this material offered a more complete picture of the Union cavalry during the Chickamauga Campaign.

I want to express my gratitude to Michael Bradley, Sean Chick, David A. Powell, Lee White, and Eric J. Wittenberg who read various sections of the manuscript prior to its completion. These readers are all authors and experts in their own right and their inputs, recommendations and expertise are greatly appreciated.

Lastly, I would like to thank George Skoch who produced the maps for this book. George is an expert in map production and I could not have completed this book without his assistance and expertise.

Foreword
by Eric J. Wittenberg

With the notable exception of the campaigns of Nathan Bedford Forrest, cavalry operations in the Western Theatre of the Civil War have received scant attention from historians. Union cavalry operations, in particular, have been almost completely disregarded. There are plenty of reasons for that—the Union western cavalry was saddled with lackluster leaders for much of the war, they had too large of a front to defend, they had little success in 1865, while the Eastern Theatre horse soldiers had far more interesting characters. Thus, there has long been a large disparity between the number of scholarly historical analyses of the operations of the Union cavalry in the Western Theatre versus the Union cavalry in the Eastern Theatre.

Dennis W. Belcher is working hard to address this disparity. In 2017, Belcher published an interesting study of cavalry operations at the 1862 Battle of Stones River (or Murfreesboro, as the Confederates called it). This followed on a well-written and useful history of the Army of the Cumberland's Cavalry Corps that was published in 2016. Belcher has now turned his considerable talents to Union cavalry operations in the Chickamauga Campaign of September 1863.

David A. Powell, the primary historian of the Chickamauga Campaign, published an insightful and useful study of the Confederate cavalry's role in the Chickamauga Campaign in 2010 titled *Failure in the Saddle: Nathan Bedford Forrest, Joe Wheeler and the Confederate Cavalry in the Chickamauga Campaign*. That study addressed the numerous failures of Forrest and Wheeler that permitted the Army of the Cumberland to seize Chattanooga, Tennessee almost unmolested. However, as one might expect, that study treated the Union cavalry as a sideline story and went into little detail regarding its role.

That's a shame, because there are great stories to tell. Many know the story of Col. Robert H. G. Minty's brigade's stand against nearly 10,000 Confederate infantry and the stand of Col. John T. Wilder's Lightning Brigade—mounted infantry armed with Spencer repeating rifles—at Alexander's Bridge on September 18, 1863. I have, in fact, written a book that provides microtactical detail of those events. But my study is just that: a portion of one day's battle. There remains plenty of remaining drama.

Fortunately, Belcher has addressed that shortfall. His new book, *The Union Cavalry and the Chickamauga Campaign*, provides a comprehensive study of the operations of the Army of the Cumberland's Cavalry Corps in this critical campaign. Hindered by the illness of the regular corps commander, Maj. Gen. David S. Stanley, who was sidelined by typhoid fever, the Army of the Cumberland's Cavalry Corps had a temporary commander with little experience with leading horse soldiers. Despite that obvious handicap, the Army of the Cumberland's Cavalry Corps performed admirably in this campaign, and, in fact, significantly outperformed its grayclad rivals from beginning to end. Just as had happened in the Eastern Theatre, 1863 proved to be the turning point for the fortunes of Rosecrans' horsemen.

Ride with Dennis Belcher as he introduces the leaders who played such an important role, and then enjoy his descriptions of the actions that occurred during the critical Chickamauga Campaign. Belcher does a fine job of telling these previously untold stories and finally does justice to their accomplishments. This book goes a long way toward righting some of that disparity that has plagued Western Theatre studies for so long and deserves a place on the shelf of any serious student of the campaigns of the Army of the Cumberland.

Civil War historian and Pennsylvania native Eric J. Wittenberg is an expert on Civil War cavalry operations. The author of more than 15 books—including The Devil to Pay: John Buford at Gettysburg, Out Flew the Sabres *and* Glory Enough for All—*he was educated at Dickinson College and the University of Pittsburgh School of Law and is a practicing attorney.*

Preface

This book is the fourth in a series focusing on the cavalry in Tennessee and Georgia with much of the emphasis on the cavalry of the Army of the Cumberland. This cavalry command provided important service and participated in some of the major campaigns in the western theater of the Civil War. On September 18, 1863, twenty-two cavalry regiments supported by two artillery batteries joined the Union infantry in the Battle of Chickamauga, the second bloodiest battle in the Civil War. These cavalry regiments originated in eight different states and included the regular army, 4th U.S. Cavalry. The campaign, the battle and the subsequent events make this one of the most difficult and misunderstood campaigns during the war. The impact of terrain, weather, and fatigue for the five-week campaign greatly impacted the events leading to the battle. Of paramount importance were the commanding generals of the armies and how they conducted their commands. The characteristics and personalities of top cavalry commanders were no less important in the outcome of this campaign. The Battle of Chickamauga was an intense battle primarily between the infantries of both armies supported by artillery, but cavalry on both sides played important roles in the campaign. The primary advantage of Civil War horsemen was mobility and a more unsuitable geography would be hard to imagine. The steep mountains, easily defensible, and the narrow valleys near Chattanooga greatly reduced this advantage for cavalry on both sides of the line. With some key exceptions, the actions of the Union cavalry during the battle are often discounted. The cavalry action at Reed's Bridge on September 18 was seen by many as the only major contribution in the battle and campaign by the Union cavalry. A more complete analysis of the contributions, both positive and negative, by Union cavalry has been long overdue.

The Battle of Chickamauga was only one part in a year-long chain of events which pitted the Union army against Bragg's Confederate army. The Chickamauga Campaign officially began on August 16, 1863, and concluded on September 20, 1863, the last day of the battle. This work expanded those dates to cover the actions of the Union cavalry immediately following the Tullahoma Campaign and concluded with the end of Wheeler's Tennessee Raid on October 9, 1863. The events from July 4 to August 16 served as a preparation for the actual advance on Bragg's army at Chattanooga; and Wheeler's raid attempted to further force General William Rosecrans to retreat from Chattanooga by destroying his supply and communications lines and is worthy to be included as a part of the Chickamauga Campaign.

The Chickamauga Campaign is a difficult campaign to understand because it occurred over such a long period of time with the initiative shifting between the Union and Confederate armies even before the battle started. Preconceived impressions by the top generals in the opposing armies complicated the campaign. Fortunately, a five-part masterful work on the

Chickamauga Campaign has been recently completed. Author David A. Powell has written this very complete and well-written history—*The Chickamauga Campaign (3 parts), Failure in the Saddle* and the *Maps of Chickamauga*. Powell's work followed Peter Cozzens' *This Terrible Sound*, another exemplary work on this battle. In regard to the Union cavalry, Powell's book, *A Failure in the Saddle*, examined the role of the Confederate cavalry and provided a detailed analysis of Joseph Wheeler's and Nathan Bedford Forrest's actions during the battle. This classic work proved to be an invaluable source when examining the actions of the Union cavalry. Most recently, Eric Wittenberg authored the insightful *The First Day at Chickamauga: September 18, 1863*, which details the actions of the Union mounted forces in what is recognized as the most direct and important contribution of the cavalry during the battle. Because of Wittenberg's excellent history of Minty's action at Reed's Bridge, this work will include only one chapter on that action and concentrates on the bulk of the cavalry on the southern flank of the Army of the Cumberland. Finally, I want to acknowledge Major John Londa's "The Role of Union Cavalry during the Chickamauga Campaign" as a well-researched and excellent analysis of the history of the Union cavalry during the campaign.

The various other events which round out the history of the Union cavalry during the campaign include:

- Robert Minty's relationship with Thomas L. Crittenden
- The importance of the September 8 Rome expedition
- The deteriorating relationship between David Stanley and William Rosecrans
- The cavalry actions at Alpine on September 9 and La Fayette on September 13
- The result of Stanley's illness and Robert B. Mitchell's subsequent command
- The Battle at Reed's Bridge
- The Battle at Glass Mill
- Mitchell's decisions at Crawfish Springs
- Watkins' defeat at Cooper's Gap
- Actions of the Union cavalry covering the retreat to Chattanooga
- Federal cavalry pursuit of Wheeler in October 1863

A few additional comments regarding the structure of the cavalry and the campaign are needed. First, the two divisions of the Union cavalry during the Chickamauga Campaign operated as a corps, but would never be designated as a corps—only as the First and Second Division. This work focuses on these two cavalry divisions. There were other mounted forces at Chickamauga, including John Wilder's mounted infantry brigade, Thomas Harrison's 39th Indiana Mounted Infantry (XX Corps), and the 15th Pennsylvania Cavalry (detached to army headquarters). Wilder's brigade would be transferred to the Second Cavalry Division after the Battle of Chickamauga, but until that time it served under the infantry command of XIV Corps. Once this brigade joined the cavalry, its detailed actions were included in this work. This history focuses primarily on the cavalry actions and does not specifically address these three other Federal mounted forces.

This history includes some of the most important Union cavalry personalities in the west—David Stanley, George Crook, Robert Minty, Edward McCook, and Eli Long. The Federal cavalry operated against a superior number of enemy cavalry as Rosecrans' Army of the Cumberland maneuvered against Braxton Bragg's Army of Tennessee which included legendary Confederate cavalry officers—Nathan Bedford Forrest, John Pegram, Henry Davidson, Frank Armstrong, Joseph Wheeler, John Wharton and Will Martin. These were cavalries at the peak of their organized lives and the stakes could not have been greater—their lives, their country, their families. These cavalries moved through mountains and valleys in some of the most beautiful scenery on earth on a deadly mission. The task was complicated by a severe drought where troopers would complain that the dust was so thick they could not see the horse in front of them, and where disease constantly plagued the troopers. Of particular importance, and often overlooked, is the five-week campaign which led up to the actual battle. While this can be plodding at time, it is important to understand this critical piece of the story of Chickamauga.

One of the most important parts of the history of the Union cavalry at Chickamauga is the story of Robert Minty. The relationship between Robert Minty and Thomas Crittenden began poorly and steadily got worse. Almost immediately after Minty fell under Crittenden's direct command the two officers were at odds with one another. Minty's intelligence would be disregarded by Crittenden, but the valorous actions of Minty and John Wilder prevented a disaster for Crittenden and Rosecrans on September 18. While Minty provided the most valuable cavalry service at the Battle of Chickamauga, he would be arrested within three weeks and subsequently court martialed for his actions during Wheeler's subsequent raid through Tennessee. Some of the more important actions of the Union cavalry are often overlooked—skirmishes at Alpine and La Fayette, and cavalry battles at Glass Mill and Cooper's Gap. During the campaign, Major General David Stanley, chief of the Union cavalry, would suffer from a severe illness which caused him to give up command of the cavalry and unfortunately, he provided no formal report on the campaign and even his memoirs are devoid of any detailed discussion of the Chickamauga Campaign. Command of the cavalry fell to Robert B. Mitchell upon Stanley's removal and Mitchell, an inexperienced cavalry commander, gained command the large number of cavalry in this a complex campaign. In addition, George Crook and Robert Mitchell also provided little details about the actions of the Union cavalry during this campaign. This campaign demonstrated the outcome of political appointments of some of the top Union commanders based on influence and not ability.

Fortunately, there were a great many primary sources available from the Union soldiers in this battle. Nothing can replace the descriptions of the events in the campaigns and battles of those who actually participated. Entries from diaries and letters were interspersed with the events to give a more complete picture of the campaign. In addition, several regimental histories offer insight into the personalities of those participating in the battle, and a fairly complete set of officers' reports are included in the *Official Records*. The National Archives Records Administration has an excellent collection of corps, division, and regimental cavalry records which offered a clearer picture of movements and orders of the various commands. Two important sources of information were found in the court martial records of Robert Minty and William Hoblitzell. These sources provided excellent details of both the Battle of Farmington and the fight at Cooper's Gap which were not included in the *Official Records*.

While the history of the Union cavalry is filled with many victories and praiseworthy actions, the Chickamauga Campaign held few accolades. However, along Chickamauga Creek in September 1863, many positive contributions came from the Federal cavalry. The officers and troopers performed their duty in the highest tradition of the United States military and many paid the ultimate price in the mountains near Chattanooga. The Battle of Chickamauga did not end the war and it was important for the top commanders in the army to assess the performance of the various units, including the cavalry. There were important lessons to be learned from this campaign but many of the top officers of the cavalry and infantry of the Army of Cumberland would be replaced and new faces would command. While some would applaud the wholescale change in the top ranks of the Army of the Cumberland after the battle, these changes resulted in the many lessons learned in the campaign, being ignored. The chief of cavalry and both cavalry division commanders would be replaced within four months of the end of the campaign. The next major campaign for the cavalry of the Army of the Cumberland was the Atlanta Campaign in 1864 and that campaign caused many in the cavalry to desire Rosecrans and Stanley back in command. In the hot Georgia summer in 1864, many in the cavalry would pay a severe price because the top commanders failed to grasp the lessons learned in the Chickamauga Campaign.

PART 1—PRELUDE

One. The Cavalry of the Army of the Cumberland (July 1863)

On July 4, 1863, the Tullahoma Campaign (June 23–July 3, 1863) was over and this campaign quietly marked the "turning point for the Union cavalry in the west" or, at least, for the Union cavalry in Middle Tennessee. The broad shouldered, and increasingly bearded, Major General David Stanley served as chief of cavalry and commanded two divisions of cavalry of the Army of the Cumberland in this campaign. This force was vastly different from the few regiments which fought in the Battle of Stones River six months earlier. The Federal cavalry dramatically improved over the intervening period through the intentional efforts of Stanley and the commanding general of the Army of the Cumberland, Major General William S. Rosecrans. When Stanley assumed command in November 1862, he initially found one division (two brigades) of cavalry and through some quick moves he assembled a third brigade of new and untried regiments just prior to the Battle of Stones River. Fortunately for the Union army, Bragg dispatched John Hunt Morgan's and Nathan Bedford Forrest's Confederate cavalry brigades on raids in December and Stanley only faced Joseph Wheeler's cavalry division during the Battle of Stones River which yielded mixed results on both sides. Since that time, Forrest's, Morgan's and Earl Van Dorn's cavalry joined Joseph Wheeler to comprise the Confederate cavalry in Middle Tennessee. To meet the challenges of the large number of Southern horsemen, the Union generals assembled a respectable cavalry command of two full divisions during the interlude preceding the Tullahoma Campaign.[1]

The Union Cavalry in Tennessee—July 1863

Since the beginning of the Civil War, the Union cavalry lagged behind the development of the Confederate cavalry. As the war began, both armies depended heavily upon the officers of the existing United States Army to train the new volunteers for the upcoming conflict. Two particular obstacles prevented the rapid development of cavalry in the North—the belief that geographic terrain was unsuitable for cavalry and the belief it took one to two years to fully train cavalry troopers. Because the high expense of maintaining cavalry and the hope that war would be over in short period of time, the Union high command did not initially focus on increasing the size of the cavalry. Early in the war, Washington restricted the number of cavalry regiments, but once the fighting started, the importance of cavalry became more apparent to Union generals. In light of the large Confederate cavalry, the North hastened to enlist and train more cavalry regiments.[2]

Union cavalry regiments generally consisted of twelve companies, each containing about one hundred men and officers, and at full strength totaled about one thousand two hundred men. In contrast, Southern cavalry regiments consisted of ten companies of about seventy-five to eighty officers and men. For better command and control, regiments were broken into four-company battalions under the command of majors. Union cavalrymen generally received their training from three manuals: *Poinsett Tactics, Regulations and Instructions for the Field Service of the United States Cavalry in Time of War*, and *Cavalry Tactics*. For the cavalry of the Army of the Cumberland, David Stanley directed that *Cavalry Tactics*, written by Philip St. George Cooke, Stanley's old commanding officer, be used. While the Union cavalry would be equipped with carbine, pistol, and saber, the revolver and saber were the weapons considered to be highly effective in close combat and during charges. By attaching sabers to the saddles of horses, they were less noisy and less cumbersome to use while being easily accessible. The newer 1860 Light Cavalry Saber replaced the 1840 "Old Wristbreaker" saber as the war began. The most common revolvers for Northern cavalrymen were Remington, Colt, and Starr revolvers. In regard to carbines, the Union cavalry used a variety of breech loading carbines and while the multi-shot Colt revolving and Spencer carbines demonstrated technological superiority, many troopers used Sharps, Smith, Merrill, Maynard, Burnside, and Enfield carbines. In addition, the method of providing horses for the cavalry varied greatly between the Northern and Southern states. Both approaches had their relative strengths and weaknesses; but by the end of the war, finding mounts for cavalry proved very difficult and resulted in many dismounted cavalry regiments. In the North, the government provided mounts for the cavalry (a system with serious problems of its own) while in the South, cavalrymen generally contracted with the government to supply their own horses. While this system resulted in better horses for the Confederate cavalry early in the war, if a horse was lost, then a replacement had to be found. This became more difficult as the war continued and as cavalry regiments traveled many miles from home. A cavalryman who could not replace his horse had to transfer to the infantry or artillery. The price of good horses skyrocketed as the war continued and many common soldiers could not afford to buy even a mediocre horse. In the later stages of the war, both armies ran perilously short of mounts.[3]

Typical Union cavalryman with saber, carbine and Colt revolver (Library of Congress).

Due to the demands of the war it was not surprising that horses remained in short supply. The lack training for cavalrymen resulted in the improper care and increased waste of mounts.

Being less familiar with horses, Union cavalrymen often carried too much weight and offered improper feed and water rations to their horses. Horses were often used beyond their endurance and needed to be replaced. David Stanley, upon gaining command, sent an order to the cavalry division directing the proper use of horses and noted that one half of the unserviceable horses were cruelly injured by careless troopers riding at "full speed" without cause or consideration for the animal. In most cases, the mounting and remounting of Northern cavalry would remain a constant problem.[4]

The Northern cavalry struggled to gain parity with their Confederate adversaries in the early part of the war. The Southern cavalry quickly became well respected and formed under the maxim: "[T]he best blood of the South rode in the cavalry." While difficult to make sweeping generalizations, the Southern cavalrymen were better and more experienced horsemen. In fact, trooper W. R. Friend, 8th Texas Cavalry, remarked at the Battle of Stones River that Federal troopers were the "poorest horsemen I ever saw." Horses were part of life in the South and those in the cavalry service were more accustomed to the saddle. Historians have argued that Southern horsemanship was part of the "gentlemanly tradition" more so than their Union counterparts because some Northerners were from urban locations and had occupations as laborers and shopkeepers. Some have observed that the Union troopers were just not accustomed to the saddle, and that the Southern cavalry also brought the finest bred horses in the south. Despite the fact over fifty percent of the Northern cavalrymen came from the farm and even though many had experience with horses, these men commonly had more experience with horses which pulled wagons and served as work animals rather than horsemanship. However, by 1863, the Union cavalrymen were accomplished horsemen and were at home in the saddle. The skill of the Union cavalry in the Chickamauga Campaign compared well to the Southern cavalrymen. For example, the troopers of the 1st Ohio Cavalry boasted they could snatch a cap or saber off the ground without dismounting.[5]

The tactics for Southern cavalry in central Tennessee in 1863 reflected the philosophy of their commander, Major General Joseph Wheeler, who had just authored *A Revised System of Cavalry Tactics, for the Use of the Cavalry and Mounted Infantry, C.S.A.* Until this time, the Confederate cavalry did not have a manual specifically for the Southern horseman. This manual was commonly used to train cavalry based on Wheeler's previous experience in the U.S. Army and after the first two years of the Civil War, he saw great value in cavalry operating dismounted.[6]

Union cavalry lieutenant, mounted with sabre (Library of Congress).

Cavalry Tactics

Tactics varied between the opposing cavalries; and, though the Union and Confederate cavalry had different approaches to their roles, the duties of cavalry in the Civil War fell into six main areas: reconnaissance, screening, covering (flank security), attack, headquarters duties, and interdiction (raids). The cavalry of both armies performed these duties at various times, but being the eyes and ears of the army described the primary role of the cavalry in the Civil War.[7]

At the beginning of June 1863, both the Union and Confederate cavalries were at the height of their game. Much had been learned and as the war began its third year, veteran troopers who knew their duties well manned most of the regiments. One of Stanley's best achievements as chief of cavalry was the reorganization of cavalry regiments into cavalry brigades which reported directly to division cavalry commanders and ultimately to him. Prior to his arrival, the Federal cavalry had been dispersed throughout the infantry corps and individual regiments reported to the infantry corps, division or brigade commanders. This latter model had been accepted throughout the west. Ulysses Grant organized his cavalry regiments in the same manner early in the war, as did William Rosecrans when he commanded the Army of the Mississippi. Stanley knew his cavalry had to be massed at brigade strength to be able to fight his Southern counterparts. Some infantry commanders did not like Stanley's plan, but Stanley insisted and Rosecrans agreed with him. This was a major achievement for Stanley and it was the right decision. This command victory demonstrated the relationship Stanley had with Rosecrans and also the respect the infantry commanders held for Stanley's leadership.[8]

The Union cavalry lagged in organization because at the beginning of the war most of professionally trained, top cavalry officers went to the Confederacy. Historian Lawyn Edwards observed: "To add to the militia organization, the new Confederate cavalry claimed most of the senior leadership and talent of the old U.S. Cavalry. As their home states seceded from the Union, Southerners in the army resigned their commissions and went home to help the war effort of the states and the Confederacy. Of the five pre-war mounted units, four of the full colonels commanding the regiments went South. Not only was this devastating to the U.S. units, but these officers were educated in and understood cavalry operations as it was." As a result, more Federal cavalry officers, particularly in the west, needed to learn their task. Stanley was an exception, being a trained cavalry officer, and he had two premier brigade commanders which would set the standard for cavalry officers in the west—Robert Minty and Eli Long.[9]

In regard to weapons, Stanley and Rosecrans worked to obtain more technologically superior weapons, including, the five-shot Colt revolving carbine. Not all of the Union regiments had this weapon and in light of the success that Wilder's Mounted Infantry Brigade had with the Spencer repeating rifle in the Tullahoma Campaign, Stanley planned to continue to arm the cavalry with multi-shot carbines. In the meantime, most of Union cavalry regiments still used breech-loading carbines. With the improved weapons for both sides, cavalry tactics also changed. The introduction of the Colt revolving rifle, which allowed the five or six shots being fired without reloading, increased the firepower dramatically despite the fact some troopers grumbled that the weapon was too long. As the war progressed, the Spencer repeating rifle would be the most effective cavalry carbine, although it remained in short supply throughout the war and in 1863 none of the cavalry in central Tennessee had this weapon. Often many different types of weapons were used within a single regiment which caused difficulty in providing and organizing the distribution of ammunition. The Federal Cavalry needed better training after Stanley's arrival, but the six-month interlude before the Tullahoma Campaign proved valuable as the Federal cavalrymen honed their skills. After the Battle of Stones River, the cavalry of both armies fought often until the Tullahoma Campaign where the training was put to the test.[10]

The method of engaging the enemy by the Union and Southern cavalry would be vastly different. Many in the Southern cavalry distained the use of the saber on which the Union cavalry would rely heavily throughout the end of the war. The Southern cavalry often relied more on the revolver which could deliver several shots without reloading. Confederate cavalry often used 1851 Navy Colt and 1860 Army Colt revolvers, but the Le Mat revolvers were common in many units. The Union cavalry was often more balanced in the weapons they carried and had revolvers, carbines, sabers and knives. The short-barreled carbines, breech loading or muzzle loading, were easy to handle in the saddle and were generally effective at several hundred yards. Muzzle loading carbines and shotguns were predominant in the Southern cavalry early in the war. The Union cavalry quickly moved to breech loading carbines as the war began, and both cavalries used knives. In addition, the Southern cavalry adapted to the role of dismounted troops more quickly and more often than Union cavalry; although, the Union cavalry fought dismounted more as the war continued. With cavalry fighting dismounted, there was an increased need for "horse holders" which reduced firepower, but the accuracy of dismounted cavalrymen often offset the loss in firepower. Generally, one man of a group of four would hold the horses while the other three troopers fought on foot. The increased dismounted fighting also introduced a modified cavalry force, the mounted infantry regiments, although dragoons were common before the war. The formal introduction of mounted infantry for the Union Army proved to be an effective innovation in the Tennessee in 1863, although some criticized this as providing inadequate cavalry and at the same time providing inadequate infantry. The proponents of this type of unit only had to point at Colonel John Wilder's mounted infantry brigade as a very successful example.[11]

Union cavalryman with Colt revolving rifle, the new technology of multi-shot weapons (Library of Congress).

Major General David S. Stanley, Chief of Cavalry

David Stanley was a professional cavalry officer. Stanley graduated ninth in his class at the United States Military Academy in 1852. He was raised in modest means at Cedar Valley, Ohio, and in his early teens he was sent to live with Dr. Leander Firestone. Stanley was training to be a physician when he was offered an opportunity to attend the United States Military Academy at West Point. He accepted this opportunity and studied with many of the men who were to play important roles in the Civil War. Thomas Casey graduated first of forty-three cadets in the class of 1852, which included such individuals as Henry Slocum, George Hartsuff, Alexander McCook, and George Crook. Stanley had a productive experience at West Point and made many significant contacts and developed relationships which were important to his career in the army. Stanley also met a life-long friend on his way to West Point—Phil Sheridan. When the war began, Stanley turned down a commission in the Confederate Army and led troops during the Wilson's Creek Campaign, Siege of New Madrid and Island Number 10, Siege of Corinth, the Battle of Iuka, and the Battle of Corinth. He was commissioned a brigadier general in command of infantry in September 1861 and accepted command of the cavalry in the Army of the Cumberland in November 1862.[12]

When Stanley arrived at the Army of the Cumberland, William D. Bickham, a correspondent of the Cincinnati *Commercial* Newspaper and member of Rosecrans' staff, described him as a "man of sanguine nervous temperament, of vehement and fiery spirit, with blazing blue eyes and a lithe figure somewhat above medium stature." Stanley faced many challenges after assuming command of the cavalry of the Army of the Cumberland in November 1862. Stanley assessed the poor organization of the cavalry and gained Rosecrans' support to improve his new command. Stanley declared, "I soon had three pretty substantial brigades formed and commanded by good officers. We made several sudden marches upon the enemy's outposts, where they were collecting provisions and running mills and we ran the enemy away."[13]

Brigadier General David S. Stanley, first chief-of-cavalry for the Army of the Cumberland (photograph taken between 1860 and 1870, Library of Congress).

The decision to form a fully operational cavalry division was met with almost universal approval by the cavalrymen under Stanley's command. They felt they had had hard service working for the infantry corps or division commanders and had accomplished very little. Small groups of cavalry had faced large Confederate forces and the Union troopers had no significant offensive role. The situation immediately changed with Stanley's arrival as he and Rosecrans began to develop a plan to build parity with the enemy's horsemen. The Federals needed to be able to mount a force large enough to meet the enemy on equal terms and this could not be accomplished under the old Union organization. In March 1863, Stanley received a promotion to the rank of major general and by July 1863, Stanley's command had swelled to two full divisions.[14]

Stanley brought years of cavalry experience to the Army of the Cumberland. After graduation, he received his cavalry training at Carlisle Barracks in Pennsylvania and then accompanied Lieutenant A. W. Whipple's Topographical Engineers expedition (July 1853 to March 1854) consisting of about 20 men. The expedition began at Fort Smith, Arkansas, and then traveled west by horse and wagon; and the engineers' task was to survey a route from Fort Smith, Arkansas, to San Diego, California. Stanley then spent years in various locations on the western frontier dealing with issues between settlers and Native Americans. While on the frontier Stanley met and served with a myriad of men who would lead troops in the Civil War. Ironically, future Confederate cavalry legend, J. E. B. Stuart, saved Stanley's life in a skirmish with Indians in Kansas.[15]

In contrast to the Southern cavalry, Stanley and other high-ranking Union officers fully supported the use of the sabers as an important tool for cavalry. Stanley wrote, "Our cavalry had been poorly instructed and depended upon their carbines instead of the saber. I insisted on the latter. I sent grindstones and had the sabers sharpened, each squadron being provided with the means for this work." This quote by Stanley generated numerous comments from historians, some positive, most not. Stanley believed the new volunteers needed as much training as possible. Granted, the cavalry tactics were rapidly changing with the effectiveness of firearms becoming more important. This was still a time of transition for cavalry tactics and Stanley never minimized the importance of firearms for his troopers. He felt the cavalry needed to be fully capable of utilizing not only pistols, muskets, rifles and carbines, but sabers too. The cavalry in 1862 still charged and in close quarters combat the saber proved to be an effective weapon of the day. The cavalry under Stanley, and fully supported by his experienced brigade commander, Robert Minty, would use the saber. Discounting some views of Stanley's over reliance on the saber, Rosecrans and Stanley armed as many troopers as possible with breech loading, revolving and repeating rifles, the new technology in weaponry at the time.

Demonstrating the importance of both weapons, on the same day Rosecrans requested revolving rifles from the War Department, he also requested three thousand sabers.[16]

Stanley successfully led infantry divisions until taking command of the cavalry in November 1862. During the advance on Corinth in May 1862, Stanley first served under wing commander, William S. Rosecrans. Rosecrans grew to value Stanley's professional attitude toward the war and despite the fact Rosecrans privately censured Stanley's late arrival at the Battle of Iuka, the two men mutually supported each other. The relationship between the two men revealed a common spiritual nature. Rosecrans was a devout Roman Catholic and his brother was a priest, later a bishop, in the church. Stanley, on the other hand, was raised in the Presbyterian Church and was also noted for his spiritual nature. Rosecrans and a serendipitous encounter with a Catholic priest, Father Jeremiah Trecy, proved instrumental in Stanley's conversion to Catholicism.[17]

Stanley's conversion occurred during the summer of 1862 and this explained much in

William S. Rosecrans, David Stanley's commanding officer, wrote "I am greatly in need of General Stanley" (Library of Congress).

regard to the relationship of David Stanley and his immediate commander, William Rosecrans. David Stanley was baptized into the Roman Catholic Church in Mississippi in 1862 and Rosecrans agreed to serve as his godfather. Rosecrans wrote to his wife about the baptism, "I had also the great joy to be God father to Genl. David S. Stanley who was baptized this morning at seven o'clock this morning previous to the Holy Sacrifice which was offered by the Rev. Father Tracy of Tuscumbia or rather of Huntsville in whose mission the region lies and who has come here to administer the sacraments to those he finds willing...." The war caused Stanley to search the core of his personal convictions. John Ireland, chaplain of the 5th Minnesota Infantry, and after the war, Archbishop of St. Paul, Minnesota, recalled Stanley's public conversion occurred during Mass held in a public square at Iuka with a very large congregation. Before this group, Stanley publicly read his profession of faith and was conditionally baptized. Word of the event swept through the army. Ireland stated, "Not many weeks later I met General Stanley, and he told me that he was most happy in realizing that he had obeyed the calling of his conscience; and that by so doing he was nearer to his God, and ready to meet Him, if death came to him in the performance of his duty on the battle field." Afterward, it was common to see Stanley kneeling on the ground with the common soldiers with his prayer book in his hand. Ireland noted, "Catholics and non-Catholics expressed their respect for him on account of his open profession."[18]

Composition of the Cavalry Divisions

The Cavalry of the Army of the Cumberland—July 5, 1863[19]

Major General David S. Stanley

FIRST CAVALRY DIVISION—*Brigadier General Robert B. Mitchell*

First Brigade

Colonel Archibald P. Campbell
4th Kentucky, Col. Wickliffe Cooper
6th Kentucky, Col. Louis D. Watkins
7th Kentucky, Col. John K. Faulkner
2nd Michigan, Maj. John C. Godley
9th Pennsylvania, Col. Thomas J. Jordan
1st Tennessee, Lt. Col. James P. Brownlow

Second Brigade

Colonel Edward McCook
2nd Indiana, Lt. Col. Robert R. Stewart
4th Indiana, Lt. Col. John A. Platter
5th Kentucky, Lt. Col. William T. Hoblitzell
2nd Tennessee, Col. Daniel M. Ray
1st Wisconsin, Col. Oscar H. La Grange

SECOND CAVALRY DIVISION—*Brigadier General John B. Turchin*

First Brigade

Colonel Robert H. G. Minty
3rd Indiana [West Batt], Lt. Col. Robert Klein
5th Iowa, Lt. Col. Matthewson T. Patrick
4th Michigan, Maj. Frank W. Mix
7th Pennsylvania, Lt. Col. William B. Sipes
5th Tennessee, Col. William B. Stokes
4th United States, Capt. James B. McIntyre
1st Ohio Artillery, Battery D (one section), Lieut. Nathaniel M. Newell

Second Brigade

Colonel Eli Long
2nd Kentucky, Col. Thomas P. Nicholas
1st Ohio, Col. Beroth B. Eggleston
3rd Ohio, Lt. Col. Charles B. Seidel
4th Ohio, Lt. Col. Oliver P. Robie
10th Ohio, Col. Charles C. Smith

Stokes' (Illinois—Chicago Board of Trade) battery, Capt. James H. Stokes

Unattached

39th Indiana Infantry (mounted), Col. Thomas J. Harrison

First Division

On June 15, the First Cavalry Division consisted of eleven veteran regiments, all fully capable in any combat situation. While Stanley seemed satisfied with his regimental and brigade commanders, the selection of division cavalry commanders deeply concerned him and reflected a deeper seeded problem in the Federal cavalry of the Army of the Cumberland. The collegial relationship between the regular army officer, Stanley, and his godfather and commander of the army seemed to be deteriorating as the summer progressed. The appointment of the two cavalry division commanders over Stanley's objections provided evidence of this fact.

In July 1863, Brigadier General Robert Mitchell commanded the First Cavalry Division, and even though there were two cavalry divisions and soon would be three, the cavalry of the Army of the Cumberland would never be formally recognized as a cavalry corps despite the fact it operated as such. Brigadier General Robert B. Mitchell, a man Stanley had known since the beginning of the war, had served with Stanley during the Wilson's Creek campaign. Mitchell, a native Ohioan, resided in Linn County Kansas at the beginning of the war. Mitchell, wounded while leading the 2nd Kansas Infantry at the Battle of Wilson's Creek, commanded the 9th Infantry Division at the Battle of Perryville and he had most recently commanded the garrison at Nashville. Stanley rightly appraised Mitchell as a political appointee; but Mitchell could ride, despite the lingering effects of his wound, and he would fight. Of the two Union division commanders, Mitchell was superior and he performed his duty during the Tullahoma Campaign in good style.[20]

General Robert Mitchell commanded the First Cavalry Division—"He is a dashing Cavalry officer if his health & wounds will allow" (Library of Congress).

Mitchell's efforts were appreciated by his men, including, men of his old command. Captain James Love, 8th Kansas Infantry serving under Mitchell, wrote, "Genl Mitchell has been removed and Genl. Wood is in command. Genl. Mitchell is home on sick leave and is assigned to the command of a Cavalry Brigade—he is a dashing Cavalry officer if his health & wounds will allow. Our Cavalry at present is doing good service all over Dixie."[21]

First Brigade

While Stanley was not pleased with his division commanders, he had good brigade commanders and these commanders handled the daily chores of the cavalry. Archibald Campbell commanded the First Cavalry Brigade in Mitchell's division. Campbell began the war serving as a captain in the 2nd Michigan Cavalry and demonstrated an exceptional ability to lead cavalry. Campbell, a 34-year-old native Scotsman, was promoted to the rank of lieutenant colonel after his actions at Booneville, Mississippi, in July 1862 and he was promoted to the rank of colonel during the Perryville Campaign. Captain Marshall Thatcher, 2nd Michigan, judged that Campbell "was from private life and advanced rapidly—too rapidly, perhaps, for his own good—had much to learn." The 2nd Michigan had distinguished service under the command of Campbell, and prior to his appointment, Phil Sheridan and Gordon Granger. And soon, Campbell gained the respect of those who served under his command.[22]

Campbell commanded six solid cavalry regiments. The 4th and 6th Kentucky Cavalry had been organized and active for several months, but the 7th Kentucky Cavalry had the dubious distinction of being involved in a major engagement—Big Hill, near Richmond, Kentucky. During the Battle of Richmond, 4,000 Union soldiers were captured and the 7th Kentucky Cavalry regiment was "shattered" resulting in 5 killed, 25 wounded, and 238 men captured. After this event, Colonel Leonidas Metcalfe resigned, although he was cited for bravery during the battle and John Faulkner assumed command of the regiment. The 7th Kentucky Cavalry was mustered into service on August 16, 1862, in Paris, Kentucky, initially was under command of Leonidas Metcalfe. Colonel John K. Faulkner commanded the regiment when it arrived for service in March 1863. Faulkner was a native of Garrard County, Kentucky, and attended Centre College in Danville. Faulkner was a farmer before the war. The 27-year-old Faulkner began rebuilding the regiment after the resignation of Metcalfe and made great strides in instilling confidence in his troops. He was described as a "gallant officer" who reestablished the fighting spirit in the 7th Kentucky Cavalry.[23]

The 4th Kentucky Cavalry was mustered into service in December 1861 with most of the troopers drawn from Louisville and the surrounding counties. Brigadier General Green Clay Smith assumed command of the regiment in May 1862 and continued in that capacity as the regiment moved to Tennessee in February 1863. Smith, 30 years old, was born in Richmond, Kentucky, and served in the 1st Kentucky Infantry in the Mexican War. Smith graduated from Transylvania University in 1850 and practiced law in Richmond and Covington prior to the war. Smith was still active in Kentucky politics while serving in the cavalry. He was a member of the state legislature and later in the year, he would be elected to a seat in Congress. When Smith served as brigade commander, the command of the regiment initially fell to Colonel Jesse Bayles, who later resigned, and subsequently Colonel Robert Wickliffe Cooper assumed command of the regiment. Cooper, 31 years old and a native of Lexington, Kentucky, was a lieutenant in the 20th Kentucky Infantry before being promoted lieutenant colonel and then colonel of the 4th Kentucky Cavalry. Cooper had been taken prisoner and paroled after the Battle of Richmond, Kentucky in August 1862.[24]

Colonel Archibald Campbell, the 34-year-old native Scotsman, commanded Mitchell's First Brigade (courtesy Archives of Michigan).

The 6th Kentucky Cavalry was organized in the summer of 1862 and was mustered into service in October 1862. Colonel Louis Watkins commanded the regiment on February 1, 1863, when the regiment arrived for duty in Tennessee. The highly regarded, 29-year-old, Watkins was a native of Florida and had joined the National Rifles, a District of Columbia volunteer regiment, until he found the men disloyal to the Union. At that point he resigned, and joined the 2nd U.S. Cavalry. He later transferred to the 5th U.S. Cavalry and participated in the Peninsular Campaign where he was severely wounded in the Battle of Gaines Mill. Next, he was ordered to report to General Gordon Granger commanding the army in Kentucky and participated in Carter's Expedition to eastern Tennessee. He was given command of the 6th Kentucky Cavalry based on his experience and performance in the war.[25]

The 2nd Michigan Cavalry was the most prominent regiment to arrive in 1863. The 2nd Michigan Cavalry was a veteran regiment, organized and mustered into service in Detroit in October 1861. This regiment produced very notable commanders—Colonel Archibald Campbell, General Gordon Granger (first colonel of the regiment) and General Phil Sheridan. Its service included action at New Madrid and Island Number 10, Siege of Corinth, the pursuit of Bragg's army in Kentucky and the Battle of Perryville.[26]

Colonel Thomas Jordan commanded the 9th Pennsylvania Cavalry. The 41-year-old Jordan, a graduate of Dickinson College, was an attorney in Harrisburg, Pennsylvania before the war. When the 9th Pennsylvania Cavalry was organized, Jordan was commissioned major and subsequently gained command of the regiment. The 9th Pennsylvania Cavalry, also known as *Lochiel Cavalry* in honor of a Scottish clan, was organized in the fall of 1861 and the officers of the regiment were: Colonel Edward C. Williams, Lieutenant Colonel Thomas C. James and Major Thomas Jefferson Jordan. The regiment served in Kentucky beginning in May 1862, sparring with Confederate cavalry and guerrillas, and it participated in actions around Perryville in October 1862, and in the east Tennessee raid in December and early January 1863. By January 1863, Thomas J. Jordan commanded the regiment after the resignation of Colonel Williams, and Lieutenant Colonel James' unexpected death on January 1, 1863. Jordan had served as an aide to Major General William Keim before joining the 9th Pennsylvania Cavalry. Jordan had been captured along with three companies of cavalry near Tompkinsville, Kentucky, in July 1862 and had been exchanged in December 1862. Since that time, he proved an exceptional cavalry commander.[27]

The final regiment in the First Brigade was the 1st Tennessee Cavalry under the command of the energetic Colonel James P. Brownlow. The 1st Tennessee Cavalry was organized from the 4th Tennessee Infantry which was mustered into service in March 1862. The regiment consisted of men from East Tennessee, primarily from Bradley, Knox, Union, Grainger, Jefferson, Greene, Hawkins and Hancock counties. The 4th Tennessee Infantry was involved in actions in eastern Tennessee and Kentucky and was part of Stevenson's retreat from Cumberland Gap. In November 1862, the regiment (1,260 troopers) was mounted and was designated the 1st Tennessee Cavalry. It was initially commanded by Colonel Robert Johnson, son of Andrew Johnson, military governor of Tennessee. The cavalry regiment's first duty was to pursue John H. Morgan during his Christmas Raid into Kentucky in December 1862 taking up position along the Salt River at Shepherdsville, Kentucky. After Morgan's return to Tennessee, the 1st Tennessee moved to Nashville in mid–January and began its service with the Army of the Cumberland.[28]

At the end of May, Lieutenant Colonel James P. Brownlow was promoted to the rank of colonel of the 1st Tennessee Cavalry when Robert Johnson resigned due to ill health. Johnson excessively used alcohol and he would finally be thrown out of the army for alcoholism. He died of a laudanum overdose in 1869. In fact, Rosecrans unsuccessfully tried to intervene to stop Johnson's drinking which "had become a subject of remark everywhere." Brownlow had been effectively commanding the regiment even before this promotion due to Johnson's incapacity. "Col Brownlow takes charge of the regt. today he is by far the best officer and the most competant to command us," noted Julius Thomas of the 1st Tennessee Cavalry in June 1863. The 6'6" tall, Brownlow was 21 years old when he assumed command of the regiment. He was the son of "Parson" William G. Brownlow, a preacher, newspaperman, and future governor and U.S. senator from Tennessee. He also had a brother in the Union Army, Colonel John Bell Brownlow of the 9th Tennessee Cavalry.[29]

Second Brigade

The ever-diligent Colonel Edward McCook, one of the "Fighting McCooks," commanded the Second Cavalry Brigade. The 30-year-old McCook commanded the First Cavalry Brigade under General Don Carlos Buell's command and he continued in that capacity under Rosecrans. Before the war, McCook was a lawyer and served in the Kansas Territory legislature. McCook enlisted without military experience and had risen in rank through his performance in the field. In September 1862, his brigade successfully captured the 3rd Georgia Cavalry near New Haven, Kentucky; and in October, McCook led the brigade in the Battle of Perryville. McCook was ill during the Battle of Stones River, but returned to command the brigade in January 1863. He sparred with the Confederates through the six-month interlude and led his cavalry in the Tullahoma Campaign. McCook was an effective and competent officer. He wasn't apt to make overly aggressive moves, but he was always on duty where he was needed, he followed orders, he protected his men and he would fight. The Second Cavalry Brigade operated in good hands of Edward McCook.[30]

Colonel Edward McCook, Second Brigade commander, commanded Mitchell's division during the Chattanooga Campaign (Library of Congress).

McCook commanded five veteran regiments. In September 1861, the 2nd Indiana Cavalry became the first complete cavalry regiment organized in Indiana, and John A. Bridgeland served as the first colonel of the regiment. Troopers enlisting in the 2nd Indiana were promised: "Good quarters, a handsome uniform and first-rate horse." At full strength, the regiment contained 1,200 men. In addition, those of the regiment received $14-$24 pay per month. In November 1862, the 2nd Indiana, a battle-hardened regiment, had service extending to the Battle of Pea Ridge and it had experience sparring with Confederate cavalry in Kentucky and Tennessee. On December 7, 1862,

John Hunt Morgan's Confederate cavalrymen captured most of the regiment in a raid at Hartsville, Tennessee. Only one company participated in the Battle of Stones; but since that time, those captured had been exchanged and the regiment returned to fight.[31]

Lieutenant Colonel Robert "Bob" Reed Stewart commanded the 2nd Indiana when it was captured and he spent several months in Libby Prison before he was exchanged. He grew up in the Wabash Valley of western Indiana and had served in the Mexican War. After the war, he traveled to California in search of gold and returned to Indiana in 1858. When the Civil War began, Stewart organized a company of cavalry which became Company I of the 1st Indiana Cavalry, and in November 1861 he became a lieutenant colonel in the 2nd Indiana Cavalry.[32]

The 4th Indiana Cavalry, a regiment of 1,223 of troopers, was organized in August 1862 in Indianapolis and this regiment joined the Army of the Cumberland in January 1863. The regiment had a little experience skirmishing with Confederate cavalry, but was involved in pursuing John Hunt Morgan during his 1862 Christmas Raid. The regiment arrived in Murfreesboro under the command of John A. Platter. One company, Company C, of this regiment served as escort for Major General A. J. Smith, XVI Army Corps, in Mississippi and Tennessee while the rest of the regiment served in the Army of the Cumberland. Platter, 31 years old, was an Indiana native and a plasterer before the war. He started the war as a captain in the 16th Indiana Infantry, a one-year regiment. Platter had been severely wounded in September 1862 with a gunshot wound to the head during a skirmish in Kentucky.[33]

The 5th Kentucky Cavalry joined the Army of the Cumberland in February 1863. The 943-man, 5th Kentucky Cavalry regiment was mustered into service on March 31, 1862, under command of Colonel David R. Haggard, but Lieutenant Colonel William T. Hoblitzell commanded the regiment when it became part of the cavalry of the Army of the Cumberland. Hoblitzell had served on Alexander McCook's staff and also as an aide to William Sherman. He was a native of Maryland, born in 1834, and was an engineer involved in railroad construction before the war. Through the influence of some high-ranking officers, Hoblitzell was given command of the 5th Kentucky; but Hoblitzell's command would be froth with controversy in the upcoming campaign. The impact of political influence seemed to resound in some of the Kentucky regiments and resulted in some violent confrontations due to perceived entitlement and political power of some of the officers.[34]

The 2nd Tennessee Cavalry was organized in eastern Tennessee and began service in September 1862; but the regiment had little combat experience before the Battle of Stones River. The regiment participated in the Union retreat from Cumberland Gap to Greensburg, Kentucky, and then served about a month in the Kanawha Valley before being moved to Nashville in December 1862. Even though the regiment had been shuttled hinder and yon for the two months prior to the Battle of Stones, it participated in that battle with disastrous results. In defense of the 2nd Tennessee, it went into the battle without a full contingent of men and was not fully organized. Since the Battle of Stones River, the 2nd Tennessee had demonstrated its ability to fight. The twenty-nine-year-old Colonel Daniel M. Ray, a North Carolina native, and son of a farmer, commanded the regiment. He resided in Tennessee and taught school for three years prior to the war. Ray served in the 3rd Tennessee Infantry before the 2nd Tennessee Cavalry was organized. Ray's younger brother, William, served as a lieutenant in the 64th North Carolina Infantry (CSA).[35]

The final regiment of McCook's brigade was the 1st Wisconsin Cavalry, a regiment which brought much energy to the Union cavalry. The 1st Wisconsin Cavalry was organized during the fall and winter of 1861 and was mustered into service in March 1862 with an original strength of 1,124 men. The regiment had extensive duty in Missouri and Arkansas skirmishing with various Confederate regiments. Part of the 2nd Battalion was attacked at L'Anguille Ferry, Arkansas, while loaded down with wagons and freed slaves; and various accounts of the engagement exist. Reportedly many of ex-slaves were "shot down in cold blood" reinforcing to this regiment the brutality of this war. In the spring of 1863, Rosecrans requested the 1st Wisconsin Cavalry's transfer to his command and the regiment arrived in Middle Tennessee in mid–June.[36]

In June 1863, the 1st Wisconsin was commanded by Colonel Oscar La Grange, born in Fulton, New York, in April 1837. La Grange's family moved to Ripon, Wisconsin, when he was a child. La Grange, an ardent abolitionist, traveled to Kansas while still in his teens to assist in the anti-slavery efforts in that state. He attended Ripon College and the University of Wisconsin. La Grange continued his strong anti-slavery actions in Wisconsin and helped an abolitionist editor to escape from a Milwaukee jail in 1860. He evaded arrest and in April 1861, La Grange aided in the organization of the "Ripon Rifles," Company D of the 4th Wisconsin Infantry. Four months later he was elected major in the 1st Wisconsin Cavalry, and in June 1862 he was promoted to the rank of lieutenant colonel. In February 1863, he was commissioned colonel of the regiment. The fiery La Grange was described: "He enjoyed nothing more than a headlong cavalry charge, when he was in the front rank." Another said, "He looked like a berserker, and was full of daring. His fixed rule was to let no man get deeper into the battle than himself."[37]

Second Division

Brigadier General John Turchin commanded the Second Cavalry Division on July 5, 1863. While Stanley had concerns about Mitchell's suitably as division commander, he had no misgivings that Turchin had to go. Turchin, a native Russian, was born Ivan Turchaninoff in 1822. Turchin had been involved in the "Rape of Athens" the previous year and had been court martialed for actions taken in the Alabama town. Immediately after the conclusion of the court martial Lincoln promoted him to the rank of brigadier general although the court recommended Turchin be dismissed from the service, and the presiding officer of the court martial was Brigadier General James A. Garfield. So disgusted by the actions being taken by Turchin, his commanding officer, Major General Don Carlos Buell, wrote that he wanted to relieve Turchin of command "in consequence of his utter failure to enforce discipline and render it efficient." Despite these concerns, on April 17 Turchin was given command of a division in the cavalry over Stanley's disapproval.[38]

More recently, Turchin's actions in May 1863 almost resulted in the death or capture of several Union cavalrymen, including Stanley himself. In May, Stanley accompanied the Second Cavalry Division on a twenty-one-day expedition to Middleton, Tennessee. On May 22, Stanley and the 4th U.S. Cavalry led an early morning surprise attack on a large Confederate cavalry position, and Turchin had orders to follow the initial attack with the remainder of the Second Division. As the attack began, Stanley turned in his saddle to watch Turchin's attack only to find him absent. When Stanley found Turchin, his cavalry just walked along a road perpendicular to the line of the attack. Stanley was indignant, but fortunately, brigade commanders, Eli Long and Robert Minty, ordered their commands forward and completed the attack. Once Stanley's rage subsided, he concluded that Turchin simply could not ride. Stanley described his riding style as one who is sitting in a rocking chair and he concluded the fact Turchin did not gallop or charge was because he was afraid he would fall off the horse. More disturbing was Stanley's description of Turchin's leadership style which called to mind the actions in Athens, Alabama the prior year. "A perfectly cold bloodied foreigner—he did not care a fig what became of me or of the few men who followed me. He did not care to be jostled in a rush of cavalry for anybody's sake.... Garfield who was everlastingly looking out for votes, had imposed Turchin on the cavalry without any inquiry as to his fitness...." Once the expedition was over, Stanley promptly marched to Rosecrans' headquarters and announced that Rosecrans would have to choose—Turchin or Stanley. Rosecrans retained Stanley and made plans to transfer Turchin back to the infantry, his original assignment. Turchin was just more suited to infantry command than cavalry. Turchin's command abilities with infantry would prove important to the Army of the Cumberland during the upcoming Chickamauga Campaign.[39]

General John Turchin commanded the Second Cavalry Division until late July (Mollus Mass Civil War Collection, United States Army Heritage and Education Center, Military History Institute, Carlisle, Pennsylvania).

First Brigade

After the expedition in May, Stanley had not forgotten or forgiven Turchin. Even though Stanley unhappily tolerated Turchin until he could be replaced, he could not have been more pleased with the two brigade commanders of the Second Cavalry Division. Colonel Robert H. G. Minty commanded the First Cavalry Brigade and was recognized as the premier Union cavalry brigade commander in the west during the Civil War. Minty had been serving as lieutenant colonel of the 3rd Michigan Cavalry before he gained command of the 4th Michigan Cavalry. Minty, born in County Mayo, Ireland, on December 4, 1831, son of an English soldier serving in Ireland, did not consider himself an Irishman. Following in his father's footsteps, Minty enlisted as an ensign in the British Army and served five years in the West Indies, Honduras, and the west coast of Africa. Minty's service in the Union Army began when he was commissioned major of the 2nd Michigan Cavalry in 1861. Stanley had great respect for Minty and his ability to command, both officers realizing the need to wield the saber when fighting in close quarters with enemy cavalry. Minty's brigade carried the nickname of the "Sabre Brigade" because of his insistence of the use of this weapon.[40]

Minty commanded five cavalry regiments, a cavalry battalion and Newell's two-gun section of 1st Ohio Artillery, Battery D. The 3rd Indiana Cavalry (West Battalion) had a somewhat unique organization in Stanley's cavalry. The 3rd Indiana Cavalry's organization resulted in four companies (G-K), the West Battalion, being assigned to the Army of the Cumberland while the other companies (A-F) served in the Army of the Potomac. The companies assigned to the Army of the Cumberland were organized after the first six companies had been sent to fight in the east. These companies generally performed escort, courier and provost duty until they were formed into an independent cavalry battalion commanded by Major Robert Klein who had served as captain of Company K. The battalion also saw action during the Perryville Campaign while protecting the army's supply train and served during the advance of Buell's army to Nashville. Klein's brigade subsequently fought at the Battle of Stones River, participating in the repulse of John Wharton's Confederate cavalry along the Union supply train, and more action over the next six months. The very capable twenty-six-year-old, German-born and ex–Prussian soldier, Klein was a resident of Switzerland County, Indiana, before the war.[41]

The 5th Iowa Cavalry arrived for duty with the Army of the Cumberland in June 1863 and the regiment saw action during the Tullahoma Campaign. The 5th Iowa Cavalry regiment, originally organized companies A-D as the "Curtis Horse" by the order of Major General John C. Frémont in Omaha, Nebraska; Company E in Dubuque; Company F in Missouri (Frémont's Hussars); Company H was organized at Benton Barracks, Missouri; Companies G, I, K as 1st, 2nd and 3rd Independent Companies, Minnesota Cavalry at Fort Snelling, Minnesota; Company L as Naughton's Irish Dragoons at Jefferson City, Missouri; and finally Company M as Osage Rifles at St. Louis. All the companies were organized from September through the end of December 1861. The various components of regiment consolidated to form the 5th Iowa Cavalry in June 1862. The regiment had several experiences during the war, including participating in the Siege of Corinth, but spent most of its time around Fort Henry, Fort Heiman, and Fort Donelson in late 1862 and into 1863. The troopers of Forrest's cavalry reportedly nicknamed the 5th Iowa Cavalry "Lowe's Hell Hounds."[42]

Colonel William Warren Lowe, born in 1841 in Greencastle, Indiana, commanded the 5th Iowa. Lowe, a West Point graduate, class of 1853, had served in 2nd U.S. Cavalry prior to the war and he spent a great deal of time in Texas after leaving the United States Military Academy. Lowe served in the defense of Washington, D. C. in 1861, and participated in the First Battle of Bull Run. Lieutenant Colonel Mathewson T. Patrick was born in Pennsylvania about 1832 and was a resident of Omaha, Nebraska, prior to the war. Patrick commanded the regiment in June 1863, due to Lowe's temporary absence.[43]

Robert Minty, Stanley's trusted cavalry commander, commanded the First Brigade, nicknamed—the "Sabre Brigade" (*Vale, Joseph. Minty and the Cavalry: A History of Cavalry Campaigns in the Western Armies. Harrisburg, Pennsylvania: Edwin K. Myers, Printer and Binder, 1886*).

The 4th Michigan Cavalry was mustered into service on July 29, 1862, and Colonel Robert Minty commanded the regiment. The 4th Michigan traveled to Louisville, Kentucky, after its organization and clashed with Forrest's cavalry near Stanford, and later escorted the infantry to Nashville. During the Battle of Stones River, the 4th Michigan experienced some highs and lows. A battalion of the regiment successfully captured an important bridge over Stewarts Creek during the advance on the Murfreesboro through the leadership of Captain Frank Mix, but while under the command of Lieutenant Colonel William Dickinson, the regiment failed to relieve the siege of the 1st Michigan Engineers. Subsequently, Dickinson resigned due to ill health and in July, Major Frank Mix commanded the regiment which saw extensive duty in the past six months.[44]

The 7th Pennsylvania Cavalry was an experienced regiment which was mustered into service during the fall of 1861, and George Wynkoop was appointed as its first colonel. The regiment contained men from various counties in eastern Pennsylvania. Wynkoop, a cavalry officer for more than twenty years, provided the much-needed experience to command the regiment. He had served in a three-month regiment prior to the organization of the 7th Pennsylvania Cavalry. Wynkoop's subordinate officer was Lieutenant Colonel William B. Sipes, a newspaper editor from Philadelphia. Sipes permanently assumed command of the regiment in 1863 when Wynkoop resigned due to disability.[45]

The prior actions of the 7th Pennsylvania included heavy skirmishing with Forrest's and Morgan's Confederate cavalry, including a particularly bloody affair near Gallatin, Tennessee, where the 7th Pennsylvania lost 140 men killed or wounded. In addition, Major John E. Wynkoop, whose brother battalion adjutant Nicholas Wynkoop had been killed in action at Gallatin on August 21, 1862, led the First Battalion during the Battle of Perryville where the regiment recorded seven casualties. Once Rosecrans gained command of the Army of the Cumberland, he told battalion commander Major William H. Jennings that the 7th Pennsylvania was the "best regiment" in the service of the United States.[46]

The 5th Tennessee Cavalry had been mustered into service as the 1st Middle Tennessee Cavalry on July 15, 1862 under the command of Colonel William B. Stokes. The 48-year-old Stokes was a farmer and had served in the house and senate in the Tennessee General Assembly prior to the war. Prior to the organization of the 5th Tennessee Cavalry, Stokes had served for a short time as a major in the Tennessee volunteer infantry. The 5th Tennessee Cavalry had been assigned to the Union garrison at Nashville until Stanley added the regiment to the Reserve Brigade. The regiment generally performed reconnaissance duties but had little combat experience except in skirmishes at Nashville and Kinderhook until the Battle of Stones River. The regiment saw action during that battle and because of its familiarity with the Tennessee countryside it had extensive action in the months since Stones River. Due to the strong personality differences of the commanding officers, Lieutenant Colonel Robert Galbraith frequently commanded part of the regiment away from Stokes' part of the regiment.[47]

The final cavalry regiment in this brigade was the 4th U. S. Cavalry, commanded by Captain James B. McIntyre. McIntyre was a classmate of David Stanley at West Point and, appointed from Texas, he graduated in 1853. After graduation, he was commissioned second lieutenant in the 7th U.S. Infantry on July 1, 1853 and almost two years later he was reassigned to the 1st U. S. Cavalry. He subsequently received a promotion to first lieutenant in 1857 and another promotion to captain in 1861. McIntyre, a thoroughly professional cavalryman, served in the army before the war and saw action during the Antietam Campaign before moving to the western theater. The 4th U. S., a professional, experienced regiment of cavalry, had extensive service in Missouri, Fort Donelson, New Madrid, Shiloh, Perryville, Stones River, Middle Tennessee and the Tullahoma Campaign. The regiment participated in a particularly intense fight with the troops of General Earl Van Dorn near Franklin, Tennessee on April 10, 1863. The aggressive 4th U. S. Cavalry captured Captain Samuel Freeman's Tennessee Battery, but the Confederate counterattack prevented the Union cavalry from escaping with the guns. The 4th U. S. Cavalry cut the spokes on the wheels and tried to spike the guns and they hastily headed back to their lines, fighting off three attacks along the way. Freeman was killed during the affair and the Confederates claimed he was murdered; but the Federal cavalry claimed he was killed in self-defense. Freeman was a favorite of Nathan Bedford Forrest and rumors abounded of a personal feud between the famed Confederate cavalryman and the men of the 4th U. S. Cavalry.[48]

Lieutenant Nathaniel M. Newell commanded the last unit in Minty's brigade, the 1st Ohio Artillery, Battery D (two guns). The main battery was captured in Munfordville, Kentucky, on September 17, 1862; but Newell's section escaped that dubious honor because it was attached to Brigadier General James S. Jackson's Tenth Division. Newell's section saw action at the Battle of Shiloh, siege of Corinth, the Union campaign in northern Alabama and Tennessee, and the Battle of Perryville. Newell's section performed commendable duty during the Stones River Campaign and throughout 1863. The battery was mustered into three-year's service in October 1861 under the command of Colonel James Barnett, who served as Rosecrans' Chief of Artillery. Newell's section contained two 3-inch rifled cannon which were noted for exceptional accuracy. The artillerymen proudly claimed the cannon could hit the end of a flour barrel at any distance less than a mile.[49]

Second Brigade

While Minty would become the premier Union cavalry brigade commander, Colonel Eli Long, also a professional cavalryman, would be a close second. Long, a Kentucky native, graduated from the Kentucky Military Institute in 1855 and served along with David Stanley in the 1st U.S. Cavalry before the war. Most recently Long held the rank of captain in the 4th U.S. Cavalry and participated in the Battle of Stones River. Long was wounded in that battle as his regiment began a series of counterattacks on the Confederate cavalry which changed the outcome of the cavalry battle. After he recuperated from his wound, Long was appointed colonel of the 4th Ohio Volunteer Cavalry and upon assuming command of the regiment, he found a demoralized regiment with officers waiting to resign; but Long made an immediate positive impact on the regiment. He stabilized this good cavalry regiment and brought it back to its full fighting potential. In March, Long's leadership resulted in his promotion to brigade command in which he commanded four Ohio regiments and one from Kentucky. The pipe smoking colonel was noted of placing his favorite pipe in his teeth prior to action with the enemy.[50]

The veteran 2nd Kentucky was one of the first new regiments to arrive at David Stanley's headquarters after the Battle of Stones. The 2nd Kentucky Cavalry regiment was organized in the fall and winter 1861 and had various assignments including service at the Battle of Shiloh, the Union campaign in northern Alabama and Middle Tennessee, and the Battle of

Perryville. The 2nd Kentucky was assigned to the Army of the Cumberland in November 1862, but it was attached to the infantry corps and was not part of the cavalry division during the Battle of Stones River even though the regiment had notable action in the fighting along the eastern flank of the army. Since that time, the regiment saw action in the skirmishes in Middle Tennessee. It was assigned duty to the cavalry division in Tennessee in January 1863 under the command Lieutenant Colonel Thomas P. Nicholas, the son of noted Kentucky judge, Samuel Smith Nicholas.[51]

The 1st Ohio Cavalry with the majority of troopers being drawn from central Ohio was one of the most experienced of Stanley's regiments. The regiment saw action in the siege of Corinth, engagements in northern Mississippi and Alabama, the Battle of Perryville, the Battle of Stones River, and the six-month campaign south of Murfreesboro. The regiment had particularly notable service during the Battle of Stones River when it made a suicidal charge into a mass of Confederate cavalry. The regiment made good initial success against the enemy but the number of Southern cavalry overwhelmed the Ohioans. As result, many were captured, and Colonel Minor Millikin and several other officers were killed or wounded during the fight. As the regiment reorganized after the Battle of Stones River, Beroth Eggleston assumed command of the regiment. The forty-six-year-old Eggleston was a native of Saratoga County, New York, and his family moved to Ohio when he was fifteen. He was a businessman, postmaster and farmer before the war near Chillicothe, Ohio. The veteran Eggleston was promoted to the rank of colonel in 1863.[52]

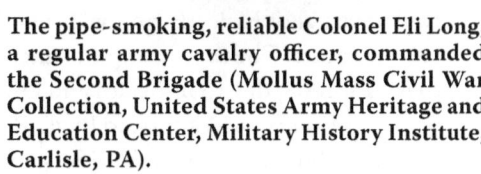

The pipe-smoking, reliable Colonel Eli Long, a regular army cavalry officer, commanded the Second Brigade (Mollus Mass Civil War Collection, United States Army Heritage and Education Center, Military History Institute, Carlisle, PA).

The 3rd Ohio Cavalry recruited troopers from northern Ohio, and was also an experienced regiment. The 3rd Ohio arrived at Shiloh on the second day of the battle, participated in the siege of Corinth, served in northern Alabama, sparred with Confederate cavalry in Tennessee and Kentucky, and participated in the Battle of Perryville. Like the other regiments, the 3rd Ohio Cavalry fought at the Battle of Stones River, the subsequent skirmishes in Middle Tennessee and in the Tullahoma Campaign. When fully mustered, 1,200 men made up the regiment which "wanted to get at it, get it done, and get home again." The first colonel of the regiment was Colonel Lewis Zahm who had been given brigade command in the fall of 1862. Next, Lieutenant Colonel Douglas A. Murray commanded the regiment. Murray, a Scotsman, was experienced and had been promoted from the 2nd U.S. Cavalry. Murray's experience in the regular cavalry made him the ideal choice for command of the regiment. Murray began training the volunteers in the skills needed to fight in the war. After the Battle of Stones River, Colonel James Paramore assumed command of the regiment. Paramore demonstrated excellent leadership of his battalion during the Battle of Stones River, but he clashed with Eli Long in June. As a result of this altercation, Paramore was relieved of command of the regiment. Coincidentally, Lieutenant Colonel Douglas Murray also left the regiment only a few weeks before. The new colonel of the regiment was Charles B. Seidel, a native of Germany. He was born in Berlin in 1835 and later immigrated to the United States where he became a carriage maker before the war. He had military service in Germany and enlisted as a private in 1861 and fought at the first Battle of Bull Run. He next joined the cavalry and quickly advanced in rank due to his leadership abilities. He was described by one of the members of his regiment: "No braver man ever drew his sword."[53]

The next veteran Ohio regiment was the 4th Ohio Cavalry, a regiment recruited from various locations across the state, primarily Cincinnati, but also from Hamilton, Dayton, Lebanon, South Charleston, Ironton, Lima and St. Marys. The 4th Ohio was an experienced regiment, being mustered into service in the fall of 1861. Like other cavalry regiments in the division, it had seen action in various engagements in Kentucky, Tennessee and Alabama. Colonel John Kennett was instrumental in its organization, and when Kennett was promoted to command the cavalry division in 1862, Lieutenant Colonel Henry W. Burdsall assumed command of the regiment. Burdsall resigned the day before Stanley arrived in Nashville in November and Major John Pugh, a 29-year-old Madison, Indiana resident, commanded the regiment through the upcoming months. As the Stones River Campaign began, the 4th Ohio was in command crisis. The week before the battle, officers were subpoenaed to testify in the court martial of Major Pugh for disobedience of orders and cowardice for actions taken the prior summer. The regiment performed its duty well at Stones River. Pugh resigned on February 25, 1863, due to ill-health and Oliver P. Robie, promoted to the rank of lieutenant colonel in February 1863, replaced Pugh. Robie was captured at Lexington, Kentucky, in October 1862 by John Hunt Morgan's raiders and subsequently paroled. Robie was born in Cumberland County, Maine, and had moved to Cincinnati by 1860 when he made a living as a salesman. He began the war in a three-month regiment, H.W. Burdsall's Independent Cavalry Company, and then enlisted in the 4th Ohio Cavalry. The twenty-nine-year-old, Robie, began his service in the 4th Ohio Cavalry as captain of Company A.[54]

Finally, the 10th Ohio Cavalry was one of newer regiments to arrive for duty. The 10th Ohio Cavalry was an inexperienced regiment, organized in Cleveland in October 1862, and its first assignment was as part of Stanley's cavalry in Middle Tennessee. The 10th Ohio arrived in Tennessee in early March and rode on its first expedition in April to Snow Hill. Colonel Charles C. Smith commanded the regiment. Smith was commissioned colonel of the 10th Ohio after serving as captain in the 2nd Ohio Cavalry where he was reported to be one of the "best officers" of the regiment. Smith was born in Lawrence County, Ohio in 1828 and later moved to Painesville where he was an engineer before the war.[55]

Eli Long also included the Chicago Board of Trade battery in his brigade. The Chicago Board of Trade Artillery was organized as a response to a call from President Lincoln for recruits. The battery was mustered into service on August 1, 1862, under the command Captain James H. Stokes. The battery initially boasted six James rifled ten-pound field artillery guns, but Stokes exchanged four rifled guns for four smooth-bore six-pound guns. The battery first met the enemy in October in Lawrenceburg, Kentucky and gained the attention of the commanders Army of Cumberland with exemplary service during the Battle of Stones River on December 31. The battery was ordered to join the cavalry effective May 16, 1863, as horse artillery, but retained its existing guns. The Chicago Board of Trade became the only battery of horse artillery for the cavalry in the Army of the Cumberland in contrast to light artillery designation of some other batteries. After the Battle of Stones River, Rosecrans made this a seven-gun battery in recognition of its performance during the battle.[56]

Born in 1814, Captain James H. Stokes was mustered in as captain of the battery. He graduated seventeenth in his class at West Point in 1835. Stokes was a Marylander by birth and served in the U.S. Army in the artillery and as a quartermaster. Stokes resigned his commission in 1843 and was involved in manufacturing and railroading prior to the war.[57]

Summary

The Federal cavalry had 10,560 men ready for duty on June 30 and this was far cry from the 3,200 which entered the Battle of Stones River. The six months pause after the Battle of Stones River provided time for Stanley and Rosecrans to add twelve new regiments and a battery of artillery. This enabled the addition of a new division which included two fairly large brigades and for the most part the regiments were veterans. Stanley's cavalry was rested and well supplied. The successes in the first six months of 1863 also boosted the morale of the men in the cavalry. They battled toe-to-toe with their Southern counterparts on equal footing and demonstrated their own abilities to meet their adversaries.[58]

However, in regard to the organization of the Federal cavalry, not everything was going well. Some changes occurred in regard to regimental officers due to various conflicts and other issues, but that was to be expected. Certainly, the four brigade commanders were experienced and highly regarded, but the selection of the two cavalry division commanders signaled trouble at the top. The ability of Stanley and Rosecrans to work well together over the past year yielded an exceptional change in the Federal cavalry. Because Stanley had the support of his commanding officer, almost immediately upon assuming command Stanley reorganized the cavalry into brigades reporting directly to him. It was Stanley's insistence and Rosecrans's agreement that provided large cavalry units to be formed which was imperative in the battle with the Confederate cavalry. In addition, more regiments and improved arms bolstered the Federal horseman, and the good relationship of Rosecrans and Stanley provided a stronger cavalry force.[59]

There were signs that cracks were forming in this solid relationship. Examples of some of initial problems included the selection of division commanders over Stanley's objections; during the Tullahoma Campaign, some of the cavalry fell under the direct command of infantry commanders with less than positive results; and finally, the battles being fought between Washington and Rosecrans resulted in some criticism of the management of the resources of the Army of the Cumberland which included the cavalry. There are always two sides to every argument, but later in life David Stanley placed the cause of many of these problems at the feet of Rosecrans' new chief of staff, Brigadier General James A. Garfield. Stanley concluded that as Garfield's and Rosecrans' relationship became closer, the politics of decisions increased. Rather than making the correct military decisions, often times, the political component influenced the military decisions. John Turchin's appointment to division command served as a prime example of this political influence. Garfield served on the court martial of Turchin and recommended his dismissal from the service. Turchin, of course, was not dismissed but six months later Garfield, in Stanley's opinion, was responsible for placing him in command of a division of cavalry for political reasons. However, Garfield had Rosecrans' ear and Rosecrans was looking toward his own future.[60]

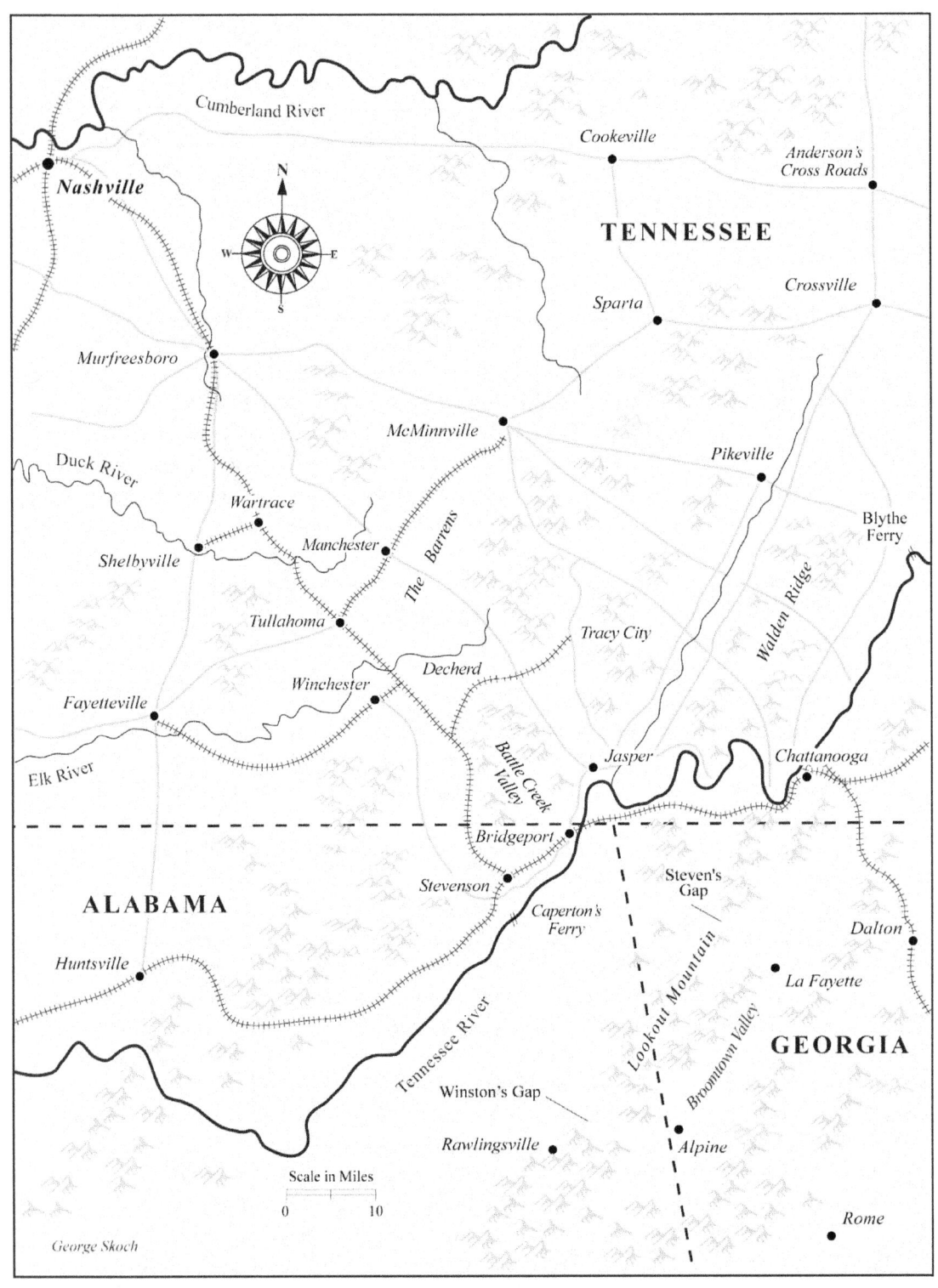

Middle Tennessee, northern Alabama and northern Georgia—summer 1863.

One. The Cavalry of the Army of the Cumberland (July 1863)

Stanley saw Garfield's hand in many of the decisions in the Army of the Cumberland and certainly as chief of staff, Garfield was very powerful. Stanley could often be a difficult personality and his own post war memoirs reflected a bitter recall of his experiences while in command of the cavalry. Stanley particularly disliked Garfield's decision to authorize Colonel Abel Streight's mounted infantry brigade to conduct a raid in April-May 1863 in northern Alabama and Georgia. The raid held disastrous results as Nathan Bedford Forrest captured 1,700 men of Streight's command. Regardless, Rosecrans liked his chief of staff and talked extensively with him on many late nights—so much that he made him his roommate. Stanley still demonstrated great loyalty to Rosecrans but he saw Garfield as a meddler interrupting the progress that had been achieved in the cavalry divisions. These appointments, and obvious battles fought by Stanley to resist them, jaded Stanley's outlook. Stanley resented Garfield's meddling which he believed, correctly, weakened the cavalry. It is important to note Stanley laid the blame of the selection of the division cavalry officers at the feet of Garfield, but this blame was made many years after the war. It was Rosecrans who made the final decision on the appointment of Turchin and Mitchell, and there was little evidence to demonstrate the full extent of Garfield's involvement in making these decisions. The brigade commanders in Stanley cavalry were fully capable of commanding divisions, Eli Long, Robert Minty, and Edward McCook, but he felt shackled with Turchin and Mitchell after making so much progress. Certainly for the remainder of 1863, David Stanley was less pleased with his time in the army than any other time in the war.[61]

Two. The Campaign So Far

If you cannot hurt the enemy now, he will soon hurt you.
—Major General Henry Halleck

On July 5, 1863, the events of the past week shocked those in the Confederacy. In the past seven days, Vicksburg fell to Grant, George Meade's army in Pennsylvania defeated Lee at Gettysburg, and William Rosecrans successfully maneuvered Bragg away from Tullahoma and out of Tennessee. While this did not sound the death knell for the Confederacy, these were disastrous events for those who supported the South. Moreover, those in Washington were jubilant. After struggling for two years, finally the momentum seemed to be on the side of Union forces. Rosecrans and those of the Army of the Cumberland happily celebrated the retreat of Bragg after an eleven-day campaign at the cost only 570 casualties; but the reaction from Washington did much to deflate the initial happiness in Tennessee.[1]

Almost immediately after the end of the Tullahoma Campaign, the ill will between Washington and Rosecrans began again. Rosecrans proudly wired Henry Halleck, General-in-Chief of the Union armies, about his victory at Tullahoma. Rosecrans felt he had just performed a remarkable piece of generalship by pushing Bragg out of middle Tennessee at a cost of less than 600 casualties, but Washington wanted more results. Secretary of War Edwin Stanton replied on July 7, "You and your noble army now have the chance to give the finishing blow to the rebellion. Will you neglect the chance?" Rosecrans, being informed of the great Union victories at Gettysburg and Vicksburg, felt his efforts had been slighted. He responded to Halleck, "You do not appear to observe the fact that this noble army has driven the rebels from Middle Tennessee, of which my dispatches advised you." Rosecrans continued, and referring to the low causality count, and urged Washington not to overlook his success "because it is not written in letters of blood." He hastened to note he had advanced to the Alabama state line and that Bragg had retreated to Chattanooga.[2]

Both Rosecrans and Washington were correct in their reactions. The position of the two opposing armies reflected a series of maneuvers and advances that began almost a year ago. In August 1862, two Confederate armies (the Army of Mississippi, commanded by Braxton Bragg, and the Army of Kentucky, commanded by E. Kirby Smith) marched into Kentucky as part of the Confederate grand offensive to take the war farther north. This campaign into Kentucky resulted in the Battle of Perryville where Don Carlos Buell's Army of the Ohio battled Bragg to a standstill. Bragg chose to retreat back to Tennessee giving the Union army a strategic victory. Next, Bragg settled his army, renamed the Army of Tennessee in November 1862, just south of Nashville at Murfreesboro. Henry Halleck ordered William S. Rosecrans to supersede Buell and renamed the Army of the Ohio as the Army of the Cumberland. The Union high command identified East Tennessee as the strategic objective for the Army of the Cumberland. One reason for Buell's removal was his inability to recognize Halleck's imperative to move his army into eastern Tennessee. Halleck felt the presence of a large Federal army there would sever the Confederates in Virginia from those in the Deep South. Rosecrans agreed but he saw the route to East Tennessee through Chattanooga, not through the Cumberland Gap, and the railroad was the key in capturing the eastern Tennessee. Rosecrans knew if no large Union army occupied east Tennessee communications, supplies and cooperation between the Confederate troops in the Mid-South and Virginia were "rapid and direct." In addition, no further movement into the Confederate territory southward was practical as long as strong Confederate forces occupied eastern Tennessee which threatened the rear of any Union army moving further south. In capturing Chattanooga, East Tennessee would be open to a well-supplied Union army which utilized the Nashville and Chattanooga Railroad; and then, the route further into the South would be within reach.

Major General Henry Halleck, nicknamed "Old Brains," General-in-Chief of all Union forces (Library of Congress).

The Federal Cavalry in the Recent Campaigns

The Union cavalry in the Western Theater had made vast strides over the past eleven months and the cavalry in Middle Tennessee in July 1863 was a far cry from the cavalry which participated at the Battle of Perryville. The Union cavalry at Perryville represented a potentially significant presence during that battle but because of its the organization, the cavalry remained dispersed throughout the army. Buell's army contained two cavalry brigades, commanded by Edward McCook and Lewis Zahm and a third provisional brigade, under the command of an acting brigadier general, Ebenezer Gay. Colonel John Kennett entered the battle as cavalry division commander, but based on Gay's rank, he commanded the entire cavalry division on paper in a very confused and convoluted command structure. While the Confederate cavalry made significant contributions during the Kentucky Campaign, the Union cavalry provided little offensive action.[3]

During the Kentucky Campaign, McCook's, Zahm's and Gay's brigades faced five brigades of Confederate cavalry—Joseph Wheeler's, John Wharton's, Henry Ashby's, John Scott's and John Hunt Morgan's. Nathan Bedford Forrest participated in the early part of the campaign but returned to Middle Tennessee to organize the Confederate positions near Murfreesboro. After the battle, the Union cavalry continued to struggle as it pursued the retreating Confederate armies and John Hunt Morgan's cavalry brigade successfully made another raid through the Kentucky countryside pursued by a provisional Federal cavalry brigade commanded by Colonel Minor Millikin, 1st Ohio Cavalry. Millikin expressed his great frustration in this task because of poor communication, incomplete orders and an unclear chain of command. He complained that he was not informed of his role in pursuing Morgan until he was "incidentally" told that his command should act independently during this pursuit. In addition, Millikin explained that his command was significantly outnumbered by Morgan and if he had, in fact, caught Morgan he would not be able to defeat him. Things were in a poor state of affairs for the Northern horsemen.[4]

Nonetheless, the commanders and troopers of the Union cavalry diligently performed their duty and led the Union advance toward Nashville after the Kentucky Campaign. Both Rosecrans and Bragg placed their armies about twenty miles apart in November 1862. The Army of the Cumberland held a line at Nashville and the newly reorganized Army of Tennessee, previously named the Army of Mississippi, claimed the territory around Murfreesboro. As the Union army moved south, Ebenezer Gay's brigade remained in Kentucky and only one cavalry division of two brigades (Lewis Zahm's and Edward McCook's) moved to Nashville. Newly appointed chief of cavalry, David Stanley, arrived at Nashville in November 1862 and immediately set about rearming, training, supplying and reorganizing the cavalry division.[5]

The Battle of Stones River—The Cavalry's First Big Test

On December 26, Rosecrans ordered the Army of the Cumberland to advance toward Bragg's Army of Tennessee and an eleven-day campaign began. In November, the Confederates boasted six strong brigades of cavalry in and around Murfreesboro. Four brigades fell under the command of Joseph Wheeler and protected the front and flanks of the Army of Tennessee. Two independent brigades commanded by Nathan Bedford Forrest and John Hunt Morgan also operated under Bragg's orders. The "raiding strategy" was a key component of the Confederate cavalry in Tennessee. The ability to swiftly strike the communications and supply lines of the Federal army brought recognition and fame to the Confederate cavalry commanders. Forrest and Morgan became heroes to many Southerners who needed this solace as Federal armies marched into the heart of the Confederacy. So, in December both Morgan and Forrest launched raids, one into Kentucky and the other in western Tennessee, on the Union armies' vulnerable supply lines. In addition, a third Confederate cavalry general, Earl Van Dorn, launched a raid in northern Mississippi and carried into western Tennessee.[6]

While these Southern cavalry raids precipitated frantic responses from Union forces in the rear, they also provided good news for the meager cavalry of the Army of the Cumberland. Instead of facing six enemy brigades, the odds improved because Morgan and Forrest operated away from Murfreesboro. In a related action, Brigadier General Samuel Carter launched a Union raid into lightly held eastern Tennessee in an attempt to draw Confederate troops away from Murfreesboro. Partly because Morgan and Forrest moved away from Murfreesboro and, largely to meet Washington's demands, Rosecrans ordered his army toward Bragg's forces in Middle Tennessee. The Army of the Cumberland moved ahead with three infantry wings, or corps, and David Stanley assembled three brigades of cavalry to screen the advance. The Union cavalry brigades were commanded by Colonel Robert Minty (while Edward McCook was away on medical leave), Colonel Lewis Zahm, and Stanley personally commanded the third. In addition, Colonel John Kennett had command of the cavalry division under Stanley who served as chief of cavalry.[7]

Both Minty and Zahm had good experienced regiments. During the Battle of Stones River, Minty commanded the 2nd Indiana (one company), 3rd Kentucky, 4th Michigan, and the 7th Pennsylvania regiments. Zahm commanded the 1st, 3rd, and 4th Ohio regiments, and also the 2nd Tennessee, although this regiment was officially part of the Reserve Brigade. Stanley commanded the greenest of the regiments in the Reserve Brigade which included— the veteran 3rd Indiana Battalion, 15th Pennsylvania, 2nd Tennessee (sometimes detached to Zahm), and 5th Tennessee regiments. Stanley scrambled to assemble enough cavalry to accomplish its task during this campaign but some events complicated this effort. For example, upon its arrival in Nashville just before Christmas, the 15th Pennsylvania Cavalry mutinied and less than a battalion actually fought in the battle. Next, the two highly regarded majors, who commanded those of the 15th Pennsylvania who did fight, were killed or mortally wounded during the advance on Murfreesboro. The 2nd Tennessee Cavalry had less than a full complement of men and had yet to be formally organized as a regiment. Finally, two days before the campaign began, the 5th Tennessee tested their Merrill carbines and found that only one half of them actually fired. Nevertheless, the Union cavalry boldly moved toward Murfreesboro beginning on December 26, 1862.[8]

The three Union cavalry brigades advanced with George Thomas,' Thomas Crittenden's, and Alexander McCook's infantry wings along different paths toward Murfreesboro. Initially, Robert Minty's cavalry provided reconnaissance and protection for Crittenden's movement directly down the Murfreesboro/Nashville Pike toward the primary concentration of Bragg's army at Murfreesboro. The Reserve Cavalry Brigade and Zahm's brigade screened McCook's and Thomas' advance along the western flank. Rosecrans discovered that Polk's infantry corps and Kirby Smith's (now only a single division) forces held the line at Murfreesboro, and Hardee's corps held the west flank between Triune and Eagleville, on the Shelbyville and Nolensville Pike with an advance guard at Nolensville. His strategy was to press Hardee. Alexander McCook's corps moved in the center of Rosecrans's army with three divisions, Thomas advanced on his right (west) with Negley's and Rousseau's divisions. McCook planned to attack Hardee at Triune and if Bragg moved to support Hardee then Thomas would join the Union attack. If McCook successfully defeated Hardee, or if Hardee retreated, and Bragg held his line north of Murfreesboro then Crittenden would attack, supported by Thomas and then McCook would, while holding Hardee in place, swing the remainder of his wing into Polk's rear. If Hardee moved to join Bragg and Polk at Murfreesboro, then Rosecrans would concentrate his army to oppose Bragg's entire force.[9]

The Reserve Cavalry Brigade got off to a slow start on the initial day of the Union advance, but Lewis Zahm's brigade rode toward Franklin with orders to neutralize a force of Confederate cavalry. Rosecrans feared the enemy cavalry at Franklin would sweep around the rear of his advancing army and sever communications, and he assigned the task of dealing with them to Zahm's Ohio cavalry. Zahm found Colonel Baxter Smith's 4th Tennessee Cavalry and the 14th Alabama Battalion at Franklin and surprised them with an aggressive attack on their position. Zahm so surprised the Confederate cavalry that he had no trouble in sending them riding for the woods and destroying their camp which had been abandoned. However, Zahm discovered the next day that the Confederates returned in force and repulsed another attack by a smaller number of Ohio cavalry. The rest of Zahm's cavalry moved forward with McCook's infantry to press Hardee's troops at Triune.[10]

Meanwhile on the eastern flank, Robert Minty's cavalry preceded Crittenden's advance, and screened, protected the flanks, and cleared the area of sharpshooters. Importantly, the 4th Michigan Cavalry made a mad dash along the Jefferson Pike and captured a bridge over

Stewarts Creek. In a heated fight, Minty's troopers held onto the bridge through a stiff counterattack by the Southern cavalry. The fight caused Captain Frank Mix, commanding the Federal attack, to exclaim, "It was the hottest place I ever got into in my life." The infantry hastened forward and secured the bridge which promised an easy crossing for Crittenden's infantry.[11]

Confederate General William Hardee withdrew to Murfreesboro when it became apparent Rosecrans' advance was real. Over the next few days, the cavalry of both armies skirmished. Wheeler promised to delay the Union advance while Bragg pulled his infantry to Murfreesboro and formed his defense along Stones River. The Federal cavalry continued to screen and skirmish with the Confederate cavalry. When Wheeler's cavalry formed a determined resistance, the Union infantry rushed ahead and joined in the fight. Both cavalries provided commendable actions during the advance.[12]

By the end of December 30, Rosecrans' army reached its objective and faced Bragg's infantry which resolutely prepared to resist the Federal advance. Ironically, both Rosecrans and Bragg decided to attack each other on the morning of December 31. Rosecrans planned to attack the eastern flank at 8:00 a.m. and Bragg planned to attack the west flank at 6:00 a.m. Bragg won the race and attacked with such fury McCook's corps was thrown into confusion and propelled rearward. Zahm's cavalry brigade, supplemented with the 2nd Tennessee Cavalry, spent five hours fighting General John Wharton's cavalry on the western flank. Finally, at eleven o'clock most of Zahm's cavalry was driven from the field and Wharton's Confederate cavalry claimed the large Union supply train at the rear of the Army of the Cumberland. At that moment, the 4th U.S. Cavalry made a determined counterattack on the Southern cavalry which failed to consider the Federals still had fight left in them. Next, the 3rd Indiana, 3rd Ohio, and 3rd Kentucky cavalries all joined in the counterattack and drove Wharton's horsemen to the rear.[13]

Later that afternoon, David Stanley and Robert Minty with about one-third of the Federal cavalry, which had been at Stewarts Creek when the morning's battle began, arrived on the field and sent Wheeler's and Buford's cavalry to rear. This secured the Union right flank which had been so badly damaged during the day. Wheeler's cavalry had just returned to the battlefield after riding completely around the Union army on December 30 attacking four supply trains along the way.[14]

Zahm commanded the defense of wagons trains and fought with Wheeler's cavalry again on January 1 and January 3. Even though, part of the Union cavalry was driven off on January 1, Zahm adapted to the Confederate attacks and successfully provided protection on both days.[15]

Despite being roughly handled during the battle, the Union cavalry provided respectable duty, but more significantly the Battle of Stones River clearly demonstrated to the Union commanders the need to improve their cavalry in numbers, organization, and armament. Because the cavalry of the Army of Tennessee was so formidable in Middle Tennessee and at the Battle of Stones River, it became a primary objective of Rosecrans and Stanley to add more cavalry that was well armed and prepared to fight.

After the Battle of Stones River

After the Battle of Stones River, Bragg retreated to the area around Tullahoma and began preparing defenses in anticipation of Rosecrans's next move. Rosecrans, for a while, became the darling of the Army, particularly, in light of the recent Federal defeats at Fredericksburg, Holly Springs, and Chickasaw Bluffs. Secretary of War Edwin Stanton wrote to Rosecrans, "There is nothing you can ask within my power to grant to yourself or your heroic command that will not be cheerfully given." But Stanton did not anticipate what Rosecrans had in mind. Rosecrans remained in the same general area around Murfreesboro from January 5 until June 24. What started as a pleasant, amiable relationship between Rosecrans and Washington ended in anger and calls for the removal of the commanding general of the Army of the Cumberland by the time Rosecrans began the Tullahoma Campaign. Rosecrans began his demands on January 14 when he explained to Secretary of War Edwin Stanton that the Confederates outnumbered his cavalry by four to one and plagued his communications and supply lines. As a solution, Rosecrans planned to mount an infantry brigade to supplement the traditional cavalry. He wanted to be able to move quickly like cavalry, but bring to bear the new technology of repeating rifles which would increase the firepower of the mounted infantry as a way to tame the Confederate cavalry. Rosecrans wrote, "I must have horses and saddles to mount some infantry, and have asked authority to buy the horses and saddles for 5,000." The brigade would be mounted under the command of Colonel John Wilder. Thus began months-long exchanges of messages from Rosecrans and Washington which demanded repeating rifles, more cavalry regiments, authority to mount infantry, and more horses to do so. Initially, Washington tried to meet Rosecrans' needs, largely based on the success at Stones River while other Union armies were stalemated; but the constant demands by Rosecrans soon became tiresome. Rosecrans' numerous requests would finally be met with a reply from Washington that enough was enough.[16]

During the intervening months after the Battle of Stones River, the opposing cavalries were not idle. The opposing armies fought almost daily and "nine expeditions, nine reconnaissance actions, and fifty skirmishes occurred in the first six months of 1863." These clashes with the enemy allowed the Union cavalry to operate in brigade-size actions where commanders tested their leadership and the various regiments gained trust and reliance on each other. Stanley and Rosecrans added thirteen new regiments, including the 39th Indiana Mounted Infantry, and the Chicago Board of Trade horse artillery to the existing cavalry division. Nonetheless, the Federal cavalry remained outnumbered throughout this period but the gap narrowed particularly as the June 24 campaign approached.[17]

While the Federal army increased its cavalry, so did the Confederates. In December, Wheeler's four cavalry brigades fought at Stones River; and Forrest and Morgan's brigades conducted their raids but these two brigades returned to duty with Bragg's army. General Earl Van Dorn would officially become part of Bragg's Army of Tennessee on March 16 and his arrival added significant numbers of cavalry to the Southern army. Van Dorn also assumed command over Nathan B. Forrest for a while. Both Wheeler and Van Dorn would formally have control of the two cavalry corps of the Army of Tennessee. In May, an outraged husband, Dr. James Bodie Peters, shot and killed Van Dorn because Van Dorn was reportedly having an affair with Peters' wife. After Van Dorn's death, Brigadier General William Hicks Jackson's division which had served under Van Dorn's command returned to Mississippi. As a result, Nathan Bedford Forrest maintained command of one of the Confederate cavalry divisions in Tennessee and Joseph Wheeler commanded the other corps. These two men did not like each other and Forrest vowed he would never serve under Wheeler after a botched attack on Fort Donelson in February 1863.[18]

Relative Strength of Union and Confederate
Cavalry in Middle Tennessee—1863[19]

Date	Present for Duty—Union	Present for Duty—Confederate
January 31	4,549	8,707
February 28	5,040	9,101
April 30	4,961	15,125
May 20	—	15,096
May 31	4,961	—
June 10	—	13,868
June 30	10,560	—

Meanwhile, Stanley reorganized the Union cavalry during the six-month interlude after the Battle of Stones River and placed four good commanders in charge of the cavalry brigades—Campbell, Long, McCook, and Minty. These men demonstrated good decision-making abilities, acceptance by the troops, skill and a willingness to fight. These officers formed the basis for Federal cavalry brigades for the next year and, for the most part, the remainder of the war. In addition, the regimental commanders generally represented good officers; but some of the regiments were plagued with political appointments. Overall, Stanley crafted two good cavalry divisions that had the objective of gaining parity with the Southern cavalry which had been so dominant in Kentucky and Tennessee thus far in the war.

The notable Federal cavalry actions during the first six month of 1863 included:

Rover, Tennessee	Jan. 31, Feb. 13, 1863	Union Victory
Bradyville, Tennessee	February 22, 1863	Union Victory
Thompson Station, Tennessee	March 5, 1863	Confederate Victory
Vaught's Hill, Tennessee	March 20, 1863	Union Victory
Brentwood, Tennessee	March 25, 1863	Confederate Victory
Woodbury, Tennessee	March 27, 1863	Confederate Victory
Snow Hill, Tennessee	April 2, 1863	Union Victory
McMinnville, Tennessee	April 17, 1863	Union Victory
Franklin, Tennessee	April 10, 1863	Union Victory
Middleton, Tennessee	May 21–22, 1863	Union Victory
Franklin, Tennessee	June 4, 1863	Inconclusive
Triune, Tennessee	June 7–9 1863	Inconclusive[20]

Arguably, command problems plagued many of the armies in the Civil War. For the Union army in Middle Tennessee, its foundations came from command problems and started when Halleck removed Buell from command because he failed to act on the desires of his commanders in Washington. Rosecrans, himself, operated under a veil of controversy even though he demonstrated his ability to defeat his opponents (Rich Mountain, Iuka, Corinth, Stones River). On the day Rosecrans accepted command of the Army of the Cumberland, Ulysses Grant concluded to remove him from command of the Army of the Mississippi. Before the Battle of Stones River, Henry Halleck told Rosecrans that some in Washington called for his removal because he was too slow in initiating an advance on Bragg. So, it is no surprise the six-month delay at Murfreesboro again resulted in threats of removal of Rosecrans.[21]

Washington continued to pressure Rosecrans to move against Bragg in June when Henry Halleck wired Rosecrans, "If you cannot hurt the enemy now, he will soon hurt you." This message followed a veiled threat from Halleck the day before, "If you can do nothing yourself, a portion of your troops must be sent to Grant's relief." Washington watched as Grant besieged Vicksburg and because the siege was lasting so long there was the threat that Confederate General Joseph Johnston could concentrate a force large enough to punch a hole in Grant's lines allowing General John C. Pemberton's army to escape. Halleck needed Rosecrans to advance and therefore hold Bragg's troops in place; but Rosecrans had finally gotten the message and realized it was time to move.[22]

David Stanley watched the quarrel between Halleck and Rosecrans as a trusted member of Rosecrans' command. Stanley observed Rosecrans' constant appeal for more supplies finally fall upon deaf ears in Washington; and Rosecrans still refused to move until the spring crops matured and could be used by the advancing army. Stanley wrote, "Rosy was powerful then, but his head was marked and it only awaited the slightest excuse to bring his dooms day."[23]

While Rosecrans delayed, James A. Garfield, Rosecrans' chief of staff, made the indiscretion of writing his dissatisfaction with the inaction of the army to

Brigadier General Nathan B. Forrest commanded the cavalry on Bragg's right flank during the Chickamauga Campaign. David Stanley wrote: "Two rebel doctors boasted ... that Forrest was coming over in a few days, and he would show us a few things" (Library of Congress).

Secretary of Treasury Salmon Chase, "I cannot conceal from you the fact that I have been greatly tried and dissatisfied with the slow progress that we have made in this department since the battle of Stone River.... Thus far the General [Rosecrans] had been singularly disinclined to grasp the situation with a strong hand and make the advantage his own." The slip on the part of Garfield would haunt both Rosecrans in the upcoming months and Garfield in the future.[24]

The politics of those in Washington and those in the army resulted in a strong dislike between Stanley and Garfield. In Stanley's opinion, Garfield's influence on Rosecrans, who seemed to identify a political future for himself, tainted the previous close relationship between Stanley and Rosecrans. Stanley, a professional soldier and one without political goals, became disillusioned. In a time of great promise for the cavalry as it increased its size and strength, deep concerns about the command and direction of the army plagued Stanley and many others.

Dates of Arrival of New Cavalry Units for the Army of the Cumberland[25]

Regiment	Arrival at Murfreesboro
4th Indiana Cavalry	January 1863
39th Indiana Mounted Infantry	April 1863 (previously assigned to 20th Army Corps)
5th Iowa Cavalry	June 1863
2nd Kentucky Cavalry	January 1863 (unattached since November 1862)
4th Kentucky Cavalry	February 1863
5th Kentucky Cavalry	February 1863
6th Kentucky Cavalry	February 1863
7th Kentucky Cavalry	March 1863

Regiment	Arrival at Murfreesboro
2nd Michigan Cavalry	March 1863
10th Ohio Cavalry	March 1863
9th Pennsylvania Cavalry	February 1863
1st Tennessee Cavalry	January 1863
1st Wisconsin Cavalry	June 1863
Chicago Board of Trade Battery, Illinois Light Artillery (Stokes)	June 1863

The six months which followed the Battle of Stones River proved frustrating for those in Washington and in Middle Tennessee as the two opposing armies held the same relative position despite a series of skirmishes and expeditions. Lieutenant W. L. Curry, 1st Ohio Cavalry, described the stalemate "...glaring at each other like two gladiators, watching for any advantage he may take over his antagonist from some weak place in his lines." The cavalry actions during this period resulted in varying degrees of success for each army. The results of the engagements of Wheeler and John H. Morgan on the east and Forrest and Van Dorn on the west of the Confederate defensive line demonstrated the Union cavalry's greater success over Wheeler and Morgan than with Van Dorn and Forrest.[26]

Historian Michael Bradley concluded the successes in the cavalry action on the eastern flank decided the route of the Union advance during the Tullahoma campaign. "Although the terrain was more challenging in the east, the success of Union cavalry probes revealed that the Confederate defenses were vulnerable in that sector and the potential rewards were much greater." The six-month interlude allowed Stanley to amass twenty-two regiments as his cavalry determined the route of the advance on the Confederates positions at Tullahoma.[27]

Part of Wheeler's corps, General John Hunt Morgan was detached during the Chickamauga Campaign (Library of Congress).

The Tullahoma Campaign

In June 1863, the Union army faced Bragg's Army of Tennessee along an impressive geographic obstacle, the Highland Rim plateau. Bragg extended his infantry from Shelbyville on the west flank to Beech Grove near Hoover's Gap on the east. The left flank of his cavalry extended to Columbia and to McMinnville on the right flank. Bragg concentrated the center of his army at Tullahoma which lay between two Rivers, the Duck River which flowed from Manchester through Shelbyville, north of Tullahoma; and south of Tullahoma, the Elk River meandered in a southwest direction about midway toward Winchester. Three main roads passed through the gaps in the Highland Rim near Tullahoma. The eastern road, the Murfreesboro-Manchester Road, passed through Hoover's Gap, a three-mile-long valley. Liberty Pike passed through Liberty Gap, two miles west of Hoover's Gap, along a southward path to Wartrace. Finally, the Murfreesboro-Shelbyville Turnpike traveled through Guy's Gap just west of Liberty Gap. Rosecrans needed to develop a plan to move through these three gaps where a determined defense by Confederate troops threatened to stall his entire advance.

Various figures have been offered for the total forces of the two armies facing each other during the Tullahoma Campaign, but Rosecrans fielded about 50,000 men including, 6,806 cavalry and 3,065 artillerymen. In addition, Rosecrans had over 12,000 men held in reserve. Bragg, on the other hand, had 46,000 men with 13,962 cavalry and 2,254 artillerymen. Facing Stanley's cavalry were the divisions of Forrest, Wharton, and William "Will" Thomas Martin; and Joseph Wheeler served as chief of cavalry over Wharton's and Martin's divisions. John Hunt Morgan's division rode on an independent raid northward and was not present during the Tullahoma Campaign.

The bulk of Bragg's army was entrenched at Shelbyville and Tullahoma. Rosecrans knew the cost of attacking well-constructed defenses and he had to find a way around the defenses. Leonidas Polk's corps was located near Shelbyville and William Hardee was near Wartrace and the Confederates also had the advantage of holding the highland passes along the three primary roads leading to Tullahoma. Rosecrans planned to push Bragg southward, and then quickly capture the bridges at Estill Springs and at Pelham trapping Bragg before he could cross the Elk River. First, Rosecrans planned to feint west and then attack the Confederate east flank which the cavalry operations over the past months suggested was more vulnerable. Rosecrans wanted to develop his full strength near Manchester and in a wheeling movement turn Bragg's right flank, placing him in the position of facing the Union infantry away from his entrenchments.[28]

Rosecrans' plan called for Thomas' XIV Corps to move along the Manchester Pike, seize and hold Hoover's Gap. Rosecrans ordered Thomas and McCook to advance, each corps within supporting distance of the other. Meanwhile, Crittenden's XXI Corps planned to advance and concentrate at Bradyville forming the east flank of the Army of the Cumberland. Eli Long's Second Brigade of cavalry under the command of General John Turchin had orders to operate in conjunction with Crittenden. David Stanley and the remainder of the cavalry advanced toward Versailles, west of the Shelbyville Road and then moved southward to unite with Mitchell's cavalry division, which had been placed under Gordon Granger's command.[29]

As the campaign began, Rosecrans sent Major General Gordon Granger's Reserve Corps and the remainder of David Stanley's cavalry to Triune in a feint to confuse Bragg as to his true plan. He hoped Bragg would send troops to an area Rose-

General Joseph Wheeler commanded Wharton's and Martin's divisions during the Chickamauga Campaign (Library of Congress).

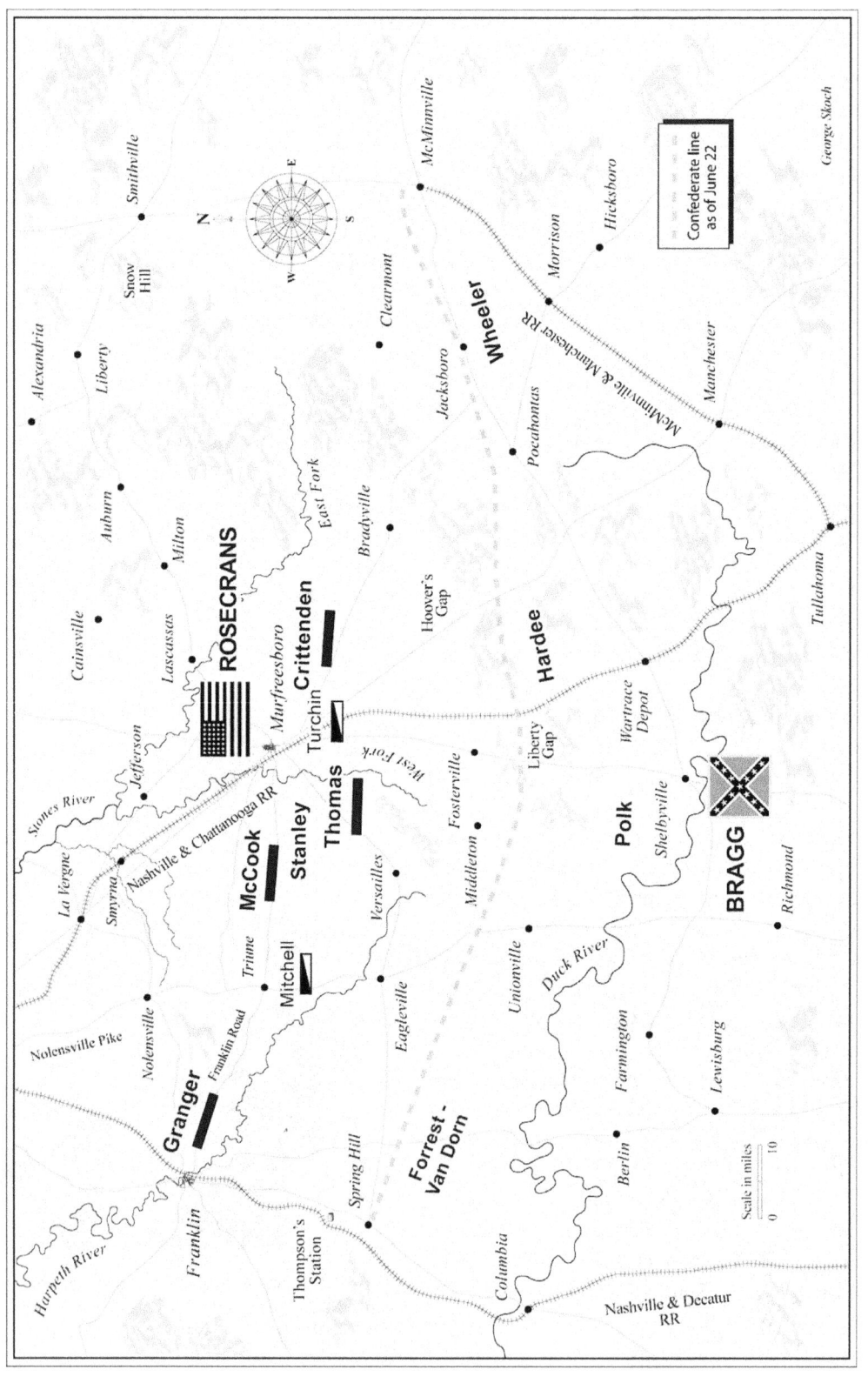

Union and Confederate positions—June 22, 1863.

crans did not plan to attack. Initially, the cavalry found and pushed back the Confederate cavalry at Eagleville, Rover, Middleton and Unionville. Interestingly, Granger commanded the Reserve Infantry Corps and Mitchell's cavalry division. Granger had overall supervisory command of all the cavalry except Long's brigade which was working with Crittenden's corps. On June 23, Granger ordered Robert Mitchell's First Cavalry Division along the Eagleville and Salem Roads pushing the enemy's cavalry and pickets in front of them. The 9th Pennsylvania Cavalry led the Union advance and battled the 2nd and 4th Georgia and 7th and 51st Alabama cavalries which fell back only to fight from hill to hill in the first action of the campaign. Due to a determined resistance by the Confederate cavalry, the 2nd Michigan Cavalry relieved the 9th Pennsylvania after the first two miles. Granger marched Brannan's infantry division to Salem and Palmer's infantry division and a brigade of cavalry to Readyville. Mitchell had sharp fights as he pushed from Eagleville and Rover.[30]

As might be expected, the Confederate cavalry provided a stiff resistance to the Granger's feint toward Triune and Middleton. Unfortunately, just as the campaign began, it began raining and rained until the end of the campaign, exhausting the soldiers and horses in the process. David Stanley recorded, "That day the rain set in, which has continued to this present date, and which, converting the whole surface of the country into a quagmire, has rendered this one of the most arduous, laborious, and distressing campaigns upon man and beast I have ever witnessed." But the feint achieved all that could be hoped. The opening actions confused Wheeler to "such as extent that for days he sent army headquarters erroneous, conflicting, and incomplete reports of enemy movements and intentions." One day before Rosecrans began his advance Wheeler moved his troopers toward Shelbyville away from the exact objective of Union advance, leaving the critical Highland Rim gaps weakly defended as Rosecrans's main thrusts moved forward.[31]

Most of Stanley's cavalry operated on the western flank of Federal army and only Turchin's division, consisting of only Eli Long's brigade, screened Crittenden's movement on the east which was almost totally unopposed. Wheeler's inability to determine the concentrations and movements of Rosecrans's army put Bragg at a great disadvantage in the campaign. Despite Bragg having excellent terrain for his defenses, Rosecrans easily maneuvered past these obstacles.[32]

The Cavalry Battle at Shelbyville

Rosecrans' plan to deceive Bragg worked so well that two Confederate divisions held a line at Shelbyville to defend against the phantom attack which never came. Instead, Thomas, McCook and Crittenden successfully moved through the treacherous gaps marching toward Manchester. Realizing Rosecrans's success, the Confederate infantry began its retreat to Tullahoma on the morning of June 27.[33]

Guy's Gap remained uncaptured and behind this gap Wheeler concentrated much of his cavalry which had been moved from the right flank. To Wheeler's credit, he resolutely planned to hold back the Union advance with just his cavalry as Polk and Hardee marched toward Tullahoma. On June 27, Stanley rode at the head of about 5,000 cavalry—Mitchell's division plus Minty's brigade. Captain Joseph Vale, 7th Pennsylvania Cavalry, recalled, "Here was presented a scene of grant military pageantry, as rare as it was inspiring. The sun, for a few hours after rising, shone out clear and bright, reflecting in full splendor the bright sabers and arms, and kissing the flags, banners, and steamers, as a harbinger of victory." Stanley sought permission from Gordon Granger to make a direct attack on the defenders at Guy's Gap and Granger "acquiesced in this, and, pushing forward, our forces deployed." Stanley ordered his cavalry forward to Guy's Gap. Stanley and Minty were ready for a fight but Mitchell's First Division was delayed. While the remainder of the cavalry waited, Minty was "raging like a chained lion" at the lack of progress. Stanley sent a rider to Minty asking him to move his brigade ahead and attack the gap, exclaiming the brigade in the lead was "so d__d slow, he couldn't do anything with it." The slowness of lead brigade was attributed to Robert Mitchell's illness and delays in sending orders to the brigade commanders.[34]

Robert Minty placed the 4th U.S. and the 5th Tennessee cavalries in front of the gap while the 7th Pennsylvania, 4th Michigan, and 3rd Indiana cavalries moved to flank Confederate defenders. Minty promptly led the attack by swinging the 4th U.S. Cavalry to the right and the 5th Tennessee Cavalry charged the lightly held gap in column of fours. Historian, Michael Bradley, noted, "Observing that not much defensive fire was coming out of the place Lieutenant Colonel Galbraith sent forward some men from his 1st Middle [5th] Tennessee Cavalry (U.S.), cleared the barricade off the road, and then charged the earthworks mounted. The few Confederates holding the place immediately scattered and for about two miles there was a horse race." The enemy abandoned their position and fled toward Shelbyville.[35]

Minty's troopers rode toward Shelbyville where Brigadier General William "Will" Martin's Confederate cavalry, about 900 strong, defended the town in entrenchments. Stanley ordered Minty to attack with his entire brigade of 2,522 men. Minty ran into the first defensive line about four miles north of Shelbyville when he came under artillery fire but Minty continued his attack. Martin had too few troopers to man the defenses and retreated again toward Shelbyville. Minty moved the 7th Pennsylvania Cavalry to the lead to replace the 4th U.S. Cavalry whose horses were fatigued. Wheeler and Martin, outnumbered and closely pursued, set up another defensive line near the courthouse square in Shelbyville centered upon Wiggins' Arkansas Battery. Minty brought artillery of his own and as he approached Shelbyville, he paused to realign his command and unlimbered Aleshire's 18th Ohio Battery. Then he ordered his cavalry to attack Shelbyville with the 7th Pennsylvania, 1st Middle (5th) Tennessee and 4th U.S. Cavalry by column of fours with their sabers drawn.[36]

"This should have been a recipe for disaster—a cavalry column charging a battery of artillery supported by a full body of cavalry," noted historian Michael Bradley. Luck favored the bold as other factors played an important part in the battle. The weather caused much of the Confederate ammunition to become wet, and rather than riding to meet Minty's charge, the Confederate horsemen received the charge at a "standstill." Further, Martin sent orders to his troopers to fire one shot and then retreat across the Skull Camp Bridge over the Duck River, swollen from the incessant rain. To complete the Union attack, the 3rd Indiana Cavalry made a flanking attack from the east.[37]

While Stanley's and Minty's insistence on training the cavalry in the use of the saber has been discounted by many, the battle at Shelbyville demonstrated the value of this weapon. This saber charge was made by troopers of the same column which had just provided effective skirmishing duty with Colt revolving rifles and carbines. The general plan called for the cavalry to fire a volley from carbines at thirty yards from the enemy and then finish the attack with sabers drawn. As one of the defenders later wrote, "On either side of the highway ... in columns of fours, they advanced at a steady gallop.... The Union troopers, with sabers high in the air, made no sound whatever, beyond the rumbling tattoo which their horses' hoofs played upon the ground.... No more gallant work was ever done by any troops than was done this day by the Seventh Pennsylvania." Lieutenant Colonel William B. Sipes, the ex-newspaper editor from Pennsylvania, commanded the 7th Pennsylvania Cavalry which charged the Confederate defenders at Shelbyville concentrated at the courthouse square. He led the 7th Pennsylvania at the walk and maintained that pace until the Confederate cannon fired and he ordered the charge. The Confederate cavalrymen unleashed a single volley and broke for the bridge. Minty's men captured one piece of artillery near a railroad depot, followed by a second taken in a sharp fight in the town and the third was captured at the Skull Camp Bridge. The pursuit did not stop at the river and the Union cavalry chased their prey for another two miles before breaking off the pursuit.[38]

In the meantime, Colonel Archibald Campbell's brigade swung around to cut off the retreat at the bridge over the Duck River. Hand-to-hand fighting took place as the 3rd Indiana Cavalry slammed into the Confederate defenders as some of the Confederates rode into the rain swollen river to escape capture with the Union troopers on their heels. So fierce was the fighting, some of the 3rd Indiana used carbines to club their enemy. Once the 7th Pennsylvania, followed by the 4th U.S., charged the cannon, the 4th Michigan Cavalry, commanded by Major Frank Mix, succeeded in riding from the flank into the escaping Confederate cavalry turning it to the left and forcing it to ride into a heavily fenced garden resulting in the capture of about 250 men.[39]

There are various accounts of this engagement but one complicating factor might have been Wheeler's belief that Forrest's cavalry was riding to his aid. Wheeler's scouts informed him that Forrest was rushing to Shelbyville with two full brigades of cavalry and he was on the north side of the Duck River. Wheeler had planned to burn the bridge and prevent Stanley's cavalry from crossing the river, but he knew this would trap Forrest and his Southern cavalry on the north side of the river. However, this was unlikely because once Wheeler had been pushed to the courthouse square he was in no position to offer any aid to Forrest on the north side of the river. More likely, Wheeler was attempting a delaying action to get his trains across the river and further to the rear. Regardless, Wheeler was in a very uncomfortable position as the Union cavalry had swung to the left and came charging directly into Wheeler's flank. Wheeler had had enough to deal with as Minty charged his front. This flanking movement proved too much. Any Confederates not across the bridge were trapped. "After a four-day downpour, Duck River was a roaring torrent, with its crest fifteen feet below the level of the streets of Shelbyville and with a nearly vertical drop from the riverbank to the water below. Wheeler 'saber in hand, shouted to his men that they must cut their way through and swim the river, ordered the charge, and, with General Martin, led in the desperate venture,'" observed Stephen Starr, author of the history of Union cavalry in the Civil War. There is no doubt Wheeler and Martin swam the river, but the 3rd Indiana followed those retreating into the same river, losing only one man, without the hyperbole of a dramatic leap into the river.[40]

After the success at Shelbyville, Stanley wanted to go after Forrest. He wanted to extend the efforts of a good day's work when at midnight he learned that Nathan Bedford Forrest's cavalry had struggled through the mud and crossed the Duck River downstream as he retreated toward Tullahoma. Unfortunately, Rosecrans had shackled Stanley to Granger. Stanley pleaded with Granger for permission to pursue Forrest, but Stanley recorded Granger

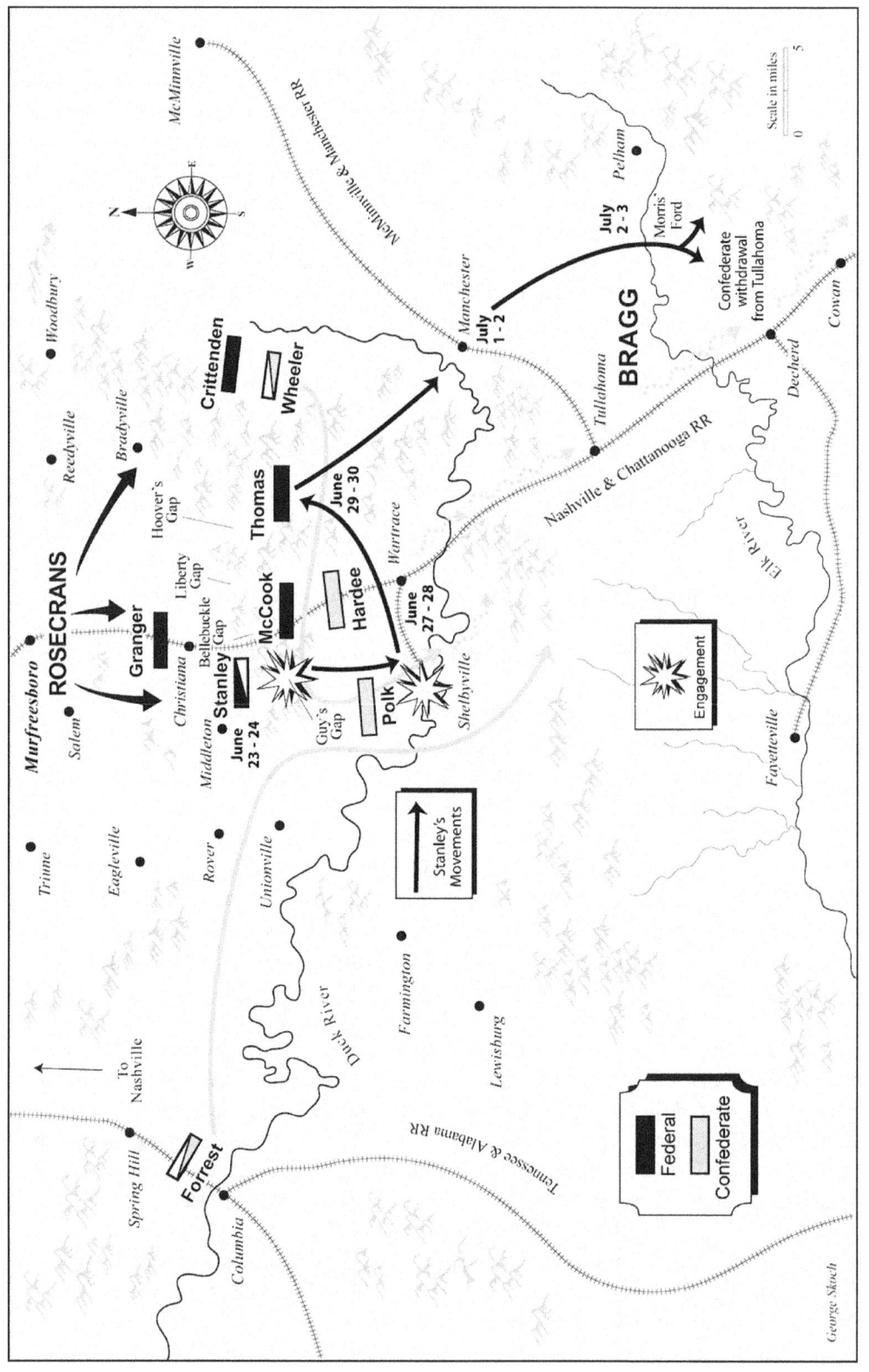

Union cavalry movements in the Tullahoma Campaign June 24–July 3, 1863.

thought the cavalry was worn out after fighting in the muddy conditions at Shelbyville. Stanley wrote, "As the matter turned out, I think it was very unfortunate that this attack was not made, as I think we could have completely routed this part of Forrest's force." Stanley had to be particularly frustrated when he received a message from Lieutenant Colonel Charles Goddard, Rosecrans' Assistant Adjutant General, who encouraged to him to take the battle to Wheeler and Forrest, "Pitch in and use them up," only to find out he had been ordered not to pursue Forrest by his new commanding officer, Granger.[41]

The engagement at Shelbyville carried great significance in terms of the strategic situation in the western theater of the Civil War. This engagement is generally recognized as a point where the dominance of Confederate cavalry over the Union cavalry in Tennessee ended. David Stanley wrote, "The Confederate cavalry never recovered from the demoralizing effect which it experienced that day of being ridden down by the Union cavalry." Rosecrans and Stanley had worked diligently to bolster the Union cavalry in terms of men, horses, training and firepower. They could now stand on their own, on equal terms, against the enemy. Stanley gave credit for the success of the engagement at Shelbyville to the confidence and training of his cavalry.[42]

Minty's brigade had the most notable service during the Tullahoma Campaign even though Mitchell's division fulfilled its role well in the deception which allowed Rosecrans to maneuver Bragg's army away from Tullahoma. Meanwhile on the eastern flank, John Turchin still suffered the displeasure of David Stanley. He operated with a single brigade, Long's, and saw little action. In the single event in which he could have made an important contribution, he was unsuccessful. Rosecrans needed Stanley to capture the bridges across the Elk River to ensure he could pursue Bragg even if he could not trap him. Under Stanley's orders, Turchin started for Hillsboro and Mitchell's division rode for Manchester. The next day, it was confirmed the route of the Confederate retreat was not through Pelham, but through Estill Springs. Upon this discovery, Stanley ordered Turchin to ride to Decherd but Turchin's advance was blocked at Morris' Ford on the Elk River by a Confederate rearguard. Turchin riding with Long's brigade made up of mostly Ohio cavalry crossed the ford and attempted to hold the crossing, but enemy artillery forced the Ohioans to retreat to the north side of the river. On the opposite side of the river the 51st Alabama Partisan Rangers and the 25th and 26th Tennessee (CSA) infantries backed by Darden's Mississippi Battery held a strong position. Stanley dispatched Mitchell's cavalry to assist in the crossing, but Eli Long got his brigade across the river first and fought a determined rearguard action by Confederate cavalry as he advanced toward Decherd. Once Long crossed the ford, Turchin and Mitchell pressed their pursuit until nightfall and Stanley's cavalry claimed a Confederate colonel killed and a second mortally wounded, in addition to another twenty soldiers killed. John Allan Wyeth, 4th Alabama Cavalry, recalled that Wheeler had set a trap for Long's brigade which led the pursuit, but Long discovered and avoided the ambush.[43]

The reports by Turchin and Stanley fairly drip with the animosity felt between the two men. Stanley stated a simple crossing of the Elk River was not accomplished by Turchin. Stanley also made almost no reference to Turchin in his overall report, except this incident. Turchin lamented the fact that his cavalry brigade "… was scattered by battalions, under command of majors and lieutenant-colonels, on the front of the two army corps." Clearly, Stanley had not forgiven Turchin for abandoning him to die in the face of the enemy earlier in the spring.[44]

Turchin's reputation continued to suffer under the pen of T. F. Dornblaser, 7th Pennsylvania Cavalry, who noted Turchin decided to take a nap before attempting to push the Confederates from the ford at Elk River. "Here we halted for a few hours. Turchin took a nap in the shade of a tree. While he was napping, the writer saw the enemy on the south side of the river, placing a battery in position. The orderly felt it his duty to wake the general, and before a 'mad Dutchman' was done growling at the unnecessary interruption, the aforesaid battery opened fire, and dropped the shells in such close quarters as to cause the general and his staff to 'get up and dust.'" A member of the 3rd Ohio Cavalry also recorded Turchin's self-importance when his coffee pot was stolen on June 27, and the brigade waited as a member of Turchin's staff tried to find the culprit and the pot.[45]

Summary

During the last eleven months and three campaigns later, the Army of the Cumberland still faced an unbeaten and dangerous foe. Neither commander had drawn the other into a decisive battle and the two armies continued to slowly maneuver southward. At the conclusion of the Tullahoma Campaign, the Federal cavalry celebrated its successes. The two cavalry divisions reported only 89 casualties in the eleven-day campaign and many recognized that the Union cavalry, for the first time in the war, had gained parity with their Confederate adversaries. One nagging item dimmed the successes of Stanley's cavalry and this returns to the command issues between army headquarters and Stanley. For an unexplained reason, Rosecrans placed Mitchell's cavalry, and really much of the bulk of the Union cavalry, under the command of Gordon Granger early in the campaign. Historian Stephen Starr wrote: "Rosecrans may have become disenchanted with Stanley's performance as an adequately aggressive cavalry commander … or he may have decided that it would be convenient to have the commander of the infantry corps with which the cavalry was to work, control the operations of all three arms." Rosecrans' reason for doing this remains unclear. However, if Rosecrans was disenchanted with Stanley's aggressiveness, this campaign should have dispelled any concerns. Stanley pushed to lead the assault on Guy's Gap, desired to pursue Forrest, and forced Wheeler and Martin to swim a rain swollen river. The campaign revealed shackling Stanley to Granger actually resulted in less action by the cavalry. Once Bragg began his retreat, Stanley was again placed in a position to "work for Thomas" in the pursuit. This strongly suggested Rosecrans intended to put the cavalry at the disposal of his infantry corps commanders as situations changed in the campaign to achieve the desired result rather than a lack of confidence in Stanley. This pattern would continue in the upcoming Chickamauga Campaign. Despite all he had learned during the past eight months, Rosecrans reverted back to the old organization which Stanley had resisted when he assumed command of the cavalry. Perhaps Rosecrans wanted to improve communications and to offer mobility should it be immediately needed, but it took command away from the chief of cavalry. This mistake on the part of Rosecrans caused little problem during the Tullahoma Campaign, but restricting the command abilities of the chief of cavalry would prove to be problematic during the upcoming Chickamauga Campaign, and then later in the Atlanta Campaign.[46]

Three. The Confederate Cavalry—Worthy Adversaries

[A] thorough solider and gentle as a woman, and as courteous as a cavalier, of the olden time, he possessed the finest courage.—Colonel Baxter Smith

During the Tullahoma Campaign, the Confederate cavalry consisted of three divisions under Wheeler's (Wharton's and Martin's divisions) and Forrest's command. At the beginning of the campaign on June 20, Wheeler's divisions totaled 8,967 men and Forrest's division totaled 4,107 men. One of the most disappointing details about the Tullahoma Campaign was the absence of Confederate records. Neither Forrest, Wheeler, nor any other cavalry officers made official reports of the campaign. So, the details and observations from the Southern point of view are minimal. Even Bragg's report, if he wrote one, no longer exists. This was a campaign which might have been better forgotten, but the good news for the Confederate high command was the Army of Tennessee remained unbeaten. It still remained intact and a dangerous opponent.[1]

One of the surviving records from the Tullahoma Campaign was preserved by Lieutenant W. B. Richmond, aide-de-camp to General Leonidas Polk. Richmond preserved a message from William W. Mackall, Bragg's chief of staff, to Polk which recorded the cavalry action at Shelbyville: "Push on your trains at once with the greatest dispatch. Martin's cavalry has been utterly defeated before Shelbyville." Clearly, the success of Minty's cavalry reverberated through the Army of Tennessee. By July 5, Bragg's army had withdrawn from the area around Tullahoma and marched for Chattanooga, and Forrest's and Wheeler's cavalry provided rear-guard action for the retreating Confederate army.[2]

By July 7, 1863, Bragg began sending orders from Chattanooga and for the next two and a half months, the cavalry of the Confederate Army of Tennessee was divided with Forrest's command patrolling the Tennessee River from Kelly's Ford/Ferry (about ten miles west of Chattanooga) eastward and northward to Kingston and Wheeler's Cavalry Corps covering the area west and south of Kelly's Ford.[3]

Comparison of Union and Confederate Cavalry Commands—July 1863[4]

Confederate Command	Total (Present and Absent)	Union Command	Total (Present and Absent)
Wheeler's Corps	6,711	Mitchell's Division[a]	5,696
Forrest's Division	3,708	Crook's Division	5,187
Total	10,419	Total	10,883

[a]Includes Corps Command and Staff

Forrest's Division and Corps

In July 1863, Nathan Bedford Forrest commanded a cavalry division consisting of two brigades. Brigadier General Frank Armstrong commanded the First Brigade and Colonel Nicholas Cox commanded the Second Brigade. Forrest was a fighter. A native of Tennessee, Nathan Bedford Forrest was born on July 13, 1821, and turned forty-two years old in July 1863. He proved to be one of the most talented Confederate cavalry officers in the war, excelling at independent actions. Forrest made a living in the Mississippi Delta before the war and when the war began he enlisted and raised a regiment at his own expense. Forrest gained national attention when he refused to surrender his cavalry at Fort Donelson and he led his cavalry through Union lines rather than surrender. He participated in the Battle of Shiloh and had caused havoc to the Union armies in Tennessee and Mississippi since.[5]

Braxton Bragg was Forrest's commanding officer and the two men did not like each other. Forrest excelled in independent operations, but struggled under Bragg's command. Forrest gained Bragg's praise and recognition during the summer of 1863 when he forced Colonel Abel Streight to surrender in northern Alabama. However, Bragg twice before sent Forrest away the main concentration of his army. The first followed the Battle of Shiloh. Next, Forrest's cavalry accompanied Bragg's Army of Mississippi in the Kentucky Campaign, but in September 1862 Bragg ordered Forrest to return to Murfreesboro to organize the Confederate defense while Bragg marched through Kentucky. Bragg placed Forrest's brigade in Kentucky under the command of John Wharton while Wheeler commanded the other cavalry brigade attached to Bragg's army. While Forrest was promoted to the rank of brigadier general in July 1862, in September Wheeler still held the rank of colonel. As Forrest reassembled new troops in Murfreesboro, Bragg took the opportunity to promote Wheeler chief of cavalry of his army. Wheeler, Forrest's junior in rank, could not have reasonably been promoted if Forrest was present with the army. In regard to Forrest, John W. DuBose, Wheeler's biographer, described: "General Bragg did not appreciate Forrest; he did not like the man. Thus, about ten days after the capture of Munfordville, he ordered the cavalry leader, the ranking officer of that arm in his army, to turn his entire brigade, except four Alabama companies and his personal staff, over to Colonel Wharton ... and proceed with the four companies and his staff to Murfreesboro, there to organize a new brigade. The ostensible reason was that the enemy were moving out of Nashville in marauding expeditions." In return, Forrest had little regard for Bragg. In December 1862, Bragg placed Wheeler in position to work with the Army of Tennessee and ordered Forrest and John Hunt Morgan to attack the Federal communications and supply lines away from Middle Tennessee. Forrest demonstrated his independence by his reaction when Bragg sent a lieutenant of artillery to accompany the expedition. When the officer presented his orders to Forrest, he declared that Captain Samuel Freeman commanded his artillery and "I don't propose to be interfered with by Bragg." Forrest was determined to act independently and the recognition of this fact probably solidified Wheeler's position and Bragg's determination to send Forrest raiding the rear of the Union armies.[6]

To complicate matters in the Confederate cavalry, Wheeler commanded two cavalry brigades, including Forrest's, in an attack on a Union garrison at Dover, Tennessee on February 3, 1863. The Union troops held good defensive positions and after a seven-hour fight, the eight hundred Union soldiers successfully repulsed the Confederate attack. Forrest's criticism directly placed the blame on the botched attack on Wheeler's command abilities and he declared he would never serve under him again. The Southern force of 2,500 men attacked 800 Union troops during the battle and at the end of the day the Confederate losses totaled 670 compared to 126 for the Federal troops. The failure of the Confederate attack, and Forrest's dislike for Wheeler, caused Bragg to divide his cavalry command between Wheeler and Earl Van Dorn. Forrest would serve as second-in-command under Van Dorn; and as promised, he would not serve under Wheeler's command. Prior to the Tullahoma Campaign, Van Dorn commanded the cavalry on Bragg's left (west) flank while Wheeler worked on the right (east) flank. After Van Dorn was killed in May, Forrest commanded a cavalry division in middle Tennessee while Van Dorn's other division returned to Mississippi.[7]

Despite Bragg's dislike for Forrest, there was no denying the cavalry commander offered a formidable command which would stand its ground. Forrest commanded a cavalry division through the Tullahoma Campaign, July and most of August. Ambrose Burnside's Army of the Ohio acting in a loosely cooperative operation with Rosecrans after the Tullahoma Campaign advanced into East Tennessee. As a result, the Confederate Department of East Tennessee formally continued only in an administrative capacity in August but the military forces of Major General Simon B. Buckner fell under Bragg's command and were added to the Army of Tennessee. On August 28, Brigadier General John Pegram received orders to move his cavalry division to join Forrest's cavalry in a cooperative effort along the Tennessee River. Five days later on September 3, Pegram's division was added to Forrest's command which elevated Forrest to corps commander.[8]

Wheeler's Corps
Martin's Division
   First Brigade—Colonel James Hagan
   Second Brigade—Colonel Alfred A. Russell
Wharton's Division
   First Brigade—Colonel Charles C. Crews
   Second Brigade—Colonel Thomas Harrison
Morgan's Division (Not present)

Forrest's Corps
Armstrong's Division
   First Brigade—Colonel James T. Wheeler
   Second Brigade—Colonel George Dibrell
Pegram's Division (Effective Sept. 1863)
   First Brigade—General Henry B. Davidson
   Second Brigade—Colonel John Scott

Frank Armstrong's Division

Frank C. Armstrong commanded the First Brigade of Forrest's division in July. Armstrong, an experienced cavalry officer before the war, shared much of Forrest's ability to act decisively and independently. Armstrong was still very young, being born in November 1835, but his prewar experience in the First Dragoons in the U.S. Army made him an ideal commander in Forrest's cavalry. Armstrong was born in the Indian Territory, the son of an army officer, and upon the death of his father, his mother married General Persifor Smith. He completed his education at Holy Cross Academy in Massachusetts. Armstrong accompanied his stepfather on an expedition to New Mexico where he demonstrated his natural abilities which subsequently gained him a commission as lieutenant in the First Dragoons. He remained in the U.S. Army and even fought for the North during First Bull Run, but he subsequently resigned his commission and offered his talents to the Confederacy.[9]

Armstrong initially served on the staffs of General Ben McCulloch, Colonel James McIntosh and General Earl Van Dorn in Missouri and Arkansas. The Confederacy needed experienced officers and Armstrong soon gained command of the 3rd Louisiana Infantry. Next, he commanded a cavalry brigade in Sterling Price's army. His cavalry brigade saw active service during the Iuka and Corinth battles and his actions demonstrated an ability to fight and act independently. However, when ordered to carry out a reconnaissance expedition into Tennessee, Armstrong decided to conduct a raid rather than a reconnaissance which resulted in his repulse at Britton's Lane. His successes far outweighed this lapse, including a successful rearguard action after the Battle of Corinth. He received a promotion to the rank of brigadier general in 1862 and served in Forrest's division while providing commendable service in the winter and spring of 1863, most notably at the Union defeats at Thompson's Station and Brentwood.[10]

Armstrong's Division

ARMSTRONG'S BRIGADE—
Colonel John T. Wheeler

3rd Arkansas: Col. A. W. Hobson
2nd Kentucky: Lt. Col. Thomas G. Woodward
1st (6th) Tennessee: Lt. Col. James H. Lewis
18th Tennessee Battalion: Maj. Charles McDonald

FORREST'S BRIGADE—
Colonel George Dibrell

4th Tennessee: Col. William S. McLemore
8th Tennessee: Capt. Hamilton McGinnis
9th Tennessee: Col. Jacob B. Biffle
10th Tennessee: Col. Nicholas Nickleby Cox
11th Tennessee: Col. Daniel Wilson Holman
Shaw's Battalion, O. P. Hamilton's Battalion and R. D. Allison's Squadron (consolidated): Maj. Joseph Shaw
Huggins' (Tenn.) Battery: Capt. A. L. Huggins
Morton's (Tenn.) Battery: Capt. J. W. Morton, Jr.

Armstrong commanded his brigade through the Tullahoma Campaign and later during the retreat to Chattanooga. When Forrest added Pegram's division to his command, Armstrong was awarded command of a division. Armstrong's two brigade commanders were Colonel James T. Wheeler and Colonel George Dibrell. The thirty-seven-year-old Wheeler, a pre-war farmer from Giles County, Tennessee, assumed command of Armstrong's old brigade. Wheeler fought in the Mexican War and enlisted in the Confederate army in 1861, commanding the 1st (6th) Tennessee Cavalry. Next, Nathan Bedford Forrest's old brigade was commanded by George Dibrell. Dibrell was born in White County, Tennessee on April 12, 1822, and he was clerk and businessman until the beginning of hostilities of the Civil War. Dibrell opposed secession but followed his home state as the war began. He enlisted and was elected lieutenant colonel in the 25th Tennessee Infantry, and later he returned to White County to organize the 8th Tennessee Cavalry. The 8th Tennessee joined Forrest's command in September 1862 and Dibrell's performance since that time earned his promotion to brigade command.[11]

Brigadier General Frank Armstrong, born in the Indian Territory, initially served in Union Army before joining the Confederacy (Alabama Department of Archives and History).

John Pegram's Division

Brigadier General John Pegram, born in Virginia, January 24, 1832, was a handsome, almost ideal symbol of the South. He was the son of a prominent Virginia family of planters, and grew up in a family at the apex of the social hierarchy in Petersburg, Virginia. His grandfather was a major general in the War of 1812 and his father was also a general in the Virginia militia and a banker. When Pegram's father died, he assumed the patriarchal role in the family. John Pegram attended West Point, class of 1854, and subsequently served in the U.S. Dragoons on the western frontier. In 1857, he became an instructor of cavalry at the United States Military Academy. In 1858, he began two years-service observing military tactics and strategy in Europe. When he returned, he resumed his military duties in the U.S. Army. At the onset of the war, he resigned his commission and offered his services to the Confederate States of America. He was promoted to the rank of lieutenant colonel of the 20th Virginia Infantry and he assumed brigade command under Brigadier General Robert Garnett in Virginia. Pegram led his troops against William McClellan and William Rosecrans at the Battle of Rich Mountain where he surrendered and was subsequently imprisoned. He was later exchanged and served as chief of engineers in Bragg's army at Tupelo in July 1862. Next, he accepted a position as Kirby Smith's chief of staff before gaining command of a brigade of cavalry in November 1862 upon recognition of his service during the Kentucky campaign.[12]

Pegram's time with the Army of Tennessee was destined to be a troubling experience for him. A letter written by Sergeant Tucker St. Joseph Randolph, a Virginian serving in the Army of Tennessee, after Pegram assumed command, described: "Genl. Pegram has taken command of the Brigade. I think the command will like him though they were very much prejudiced against him." Controversy seemed to swirl around Pegram. In the Battle of Stones River, Pegram's brigade saw little action and historians have cast blame on him for poor reconnaissance. However, a more thorough examination of the records demonstrated that Pegram and his cavalry provided satisfactory duty during the battle. After the battle, another difficult campaign into Kentucky further alienated Pegram and John Scott, one of Pegram's brigade commanders. It was somewhat ironic that the Virginia gentleman soldier, and perhaps one the most experienced commanders in the Southern cavalry, struggled in the rough and tumble cavalry of the western theater.[13]

Brigadier General John Pegram commanded a cavalry division in Forrest's corps—The Virginia cavalryman in Tennessee and Georgia (Library of Congress).

Pegram's Division

DAVIDSON'S BRIGADE—
General Henry B. Davidson

1st Georgia: Col. James J. Morrison
6th Georgia: Col John R. Hart
6th North Carolina: Col. George N. Folk
Rucker's Tennessee Legion: Col. E. W. Rucker (12th Tennessee Battalion and 16th Tennessee Battalion)
10th Confederate: Col. C. T. Goode (detached from Scott's Brigade)
Huwald's (Tennessee) Battery: Capt. Gustave Huwald

SCOTT'S BRIGADE—
Colonel John S. Scott

Detachment of John H. Morgan's command:
   Lt. Col. R. M. Martin
1st Louisiana: Lt. Col. James O. Nixon
2nd Tennessee: Col. Henry M. Ashby
5th Tennessee: Col. George W. McKenzie
Robinson's (Louisiana) Battery (one section):
   Lt. Winslow Robinson

Brigadier General Henry Brevard Davidson commanded Pegram's First Brigade. Davidson, born on January 28, 1831, was appointed to the United States Military Academy from Tennessee and he graduated in 1853. He was commissioned lieutenant in the 1st U.S. Dragoons and served for two years at Jefferson Barracks in Missouri. Next, he served on the frontier at Fort Union in Albuquerque and later at Fort Stanton in New Mexico before traveling to Ft. Vancouver, Washington, then to Ft. Dalles, Oregon, in 1856, and finally to San Francisco, California, in 1857–58. His time on the frontier included several military clashes. As part of his pre-war experience service, he served as a quartermaster and when the Civil War began he initially served as a staff officer. While he served in Virginia, Davidson received his orders to assume his command in Tennessee on August 18, 1863. Pegram's other brigade commander was Colonel John Sims Scott, the first colonel of the 1st Louisiana Cavalry. John Scott was a controversial commander of the regiment and his actions at Athens, Alabama in May 1862 and at the Elk River caused much upheaval within the officer ranks of the regiment. Many believed Scott's orders were reckless which endangered the men and allowed the Union cavalry to successfully capture the ferry. As result of what was deemed to be Scott's incompetence, nine captains marched to P. T. Beauregard's headquarters in Corinth and preferred charges against Scott. But, Beauregard, displeased with the captains' actions of leaving their commands and riding to his headquarters, ordered the arrests of all the captains, except two, who were not with the regiment at that time, for abandoning their posts in the face of the enemy. Ultimately no charges were made against these officers and they returned to duty, but there was little doubt the command situation within this regiment was stressed.[14]

Colonel John S. Scott, 1st Louisiana Cavalry, "good judge of horse flesh, a bold rider and a brilliant shot" (Howell Carter, *Cavalryman's Reminiscences of the Civil War, 1900*).

The 1st Louisiana Cavalry joined in Bragg's and Smith's Kentucky Campaign where John Scott was rewarded with command of a cavalry brigade, but he was arrested for disobedience of orders during the retreat to Tennessee. Scott personally missed the Battle of Stones River and had been assigned to the Department of East Tennessee afterward. There, he clashed with his commanding officer, Pegram, and subsequently Pegram charged him with disobedience of orders in March 1863. Scott was court martialed, and later returned to duty. At the time of the Chickamauga Campaign, Scott was subordinate to Pegram and Forrest, and he seemed to continue his contentious personality. A member of his regiment wrote in regard to both of his commanding officers: "neither of whom he had any love for."[15]

The controversial John Sims Scott was a planter from East Feliciana Parish, Louisiana. Scott began the war serving in Magruder's cavalry in Virginia and then returned to Louisiana to raise a cavalry regiment from his home state. Despite his aggressive nature in the Confederate cavalry, Scott was known in Louisiana as "genial companion and intelligent gentleman, distinguished especially as a good judge of horse flesh, a bold rider and a brilliant shot." Scott's reputation within the army was one of concerns about his command ability and his quarrelsome nature toward other officers. Scott would remain a controversial member of the Confederate cavalry receiving the highest praise while his relations with others in the Confederate army resulted in volatiles exchanges.[16]

Wheeler's Cavalry Corps

When Bragg reached Chattanooga in July 1863, Wheeler had just ended his ninth month as commander of a division, and later a corps, of Confederate cavalry. Wheeler had a dismal experience during the Tullahoma Campaign. This followed a mixed performance by Wheeler at the Battle of Stones River. Early in 1863, Wheeler commanded Bragg's expanded cavalry on the eastern flank of the Confederate army at Tullahoma while Van Dorn/Forrest covered the western flank. During the Tullahoma Campaign, Wheeler's corps struggled to deal with the revitalized Union cavalry and infantry. Of course, Minty's victory at Shelbyville dramatically boosted the morale of the Federal cavalry after shattering Martin's division. After the campaign, Wheeler's cavalry was so worn down that much of his command had to spend the next two months recuperating.[17]

Joseph Wheeler was born in Augusta, Georgia on September 10, 1836, the youngest son of Joseph and Julia Wheeler. His parents were native New Englanders who had moved to Georgia after the War of 1812. The senior Joseph Wheeler had been a merchant, banker and landowner but had lost most of the family's wealth in the Panic of 1837. Afterwards, the younger Wheeler was sent to Connecticut to complete his education while living with two of his aunts. At seventeen, he graduated and received an appointment to West Point on June 8, 1854, most likely through the influence of the Wheeler family and extended family. But, Wheeler's experience at West Point was not a success. His biographer wrote that Wheeler had "a rather dismal record at the Academy, one that started poorly, and then went downhill." Wheeler performed poorly in just about all areas of study, but he was not disruptive and recorded no large number of demerits. Neither was Wheeler one to excel in sports. He received the nickname "Point" because of his small stature and because he had "neither length, breadth, nor thickness." Wheeler was just an introvert, but one which was recognized as gentlemanly and quiet. He graduated 19 in a class of 22 in 1859 in a class in which he was the only one to achieve recognition for military success.[18]

Upon graduation, Wheeler was initially appointed lieutenant in the First U.S. Dragoons, but after the completion of his training for mounted duty at Carlisle Barracks, he was assigned to the Mounted Riflemen at Fort Craig in the New Mexico Territory. On the way to his new posting in 1860, he was assigned to duty as escort to a wagon carrying a surgeon and the pregnant wife of an army officer. When the woman went into labor, Wheeler, the doctor and the teamster remained behind the column to deliver the child. Immediately after giving birth, an Indian war party attacked the small group. Wheeler charged the party, firing a carbine which was immediately discarded, and attacked with his Colt revolver, supported by the teamster. He successfully drove off the attacking Indians. Because of his aggressive action, he lost the nickname "Point" which was replaced by "Fightin' Joe," a name which remained with him for the remainder of his life.[19]

Wheeler had a relatively quiet life in his short stay at Fort Craig. The fires of rebellion were burning in the east and Wheeler faced a life changing decision. Although he had connections to the South, he also had connections in the North. Wheeler's home state of Georgia followed the other Southern states of South Carolina, Mississippi, Florida and Alabama and voted for secession on January 19, 1861. Wheeler's brother, William, immediately began organizing an artillery battery and interceded with authorities in Georgia for a commission for Joseph. On February 27, Wheeler offered his resignation to the United States Army and traveled to Georgia to take up arms against his country as a lieutenant in an artillery battery in the Confederacy. He was initially assigned to Pensacola where the Southern troops were commanded by Braxton Bragg, and shortly thereafter, he was given command of the 19th Alabama Infantry in Mobile in September 1861.[20]

Wheeler was a dedicated and diligent commander of the new regiment and worked tirelessly to make the 19th Alabama a premier fighting unit. In February 1862, Wheeler's regiment joined Albert Sidney Johnston's army at Jackson, Tennessee. During the Battle of Shiloh, the months of training paid off for the 19th Alabama which maintained its integrity and cohesion throughout the battle. In July, Wheeler assumed command of a cavalry brigade and began to organize his troops which were scattered across a large geographic area without much organization. His 1,000-man brigade consisted of Colonel William "Red" Jackson's, Col. W. F. Slemons', Colonel R. A. Pinson's and Lieutenant Colonel William B. Wade's cavalry regiments. Based on his experience, Wheeler concluded to utilize his cavalry primarily as mounted infantry. One of his initial efforts was a raid through Union-held outposts at Grand Junction, Bolivar and Middleburg, destroying supplies, and communications along his path.[21]

Next, Wheeler, a mere 5'5" and 120 pounds, was ordered to eastern Tennessee in August in preparation for Bragg's Kentucky Campaign and ultimately Wheeler's and Wharton's brigades performed duty during the Battle of Perryville and then returned to Middle Tennessee. Wheeler's promotion to chief of cavalry was based on Bragg's assessment of his ability to train and lead cavalry. Colonel Baxter Smith wrote of Wheeler: "[A] thorough solider and gentle as a woman, and as courteous as a cavalier, of the olden time, he possessed the finest courage." Bragg saw in Wheeler a commander who could adapt to rapidly changing situations, one who was serious and dedicated, and a commander that followed orders. Certainly, Wheeler's West Point education was appreciated by Bragg, and with Bragg's tendency to alienate others, he needed a commander loyal to him. He believed Wheeler was such a commander. One of Wheeler's biographers wrote: "He never displayed the audacity and flash of

Forrest and Stuart, but in performing the true functions of cavalry attached to the flanks of an army he was unsurpassed." Wheeler was well-liked by his troopers and he often shared camps and food with them. Sir Arthur Fremantle, a British military observer, traveled with the Confederate army in 1863 and described Wheeler as a "little man" but a very "zealous officer."[22]

John Wharton's Division

Brigadier General John A. Wharton was Wheeler's most aggressive division commander. Wharton served as brigade commander with Wheeler during the Perryville Campaign and the Battle of Stones River. He was born a short distance from Nashville on July 3, 1828, when his parents were on a shopping trip to buy furnishings for their plantation in Texas. He was the only son of William H. and Saran Ann Wharton. William Wharton was an attorney who moved to Texas in 1827, and his son, John Wharton, grew up on a plantation, Eagle Island, between the Brazos River and Oyster Creek and only twelve miles from the Gulf of Mexico. He was privately educated in the home of his uncle, and when he was fifteen he went to Columbia, South Carolina to complete his education, which he did at the age of twenty. While at Columbia, Wharton read law under William C. Preston, a noted South Carolina attorney. Wharton's support of states' rights was solidified during his time in that state and determined his political position as the Civil War began. While studying law, John A. Wharton met and later married Penelope Johnson, the only daughter of the governor of South Carolina, in 1848. Wharton and his bride moved to Texas where Wharton completed his legal training and became an attorney. He was active in the secession of Texas, and he was credited with introducing the resolution calling for Texas to leave the Union.[23]

Wharton enlisted in the 8th Texas Cavalry, also called Terry's Texas Rangers, and was elected captain of a company. The regiment moved to Bowling Green, Kentucky after its organization and Wharton fell ill to a severe case of measles. When Colonel B. F. Terry was killed in Kentucky, Wharton became colonel of the regiment. Wharton was severely wounded in his leg at the Battle of Shiloh and again wounded in the fighting at Murfreesboro in July 1862. Wharton had commendable service during the Battle of Stones River early on the morning of December 31, only to be repulsed later in the morning by fragments of the Union cavalry and again on January 1 at the hands of 1st Michigan Engineers and Mechanics. Wharton was aggressive and ambitious. He wanted higher rank and was an important rival for Wheeler.

Brigadier General John Wharton, cavalry division commander in the Army of Tennessee, was aggressive, effective and ambitious (Alabama Department of Archives and History).

Wheeler's less than stellar performance during the recent campaigns convinced Wharton he should be commanding the cavalry corps.[24]

Wharton's Division

FIRST BRIGADE—Colonel C. C. Crews	SECOND BRIGADE—Col. Thomas Harrison
7th Alabama: Col. J. C. Malone, Jr.	3d Confederate: Col. W. N. Estes
2d Georgia: Lt. Col. F. M. Ison	1st [3rd] Kentucky: Col. J. R. Butler
3d Georgia: Lt. Col. R. Thompson	4th [5th] Tennessee: Lt. Col. P. F. Anderson
4th Georgia: Col. L W. Avery	8th Texas: Lt. Col. Gustave Cook
	11th Texas: Lieut. Col. J. M. Bounds
	Tennessee Battery: Capt. B. F. White, Jr.

Charles Constantine Crews was a pre-war physician who helped organize the 2nd Georgia Cavalry. He served as lieutenant, captain, lieutenant colonel and finally colonel of the regiment; and in the fall of 1862, he was captured at Glasgow, Kentucky. Crews was exchanged within a month of his capture and he returned to his regiment. After the Battle of Stones River, he is given command of a brigade of cavalry. He was wounded in the hip during the Battle of Dover in February 1863 and commanded the First Brigade during the Tullahoma Campaign. Colonel Thomas Harrison commanded the Second Cavalry Brigade under Wharton's command. John Wharton, the late colonel of the 8th Texas Cavalry, was appointed to brigade command in the fall of 1862 and Colonel Thomas Harrison assumed command of the 8th Texas regiment in December 1862. Harrison led one of three cavalry wings in the Battle of Stones River under Wharton's command. After the battle at Murfreesboro, Harrison received a permanent assignment as brigade commander and commanded a brigade during the Tullahoma Campaign. Harrison, born in 1823 in Alabama, moved to Texas in 1843. He lived in Waco at the outset of the war; and Harrison was described as "of a somewhat grumpy disposition, at times irascible, and not easily understood. He got off to a rather slow start in gaining confidence of the men." Harrison won the confidence of the men when he led a cavalry charge during the Battle of Shiloh, and troopers agreed: "He was a worthy successor of Wharton."[25]

William Martin's Division

William "Will" T. Martin was a Kentucky native, born in Glasgow on March 25, 1823. Martin graduated from Centre College in Kentucky and moved to Natchez, Mississippi where he was admitted to the bar in Mississippi. He opposed secession, but he organized a company of cavalry and joined the war in Virginia. His company became part of the 2nd Mississippi Cavalry Battalion and Martin was elected to the rank of major. The battalion subsequently became part of the Jefferson Davis Legion and Martin was promoted to the rank of lieutenant colonel in February 1862. While serving in Virginia, Martin participated in the Peninsula Campaign, Stuart's ride around McClellan's army in June 1862, and the Maryland Campaign. Martin, having performed well under J.E.B. Stuart's command in Virginia, received a promotion to the rank of brigadier general in December 1862 and in March 1863 he was transferred west to division command in Wheeler's corps. Martin made an initial positive impact with his actions in the west, but he was handily defeated at Shelbyville during the recent Tullahoma Campaign by Minty's Federal cavalry.[26]

Martin's Division[27]

HAGAN'S BRIGADE—*John T. Morgan*
1st Alabama: Maj. A. H. Johnson
3d Alabama: Lt. Col. T.H. Mauldin
51st Alabama: Capt. M. L. Kirkpatrick
8th Confederate: Capt. J. H. Field

RUSSELL'S BRIGADE—*Colonel A. A. Russell*
4th Alabama: Lt. Col. J. M. Hambrick
1st Confederate: Capt. C. H. Conner
Wiggins' (Arkansas) Battery: Lt. A. A. Blake

Note: John Hunt Morgan's division was on detached duty

John Tyler Morgan commanded the 51st Alabama Partisan Rangers when he joined the cavalry. Morgan, a native of Athens, Tennessee, was born in 1824, the son of a merchant. His family moved to Calhoun County, Alabama when he was nine years old. He prepared for a career as an attorney by studying law at a private school in Tuskegee under the guidance of the Honorable William P. Chilton. He began practicing law in 1845 and in 1855 he moved to Dallas County, Alabama where he settled in the community of Cahaba. Morgan participated in the Alabama state constitutional convention that decided upon Alabama's secession from the Union. In April 1861, he enlisted for twelve months and was elected as major in the 5th Alabama Infantry. He spent his time with the 5th Alabama in Virginia and returned to his home state with authority to raise a mounted regiment. He successfully raised, and personally helped to equip, the 51st Alabama Partisan Rangers in the fall of 1862. After the Battle of Stones River, Morgan gained command of a cavalry brigade and was promoted to the rank of brigadier general in June. Colonel A[lfred]. A[lexander]. Russell commanded the other brigade in Martin's division. Russell, like Charles Crews, was a pre-war physician and when

Left: **Colonel John Tyler Morgan commanded the First Brigade of Martin's cavalry division (Alabama Department of Archives and History).**
Right: **Colonel James Hagan, 3rd Alabama Cavalry—"An imposing figure, a notable horseman" (Library of Congress).**

the war began he enlisted in the 7th Alabama Infantry. He was elected major in the regiment, but after the Battle of Shiloh he transferred to the cavalry and gained command of the 4th Alabama Cavalry. After the Battle of Stones River, Russell became a brigade commander in Martin's division.[28]

Roddey's Brigade

Brigadier General Philip Dale Roddey's cavalry brigade patrolled northern Alabama and when Bragg moved to Chattanooga, Wheeler gained command of Roddey's cavalry. Roddey was born Moulton, Alabama in 1820. Roddey had various trades before the war including tailor and sheriff, and he finally settled on the occupation of a steam boatman on the Tennessee River. When the Civil War began, Roddey organized a company of mounted men and entered the war. Roddey's men initially performed scouting duty and received Bragg's praise for their actions at Shiloh. After that battle, Roddey acted as detached cavalry in a partisan role with orders to strike the enemy whenever possible. By the close of 1862, Roddey maintained his position at Tuscumbia with his cavalry regiment. His cavalry saw action at Tuscumbia in February and at Columbia, Tennessee in March 1863. He also found a strong force under the command Brigadier General Grenville Dodge, which participated in the failed Abel Streight's raid, and fought it stubbornly during its advance to Courtland. Soon afterward, he was promoted to the rank of brigadier general and gained command of three cavalry regiments, one unorganized regiment, and Ferrell's Georgia Battery. While Roddey's brigade remained in northern Alabama, it provided additional manpower and protected the far west flank of Bragg's army, and he was available to be called upon to join in cavalry operations near Chattanooga.[29]

Cavalry in the District of Northern Alabama

RODDEY'S BRIGADE—Brig. Gen. P. D. Roddey

5th Alabama Cavalry: Col. Josiah Patterson
53d Alabama Cavalry: Col. M. W. Harmon
Roddey's Cavalry Regiment: Lieut. Col. W. A. Johnson
Unorganized troops: Capt. W. R. Julian
Georgia Battery: Capt. C. B. Ferrell

Confederate Cavalry After the Tullahoma Campaign

After the Tullahoma Campaign, the Confederate cavalry moved to the complex mountainous terrain which surrounded Chattanooga. These troopers rode in their own country and believed they faced an invading army which would show no mercy on those supporting the rebellion. They tirelessly sought to block their foes at every step. Undefeated, their will to fight remained strong. The lack of mounts, equipment and arms plagued the Confederate cavalry and would throughout the war. Cavalry was an expensive prospect during the Civil War, but it remained an indispensable component in the strategy to thwart the advances of the Northern armies.

Within the cavalry, the two cavalry corps commanders had issues of their own. Nathan

Bedford Forrest, during the time of the Civil War and perhaps more so today, carried an almost holy persona for those in the South. He was relentless, he was merciless, and he won battles. This description should be tempered with the acknowledgment that Forrest's greatest accomplishments in the war at this point occurred through his exemplary independent actions. Forrest's partisan-like and raider abilities made him a cherished figure in the South, but the ability to cooperate and work in unison with the rest of the large Army of Tennessee, and particularly with Bragg, had yet to be fully tested. Working on the Confederate right flank in conjunction with infantry corps on mundane reconnaissance and security duty would be challenging to Forrest. He needed to hone new skills and put these to work as the Army of the Cumberland began its march toward Chattanooga.

Forrest, who did not like Braxton and Bragg in return did not like Forrest, seemed to realize he now held a position unsuitable to him. As a result, Forrest wrote to General Samuel Cooper, Adjutant General of the Confederate Army in Richmond, on August 9 with a request that would release him from his duties with Army of Tennessee and allow him to use his more natural talents. Forrest told Cooper he had been contacted by many friends and important figures in western Tennessee and northern Mississippi who requested his services to fight in that geography. Forrest proposed to take just 400 men of his current command and be given the authority to operate between Cairo and Vicksburg. He further wrote he would be able to enlist between 5,000 and 10,000 men, and with this command he could stop river traffic and cause havoc to the Federal communications and supply lines. He closed by saying he only desired this for the good of the service, but that he lived in this area before the war and would make an immediate and dramatic impact with this new command. So, while there were some concerns about Forrest's command abilities in the association with the Army of Tennessee, Forrest seemed desirous of his own removal; but Bragg refused to allow him to leave even when Forrest went over Bragg's head and appealed directly to Richmond. Before the completion of the new campaign Forrest would be granted his request, but not in the manner in which he hoped.[30]

In regard to Joseph Wheeler, many in the Army of Tennessee liked the diminutive cavalry corps commander. He was quiet, thoughtful, and brave to a fault. But, there were nagging issues lingering about Wheeler which remained from the Battle of Stones River and the recent Tullahoma Campaign. At Stones River, Wheeler chose to act as a brigade commander and led a raid around the rear of Rosecrans's army in fulfillment of the "raiding strategy" of the Confederate Army. While he remained away on the raid much of the cavalry battle occurred on the Union right flank without his presence. When he arrived on the battlefield, David Stanley's and Robert Minty's outnumbered cavalry sent Wheeler's brigade to the rear. Finally, in regard to the very important and necessary reconnaissance on January 1 and 3, Wheeler missed on both occasions and delivered the wrong assessment of the Union army's situation. Wheeler appeared to do no better during the Tullahoma Campaign, being fooled into believing the thrust of the Federal army was directed at Shelbyville. He was ingloriously defeated at Shelbyville by Minty's cavalry and had to take to a rain-swollen river to avoid capture. The last nine months had been difficult ones for Wheeler, but he still had Braxton Bragg's support. Bragg who was faced with a group of subordinates desirous of his removal appreciated Wheeler and he supported him. The new campaign was of upmost importance to the still very young Wheeler as he tried to improve his command abilities.[31]

Part 2—The Advance on Chattanooga

Four. The Two Armies Prepare for the Campaign (July 5–August 15)

> *Our gallant boys raised the yell as they poured volley after volley into them.*—Colonel George Dibrell

In July, both the Union and Confederate commanders focused on Chattanooga, a town with a peace-time population of 2,500. Before the war, the town had been a prosperous, active commercial center with an increasing population. Chattanooga served as a strategic center for transportation for the Confederacy, and the Union high command had its sights on Chattanooga as a critical part of the overall strategy to isolate the Deep South from Virginia. To the north lay Knoxville and Cumberland Gap and the Confederate Department of East Tennessee with troops under the command of Major General Simon Bolivar Buckner. To the east lay North Carolina and the opportunity for the Union armies to cut Lee's army in Virginia from the rest of the South. To the south was Atlanta and Montgomery in the heart of the Confederacy. Important railroads ran through Chattanooga connecting the various parts of the Confederacy and the location was vitally important for the transport of supplies, raw materials and food from one section of the South to another. Chattanooga offered many excellent defensive positions because the mountain gaps and narrow roads could be easily defended with an economy of troops. The Union army risked congestion in its movement if Rosecrans chose to keep his army concentrated. If Rosecrans decided to disperse his command and move independently over the various mountain passes and roads, then Bragg had the opportunity to defeat the Union army in detail. The key factor which faced the armies in the Chickamauga Campaign was the terrain—the all-important and difficult variable which could hide an enemy and result in disaster for the unwary. For the cavalry, a more unsuitable geographic area was hard to imagine. The challenge of maneuvering, scouting and fighting by large bodies of mounted men proved difficult for both sides.[1]

Gloom fell like a pall over the Army of Tennessee after the Tullahoma Campaign. Bragg was a weary general and a man with many problems. He retreated from Tullahoma to Chattanooga after the recent campaign as a broken man. In addition to the many problems he had with his army, he was physically a wreck to such an extent that he continued on to Ringgold, Georgia and entered a hospital. Bragg had a history of maladies that plagued him, including stomach problems and migraine headaches. In the spring and summer of 1863, he added boils to the headaches and chronic diarrhea, and the added stress of the recent Tullahoma Campaign proved too much for the Southern general who was appearing even more cadaverous than usual. If his health problems were not enough, he continued to be to an unpopular general with his subordinates, an unpopularity which continued to increase after the Perryville Campaign almost a year earlier. Polk and Hardee, Bragg's two most important infantry corps commanders, had long since wearied of Bragg's command, and in 1863 Bragg had added John C. Breckinridge, Benjamin Cheatham, William Preston, as well as others, to the list of those commanders who mistrusted their commanding general. By mid–July, Lieutenant General Daniel Harvey Hill arrived in Chattanooga to assume command of William Hardee's infantry corps in the Army of Tennessee and Hill immediately became disturbed by the conditions of his new army. The Confederate army had retreated to Chattanooga and without a fight forfeited almost all the territory west of the town to the Union army, should it decide to continue the pursuit of the Army of Tennessee. In Hill's opinion, the energetic and organized armies in the east contrasted greatly with the army at Chattanooga. In his eyes, his new command contemplated only one thing—defense.[2]

Bragg's retreat and the low morale of his army would prove helpful to the Army of the Cumberland. Even the defense Bragg prepared in Chattanooga did little to ameliorate D. H. Hill's concerns about giving up the territory west of the Tennessee River. Hill's corps had been ordered into position on the eastern flank of the army and extended northward to Loudon and Polk's corps remained near Chattanooga. Only Brigadier General Patton Anderson's brigade maintained position at Shellmound, about fifteen miles west of Chattanooga, from which to observe the movement of the Union army. On July 15, Anderson reported the Confederate defenses at the various crossings of the Tennessee River—"I find that there is a guard of 52 men at Running Water Bridge, 1 mile west of Whiteside Station, furnished from Brigadier-General Jackson's command; also, a guard of 13 men at bridge over Lookout Creek, and one of [only] 11 men at Chattanooga Creek, near the city of Chattanooga." Should Rosecrans pursue Bragg, there were frightfully few Confederate soldiers to contest a crossing of the Tennessee River.[3]

In addition to Bragg's Army of Tennessee retreating to Chattanooga, Major General Simon Bolivar Buckner commanded the Confederate forces headquartered at Knoxville in the Department of East Tennessee. Not only did Rosecrans threaten Bragg, Ambrose Burnside, commanding the recently resurrected Army of the Ohio, had orders to march on Knoxville. The Union high command reasoned two Federal armies descending on East Tennessee would effectively remove the resistance there. This two-pronged advance into East Tennessee caused Buckner's troops to be placed under the command of Bragg so that a coordinated defense could be prepared. The threat to Knoxville as well as Chattanooga added to the concerns of Bragg.[4]

The railroad, such a critically important part of Rosecrans' strategy, aided the retreat of the Army of Tennessee to Chattanooga. Bragg's retreat from Tullahoma proved so effective that Wheeler's cavalry had moved to Bridgeport, Alabama by July 5 and by July 22, Wheeler made his headquarters at Gadsden, Alabama, eighty miles southeast of Huntsville and about 120 miles from Chattanooga. In only seven days, Bragg moved his entire army from Tullahoma to their positions around Chattanooga. In addition, Phillip Roddey's cavalry extended even farther west into Alabama. Joseph Wheeler contemplated his situation along the west flank in mid–July and devised a plan to prevent damage to the areas in the rear of the army. Upon reaching Chattanooga, the generals in the Confederate army wisely foresaw the threat to areas in the rear—Atlanta and Rome, Georgia. Wheeler recommended increasing the defenses at these locations and others. Two months before Rosecrans would order a raid on Rome, the Confederate high command had already considered the threat and moved to protect the railroad running from Atlanta to Chattanooga. Wheeler wrote that it was important to plan for an attack on Rome and Atlanta now. He wanted a contingent of Confederate troops, supplemented by state and local troops to defend the railroad and bridges between Bragg's army at Chattanooga and Atlanta. He knew that Rome was a very important position along the link and he believed that a large force of troops, in particular a division of cavalry, needed to be stationed there. Wheeler explained that a system of stockades or blockhouses would aid in the defense and that in the event a raid did occur, all the troops along the rail system would be mobilized and moved to defend against an attack. He concluded: "The moral effect of fortifications and artillery in position would be very beneficial in deterring raids." With this plan, he correctly anticipated Rosecrans's desire to attack Rome two months hence and at the same time, justified sending John Wharton's division to Rome to rest after months of hard campaigning. As a result, Will Martin's division of Confederate cavalry remained near Wheeler's headquarters while Wharton's division moved to Rome to recuperate while remounting his division.[5]

The Politics of War

Rosecrans' delay in mounting an aggressive pursuit should have been intriguing to Bragg and also an opportunity for the Army of Tennessee. By July 19, Confederate scouts reported that the full extent of the Union pursuit amounted to Federal cavalry probing forward and along the flanks and infantry working on repairing the railroad. Certainly, the Tullahoma Campaign was wet and an exhausting ten days, but the Confederates expected an active pursuit which didn't come. Rosecrans did contemplate a pursuit of the Confederate army by sending his cavalry to destroy the Memphis and Charleston Railroad. Rosecrans planned for Stanley to lead his cavalry over the Tennessee River near Bridgeport, Alabama and sever the railroad connecting Chattanooga to Huntsville and Decatur. Rosecrans cancelled the raid when General Phil Sheridan reported that the bridge over the Tennessee River at Bridgeport had been destroyed, effectively preventing the cavalry from crossing. Rosecrans simply concluded without the bridges in place the effort would be futile.[6]

Instead of pursuing Bragg, Rosecrans settled his army around Middle Tennessee. The Nashville and Chattanooga Railroad was a critical source of communications and supplies for his army and he set his infantry and engineers the task of making it operational. Rosecrans desperately needed the rails as he contemplated his next advance on Bragg's army. Fortunately, when Bragg retreated he did not destroy the Cumberland Mountain Tunnel, an important link in keeping the supplies moving south through the mountains. In addition, as the Union troops moved forward along the railroad they found the Confederate cavalry did not burn all the railroad bridges leading to the Tennessee River, leaving several still intact. However, the roads in the trail of the Army of Tennessee remained in terrible condition because of the excessive rains in July and Rosecrans chose to improve the rail systems and allow the roads to dry before contemplating another advance.[7]

While Bragg had trouble with his health and his subordinates, William Rosecrans had problems of his own. Almost immediately after the end of the Tullahoma Campaign, the ill

Four. The Two Armies Prepare for the Campaign (July 5–August 15)   65

will between Washington and Rosecrans began again. Rosecrans proudly wired Halleck about his victory at Tullahoma, but Bragg's army had again escaped destruction. Washington wanted more action from Rosecrans and they wanted it quickly. Those in Washington had lost their patience with Rosecrans after the six-month delay after the Battle of Stones Rivers and repeatedly demanded that he advance on Bragg. Although Rosecrans had just maneuvered Bragg out of Middle Tennessee, Washington had little confidence that Rosecrans would aggressively pursue and battle Bragg. Secretary of War Henry Stanton revealed his thoughts about Rosecrans when General Lovell Rousseau and Colonel J. P. Sanderson traveled to Washington to discuss with Stanton and Halleck the plan of re-enlisting veterans. Stanton was overheard stating he would rather they had asked to command the Army of the Cumberland themselves. Making reference to Rosecrans, he said, "He shall not have another damned man." Rosecrans had exhausted the patience of his superiors.[8]

Although Rosecrans had a good series of victories, his delays caused more frustration in Washington and this frustration was enhanced by the equally tardy movement of Ambrose Burnside's Army of the Ohio which was causing problems of its own. The overall strategy from Washington envisioned two strong Union armies marching into East Tennessee. While Rosecrans dealt with his own political issues, he faced both the Army of Tennessee and potentially the Confederate forces of Buckner in the Confederate Department of East Tennessee. Ambrose Burnside's army was supposed to be acting in conjunction with Rosecrans and alleviating some of the pressure from his left flank, but Burnside also delayed. Henry Halleck wrote to Rosecrans on July 13 that he had urged Burnside to move forward and cover Rosecrans' left flank while pushing toward Knoxville. Halleck impotently declared: "I do not know what he is doing. He seems tied fast to Cincinnati." Despite Burnside's tardiness, Halleck demanded Rosecrans move forward.[9]

Rosecrans' primary concern focused on the supply line from Nashville to his army and he determined not to move until he was ready. This delay set off another series of demands from Washington to move, but Rosecrans remained in Middle Tennessee for six weeks as he prepared his army for another move against Bragg. On July 24, Henry Halleck wrote to Rosecrans stating: "You must not wait for Johnston to join Bragg, but must move forward.... There is great disappointment felt here at the slowness of your advance. Unless you can move more rapidly, your whole campaign will prove a failure, and you will have both Bragg and Johnston against you." In a personal and confidential letter to Rosecrans, Halleck, in the role of offering personal advice to a friend, urged, "[Y]our army should remain no longer inactive. The patience of the authorities here has been completely exhausted, and if I had not repeatedly promised to urge you forward, and begged for delay, you would have been removed from the command. It has been said that you are as inactive as was General Buell and the pressure for your removal has been almost as strong as it has been in his case." The fact that some congressional elections would be held in November certainly had an impact on those in Washington.[10]

Rosecrans responded to Halleck on July 25 about the concerns in Washington regarding the lack of progress of his army and he believed he was justified due to the obstacles he faced. To Halleck's credit, he knew the low regard many in Washington held for Rosecrans and he knew if Rosecrans wanted to remain in command, he needed to move. After receiving Rosecrans' reply of July 25, he gave up his attempt to advise Rosecrans to begin an advance and simply wrote that he would not again refer to this matter. From Rosecrans's standpoint, he faced thirty miles of the Cumberland Mountains between Tullahoma and the Tennessee River. This was barren ground with little hope as a source of forage for his army or his animals. He needed to rely on the Nashville and Chattanooga Railroad for his supplies which amounted to sixty rail cars per day for the army. Before Rosecrans could realistically advance, as Washington urged, this lifeline needed to be secure and fully operational. Rosecrans wanted to repair the railroad to Bridgeport to support any advance made on the other side of the river by the Army of the Cumberland. Next, there were ferries and fords along the Tennessee River that were guarded, Rosecrans believed, with detachments of Confederate infantry. In preparation of an advance, Rosecrans sent parts of his army forward. Alexander McCook sent three regiments to Stevenson and Major General Philip Sheridan approached Bridgeport with a construction train on July 19. The 2nd Tennessee Cavalry (U.S.) worked with McCook's corps to protect the existing bridges and rails from further damage near Bridgeport.[11]

Lieutenant John Andes, 2nd Tennessee Cavalry, recorded in his diary that his regiment passed Sheridan's infantry division on July 11 and became the first Union troops over the Cumberland Mountains screening the Federal advance. The Tennessee cavalry discovered the bridge over the Tennessee River at Bridgeport had been destroyed and the cavalry began scouting the area for lingering Confederates. The regiment was active at Caperton's Ferry near Stevenson, Alabama on July 26 and occupied the attention of the Confederates on the other side of the river. As a result, Patton Anderson ceased using a steam boat near Bridgeport when the Union advance reached the river. Anderson wrote: "A small party of the enemy's cavalry made a dash this morning about 10 o'clock at the steamer *Paint Rock*, while loading at Bridgeport, but was quickly repulsed by the company of sharpshooters…." Despite the fact no damage was done to the steamer, Anderson ordered the boat away from the area and back to Chattanooga. The cavalry returned the next morning, found the steamer gone and exchanged a few shots with the enemy across the river.[12]

By July 23, Rosecrans knew that Bragg's Army held Chattanooga and Forrest's cavalry stretched northeast from Chattanooga, and Wheeler's cavalry extended southwest of Chattanooga. In fact, Wheeler's cavalry was positioned on the left flank of Bragg's army from Chattanooga along the Tennessee River and extending as far west as Decatur, Alabama. Forrest's cavalry held the right flank and stretched from Chattanooga toward Kingston, Tennessee. In regard to the Confederate expectation of Rosecrans' pursuit, they needed patience because Rosecrans remained stationary across Middle Tennessee. He positioned his army with Thomas' XIV Corps at Decherd, and Alexander McCook's XX Corps had headquarters at Winchester. David Stanley moved his cavalry headquarters

Major General Alexander McCook, a classmate of David Stanley at West Point, commanded XX Corps during the Chickamauga Campaign (National Archives).

Four. The Two Armies Prepare for the Campaign (July 5–August 15)

to Salem and Robert Mitchell's cavalry division was at Fayetteville. Major General Thomas Crittenden, whose XXI Corps headquarters was at Manchester, had three divisions nearby and one division at McMinnville. Soon good news arrived for the Union army, the railroad was open and carrying supplies, to Bridgeport and Tracy City, and the engineers planned to send pontoons forward.[13]

Union Cavalry Activities in July

While Rosecrans and those in Washington argued about the next advance on Bragg, the Union cavalry remained busy with the day-to-day activities. Immediately after the Tullahoma Campaign, Stanley concentrated his cavalry near Salem, Tennessee (about ten miles southwest of Winchester). On July 8, Stanley reorganized the First Cavalry Division to include a third brigade. While no new cavalry regiments joined the corps, Colonel Louis D. Watkins assumed command of the Third Cavalry Brigade which consisted of the 4th, 5th, 6th, and 7th Kentucky cavalries. Watkins, who would marry the daughter of Major General Lovell Rousseau the following year, positioned his cavalry at Winchester. Less than a month later, a third brigade was added to the Second Division, commanded by Colonel William Lowe of the 5th Iowa Cavalry. Lowe's new brigade included the 5th Tennessee, 5th Iowa, and 10th Ohio cavalries.[14]

Left: Colonel William W. Lowe, a regular army cavalry officer before the war, commanded a newly formed cavalry brigade in Crook's division (Mollus Mass Civil War Collection, United States Army Heritage and Education Center, Military History Institute, Carlisle, Pennsylvania).
Right: Colonel Louis Watkins, severely wounded in the Battle of Gaines Mill, gained command of a newly formed cavalry brigade in July (Library of Congress).

For the Union cavalry, the ten-day Tullahoma Campaign of continuous rainfall and the subsequent mud had taken a toll on horses and men. After Stanley had time to fully appraise the condition of the cavalry, he summarized from his headquarters in Winchester: "The incessant rain and consequent condition of the roads rendered the operations of the cavalry difficult and exceedingly trying to men and horses. The impossibility of bringing up forage in wagons, and the absence of feed in the 'Barrens' of the Cumberland Mountains, the constant rain depriving our poor beasts of their rest, has reduced the cavalry considerably." Stanley wanted some time to recondition his men and mounts.[15]

Upon its arrival at Bridgeport, the 2nd Tennessee Cavalry behaved badly. The lack of discipline in the 2nd Tennessee Cavalry resulted in scrutiny and disapproval by Sheridan and Stanley. Stanley's adjutant general, Major William Sinclair, threatened to send the regiment back to Colonel Edward McCook for discipline. Sinclair told McCook the regiment was unsuitable for its duty and wrote: "Since they have been with Genl. Sheridan's division the regiment has been going to the ___ as fast as possible. They have been drunk most of the time. One of the Capts. in a drunken fit threw a canteen of whiskey at Surgeon [Dr. Anthony] Carrick & threatened to murder him if he does not leave the regiment as he does not happen to be one of the 'Royal Blood,' an East Tennessean."[16]

After the Tullahoma Campaign, Stanley worried about discipline, not only with the 2nd Tennessee Cavalry, but with the discipline throughout the Union army. He also tried to maintain the peace as much as possible with citizens, but in some cases, he resorted to fear tactics. Stanley even tried to scare some citizens into keeping the peace by his "savage threats." Stanley, while he strove to make life as good as possible for his men, was a strict disciplinarian and was ever aware that lack of discipline could quickly turn into chaos and pillaging. To demonstrate he would not allow this type of behavior on the part of his troops, he endorsed the verdict of a court martial of Corporal George W. Mercer, 1st Ohio Cavalry, who had been found guilty of setting fire to a cotton factory. A member of the 4th Kentucky Cavalry had his head shaved and a sign placed on his back with the words "thief" after his court martial for horse theft. He received a two-year prison sentence for the crime. Discipline issues in the Union cavalry ranged the gambit of thievery, intoxication and being absent without leave.[17]

Stanley's mandate for discipline was communicated to his subordinates. He reminded his two division commanders, Mitchell and Turchin, of the importance to maintaining a tight rein on their soldiers. He wrote in a very thinly veiled jab at Turchin who was involved in the "Rape of Athens" in 1862: "Irregularities and insufferable outrages in the war of foraging having been practiced by soldiers on former expeditions," and he issued orders that if a soldier was found inside a civilian's house or acquiring a horse or mule in a method not according to regulations, the soldier "will be whipped, the uniforms stripped from him, and be drummed out of camp." In addition, Stanley reminded his subordinates of two recent events—one which resulted in the severe wounding of a cavalry trooper and the other which resulted in the two-year conviction of a trooper after "having one half of his head shaved as a mark of disgrace." While Stanley was not as severe a disciplinarian as Gordon Granger, he insisted and required his soldiers to act like soldiers and not like bandits. David Stanley had long felt discipline was essential to the efficiency of his command. Julius Thomas, 1st Tennessee Cavalry, recorded, at least one unpleasant event which probably prompted Stanley to reinforce discipline after the Tullahoma Campaign. Thomas wrote, "[A] complaint was given in by two women that some of our men had ravished them the charge was laid to the Col of the

7th Penn. and a Capt. of the 4th regular Cav. in consequence of which very stringent order was issued by Gen. Stanley." General Robert Mitchell heartily joined Stanley in enforcing discipline on the troops, and was also called a rigid disciplinarian by some of his subordinates.[18]

Discipline was not pleasant, as many of the men did violent and unacceptable acts. George Kryder, 3rd Ohio Cavalry, recorded, "Last Friday there was a man hung in Murfreesboro for deserting and murder. He deserted our army and went to bushwhacking and robbed a union man of his money and then shot him in the face and then cut the man's tongue out before he was dead. Horrible! Horrible!" John McLain, 4th Michigan, also noted in February, "5 of our soldiers were whipped, heads shaved, and drummed through camp" for violating military regulations. W. R. Carter, 1st Tennessee Cavalry, wrote of a violation of ignoring the "lights out" rule, "And if a soldier was found with a light burning in his tent, he was taken to the provost-marshal's headquarters and there either tied up by the thumbs or made to carry a rail from three to five hours." Charles Goodrich, 1st Wisconsin Cavalry, noted, "We are subjected to a much more severe discipline than we were in Missouri. We are on the march, and no one is allowed to fall out of the ranks to get water or for any other purpose, without permission from the General. In a column of five to eight miles in length, he cannot be everywhere present to give permission, if he were so disposed. If one does fall out, he is in danger of being dismounted and performing a day's march on foot. No soldier is allowed, on pain or severe punishment, to enter any house.... All this strictness is right and necessary. In the army, there are so many undisciplined and evilly disposed men to prevent our army from being converted into a marauding rabble, scattered all over the country, committing the most brutal and disgraceful outrages." W. R. Carter summarized the philosophy of Stanley's cavalry—there were three things necessary to make a good solder—discipline, discipline, and finally, discipline.[19]

Huntsville, Alabama, Expedition—July 11–July 22, 1863

Rosecrans scrapped his plan to have the cavalry cut the railroad on the east side of the Tennessee River near Bridgeport but on July 10, Rosecrans ordered Stanley to limit his expeditions and prepare the Union cavalry horses for future action. Three days later the cavalry rode to Huntsville, Alabama (about forty miles south of Winchester), with both Turchin's and Mitchell's divisions on an expedition which lasted from July 13 through July 22 to secure Union possession of the territory north of the Tennessee River and to collect as much forage, horses and mules as could be found. In addition, Stanley had orders to send cavalry to the west and to secure Pulaski and Lawrenceburg, Tennessee; and at the last minute, Tuscumbia was added to list of towns to be temporarily occupied by the Union cavalry. Stanley's expedition began at Winchester, traveled south through New Market, then to Huntsville. While Rosecrans contemplated the destruction of the railroad leading to Chattanooga only a few days earlier, he gave different orders to Stanley on his expedition to Huntsville. Rosecrans wanted Stanley to find out the condition of the railroad system in north Alabama which might be used by the Union army. As a show of force, the cavalry planned to occupy Huntsville and the objective of the movement was to let the citizens in Middle Tennessee and northern Alabama "realize that we have actually taken possession of the country." Rosecrans also hoped to coordinate his cavalry's effort with that of Major General Stephen A. Hurlbut, commander of the XVI Corps in Western Tennessee and Mississippi, who was moving troops to Tuscumbia. Stanley burnt one railroad bridge fifteen miles east of Huntsville on July 12 insuring that supplies were not sent directly to support Bragg's troops in Chattanooga. Instead of destroying additional Confederate infrastructure which might soon be needed, Stanley planned to retain as much of the railroad system as possible. In addition, Rosecrans ordered Stanley to gather ex-slaves for the purpose of employing them as teamsters and laborers for the preparations of defenses at Nashville and Murfreesboro. The cavalry provost marshal decided the best way to accomplish its task was to converge on churches and to collect the ex-slaves at the end of services. Stanley collected 600–1,000 ex-slaves during various cavalry expeditions in the Huntsville area. Brigadier General John Beatty recorded in his diary, "General Stanley has returned from Huntsville, bringing him about one thousand North Alabama negroes. This is a blow at the enemy in the right place. Deprived of slave labor, the whites will be compelled to send home, or leave at home, white men enough to cultivate the land and keep their families from starving." Stanley's actions from the Southern point of view seemed to be achieving the desired effect. Local Huntsville resident, Mary Jane Chadwick, wrote, "They are stealing all the Negroes and confining them in the Seminary building. Seventy have just passed by under a strong guard. All the good horses have been taken." Stanley promised the local civilians that he would keep the ex-slaves overnight and if any wanted to return to their old masters, he would allow them to do so. None chose to return to their old way of life.[20]

Huntsville boasted a prosperous cotton and transportation industry prior to the war

Stanley's cavalry "rode about the streets in all directions"—People and wagons outside a clothing store during the Union occupation of Huntsville, Alabama, circa 1863–1865 (Alabama Department of Archives and History).

Four. The Two Armies Prepare for the Campaign (July 5–August 15) 71

and it served as a resort town for some in Alabama. W. R. Carter, 1st Tennessee, wrote: "Huntsville is a beautiful little town, surrounded by rich and fertile fields, while from its center a large, magnificent spring furnishes not only the inhabitants with pure, crystal water, but in addition furnishes the power that forces the water to the people." Perry Goodrich, 1st Wisconsin Cavalry, also liked the appearance of Huntsville. In a letter written from Huntsville, he wrote it was a "beautiful town of ... five or six thousand inhabitants. The streets are broad and thickly lined with large, wide spreading shade trees." Stanley's cavalry remained in Huntsville for six days and he sent regiments scouting in all directions. Stanley's expedition included greater than 5,000 troopers and as a result the Confederate cavalry remained in place on the south side of the river, content to watch the activities of Stanley's men. On July 17, General Robert Mitchell took his division toward Guntersville accompanied by a section of artillery. Goodrich noted that Mitchell's artillery "knocked their fortifications flat" on the southern bank and the Confederate troops moved away from the river, out of range.[21]

The newspapers reported Stanley's actions at Huntsville. The *Alexandria Gazette* (Virginia) reported on July 18 that Stanley immediately captured 1,200 horses and mules. "He does not intend to be idle, and you may expect to hear from him again," exclaimed the *Washington City Evening Star* on July 25. The *Staunton Spectator* July 28 compared Stanley's expedition to that of John Turchin's possession of another Southern town, Athens. The editorial offered the feeling of many Southerners regarding John Turchin's role in the previous expedition and observed that Turchin had been court martialed for his role in the actions at Athens earlier in the war. It declared that Turchin allowed his troops unfettered liberties with the population in the town. According to the newspaper, Turchin reportedly told his men to proceed with their actions stating, "I shut my eyes for one hour." When his men replied that one hour was not enough time, he reportedly declared, "I shut my eyes for two hours."[22]

A first-hand account of the raid by a resident of Huntsville appeared in the *Abingdon Virginian*, August 7, 1863. An unidentified author of the letter wrote that the citizens of Huntsville awoke on the morning of July 18 to sound of hoof beats and soon found the town full of "blue-coats." The cavalry entered the town during the early morning hours and quietly waited for the residents to begin their day. David Stanley announced to the local authorities that he commanded the cavalry in possession of the town and the resident wrote: "We were surprised and greatly relieved at the quietness and order which they observed in the taking possession of the place. They rode about the streets in all directions, but entered no private lots or grounds. The citizens were wholly unmolested in person or property, no insulting word or act made use of to any one ... in the afternoon they came pouring in, regiment after regiment, in formidable column.... We all slept quietly, and awoke in the morning hardly conscious of their presence." Later in the day, Stanley made a great show of the strength of his cavalry accompanied by music played by the Union band and he explained that the cavalry planned to begin foraging the area. "We were told by the General that he had instructions to take all the mules, horses, and able-bodied negroes between the ages of 17 and 45.... From many plantations they took every negro man and boy, and every horse and mule of any worth. The people poured into the General's headquarters to get some of their negroes and horses. To all he was polite, considerate, and, as far as he could be, accommodating. Had negroes and mules returned, at least in part, but held on to all the young men and good animals." While some of the slaves hid themselves, "[m]any came willingly, and left gladly." On the return to Tennessee, Stanley sent some of the cavalry through Athens and Pulaski while others returned along the same route they had taken to Huntsville. After the expedition, the cavalry encamped at Salem and Fayetteville, Tennessee.[23]

Other Cavalry Actions

While Stanley's cavalry rode south to Huntsville, the 2nd Tennessee Cavalry, after being censured by headquarters, returned to its duty screening Phil Sheridan's division which repaired the railroad. By July 19, Sheridan had the railroad repaired to within five miles of Bridgeport and the few Southern defenders observed the Federal approach and tried to destroy the progress which was being made. The 2nd Tennessee made its headquarters at Stevenson, Alabama (about ten miles southwest of Bridgeport) and effectively repulsed the attempts to stop this progress. In the meantime, the troopers of the Union cavalry also met some of the local citizens. Trooper George Wood, 2nd Michigan Cavalry, recorded on July 23 his enjoyment of talking to the young women in Tennessee. "They are all full of fire (p___s & vinegar) for the southern cause. If I wished to know the sentiments of the people, I would talk to the female portion. They seldom keep anything back."[24]

While Stanley made his expedition to Huntsville, Lieutenant Colonel Robert Galbraith's 5th Tennessee Cavalry moved to Pulaski (seventeen miles to the west) and Athens on July 12. Galbraith, accompanied by an unidentified regiment, occupied Pulaski on July 15 before joining Stanley in Huntsville on July 18. Galbraith found no threats during the initial part of his expedition but one trooper and one officer were wounded during the expedition. The 5th Tennessee Cavalry was a rowdy group of men and had the unenviable task of dealing with guerrillas and bushwhackers. As result, they caused a lot of problems along the way. Brigadier General Walter Whitaker reported on August 2: "The Tennessee cavalry of Colonel Galbraith is giving me excessive trouble and worrying and plundering through the country whenever they go out. They are under no control or discipline, as far as I can learn." John Brandon, 5th Iowa Cavalry, also agreed that the 5th Tennessee earned their reputation. Brandon explained the men of the regiment had been hunted by the enemy and driven from their homes. In return, they bitterly hunted the enemy whenever they could. Brandon wrote: "'Stokes Cavalry' is the worse I ever met … they … have proven themselves devoted to our cause without regard as to the consequences."[25]

On July 22, David Stanley sent Rosecrans a summary of the situation from his cavalry after the expedition to Huntsville. He explained that the Confederates guarded the fords across the Tennessee River with only small numbers of troops. Some citizens reported that Gideon Pillow had retreated to Rome, Georgia and bushwhackers awaited Union troops as they advanced into the mountains near Chattanooga. Despite the strong Southern sentiment in Huntsville, the citizens opposed the use of bushwhackers. Stanley also discovered a strong contingent of pro–Union citizens in Huntsville. Stanley asked, "What policy will you adopt with Tennessee rebels?" He planned to obtain oaths of allegiance from the citizens or force them south of the Tennessee River. The only local rumors revealed that Confederate officers recently attempted to enlist more cavalry from the Huntsville area. Stanley wrote: "Two rebel doctors boasted on Monday that Forrest was coming over in a few days, and he would show us a few things. I would like to see him try it. News is hard to get, as the refugees avoid the rebels."[26]

The local citizens would have a long wait for relief by the Confederate cavalry even though Wheeler had his headquarters only 25 miles southeast at Guntersville. The Union cavalry in Alabama troubled some citizens and therefore troubled the politicians. The local civilians expressed concern, as early as December 1862, about the ability of the Confederate forces to protect them from the invaders from the North. Jefferson Davis visited Murfreesboro just prior to the Battle of Stones River and wrote: "The feeling in East Tennessee and North Alabama is far from what we desire. There is some hostility, and much want of confidence in our strength." More immediately the Confederate generals worried about the intent of the Union cavalry in regard to the destruction of the railroad which brought supplies directly from Alabama and whether Stanley intended to strike the rear of Bragg's army. General Phillip Roddey had the primary cavalry responsibility for the affairs in northern Alabama but his brigade was no match for the two approaching Union divisions and he sent an appeal for assistance. Remarkably, Wheeler, headquartered at Guntersville, had only two cavalry regiments patrolling the Tennessee River and he made no attempt to resist Stanley's moves. After the Tullahoma Campaign morale was low for Wheeler's men. Only the 8th Confederate Cavalry watched the river from Guntersville to Decatur and the 3rd Confederate Cavalry covered the river from Bridgeport to Guntersville.[27]

The purpose of Stanley's expedition was to push the enemy south of the Tennessee River which was important in regard to Rosecrans' overall strategy. Henry Albert Potter, 4th Michigan Cavalry, wrote in a letter to his sister that the expedition was successful: "There are no rebels this side of the Tennessee River." After returning to Fayetteville and Salem most of the cavalry rested and recuperated while enjoying the numerous blackberries found throughout the countryside. But, the war was never far away. A member of the 4th Indiana Cavalry was found hanged from a tree just outside the cavalry camp on July 24. Trooper Goodrich, 1st Wisconsin, wrote, "I suppose he had been pillaging and plundering from the citizens...." In addition, the cavalry commanders began efforts to gather up as many troopers for active service as possible. The war took a terrible toll on regiments through the loss of men to battles and due to the attrition of illness and exposure. In many cases, the various duties in the army sapped the cavalry of manpower, including, hospital duty and duty at convalescent camps. Colonel Robert Minty exclaimed that at least twenty to thirty troopers in his command were in Louisville and in every "town from Louisville to Tullahoma ... detained on petty details." The drain on manpower became important after the previous campaign and the realization that further fighting was likely. Minty needed to bring his regiments back to full fighting strength. The efforts of maintaining a full complement of fighting men was frustrated through the efforts of those recruiting new regiments back in the Northern states rather than seeking recruits for the older regiments. Minty even appealed to the governor of Michigan to assist with recruits for the 4th Michigan cavalry before filling new regiments.[28]

Final Actions of July

The month which began with the Union army pressing Bragg at Tullahoma ended with the same army stationary in central Tennessee. In a final personnel change for the cavalry, John Turchin was relieved of duty with the cavalry on July 29. The historian of the 7th Pennsylvania Cavalry wrote of Turchin, "General Turchin, as a cavalry officer, was not a success.

He was personally brave, and had a good deal of dash in his mental make-up, but was physically out of place on horseback, the circumference of his body being equal to his height. His failure as a commander of cavalry was due, more than anything else, to the fact that he marched with too long a tail, orderlies and escort numbering nearly four hundred men...." George Crook, a West Point classmate of Stanley, assumed command of the Second Cavalry Division upon Turchin's removal. Crook served early in the war in western Virginia, at the Second Battle of Bull Run and the Battle of Antietam. He and his division had been transferred west to the IX Corps of the Department of Ohio, and Crook commanded an infantry brigade in XIV Corps during the Tullahoma Campaign.29

Brigadier General John Beatty's diary entry for July 31 recorded some important observations about the recent changes in the cavalry, "Met General Turchin for the first time since he was before our court-martial at Huntsville. He appeared to be considerably down in spirit.... General Crook, hitherto in command of a brigade, succeeds Turchin as commander of a division. In short, Crook and Turchin just exchange places. The former is a graduate of the West Point Military Academy, and is an Ohio man, who has not, I think, greatly distinguished himself thus far.... General R. B. Mitchell is, with his command, in camp a little over a mile from us. He is in good spirits, and dwells with emphasis on the length and arduousness of the marches made by his troopers since he left Murfreesboro. The labor devolving upon him as the commander of a division of cavalry is tremendous; and yet I was rejoiced to find his physical system had stood the strain well. The wear and tear upon his intellect; however, must have been very great." Despite Beatty's disparagement of Mitchell, Mitchell received medical leave after the Tullahoma Campaign. First Lieutenant I. R. Conwell, 2nd Indiana Cavalry, noted in his diary on August 2 that Mitchell took a "short leave" and left the army to recuperate. Mitchell's short leave would extend for a month and a half and keep him away from the action until mid–September. In the meantime, Edward McCook assumed command of the cavalry division.30

Brigadier General George Crook, replaced John Turchin, as Second Division commander of cavalry (Library of Congress).

Eli Long's brigade returned from an expedition where he had citizens sign loyalty oaths, and he could not "make out oaths and bonds as fast as the rebs want to take them." He felt seventy-five percent of the citizens in the area supported the Union, but some of the Ohio cavalrymen were less than impressed with the local population signing oaths of allegiance. The Union cavalry couldn't confiscate horses and mules from loyal citizens and some cavalrymen felt the oaths were signed just as a way of preserving livestock. W. L. Curry, 1st Ohio Cavalry, recorded: "We remain here until the first of August, and during our stay about 6,000 persons came in and took the

Four. The Two Armies Prepare for the Campaign (July 5–August 15)

oath of allegiance to save their mules, and then went immediately home, took their shot-guns and went to bushwhacking."[31]

Elsewhere, rumors abounded, and those Federal troops in Kentucky worried about another cavalry raid into the state. John Hunt Morgan, commanding a brigade in Wheeler's cavalry corps, just completed a raid in July which drained much of the energy and reserves of the troops in the rear, although Morgan's raid was less than the Southern general had hoped. The new rumors predicted that Nathan Bedford Forrest intended to ride out of East Tennessee and into Kentucky. To counter this move, Stanley ordered Robert Minty to move his brigade to Sparta, a pro–Southern town about 25 miles from McMinnville, to counter any move made by Forrest. The rest of Stanley's cavalry remained relatively stationary.[32]

Communications from Washington continued to urge Rosecrans to start his advance on Chattanooga. Halleck, in reply to Rosecrans' concern about an extended supply line, urged Rosecrans to tell his infantry to carry the necessary supplies, but to move forward. "There is great disappointment felt here at the slowness of your advance." Halleck explained that Rosecrans needed to continue his pursuit of Bragg or his earlier successes would be lost because Joseph Johnston, Bragg's commanding officer, would reinforce the Army of Tennessee. Halleck, in a conciliatory tone, wrote that Rosecrans seemed to think that he was being unnecessarily ordered to move against Bragg. Halleck told him that the country, and Rosecrans' reputation, required an active pursuit. Halleck wrote, "The patience of the authorities here has been completely exhausted, and if I had not repeatedly promised to urge you forward, and begged for delay, you would have been removed from the command." While acknowledging the problems Rosecrans faced, many in Washington thought his actions resembled those of Don Carlos Buell, whom Rosecrans replaced. Halleck concluded that, as a friend rather his commanding officer, he felt obligated to explain the political pressures "whether well founded or without any foundation at all, the dissatisfaction really exists...." Rosecrans was not the only person receiving the message to advance. On the same day, Halleck wired Burnside and told him that he needed to move immediately toward Knoxville along Rosecrans' flank. Despite these urgings, Burnside would not move for some time.[33]

One of the final events of the month occurred on the Confederate side of the Tennessee River. With Bragg trying to regain his health, corps commander Leonidas Polk offered a strategy for a campaign which would deal with the Army of Cumberland. Polk wrote to William Hardee, who had recently transferred to Mississippi, and told him that Joseph Johnston should move to Chattanooga and command a very large Confederate army which would include Bragg's army, Simon Bolivar Buckner's Department of East Tennessee and all other forces which could be quickly moved to Chattanooga. Polk reasoned that the Confederate forces in the Deep South were scattered in smaller units, each of which was outnumbered and which had to operate defensively rather than offensively. The areas at risk in the summer of 1863 included Mobile, the Red River area of Louisiana, Mississippi and, of course, Knoxville and Chattanooga. Polk envisioned an army of 80,000 or more men overwhelming Rosecrans, and Burnside if he ever arrived in the field, and shifting to the west reclaiming Island Number 10, Memphis and control of the Mississippi River. Polk told Hardee that he had already discussed this plan with President Davis and asked for Hardee's agreement and support. Even though the Union armies had much success in the summer of 1863, the South was clearly not defeated and Polk felt the Confederacy needed another grand offensive.[34]

As the month of August began for the Confederate generals, the telegram wires hummed for those contemplating Polk's idea about initiating a new offensive and the decision fell on Bragg. General Samuel Cooper, who reported directly to Jefferson Davis, asked Bragg on August 1, "If we can spare most of Johnston's army, temporarily, to re-enforce you, can you attack the enemy?" Bragg vacillated and replied that before he answered he would need to discuss this with Johnston; and Johnston simply replied that he would gladly meet Bragg at a time convenient for him. However, Bragg replied to Cooper on August 5 and quashed Polk's plans. Bragg reasoned that, even with reinforcements, he would need to leave behind many of his troops to secure his communication lines and that Rosecrans still outnumbered his command two-to-one. It seemed now and for the next thirty days, the Southern general only had defense on his mind. He replied; "[I]t would be rashness to place ourselves on the farther side of a country rugged and sterile, with a few mountain roads only by which to reach a river difficult of passage. Thus situated, the enemy need only avoid battle for a short time to starve us out. Whenever he shall present himself on this side of the mountains the problem will be changed." Jefferson Davis sustained the decision stating: "It would be unwise to order its execution by one who foretold failure." With this decision, the status quo returned to the Confederate troops at Chattanooga and the hopes for a grand offensive faded away. Even Polk finally concluded that his suggestions were impossible upon learning of the impracticability of obtaining the troops needed for this type of a campaign.[35]

Lieutenant General Leonidas Polk, "The Fighting Bishop" (Library of Congress).

The Opening Moves—August 1–15, 1863

For the average Federal cavalrymen, the war progressed through daily movements on horseback and the grand strategies remained a mystery. A trooper in the Michigan cavalry wrote in a letter, "Where we go from here now God only knows." John Lynch, 2nd Michigan Cavalry, echoed this thought: "It is hard for a private to form an opinion of future movements—but we are satisfied that 'Old Rosy' knows best when & how to move & when he starts we have no fears for the result."[36]

While the Confederate high command contemplated the next move, Washington continued to push Rosecrans to make an active pursuit of Bragg's army. Rosecrans wrote to Henry Halleck and outlined seven problems he faced. These included the base of his supplies was 264 miles away, and he was 83 miles from his closest depot at Nashville. His basest needs had to be transported overland or by raft. Next, he pointed out the mountains to his front were difficult to travel with poor roads and little hope of forage opportunities. Once he made it to the Tennessee River, he faced an obstacle 400–800 yards wide defended by Confederates. Rosecrans also faced an undefeated foe that was likely to be reinforced by Johnston's army. Finally, he noted, "We must so advance as never to recede. The citizens say, and not without justice, 'Whip our armies, and then, when we no longer fear their return to power, we will show you that we are satisfied to be in the Union; but until you do that, we are not safe from proscription.'" Fortunately, the railroad was finally open to Bridgeport but Rosecrans still worried about crossing the Tennessee River. Despite these obstacles in Tennessee, Halleck felt he faced two generals who seemed determined to march at their own pace. Ambrose Burnside also seemed reluctant to advance on Knoxville; but in the case of Rosecrans, his last delay extended for six months and those in Washington would not allow him to pursue his enemy at a snail's pace this time.[37]

On August 3, Halleck's patience was exhausted and he inquired about the positions of both Rosecrans' and Burnside's commands. Rosecrans responded with a description of the location of his army—his reserve corps stretched from Nashville to Shelbyville, Thomas' XIV Corps was in the vicinity of Decherd, Crittenden's XXI Corps extended from McMinnville to Pelham and McCook's XX Corps was located at Tullahoma and Winchester with brigade at Bridgeport. The First Cavalry Division (Edward McCook's) was in position at Fayetteville and Salem, Crook's division occupied Winchester, Minty's brigade was at McMinnville and Watkins' brigade was at Winchester. Further to the north Burnside responded to Halleck's call to begin his march, and promised to be on the move soon. He explained that his command was scattered over a large geographic area and he needed time to concentrate his army for the advance to the south. Halleck had had enough of delays and responded to Rosecrans: "The orders for the advance of your army, and that its movements be reported daily, are peremptory." Halleck's orders to Burnside also directed him to move forward and unite his command with Rosecrans.[38]

Rosecrans acknowledged this preemptory order and he considered the challenges he faced. It proved impractical to attempt to cross the Tennessee River between Bridgeport and Chattanooga, but he thought he would be successful if he fooled Bragg into thinking he intended to cross the river north of Chattanooga when he really planned to cross west of the town near Bridgeport. While this would get the Army of the Cumberland across the river, it still meant that supplies had to be moved over the mountains and the troops would have to sustain themselves after the crossing of the river and during any battles thereafter. But, Rosecrans understood orders and then, he sent orders of his own to Thomas, Crittenden and Alexander McCook to prepare to move forward. On August 7, Rosecrans wired Burnside about his plans to begin his advance against Bragg and offered to set up a supply depot in McMinnville to assist with Burnside's movement across the mountains into Tennessee.[39]

The Condition of the Cavalry of the Army of the Cumberland

Almost a month had passed since the Tullahoma Campaign ended which gave the Federal cavalry time to recuperate after the grueling ten-day campaign. Almost no fighting or movements, except the Huntsville expedition, had occurred over the past thirty days. David

Stanley described the state of the cavalry divisions in a long letter to Major General George Stoneman, who had just been appointed as the Chief of the U.S. Cavalry Bureau in Washington in July. Stoneman had been active in the eastern theater and Stanley wanted to bring him up to date on the situation with the Army of the Cumberland. Stanley told him that one of his top accomplishments was the reorganization of the cavalry into active brigades. Stanley now had twenty-two regiments and he also had command of the 3rd and 4th Tennessee cavalries as these units tried to gain enough men to form full regiments. The arms of his cavalry troubled him. Of the full complement of regiments, only the 1st, 3rd and 4th Ohio regiments had uniform arms for all the troopers. All the other regiments had various types of carbines which made the process of acquiring and distributing ammunition confusing and difficult. In addition, the 2nd and 4th Michigan cavalries had Colt revolving rifles, "infantry pattern," which could not be accurately used in the saddle. While these weapons added significant firepower, the troopers had to be dismounted to fully utilize the rifles. Stanley told Stoneman that his priority for carbines was: (1) Sharps, (2) Colts, (3) Burnside's, and (4) Smith's carbines. All other carbines would be rejected. In regard to revolvers, Stanley would only accept Colts.[40]

Next, Stanley addressed the distressing condition of the McClellan saddles which had been in use for about six months. The saddles used by the Union cavalry, particularly during the Tullahoma Campaign and afterward, were ruined by the active campaigning in the rain. Two problems plagued the saddles—first the iron used to hold the components of the saddle together was badly tempered and caused the saddles to flatten. Secondly, the rawhide protecting the horses back from the wooden parts of the saddle rotted in the excessive moisture during the July campaigning. Stanley complained that the saddles damaged the horses' backs resulting in not only bad saddles, but also injury to the valuable mounts. Washington promised to immediately dispatch 2,000 replacements but these poor saddles would continue to plague the cavalry throughout the campaign. The bridles were also flimsy and of poorer quality than those previously received and Stanley expected 4,000 sets needed to be replaced. Certainly, the request came at a poor time just as the army began to move forward but cavalry commanders had no choice. The average cavalryman would lament the condition of saddles and horse equipment through October.[41]

Louisville had been chosen as the closest cavalry depot to Stanley's cavalry and while the location in the rear, and along the Ohio River, proved convenient, it was a long way away from Winchester, Tennessee. Also, Stanley did not have enough horses to mount his command. To make matters worse, Louisville was technically in the territory commanded by Ambrose Burnside who had 8,000 mounted troops of his own. Often times, Stanley explained, Burnside ensured his command was supplied at the expense of those further south.[42]

Despite these concerns, Stanley spoke highly of his troops: "Some of them are all that could be expected of a volunteer cavalry and perhaps quite equal to any regular cavalry now in service. They are equal to any emergency and do not hesitate to charge anything sabre in hand." The importance of the recent cavalry action at Shelbyville was not lost on Stanley who proudly described the increased élan of his troops. But, he did express concerns about mounting too many Tennessee regiments: "[The] men are brave and willing but the officers lack education and are wanting in industry." The discipline of the 2nd Tennessee and 5th Tennessee cavalries, in general, caused him concern. In regard to the cavalry of the Army of the Cumberland, Stanley went so far as saying the farther north the trooper came from, the better the cavalryman. Next, Stanley appraised his division commanders, Crook and Mitchell. Mitchell's health was a concern for Stanley and he asked Stoneman to contemplate a good officer to replace him. Crook, on the other hand, was seen as a good division commander. Stanley concluded that he intended to make this cavalry the most respected in the army.[43]

Minty Fights Dibrell at Sparta, Tennessee—August 5 and 9, 1863

While Wheeler seemed to be willing to remain in position and wait for the Union army to advance, Nathan Bedford Forrest wanted more action. At the end of July, he sent Dibrell's 8th Tennessee Cavalry (CSA) across the Tennessee River to the area around Sparta. Major General Horatio Van Cleve's infantry division held a position in McMinnville, twenty-seven miles southwest of Sparta. Anticipating an aggressive move from Forrest, Stanley had ordered Robert Minty's cavalry brigade to McMinnville. The concern about Forrest's move was just one additional action of many by the Confederate cavalry in July and early August. Of note was the raid of John Hunt Morgan which took place in July, and although it had little impact on the overall situation in the west, it did strike terror into the hearts of the citizens of Indiana and Ohio before Morgan's command was finally caught. Dibrell's rather innocuous move to Sparta prompted an immediate response from Stanley and he dispatched his most capable brigade commander forward to address the situation.[44]

Minty's cavalry brigade left Salem on August 1 and arrived in McMinnville on August 3 and began to work in cooperation with Horatio Van Cleve's infantry division. Van Cleve held the extreme eastern flank of Rosecrans' army and, ideally, once Burnside's Army of the Ohio began it advance on Knoxville, Van Cleve would operate in some manner to present a solid front. Already Morgan's raid into the North caused problems for the Union forces in Kentucky, Indiana, and Ohio, and, more recently, Colonel John Scott's cavalry brigade from Simon Buckner's Department of East Tennessee initiated a raid into southeastern Kentucky on July 25. Scott's raid continued into central Kentucky, but Burnside commanded 8,000 mounted troops and had little trouble in sending Scott back into eastern Tennessee. Simon Buckner wrote that Burnside's forces "converted Colonel Scott's success into a partial disaster. The conduct of some of the subordinate commanders seems to be reprehensible." As a result, the action of Forrest sending Dibrell's cavalry along

Colonel Minty's cavalry supported General Horatio Van Cleve's division on the left flank of the Union army (John Fitch, *Annals of the Army of the Cumberland, 1864*).

that same front was greeted with concern from the Army of the Cumberland. The Union commanders did not need Forrest slipping between Rosecrans and Burnside on a raid of his own.[45]

Dibrell's 8th Tennessee Cavalry reached Sparta on July 29 and camped on Dibrell's own farm about two miles north of the town. In 1860, Sparta had a population of 472. It is located just west of the Cumberland Mountains and about fifteen miles south of Cookeville, Tennessee. The Calfkiller River, named for a Cherokee chief, ran approximately north and south on the west side of the town and about a mile north turned sharply to the east. The town was about 65 miles west of Kingston, Forrest's headquarters. Dibrell had not planned a raid as feared by the Union commanders, but he intended to forage the area while observing Rosecrans' movements and at the same time offered the troopers an opportunity to visit their home community. Dibrell diligently set scouts as far as eight miles away from his headquarters. General Horatio Van Cleve knew the Southern cavalry was active at Sparta, and he sent Minty's brigade to Sparta on August 4 to deal with Dibrell's cavalry. Minty's expedition totaled about 1,100 men and he correctly suspected Dibrell was encamped, about a mile north of Sparta. To reach Sparta from McMinnville, Minty needed to cross the Caney Fork River about eight miles southwest of the town. At the mouth of the Collins River was the Rock Island Ferry where Dibrell wisely posted about seventy troopers to delay any Federal movement from McMinnville. To surprise Dibrell, Minty needed to capture this enemy force and then proceed to Sparta, but this proved a difficult task. Minty ordered Lieutenant Colonel Robert Klein's 3rd Indiana across the Caney Fork River a few miles west of the ferry at 9:00 a.m. and then Klein planned to circle behind the guards at Rock Island Ferry and at a second ford, Dillon's Ford. At noon, Minty planned to charge the remainder of his cavalry across the river in conjunction with Klein's encirclement. When Minty saw the area that he had to attack, he was not pleased. Dibrell had chosen this location well. Minty wrote that the "fords were represented to me as being practicable, in fact, good, whereas they were so impracticable that 5 men could hold either of them against any cavalry force that could be brought against them; they could shoot men down faster than they could enter the river." The joint attack began at noon, but rather than resisting the Federal attack across the river, the Southern cavalry fled after firing only one shot. Klein's cavalry could only manage to capture fourteen prisoners while another forty-fifty enemy cavalry made their escape. Being unable to surprise Dibrell, Minty returned to his camp at McMinnville.[46]

After Minty's seventy-mile trek north from Salem to McMinnville and then the twenty-five-mile ride to the Rock Island Ferry, his horses were exhausted. At McMinnville, Minty began a good relationship with Horatio Van Cleve and these two commanders would work together for the next month with both men showing mutual respect for the other. Although Van Cleve was disappointed that Dibrell still remained in Sparta, he was confident Minty would move him out after his horses rested.[47]

Sparta was a pro–Southern town, and the Confederates made life difficult for those in support of the Union. Dibrell's secondary purpose in Sparta, according to the Union-supporting citizens, included the removal of all resources which would prove useful to Rosecrans' army. The locals reported that Dibrell had orders to avoid a fight with Minty's cavalry, if possible, and in the meantime, capture all the horses and mules which could benefit the Union army. In addition, the local citizens told Minty that Dibrell had instructions "to secure all the beef, all the wheat, and to use and destroy all the oats and corn in White and Van

Buren Counties they cannot carry off, so as to subject the Federal army to all the inconveniences possible when they come to occupy."⁴⁸

Minty made another expedition to Sparta on August 8 with 774 men to find George Dibrell's 8th Tennessee of about 300 men. The Union cavalry rode at 3:00 p.m. due east from McMinnville to Spencer after discarding the previous route with the easily defendable fords. Minty reached Spencer at 11:30 p.m. and then proceeded north across the Caney Fork River which had caused him problems a few days before. He was in position as the sun rose and he charged the enemy pickets about four miles south of Sparta. The pickets turned and rode for the town. When Minty reached the town, he found no sign of Dibrell's regiment but he discovered that the Confederate camp was a few miles north. Minty pushed northward and by this time, Dibrell was prepared to meet the Union column. Upon the arrival of his scouts, Dibrell quickly mounted his command, moved east across the Calfkiller River at the confluence of Wildcat Creek and left a single company to delay Minty's advance. Dibrell, familiar with terrain, selected this location "with its deep banks and a mill pond above the bridge, was only passable at the bridge. The enemy were in full speed, and before we could get into position were pressing our rear, having met and routed McGinnis and his company." Captain Hamilton McGinnis had the unpleasant chore of delaying Minty's attack with the 4th Michigan Cavalry leading the way.⁴⁹

Minty's account of the skirmish described that Dibrell moved his cavalry across the Calfkiller River and held a strong defensive position on a hill which offered a clear field of fire. For the Union cavalry to attack, it had to move across a "narrow rickety bridge" which was the only way to reach the Confederates behind their defenses on the hill. Captain James McIntyre, 4th U.S. Cavalry, found a rough ford across the creek about a quarter mile south of the bridge. Minty ordered McIntyre to lead the 4th U.S. across the ford and to attack the flank of Dibrell's line. Then, the 7th Pennsylvania moved to support the attack of 4th U.S. Minty's attack focused on the Confederate flank while the 4th Michigan and 3rd Indiana moved forward to face the Confederates on the hill. The flank attack settled the fight and Minty wrote that although the Confederates held "a strong position, difficult of access, would not wait for the attack, but scattered in every direction. The Fourth Regulars, Seventh Pennsylvania, and Third Indiana scoured the country for about 3 miles, but their horses were too tired to overtake the freshly mounted rebels."⁵⁰

In contrast, Dibrell's account was quite different. He agreed the bulk of his regiment was on a hill facing the narrow bridge he expected Minty to cross and he formed a line which extended to the Calfkiller River. He told his men to hold their

Colonel George Dibrell, opposed to secession, knew the territory around Sparta well and put his knowledge to good use (Alabama Department of Archives and History).

fire until the Union cavalry attempted to force a crossing at the bridge. Dibrell positioned his men with 200–300 yards of open ground between the streams and the Confederate line. In addition, a large fence prevented a rapid attack by the Union cavalry once they crossed the creek. Dibrell described that once the 4th Michigan reached the bridge, he ordered his men to open fire. "They were yelling and charging at full speed, and the open space above referred to was full of them. Our gallant boys raised the yell as they poured volley after volley into them, until they retreated in great confusion out of the trap into which we had drawn them. They soon rallied and charged us again, said to be by the Fourth Regulars, but we soon repulsed them. They then attempted a charge on foot, but were again repulsed. They then sent a party across the Calfkiller River to gain our rear, but I had anticipated them, and they were soon driven back." Despite Dibrell's exclamation of victory, he conceded that his command was too small to withstand Minty's attack and he withdrew under the Federal advance. Once Minty called off his pursuit, Dibrell sent scouts to observe the Federal movement back to McMinnville. Dibrell claimed a loss of four wounded and eight captured."[51]

Minty agreed that this was a heated skirmish and all his losses came from the 4th Michigan Cavalry of which only one hundred fifteen men participated in the fight. Minty reported that he captured eight prisoners and killed or wounded fourteen more. The Union colonel did not report his total losses, but one Union cavalryman was killed and three others were mortally wounded. After the skirmish, Minty remained at Sparta until 1 p.m. and then rode back to McMinnville. Minty had not faced Dibrell alone during the skirmish and a company from Champ Ferguson's command, partisans operating in the area, joined in the fight. After Minty left, Dibrell returned to his camp and the pro–Confederate citizens cooked a meal for his troopers. Despite the heated skirmish, Dibrell did not return to Kingston but remained in the area. A few days later, small groups of Southern cavalry began foraging in the area and Minty returned to try to find them.[52]

Minty's actions at Sparta provided some much-needed offensive action for Rosecrans to satisfy his masters in Washington. Rosecrans used the skirmish to show Washington that he aggressively dealt with the enemy. While not exactly true, he wrote: "Minty's cavalry whipped General Dibrell's brigade of rebels out of Sparta." Rosecrans could not help but send a small barb in his message to Washington that while he sent his cavalry ahead, the railroad could not provide sufficient supplies for his army.[53]

Meanwhile on the other flank, Edward McCook's cavalry division rode to deal with Confederates along the Tennessee River. McCook, a worthy replacement for Mitchell, dispatched Colonel Louis Watkins' brigade to deal with a body of about three hundred Confederates who had moved across the Tennessee River and occupied Athens, Alabama—about fifteen miles west of Huntsville. Watkins moved two regiments to Athens and attempted to swing the third around the rear of the Confederates on August 6 without success. Reportedly, the Confederates had a small steamboat which pulled barges loaded with Confederate cavalry across the river wherever they wanted to attack.[54]

Stanley Reorganizes the Cavalry

After the Tullahoma Campaign, Stanley formally shuffled the regiments of the two cavalry divisions to include an additional brigade in each division. His new organization included six brigades instead of the four brigades in the old organization.

Cavalry, Army of the Cumberland—August 31, 1863[55]

Major General David S. Stanley

Escort
4th Ohio Cavalry, Company D, Captain Philip H. Warner

FIRST DIVISION—*Colonel Edward M McCook*

First Brigade
Colonel Archibald P. Campbell
2nd Michigan, Maj. John C. Godley
9th Pennsylvania, Lt. Col. Roswell M. Russell
1st Tennessee, Lt. Col. James P. Brownlow

Second Brigade
Colonel Oscar H. La Grange
2nd Indiana, Maj. Joseph B. Presdee
4th Indiana, Col. John A. Platter
2nd Tennessee, Col. Daniel M. Ray
1st Wisconsin, Lt. Col. Henry Pomeroy

Third Brigade
Colonel Louis D. Watkins
4th Kentucky, Col. Wickliffe Cooper
5th Kentucky, Lt. Col. William T. Hoblitzell
6th Kentucky, Maj. Louis A. Gratz
7th Kentucky, Lt. Col. Thomas T. Vimont

Artillery
1st Ohio, Light, section Battery D (2nd Brigade), Lieutenant Nathaniel M. Newell

SECOND DIVISION—*Brigadier General George Crook*

First Brigade
Colonel Robert H. G. Minty
3rd Indiana (battalion), Lt. Col. Robert Klein
4th Michigan, Maj. Horace Gray
7th Pennsylvania, Maj. James J. Seibert
4th United States, Capt. James B. McIntyre

Second Brigade
Colonel Eli Long
2nd Kentucky, Col. Thomas P. Nicholas
1st Ohio, Lt. Col. Valentine Cupp
3rd Ohio, Lt. Col. Charles B. Seidel
4th Ohio, Lt. Col. Oliver P. Robie

Third Brigade
Colonel William W. Lowe
5th Iowa, Maj. Alfred B. Brackett
10th Ohio, Lt. Col. William E. Haynes
5th Tennessee (1st Middle), Col. William B. Stokes

Artillery
Chicago (Illinois) Board of Trade Battery, Capt. James H. Stokes

To supplement his two current cavalry divisions, Rosecrans wanted more cavalry although at this point whatever good will that existed between Washington and Rosecrans was gone; but he did write a detailed letter to Secretary of War Edwin Stanton in August, requesting another 10,000 mounted forces. Washington simply ignored this request and continued to press Rosecrans to begin his offensive, but Rosecrans had gotten the message and showed no further reluctance in beginning his movement. He attempted to coordinate his movement with Burnside who planned to start his march on August 18 from Stanford, Kentucky—one hundred fifty miles from Sparta. Halleck added a personal, unofficial, message to Rosecrans on August 9 which stated that the despite the orders from the War Department, those in Washington only wanted success for Rosecrans' army. Halleck directly stated, "It is said that you 'do not draw straight in the traces, but are continually kicking out or getting one leg over.' No one doubts your good intentions and your great interest in the cause, and your desire to secure its success."[56]

Cavalry—Present for Duty—August 10, 1863[57]

Confederate Cavalry[a]		Union Cavalry	
Forrest's Division	3,842	Mitchell's Division[b]	5,540
Wheeler's Corps	7,143	Crook's Division	4,433
Pegram's Division[c]	5,758	15th Pennsylvania[d]	427
Total	**16,743**		**10,400**

[a]—Includes cavalry and artillery; [b]—Includes corps staff;
[c]—Part of the Department of East Tennessee; [d]—Detached to army headquarters

Facing Stanley in August was a formidable cavalry force. Wheeler's division officially included John Hunt Morgan's cavalry brigade that had participated in the ill-fated raid into the north. Wheeler's total would technically be about 2,500 men less than he reported because Morgan's raid resulted in about 2,000 Southern cavalry being captured. On a more positive note for Bragg, he successfully integrated Simon Bolivar Buckner's troops from the Department of East Tennessee into his Army of Tennessee as a third corps in August. Along with infantry, Bragg gained more cavalry, which increased his cavalry by an additional division. The cavalry from the Department of East Tennessee included John Pegram's and John Scott's cavalry brigades. Forrest gained the new cavalry which allowed him to increase his division into a cavalry corps in early September. The addition of the new cavalry resulted in Brigadier General John Pegram maintaining division command under Forrest.[58]

Rosecrans Prepares to Move Toward Chattanooga

Rosecrans, obeying his direct orders from Washington, prepared to move his army forward. Major General Joseph Reynolds' division of Thomas' XIV Corps reached Tracy City on August 11 but no other Union forces advanced due to lack of provisions. For the most part, the bulk of Stanley's cavalry held a line between Fayetteville to Salem to Winchester until August 11. According to orders, Rosecrans sent messages daily to Washington about his actions during the day. On August 12, Absalom Baird's division, XIV Corps, reached Stevenson, Alabama and Rosecrans developed his plan to confuse Bragg about his line of march. Because Rosecrans still had the task of crossing the Tennessee River which could be easily defended, Rosecrans planned to feint a crossing at or north of Chattanooga with Crittenden's XXI Corps and Minty's cavalry brigade, when he really intended to cross to the west of the town at Bridgeport. Rosecrans simply wrote to Washington: "Rebels expect us above Chattanooga."[59]

As Rosecrans prepared his march, Edward McCook moved his division to Larkinsville, Alabama on August 13 to scout and screen the southern flank of the Federal army. Daniel Ray's Second Brigade led the advance to Larkinsville, followed by Louis Watkins's Third Brigade and Archibald Campbell's brigade brought up the rear. With the Federal army in control of the geography north of the Tennessee River in Alabama, the existing railroad became important as a future route of re-supply. McCook's movements were of particular importance because it secured Rosecrans' flank along the south from the Tennessee River back to the west of Huntsville. Archibald Campbell's First Brigade moved past Maysville and set up camp on the Flint River intent on protecting the Memphis & Charleston Railroad. Watkins was also given the task to guard the railroad east of Huntsville to ensure no enemy actions succeeded in destroying the tracks. Watkins planned to make his headquarters along the Flint River, about five miles east of Huntsville once Campbell moved farther east.[60]

While Rosecrans prepared his advance, he kept in constant communication with Burnside as the two armies prepared to sweep from the west and north in a unified front into East Tennessee. Burnside wired Rosecrans that he planned to begin his offensive on August 15. In addition, Major General Stephen A. Hurlbut's XVI Corps troops to the west, although stretched thin, attempted to link Rosecrans southern and western-most troops to provide a solid line to the west. As the infantry advanced, the 2nd Tennessee Cavalry continued to cover the flanks of Sheridan's infantry which worked near the Tennessee River at Bridgeport. The 2nd Tennessee scouted northward toward Shellmound where Patton Anderson's Confederate infantry still held it position. Cavalry scouts found an estimated 400–600 Southern infantry supported by artillery, and succeeded in capturing two Confederate couriers near Jasper along with their dispatches.[61]

Summary

While perhaps inglorious, the history of the Federal cavalry during the Chickamauga campaign must include the preparation and the advance on Chattanooga. This period began after the Huntsville expedition concluded and would carry forward until September 17, 1863. The cavalry of the Army of the Cumberland would be sorely tested during the campaign. The role of Union cavalry became defined by the personalities of the commanding general and the chief of cavalry, as well as the tasks that James A. Garfield envisioned for the cavalry. Also, the stress experienced by Rosecrans during this extended campaign caused him to lash out at many of the top commanders of his army, including David Stanley. Paramount in Stanley's vision for the cavalry was the ability of the chief of cavalry to direct his cavalry as divisions and brigades and not as small units interspersed with many objectives under the control of the various infantry commanders. Certainly, Stanley had come to expect that his voice should be important to the decisions made regarding the cavalry. Unfortunately, many of the things that worked so well for Stanley and cavalry over the past nine months would be cast aside during the upcoming campaign.

On August 14, the Army of the Cumberland became a flurry of activity and the soldiers prepared to begin their advance. Rosecrans sent a series of communications for the commanders of the various corps to insure they were supplied, the wounded and sick dealt with, and that adequate rations and ammunition had been provided. The major exception was Minty's cavalry brigade which had only one day's forage and just a few days' rations available. About eight to eighteen days' rations and three to ten days' forage were provided for the other commands. While the communications on the Union side were excited and full of energy, almost no communications came from Bragg. The greatest energy came from Johnston's activities in Mississippi while Bragg's army remained quiet. Finally, on August 15, Rosecrans wired Washington: "It begins tomorrow morning."[62]

Five. The Advance to the Tennessee River (August 16–September 1)

The bullets whistled and sung altogether too close to be pleasant.—Captain Robert Burns

As Rosecrans began his advance on Bragg's army at Chattanooga, the Union cavalry stretched along the flanks of the Army of the Cumberland. Edward McCook's cavalry division extended from Huntsville, Alabama to Bridgeport along a seventy-five-mile front. In front of his cavalry waited Wheeler's cavalry corps supplemented with Brigadier General Phillip Dale Roddey's cavalry brigade. Thus far in the campaign, Roddey's cavalry had shown more energy than Wheeler. In fact, only a couple of Wheeler's regiments provided duty of securing the fords at Guntersville and northward to area around Bridgeport. On the other flank, Nathan Bedford Forrest had his headquarters at Kingston, Tennessee and his division concentrated in the area from Kingston to Chattanooga. On the north flank of the Union army, Minty's cavalry brigade remained in McMinnville trying to locate and draw Dibrell's cavalry into a fight. The remainder of Crook's division was still in Middle Tennessee—Long's brigade remained in Winchester until August 19 and Lowe's brigade prepared to protect the supply lines of the advancing army.

Rosecrans issued orders to respect the rights of the local citizens as the Army of the Cumberland moved further into Confederate territory, but he issued a stern warning to the Southern sympathizing citizens—"In enforcing this duty the general commanding will follow the old rule of common law, and hold the inhabitants of each locality responsible for the guerrilla warfare practiced in their midst, and unless satisfied that they have done their full duty and used their utmost efforts to stop it, will lay waste their country and render it untenable for robbers."[1]

On August 15, Rosecrans issued his orders for his army to begin moving the next morning and he made his assignments:

> (A) George Thomas' XIV Corps was ordered to move two divisions to Stevenson and his remaining two divisions needed to march into the Sequatchie Valley (the valley just east of the Cumberland Mountain and west of Walden's Ridge). These divisions needed to remain within supporting distance of one another and the center of the corps would be located near Jasper. Rosecrans also told Thomas to reach his appointed destinations by August 26. Thomas gave one division special orders, Major General Joseph Reynold's Fourth Division, which included Colonel John Wilder's Mounted Infantry Brigade. Because of Wilder's mobility, exceptional record and aggressiveness, he received orders to make one demonstration directly from the north on Chattanooga and another a few miles north at Harrison's Landing. This was necessary to direct Bragg's attention to Wilder (and Crittenden's corps) while allowing the remainder of the army

to cross the Tennessee River to the west, near Stevenson and Bridgeport.[2]

(B) Crittenden's XXI Army Corps was ordered to operate north of Chattanooga and serve as a feint in cooperation with Wilder in the effort to make Bragg think Rosecrans, in conjunction with Burnside's army, planned to unite and cross the Tennessee River somewhere between Knoxville and Chattanooga. All three of Crittenden's divisions were ordered into the Sequatchie Valley, and Van Cleve's division would hold the extreme left flank of the army until Burnside secured the flank. Robert Minty's cavalry brigade was assigned to Crittenden's corps, specifically to protect Van Cleve's northern flank. As Van Cleve's march began, Minty was ordered to return to the Sparta and drive Dibrell's, and any other Confederate mounted forces eastward, back toward Forrest at Kingston. Rosecrans ordered the 3rd Indiana Cavalry to remain in the Sparta area after Van Cleve moved forward to prevent further activity from the Confederate cavalry. Once Van Cleve reached his destination, Minty's cavalry was given the duty of pushing forward toward Blythe's Ferry and the town of Washington where a strong force of Forrest's cavalry held a strong position on the opposite shore of the Tennessee River. Crittenden's remaining two divisions would work in conjunction with Wilder's mounted infantry near Chattanooga.[3]

Major General George Thomas commander of the Union XIV Corps (Library of Congress).

(C) Alexander McCook already had Sheridan's and Brannan's divisions in possession of the area around Stevenson and Bridgeport. Rosecrans specified that Richard Johnson's division move to Bellefonte, and Jefferson C. Davis' division march to the area south of Bolivar and north of Bellefonte. McCook's XX Corps also needed to be fully in place by August 26.[4]

(D) Rosecrans' orders for his cavalry proved to be somewhat non-specific other than Minty's brigade. The only other orders for the cavalry were: "The chief of cavalry with the reserve brigade will follow the general headquarters, and will have special instructions for the remainder of the cavalry, which will be given him by the general commanding." As the campaign unfolded, it became clear Minty would be assigned duty with Crittenden, Eli Long's brigade would work with Alexander McCook's corps, and William Lowe's brigade protected the rear of the advancing army. Only Edward McCook's cavalry division would have the flexibility for offensive action and would operate along Alexander McCook's right flank.[5]

(E) Finally, Gordon Granger's Reserve Corps, 25,000 strong, marched at the rear of the advancing army and initially concentrated at Fayetteville. Granger would send some of Lowe's cavalry brigade to Athens and then extended a line of cavalry to Decatur. He had orders to

Major General Thomas L. Crittenden commander of the Union XXI Corps (Library of Congress).

protect the communications and supply lines as he marched forward by leaving sufficient troops for this duty. Granger had the responsibility of covering those important locations which had just been vacated by the advancing army.[6]

(F) In miscellaneous instructions, Stokes' 5th Tennessee Cavalry (headquartered at Carthage), which was adept at fighting the enemy in the countryside within Tennessee, planned to move to McMinnville and relieve the 3rd Indiana Cavalry which would re-join Minty's brigade. Stokes would be part of the "Carthage brigade" which had the duty of protecting the supply lines in that part of the state. Meanwhile, Rosecrans would establish his headquarters at Stevenson on August 25. Rosecrans admonished his commanders to move quietly, quickly and efficiently. Rosecrans had two objectives in mind—claim Chattanooga and defeat Bragg's Army of Tennessee in the process.[7]

The Advance Part I: On to the Tennessee River—August 16–29

The bridge over the Tennessee River at Bridgeport spanned 2,700 feet, but the Confederates destroyed the bridge leaving the Union generals with the question of how to cross the wide Tennessee River. The activity of the enemy on the other side of the river was of paramount importance for the Union commanders. The river was such a formidable obstacle and so easily defendable that the challenge of its crossing vexed Rosecrans. Therefore, the Union troops carefully watched for lightly held crossings, but little did the Union commanders realize only Brigadier General Patton Anderson's brigade of Mississippi infantry supplemented by Wheeler's less than aggressive cavalry had the responsibility of covering the Tennessee River near Bridgeport and Stevenson. Wheeler's cavalry had yet to respond to a potential Union advance. In addition, only small work parties were seen on the opposite shore. The 2nd Tennessee Cavalry (U.S.) observed the enemy movements on the other side of the river, but neither the enemy infantry or cavalry seemed to be too concerned about the Union troops moving on the west side of the river.[8]

Major General Gordon Granger commander of the Union Reserve Corps (Library of Congress).

On the southern flank of the Army of the Cumberland, Edward McCook's brigade remained busy and he moved his headquarters to Larkinsville, a small railroad village boasting only a handful of businesses. McCook's primary responsibility was covering the railroad and the southern flank. McCook knew Will Martin's cavalry division was just across the river near Guntersville. On August 14, McCook sent the 1st Tennessee Cavalry scouting over the Cumberland Mountains along the Bellefonte Road to insure there were no large bodies of enemies lurking there and finding no guerrillas, the regiment arrived at Larkinsville on August 15. The movement to Larkinsville proved difficult due to the extreme heat and increasing dustiness, a pattern of weather which lasted throughout much

Five. The Advance to the Tennessee River (August 16–September 1) 89

of the Chickamauga Campaign. In weather so hot and dry, many "horse[s] fell dead by the road" remarked First Lieutenant I. R. Conwell, 2nd Indiana Cavalry.[9]

Edward McCook's cavalry reached its destination on August 16, and found an extensive front to cover. Archibald Campbell's brigade moved forward and guarded the shore from Guntersville to just north of Stevenson. Daniel Ray's Second Brigade covered Larkinsville and Paint Rock (about ten miles east of Huntsville). Louis Watkins' Kentucky cavalry brigade settled in the area just east of Huntsville along the Flint River. McCook told his brigade commanders to watch all the fords on the Tennessee River with patrols sent out as often as possible to determine the position and concentrations of the enemy on the other side of the river. Eli Long's brigade (of Crook's division) which was assigned to follow army headquarters had the same duty from Stevenson to Bridgeport. Finally, McCook ordered his division to clean out all the bushwhackers in their vicinity; and, above all, communicate with his headquarters in Larkinsville if any problems occurred.[10]

Almost immediately Colonel John A. Platter, 4th Indiana Cavalry, stationed near Paint Rock Station, reported the good news that no Confederates were found on the north side of the river and the other side of the Tennessee River was only lightly defended. Brigadier General William Lytle, commanding the First Brigade of Phil Sheridan's division, received a deserter on the evening of August 15 who confirmed the Confederates did have work crews in action but they were not constructing works to repel a Federal crossing around Bridgeport. Lytle even resorted to sending his scouts in dugout canoes to float past the Confederate positions during the evening to determine the positions of the enemy.[11]

As Edward McCook followed his orders, the 2nd Tennessee Cavalry which had worked in conjunction with Sheridan's division became temporarily missing in action. Both Edward McCook and William Lytle looked for the regiment and couldn't find them. Lytle wrote on August 18, "I have had no reports from the Second Tennessee for a day or two, in violation of their instructions. Shall I send Ray up toward Jasper tomorrow?" The 2nd Tennessee's lack of discipline irritated both commanders and McCook contemplated sending Daniel Ray, Second Brigade Commander and old colonel of the regiment, to instill discipline in the regiment. In the meantime, Edward McCook set about the task of the clearing the area of the pesky bushwhackers along his flank. "Am killing off bushwhackers gradually, and have taken about 20 Confederate prisoners." A trooper in the 2nd Indiana Cavalry wrote: "Soldiers hate these bushwhackers" after a member of the 2nd Michigan was captured on August 15. Joseph Shelly, 2nd Indiana Cavalry, wrote to his wife: "The surroundings are filled with bushwhackers, and one is quite sure to hear the bullets whistle if he goes half a mile from camp, just to let you know where they come from. But we often catch them whereas their procedure is a short one." John Large, 3rd Ohio Cavalry, described to his father in a letter the anger the Union cavalry held for bushwhackers: "I don't know what this ware is a coming to. They got so that thay wont stand and fite but thay lay around in the woods and when thay git a few men together thay lay behind the bushes and murder."[12]

To add to the discomfort of McCook's cavalry, Louis Watkins found the conditions around the Flint River low, swampy and unbearable. Because so many of his soldiers became sick, he requested permission to move closer to Huntsville while covering his assigned territory. Watkins wrote: "The location of my present camp is a very unhealthy one indeed, and already several men in the command are suffering with chills and fever. The country all around is either of a low, swampy character or too rough and hilly for cavalry to camp on, and I

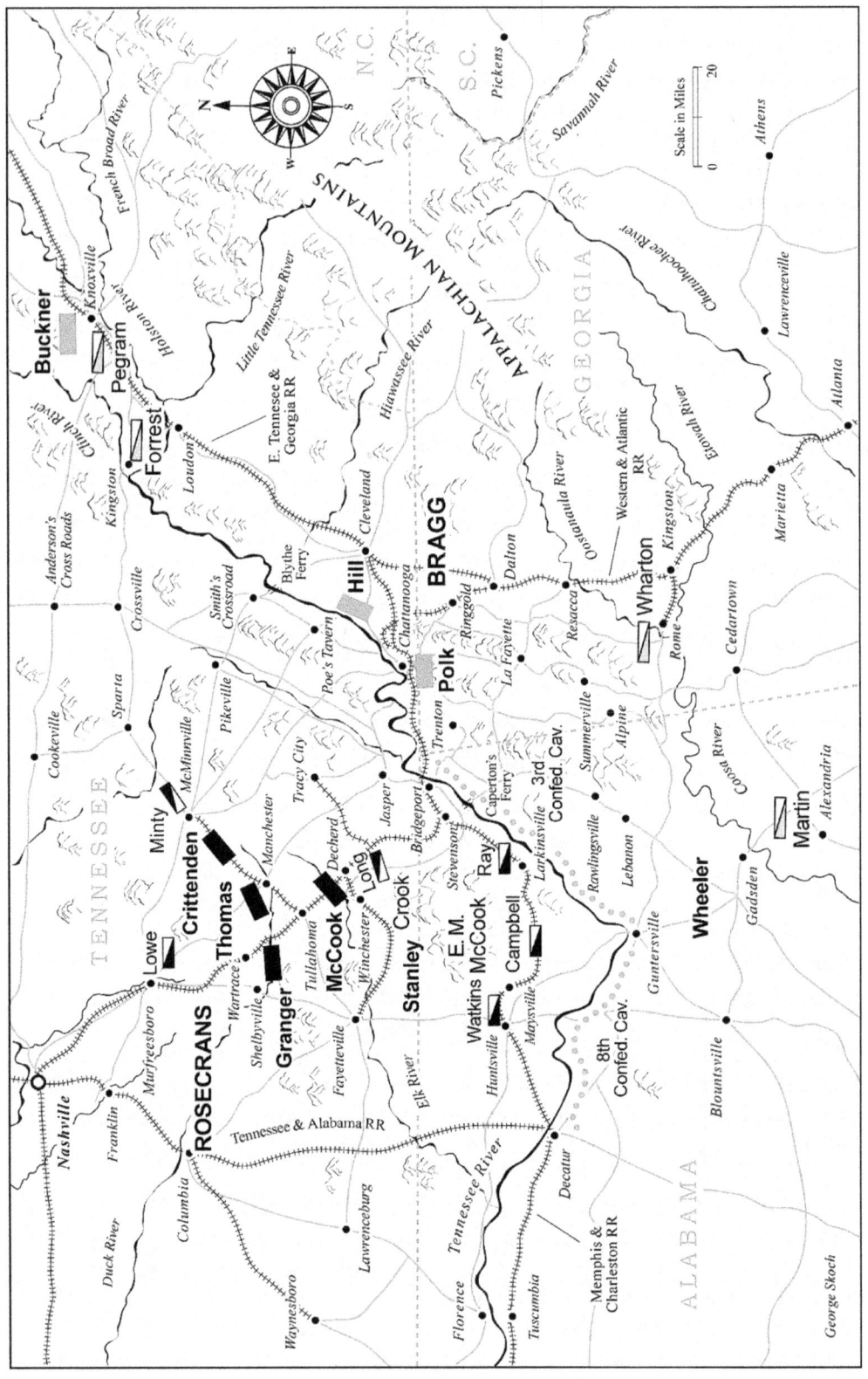

Opposing forces in mid–August 1863.

should like very much to move out of it." He finally moved his camp to Maysville where the environment was more conducive to good health and still in the center of his assigned territory.[13]

Operating along the wet lowlands near the Tennessee River in late-summer was periodically unhealthy for soldiers. Medical Inspector Frank H. Hamilton filed a report about the sickness many of the cavalry troopers: "The troops encamped at Stevenson, Bridgeport, and other points which I have visited in the valley, are already beginning to suffer from malarial fevers, both remittent and intermittent, generally of a mild character." Hamilton saw so many new cases that he became concerned the army might stay in this location too long. He consulted Dr. Thomas Maddin of Nashville, a former resident of north Alabama, and found that the malarial diseases were common in the area, particularly late in the summer. Maddin prescribed a treatment: "the cold-water effusion, or dash, as the most effectual method of arresting the chill, (a) and, as an internal remedy, he recommends a powder composed as follows: Take quinine, 1 drachm; calomel, ½ scruple; opium, 5 grains; cayenne pepper, 12 grains. Divide into six powders. Take one powder every 2 hours...."[14]

Archibald Campbell reached his assigned position on August 18 at the various ferries and crossings along the Tennessee River. The 9th Pennsylvania had the duty of guarding Gunter's Ford and protecting the countryside and railroad bridge over Mud Creek, a stream about ten miles south of Stevenson which emptied into the Tennessee River. The 2nd Michigan and 1st Tennessee Cavalry encamped at Bolivar (a couple of miles north of Stevenson) and guarded Caperton's Ford, Cox's Ford, and Shallow Ford, the primary crossings between Stevenson and Bridgeport. In addition, the two regiments picketed the roads in the vicinity.[15]

Despite the initial movements of the Federal army, no immediate alarm bells sounded for the Confederate army stretched in both directions at Chattanooga, but Bragg's chief of staff wrote to Wheeler to increase his vigilance in guarding the fords and connecting roads, although these orders concerned deserters rather than the enemy. Even Minty's attack on Dibrell on August 17 caused no immediate reaction from the Confederates.[16]

Minty Skirmishes with Dibrell's Cavalry at Sparta

Robert Minty had difficulties with George Dibrell's Confederate cavalry at Sparta. Since the beginning of the month, Minty made two expeditions to the town and except for the skirmish on August 9, Minty had failed to draw Dibrell into a decisive fight. Even though outnumbered, Dibrell knew the territory and tactically placed his troops in almost unassailable positions. When the advance on Chattanooga began on August 16, it became imperative for the Union cavalry to drive Dibrell back across the Tennessee River. But, Rosecrans' decision to begin his advance was abrupt for Minty who had only one day's forage for his mounts and Minty requested that Galbraith's 5th Tennessee cavalry be moved to McMinnville so that Minty's entire command could advance with the army. And so, began a tough month for Minty who operated away from Stanley's direct command and away from the main body of the Federal cavalry. Minty would remain on the left (east) flank of the advancing army as Rosecrans approached Chattanooga and as a result, he would report to infantry commanders. Stanley had broken this model when he assumed command of the cavalry and for good reason as would be demonstrated in Minty's case. Minty had two things going in his favor—the first was General Horatio Van Cleve. The bespectacled and thoughtful Van Cleve was one of the oldest generals in the Union army but he was very supportive of Minty over the next thirty days and he would intercede on Minty's behalf with Crittenden on numerous occasions. Secondly, Minty would share duty of the mounted forces on the left flank with Colonel John Wilder's mounted infantry brigade. As the march began, John Wilder's brigade moved to Tracy City, about forty miles south of Minty's position.[17]

Minty advanced with his three regiments—4th U.S., 4th Michigan and 7th Pennsylvania, and almost immediately Rosecrans ordered Crittenden to appropriate some of Minty's cavalry for his use. On August 18, Van Cleve responded to the request to send some additional cavalry for Crittenden's use. Van Cleve explained that he could not appropriate any more cavalry for Crittenden because he had one cavalry battalion already attached to his division, another battalion advanced to Spencer, and the remainder of Minty's brigade moved toward Sparta to fight with the Southern cavalry ensconced there. Rather than directly denying Crittenden's request, he explained that Minty would not join his division until the actions at Sparta were complete, but Minty expected rejoin the infantry column at Pikeville the next day. Van Cleve further reminded Crittenden that Minty's full contingent of cavalry was less than 1,700 men. Already, the problems of placing cavalry under the direct control of infantry commanders resulted in plans to disperse Minty's cavalry into smaller, less effective units, a style of command David Stanley abhorred.[18]

Minty's brigade left McMinnville in the early morning hours of August 17 in his next expedition to Sparta to fight with Dibrell's Southern cavalry. Since his last expedition, Dibrell's 8th Tennessee Cavalry camped at a mill along the river north of the town and had been reinforced with the 4th Tennessee Cavalry (Starnes) under the command of Colonel William S. McLemore. Minty arrived at 2:00 p.m. and he fought the enemy along Calfkiller River until dark. By the next morning, Dibrell and McLemore could not be found. Minty did not have a good estimate of the casualties he inflicted but reported: "Cannot say what their loss was; saw only 2 dead, but a good many wounded; a few by sabers." Minty's horses were shot twice from under him during the fighting in the skirmish. Minty reported his losses:

Casualties of Minty's Briagade at the Skirmish of Calfkiller River, August 17, 1863

Regiments	Killed	Wounded		Total	
		Officers	Men	Officers	Men
Brigade headquarters	...	1	1	1	1
4th Michigan	...	...	3	...	3
7th Pennsylvania	...	2	5	2	5
4th United States	1*	...	3	...	4
3d Indiana	...	...	...	...	...
Total	1	3	12	3	13

*one man drowned while crossing Calfkiller River[19]

In Dibrell's report, he explained that his scouts detected Minty's advance as it passed Rock Island and he estimated that Minty's command moved with seven regiments and a total of 3,500 men, greatly exaggerated. Minty's advanced force chased the scouts back to Dibrell's camp along Calfkiller River before returning to Sparta. Minty divided his command at Sparta

Five. The Advance to the Tennessee River (August 16–September 1) 93

to attack Dibrell's camp two miles north of town, just north of the confluence of Wildcat Creek. Minty split his command with the 7th Pennsylvania and 4th Michigan moving up the east side of Calfkiller River while the 3rd Indiana and 4th U.S. advanced up the west side of the stream to Sperry's Mill where they encountered Dibrell's 8th Tennessee Cavalry which had moved from the east to the west side of the river. McLemore had 200 troopers of the 4th Tennessee camped at the mouth of Wildcat Creek. Dibrell recorded: "[M]any efforts on their part to charge us and force a crossing was repulsed with heavy loss. We could only defend ourselves, owing to the smallness of our forces. At least half of the Eighth was absent on leave to get up supplies. But we held our ground and punished them severely." Dibrell utilized the terrain to his advantage, just as he had done earlier in the month, and escaped Minty's attack by riding to the north, to Yankeetown.[20]

William Van Antwerp, 4th Michigan Cavalry, described the fight in a letter to his wife. "We could not do much with them, the ground was so unfavorable to us and advantageous to them. We had to fight dismounted, our regiment were lying flat on their bellies all the time." Van Antwerp explained that Dibrell's troopers had better cover behind trees and the Calfkiller River lay between the two forces. For Minty's men to reach the Confederates they would need to cross open ground, then cross a creek. John McLain, 4th Michigan, recorded in his diary: "Found some rebs about 6 miles from town. Charged on them and took a few prisoners.... The rebs fired on us and we fell back to cover and had an Indian fight ... went around in the rear of the rebs and drove them into the mountains." McLain paid Dibrell a high complement in his diary, writing that the 8th Tennessee was the best regiment they had fought in the war. Othiel Gooding, 4th Michigan, described the fighting in a letter: "[T]wo out of our company ware wounded thare one of them was shot from his horse the other was dismounted and stood but a few feet from me he was shot through the thigh he is like to get well, the other one was shot in the neck the ball going down back of his lung, he is able to walk round and is like to get well, it looks hard to see men shot down in this way yet it dont give one such bad feelings as you would think it would."[21]

At the end of the skirmish, Dibrell withdrew his regiment back two miles to the crest of the Cumberland Mountain because he believed he was greatly outnumbered and expected the fighting to continue the next day. "As McLemore was withdrawing his men under Captain McGregor the enemy in his front made a fierce charge on him. His men rallied promptly near the barn of the Widow Fisk and repulsed them handsomely, killing 6 men and 6 horses." Dibrell reported his loss as 2 killed, 6 wounded, and 4 captured. "The enemy's loss was heavy, as we had every advantage in position...."[22]

Minty's report also included an account of an ambush at the conclusion of the day. Both Robert Minty and Captain Joseph Vale of Minty's staff refuted Dibrell's report that only two Confederate regiments participated in the fight and wrote that during the day the Union cavalry captured twenty-five prisoners from four different regiments. As the initial fighting ended, Minty's cavalry pursued Dibrell's cavalry to Yankeetown and this might have led to the account of McLemore's actions although the Union and Confederates accounts are very different. After Dibrell's retreat, Minty ordered his men back to Sparta to camp for the evening. Minty's cavalry traveled down a road along the heavily wooded Calfkiller River which had a bluff on the east side of the river. Two hundred Confederate cavalry hidden in the woods on the bluff ambushed Minty's column resulting in the wounding of Joseph Vale, two orderlies and the brigade inspector. In a letter, Robert Burns of Minty's staff explained that the Confederates moved into position on the opposite side of the Calfkiller River and occupied a position that had been cleared out by the 7th Pennsylvania and 4th Michigan on the advance up the creek. As the column advanced, Burns exclaimed, "an infernal fire was opened on us.... Their object was to kill Col. Minty by whose side I was riding.... The bullets whistled and sung altogether too close to be pleasant." Burns found no immediate cover and a high fence blocked the other side of the road. The head of the column faced a line of two hundred Confederate cavalry and the only way out was to ride through a gauntlet of fire. The Federal cavalry dismounted and returned fire as the enemy musket balls were "popping into the fence and earth." Then Minty's troopers pushed down the fence and found cover. Next, part of the 4th Michigan and a squadron the 4th U.S. Cavalry dismounted and returned fire while the remainder the 4th U.S. attempted to cross the creek north of the ambush without success, but the 7th Pennsylvania and 3rd Indiana successfully chased the attackers away after crossing south of the ambush. Minty arrived at Sparta at dusk and settled in for the night. The next morning the Confederate cavalry could not be found. Dibrell's familiarity of the territory proved to be a great advantage and Minty noted "[E]very foot of the ground over which we fought was familiar to them. It was wooded, hilly, broken, and intersected by half a dozen branches or creeks, with plenty of good positions, all of which they were able to take advantage of ... the country was to us terra incognita, notwithstanding which we drove them at a gallop. I had 1 man drowned, and 15 wounded, including 3 commissioned officers. I took 23 prisoners, including 1 lieutenant and representing four regiments." Due to the mobility of the Confederate cavalry, Minty was unsuccessful in driving Dibrell back to Kingston.[23]

After remaining in the Sparta area overnight, Minty followed his orders to advance to Smith's Crossroads, Tennessee, to his position along Crittenden's flank. He also left about two hundred men who had no mounts in McMinnville until Granger's Reserve Corps relieved them. The 3rd Indiana Cavalry remained at Rock Island and despite Minty's best efforts to include this battalion into his brigade, it would remain detached throughout the campaign. Minty rode forward with about 1,200 men. After the ambush along the Calfkiller River, Captain Joseph Vale found the Southern sympathizing Chattanooga *Rebel* newspaper erroneously reported that the ambush had killed "General" Minty, but when Captain Vale read the article, he pledged to shave his beard. He said he didn't mind being killed as a captain, but he wasn't ambitious enough to assume the rank of general.[24]

Dibrell unsuccessfully attempted to ambush the Union cavalry the next morning, and Minty proceeded unhindered on toward Pikeville.

The Army of the Cumberland Moves Over the Mountains

On marched the Army of the Cumberland over the Cumberland Mountains and Rosecrans, as ordered, sent daily updates to Washington. Two days into the march, Rosecrans' army progressed well with about half the army already on the Cumberland Mountains; but the roads were in terrible condition after the heavy July rains. Lieutenant W. L. Curry, 1st Ohio Cavalry of Long's Brigade, and his regiment initially had duty of escorting the wagon trains over the Cumberland Mountains and he described it as an arduous process. His diary recorded: "This is a day long to be remembered as the wickedest day on record, as the swearing of the 'mule whacker' would rival the demons of Hades." The importance of the railroad to

Rosecrans' plan became clear as his vast army marched over the barren mountains. In addition, on August 17, the Union engineers began sending the pontoon bridges forward on the railcars. And while Rosecrans was already two days into his march, he received a wire from Burnside (about 130 miles from Knoxville) that he had been delayed and planned to move from Crab Orchard, Kentucky on August 18.[25]

For the next few days, the Army of the Cumberland made its slow journey over the Cumberland Mountains (also referred to as the Plateau of the Cumberland which reached an elevation of 2,200 feet in certain locations) and on August 19, Wilder and Crittenden reached Dunlap, Tennessee about twenty miles due north of Chattanooga. North of Chattanooga and east of the Cumberland Mountain, the mountainous terrain gave way to the long and narrow Sequatchie Valley and immediately east of that valley was another steep elevation, Walden's Ridge, which reached an elevation of about 1,250 feet just north and east of Chattanooga. The newspapers of the time reported that Sequatchie translated as "very much possum" in honor of the large number of those animals in the valley. Dunlap was located between the elevations in the three to four miles wide Sequatchie Valley. Beyond Walden's Ridge lay the Tennessee River. Rosecrans hoped that by moving Crittenden to the north, Bragg would believe that Burnside and Rosecrans planned to march together into East Tennessee near Knoxville and the main thrust of the Army of the Cumberland would come from the north. Wilder moved his brigade directly for Poe's Tavern about 10 miles north and slightly east of Chattanooga and then split his command and with one half of his brigade advancing directly on Chattanooga and one half moving to Harrison's Landing about five miles north along the Tennessee River. With Crittenden pressing Chattanooga from the north, Bragg's attention would be directed there and not at the remainder of the Union army seeking to cross the Tennessee River to the west, near Bridgeport. Robert Minty's role in this maneuver was to ensure that Forrest did not break out into the Federal rear or circle around Crittenden's flank until Rosecrans' army united with Burnside's army.[26]

Major General Ambrose Burnside, commanding the Army of the Ohio, had orders to move in cooperation with Rosecrans' army (Library of Congress).

On August 19 Confederate scouts from Cumberland Gap discovered the progress of Burnside's column as it marched toward East Tennessee. While Burnside's exact intent was unknown, this alerted the Southern forces to a general movement of Union forces, even though Rosecrans' movement still had not produced reactions from the Confederate troops at Chattanooga. John Pegram, commanding Simon Buckner's division of east Tennessee cavalry, sent his troops ahead to bolster the infantry defenses in the gaps west and north of Knoxville and Buckner sent the question to Bragg—hold and fight Burnside in the mountains near Knoxville or withdraw to concentrate with Bragg's army in Chattanooga? Buckner faced

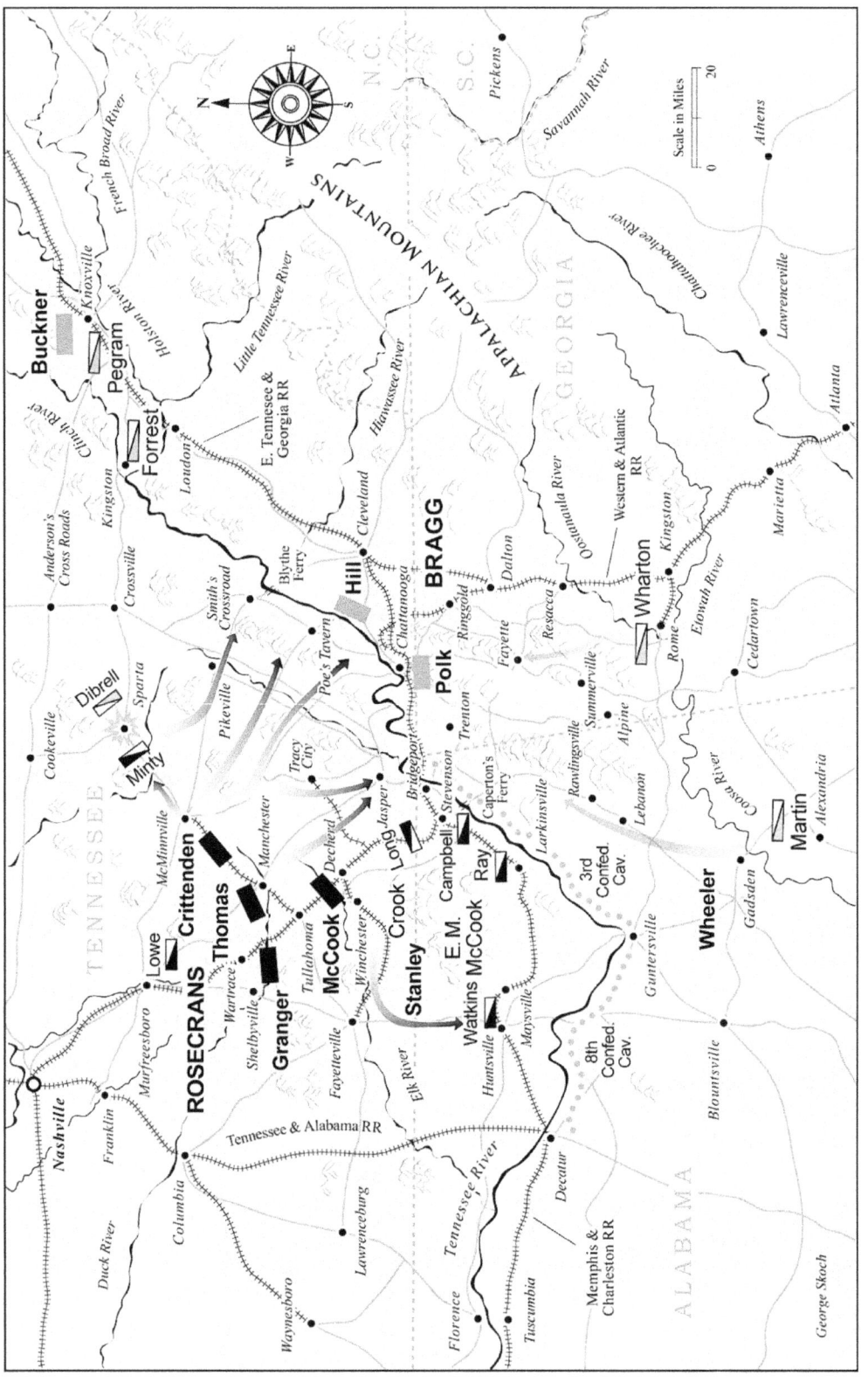

The advance begins (August 16–August 30, 1863).

forty-three gaps from which Burnside could choose to advance his army and without reinforcements he felt could not delay the Union army.[27]

Van Cleve's division of Crittenden's corps continued eastward along a line north of Dunlap and arrived at Pikeville, Tennessee about ten miles north of John Wilder's brigade on August 19. After the initial fighting and the movement, Minty's command was already reduced, through detachments, losses and "broken down" horses, to about 1,200 troopers. Minty, aware that Forrest was active near Kingston with about 4,000 cavalry, planned to make a mounted reconnaissance in force with about 1,000 men the next day. In the meantime, Gordon Granger sent his Tennessee troops eastward to bolster the connection between Rosecrans and Burnside. Because Rosecrans intended to swing south to attack Bragg, he needed to be sure he had some connection with the Union forces advancing on Knoxville.[28]

The march of Minty's brigade and Van Cleve's infantry division proved a difficult endeavor filled with some unexpected challenges. A member of the 4th Michigan Cavalry described the trek "as one of the hardest trips I ever had, it took me two or three days to get rested." Captain William Van Antwerp also experienced the dangers of traveling in Southern controlled territory. Van Antwerp's company became separated from the main cavalry column and rode into the night. Seeking to determine if he was in friendly territory, Van Antwerp stopped at house and had one of his troopers play the role of a Confederate cavalryman. The Union trooper yelled to the civilian in the house and told him he was a Confederate cavalryman. He asked the civilian if he had seen any "Yanks" and the man replied, "No." Then, he asked if the Confederate cavalry was nearby and the man replied that they had been there earlier, had supper, and had a camp a short distance ahead. Then, Van Antwerp knew he needed to backtrack and take another road.[29]

In contrast to Van Antwerp's experience, Minty's main column found plenty of loyal citizens in eastern Tennessee. Captain Joseph Vale described an incident in which a column of cavalry rode to house and found the occupant afraid that the men were Confederate cavalry. When he discovered the column was Union cavalry, the civilian exclaimed, "Delivers had come!" and he "praised the Lord that long-looked-for-day of the advent of the National army was come." Vale also recalled that many loyal citizens accompanied the column eastward and cheered the first Union soldiers they had seen so far in the war.[30]

A few days later, the Union cavalry's presence was still greeted with pleasure by the citizens in East Tennessee. George Clark, 4th Michigan Cavalry, wrote that his regiment participated in a flag-raising by the local citizens who cheered the cavalry in blue. Many of the citizens had never seen any Yankees and they came in from the mountains. Clark wrote: "They actually believed we 'Yanks' had enormous horns and long tails." James Wiswell, 4th U.S. Cavalry, described being greeted by an elderly lady who immediately grabbed him in a warm embrace, declaring he was the first Union soldier she had ever seen. Wiswell merely stated that she would probably see more Union soldiers than she ever wanted to see. At that point, a Union foraging party arrived and stripped the lady's vegetable garden despite Wiswell's protests. While many welcomed the Yankee cavalry, many pro–Southern citizens in East Tennessee traveled south, away from their homes, to avoid them.[31]

The next day (August 20), the Union trains arrived with the pontoon bridges near Anderson (about ten miles north of Stevenson), but little else happened of importance, except the various infantry regiments continued to move forward and many reached their assigned positions. This allowed for some time to resupply and rest after the march over the mountains.

Horatio Van Cleve also sent a message to Crittenden in defense of Minty and this would be one of several in which Van Cleve would intercede on Minty's behalf. Minty followed his orders and held the isolated position on the extreme flank of Crittenden's corps and opposite a superior number of the enemy. Van Cleve described Minty's shortage of rations: "He is short of forage. His train arrived today from McMinnville with but two days' forage, bringing all that could be had at McMinnville." Van Cleve told Crittenden that his orders to begin moving to the east arrived only an hour and a half before he began his movement from McMinnville. Minty had no time to prepare for the advance because he was already in motion in his efforts to drive Dibrell from Sparta. Van Cleve explained: "Colonel Minty could not have made his march by way of Sparta and accomplish what he was required to do in less time than he did it. He is certainly an able and efficient officer…." Van Cleve sent some of his supply wagons and all of Minty's supply train to the rear the next day to obtain supplies. In the meantime, Minty's brigade had little in regard to rations and only a small amount of forage. It was apparent from the communications from Van Cleve that Crittenden was critical of Minty's performance. Whether this was a continuation of some prior dislike or whether the result of this campaign was unclear, but Crittenden and Minty would spar verbally during and after this campaign. Minty's cavalry would be appropriated without his approval, and the welfare of the cavalry would be disregarded by Crittenden who had the services of the premier brigade commander of the Union cavalry.[32]

The Advance Part II—August 21–25

At mid-day on August 21, Rosecrans, from his headquarters at Stevenson, wired Washington that Crittenden's XXI Corps had moved into the Sequatchie Valley and Thomas' XIV Corps reached Battle Creek. Rosecrans proudly declared a victory for Minty at Sparta, although Dibrell would not return to Forrest's command until a week later. Rosecrans still needed some positive offensive results for those in Washington and Minty provided it. "Minty's cavalry had a fight with Dibrell's brigade, of Forrest's, at Sparta, on Monday night; whipped and drove them to Yankeetown and Kingston." Rosecrans also reminded those in the east that he still faced the formidable Tennessee River and he wanted his superiors to know that the crossing could be a bloodbath if he did not plan well. Fortunately for Rosecrans, the hot dry weather reduced the flow of the river and in places the river did not exceed four feet deep. His chief engineer, Lieutenant George Burroughs, recommended the crossing at Caperton's Ferry which had a good approach and the river was only 400–500 yards wide. In addition, the bank on the west side of the river "commands that opposite," so that infantry and artillery would have the advantage if the Confederates resisted the crossing. Finally, the river meandered at this location without a strong current. Burroughs also gave Rosecrans an option for a second location to cross—Cox's Ferry, which was two miles north of Caperton's Ferry and more unsuitable. Rosecrans, Alexander McCook and Stanley scouted together toward Bridgeport and after looking at the alternative concluded that Caperton's Ferry was the best location.[33]

At 11:00 a.m., John Wilder sent a message to General Joseph Reynolds informing him that his brigade arrived opposite Chattanooga. Wilder found two steamboats which he began to shell with his artillery and he noticed a pontoon bridge in the river, assembled and ready to be moved into place to the cross the river. The local citizens and deserters told Wilder that Bragg had a

Five. The Advance to the Tennessee River (August 16–September 1)   99

A view of the Tennessee River, a wide and imposing obstacle to Rosecrans' army (National Archives).

total of 30,000 infantry and cavalry at Chattanooga. Wilder delivered even better news—there were only two forts west of the town and no large enemy force prepared to meet the advancing Union army. Wilder initially observed no large caliber artillery at Chattanooga, but soon he received a shot from a 32-pound gun directed at Lilly's 18th Indiana Light Artillery battery. In all, Wilder counted nineteen cannons protecting Chattanooga. After scouting Chattanooga, Wilder sent half of his brigade to make a demonstration at Harrison's Landing, while observing the enemy, and continued drawing attention to a potential crossing north of the town.[34]

When Wilder's artillery began firing, the entire Confederate force in the town quickly moved into position to deal with the Union threat. Wilder returned on August 22 and again shelled Chattanooga from 10 a.m. to 5 p.m. and withdrew outside the range of the Southern guns. Brigadier General Thomas Wood observed the action from the heights opposite Chattanooga and noted: "They filled their works with men, and seemed to be very busy marching and countermarching. Evidently they had a great number of troops, or they kept what they had marching all the while for effect. For four hours troops could be seen moving about." Confederate officers reported that cavalry supported by artillery arrived on the north side of the Tennessee River and that Wilder shelled the town "without material damage." The Union attack gained the attention of the Confederates at Chattanooga who now recognized that a real attack was imminent. Leonidas Polk wrote to Major General Thomas Hindman guarding Kelly's Ford to keep a close eye on the Union activity ahead of him. Hindman also noticed cavalry, probably the 2nd Tennessee (U.S.) Cavalry, and reported without concern that the crossings and fords remained lightly guarded—"Brown's Ferry, one regiment, 300 men; Kelley's Ferry, 60 men; Running Water bridge, 60 men; Lookout bridge, 30 men." In fact, Patton Anderson withdrew back toward Chattanooga on August 21 in light of the increased size of the Union infantry on the opposite side of the river. On the Union-held side of the river, General William Lytle, at Bridgeport, also sent good news to headquarters—deserters reported that the Confederates on the other side of the river at Bridgeport were becoming more demoralized as they observed the increased Union activity. Union scouts also found that the enemy of the other side of the river at various location had not been reinforced which gave hope that a crossing might be successful.[35]

Finally, the movement of both Union armies toward Knoxville and Chattanooga dispelled the apparent lethargy at Chattanooga and forced Bragg to act as he realized the two armies marched directly toward his forces. After the artillery attack from Wilder, Bragg asked for help from Joseph Johnston and told him he expected Rosecrans to begin crossing the Tennessee River soon. He appealed, "If able to assist us do so promptly." Johnston responded that he would send him two divisions (Walker's and Breckinridge's) by train as soon as possible. Facing two Union armies, Bragg simply waited, but he told D. H. Hill that his reaction would depend on the further movement of the Union forces. So, he waited, and while he waited, the reports from his men in the field gave the impression that Rosecrans desired— the Union army was preparing to attack north of Chattanooga.[36]

Accordingly, the Confederates began to prepare should the Union army attempt to cross the river north of Chattanooga. Alabaman, Brigadier General Henry D. Clayton of General A. P. Stewart's division, wrote that he felt Blythe's Ferry was secure because he had rifle pits for six hundred men and the bluff on the east of the river commanded the river and the shore opposite. Clayton worried more about Doughty's Ferry, a few miles south. The west side of the river commanded his position at this location and, at present, he had only rifle pits for one hundred men. The concerns of the Confederate officers meant Van Cleve, Minty and Wilder were doing their jobs well. On August 21 Minty established his headquarters in a church at Smith's Crossroads (currently named Dayton) about ten miles north of Poe's Tavern and General Clayton's scouts immediately detected his presence. Clayton observed that five hundred Union cavalry took up position near Blythe's Ferry while the main body was encamped at Smith's Crossroads. In addition, Major General A. P. Stewart reported that he expected a crossing near the mouth of the Chickamauga Creek the evening of August 22. Further north, the Confederate action continued when Buckner began moving much of his command from Knoxville to Kingston and he placed Pegram's cavalry division under Forrest's direct command. So effective were the Union activities, Buckner also reported that Rosecrans apparently intended to cross the Tennessee River between Knoxville and Chattanooga. While Buckner moved the bulk of his command southward, he left some two thousand infantry guarding Cumberland Gap under the command of Brigadier General John Wesley Frazer with orders to hold the gap at "all hazards."[37]

Minty's Cavalry at Smith's Crossroads

The friction between Minty and Crittenden continued on August 21 when Van Cleve sent a sharp reply on behalf of the corps commander to Minty that despite being low on rations and forage that his orders required to him to remain on the flank until further notice. If Forrest was, in fact, at Kingston, Minty was in position to receive a severe blow if Forest's cavalry surged ahead. Van Cleve's adjutant general explained the orders "received from General Crittenden last evening ... required you to remain in the valley of the Tennessee until further orders. The general thinks you had better select some strong position near Morganton [just west of Smith's Crossroads], and send back to this place for rations and forage." Van Cleve cautioned Minty that he had no forage in his vicinity, but Minty would need to find feed for his horses in the local communities. Crittenden thought there would be sufficient grain in the hands of citizens, a supposition Minty would soon dispute.[38]

When Minty's cavalry arrived at Smith's Crossroads, his troopers secured the west bank of the Tennessee River at Washington by driving about one hundred fifty enemy cavalry to east side of the river. Minty's men found the other side of the river, at Blythe's Ferry, occupied with two firmly entrenched Mississippi infantry regiments of Brigadier General Mark Lowrey's brigade. Minty estimated that 900 infantry were positioned at Blythe's Ferry supported by artillery. The river was 700–800 yards wide at the ferry location. John McLain, 4th Michigan, recorded in his diary: "Our Company and Company B went in advance of the 7th Penn. to Washington, near ½ mile, the Tenn. River. No fighting except firing a few shots across the river ... Washington ... 7 miles northeast of Smiths Crossroads. Not much of a place." Many of Crittenden's men had low rations, but Minty's brigade alone, unlike many of the other commands, had not been supplied when the march began. So, Minty's cavalry suffered disproportionately and he voiced his unhappiness: "My rations run out in the morning. I must depend upon you to supply me. Forage is not so plentiful as you appeared to think. There is very little corn to be had. The position here is not good." Minty's cavalry had no supplies except what the cavalry carried on their horses. Robert Burns explained "We are again without tents, clothing baggage or wagons and have to go shirtless while one is being washed and dried ... we are accustomed to sleep shelterless on the ground."[39]

The Confederates suddenly became active near Minty's position on August 22 which resulted in another subdued clash between Minty and Crittenden. From Minty's headquarters at Smith's Crossroads, he observed the enemy crossing Blythe's Ferry after a day of increased activity on the southern side of the river. Due to the size of the forces, the Confederates moved across the river almost at will. Some enemy troops moved back across to the east side of the river while others moved west to develop the position of the advancing Union army. This action came on the heels of a Confederate attack on Minty's forage party near Washington the day before. Minty had posted six sentries at Blythe's Ferry and the men hurriedly returned the next morning after observing the enemy cavalry crossing the ford. Minty realized a large enemy force could push their way between Minty's brigade and the Union infantry at Poe's Tavern. This could isolate Minty and doom his brigade. Minty wrote: "My position here is, as I stated in my last, not good.... Forrest can take me in flank and rear, completely surrounding me." Minty prudently moved southward to prevent from being encircled. Crittenden insisted: "[H]e must reoccupy his position.... I am much annoyed at this movement of Minty's." But, General William B. Hazen, commanding infantry at Poe's Tavern, echoed Minty's concern, writing: "I have reports today, which I believe reliable, that all the crossings near here and above have been considerably reenforced. The conscript says they are expecting an attack above." Despite these problems, this increased Confederate activity north of Chattanooga boded well for Rosecrans. Burnside's advance and Crittenden's division had the desired effects on the Confederate army. In regard to the cavalry at Smith's Crossroads, Van Cleve wrote, "Colonel Minty has every available man and horse with him, and urges sending him more." Minty still operated with only three regiments while the 3rd Indiana Cavalry remained detached from his command.[40]

The inflexible Crittenden retorted through Van Cleve that if Minty had moved from his positions that he had done so without orders and that "he has acted very imprudently and must return to watch the enemy, and if forced to retire must do so on Pikeville. If by this fatal step he cannot reoccupy his position he must in some way rejoin you without fatiguing his horses. Being on the ground you must act on the above by your own judgment, and always have in mind the exposed condition of your left." Van Cleve responded that Minty moved back because he felt threatened by a superior force. Van Cleve declared Minty "no doubt found it absolutely necessary to save his command." Certainly, the driving force behind Crittenden's harshness was his concern about Van Cleve's left flank. Crittenden's position was tenuous and the same concern Minty had for his brigade extended to Crittenden's corps which could be exposed to attack from multiple directions. If Minty needed to withdraw, Crittenden wanted him to withdraw to the west and take up a blocking position on Walden's Ridge. On August 24, Crittenden wrote to Garfield; "I am all the time uneasy about Van Cleve's exposed left."[41]

Army headquarters tried to reassure Crittenden while giving him *carte blanche* command over Minty. Rosecrans told Crittenden that Burnside would soon be arriving to secure the left flank. In the meantime, Crittenden needed to hold his position to assure Rosecrans' plan of moving the army across the river. But Crittenden assumed Minty had abandoned his position while, in fact, he had just withdrawn a short distance while protecting his command. Minty explained that he moved his command about five or six miles south of Smith's Crossroads at 5 a.m. and established communications with infantry headquarters at Poe's Tavern, another five miles south. While Minty secured his position, he had scouts out in all directions to determine the movements of the enemy. Minty was correct about the increased Confederate activity and Van Cleve supported his concern. On August 24, Van Cleve informed Minty that two enemy infantry brigades moved hastily from Harrison's Landing in the direction of Blythe's Ferry. In addition, all the ferries and crossings from Harrison's Landing northward had been reinforced. While this response was exactly what Rosecrans had hoped, Minty faced a large force of enemy infantry, artillery and cavalry.[42]

The drama between Crittenden and Minty continued to play out when Minty attempted to set Crittenden straight about his movements. Minty wrote "The general is evidently under the impression that I abandoned Morganton and Smith's Cross-Roads; this is not the case. So far as watching the enemy goes, I was under the impression that I was using a good deal of vigilance." Since moving away from Smith's Crossroads his scouts determined that no general movement was directed toward crossing the river near Washington and Blythe's Ferry except for some small scouting expeditions. Minty chafed under Crittenden's expectation that his small cavalry brigade would stop a concentrated Confederate attack on his position; but Minty explained he had not abandoned his position and he still had troops in Washington and near Blythe's Ferry. Minty observed that two new enemy infantry regiments arrived at Blythe's Ferry the previous night making a total of four infantry regiments supported by artillery. Van Cleve, yet again interceded on Minty's behalf, while trying to counter Crittenden's dislike for the cavalry commander: "I have every confidence in Colonel Minty's vigilance and judgment, and believe you will be perfectly satisfied with his movements."

The Army of the Cumberland continued to receive little direct benefit of Burnside's advance. If Rosecrans expected Burnside to be pressing on Knoxville at the same time he approached Chattanooga, he was destined for disappointment. Despite Burnside's plan to begin his advance on August 15, his last message told Rosecrans that his army was still preparing to move forward on August 21; but much of his army was still at Columbia and Somerset, Kentucky—still over a hundred miles from Knoxville. Rosecrans was definitely on his own, although at this point in the campaign he expressed little concern about Burnside's progress.[43]

The Army of the Cumberland Inches Forward

On the morning of August 22, Rosecrans had about one-half of his pontoon bridge ready to be assembled. Another bit of good news reached his headquarters—the Confederate troops picketing the opposite side of the river near Bridgeport had withdrawn by the afternoon. General Lytle also sent a group of twenty-five sharpshooters to verify the absence of enemy troops. Patton Anderson's men by all indications had moved east beyond Shellmound. As a result, Joseph Reynolds' troops crossed the river and burned the railroad bridge there during the evening of August 22 without resistance. Reynolds claimed the ferry, three skiffs and a large flat boat.[44]

The Federal cavalry continued in its role of providing security for the flanks and advance of the army. George Crook left a poor record of the actions of his cavalry division. In fact, each cavalry division commander was required to keep a log book of letters and orders sent. The last entry in the Second Division log book ended the day John Turchin was relieved of command in July and no entry was made until Kenner Garrard assumed command after Crook was transferred in 1864. But some additional records show that Eli Long's brigade left Winchester on July 19 and spent the next two days assisting the wagons trains over the Cumberland Mountains. Crook settled his command near Stevenson on August 22. The next morning the 2nd Tennessee Cavalry of Edward McCook's division stretched along a twenty-mile front from Bridgeport to Jasper and some of the regiment served as couriers to establish communications from Joseph Reynolds' position opposite Shellmound with Wilder's mounted infantry located north of Chattanooga. Meanwhile, Rosecrans ordered David Stanley to bolster security in the rear of the army with Lowe's brigade. The 5th Tennessee was dispatched to McMinnville and a small overnight raid at Winchester sent some units of the cavalry toward that point also. Along the southern flank, the 4th Indiana Cavalry had a lively skirmish on August 24 and Major Joseph Lesslie led a scouting expedition to Deposit, Alabama on the Tennessee River. The 4th Indiana surprised a ferryboat crossing the river. Lesslie first noticed a man "beckoning" from the other side of the river and found a ferryboat trying to reach the other shore. When Lesslie's troopers arrived at the river, they received gun fire from about thirty Confederate troops on the other side trying to cover the movement of the ferryboat. Lesslie returned the fire, killing or wounding everyone in the boat except for one man who reached the other side. Lesslie captured one of the men who swam to shore and discovered that his men killed a fellow named Cooper, "a notorious conscript agent." In addition, Lesslie promptly arrested a preacher by the name of Poarch who had alerted the Confederates that the Union cavalry had arrived.[45]

Discipline again reared its head on August 21, when Lieutenant Benjamin F. Bailey, 2nd Michigan Cavalry, was arrested for allowing his men to engage in "house robbing" and to make matters worse when the action was brought to the attention of authorities, Bailey was found with some of the loot. David Stanley acted swiftly and decisively by depriving Bailey of his rank as an officer and placed him under guard until a preliminary hearing was held. To emphasize this point, Stanley ordered the details of the event to be read to the men of each of his regiments. Discipline would not be weakened.[46]

While discipline became an issue for some, for those troopers of Archibald Campbell's brigade who had reached their destination and patrolled the Tennessee River, there was time for a little relaxation. One of the most remarkable regimental commanders in Stanley's cavalry was Colonel James Brownlow, 1st Tennessee Cavalry. Brownlow was 6'6" tall and a favorite of his men. To alleviate some of the boredom, Brownlow challenged one of the enlisted men to a foot race and the very tall Brownlow, by 1863 standards, won the race. A few days later a friendly, unsanctioned competition started up between the 2nd Michigan and 1st Tennessee to see which regiment could steal the most pistols of the other regiment. Trooper Julius Thomas, 1st Tennessee, recorded in his diary: "there is quite a time amongst the boys of ours and the 2d Michigan regt. stealing pistols and selling them."[47]

Colonel James Brownlow, 1st Tennessee Cavalry, "is by far the best officer and the most competant to command us" (Mollus Mass Civil War Collection, United States Army Heritage and Education Center, Military History Institute, Carlisle, Pennsylvania).

Rosecrans Awaits Burnisde and Inches Closer to the River

On August 24, few new actions were undertaken but Rosecrans worried about the enemy along his Minty's flank. Rosecrans wired Washington: "Nothing further from the left, excepting that enemy are reported as having moved up two brigades to Blythe's Ferry, Tenn. Have heard nothing from Burnside. Would like to know if Grant is to do anything to occupy Johnston's attention. No changes in position today."[48]

Since the arrival of the Union forces at Chattanooga, the Confederates continued their increased vigilance and Major General Patrick Cleburne joined in the activity by securing the infantry line north of Chattanooga at the various fords. The flurry of Confederate activity ceased by August 24 when better intelligence and decisions ruled the day. Meanwhile, Buckner's corps remained about 20 miles south of Knoxville with about 8,000 men concentrated at Loudon and in proximity of Forrest's cavalry at Kingston. As Buckner withdrew southward, he gave orders for General John Pegram and Colonel John Scott to delay Burnside's approach, but reinforced his orders placing them under Forrest's overall command. While the Confederate forces north of Chattanooga reacted to the presence of the Union armies, Joseph Wheeler's cavalry continued to demonstrate little energy. Wheeler's cavalry provided little information regarding the Union army's movements across the Tennessee River and he used the excuse of refitting his horses as an explanation. Wharton's division remained in Rome, Georgia (75 miles south of Chattanooga) and Wheeler remained at his headquarters at Gadsden, Alabama, 90 miles southwest of Chattanooga. A member of the 8th Texas Cavalry recalled after the Tullahoma Campaign "I don't remember seeing another blue coat until ... [September] 19th and 20th." Despite the fact that Major General Thomas Hindman's infantry, as well as some of Wheeler's own cavalry, detected increased enemy activity two days before, Wheeler registered little concern along his flank. Will Martin's division waited far from the action of Rosecrans' army along the river.[49]

Burnside's cavalry finally reached the vicinity of Knoxville and the Confederate presence at the fords and ferries north of Chattanooga again strengthened overnight. With Rosecrans's left flank now more secure, he ended August 26 anticipating what Bragg's next move would be. Would Bragg move toward the massing Army of the Cumberland? Would Bragg attempt to repel Rosecrans' crossing of the Tennessee River? Or, would Bragg withdraw from this secondary place of importance and move to the more important location of Atlanta? Rosecrans thought he had enough intelligence reports to conclude that Bragg would dig in and attempt to hold Chattanooga; but this would be just one in many days of attempting to guess Bragg's next move. Of more immediate concern, Rosecrans needed to decide how to cross his army over the Tennessee River. Rosecrans' engineers determined that ropes 2,000 feet long were needed in some places to aid the infantry marching across the river while boats were needed in other areas. The Union engineers also prepared for the construction of a pontoon bridge to cross the river. In the meantime, Union soldiers swam to the other side of the river fairly commonly to determine the exact concentration and locations of the enemy, and Bragg still made no preparations to repel the Union army's crossing of the river.[50]

George Dibrell's cavalry finally rejoined Forrest and Forrest crossed some of his cavalry to the west side of the Tennessee River at Kingston raising concerns about a possible raid, but no further actions were made by the Confederate cavalry. Deserters told Minty that the Confederates were fully aware of the progress of Burnside's main column of infantry still located at Jamestown and that some of Pegram's and Scott's cavalry manned the gaps in hopes of slowing their progress. The rest of Pegram's cavalry provided a screen for Buckner's corps which stretched from Knoxville to Kingston. Minty made yet another unsuccessful appeal to Crittenden to understand this situation and allow him to add the 3rd Indiana Cavalry to his brigade: "I have made my pickets as small as possible—12 men on each road, except Blythe's, and there only 24—but yet the picket duty is very heavy. Can you not send me the men of my brigade that you have in Sequatchie Valley?" The next day Minty's patience had given out and he exclaimed to Crittenden that his men had no rations. "Rations ran out last night. You ought to keep me supplied with coffee, sugar, and salt. The men are constantly at work, and should be fed." Despite Crittenden apparent disregard for Minty's cavalry, Van Cleve, ever helpful, authorized the release of some of his rations for Minty's men.[51]

Burnside Moves Forward

Burnside optimistically reported that his column reached Tennessee, but other communications showed that he still had troops just leaving Crab Orchard, Kentucky on August 27. Despite this fact, Burnside's presence effectively forced Buckner southward. So, without firing a shot, Burnside seemed poised to claim Knoxville. Cumberland Gap appeared to be the only point that would be contested. Of the two armies converging in East Tennessee, Burnside appeared to have benefited the most. When Buckner had moved south, Bragg gained another corps of infantry and another division of cavalry which would face Rosecrans while Burnside marched ahead virtually unopposed. The combinations of the two armies marching into East Tennessee caused Rosecrans to a face stronger foe and now Rosecrans needed Burnside to continue southward to unite the two armies.[52]

Ambrose Burnside had a frustrating start with the Army of the Ohio. Burnside commanded the Union Army of the Potomac during the Battle of Fredericksburg in which Robert E. Lee's Confederates soundly defeated his army. After being relieved of command in the east, Burnside received command of the Department of Ohio in March 1863. In May, he arrested the anti-war, Ohio congressman, Clement L. Vallandigham, who had violated Burnside's directive forbidding the public expression of anti-war sentiments. Burnside even shut down the *Chicago Times* which had published anti-war editorials. Both of these events ran contrary to Lincoln's directives and the President interceded to rectify Burnside's action. In regard to the army, Burnside also ran into problems. In May 1863, he had only 31,000 troops available to cover four states. He initially placed 5,000 troops in Ohio, Indiana and Illinois and the remainder was stationed in Kentucky.[53]

When Rosecrans began his Tullahoma Campaign, Henry Halleck intended Burnside's Army of the Ohio to sweep south past the Cumberland River, but Rosecrans delayed his advance until late June. In the meantime, Grant besieged Vicksburg and requested more troops. While Rosecrans waited, Burnside sent 8,600 troops of the IX Corps to Vicksburg and this diminished the size of his command such that he could not cooperate in the Union advance on Tullahoma. To complicate things for Burnside, John Hunt Morgan initiated an audacious, but ultimately disastrous raid, in Kentucky, Indiana and Ohio. Morgan's raid began on June 11 and ended on July 26, and the raid required much of Burnside's cavalry to pursue him. In the meantime, Burnside initiated a raid of his own under the command of Colonel William Sanders. Sanders began his raid in mid–June and ended on June 23 as the Union force penetrated to Knoxville destroying bridges and tracks along the way.[54]

Once Morgan's cavalry was neutralized, Halleck turned his attention to Rosecrans' army which had been peremptorily ordered to advance. On August 5, Burnside received abrupt orders, in his mind, to advance his army in conjunction with Rosecrans. Burnside received these orders with anger and resentment. Burnside felt his army was too small for the territory it covered already, and therefore, Burnside felt his political enemies were working against him. They had placed him in a position to fail because his enemies wanted him to resign. From Halleck's standpoint, he felt Morgan's raid to be more nuisance than threat, and Burnside had received the return of the two divisions of the IX Corps which had been sent to Vicksburg, albeit smaller in size and tired after the recent campaign. Finally, Burnside understood his orders, but he was not prepared to march. He reached Crab Orchard, Kentucky on August 18 and remained there for three days as he tried to assemble horses and forage for the expedition. Finally, on September 3, Burnside rode into Knoxville and accomplished his initial objective.[55]

One final and yet significant event occurred in August. On August 30, Secretary of War Edwin Stanton announced he was sending one of his assistants, Charles A. Dana, to the Army of the Cumberland. Earlier in 1863, Dana had been sent to observe Grant during the Vicksburg Campaign. Little did Rosecrans or David Stanley know the impact of having this person in their midst would affect both their careers in the Army of the Cumberland. Stanton wrote: "Mr. Dana is a gentleman of distinguished character, patriotism, and ability, and possesses the entire confidence of the Department. You will please afford to him the courtesy and consideration which he merits, and explain to him fully any matters which you may desire, through him, to bring to the notice of this Department." The purpose of Charles Dana with the Army of the Cumberland was not fully known, but those in the army perceived Dana to be there to judge the progress of the campaign and received him as a "bird of ill-omen."[56]

Charles Dana was seen as "bird of ill-omen" for the Army of the Cumberland (Library of Congress).

The Cavalry Crosses the Tennessee

While Minty was active north of Chattanooga, Edward McCook received an influx of Union men wanting to enlist. He added twenty newly enlisted troopers to the 4th Indiana cavalry and another 76 partisans waited as a unit to enlist. McCook would be told not to enlist the partisans, because only Washington had the authority to integrate these men into the Union army. McCook also continued his task of cleaning out pockets of irregulars and bushwhackers and Louis Watkins' Kentucky cavalry seemed particularly adept at this task. Watkins also received several refugees and deserters. The deserters told Watkins that desertions were common in Bragg's army which was becoming more demoralized. Despite the good efforts of Louis Watkins in dealing with bushwhackers, the enemy struck back on the evening of August 26 burning bridges at Indian Creek (eight miles from Huntsville), Limestone Bridge (six miles from Huntsville), and Piney Bridge (nineteen miles from Huntsville). In addition, five troopers of the 6th Kentucky Cavalry were surprised and taken prisoner on the Maysville Road during the day. In retaliation, Edward McCook sent a regiment in pursuit of the enemy and had all the property in the area of the attack burned.[57]

To the east, Edward McCook joined with some of his troops in search of ways to cross the Tennessee River and was initially stymied; but the cavalry soon found new ways across the Tennessee River near Bellefonte, about five miles south of Stevenson. Captain James

Hawley of Stanley's staff found a new ford across the Tennessee River at Hart's Bar. Hawley gained the assistance of a local civilian who told him he might be able to cross at that location. Hawley took a chance and moved toward the sand bar in the middle of the river. He soon became too visible to the enemy on the other side of the river but concluded it could be crossed by cavalry. Hawley explained: "In crossing the channel I found in no place it was over 4 feet deep. I sent a mounted man 100 yards in as deep and heavy a current as in the distance I forded. The horse moved firmly through the current, the water coming half way up his sides. I believe the river fordable for either mounted or foot men, and am willing to take 50 men and cross, if the general commanding desires. I had 2 men with me, one of them 5 feet 5 ½ inches in height; still experiencing no difficulty in crossing. The roads on this side of the river would have to be improved, but good ones could be made." During the day, the axes rang on western shore as the cavalry began cutting improved approaches to the river at various locations in preparation for the crossing.[58]

At nine o'clock on the evening of August 28, Rosecrans began crossing the Tennessee River by sending the cavalry across first. His infantry moved into place and the pontoons for the first bridge were concealed but ready to be assembled the next day. He wrote to Halleck: "The cavalry will begin to cross tonight." Eli Long's cavalry brigade which had had duty at army headquarters pushed ahead, and 1st Tennessee Cavalry of Archibald Campbell's brigade moved across a ford and secured the other side of the river from Stevenson. Long encountered a portion of the 3rd Confederate Cavalry and some of the Southerners withdrew toward Chattanooga and others rode toward Trenton. General Phil Sheridan requested his old regiment, the 2nd Michigan Cavalry under the command of Major Leonidas Scranton, to lead

The ruins of Bridgeport bridge and pontoons can be seen partially across the river (Library of Congress).

the crossing of his division and the regiment crossed at Bridgeport and secured the other side of the river for the crossing of his infantry.[59]

Thus, began the crossing of the Tennessee River by the Army of the Cumberland, and what could have been a blood bath for the Union army passed with scarcely a whimper. About one hundred Confederates soldiers were captured as the crossing began. George Thomas' and Alexander McCook's troops quickly began to move across the river and secured the crossings after the cavalry made the first move. Brigadier General John Brannan's and Major General Joseph Reynolds' troops crossed the river according to Thomas' orders on August 29 at Jasper and Shellmound. Meanwhile, the pontoon bridge was completed at Caperton Ferry and two of Alexander McCook's brigades safely marched to the east side of the Tennessee River—Colonel Hans Heg's being the first across. When the 2nd Michigan Cavalry crossed over the river, the troopers found only a few pickets and then Sheridan sent the regiment scouting the area to find any potential threats and found nothing that would suggest that the crossing of the entire army would be challenged. The lack of resistance by the Confederates at the crossing even suggested that the Confederates might be evacuating Chattanooga.[60]

Henry Mortimer Hempstead, 2nd Michigan Cavalry recorded the crossing in his diary: "First we had to make a passage down a steep bank, about 15 feet to the bed of the river, then before us lay the head of an island covered thickly with a cane brake ... the troopers of the column were very busy securing things on their saddles, unbuckling revolver and cartridge boxes to carry over their heads.... But the crossing was not as bad as expected and the whole column reached the island without serious accident.... The 1st and 3rd Batt. were drawn up in line of battle along the shore of the island and the 2nd Batt. Company M leading ordered forward. For my part I expected every minute a deadly shot from the sheltered bank of the Southern shore but none came and we moved on unmolested." Hempstead noted that the cavalry swam the river, and the infantry passed over on a pontoon bridge the next day. Daniel Prickitt, 3rd Ohio Cavalry, recorded in his diary that the movement so surprised the few pickets on the eastern shore that they "struck terror" causing the men to retreat leaving their weapons behind.[61]

While the crossing proceeded from Shellmound to Jasper, Crittenden's corps continued to harass those in Chattanooga, and the efforts of the enemy to fortify the crossings north of Chattanooga continued. Rosecrans' feint worked perfectly, but not everyone was surprised by the crossing. Confederate soldier John W. Harris had written to his mother: "The enemy ... have batteries immediately opposite the town, from which they can easily throw shells anywhere in Chattanooga, and beyond it even." As the Union army moved toward Chattanooga, the Confederate supplies had been moved a few miles to the rear and the families who resided in the town had been sent away. Harris climbed to the position of a Confederate battery and looked at Crittenden's forces on the north side of the river and concluded: "I don't think the force there is a very large one though for I believe that the larger portion intend crossing somewhere below here."[62]

The Condition of Wheeler's Cavalry

The first crossings of the Union cavalry sent the thin line of the 3rd Confederate Cavalry to the rear. To the Confederate cavalrymen watching the crossing, Union troopers swimming their horses across the river looked like a "mass of moving centaurs." Colonel William Newton Estes of the 3rd Confederate Cavalry wrote to Wheeler, "Enemy crossed the Tennessee River 10 miles below Bridgeport this morning, by fording, in a large cavalry force. We are gradually falling back on Trenton. We have fallen back 1 mile since last skirmish." Estes, a native of Tennessee, resided in Alabama before the war. Unfortunately, Estes would not survive the campaign and would be killed in a skirmish with the 39th Indiana Mounted Infantry on September 17. So, effective were the actions of the Federal troops north of Chattanooga and so weak were Wheeler's reconnaissance efforts that this appeared to be the first indication that Rosecrans planned to cross the Tennessee River at Bridgeport instead of Chattanooga. The fitness of Wheeler's cavalry might have been the cause for his lethargy. His command ended the Tullahoma Campaign in very poor condition with Martin's division shattered and Wheeler seemed to show little energy in revitalizing his command. In addition, the Union infantry and cavalry were not impeded at all in their advance prior to, or during, the crossing, nor did Wheeler excel in providing intelligence to army headquarters about the movements of the Federal troops.[63]

Once the crossing began, Wheeler finally began to take some action. On August 29, Wheeler ordered Wharton's division, which had been at Rome since July, forward to meet the impending threat of the Union advance. Wheeler also ordered Will Martin's division northward from its position in Alexandria, Alabama—eighty miles southwest of Chattanooga. Bragg's chief of staff, William Mackall, wrote there was really only one "division of Wheeler fit for the field." The day before Mackall wrote, "No other news except inspection of Wheeler's cavalry shows it worse than even we thought." Deserters from the 51st Alabama Rangers reported: "They had been … recruiting men and horses; half of them only being armed, the others having lost their arms at Shelbyville." Despite the poor condition of his corps, Wheeler initially ordered Martin to move a short distance to Round Mountain, Alabama—and 20 miles northeast of Gadsden and 30 miles west of Rome. When the Union crossing continued, Martin moved on to Trenton.[64]

The full extent of Wheeler's defeat at Shelbyville and Wheeler's failure to instill discipline in some of his cavalry became problematic. The threat of Burnside and Crittenden converging on Chattanooga occupied Bragg's mind and as a result he ignored Wheeler's cavalry, and Wheeler seemed content to be ignored. A member of Wharton's division explained the horses were exhausted and the troopers needed time recuperate. Bragg would later explain that his cavalry suffered due to months of service with poor rations. Mackall's message seemed to indicate that the poor condition of Wheeler's corps was common knowledge at army headquarters, but perhaps the full extent was not known. Wharton was in Rome to recuperate and to enlist men to fill the depleted ranks, and Martin's division had the duties near the Tennessee River, but Wheeler was not vigilant in his duties in August. Security was lax. A Confederate army inspector rode from Lookout Mountain into Chattanooga without being challenged by a single picket. In addition, Wheeler had been reprimanded twice in July by Bragg for reporting inaccuracies because he often reported more officers and men available for duty than he really had. His second reprimand identified a major problem with Wheeler's men and that was discipline. Citizens, both pro–Confederate and pro–Union, made numerous complaints about the Southern cavalry, particularly those of Wheeler's corps. Even Wharton's cavalry at Rome was the source of "all sorts of depredations" and Forrest who gained new troopers expressed his unhappiness because the men had no discipline. The lack of discipline at Rome seemed to arise because of the low regard that the cavalry and the citizens held for one another. One of Wheeler's cavalrymen expressed the disregard of some of the Southern cavalry for the citizens near their location, "The Georgians are held in contempt by our soldiers because of their parsimoniousness—they are *the* Yankees of the south." Private Benjamin Burke, 8th Texas Cavalry, also wrote in a letter that the interaction between the citizens near Rome and Wheeler's cavalry was difficult: "The citizens here are a great more stingy than they are in Tenn. They ask very extravagant prices for everything." While the lack of discipline caused many problems, it was Wheeler's lack of vigilance in regard to security, and Bragg's lethargy, which allowed the Union forces easy access to the eastern bank of the Tennessee River.[65]

Eli Long's Trenton Expedition

Eli Long's brigade (2nd Kentucky and 1st, 3rd and 4th Ohio regiments) crossed the Tennessee River and, finding the east side of the river only lightly defended, aggressively set out on an expedition to determine the location of the enemy in the area. Long's brigade advanced over the river at Island Creek Ford under orders to silently cross the river. Once on the other side, the men had orders to capture the rebel pickets. In the case of the 3rd Ohio the surprise was thwarted when one of the officers' revolver accidentally discharged wounding one of the men. Once across, Long's regiments dispersed and scouted the east side of the river to the north and south to ensure there were no large concentrations of enemy soldiers. Long with the 2nd Kentucky Cavalry proceeded toward Caperton's Ferry and captured a Confederate courier with dispatches for Colonel Estes, 3rd Confederate Cavalry. According to the dispatches, only fifty of Estes' troopers guarded the crossing and Long set out in an attempt to capture them, but was unsuccessful. Next, Long ordered his brigade over Sand Mountain in the direction of Trenton and he found the ascent of the mountain along a poor road. At the top of the mountain, the Union cavalry captured four soldiers, three from the 3rd Confederate Cavalry.[66]

Traversing Sand Mountain was no easy feat. Geologically, the impressive sandstone plateau was a continuation of Walden's Ridge from the north side of the Tennessee River. The mountain rose over two thousand feet above the valley floor and a plateau, ranging from one to seven miles wide, crowned the elevation. Sergeant Daniel Prickitt, 4th Ohio, placed his field glasses to his face and looked up the mountain and saw men moving four miles away. As the 1st Ohio proceeded initially across the river they observed picket posts which had just been deserted. The 1st Ohio Cavalry also proceeded up the mountain via the road from Moore's Springs and found a citizen who reported that one hundred fifty of the 3rd Confederate Cavalry bivouacked on the side of Sand Mountain and another four hundred cavalry encamped two miles further along toward Trenton. As the 1st Ohio moved ahead they were fired upon by enemy vedettes but these quickly dispersed after a few returned shots. Lieutenant Colonel Valentine Cupp commanded the regiment and found several weapons and other equipment abandoned as the Union cavalry advanced. Cupp finally reached the top of the mountain and found Estes' camp. The 1st Ohio charged the pickets and then rode directly into the camp only to find their quarry gone. Cupp wrote, "[T]he colonel had left with his command a few moments before my advance reached the camp, leaving clothing, cooking utensils, commissary stores, and their dinners cooking on the fire; everything indicating a very hasty evacuation.... I destroyed 20 stand of arms (short rifles), killed 1 man, and captured 6 prisoners."[67]

Union Cavalry Supports the Crossing of the Tennessee

The initial steps for Federal infantry brigades across the river secured the fords and the all-important crossing occurred without a hitch. On August 30, full divisions of Thomas' and McCook's corps crossed the river. Also, Crittenden's corps which had done a splendid job of occupying Bragg's attention marched down the Sequatchie Valley and began crossing at Shellmound, Jasper and Bridgeport. Only William Hazen, George Wagner, John Wilder and Robert Minty would remain on the north side of the river to guard the crossings.[68]

Meanwhile to the south, Edward McCook began moving his division in preparation of a crossing near Bellefonte on August 30 and he ordered Louis Watkins' brigade forward to Caperton's Ferry from his position at Huntsville. All the cavalry was on the move, and this was time of excitement. Once the army crossed the river, then all focus would be directed on the Confederate forces at Chattanooga and Rosecrans' broad sweeping movement by McCook and Stanley south of the town.[69]

With the army pushing ahead, Gordon Granger's reserve corps marched behind, securing the vulnerable links in communications, transportation and supply. Colonel William Lowe's

The Union cavalry moved across the river like a "mass of moving centaurs" to secure the opposite bank for the infantry (from *Frank Leslie's Illustrated Famous Leaders and Battle Scenes of the Civil War* [New York: Mrs. Frank Leslie, 1896]).

Third Cavalry Brigade supported Granger's infantry and was dispersed in different areas of the rear. When the Third Brigade was formed in July, Lowe received this information in a rather off-handed manner. His headquarters remained at Murfreesboro throughout most of July and August and he had various mounted regiments under his command at different times, including his three regiments, but also the 7th Kentucky Cavalry and the 3rd Tennessee Cavalry. On August 27, Lowe's cavalry regiments were spread out in the rear—5th Iowa at Murfreesboro; a detachment of cavalry at Alexandria (5th Tennessee), Galbraith's cavalry (5th Tennessee) at Shelbyville; and two battalions of the 10th Ohio Cavalry *en route* to Athens.[70]

On the last day of the month, Rosecrans had his infantry corps in place and continued with the general crossing of the Tennessee River. The initial actions of the cavalry in reconnaissance and establishing beachheads brought positive news for Rosecrans, particularly Long's expedition to Trenton, which revealed no immediate threats for the advancing Union army at Sand Mountain. One of the Union cavalrymen poetically remarked about the march across the Tennessee: "It was a beautiful sight to see the cavalry file across the river in a semicircle three-quarters of a mile in length, just as the sun on that bright clear morning threw his luminous smiles across the frowning peak of Lookout mountain." Rosecrans initially concluded that with his crossing and the threat this posed to the Confederate flank would probably cause Bragg to begin evacuating from Chattanooga.[71]

In addition to Long's expedition, Colonel Edward King infantry brigade's movements were assisted through the efforts of 375 troopers of the 2nd Tennessee Cavalry who vigorously participated in scouting ahead of the infantry—"I sent Colonel Ray in advance, with instructions to proceed to toward Chattanooga, and if he could, without exposing his regiment too much, to go within view of the enemy at Lookout Mountain, falling back upon my brigade if hard pressed.... Colonel Ray carried out his instructions very handsomely, driving in the enemy's pickets at daylight, and approaching within view of a five-gun battery at Lookout Mountain, he captured a rebel acting commissary of subsistence...." Daniel Ray apparently had moved from his brigade command to lead the regiment which had discipline problems, but the troopers concentrated on the task at hand and performed the mission well.[72]

At 8 a.m. on August 31, the army was in full movement, unimpeded by the enemy. "Things are moving," wrote General Joseph Reynolds. Most of McCook's XX Corps had already crossed a pontoon bridge at Stevenson and second bridge was almost completed at Bridgeport. Thomas' divisions were also crossing at various locations. John Brannan moved across at Battle Creek, and the Federals claimed Shellmound. Reynolds wrote: "We have had possession of Trenton since yesterday morning. As I am informed, a brigade of cavalry [Long's] holds it.... Should any point develop itself during the day, will notify you. In the mean time, as the *New York Herald* has it, 'Watch and pray.'"[73]

The Federal crossing of the river caused action within the Confederate ranks. Leonidas Polk wrote a warning to army headquarters, which seemed to be too focused on the action north of Chattanooga rather than the threat which loomed west and south of the town. "I am just in receipt of your note advising me of the approach of the enemy's cavalry within 5 miles of the junction of the Trenton and Bridgeport roads, and suggesting the withdrawal of my guards and pickets to the intersection of those roads. In reply I have to state that I have not nor have I ever had any troops beyond Lookout Creek." D. H. Hill remarked that the lack of knowledge regarding the enemy's movement proved a "worse portent of calamity."[74]

The Army of the Cumberland marched ahead, and the Confederate commanders soon knew the extent of the movement. The reports of the opposing forces at this location are contrary. Lieutenant Colonel T. H. Mauldin, 3rd Alabama Cavalry, reported from Trenton on August 31, 1863, to Wheeler: "I arrived at this point 5 o'clock this morning, after a march of 35 miles yesterday and 10 this morning. The enemy were here yesterday with considerable force; came in about 8 o'clock and left in the evening. Did no damage. This morning about 9 o'clock the enemy attacked my scouts on top of the mountain, drove them down, and charged them and the picket." Mauldin had just been hurriedly ordered from its position forty-five miles away to assist the 3rd Confederate Cavalry, but his command was too small to stop the flow of Yankees. A short time later, thirty of the 1st Tennessee Cavalry (U.S.) accompanied some of the infantry to Trenton and found evidence that Alabama cavalry had recently camped at that location.[75]

Mauldin realized the thrust of the Union army was from the west and wrote to Wheeler on August 31 from Trenton. He told Wheeler that the thin line of the 3rd Confederate cavalry had been scattered with the crossings of the Union army and, more concerning, a heavy force of Federal cavalry led the advance. To meet this threat, the Confederates still had no large concentrations in position to delay the advance. By the time the Confederate cavalry could react, the Federals already had possession of Sand Mountain. Mauldin sent out a scout during the day and it came scampering back to headquarters after running into a strong force of Union cavalry. Mauldin declared: "I am looking for an attack in the morning. I shall soon be short of ammunition and rations. If a large force attacks me I can see no chance to save my train, as there is no gap here where I can go up Lookout Mountain. I shall do the [best I] can under the circumstances, and await your orders." Mauldin clearly felt the Confederate army was unprepared to deal with Rosecrans' army and Stanley's cavalry.[76]

Summary

The Union cavalry secured the flanks and marched ahead over the Tennessee River in this part of the campaign. Rosecrans' success in crossing the Tennessee resulted from good planning, excellent execution by Wilder, Crittenden and Minty and also, in a great part, by the lack of energy of both Bragg and Wheeler. The Union commanders worried about a determined defense on the east side of the River and as historian Peter Cozzens observed: "Had the Confederates been on the opposite bank in force, few Yankees would have gotten across alive...."[77]

Six. Bragg at Bay (September 1–8)

So far your command has been a mere picket guard for our advance—General William S. Rosecrans

Across the Tennessee—September 1–5

September arrived "dry, hot, dusty," wrote Marshall Thatcher, an officer in the 2nd Michigan Cavalry, and these conditions would generally continue throughout the campaign. The crossing of the Tennessee River by the Army of the Cumberland went without a hitch. By the end of September 1, half of both XIV and XX Corps had crossed the river and Crittenden's XXI Corps marched toward Jasper to begin its movement across the river. On the southern flank, Edward McCook's full cavalry division began scouting and establishing security of the east side of the river on September 2. While some of the cavalry forded the river, the 2nd Indiana and 1st Wisconsin cavalries crossed the river on the pontoon bridge that contained sixty pontoons. McCook initially established his headquarters on Raccoon Creek and then moved to Allen's House four miles north of Rawlingsville in Will's Valley. The crossing went so well Rosecrans wondered about the lack of a reaction from Confederates and wrote to Halleck: "Nothing more definite from the enemy."[1]

As Rosecrans might have expected, Bragg began to shift his forces to meet the new threat but he still took no offensive actions to delay the Union advance. Bragg had been blind to Rosecrans' crossing of the Tennessee River due in large part to Wheeler's failure to adequately monitor and communicate the Federal actions along the Tennessee River west of Chattanooga. Initially, the thin line of Confederate cavalry pickets along the river withdrew and returned to their commands and Major General Thomas Hindman's infantry troops at Shellmound moved back toward Chattanooga. Also on September 2, Bragg wired Secretary of War, James Seddon, about his situation but told him Rosecrans was still sixty miles away, and this probably gave the commanders in Richmond a false sense of calm. He explained: "Rosecrans' main force has crossed the Tennessee below Bridgeport opposite Stevenson. He is 60 miles from us, with two ranges of barren mountains interposed. Unable to hold so long a line without sacrificing my force in detail, Buckner has been drawn this way so as to insure a junction at any time. Burnside was 60 miles from Knoxville at last accounts." Bragg's lack of offensive actions increased Rosecrans' confidence and belief that Bragg would not fight at Chattanooga.[2]

Bragg's chief of staff wrote to Wheeler on September 2 with a much different tone than

Bragg communicated with Richmond. Brigadier General William Mackall wrote to Wheeler about the importance of communicating and expressed concern about the movements of Rosecrans' army. The Union army had crossed two corps without that information being sent to headquarters and Mackall needed details. Also, Mackall, clearly nervous about the lack of Confederate response to the Union movement, questioned whether infantry should be bolstering the cavalry's positions in the mountains. "I am uneasy about the state of affairs. It is so vitally important that the general should have full and correct information. One misstep in the movement of this army would possibly be fatal. Your line of pickets now occupy on Lookout Mountain about the same advantages they possessed on the river or Sand Mountain. The passage at Caperton's Ferry broke the line, and a week has passed and we don't know whether or not an army has passed. If this happens on Lookout, say tonight, and the enemy obtain that as a screen to their movements, I must confess I do not see myself what move we can make to answer it. Ought not there be an infantry force to sustain your line on the mountain?" In response, Wheeler became more active and hurried Wharton's division forward to picket the passes on Lookout Mountain east of Will's Valley, the deep narrow valley between Sand Mountain and Lookout Mountain, and he also established a line of scouts south from the Tennessee River; but he did not order a determined defense at the gaps over the mountains. One of Wharton's brigades moved to Alpine and the other to La Fayette. Likewise, Bragg did not order Wheeler to block any of the routes over Sand Mountain and not until two days later did Bragg send Wheeler any specific orders to observe the Federal movements east of the Tennessee River. Because of the large territory, Wheeler assigned only small forces to guard the major gaps over Lookout Mountain in front of McCook's XX Corps and Stanley's cavalry, ranging from three men to a maximum of forty men. These units would not be able to offer a significant defense to a large Union force but Wheeler wanted these men merely as scouts and observers of the enemy's movements. In the meantime, Wheeler particularly needed to know what Stanley's cavalry was doing and ordered increased communications in regard to the Union cavalry. Wheeler also turned his attention to Will Martin's division, but he merely relocated the bulk of this division to an undesignated location near La Fayette, probably Summerville. Wheeler continued to have special duty for the 3rd Alabama Cavalry and he ordered this regiment to set up pickets from the Tennessee River to Raccoon Mountain, then forward a mile west of Kelley's Ferry, and even further south onto Lookout Mountain extending into Will's Valley. All of the gaps designated by Wheeler covered the southern part of the Federal advance should the cavalry decide to initiate a raid toward Rome.[3]

Minty's Cavalry Brigade and Burnside Reaches Knoxville

Robert Minty's cavalry brigade, except for the 3rd Indiana Cavalry, which was assigned security duty at Dunlap, remained at Smith's Crossroads and had a tenser day than the rest of the cavalry, which had crossed the Tennessee River near Stevenson and Bridgeport. Minty reported that his scouts observed five brigades of Confederates at Blythe's Ferry, and General Thomas Wood also received some deserters who reported the enemy planned to attack and gain the rear of Crittenden's XXI Corps. Even William Hazen, headquartered at Poe's Tavern, who had been making demonstrations on the enemy on the opposite shore, expected an attack during the evening. The consideration of a Confederate attack on Crittenden's corps had not been missed by the Union commanders. Crittenden boldly wrote to Rosecrans: "If Bragg should make a dash at Burnside and Burnside retire slowly, declining to fight, I think we can destroy his [Bragg's] army." Crittenden, who remained remarkably over-confident during the campaign, showed little concern for a concentrated attack on his dispersed infantry.[4]

Ambrose Burnside sent welcome news to Rosecrans on September 2 from Kingston that his columns were pushing for Loudon and Knoxville. On the same day, Robert Minty's brigade worked for the first time in conjunction with troops of the Army of the Ohio. Minty's cavalry led the advance of Burnside's troops into Kingston, captured twelve prisoners and had one trooper mortally wounded during the skirmish which resulted. The action effectively drove the last Confederate cavalry across the Tennessee River. Forrest's cavalry burned all the boats in the area as they retreated so they would not be used by the Federals. Three riverboats, the *Tennessee*, the *Holston*, and the *James Clover*, steamed closer to Loudon for use by Bragg's forces; but all of the crossings south of Kingston remained heavily guarded by Confederate troops. Frank Armstrong's Confederate cavalry division supported the infantry guarding the crossings, but morale was low. Minty's command, now about 1,100 men strong, collected eighty-seven deserters over the last ten days. There were numerous fords and ferries along his sixty-mile long portion of the river and while keeping an eye on the enemy, he found the opposite shore firmly defended by infantry and cavalry; but he observed that the supporting artillery had been withdrawn. Minty felt more confident with his flank secured by Burnside's troops and his reports reflected this. Frank Wofford's cavalry brigade of the Army of the Ohio held the line at Big Emery, Tennessee, just outside Kingston and aided in keeping Forrest on the east side of the Tennessee River.[5]

The remainder of the Army of the Cumberland continued its advance. Upon reaching the eastern shore of the Tennessee River at Bridgeport and Stevenson, the infantry and cavalry began pushing ahead and over Sand Mountain. Jefferson C. Davis' infantry division stopped for the night on September 2 in Lookout Valley after traversing the imposing Sand Mountain. He reported, "Wheeler's headquarters were in this neighborhood a few days ago, but now he has gone down Will's Hollow (or valley) to Lebanon and Gadsden, Ga. [Ala.] and is occupying that part of the country with a large cavalry force." In more accurate intelligence, Davis reported that five hundred of Will Martin's cavalry held a position near at Trenton. Alexander McCook's southern-most infantry corps continued to implement its orders and marched forward into Will's Valley to Winston's Gap. Thomas' and Crittenden's corps also moved easily across the river and then pressed ahead.[6]

Lowe's Cavalry Brigade in the Rear

At the rear of the Rosecrans' army, Colonel William Warren Lowe's Third Cavalry Brigade continued its inglorious duty of assisting with the security of the communications and supply lines that linked the army at Chattanooga to Nashville. This was important duty but duty which received very little recognition. Lowe was a West Point graduate and was recognized as an able, professional officer. Lowe's brigade worked in conjunction with Gordon Granger's Reserve Corps which assumed the positions previously held by infantry marching to the front. Granger, an infamous stickler for discipline and detail, was the perfect choice for this duty. Granger watched over the communication lines from McMinnville to Huntsville, Alabama—a very large task. The vitally important McMinnville supply depot proved a source of trouble for Granger. In early September, the 3rd and 6th East Tennessee Infantry and the 5th Tennessee Cavalry arrived to provide security, and Rosecrans considered that Lowe should command all the forces there due to his experience. While this was a good decision, the removal of the 5th Iowa from Murfreesboro left the railroad in that area without cavalry protection and the other problem was Brigadier General James Spears who had accountability for the forces at McMinnville. Spears held a superior rank to Lowe which made it impossible to assign Lowe, even though many wanted Lowe, or anyone except Spears, to command the depot at McMinnville. Spears was so un-liked that twenty-seven officers at McMinnville, including cavalry officers, wrote to Rosecrans urging Spears removal: "We, the undersigned officers composing the Third Brigade, Third Division, Reserve Corps, Army of the Cumberland, would most respectfully beg that you would relieve us of Brigadier General Spears, who, we are informed, is to command us, who, by his former tyranny and ungentlemanly conduct toward us, his subordinate officers, rendered him more than useless for doing good in that cause which you have done so much to bring to a successful issue. Since his return to Carthage the dissatisfaction is so great that, in the opinion of your humble petitioners, six weeks with him commanding will deplete the brigade by demoralization. He has also threatened that any officer offering his resignation shall be placed under arrest and the communication stopped: also that the Tennesseans (loyal soldiers) would see hell. We would therefore humbly pray that you in your official capacity may see proper or fit to assign the command to either of our colonels, or should you think it best to send us some other officer and gentleman, we will cheerfully discharge our duties as officers and soldiers. We have the utmost confidence in your judgment and discretion after the fact is known to you that Brig. Gen. James G. Spears does not enjoy the confidence of either officers or soldiers, feeling that from your well-known philanthropic and Christian principle we will not have plead in vain." The decision to send the 5th Iowa to McMinnville was approved, whether a result of the letter complaining about Spears or not. The 5th Iowa Cavalry reached the town on September 8, 1863; however, the regiment did not remain long in McMinnville and after a few days, rode to Tracy City, only to return by September 15.[7]

Lowe also had other regiments spread across Granger's assigned territory, and the 10th Ohio Cavalry, which recently arrived in Athens, rode to Huntsville as Granger's Reserve Corps moved forward. The 10th Ohio Cavalry regiment would be dispersed along a line from Huntsville to Larkinsville, the territory Watkins' cavalry brigade previously held. Initially, four companies were assigned duty at Huntsville and another three companies were sent to Flint River. Upon the arrival of the Ohio cavalry, Watkins' Kentucky cavalry moved forward with McCook's division into Georgia. The 7th Kentucky Cavalry, although part of Louis Watkins' brigade, also moved with Granger's corps and would remain near Bridgeport throughout the campaign.[8]

Rosecrans Issues New Orders

Now that Rosecrans' army had successfully crossed the Tennessee River, it was time for the next part of his plan to be unveiled. The campaign so far had unfolded beyond Rosecrans' expectations. Alexander McCook summarized: "All goes on swimmingly…." The cavalry had done valuable service during the first phase of the campaign, but its duty was primarily defensive. Now, Rosecrans needed to make a decisive advance to draw his adversary into battle and this required important duty for the cavalry.[9]

Rosecrans issued new general orders on September 3. First, Thomas' corps was ordered to march for Trenton, while a regiment was sent north to form a connection with Crittenden's advancing corps. Then, a division was ordered to move to capture Frick's Gap and Stevens' Gap. Thomas would retain only a single regiment of Wilder's Mounty Infantry for his use and the remainder of the brigade would continue working with Crittenden. Meanwhile, Crittenden planned to march directly for Chattanooga, protecting the railroad along the way. There remained a real likelihood that Bragg intended to fight at Chattanooga and the railroad remained a valuable part of the Union supply line. Alexander McCook needed to advance his corps to Valley Head and then, over Lookout Mountain. McCook's orders directed him to capture Winston's Gap and then open communications with Thomas on his left flank.[10]

In regard to the cavalry, Minty's cavalry remained detached from Stanley's command, as was Lowe's brigade, which remained in the rear, leaving Stanley with four cavalry brigades on the right flank. Stanley ordered Long's brigade and Edward McCook's entire division to advance to Valley Head and Rawlingsville on the extreme southern flank of the army. Then, Eli Long's brigade was ordered to cooperate with Alexander McCook's advance and with the remaining cavalry, Stanley was ordered to make an advance on Rome. Specifically, in regard to the Rome expedition the orders stated: "General Stanley will send such force from Rawlingsville as he may deem sufficient for the purpose to Rome, Ga., or as far in that direction as practicable, to ascertain the position and intentions of the enemy. This force should push forward with audacity, feel the enemy strongly, and make a strong diversion in that direction." These orders were critical to the subsequent actions along the southern flank and specifically stated the need to "feel" the enemy with a force sufficient to accomplish the task. As the campaign continued, these orders would serve as a major point of disagreement between Rosecrans and Stanley.[11]

Rosecrans' orders clarified how the cavalry would be used. Only Edward McCook's three brigades had the flexibility of independent action and Rosecrans and Garfield had definite plans for them. In regard to other mounted troops, Crittenden would also have the use of most of Wilder's brigade throughout the advance on Chattanooga and Thomas would have only a single regiment of mounted infantry. Alexander McCook would have use not only of Eli Long's brigade, but also Colonel Thomas Harrison's 39th Indiana Mounted Infantry.

Cavalry Moves Over Sand Mountain

David Stanley reached Winston's, the home of Colonel William O. Winston, on the evening of September 3. The Union cavalry was welcomed by Winston, a public figure in DeKalb County, opposed to succession and loyal to the Union. Specifically, Edward McCook's division moved into position in Will's Valley near Allen's House, north of Rawlingsville, and Crook and Eli Long remained near Stanley's headquarters at Winston's. The cavalry trains still lagged two days behind due to the slow pace of getting wagons over the mountains. The local citizens reported, incorrectly, that Wheeler's cavalry was only twenty-four miles away at Lebanon.

Stanley prepared to meet the enemy and boldly stated: "As soon as I get the cavalry well together I will move Wheeler." The Army of the Cumberland had poor maps and Stanley told Garfield that Winston's was twice as far from Trenton as the maps indicated—twenty miles south instead of ten. Stanley, while happy with the ease of movement of his cavalry, knew that the Federal cavalry faced two corps of enemy cavalry, Forrest's and Wheeler's. Granted Forrest's cavalry remained north of Chattanooga and Stanley primarily faced Wheeler's corps, but Stanley faced Wheeler's corps with a division. Edward McCook's division (three brigades) had the primary task of dealing with Wheeler.[12]

When Edward McCook prepared his cavalry for movement into Georgia, he ordered his men to advance with little encumbrances—three days' rations in haversacks, no "led horses," no baggage and no dismounted troopers. McCook also permitted only one ambulance for each regiment and he told his brigade commanders to assign the weakest regiment to escort the cavalry baggage train over Sand Mountain, a difficult enterprise. The 2nd Indiana Cavalry crossed the eighteen-mile path over Sand Mountain on September 3 and Sergeant G. W. Baum wrote that the "land is poor you could not raise beens." The 2nd Indiana stopped for the night near Jefferson C. Davis's division in Little Wills Valley after an arduous trek. Baum exclaimed that after passing over the mountain he lost his desire to ever climb mountains again. First Lieutenant Isaac Conwell of the same regiment wrote that the movement was complicated because the narrow roads were blocked by wagons and infantry. He wrote: "Had an awful time." Marshall Thatcher, 2nd Michigan Cavalry, observed the mountain seemed more rock than sand and even the mule drivers had difficulty getting their teams over this imposing obstacle. Accidents occurred while moving over the mountains and troopers observed mules still hitched to wagons tumble over the mountainside. Certainly, topography and terrain became important parts of the campaign in the mountains near Chattanooga for the cavalry and infantry alike. The route was "rough and mountainous and was almost destitute of water, as well as forage. Sand and Lookout Mountains, with their steep and rugged sides, with bad roads, presented a barrier almost too great for an army to undertake," wrote W. R. Carter, 1st Tennessee Cavalry. The passage over the mountain was equally difficult for the artillery. Benjamin Nourse, whose section of the Chicago Board of Trade Artillery traversed the mountain, had a difficult time and while encouraging the horses up the mountain, his horse fell and landed on his leg. He made the remainder of the passage over the mountain in the rear of an ambulance.[13]

Stanley's initial chore was locating Wheeler's cavalry and any concentrations of infantry on the southern flank. Although a superior force which had the opportunity to strike severe blows to the dispersed Union cavalry which inched over the mountains and valleys, so far, Wheeler offered no resistance. As Edward McCook scouted ahead he soon discovered that Wheeler was not in Rawlingsville or Lebanon, nor was there any enemy infantry at Gadsden, which was good news for the Federal cavalry. Edward McCook brought better intelligence regarding Wheeler's location than the earlier reports and explained that one of John Wharton's brigades, was located at Alpine, not Lebanon. His intelligence also indicated that Will Martin with five regiments (1st Alabama, 3rd Alabama, 51st Alabama, 1st Confederate, and 4th Alabama) of 2,000 troopers concentrated near Trenton. While McCook gathered intelligence about the Confederates in the area, the enemy observed the Union movements from atop the imposing Lookout Mountain. Confederate observers reported McCook's and Thomas' movement on Sand Mountain included about 40,000 troops.[14]

Six. Bragg at Bay (September 1–8) 121

The breath-taking view from Lookout Mountain (Library of Congress).

Throughout the next phase of the Chickamauga Campaign (September 6–September 17), David Stanley and Alexander McCook worked very closely together. Stanley was separated from army headquarters by sheer distance and by the complex geography of the area. Often Stanley sent his messages to Rosecrans via McCook, who was closer. In addition, their joint actions required that McCook and Stanley operate in a cooperative manner. They often moved units in conjunction, McCook supporting the cavalry which provided security along the flank; and together the two Union forces intended to make a large wheeling movement from the west and south to cut Bragg's communications and supply lines to Rome and Atlanta. The relationship between Stanley and Alexander McCook was a good as would be demonstrated throughout this campaign. The two men were classmates at West Point and worked well together. Alexander McCook wrote to Stanley on the evening of September 3 explaining which of the gaps Garfield had assigned for him to capture (Winston's and Stevens' gaps), and that Stanley had been assigned the duty of capturing Dougherty's Gap. McCook concluded his message with perhaps the most important item: "I hope you are better. Have you

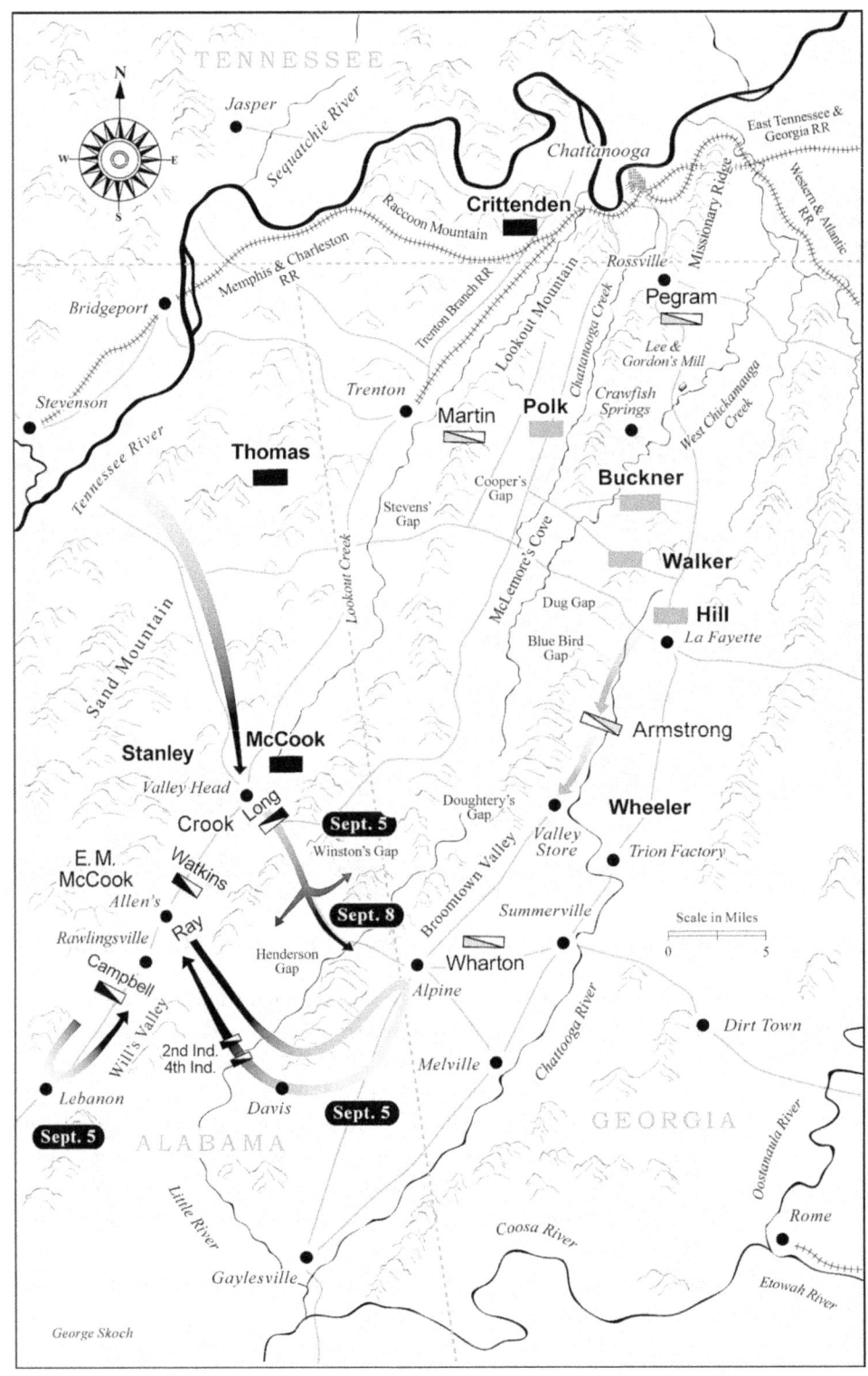

Union cavalry movements: September 2–8.

any news?" Stanley had dysentery and this was the first record of his illness. Although many in the army fell ill, this was important because it impacted and clouded the cavalry actions during the campaign.[15]

Edward McCook continued to scout the immediate area and funnel intelligence reports to Stanley's headquarters. McCook sent his troops up Lookout Mountain and the large mountain offered an opportunity to watch enemy troop movements in the valleys below. It had been so dry any large troop movements produced clouds of dust and McCook sent scouts to observe the Chattanooga-Rome Road. They observed a continuous cloud of dust from a supply train or troop column moving along the road. Edward McCook had not yet reached Rawlingsville, but he promised to sound reveille at 3:00 a.m. and have the men in the saddle by four o'clock. The cavalry remained at its location and scouted the immediate area, because one regiment from each of the brigades still remained with the cavalry train trudging over Sand Mountain.[16]

Those advancing over the mountains and valleys soon lost confidence in the maps which had been provided. Stanley and Alexander McCook corrected the distances which had been incorrectly recorded on the poor maps. Alexander McCook bitterly wrote to army headquarters about his line of march and explained there was no Winston's Gap as specified on the map. Colonel Winston lived at the base of the mountain and the eight-mile trail leading over the mountain was poor. He also clarified the distances from his location which were also incorrect on his map—"25 miles from La Fayette, 23 miles from Trenton, 9 miles from Rawlingsville, 25 miles from Caperton's Ferry, 48 to Rome, 42 to Chattanooga, and 45 to Dalton." David Stanley had set up his headquarters there, too. "All goes on well. The rebel cavalry has all moved toward Chattanooga."[17]

McCook also sent a message to George Thomas, to the north, that he received two deserters from the 51st Alabama Partisan Rangers from Wheeler's cavalry corps. They told McCook that Wheeler had two thousand cavalry at Alpine and they were planning to move toward Chattanooga. The information McCook gathered from prisoners led him to believe that Bragg planned to concentrate his forces at Chattanooga. McCook also heard rumors that Joseph Johnston had arrived in Chattanooga and that Longstreet would reinforce Bragg.[18]

The Cavalry Crosses Lookout Mountain into Broomtown Valley

On September 4, Crook's cavalry brigade moved into Broomtown Valley just west of Lookout Mountain. The cavalry commanders discovered the road forked with one route leading to Alpine and the other to Summerville, two towns that would receive much attention in the upcoming days. McCook and Stanley decided to send Long's cavalry along a route which reached eight miles north of Alpine. McCook optimistically wrote: "I do not know what Stanley's instructions are, but he wrote me that he could carry them out as well on that, side of Lookout Mountain. He has 5,800 sabers and can whip all before him."[19]

Stanley sent word to Garfield on the morning of September 4 that Eli Long's brigade took possession of the gap over Lookout Mountain. In the meantime, Edward McCook had his cavalry in the saddle and riding further south toward Rawlingsville to ensure that no enemy troops lingered along his southern flank. The trails and roads over the mountain proved to be a problem and Stanley described: "Four miles this side of Rawlingsville a road

McCook's cavalry scouting the mountains caused him to report—"This movement of these regiments and their return after night ... will lead the enemy to think that we have moved in the direction of Rome" [Alfred Waud drawing—"Scouting in the Blue Ridge" (Library of Congress)].

crosses the mountain, but it is a bad road. The crossing here is also bad; no depression in the mountain. Between this and Easley's are traces every 4 or 5 miles which cavalry may cross, single file." Stanley often relied on citizens for intelligence and they told him that the Confederate cavalry had been in the area and Martin's division was rumored to be moving to Chattanooga and that Wharton's division was directly east in Broomtown Valley. Stanley also clarified the accurately identified the distances on the inaccurate Union maps and he told Garfield the distance to Rome as 48 miles, Dalton 45–50 and La Fayette 25 miles. "I will send a force to Broomtown Valley tomorrow. I am satisfied we can learn nothing of the enemy's movements until we cross the mountain." Stanley also alluded to an upcoming expedition to Rome by the cavalry planned for September 8. During the day, Edward McCook's cavalry scouted the area and McCook identified the best route to Rome utilized the Winston's Gap road. After finding no concentration of enemy troops in Will's Valley, no further movement southward was needed and Rome was almost directly east of his current location. Stanley also sent McCook to scout the mountain to the east of Rawlingsville to ensure there were no enemies there. Stanley also reminded Garfield that his supply trains and escorting regiments had not passed over Sand Mountain. At least, two regiments of McCook's division had yet to reach his headquarters—2nd Michigan and 2nd Tennessee, and McCook expected them to arrive the next morning.[20]

Supply trains were not a glorious aspect of the Chickamauga Campaign for the Army of the Cumberland, but these trains were all important. The wagon trains would roll back and forth and brought the valuable ammunition and rations to the army from the supply depots at the Tennessee River and carried the sick back to the hospitals. The roads were poor and narrow particularly over the mountain gaps. While the cavalry also had a large supply train, this train remained with XX Corps which progressed more slowly than the cavalry but this allowed the cavalry greater mobility.[21]

Bragg Contemplates Rosecrans' Advance

Bragg called a meeting of his top commanders on September 2 and announced that the bulk of Rosecrans' infantry and cavalry had crossed the Tennessee River; but the meeting achieved very little else in regard to stopping the Federal advance. Daniel Harvey Hill assumed the role of confidant and advisor to Bragg and Bragg encouraged Hill's view of the situation. Hill told Bragg on September 3, "If the Yankees have really crossed in force at Caperton's, it seems to me plain that the movement is for Chattanooga, in order to secure the railroad as an entirety. They will work their way up Will's Valley until they get in position to drive us from Chattanooga. The [rail]road will then be put in operation from Bridgeport." Hill had surmised Rosecrans' plan accurately and immediately. Bragg responded the next day and explained that Thomas' and McCook's corps were on the east side of the river and he believed the Union objective was Rome or Atlanta. Hill's corps occupied the opposite shore from the remaining troops of Crittenden's corps still north of Chattanooga. Bragg asked Hill if he could cross the river and attack the Federals on the north side of the river: "There is no doubt of the enemy's position now; one corps opposite you, and two this side of river from Shellmound by Bridgeport to Caperton's, the point of first crossing. A part of the latter are reported moving down Will's Valley toward Gadsden or perhaps Rome; Wheeler is gone to develop them and Walker goes by railroad to Rome to head them off from our communications.... The crushing of this corps would give us a great victory and redeem Tennessee. Can you be the instrument to do it?"[22]

Bragg's messages were not consistent. After urging Hill to take the offensive, he wrote to Jefferson Davis the next day explaining why he could only consider defensive actions. He told Davis that if the opportunity presented itself, he would attack Rosecrans. He continued: "My position is to some extent embarrassing in regard to offensive movements." Bragg told the president the terrain made communications difficult and that he had the disadvantage of maintaining an extended supply line which needed to be guarded by his troops. Guarding the supply line would diminish his available force and prevent him from attacking Rosecrans' army. Alexander McCook's and Stanley's movements already threatened the rail line south of Chattanooga. Bragg promised: "No effort will be spared to bring him to an engagement whenever the chances shall favor us."[23]

Minty at Smith's Crossroads—Conflicts with Crittenden Continue

Rosecrans continued to attempt to coordinate his actions with Burnside and over the next three weeks there would be several other attempts to encourage Burnside to actively aid in his advance against Bragg, but with little success. He told Burnside "I hope you will close down upon our left as soon as possible, and at once throw cavalry in that direction to cover our flank. I have much evidence to show that Johnston is re-enforcing Bragg with a considerable force." On September 5, Rosecrans continued his advance unimpeded.[24]

Then, Colonel John Wilder reported disturbing news. Bragg was still alive at Chattanooga and appeared to threaten a movement northward across the river at Chattanooga. Wilder discovered a pontoon bridge, partially assembled and ready to be moved into place. On September 5, Brigadier General George Wagner agreed with Wilder about the threat across the river and Wilder's artillery fired on the pontoon bridge and sank two floats. To Wilder, it appeared the Confederates contemplated an attack to the north across the Tennessee River, just as Bragg has suggested to D. H. Hill, although Hill would never initiate the offensive. Wilder explained: "Nothing would be easier than for the rebels to ferry a force across the river at the base of Lookout Mountain, as their artillery completely covers the long promontory below Chattanooga formed by the bend in the river, and if they could throw their whole army between Burnside and Rosecrans...."[25]

After a month of very active service, Robert Minty's brigade had a respite because of Burnside's arrival at Knoxville. As part of Van Cleve's division moved south to cross the river, Minty came under the command of William Hazen. Hazen, like Van Cleve, worked well with Minty and told the cavalry colonel to keep contact with Burnside's cavalry and maintain his position. If Minty were to rage, he had to rage at the next orders which came from Crittenden. Minty had operated with only three of his four regiments during the past three weeks. Now, word came from headquarters that another regiment needed to report to Crittenden at Shellmound for duty as directed from headquarters. This effectively would leave Minty with two regiments to cover sixty miles of Crittenden's flank. In regard to giving up additional cavalry, Minty told Hazen, "I have received no order to send a regiment to General Crittenden; if I do, I shall protest against it; the effective force of my brigade does not exceed the original strength of my own regiment." Minty told Hazen that Crittenden had already appropriated a battalion of 4th Michigan for duty at headquarters. Later that day William Hazen reported that the Rebel pickets had been removed from Blythe's Ferry and Sulfur Springs; and it appeared that the Confederates were pulling back toward Chattanooga. So convinced was Hazen of his intelligence that he ordered Minty to join him at Poe's Tavern; but Minty balked at Hazen's request. Minty told Hazen that if Burnside's cavalry would only show some effort in cooperating by unifying with Rosecrans then he would be able to move in closer proximity to Hazen's infantry. By moving further south, Minty's train at Pikeville was exposed to a sudden Southern attack. In a sobering message, Minty explained the full extent to Burnside's cooperation during the campaign—meeting the letter of his orders, he extended a cavalry force to the area near Minty and would move no further southward.[26]

William Van Antwerp, an officer in the 4th Michigan, described the situation Minty's cavalry faced. "There is quite a force of rebels on the other side of the river at Blyth's Ferry, six miles from our camp. The river is just six hundred yards wide at that point, and the rebels have thrown up earthworks all along close to the edge of the river for some distance, from behind which they fire at our men whenever they make their appearance on this side." In an interesting turn of events, the men of the 4th Michigan received permission from Minty to serenade the Confederates on the other side of the river on September 3. The regimental band, accompanied by some officers of the 4th Michigan, walked to the edge of the Tennessee

River under the protection of a white flag. Then, the band played "Bonnie Blue Flag" and then a few heads popped up above the Confederate defenses and soon a boat carrying an officer and three oarsmen rowed across the river under a flag of truce. The officer shook hands with the Union men and asked what was the purpose of the music and flag. The Union cavalrymen explained there was no purpose except to serenade them. After a half an hour's conversation, the Southern soldiers returned to their side of the river. Soon afterward, shouts came from the east side of the river to play "Home Sweet Home" and then "Dixie" and the band replied they had no music for either of the songs. Then, a Southern soldier asked for "Yankee Doodle" which the band played, followed by an encore of "Bonnie Blue Flag" and finally "Van Dorn's Waltz"—and so ended an act of civility in such a terrible war. After the serenading, it was back to the war.[27]

Rosecrans Changes the Plan

A battle of wills began on September 5 between David Stanley and headquarters. Stanley's new orders required him to execute a raid on Rome, and instead of "feeling" the enemy as previously ordered, Rosecrans and Garfield wanted Stanley to make a raid to disrupt the communication lines in the rear of Bragg's army. The change of orders shifted from a diversion to a full-blown raid; but Stanley balked. Stanley wrote to Garfield and told him, "I do not want to start to interrupt the enemy's communications until Minty joins, unless the general desires me to go sooner. Ask the general to let me know tomorrow by cipher how far I am to regulate my movements by those of the infantry." The new focus for the cavalry on the southern flank of the army centered on Rome and despite Stanley's desire to obtain Minty's command, he prepared to carry out his mission even though he felt he was outnumbered. Stanley's chief of staff, William Sinclair, wrote to Edward McCook to prepare for the new mission. He inquired if McCook had the tools with him to destroy the railroad tracks, including, crowbars and even torpedoes.[28]

The change in the objectives for the raid caught Edward McCook unprepared. He replied that he had none of the tools, explosives, or even personnel to deal with the explosives in his command; but ordered Captain John Kessler, 2nd Indiana, to ride with the ordnance train which has not yet come up. McCook explained: "He is a man who will not sleep until his mission is accomplished, and will enforce to the letter any order you may give." Meanwhile, McCook's scouts found little during the day. They found no enemy cavalry at Lebanon and the 4th Kentucky Cavalry moved over the mountain near McCook's headquarters and found only enemy pickets which his cavalry chased to within six miles of Alpine, capturing a sergeant and ten men along the way. McCook extracted some fairly accurate information from the prisoners that Colonel C. C. Crews' Confederate cavalry brigade was positioned at Alpine with the 2nd, 3rd, 4th Georgia and a regiment of Tennessee cavalry. McCook also found out the Crews' brigade was the most southern of Wheeler's force.[29]

Edward McCook received his first supply trains which had traversed Sand Mountain and also received some troops which had been on duty at the Tennessee River during the day—2nd Michigan which had been detached with duty with Sheridan's division and Daniel Ray's 2nd Tennessee Cavalry. On September 5, Colonel Archibald Campbell's First Brigade rode southward down Will's Valley toward Lebanon and destroyed the salt works used by the enemy while scooping up a few Southern troops along the way. Colonel James P. Brownlow's 1st Tennessee Cavalry led the advance and found a group of Southern cavalry a mile south of Rawlingsville. The Southern cavalry took to their saddles and fled with Brownlow on their heels; but he couldn't catch them. Brownlow proceeded to Lebanon and then returned to camp after a thirty-mile expedition, but the actions effectively drove the entire enemy force out of Will's Valley. Now, the cavalry focused on Broomtown Valley.[30]

In preparation for the raid to Rome, McCook sent two regiments, 2nd and 4th Indiana cavalries, to scout toward Rome. These regiments reached about seven miles south of Alpine and within thirty miles to Rome. McCook's cavalry encountered a sizeable force of Colonel Charles Crews Confederate cavalry brigade but enemy did not pursue the Federal regiments. McCook concluded: "This movement of these regiments and their return after night, when their movement could not be discovered, will lead the enemy to think that we have moved in the direction of Rome, and I suppose cause them to send at least part of their infantry from Summerville to re-enforce that place." The shift in headquarters' desire for a raid rather than a diversion and reconnaissance to Rome had yet to be communicated to all the cavalry commanders. McCook, consistent with the initial orders, seemed content that his actions might draw some infantry farther south.[31]

Colonel Charles C. Crews, commander of the First Brigade in Wharton's division, a "brave and faithful" commander of cavalry (Mollus Mass Civil War Collection, United States Army Heritage and Education Center, Military History Institute, Carlisle, Pennsylvania).

In addition to McCook's reconnaissance during the day, Crook moved his cavalry into Broomtown Valley. George Crook sent two regiments, the 1st and 3rd Ohio, from Winston's on an expedition over Lookout Mountain on their way to Broomtown Valley. The civilians in the area told Crook that three companies of Wheeler's cavalry had just moved forward to attempt to block the road over the mountain. Crook found the first of Wheeler's vedettes three miles from the top of Lookout Mountain and five miles from the valley floor. The Federals skirmished with the enemy on top of the mountain before pushing the smaller force to the rear. Crook found the road leading to the valley blocked incompletely with felled trees, but the Union cavalry surprised the enemy which had not completed their task. The 1st Ohio Cavalry ran into the first enemy pickets at noon and the Ohioans raised their carbines—"bang! bang! and away we go at a sweeping gallop." Because he needed to clear the obstructions, primarily pine trees and large boulders, Crook sent one hundred men on foot to scout the valley, but the men found no enemy waiting at the foot of the mountain. He not only found no forage on the mountain but also discovered a good source of water, the Little River, and he returned to camp at Winston's.[32]

W. L. Curry's 1st Ohio troopers found more

than the good water on Lookout Mountain. The troopers discovered a manufacturer of peach brandy. Curry humorously noted that he could well understand why the rebel cavalry had made such a strong defense for the mountain. The possession of the brandy factory provided an excellent incentive to fight. Colonel Long sent a captain of the regiment to return the men to duty and when that officer did not return, he sent another officer to gain control of the men. The first officer by that time had already succumbed to the effects of the brandy. Long concluded the best thing to do was to just move away from the source of the problem. Soon, many of the regiment had their canteens filled with the brandy and enjoyed their ride over the mountain that night. Curry noted by the next morning, "Those that could not ride down or walk down, just fell down."[33]

While Rome became the focus of Rosecrans and Stanley, the town also became a focus for the Confederate high command. On September 4, Bragg ordered Major General William H. T. Walker's infantry division to Rome to protect the communication lines of the Army of Tennessee. Bragg ordered Walker—"The general commanding directs that you ... will so maneuver as to prevent any force of the enemy from interposing between you and your connections with this army." While Rosecrans planned for Stanley to lead an expedition on Rome, the enemy had already anticipated this move and was prepared for it. In fact, the Confederates had contemplated a threat to Rome since July. Bragg also told Walker that Wheeler would keep an eye on Stanley's cavalry and assist in the defense of the railroad from Rome to Chattanooga. Ironically, and unfortunately for the Union army, Bragg had copies of Northern newspapers, the *Chicago Times* and the *New York Times*, which detailed the movements of Rosecrans and Burnsides very accurately including the threat to Rome. So, whatever illusions Rosecrans had hoped to weave for Bragg regarding Rome had come undone. As a result, Wheeler received his new orders. Bragg wanted more aggressive action from Wheeler including pushing into Will's Valley and, in regard to the Union cavalry, "assail him so as to develop his designs, strength, and position. This must be done even at the sacrifice of troops." Bragg seemed to finally realize that he could not remain stationary in Chattanooga. He had two choices—move forward, which he seemed unable to do, or move backward.[34]

In what would prove to be a disappointment in the campaign, Burnside continued to fail to grasp the importance of moving his force further south to offer support for Rosecrans. Burnside seemed content with his occupation of Kingston, Knoxville and the other towns in East Tennessee. The Federal column had an easy march into Knoxville and faced "no serious opposition," wrote assistant secretary of war, Peter H. Watson, on September 6. Rosecrans' still had not heard directly from Burnside, and for those in Washington, this was disappointing news. Henry Halleck fully expected Burnside and Rosecrans to be marching as a united front. Halleck feared exactly what Bragg had encouraged D. H. Hill to do—attack Rosecrans' army in detail.[35]

Preparation for the Rome Raid Continues

In regard to the Rome raid scheduled for September 8, James Garfield gave David Stanley clear expectations from army headquarters: "Rush the enemy sharply, and if possible strike the railroad." Garfield told Stanley that Minty would not be available to him for another week. He also told Stanley that Bragg intended to make a stand at Chattanooga and the raid would sever his communications and supply lines. Then, he erroneously told Stanley that Forrest and part of Wheeler's cavalry were positioned at Chattanooga and therefore, he would have no problem in executing the raid "with impunity…. The general commanding hopes soon to hear that you have struck a heavy blow." Garfield's report that all the Confederate cavalry moved to Chattanooga was clearly wrong and potentially held deadly consequences for Stanley's men.[36]

Edward McCook's cavalry remained active during the day in preparation of the raid on Rome scheduled for September 8. McCook's troopers again scouted Davis Gap, the rough trail and gap, southeast of Rawlingsville, and chased the enemy pickets away again. The prisoners reported that Wharton's cavalry held a line between La Fayette and Rome with Crews' Confederate cavalry brigade in position at Alpine and Harrison's brigade concentrated at La Fayette. Stanley and McCook agreed that the best route to Rome would be through Winston's Gap. Stanley told Garfield the prisoners had seen Joseph Johnston in Chattanooga in Chattanooga and reinforcements from his army were expected at any time. In contrast, a reliable civilian had been to Chattanooga and told Stanley that Bragg had ordered a retreat from the town. Stanley merely stated: "I give this for what it is worth. We will try and prevent this, blocking the descent from the mountains…." As the raid was being contemplated, the rumors drifted over to the infantry, and James Love, 8th Kansas Infantry, wrote in a letter: "Stanley's boys are regular dare devils and avengers, and are going if not gone to the heart of Georgia—bent on destruction to railroads there."[37]

Bragg Considers Evacuating—Confederates Receive New Orders

Bragg began to show more energy as he realized he needed to evacuate Chattanooga and he sent an urgent request to Richmond for reinforcements. The concern which prompted his withdrawal proved to be McCook's, Thomas' and Stanley's movements. Bragg told Jefferson Davis that Rosecrans' main force concentrated behind the mountains to the west, threatening his communications and supply lines. Despite the mixed messages Bragg sent, this threat convinced him he needed to withdraw from Chattanooga. Although Bragg had successfully pulled Buckner's troops into his army, he wanted more men. On September 6, William Hardee sent two brigades to Atlanta (McNair's and Gregg's) and replied he had no more men to send; but, two additional divisions (Hood's and McLaw's) under the command of James Longstreet had been approved to be sent from Virginia to bolster Bragg's troops. Breckinridge's and Walker's divisions had been previously dispatched from Hardee.[38]

On the same day, Bragg issued orders for the withdrawal from Chattanooga and he ordered the movement to begin on the evening of September 7. Rather than retreating, Bragg told his commanders that he was maneuvering to be in position to attack and defeat Rosecrans in detail. The orders stated:

> "The troops of this army will move immediately toward Rome in four columns. Lieutenant-General Polk will move on the La Fayette road via Rossville, Snow Hill, and La Fayette to Summerville. He will, however, leave a regiment at Chattanooga and one at the foot of Lookout Mountain until the column of General Hill shall pass, when General Hill will order them to move with him. General Hill will follow Polk's column. General Walker will move via Graysville to the intersection of the Federal or State road; thence with that road to the intersection of the Ringgold and Pea Vine Church road; thence with that road to its intersection with the Summerville road to a point nearly opposite La Fayette; thence turning to the left on the Villanow

road to the eastern slope of the ridge; thence turning to the right to Mount Hickory via Subligna. General Buckner will follow General Walker.

General Forrest will, with Dibrell's brigade and such other cavalry as he may deem necessary, move rapidly to the front in advance of Polk's column, leaving a sufficient force to picket the river, and bring up the rear, with all other cavalry marching on different roads, so as to cover all. The detachment of Wheeler's cavalry on picket between the foot of Lookout and Kelley's Ferry will report to and receive orders from the officer commanding the rear cavalry, who will take charge of all detachments."[39]

Joseph Wheeler received orders on September 6 to push his cavalry into Will's Valley and Lookout Valley but he refused to do so. He offered his explanation and described the proposed duties for his cavalry in a very long and detailed response. Wheeler explained that his cavalry had been already been assigned security duty in the mountain passes and covered an area forty miles long. Because of the movement and the size of the Federal cavalry and infantry, any of the passes were vulnerable to attack from the army of blue moving eastward. The Southern cavalry had worked hard over the past days to fell trees to impede any swift movement through the mountains. Wheeler reasoned that the orders received must have been sent before realizing there were 4,000–5,000 Union cavalrymen in Will's Valley supplementing McCook's and Thomas' infantry. Wheeler faced two army corps and a division of cavalry, and he retorted: "As your dispatch stated that the object of moving my command into the valley was to ascertain the 'enemy's strength, design, and position,' I conceived that if these points could be learned better by other means you would not desire great risks run and almost insuperable difficulties overcome in order to comply with the letter rather than the spirit of orders." He explained that to comply with his orders he would have to clear the obstructions in the various gaps that his cavalry had spent so much time blockading over the previous days.[40]

Most importantly, Wheeler explained that moving his cavalry back to "Will's Valley would leave Rome entirely uncovered, while the enemy might cross at some point lower down or higher up, and be well in advance on the road to Rome or Atlanta before I could get back, and when I did get back the horses of my command would be in no condition for a vigorous pursuit." Rosecrans should also have been aware that the Confederates with the substantial number of cavalry would not have left their rear open to an unopposed expedition to Rome. Wheeler continued to explain why he could not, or would not, follow these orders. Wheeler told army headquarters that it was imperative to have the cavalry in good condition for the upcoming campaign and "as it would be indispensable to protect our lines of communication." He consulted "General Wharton, Major Lee, of General Bragg's staff, and Captain Steele, formerly engineer of General Bragg's staff, all of whom fully concurred with me in the matter.... They also concurred with me in the opinion that this movement would leave our lines of communication very much exposed as the enemy might easily throw a column of cavalry over the mountain and strike the railroad." Historian, David Powell, concluded that despite Wheeler's reasons for not following his orders, he had forgotten his primary responsibility—"discover what Rosecrans was up to and promptly inform Bragg." All his other concerns were secondary to this. The more active commander, Forrest, was also on the move on September 6. His sent a brigade of cavalry from Ringgold toward Rome that morning and the remainder Armstrong's command left at mid-afternoon. Forrest brought ten artillery pieces and planned to move within five miles of La Fayette.[41]

Regardless of the other actions of Bragg's cavalry, there can be little doubt that the failure of the Southern cavalry to adequately observe the Federal movements kept Bragg and other Confederate commanders in the dark regarding Rosecrans' movements. This had resulted in holding much of the Army of Tennessee at Chattanooga expecting an attack there while Rosecrans slowly moved two-thirds of his army into position to sever his escape route southward.[42]

The Climate Within the Army of the Cumberland Changes—September 7

The whole tenor of the Army of the Cumberland seemed to change on September 7. Certainly, friction occurred daily and was expected in an army as large as the Army of the Cumberland, but the new tension of closing on the enemy increased irritability to a new level. Perhaps the next two days' internal conflicts set the theme for the campaign for the Union army—when and how do you obey an order?

Burnside communicated with Rosecrans at 6 a.m. "Our cavalry now joins on your left. We have full possession of East Tennessee except Cumberland gap, which is still held by the enemy. I have a force moving against it from the Kentucky side, and I move from here at once in person with a force to attack it from this side." After receiving this message, Rosecrans snapped at Halleck in an "I told you so" message at midnight on September 7. It was too much for Rosecrans to listen to Halleck in Washington and to find out from Burnside that his cooperative advance stalled because of a single enemy brigade holding Cumberland Gap. "Your dispatch of yesterday received with surprise. You have been often and fully advised that the nature of the country makes it impossible for this army to prevent Johnston from combining with Bragg. When orders for an advance of this army were made, it must have been known that those two rebel forces would combine against it, and, to some extent, choose their place of fighting us. This has doubtless been done and Buckner, Johnston, and Bragg are all near Chattanooga. The movement on East Tennessee was independent of mine. Your apprehensions are just, and the legitimate consequences of your orders. The best that can now be done is for Burnside to close his cavalry down on our left, supporting it with his infantry, and, refusing his left, threaten the enemy, without getting into his grasp, while we get him in our grip and strangle him, or perish in the attempt." While the Confederate high command agreed about the importance of reinforcing Bragg, Rosecrans unhappily told Halleck he faced a reinforced Bragg alone, not in conjunction with Burnside, as Halleck had expected. As a result, Burnside calmly stopped his entire movement south to deal with a single Confederate brigade, except for extending some cavalry south to Smith's Crossroads. The Confederates were already moving further south. Still, Rosecrans' three corps moved through the mountain passes meeting only minor resistance. The atmosphere of uncertainty and tension pervaded headquarters as Rosecrans tried to anticipate Bragg's next move and commanders started snapping at each other.[43]

In the most fateful clashes of the day, Brigadier General Thomas Wood refused to fully obey an order given by Rosecrans to conduct a reconnaissance in force on Lookout Mountain. Crittenden ordered Wood to take his division along a railroad track to the base of Lookout Mountain to demonstrate toward Chattanooga. The Union commanders had already spotted artillery on the mountain while the full force of the Confederate army lay a few miles ahead, yet to reveal itself. Wood explained that his division held a highly vulnerable position: "I cannot believe General Rosecrans desires such a blind adherence to the mere letter of his order for the general disposition of his forces as naturally jeopardizes the safety of the most salient portions of it, and certainly cripples the force and vigor and accuracy of its reconnaissances." In an attempt to carry out his orders, he ordered Charles Harker's infantry brigade to march two miles ahead to a spot across from Lookout Creek, supported by the remainder of Wood's division. At the end of the day, Wood pulled his entire division back four miles to a place of apparent safety nearer to the main Federal line.[44]

Wood failed to carry out the orders given him and he was chided by Crittenden for failing to do so as prescribed by army headquarters. Crittenden's comments regarding Wood's movements resulted from the rigid guidelines Rosecrans had set for his various commanders. Wood's response seemed to exacerbate the situation. Wood spent too much of his report explaining why he took the action he did rather than reporting what Harker found out. When Crittenden forwarded Wood's report, headquarters wanted to know more about the results of the reconnaissance. Wood response was a very long, multi-page response complaining about the disparaging remarks about Wood's actions during the day. He also explained his comments about the "blind adherence" to orders. "I respectfully submit that, according to my experience, there is a wide difference in the opinion of military men between the duty of obedience to a specific order and adhesion to the details of a general plan announced in orders, and which admit of latitude and discretion in their execution." Crittenden then explained he had no charge against Wood: "General Wood has at great length vindicated himself from charges which I claim never to have made, and very imperfectly, in my judgment, attempts to refute the only charge I did make." Later in the day, Wood finally gave the report of the reconnaissance.[45]

But the matter wasn't quite finished. Wood receiving Crittenden's explanation of his understanding of the events, again wrote another long letter to Rosecrans. Then Rosecrans shut the door on the matter while expressing disapproval of Wood's unwillingness to let the matter rest. Garfield responded to Wood: "The general commanding was disappointed that your reconnaissance was not made earlier, and he is still uninformed of the place where you found the enemy, the strength of force which you encountered, and the distance to which you pushed the reconnaissance." Of course, this exchange set the stage for an order given to Wood by Rosecrans on September 20 which would determine the fate of the battle.[46]

"Blind Adherence" to Orders

Still, there was one remaining exchange which would result in an outburst of anger from the commanding general of the army directed at the chief of the Union cavalry because an order was not carried out the next day to the satisfaction of Rosecrans and Garfield. David Stanley wrote to Garfield on the morning of September 7 that he would begin his raid to Rome. He cautioned, "I regret exceedingly that I cannot have the aid of Minty's brigade, as I deem my present force entirely inadequate to the work to be performed. I fear the general is not aware that I have but thirteen small regiments here, reduced by battalions guarding the Nashville and Huntsville Railroad. To seriously affect the railroad we should be able to hold it for at least half a day. My force is so small that I cannot make proper detachments for striking the road and at the same time fight the force of the enemy. The entire force of Wharton's and Martin's divisions lie between me and the railroad. I will do the best I can. If the general wishes any modification, send a courier through tonight." Stanley stressed he needed assistance from both Minty and Wilder to occupy the enemy's cavalry. He flatly stated that he needed his entire cavalry force to successfully make the raid. And Garfield replied at 8:30 p.m. that Rosecrans felt Stanley would be successful with just the force he had, in light of the fact that bulk of Wheeler's and Forrest's cavalry were located at Chattanooga—a critical error on the part of headquarters. Garfield wrote that the enemy cannot "be brought to bear against you, he has the more confidence in your ability to succeed in the expedition." While unable to give Stanley any additional support in occupying the enemy cavalry, Garfield told Stanley that Alexander McCook would hold the mountain passes and secure Alpine. Neither of these held any immediate benefit in occupying Forest or Wheeler, both of these commands now on the southern flank of the Confederate army. Garfield continued, "The general commanding directs you to push forward rapidly and with audacity. The severing of the enemy's railroad communication with Atlanta will be the most disastrous to him." The stage was set and Rosecrans expected Stanley's cavalry riding to the east the next morning.[47]

Edward McCook's division prepared to make the raid on Rome and McCook sent the message to all his brigade commanders (Campbell, Watkins, Ray): "You will prepare your command and have it in readiness to march at daylight tomorrow morning." The 2nd Indiana Cavalry arrived at Edward McCook's headquarters the day before after escorting the cavalry train over the mountain. Then, McCook's division spent much of the day re-shoeing horses. It is also important to note that there continued to be a large number of sick soldiers and this included David Stanley who continued to command despite his malady. The 2nd Indiana Cavalry arrived with several troopers ill, including the Colonel John A. Platter, the regimental adjutant, the chaplain, and several other enlisted men. Lieutenant Isaac Conwell, 2nd Indiana also fell ill, and described the plight of the sick troopers: "I think it a most inhuman way of treating sick men. To turn them out in the woods without shelter and a great many without even blankets or anything to eat…. I watched as the train came up for some of our men but could not find any of them…. Have had a steady fever all day." Many were sent to the hospital and would ultimately be moved to the rear to convalesce, including Platter who was so ill he submitted his resignation on September 9. Even the 2nd Michigan Cavalry reported a number of sick troopers. Henry Mortimer Hempstead noted: "We have a great many sick with diarrhea, a heavier sick list than we have shown before in months." Marshall Thatcher, 2nd Michigan Cavalry, estimated that nearly one third of the troopers were sick. Thatcher recalled that sick soldiers were found wandering away from their beds and as they were gently returned to the hospital he thought that "rough soldiers sometimes have hearts of women." First Lieutenant Peter Williamson, 1st Wisconsin Cavalry, also wrote in a letter that while his health was good, many of the other officers were in "feeble health." Trooper George Healy, 5th Iowa Cavalry, also reported the extensive illnesses in the cavalry, "There are a great many sick nowadays—fevers of all kind and ague."[48]

Edward McCook sent his final orders to his division before embarking on the expedition to Rome. He told his brigade commanders to have the troopers carry three days' rations which needed to last for six days. Twenty men from each regiment carried axes and planned to lead the Federal column to deal with any obstructions along the way. Each cavalryman carried sixty rounds of ammunition and McCook explained the seriousness of the expedition. Nothing would impede the success and movement of the column.[49]

Meanwhile the remainder of Rosecrans' army moved forward slowly pressing toward Chattanooga. Of particular interest, James Negley's division marched with orders to claim Stevens' Gap, the gap which led into McLemore's Cove. This line of march would lead into an ambush by the Confederate infantry and the first offensive action for Bragg's army in the campaign, but not until three days later. On the left flank and despite the verbal clash with Thomas Wood, Crittenden moved forward and found Kelly's Ford manned by only about 300 Confederate cavalry.[50]

Bragg Decides to Evacuate Chattanooga

At last, Bragg was gone from Chattanooga on September 8, and after realizing the threat to his flank, he re-positioned his army south of the town. By nightfall, D. H. Hill had moved his corps to La Fayette, Buckner's corps and W. H. T. Walker's reserve corps also marched south, and Polk moved into Crawfish Valley. John Pegram's cavalry division screened the retreating Confederate infantry during its withdrawal and Wheeler's cavalry remained picketed at the Lookout Mountain passes from Chattanooga to Alpine. Wheeler also kept a close eye on the route to Rome should the Union army initiate a raid in that direction.[51]

With Bragg withdrawing his army, the tension which was so palpable a few days ago at Minty's location was gone. He was in communication with Burnside's cavalry and he found no enemy in front of his brigade. Minty continued to watch the various ferries and fords but finding no enemies, he believed that it was unlikely that a Confederate cavalry attack would occur. Minty, who had moved his brigade further south just the day before, also had important orders to implement the next morning from Hazen—because the enemy had withdrawn, Hazen told Minty to cross over the Tennessee River at Sale Creek, a few miles south of Smith's Crossroads and to ride for Harrison's Landing.[52]

September 8—A Cavalry Raid Which Never Started

In an optimistic and professional summary of the events of September 8, Rosecrans wired Halleck: "Information tonight leads to the belief that the enemy has decided not to fight us at Chattanooga. Our reconnoitering today shows that he has withdrawn his pickets on Lookout Mountain, opposite and below us, and Winston's Gaps." Rosecrans explained that Alexander McCook and Stanley would advance further into Broomtown Valley the next day and Crittenden would march south through Chattanooga in pursuit of Bragg. Granger's trailing corps continued to move forward. Rosecrans' staff wrote to Thomas to send his most reliable men to confirm that Bragg was retreating and in which direction.[53]

However, Rosecrans raged at his cavalry in private. Stanley failed to make the raid on Rome during the day as Rosecrans had expected and for which he even moved his infantry to assist in the movement. Perhaps the greatest error was the fact that Rosecrans found out that the raid did not take place before Stanley told him. Rosecrans wrote to Stanley: "I have a messenger from General Crook asking for turpentine, but whether for horse medicine or bridges does not appear. The messenger brings nothing from you, but I learn from him that your command lies at the foot of the mountain on this side, intending to move in the morning. I am sorry to say you will be too late. It is also a matter of regret to me that your command has done so little in this great movement. If you could do nothing toward Rome, nor toward the railroad, you might at least have cleared the top of Lookout Mountain to Chattanooga and established a patrol and vedette line along it, which I should have ordered had I not trusted to your discretion, expecting something more important to be done. But what is worse than this, you had peremptory orders to move, which were reiterated yesterday, expecting you would move this morning. It appears that the enemy have sent a large infantry and cavalry force to Alpine. Your cavalry ought to have full control from your position to that place. This you do not appear to have done. Had you gone according to orders you would have struck the head of their column, and probably inflicted on them irreparable injury. So far your command has been a mere picket guard for our advance. Orders accompany this, which I hope to see effectually executed. Let me always hear from you fully. Why have you not supplied your command with means of burning bridges and destroying railroads?" Stanley responded to Rosecrans's at 7:00 p.m.: "I could not get off this morning on account of deficiency of horseshoes. I am in pretty good trim now, and gain 600 men by delaying today." Stanley reassured the commanding general that Crook and McCook would press ahead the next day with the objective of capturing Alpine. Stanley had discovered that both Wheeler and Wharton were at Alpine the day before, and that Will Martin's cavalry was positioned just north at La Fayette. "I expect to fight them at Alpine. Wharton has with him a full battery. If he can get them on good ground you need not fear the result.... I expect we will have a pretty sharp affair." Certainly, horses needed to be shod; but Stanley had been shuffling dismounted troopers to Nashville to be mounted and those men were just returning to the cavalry. With the absence of detached troops and without Minty, Stanley chose not to begin the expedition.[54]

The exact cause for the failure to order the expedition remains a mystery and controversy. All the individual accounts from the troopers indicated the intention of making the raid on September 8. Sergeant G. W. Baum, 2nd Indiana, recorded in his diary that he expected the marching orders on September 7 and finally them received on September 8, but "for some cause or other we did not move." Trooper Robert S. Merrill, 1st Wisconsin Cavalry, wrote in his diary on September 7, "Rec'd orders to march in the morning." and the next day, "Saddled up but waiting most of the forenoon we did not move. We drew new horses this P. M." Peter Williamson of the same regiment wrote his wife on September 7 that the regiment would move the next morning to destroy the railroad south of Chattanooga. Lieutenant Isaac Conwell noted in his diary the same message: "This Cavalry Division had orders to march this morning at daylight but for some reason the order was countermanded and it is now to move this evening." Henry Hempstead, 2nd Michigan Cavalry, recorded in his diary that orders were issued to begin the expedition at 4:30 a.m. but the expedition did not begin. Instead, a battalion of that regiment scouted about eleven miles in a southerly direction. Interestingly, Stanley's itinerary of the cavalry recorded that September 7 was spent horseshoeing the command after the cavalry trains arrived. Edward McCook's headquarters records show a request was made to Stanley on September 7 to continue the shoeing of the horses in his command, but McCook's orders also specified that the troopers be prepared to march at daylight the next day.[55]

Edward McCook's division shoed their horses in preparation for the raid on Rome (Alfred Waud drawing—Library of Congress).

The only insight into the delay came from Stanley's message to Garfield that the delay was necessitated due to poorly shod horses. Stanley told Garfield that he believed he had inadequate number of men to accomplish his task without Minty's brigade and he explained that delaying the raid by a single day allowed him to gain another six hundred men for the raid. Stanley most likely decided that the additional number of cavalry was vitally important for the raid. Stanley could also have been delayed as the tools needed to the destroy the railroad were retrieved. All evidence points to the fact that Stanley planned to delay the raid for a day to get his command fully prepared before initiating the raid on September 9.[56]

Despite Rosecrans' anger, Stanley's decision not to move on Rome was a good one. He faced too enemy cavalry in terrain that was too easily defended by a relatively small force, either on Stanley's way to Rome or on his return. Forrest's biographer, John Allan Wyeth, agreed with Stanley's decision: "Stanley was correct and Garfield was mistaken. The latter was a better politician than soldier.... On September 6, Forrest was at Ringgold, but, having heard of Stanley's movement, by morning of the 8th he was at Alpine." Frank Armstrong's division had moved south to prevent the raid that Rosecrans so earnestly desired; and supported by Wharton's division, which had regiments at Summerville just a few miles from the proposed route of march, this made Rosecrans' and Garfield's plan to cause havoc on the Confederate rear a poorly designed expedition with little chance of success. Also, Brigadier General States Rights Cist's brigade of infantry waited in Rome for any attempt to destroy the railroad. Even if Stanley could reach Rome, it was unlikely he would have had a path back to the Union lines.[57]

Rosecrans operated under the misconception that Bragg's army retreated as a weak column which was unprepared to fight. This was not the case and the Confederate army had plenty of fight. Bragg and Wheeler were aware the enemy might plan to attack the communications between Chattanooga and Rome and had prepared for this. Numerous communications from Wheeler explained that he had planned for this contingency and Confederate infantry awaited any force which penetrated that far. Despite this failed raid, the most important result of the moves of both armies on September 8 resulted in losing contact with one another. The factor of terrain complicated the movements of both generals, and now, Rosecrans became blind to the location of the bulk of Bragg's army once it began its evacuation.

New Orders for the Cavalry on the Southern Flank

In the meantime, Garfield sent a more reasonable response to Stanley at 11:00 p.m. in which he simply responded regarding the unavoidable delay in beginning the cavalry raid. "The general commanding learns that your expedition against the railroad has been delayed and the movement not yet begun. If this be so he directs the following as a substitute for the last order sent to you." With Bragg evacuating Chattanooga, Garfield realized the importance of Stanley's raid to Rome was no longer necessary. Instead, the Union generals needed to find the route of Bragg's army. Crook was ordered to advance ahead over Lookout Mountain from the south until he reached the southern tip of Missionary Ridge if necessary. Then, Garfield told Stanley to send another brigade into Broomtown Valley and move northward toward Summerville in an effort to find the Confederate infantry. Garfield also told Stanley to push forward vigorously without delay and there was "not a moment to lose in starting these expeditions" because army headquarters believed Bragg was in full retreat. The urgent and all-important raid on Rome evaporated during the day and the cavalry returned to its important role of finding Bragg.[58]

Edward McCook sent a message to his division to begin moving toward Alpine: "The command will be held in readiness to march at any moment, as previously ordered.... The command will move tomorrow morning promptly at 4 o'clock Reveille at, 2.30; boots and saddles, 3.30; to horse immediately after." The next day, Edward McCook planned to scout further south with a brigade and then move to Alpine with his division to deal with Wharton's cavalry there as reported by deserters. For the remainder of the cavalry corps, Garfield told Crook he needed to move his cavalry quickly the next morning to the Chattanooga Road and then move northward until he found the main column of Bragg's army. The reconnaissance should be thorough "ascertaining the whereabouts and direction of the enemy. In view of the delay in the expedition which the cavalry was ordered to make, the order directing it is revoked, and the consequent modifications are made ... to support the cavalry movement."[59]

Robert Mitchell authored the cavalry report at the end of the campaign and recorded that September 7 was spent re-shoeing the horses and the next day Crook's brigade moved with artillery and ambulances up Lookout Mountain at Winston's Gap. Once on the mountain, Crook bivouacked for the night and the cavalry train was moved to the proximity of McCook's infantry trains. Finally, those troopers whose horses had given out were sent on their way to Nashville to be remounted. This was such a small report for the happenings of that day and the preparations for the actions yet to come. Mitchell, nor any other cavalry report, made any mention of the failure to initiate the raid on Rome.[60]

Rosecrans Misreads Bragg's Retreat

The good news of Bragg's evacuation from Chattanooga also brought new concerns for Rosecrans, but Rosecrans underestimated Bragg's will to fight and continued to imagine Bragg retreating to Rome or Atlanta. Rosecrans failed to perceive that Bragg had just shifted his strategy. Brigadier General Will Martin brought word which helped Bragg gain the offensive when he reported that James Negley's Union division advanced alone near McLemore's Cove. Rosecrans had yet to catch his prey and his own army was stretched across a vast geography without support among the various corps. If Bragg moved on the offensive, Rosecrans could be defeated in detail as his divisions moved through the mountain gaps. Martin's reconnaissance suggested that Negley's division moving toward McLemore's Cove was vulnerable to attack. The Federal division moved closer to Cooper's Gap and Stevens' Gap and found the enemy had obstructed the passes by felling trees across the passes and roads making the journey slow and in some cases impossible for the wagons to pass. In an ominous reminder that Bragg remained a dangerous foe, Negley observed 2,000 rebel cavalry of Will Martin's division in front of his line of march. As Negley moved forward during the day he faced primarily enemy cavalry and he drove them from Stevens' Gap. He discovered the cavalry was from Wheeler's corps headquartered at La Fayette and identified the location of John T. Morgan's brigade of the 1st, 3rd, 4th and 51st Alabama cavalries, the 4th Georgia, the 1st and 8th Confederate cavalries and one artillery battery. But, Rosecrans still failed to realize the threat he faced.[61]

Brigadier General William T. Martin's division spotted Negley's vulnerable division at McLemore's Cove (Library of Congress).

While events were intensifying for the Southern army, Crittenden's remaining infantry on the north side of the Tennessee River was alerted that Union troops planned to occupy Chattanooga the next morning. Crittenden told his troops to begin a "vigorous" pursuit of Bragg's retreating army. Brigadier General George Wagner supported Rosecrans' perception of a full Confederate retreat after questioning a deserter. The deserter told Wagner that the Confederate artillery pulled out from Lookout Mountain last night and no infantry remained in the area. Buckner's most northern division marched south through Chattanooga the day before headed for Rome. The deserter reported that Confederate cavalry colonel, James Starnes, was quoted: 'We are going to Rome, Ga.; will have to go through in three days.'"[62]

While the news that the Confederate army withdrew from Chattanooga was well received, the ever-present threat of a Confederate cavalry breakout between Rosecrans' and Burnside's armies again became a real threat. Minty's confidence from the day before evaporated when he discovered that Confederate cavalry had moved back to Blythe's Ferry and threated to drive to the west. In addition, John Scott's brigade engaged some of Burnside's cavalry near Sweetwater, about fifteen miles north of Minty's positions two days before. Still only Burnside's cavalry pickets connected with Rosecrans' army. Wagner reported the threat to William Hazen: "If you think there is a probability they will cross, Colonel Minty must be re-enforced, so as to prevent it, for it will not do to have a raid made upon the railroad at this time." The threat proved real enough for William Hazen to delay Minty's movement southward. He wrote to Minty that John Pegram's cavalry occupied the other side of the river with a force twice the size of Minty's. Then, Hazen told Minty not to cross the river with anything larger than scouting parties, which Minty did without finding any of Pegram's cavalry.[63]

Summary

During this part of the Chickamauga Campaign, the Federal cavalry performed its duty well, but much of the success of Stanley's cavalry resulted from the lack of offensive action on the part of the Confederate cavalry. Wheeler and Forrest commanded formidable troops, but the lack of energy on the part of Bragg kept these two mounted commands in a defensive role. Forrest remained on the northern flank preparing for the joint attack of Burnside and Rosecrans north of Chattanooga. Because of this, Rosecrans, Minty, Wilder, Van Cleve and Crittenden deserve credit for providing such a creditable feint that the rest of the Army of the Cumberland easily crossed over the Tennessee River. In regard to Wheeler's actions on the southern flank, it remains remarkable that he offered no resistance to the advance of the Federal army even as it moved into Georgia. This resulted in easy and successfully service for McCook's and Crook's cavalry.

In regard to Minty's brigade, his men had the most difficult duty during the initial part of the campaign, and the relationship between Crittenden and Minty deteriorated during this time. Minty skirmished with Dibrell, operated without adequate provisions, and provided security to the Union left flank. Both Van Cleve and Hazen recognized Minty as an exemplary cavalry commander while Crittenden did not, much to Crittenden's discredit. Overall, Minty's cavalry held its position although it would have been in a difficult position had the Confederates decided to offer any kind of offense in the first part of the campaign.

Along the southern flank, Crook's cavalry had been called for very little action but worked well with the advancing army. Once across the Tennessee River, Eli Long's brigade quickly moved forward to Trenton and captured the town and a route over Sand Mountain. Surprisingly, Long and the rest of the army met almost no resistance. Once over the mountain, Long began to actively seek the enemy in front of the army. Still farther on the south, Edward McCook's division also began the campaign in good form. McCook successfully established a secure flank from Huntsville to Bridgeport until the crossing of the Tennessee River without a problem. Once across the river, McCook began securing the southern flank and found no enemy cavalry to the south; but he did discover the enemy ahead. Stanley planned to use Edward McCook's division in the raid on Rome but the raid did not occur on September 8. There is no evidence to suggest that the failure to initiate the raid resulted with Edward McCook.

David Stanley did not author a report about the cavalry operations during this campaign, but Robert Mitchell did. Mitchell offered no explanation for the failure to initiate the raid. In his memoirs, Stanley also refused to offer any details about the campaign. The only insight in the raid comes from a single letter Stanley wrote to Rosecrans after the battle and the official records. None of the other cavalry officers referred to his event, except to Crook. George Crook wrote in his memoirs: "The officers were together when Gen. Stanley received a letter from Gen. Rosecrans, accusing him unmercifully of procrastination, unnecessary delays, and of wants of appreciation of situation, etc. stating that the enemy was in full retreat, and that instead of his cavalry being on their flanks, destroying them, he had by his delays lost the fruits of all the campaign, etc. Gen Stanley was taken sick. In fact, he was sick then. He was shortly afterwards compelled to go off duty." In Stanley's letter to Rosecrans after the battle, he simply wrote: "Upon my return I think I can give you very satisfactory reason for my delay in moving the cavalry of the right wing further south at an earlier day than I did." What those reasons were, are not known.[64]

Six. Bragg at Bay (September 1–8)

Regardless of the reasons, Stanley made a good decision in not moving a division to Rome which was unlikely to have succeeded. In a serious misinterpretation of intelligence, Garfield and Rosecrans insisted that Bragg concentrated the Confederate cavalry at Chattanooga when just the opposite occurred. The Confederates had just concentrated in the area where the raid was supposed to have occurred and on the exact date. Wheeler repeatedly made reference to keeping a defense in place to repel a raid on Rome; and the position of Edward McCook's cavalry was so well known that the *Rome Tri-Weekly Courier* published the location and the size of McCook's cavalry just a few days later. States Rights Cist's infantry brigade was already at Rome, Wheeler's division was far enough south to respond to a raid, and part of Forrest's cavalry had been moved to La Fayette on September 8 to deal with a raid toward Rome. How all these forces would have aligned if Stanley ordered Edward McCook forward will be forever unknown, but based on the Union cavalry raids during the Atlanta campaign, McCook would have needed at least a half a day to make any impact on the communications link between Rome and Chattanooga. If McCook ever reached Rome, it seems unlikely he could have ever found a route back to the Union lines. Had Bragg not evacuated on the day he did, Stanley would have likely initiated the raid on September 9. In the meantime, Rosecrans's anger toward his chief of cavalry was real and would be again revealed later in the campaign.[65]

Finally, there were two important points about the activities at headquarters which clouded the campaign. The first was Rosecrans' mistaken impression of the condition of Bragg's army. As will be revealed, Rosecrans misunderstood Bragg's reason for evacuating Chattanooga. Rosecrans believed a battered, demoralized army rapidly retreated toward Rome. The need for Stanley's raid was two-fold: first, to sever the communications and supply route to force Bragg's evacuation and secondly, once Bragg began to retreat, Stanley could have struck a blow to this demoralized band of retreating Confederates. Neither of these were true. The second important point was the hope that Burnside's army would play a role in the campaign. In the final assessment, Burnside's greatest contribution would be in favor of the Confederate army. His march to Knoxville essentially added a division of cavalry and an infantry corps to Bragg's Army of Tennessee.

Seven. Bragg Gains the Initiative (September 9–17)

Jonesborough? Jonesborough? Damn Jonesborough—Abraham Lincoln

The next phase of the Chickamauga Campaign began when Bragg evacuated Chattanooga. The Confederate general finally took action after being threatened by the movements of XIV Corps, XX Corps, and Stanley's cavalry to the south. The Union cavalry also began a new phase of the campaign focused on its more traditional role. Overnight, the emphasis on the raid on Rome diminished and the cavalry's new role focused on finding the enemy which had escaped behind a screen of Forrest's and Wheeler's cavalry in the mountainous terrain. Stanley would finally complete an expedition to Rome during this period and he would gain the authority to command his own force. Rosecrans would continue to mistakenly believe that Bragg was in full retreat for the next few days, but he would soon discover that initiative had shifted to the Confederate army. Over the next nine days, the cavalry skirmishes increased and the battle would finally erupt at Reed's Bridge on September 18.

Cavalry Gains Its Own Discretion

On the morning of September 9, the Confederate forces marched toward La Fayette, but no farther. La Fayette was a small town and county seat of Walker County with a prewar population of 300–400. The town had two academies, a few churches, a hotel, a courthouse and ten to twelve streets and cross streets. Both D. H. Hill and Joseph Wheeler received direct orders to proceed to La Fayette and Wheeler relayed orders to Forrest to bring his cavalry there also. Bragg could not allow his army to be cutoff and isolated at Chattanooga and his movement to La Fayette allowed him to neutralize Thomas' and McCook's forward movements which threatened his communication lines. The average Confederate soldier was told that the march to La Fayette was made to protect that town from the Yankees, but the news of the evacuation "fell like a wet blanket" on many Tennessee cavalrymen. As Bragg shifted his strategy, he had a surprise in store for James Negley.[1]

At last, Wheeler energetically ordered his cavalry to prepare to defend the territory around Alpine and La Fayette and resist any further Union advance. At 8 a.m. on September 8, Forrest wrote to Wheeler from Gower's and told him Bragg instructed him to delay the Union advance as much as possible. He told Wheeler, "If the enemy does not advance we

Seven. Bragg Gains the Initiative (September 9–17)

must move on them." Granted Forrest was still some few miles north of the proposed route of Stanley's ordered raid upon Rome, but the belief that a beleaguered, defeated army, vulnerable to a flank attack by a single Union cavalry division could not have been further from the truth.[2]

On the northern flank, Crittenden's troops marched into Chattanooga and raised the United States flag. As the Union troops entered the town, the last of the Confederates rode away. Rosecrans' wanted his troops pushing ahead at daylight on September 9. His orders for the Army of the Cumberland resulted in Thomas' infantry seizing the gaps on Lookout Mountain and McCook's corps and Stanley's cavalry pushing further into Broomtown Valley. Crittenden's XXI Corps intended to gain the top of Lookout Mountain south of Chattanooga and Granger's Reserve Corps planned to occupy Bridgeport and Stevenson.[3]

After the failure to begin the cavalry raid on Rome on September 8, Stanley's cavalry began its reconnaissance duties and moved into Broomtown Valley. Alexander McCook reinforced the claims of the size of Stanley's adversary, which headquarters seemed to have forgotten. He wanted Stanley to drive back the Confederate cavalry which seemed to be massing along his line of march toward La Fayette. Reflecting on the Union cavalry, McCook wrote, "I fear the force engaged in making the reconnaissances ordered may prove too small, as I believe all of Wheeler's cavalry is in the vicinity of Summerville." George Crook led the reconnaissance into Broomtown Valley the same day and as expected ran into large numbers of Southern horsemen.[4]

At 9:30 a.m. Garfield wrote to Stanley regarding the situation with the infantry in light of Bragg's evacuation of Chattanooga. In this order were two paradoxical issues. One was what Stanley had striven for—the ability to design his operations for the cavalry because he was on the scene and had a better ability to determine the extent and practicality of offensive action. After Rosecrans' tirade the day before, Garfield gave Stanley the latitude to operate depending upon the unfolding situations he faced and secondly, Garfield just assigned Stanley the duty for which he was severely criticized the day before. These orders supplemented the orders from the prior evening which assigned Crook and Edward McCook to reconnaissance missions to find Bragg's army. Rosecrans and Garfield still believed Bragg's retreat reflected a disordered and demoralized army, but Stanley, Thomas, and Alexander McCook increasingly knew this was not the case. Garfield knew that Stanley needed Minty and that he had repeatedly requested him to join the cavalry in the south. He told Stanley that Minty remained attached to Crittenden's corps but he "will join you in a few days." Stanley held Edward McCook's division in readiness and ordered Crook to begin a reconnaissance. Edward McCook still intended to fulfill the orders to press toward Rome but in the meantime, he moved his division into Broomtown Valley hoping to find the retreating Southern army.[5]

While Stanley's cavalry began reconnaissance expeditions, the infantry corps also marched forward. After claiming Chattanooga, Crittenden began to pursue the retreating enemy. Garfield told Thomas to join in the pursuit: "The general commanding directs you to move your command as rapidly as possible to La Fayette and make every exertion to strike the enemy in flank, and, if possible, to cut off his escape." Little did the Union generals realize that Bragg began his first offensive movements of the campaign. Bragg's greatest advantage was the opportunity to attack the Union columns in detail as they came through the mountain gaps. McCook's corps moved on the extreme southern flank near Alpine about fifteen miles south of Thomas' center position. McCook also had orders to push ahead and hopefully find the flank of the retreating Confederates and attack it. Negley's division moved into McLemore's Cove, trailed by Absalom Baird's division still crossing Lookout Mountain. Negley's advanced division was vulnerable but he had detected the increased Confederate activity in the area. George Thomas wrote on the evening of September 9 that he observed the enemy cavalry, Martin's division, in front of his line of march. Further, Thomas determined from the local citizens that three or four infantry divisions, supported by the enemy cavalry and artillery were concentrating near Dug Gap, just ahead of Negley's line of march, in preparation to resist the Union advance. In return, Martin's cavalry closely watched the advance of Negley's division, as it moved toward McLemore's Cove, from atop Pigeon Mountain, a spur of Lookout Mountain and the last mountain west of the La Fayette and the repositioning Confederate army. To assist in re-positioning the Confederate army, Wheeler received stern messages from Bragg to develop the Union positions and strength but "divert no force except to protect our rear."[6]

Rosecrans wrote to Halleck at the conclusion of September 9: "Chattanooga is ours without a struggle, and East Tennessee is free. Our move on the enemy's flank and rear progresses, while the tail of his retreating column will not escape unmolested.... Messengers go to Burnside tonight, urging him to push his cavalry down. No news from him or his cavalry." By the end of the next day, Rosecrans planned for Crittenden to reach Rossville expanding his front to Ringgold, Thomas to reach La Fayette and McCook to be at Alpine and Summerville. As Rosecrans maneuvered the Confederates south out of Chattanooga, the bulk of Burnside's army held positions within fifteen miles of Knoxville. The exception was a mounted brigade at Athens, Tennessee and cavalry pickets which extended to Smith's Crossroads. The next morning Rosecrans explained to Halleck the need of assistance from Burnside: "I did not, in my last telegram, lay enough stress on uniting Burnside's cavalry with mine." Rosecrans' cavalry was moving south and a new, wider gap formed with Minty's movement further south. The capture of Chattanooga resulted in Rosecrans sending a message to Burnside he would regret a few days later. In this message, Rosecrans only asked for Burnside's cavalry to connect with his.[7]

The Cavalry Fight at Alpine—September 9

David Stanley replied to orders from Garfield at 6:30 p.m. from Henderson Gap, a couple of miles west of Alpine. When he received Garfield's earlier orders, his cavalry was already fighting Confederate cavalry the mountain gaps and the valley below. This cavalry action formed the first notable cavalry fight during the campaign and it proved Alexander McCook to be correct in the size of the enemy facing Stanley. Crook's brigade camped on top of Lookout Mountain on September 8 and the next morning he led the Union cavalry advance on Alpine that scouts determined to be defended by infantry, cavalry and artillery. As Crook approached Henderson's Gap (the gap directly east of Valley Head), he drove enemy pickets to his front. Immediately he found the gap, which was narrow, obstructed with timbers felled across the road and with boulders which had been rolled onto the road. Lieutenant Colonel Elijah Watts, 2nd Kentucky Cavalry, moved his men forward and found some recent campfires, still warm, which "showed plainly enough that we were fairly in presence of the enemy." After an hour of clearing the road, Crook continued down into Broomtown Valley. The cavalrymen

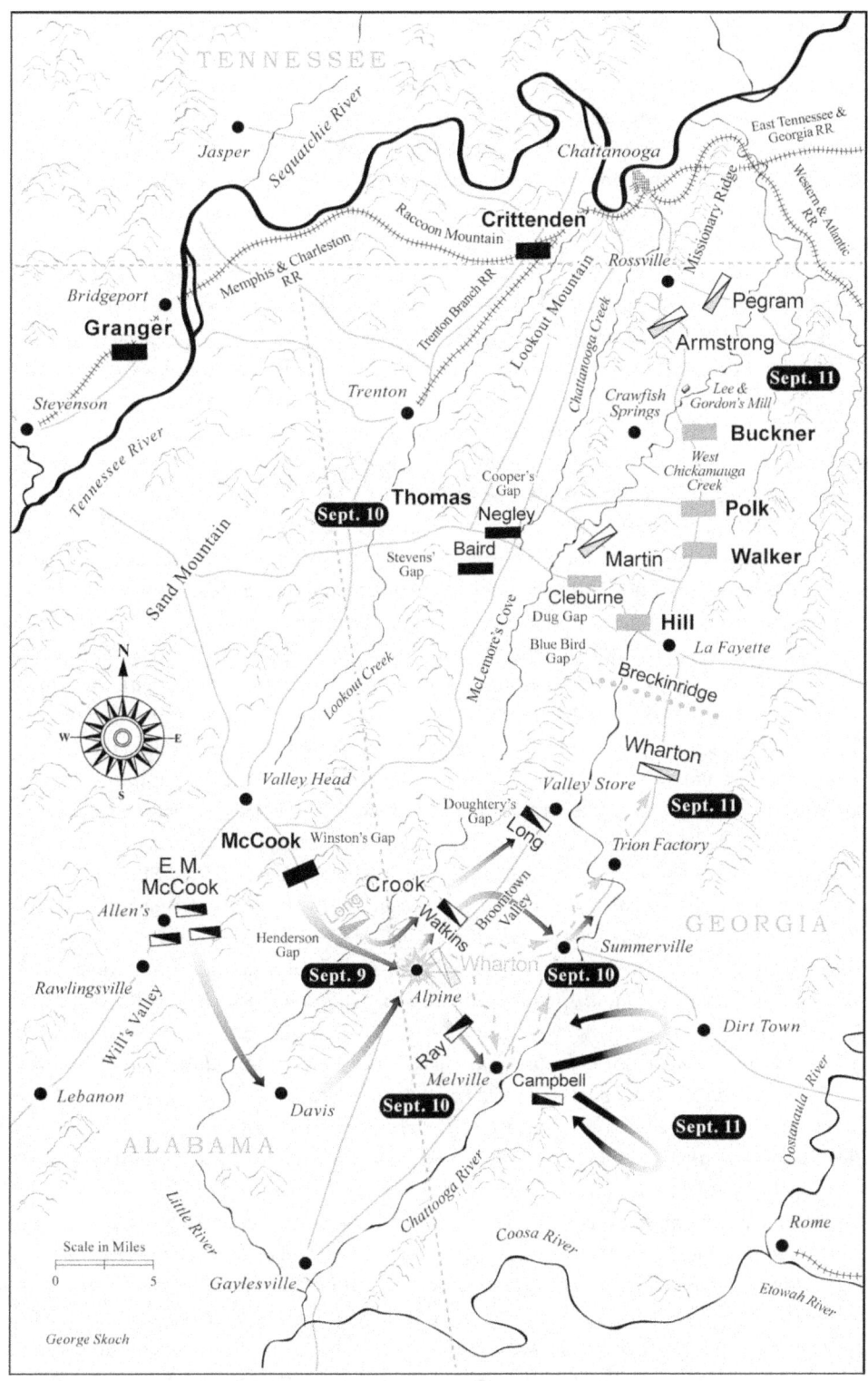

Union cavalry movements: September 9–11.

dismounted at the base of the mountain and allowed their horses to drink from a stream, but suddenly, gunfire erupted as scouts discovered a strong force of four regiments of enemy cavalry. Near Alpine, Crook approached the enemy across a large field, and his command engaged John Wharton's cavalry occupying a tree line. The Union cavalry returned the fire and a bloody fight resulted. The arrival of Edward McCook's division decided the contest. McCook's line of march took his division from Allen's House near Rawlingsville and then over Lookout Mountain and descended at Davis. McCook attacked from the south while Crook attacked from the west. McCook flanked the Confederate cavalry which was "forced to retire, fighting us, however, from the time we struck them in the valley until we drove them through Alpine, some retreating on the Rome road, but most of them on the road to Summerville," recorded Brigadier General Robert Mitchell. Sergeant G. W. Baum, 2nd Indiana Cavalry, explained the path over Lookout Mountain was fourteen miles long and McCook's cavalry initially found some pickets on the mountain and upon hearing Eli Long's battle McCook charged into a "brigade of rebs, driving them in every direction." Crook reported his losses at three killed and eleven wounded during the fight. After capturing Alpine, the Union soldiers found an unremarkable settlement of only three houses.[8]

Elijah Watts, 2nd Kentucky Cavalry, described the battle in detail: *"Col. Eli Long, commanding our brigade passed to the front, and a moment later sent for the hundred dismounted men, Nicholas* [colonel of the 2nd Kentucky] *taking them forward at once and we became aware that there must be a strong force of the enemy present by the volume of firing, by this time sharp and continued. Having command of what remained of the regiment, and obstructed in front by the horses led by 'Number four' I held the command in readiness waiting orders. Meantime, the other regiments of the brigade, the 1st, 3rd, and 4th Ohio Cavalry, passed to the front. Orders arrived, and moving forward we met a stampede of Headquarters, servants and orderlies and other non-combatants, all of whom had (illegible) followed Col. Long down the mountain,—and hastily taking measures to have the led horses sent to one side to wait the call for them, one of the aides, Capt. Crane galloped up to where I was, calling out as he came to let go of the led horses. '[T]hey are charging!!,' he exclaimed … with all the others in the command hurried into the open, went into line—but immediately saw there was no fear of a charge by the enemy, for he had already been repulsed…. The situation was intensely dramatic, the scene inspiring. In our immediate front, to the right and left, were large grain fields covered with stubble only, undulating—slightly rolling, and three hundred yards away a slight incline; another hundred yards began a heavy timber it edges slightly irregular. Farther to the right, and the left were harvested cornfields, with a clear space beyond to the timber. On first observing the situation in our immediate front, a regiment of rebel cavalry was confused and broken, moving back to the woods. They had charged, been repulsed, and were to retiring to shelter. The woods was alive with rebels. Halfway between us and the enemy, Lieutenant Hosmer and his gallant troop held a position on a light knoll, sustaining themselves as they always know how to do it, and Gen. Crook comdg. the Division and his escort behind him, hastily making formations for a regular attack. The led horses were taken forward, and the regiment all remounted and together excepting Hosmer and his troop, still holding the position he won in the preliminary encounter. The Ohio regiments were placed in line of battle off to the right, rapidly taking their position behind a crest in point blank range of a heavy force of the enemy. Rising to the crest in excellent style, they opened fire effectually as shown by the disturbance among the rebels and slowly advancing toward them. In the meantime, the 2nd Kentucky was not idle. Joined by Col. Long, the regiment entered a field to the left, called in troop 'A,' and the command was given: 'Pre-*

pare to fight on foot!' Then a reformation and advance through the cornfield toward the timber, up to its very edge steady and without a halt, the resistance being only scattering shots, a rush and loud hurrah into the woods completed the work, the enemy men driven away and the field was won." Watts' account did not include the actions of McCook's cavalry on the opposite flank, but Watts found out later in the day the part that unit played. Crook told Watts that McCook attacked from the south striking Wharton's cavalry in the flank and rear while Long's brigade held the Confederate cavalry with a frontal attack. Watts acknowledged the part McCook's division made in the fight. "They had not fled from us so much as from fear of the flank movement. This it as ever, we learn the particulars of campaigns and battles after they are over!"[9]

Some of the details missed by Watts occurred with the 1st Ohio Cavalry which was positioned away from the 2nd Kentucky. Two companies of the 1st Ohio pushed forward as skirmishers and due to some confusion, the remainder of the regiment halted and this left the two companies exposed to enemy fire for twenty minutes without any support. Lieutenant W. L. Curry of the 1st Ohio recorded casualties of thirty men during this fight; but David Stanley reported a significantly smaller number in his daily report. In addition, the action of the Chicago Board of Trade Artillery helped turn the fight in favor of the Federal cavalry. When Crook's initial advance began against the line of Confederate cavalry, the momentum shifted in favor of the Colonel Thomas Harrison's Confederate cavalry. Benjamin Nourse described that his section joined the fight after hurrying forward and "opened on them sharply,

"[T]hey are charging!!," echoed during the cavalry fight at Alpine on September 9 (Library of Congress).

checking them." When McCook's cavalry joined in the fight, the Union artillery was lobbing shells into the tree line until the enemy withdrew.[10]

Among the Confederate cavalry in the fighting at Alpine were the 8th Texas and 4th Georgia Cavalry regiments. Chaplain Robert F. Bunting wrote in a letter that the regiments tried to hold the line against the Crook and McCook but they were just outnumbered and compelled to retreat. Crook sent a detachment of cavalry to follow up his victory but after following the enemy a few miles past Alpine toward Melville, the pursuers found a strong force of Wheeler's cavalry and stopped the pursuit.[11]

The prisoners told Stanley that Confederate infantry held Summerville and reinforcements were expected from Virginia. Among the prisoners was a courier with dispatches from Wheeler which indicated the Confederate army intended to concentrate at La Fayette. The day's action was long and laborious as the Union cavalry had to ride through the elevations of Lookout Mountain and make the descent all the while dealing with a fighting retreat of Wheeler's cavalry. It took the entire Federal cavalry on the Southern flank to accomplish this but in the end Alpine remained in Federal possession. Upon the capture of Alpine, Stanley sent another scouting expedition toward Summerville to determine the strength of the enemy there. Soon, Brigadier General Jefferson C. Davis arrived at his headquarters and the two generals concluded to work together for a safe descent of the infantry into the valley the next day. Stanley passed along some rumors from the prisoners to army headquarters. The first suggested "that Bragg is retreating south of the Oostanaula; I have not definite information. The enemy fought stubbornly from the foot of the mountain. The country is well adapted to their mode of warfare." The second offered some support to the delay in the Federal expedition to Rome: "One of the enemy captured today says Forrest was here today, and that he saw him and knows him." This confirmed that a single cavalry division riding for Rome would have faced not only Wheeler's corps, but Forrest's as well. In addition, Stanley's cavalry had also just missed a significant battle at Alpine with not only Wharton's cavalry, but also with Armstrong's full division, had it not been ordered the night before to move to La Fayette.[12]

Minty's Actions with XXI Corps—Bragg Prepares an Attack

Crittenden continued to move past Chattanooga on September 10 hoping to locate Bragg's army. Major General John Palmer, Second Division, ran into a screen of Confederate cavalry and he had the support of Van Cleve's division as his infantry pressed to within five miles of Ringgold. Thomas Wood's division remained two miles to the rear near Chickamauga Creek. To the chagrin of Palmer, a Confederate cavalry force of 300–600 troopers sent one of Charles Cruft's regiments, the 1st Kentucky Infantry, scampering to the rear. Palmer's scouts reported that a cavalry brigade remained in close vicinity of his division looking for an opportunity to inflict damage on unsupported infantry. Palmer further described: "The affair of today annoys me very much" because it resulted in the loss of two officers and fifty-eight men as casualties—killed, wounded or captured. The attack on the 1st Kentucky Infantry was prompted by an attack by the 4th Michigan Cavalry which probably embarrassed some Southern horsemen, of which the 6th Georgia Cavalry was one regiment. Palmer described that a detachment of the 4th Michigan Cavalry had been ordered to drive off some lurking Confederate cavalry. "This small party attacked with great spirit, drove the enemy a mile, and as it was quite obvious that the parties of the enemy near were numerous and comparatively strong, it rejoined the column. A few minutes after the return of our cavalry, a force of the enemy, under cover of a cloud of dust, charged the advance guard (four companies, First Kentucky) at full speed, threw it in confusion."[13]

While the 4th Michigan fought the Confederate cavalry, five miles east of Ringgold at Graysville, Colonel William Grose, Third Brigade of Palmer's division, confirmed that Buckner's and Walker' troops had just marched through the town along the La Fayette Road. "A large amount of cavalry left there today, the last since noon. Most of that tends toward La Fayette." The cavalry Crittenden's troops encountered was Pegram's division operating in front of Polk's Corps. As Crittenden moved south, Wilder's mounted infantry joined in the pursuit and by the end of the day reached Palmer's position. Wilder sent a scouting party ahead to Ringgold and found no enemies in the town, but reported that Scott's and Davidson's cavalry remained in the area providing rearguard duty while the infantry withdrew toward Rome. Crittenden began to fan his corps out and move southward, marching toward Thomas' corps near La Fayette and extending eastward along the Dalton road.[14]

The most important event of the day involved James Negley's division at McLemore's Cove. He was startled when he found a large Confederate force directly ahead at Dug Gap. Negley also found a second concentration of enemy troops which he estimated to be a division with two batteries of artillery only three miles to the north. To make things worse, Martin's cavalry division also approached his position and he suspected the cavalry would attempt to swing to his rear and cut off any effort to retreat. Negley knew he held a precarious position and felt that the Confederates were maneuvering to attack. He had also received reports that morning of a concentration of Confederate infantry at La Fayette. Negley sent a message to Absalom Baird, the closest supporting Federal infantry, explaining that his division was exposed by two roads on the flank, but Negley felt he had a good position to fight if needed. Negley needed reassurance that Baird would be in position to support him in the fight and he urged Baird to march forward through the night to reach his position.[15]

Negley's position was indeed advanced and while he thought he was prepared to fight, he had no idea the welcome that Bragg prepared for him the next morning. Bragg, who moved his headquarters to La Fayette during the day, began moving troops to attack Negley's division on September 10, but the attack stalled because Thomas Hindman's and Patrick Cleburne's divisions could not get into position. Instead, the attack was delayed until the next morning. Negley was twelve hours ahead of his nearest reinforcements. Rosecrans, still believing that Bragg marched southward toward Rome, demanded his infantry and cavalry to drive ahead causing damage to the vulnerable flank of the withdrawing army. Negley wisely slowed his advance because of the concentrations of the enemy in front of his line of march. Just as Rosecrans had unleashed a tirade on Stanley two days before, he now turned on Thomas. Rosecrans told Thomas he was "disappointed to learn ... that his forces move tomorrow morning instead of having moved this morning, as they should have done, this delay imperiling both extremes of the army. Your movement on La Fayette should be made with the utmost promptness. You ought not to encumber yourself with your main supply train. A brigade or two will be sufficient to protect it. Your advance ought to have threatened La Fayette yesterday evening." Rosecrans' anger, toward Stanley and now Thomas, resulted from his mistaken belief that "the Confederates were in panic-stricken retreat, their army disintegrating," wrote historian Peter Cozzens.[16]

Meanwhile on September 10, Stanley had scouting expeditions out along three different routes. Louis Watkins' brigade rode to Summerville and saw the most action during the day. Watkins narrowly missed a difficult morning and only had to deal with a small body enemy cavalry. From the prisoners, Watkins learned that Wharton's and Armstrong's divisions were all in the vicinity. They had just left a small cavalry force at Summerville as they moved north on the La Fayette Road. Watkins' Third Brigade gained possession of Summerville and in the process of capturing the town, Watkins claimed one captain and 11 privates mostly from the 3rd Georgia Cavalry, although Watkins' earlier report indicated two companies of the 2nd Georgia were in the town. After questioning the prisoners, Watkins found there were two other regiments encamped about three miles north on the La Fayette Road. Major Christopher Cheek, 5th Kentucky Cavalry, attacked the camp as the enemy prepared for the skirmish. The Confederate cavalry, having received word after the attack at Summerville, prepared to meet the Kentucky cavalry, but the 6th Kentucky Cavalry also joined in the fight. The Southern cavalry withdrew and left a supply depot in the hands of Watkins. The depot had some baled cotton and miscellaneous food supplies. The 6th Kentucky lost one trooper killed and four wounded, including a member of Stanley's escort who was shot in the shoulder. In return, Watkins was unsure of the total enemy casualties but found two dead lying in a field.[17]

Along a parallel road to the west, Crook's lone brigade under the command of Eli Long scouted in the direction of La Fayette and scooped up a few prisoners who confirmed Watkins' intelligence about the Confederate cavalry. Finally, Archibald Campbell and some of the second brigade scouted toward Rome in preparation for a reconnaissance in force the next day. Campbell's brigade rode to Melville without resistance but determined that Rome was well protected with "a large force of all arms."[18]

Stanley made his report to Garfield on September 10 and he told him that Edward McCook's division scouted toward Rome and it ran into no large concentrations of the enemy, but the local citizens told the cavalrymen that a strong force of W. H. T. Walker's infantry was positioned at the town. The diary of a member of the 2nd Georgia Cavalry revealed the movement toward Rome by McCook was immediately known and Wharton's cavalry division closely observed the movements of the Federal Cavalry. Wharton's division received instructions to prepare to defend Rome, but the Federal expedition was tentative and required no response from Wharton. Stanley also described the third reconnaissance mission—Louis Watkins' efforts during the day which heralded the capture of Summerville. Watkins determined from his prisoners that movements of the Confederate cavalry to La Fayette was due to approach of Thomas' infantry at that location. Finally, Stanley reported to headquarters about his deteriorating health. "I have been very sick and confined to my bed all day, but hope to be up tomorrow or next day."[19]

Bragg Takes the Offensive—The Attack at McLemore's Cove

Despite the shifting initiative in favor of the Confederate forces south of Chattanooga, the overall confidence of the Army of the Cumberland's headquarters went unabated and extended to Halleck in Washington. Bragg's lack of offensive action over the past thirty days indicated the Confederates would not fight and when Chattanooga was abandoned without a fight, it appeared Bragg planned to continue his retreat. Halleck told Rosecrans that intelligence gathered in Virginia (which proved to be erroneous) suggested that Bragg was even sending troops to reinforce Robert E. Lee. Unfortunately, Halleck wrote to Burnside on September 11 that it wasn't necessary to extend further south other than establishing a line of cavalry to connect with Rosecrans. In reality Bragg was receiving reinforcements from other locations; but the Army of Ohio received orders to remain near Knoxville and not march to assist Rosecrans as he unknowingly faced the increasing lethal Army of Tennessee. From Rosecrans' optimistic messages that Bragg retreated for Rome, Halleck concluded Burnside was no longer needed at Chattanooga. To support the erroneous opinions of the Union high command, newspaper correspondents sent "to the world joyful accounts of the utter demoralization of Bragg's army, of his weakness and retreat.... In their mistaken zeal, they already pictured Rosecrans at Dalton and Atlanta," wrote John Fitch, judge advocate of the Army of the Cumberland.[20]

But, Rosecrans soon found that the resistance by his enemy, now south of Chattanooga, intensified throughout the day. Negley's division would narrowly escape disaster through the bungling of a Confederate attack. Bragg ordered Major General Thomas Hindman's division south into McLemore's Cove while Cleburne's Division was positioned on Pigeon Mountain defending Dug Gap. Through a series of blunders, D. H. Hill did not move Cleburne's division into the valley and Hindman failed to attack, despite being reinforced with two additional divisions. Due to these delays, Negley successfully withdrew his vulnerable division from McLemore's Cove with minor losses. The Confederates finally attacked at 4:00 p.m., but the delay allowed Negley time to withdraw to a more secure location and await reinforcements which arrived the next morning. The belated Confederate attack echoed throughout the mountains and Crittenden heard the fighting from his position to the north. Despite this misstep, Bragg had just shifted from a defensive to offensive strategy.[21]

Confederate cavalry general Will T. Martin operated under the command of Hindman and he felt Negley remained unaware of the impending attack but that "[h]ours were lost in consultations." Martin thought the attack should have been carried out much earlier. "The delay was inexplicable to me," remarked Martin. For some reason, Hindman stopped his command within striking distance of Negley's Union troops. Martin's cavalry remained behind Hindman's infantry as Hindman waited to attack, but by noon, Negley's scouts had detected the threat and Negley began to withdraw his division. As Negley withdrew, Hindman ordered Martin to charge the enemy's rear while some of the infantry charged the front. Martin recalled that he did so with some Alabama cavalry, about 150 strong, all that he had in that part of the field. "I was repulsed after sharp loss inflicted by infantry and artillery," wrote Martin.[22]

Rosecrans, unaware of the near miss at McLemore's Cove, criticized Thomas' failure to reach La Fayette the evening before, but Thomas wrote to Rosecrans that Negley "has received information from several independent sources that the enemy are prepared to resist his advance with a large force, and are also endeavoring to flank him. You will see by my instructions to General Negley of 3 o'clock this a m. what disposition I have made to support him and to dispose of the force threatening his flank. I am satisfied that if the information he received was correct, his division would have suffered very severely had he attempted to march on La Fayette yesterday." Thomas and Negley both were right and had just missed a massive attack.[23]

In the meantime, Crittenden, who moved southward in three parallel columns, ran into increased resistance from the Confederate cavalry as he inched southward from Chattanooga. Forrest's cavalry screened the Federal advance and shielded the location of the Confederate main force from Rosecrans, although by the end of the day the Union commanders concluded that Bragg had withdrawn to La Fayette and not to Rome. Colonel William Palmer, 15th Pennsylvania Cavalry, discovered that two divisions of Confederate infantry had been at Lee and Gordon's Mill the day before. The 15th Pennsylvania Cavalry was a detached cavalry regiment assigned to headquarters duty and Rosecrans utilized all his mounted forces to determine the location of Bragg's army, including this regiment. Major General John Palmer, who reached Lee and Gordon's Mill by late afternoon, also observed Pegram's and Armstrong cavalry divisions throughout the day. Some of Wilder's troops also skirmished with about eight hundred of John Scott's Confederate cavalry of Pegram's division near Ringgold during the day. In light of increased skirmishing, Rosecrans, sensing the vulnerability of his infantry, reconsidered his plan of advance. He ordered Crittenden to push toward La Fayette from the north but no farther than Ringgold; and he ordered Thomas and McCook to proceed from the west. Thomas told Rosecrans he faced a concentration of the Confederate infantry and could not reach La Fayette until at least the next day. Alexander McCook established communications with Thomas and reported that he had issues of his own—at least, a brigade of cavalry between Alpine and La Fayette. Rosecrans, returning to the consideration that Bragg could produce offensive actions, began to move his infantry corps to within supporting distance of each other; and for the second time during the week, Rosecrans left McCook's, as he had with Stanley a few days before, movements to his own discretion.[24]

Union Cavalry Searches for Bragg—McCook Rides for Rome

One of the basic principles during the Civil War defined that the cavalry would be the eyes and ears of the army, but this principle proved difficult in the terrain near La Fayette. Stanley sent out three expeditions to develop enemy concentrations the day before, but still had not located Bragg's army. In absence of direct orders from headquarters and without a clear picture of what lay ahead, Alexander McCook planned to march on Summerville on September 11, which had been captured by Stanley's cavalry, until he could determine the position and number of enemy troops at La Fayette. McCook requested assistance from Stanley to cooperate with Colonel Thomas Harrison's 39th Indiana Mounted Infantry in determining the locations and concentration of Confederates along his intended path of march. Harrison's single regiment proved inadequate to penetrate Wharton's cavalry screen in front of La Fayette and Louis Watkins' cavalry brigade moved to join in this duty.[25]

Watkins moved his brigade along with one cannon of Newell's artillery over the La Fayette Road to open the road between Alpine and Harrison's 39th Indiana Mounted Infantry, about ten miles away. Wheeler's Confederate cavalry blocked the road and Thomas Harrison's regiment was not strong enough to push past the enemy. Watkins had his three Kentucky regiments in the saddle and riding ahead at 5:30 p.m. The two colonels met at midnight, and decided to begin their joint action the next morning, but a rider arrived at 4:00 a.m. with a message from headquarters. Realizing after the near miss at McLemore's Cove that Bragg was not withdrawing but preparing to strike the Union army near La Fayette, the two mounted forces were also probably outnumbered and vulnerable to attack. Upon receiving new orders,

Seven. Bragg Gains the Initiative (September 9–17)

they returned to Watkins' old camp at Alpine. There, local citizens told Watkins that Wheeler and Forrest both were just ahead of where Harrison and Watkins stopped for the night. Watkins felt lucky to have returned in one piece.[26]

Edward McCook's cavalry finally made the long-delayed expedition to Rome. McCook scouted ahead with two brigades on September 11 just south of Wheeler's headquarters located at Trion Factory, a small town established around a set of cotton mills. The location was a good one for Wheeler and it allowed Wheeler quick access to Summerville and La Fayette. The town was also situated on the Chattooga River, a good source of water for horses and men. Wheeler's scouts watched McCook's Union cavalry cross the Chattooga River, disperse and then return. McCook's expedition was tentative and posed no real threat but Wheeler had seven regiments of Wharton's division at Trion factory available to attack the Federal flank or rear had McCook taken action against the railroad or Rome. In addition, the infantry presence in Rome was sufficient to deal with this reconnaissance. Wheeler who had been concerned about a cavalry flanking movement throughout the campaign and explained, "I have several scouts in among the enemy this side of the mountain."[27]

Archibald Campbell and Daniel Ray made their probe as far as the Coosa and Chattooga rivers before running into concentrations of infantry and artillery. Campbell reported that some of his brigade reached Melville and then he sent out scouts to within a few miles of Rome and found a large concentration of infantry six miles away. One of the 2nd Michigan was lost during the day due to unknown reasons. "Private Bernard Bourassa, missing, having stopped to attend to calls of nature, was not seen or heard from after." Campbell held his position at Melville for a few hours and returned to Alpine. The 1st Tennessee Cavalry made the greatest progress during the expedition. Colonel James Brownlow's 1st Tennessee rode five miles toward Rome and then split his command. Two battalions rode toward Rome where "they drove in the pickets, capturing and destroying all the arms and equipments of one company." Brownlow sent the other battalion to the small village of Dirt Town which was built along a trail used by Native Americans. Brownlow's troopers moved between two enemy cavalry forces and his men skirmished with the enemy for two hours before returning to the Alpine about midnight.[28]

During this expedition, some of the pro–Southern citizens sent less than subtle messages to the Federal cavalry. The 27-year-old Huntingdon County Pennsylvania native, Captain Thomas McCahan, led a company of the 9th Pennsylvania Cavalry during the expedition to Rome and his men rode past a house with a human skeleton suspended on a pole with its head in a noose. The Pennsylvanians returned the sentiment and totally destroyed the brick house in five minutes from which the skeleton was suspended. McCahan explained this was a "black flag" to the Union cavalry and the men responded in kind.[29]

W. R. Carter, 1st Tennessee, recorded his experience with a battalion of cavalry which captured some enemy pickets during its expedition toward Rome: "If the sun had suddenly ceased to shine, it would have been no greater surprise to our captives than the sight of bluecoats. They did not believe at first that we were 'Yankees,' but when they saw the flags they became convinced, and wanted to know what we were doing down in 'Dixie,' the land of cotton. With this information we pushed ahead, and at dark attacked and drove in Wheeler's pickets. Colonel Brownlow now ordered forward his detachment, and a running fight was kept up for a mile or two, only halting when we heard Wheeler's buglers sounding 'boots and saddles.' We captured fifteen prisoners, and on our return destroyed a small bridge that we supposed spanned Chattooga river." Brownlow reached to within a few miles of Rome and determined it was impractical to advance any further. Thus ended the long-desired expedition to Rome.[30]

As the day drew to a close, Alexander McCook felt more isolated and told Stanley to keep a close eye on the enemy. "[O]ur troops here are exposed to the entire force of the rebel army." And the final message of the day came to Stanley from Garfield who conceded that Bragg had concentrated his army at La Fayette. Bragg appeared to be ready to fight at La Fayette and this put Rosecrans in a dangerous situation with his various corps still widely separated. Garfield wanted Stanley's cavalry to stop probing ahead and to move in close proximity to Alexander McCook's flank. Upon moving into position Garfield emphasized the highest priority should be the determination of location and the size of the enemy concentrations, as soon as possible. Garfield sent two additional bits of information—first, it was unlikely that Minty would be allowed to rejoin the main body of cavalry anytime soon, as previously promised, and secondly, Robert Mitchell, Stanley's second-in-command had just returned to duty at army headquarters.[31]

Edward McCook settled into camp near Alpine because he felt this was the only safe location for the night. He was concerned about moving closer toward La Fayette because the local citizens told him Polk's entire infantry corps awaited twelve miles ahead at Trion Factory screened by Wharton's cavalry division only two miles ahead at Mitchell's. McCook planned to move toward Wharton's cavalry the next morning, writing: "I will feel Mr. Wharton a little." Then, McCook sent scouts out in all directions trying to determine concentrations of the enemy. Crook agreed with McCook's plan and wrote to McCook at 5:00 p.m. from the Trion Factory and La Fayette Road requesting that McCook move toward Trion Factory the next morning to occupy Wheeler's attention. Crook needed to complete a reconnaissance mission of his own the next morning toward La Fayette and he felt the more enemy cavalry watching McCook, the greater chance he had for success. Crook told McCook to occupy Wheeler as much as possible until he could complete his reconnaissance.[32]

The Momentum Swings in Favor of Bragg

Upon learning of Halleck's orders for Burnside to concentrate his attentions around the Knoxville area and assuming Rosecrans had an open field ahead of him, Rosecrans reminded Halleck that he still faced Bragg's army and that he was pushing southward. Rosecrans, probably over confidently, explained that he had sufficient troops to deal with Bragg but he still needed someone, either Burnside or part of the Army of the Tennessee, to cover the gap developing between the Army of the Ohio and the Army of the Cumberland. The optimism of earlier messages to Washington was now gone as Rosecrans considered the reality of the unfolding situation. Later in the day, he told Halleck that Bragg was receiving reinforcements and that Thomas had been attacked the day before by overwhelming numbers of enemy troops. Rosecrans now grasped that Bragg was not in full flight to Rome or Atlanta, but he concentrated near La Fayette and prepared to fight. He urged Halleck: "Burnside ought to send his infantry down in this direction." On the day Rosecrans made the appeal to hurry Burnside toward Chattanooga, General Sam Jones, now in charge of the Confederate defense of East Tennessee including Knoxville, wrote to James Seddon, Secretary of War, and

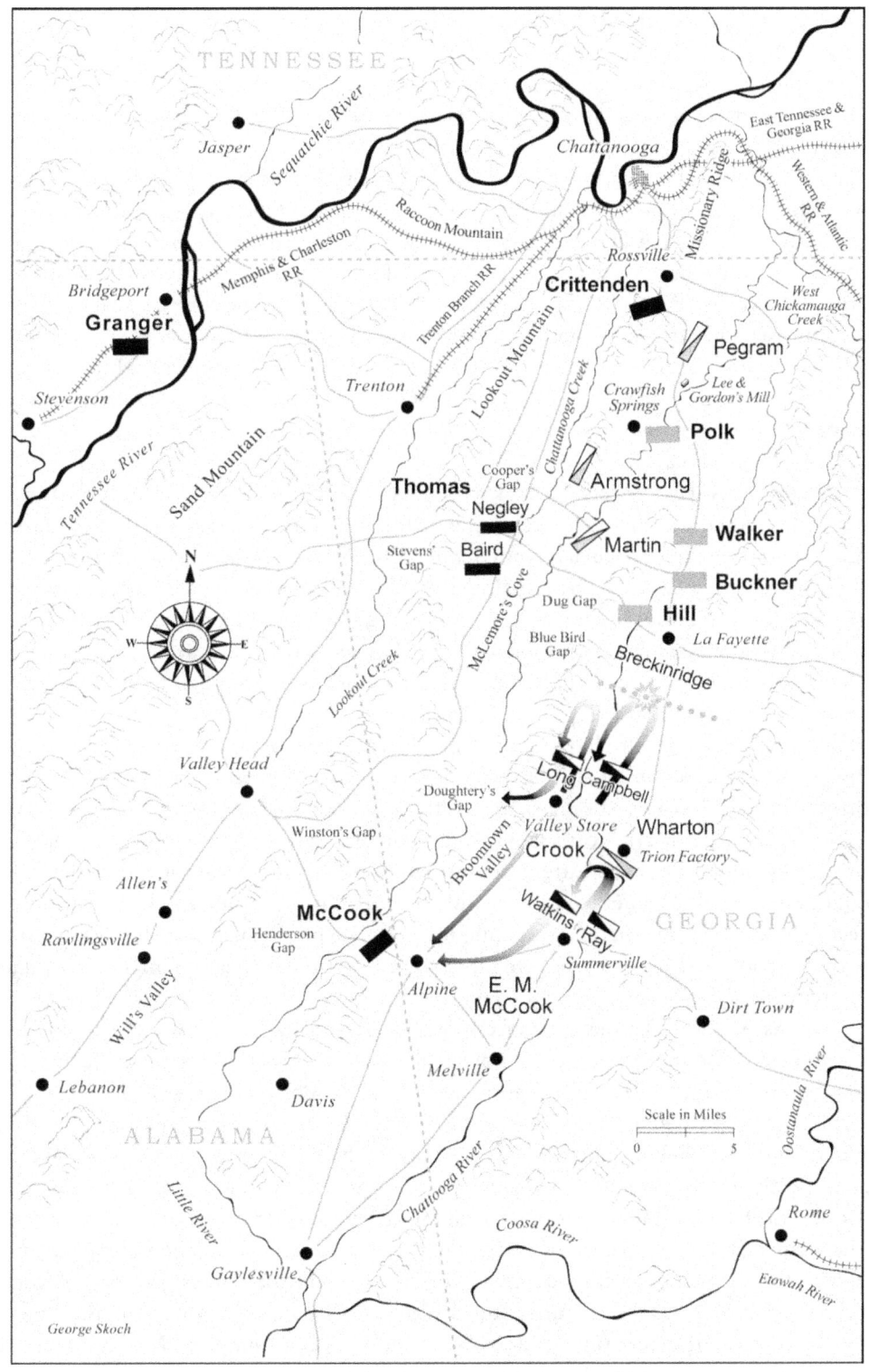

Union cavalry movements: September 12–13.

exclaimed that he had only two regiments and a battalion of infantry, one cavalry regiment and one battery in which he had any confidence. "If the enemy operates with vigor I cannot hold any part of East Tennessee." While Burnside lingered near Knoxville, he faced no large concentration of Confederate forces, and Rosecrans finally realized he still faced a dangerous foe.[33]

Both Jefferson Davis and James Seddon commented on Bragg's strategy, and both still believed that Burnside would march to assist Rosecrans at Chattanooga. Jefferson Davis wrote: "The case demands great activity, with which it is hoped the enemy's purpose may be defeated by fighting his two columns separately. If the weaker can be beaten first the stronger will be attacked afterward with the advantage which success and re-enforcements will give." Seddon agreed and offered support to Bragg's recent shift to the offense. He told Bragg to avoid fighting both armies together and it seemed "to necessitate a prompt blow at Rosecrans.... It may yet be safe and pardonable in me to express the conviction that early and decisive action against one or the other of the advancing columns of the enemy is essential to success in the campaign."[34]

The previous day's botched attack at McLemore's Cove caused the Federal army to pause. So, despite the many earlier reports which suggested that Bragg would fight further south, the new reports, particularly from Stanley and Thomas, indicated that Bragg concentrated his army at La Fayette. The remainder of Thomas's corps moved forward to support Negley's position and Alexander McCook, concerned that he was alone along the flank, cautiously sent reconnaissance expeditions ahead. Thomas wanted the cavalry to scout ahead and he wanted Wilder's brigade back with his corps. McCook, on the other hand, relied on Harrison's 39th Indiana Mounted Infantry in addition to Stanley's cavalry.[35]

Because Thomas faced a large Confederate force in front of his corps and because much of Bragg's army seemed to be at La Fayette, Thomas urged Rosecrans to move Crittenden directly south and threatened Bragg's rear. Although Thomas' caution was vindicated after the abortive attack at McLemore's Cove, Rosecrans still appeared unhappy about Negley's actions and wrote to Thomas: "After maturely weighing the notes, the general commanding is induced to think that General Negley withdrew more through prudence than compulsion." Rosecrans told Thomas to maintain communications with headquarters and he also reminded Thomas to report on McCook's movements so that Crittenden's position might be regulated by the remainder of the army.[36]

Thomas' XIV Corps remained in front of Dug Gap during the day with Reynolds' division extended to Cooper's Gap, to the north. Thomas also reported the force Negley faced the day before included all of Hill's infantry corps, part of Buckner's corps and Martin's 2,000 cavalry. Thomas pushed as far as Widow Davis' crossroads and found no enemy in front. General Robert Mitchell, commander of the First Cavalry Division, arrived at Negley's headquarters with verbal orders from Rosecrans for Thomas. Rosecrans wanted Alexander McCook and Stanley to move northward to support Thomas' corps so that a joint movement on the enemy at Dug Gap and La Fayette could begin. Mitchell brought a complaint from headquarters: "General Rosecrans complains of a want of information in regard to your movements and position, and of the numbers and position of the enemy." The need for information remained a critical need for army headquarters and Thomas, Stanley, and McCook would be criticized during the day regarding their communications.[37]

If the Confederate army concentrated at La Fayette, Thomas' corps risked a major battle.

La Fayette lay approximately five miles to the east and at the foot of Pigeon Mountain. If Bragg intended to attack and destroy the Army of the Cumberland in detail, he had a good opportunity to do that. Thomas planned to march over Pigeon Mountain through the three gaps near La Fayette—Blue Bird Gap, Dug Gap, and Catlett's Gap. In the meantime, he fulfilled his orders to tell McCook and Stanley to close up on his right flank. Thomas suggested that XX Corps and Stanley's cavalry should move directly north and secure the passes on the mountain. This was good strategy because the Union officers did not know what lay behind Pigeon Mountain and the screen of Confederate cavalry at La Fayette.[38]

The cavalry actions of the prior two days had yielded important intelligence for Alexander McCook's southern-most corps. James P. Brownlow's 1st Tennessee Cavalry's penetration to the vicinity of Rome provided the important information—Bragg's army was not there and this reinforced Thomas' intelligence that he faced the bulk of the Confederate army at La Fayette. In addition, Wheeler's cavalry increased its activity; and as Edward McCook's cavalry scouts pressed toward Trion Factory, they were chased away by large concentrations of Confederate cavalry reported to be "brigade sized." Edward McCook picked up a prisoner who confirmed the intelligence being gathered by the Federal cavalry and the prisoner told McCook that both Wharton's and Martin's cavalry divisions were operating in the area. McCook also boldly stated: "[T]hey have no idea we can whip them." McCook flatly reported after his past two days of reconnaissance that Bragg was not retreating, but there was a significant enemy force at Rome. He concluded that the enemy cavalry appeared to be headed in his direction and said," I think they may try me in the morning." Realizing the need to fully assess the situation, David Stanley decided to send his entire cavalry division to determine the enemy's position and numbers at La Fayette on September 13.[39]

While Thomas believed that a fight lay directly in front of him, Alexander McCook felt no better and told George Thomas: "I am not desirous of fighting Bragg's whole army, and in case he is concentrated at La Fayette I am in a false position, for I could not reach you." While Rosecrans urged his corps commanders to send information, headquarters seemed to be lax in return. McCook felt very exposed and he decided to keep his wagon train well in the rear on top of Lookout Mountain and his troops in the valley. McCook also realized the advantage La Fayette held for Bragg. He was hidden behind Pigeon Mountain and Wheeler protected the southern approach to this location. In addition, Bragg had the option of simply withdrawing to Dalton or Rome if he was pressed. McCook wisely wrote to Thomas that Bragg wanted to concentrate his entire force and attack the widely-separated Union divisions. "All citizens here, both Union and secession, say that he will fight, and with the advantages he has I think so also. I have no doubt that the rebel army is concentrated at or near La Fayette." Alexander McCook's XX Corps was still twenty-three miles south of La Fayette and he knew the most important task centered on finding the Confederate forces in front of him.[40]

Stanley Again Criticized—Cavalry Prepares to Ride to La Fayette

The final tirade against Stanley from Rosecrans came on September 12 via a message from Frank Bond, Rosecrans's aide-de-Camp: "The general commanding directs me to say that after the most explicit order to connect with and keep open courier lines, he finds that neither your own nor General McCook's headquarters are connected with the headquarters of the department or of General Thomas. He directs me to say there is no military offense, except running from the enemy, so inexcusable as a neglect to keep up communications with headquarters. Our lines are now much extended, and we must husband our resources. The general commanding therefore directs that you at once establish courier lines to General McCook's headquarters and to Easley's, there to connect with our lines, via Winston's up the valley, or by the mountain road—the latter believed to be the most preferable. It is of the greatest importance that our dispatches should be forwarded with promptness." The choice of words in this message could not be interpreted as anything other than a severe rebuke. This rebuke follows a similar statement of disappointment to George Thomas earlier in the day, but clearly this one carried a bitterness absent from the one sent to Thomas. It is unclear when Bond sent this message, but Alexander McCook had information early on the morning of September 12 regarding the previous day's cavalry activities and he forwarded the intelligence onto army headquarters later during the day.[41]

Stanley sent his daily update at 3:00 p.m. to Garfield about the results of the actions of the cavalry on September 12 and he summarized the results of the long-awaited expedition to Rome, which for the most part no longer held much value to army headquarters. Stanley told headquarters that there were at least two infantry divisions at La Fayette -Withers' and Breckinridge's. This ominously supported the belief that Bragg was being reinforced from other Confederate armies. In addition, he determined large numbers of enemy cavalry present in the vicinity of La Fayette. Stanley told Garfield that he planned to send all his cavalry toward La Fayette in a forced reconnaissance the next day. Then, Stanley told Garfield about his physical condition. There was no reason army headquarters should have known of this, because Stanley seemed intent on weathering the malady and continuing with command. "My dysentery, which has been working on me for a week, has completely prostrated me, so that I am not able to be out of bed but a few minutes at a time. I am a little better today, and hope to be up in a few days." Would headquarters have been more tolerant of Stanley's actions had they known how ill he was? It is unknown, but Stanley was very sick. He bravely fought to stay in command and as a veteran campaigner, he knew chronic diarrhea often occurred during extended periods in the field.[42]

After examining the existing records, Stanley did not appear to have been tardy in sending his updates to headquarters. In addition, Rosecrans was clearly wrong in his severe rebuke of Stanley because the process of getting messages from the southern flank to headquarters was so difficult. Historian Peter Cozzens would write of the communications between headquarters and Alexander McCook "who seldom knew from one moment to the next where army headquarters was." Stanley had a more severe disadvantage and often relied on yet another link in the communication chain by sending his messages first to McCook who then sent them to headquarters. Historian, David Powell, wrote that with La Fayette in the hands of the enemy, the communications often took sixty hours to reach headquarters. Trooper A. D. Frankenberry, 15th Pennsylvania Cavalry, performed courier duty from Rosecrans' headquarters to Stanley and just a few days before had an arduous trek of carrying messages to the cavalry on the southern flank. It took three days to complete the task. Frankenberry had an escort of mounted infantry and still ran into the enemy along his path. He described his trek: "During the march we were fired on often, and the men were very bitter because they were not permitted to return the fire." Stanley had no telegraph service available to him and all the messages needed to go by courier. Messages to George Thomas generally took twelve to fifteen hours to reach him from Rosecrans and McCook was twenty-three miles further south, and Stanley yet further. W. R. Carter, historian of the 1st Tennessee Cavalry, noted: "General Stanley was unable to communicate with Rosecrans by the valley road, it being held by Bragg." These facts added a dimension to this rebuke, which perhaps reflected the stress and tension at headquarters, rather than a failure on the part of Stanley to perform his duties; but Stanley never directly responded in his own defense or acknowledged any blame.[43]

Crittenden Remains Confident

While McCook and Thomas were anxious about their situations, Crittenden continued to confidently press southward during the day. Thomas requested Wilder's brigade be returned to XIV Corps and Rosecrans initially agreed to send the mounted infantry back. As a result, he further dismantled Minty's brigade by sending the 4th U.S. Cavalry to the direct command of Crittenden and then ordered the remainder of Minty's brigade (now only two regiments) to replace Wilder. As the day advanced, Crittenden reached Lee and Gordon's Mill around 11:00 a.m. and he received information that Confederate cavalry remained active to the east of his advance.[44]

Three miles east of Lee and Gordon's Mill, Crittenden's infantry continued its march southward and the over confidence from the Union high command still resonated with Crittenden. He wrote to Rosecrans: "Should General Thomas be in the vicinity of La Fayette, as stated in your order of yesterday morning, I think that between him and Colonel Wilder, all the enemy north of La Fayette will be effectually bagged." Crittenden planned to get his corps into position and remain near Lee and Gordon's Mill that evening. Later in the afternoon, the Southern cavalry provided stiff resistance to the advanced elements of the Union column. Crittenden heard artillery fire to his left and—"The audacity of the rebel cavalry surprises me, and I can hardly realize that Generals Thomas and McCook are in the positions supposed, or at least that the former is not at or near La Fayette.... I still believe that the enemy is running, and that he will make no stand short of Rome."[45]

That evening, Garfield tried to temper Crittenden's confidence with some sobering information and presented to him the increasingly serious situation of the disconnected Federal army. Garfield cautioned Crittenden not to be over confident, because Thomas still languished in McLemore's Cove facing a large Confederate force. In regard to Wilder, Garfield directed Crittenden to draw him back to the front and left flank of XXI Corps. Wilder needed to provide intelligence and security because army headquarters still did not know Bragg's intentions. Garfield also wanted Minty on the right flank of Crittenden, again providing security along that flank even though the 4th U.S. cavalry had been detached to Crittenden's headquarters duty. Garfield concluded, "Examine the character of the creek, and see that your command has free communication both to the front and rear. Take up a defensible position...." Garfield sent a subsequent message at 9:30 p.m. that there was no doubt Bragg was concentrating his army at La Fayette. Then, Garfield directly told Crittenden that there a greater likelihood of Bragg attacking them than Bragg retreating any further south. "Get your command well in hand, and be ready for defense or advance, as may be necessary."[46]

Crittenden still had not grasped the situation near La Fayette by the end of the day and he sent Garfield the results of a heavy skirmish between Wilder's mounted infantry and

Pegram's Confederate cavalry at Leet's Tanyard. Wilder had seven men killed, another twenty-three wounded. The major fighting included Pegram's and Armstrong's cavalry but Wilder estimated a brigade of infantry (Brigadier General Otho F. Strahl) defended the wooded area he attacked. Pegram reportedly employed four regiments and five artillery pieces, and Wilder's troops moved steadily ahead until it reached the wooded area where infantry was observed. Crittenden discounted Wilder's observation of infantry explaining, "It has always been the plan of the enemy to make stubborn defenses on a retreat, and I do not yet believe that there is a strong force of infantry in the vicinity of La Fayette." He was confused about the heavy resistance he faced if Thomas faced the bulk of the Army of Tennessee at La Fayette. "[I]t is unaccountable to me that the rebel cavalry should make such demonstrations as they do. I am not, however, given over blindly to my opinion, and shall be cautious, occupying a position here that I think I can defend."[47]

Crittenden had just encountered some of the Confederate forces which planned to attack his corps under orders from Bragg. Bragg remained very frustrated at the missed opportunity at McLemore's Cove where Negley's division barely missed a crushing blow, but Bragg still saw great opportunity if he could defeat Rosecrans's scattered corps in detail. While Rosecrans focused on the Confederates at La Fayette, Bragg intended next to strike Crittenden's XXI Corps. Bragg directed Leonidas Polk to move Cheatham's division, reinforced by Hindman's and Walker's divisions, to crush at least John Palmer's Union division. The morning of September 12th was selected as the time for the attack. Strahl's presence with the Southern cavalry was part of the intended attack. Again, the attack never came because instead of just facing Palmer's division, Polk faced Crittenden's entire corps while the remainder of his corps was still marching from its position in McLemore's Cove. Bragg urged Polk to make the attack on Crittenden in a late-night message, "General, the enemy is approaching from the south, and it is highly important your attack in the morning should be quick and decided. Let no time be lost." Again, on the morning of September 13, no attack came much to the displeasure of Bragg. Polk probably received an order which he could not execute due to the various positions of the Union and Confederate troops, and instead of attacking, he established a defensive position in preparation to receive an attack from Crittenden. "Twice in as many days the Army of Tennessee had allowed certain victory to slip through its grasp," noted historian Peter Cozzens.[48]

Frustrations mounted on Union side of the line too. Robert Minty felt Rosecrans dismantled much of his brigade. The 3rd Indiana Cavalry fell under the command of George Wagner who garrisoned the town of Chattanooga and the 4th U.S. rode away to report to Crittenden. Minty, himself, was summoned to army headquarters, further revealing his many masters. From his headquarters at Stringer's Creek, at 10:30 p.m., Minty dejectedly responded to Goddard's message that he had sent the 4th U.S. Cavalry as directed. "With the remainder of the brigade I will be at the river at daylight. I have a large train, and the mules are tired out by today's march (27 miles).[49]

On the southern flank, Edward McCook's two brigades rode toward La Fayette at 1 p.m. with some of the cavalry stopping at Summerville and others moving along the La Fayette Road to within seven miles of that town. The troopers described the movement during the day as the dustiest they had encountered, often unable to see the horse in front of them. McCook also pushed his brigade to Trion Factory where they met a concentration of Wheeler's Confederate cavalry which withdrew upon their arrival. At the end of the day,

McCook bivouacked at Summerville and Valley Store and then, he coordinated the next day's actions with Crook. The Union cavalry needed to determine what enemy forces were at La Fayette which faced Thomas' and McCook's infantry corps.[50]

Stanley's illness took a turn for the worse and he had already been too ill to ride with any of the cavalry for several days. George Crook, being the next senior officer in the absence of Mitchell, took command of the cavalry's effort to determine the enemy's position and concentration at La Fayette. At 10 p.m., Crook sent a message for Edward McCook to coordinate his division with the actions of Long's brigade the next day. "I have a battalion just returned from Trion Factory, which has met with no enemy in that direction. If your horses are not too tired, I would like to have you move toward La Fayette at daylight in the morning. I will move in that direction at that time on this road."[51]

September 13—Stanley's Illness Worsens

As the sun rose on September 13, Rosecrans suspected that the momentum of the campaign had shifted to Bragg. Rosecrans' three corps remained separated in the mountains and valleys south of Chattanooga and his Reserve Corps slowly moved forward. He desperately needed to concentrate his army before Bragg attacked one of the isolated corps and his orders clearly reflected this shift in strategy. McCook and Stanley planned to march northward to support Thomas' XIV Corps and Crittenden's XXI Corps stopped and held a line near Lee and Gordon's Mills. Ominous columns of dust, and even smoke, were observed during the day, signaling more movement by the Confederate forces which Rosecrans now believed concentrated near La Fayette.[52]

Thomas did not want to continue his advance toward La Fayette until the three Federal corps united and so, he held a line in McLemore's Cove. At 7 a.m., Thomas had a strong position at the gaps in front and in the rear of his corps; but he balked at the suggestion that he should advance any farther eastward without Crittenden and McCook in support. As a result, Thomas' infantry remained in place content to watch the gaps leading over Pigeon Mountain in case Bragg again attempted to attack his corps. Thomas, who had been chastised the day before directly and indirectly when Robert Mitchell arrived at his headquarters, sent Rosecrans a detailed message of the geography he held and wrote: "I have been thus particular in thus describing the valley and the roads leading across it because I inferred from what General Mitchell told me that you were dissatisfied with the little information I had given you of the country." Obviously, Thomas had detected the irritability of the commanding general from his earlier message.[53]

Alexander McCook wrote to Thomas at 8:15 a.m. that he was moving his corps directly from Alpine to link with Thomas' XIV Corps. He planned a forced march through Dougherty's Gap into McLemore's Cove. McCook, too isolated at his position, wanted to remedy the situation as soon as possible. He wrote to Garfield regarding the chastisement by Frank Bond sent to David Stanley and himself. "I saw a letter to General Stanley, written by Major Bond, in which I am charged of being guilty of offense—classified by the general commanding as the next worst thing to running from the enemy. I have always had a courier line between my headquarters and department, headquarters, with the exception of a few hours, since I left Will's Valley, therefore Major Bond's charges are without foundation. The headquarters of the department were moved away from Stevenson to Trenton without my knowledge. They were moved from Trenton to Chattanooga without my knowledge. I cannot be responsible for the courier line of the Anderson Cavalry. It took them nine hours to convey an order to me a distance of 20 ½ miles. In another instance, it took them from 7 p.m. till 3 a.m. to convey a dispatch from me to General Sheridan, a distance of 7 miles (dispatch marked gallop). Such conduct as this explains the delay in communicating with department headquarters." While Stanley seemed no less tardy than Thomas or McCook in sending his message, he chose not to retaliate in the form of a message to Rosecrans. Alexander McCook's defense of the problems with communication provided an excellent explanation to the lack of timely messages across so many miles.[54]

Alexander McCook wisely chose to gain additional intelligence regarding the Confederate army at La Fayette before making any dramatic moves. McCook wrote again to Garfield about his position and offered intelligence from a captured enemy soldier. A prisoner captured by the Kentucky cavalry told his captors, "he has never seen so large an army together as the one now concentrated at La Fayette." He saw the top generals in the Confederate army there, including "Bragg, Polk, D. H. Hill, Forrest, Wharton, Harrison, Pegram, Scott, Breckinridge, Preston, Hodge, and Wheeler." He also told the Union officers that Bragg had been definitely reinforced by troops from Virginia. McCook also told Garfield about Stanley's condition. He knew Stanley was ill and tried desperately to continue in command; but he was so sick that he was transported by ambulance. McCook ended his message expressing his confidence that the cavalry along his flank would fend off any surprises until he reached Thomas.[55]

Campbell's Charge at La Fayette

Edward McCook, at Trion Factory, began the day working in conjunction with George Crook and the day would be a frustrating, but productive, one for the Union cavalry. Crook took control of the cavalry in the field, and he divided the Union cavalry into two columns of two brigades each. (Archibald Campbell brigade of McCook's division would cooperate with Eli Long's brigade in Crook's reconnaissance to La Fayette.)[56]

At 10:00 a.m., McCook reported to Major W. H. Sinclair at cavalry headquarters that his cavalry chased away the Confederate cavalry pickets in front of his division and then he sent the 4th Indiana Cavalry to the eastern side of the Chattooga River. The 4th Indiana attempted to eliminate the troublesome, but strong, screen of Wharton's cavalry which fired on the Union cavalry on the west side of the river. McCook anticipated this action would take until one o'clock in the afternoon and then he would join Crook in his mission. McCook reasoned that due to the mountains and the proximity of river next to the mountain, only a regiment-sized force would be able to maneuver against Thomas Harrison's Confederate brigade along the eastern side of the river: "[T]he country there is bad to handle a large force in, and the force in front of me as I stated in my last dispatch—is larger than I could whip." He was blocked by a large concentration of enemy cavalry in front of his advance. McCook accurately described the situation: "One regiment can accomplish all that the whole division could.... I am still impressed with the belief that the enemy's infantry are in force the other side of the Coosa, at La Fayette, and their cavalry on this side." At 2:00 p.m., Wheeler's cavalry held a position in the crossroads in front of McCook's advance at the Ringgold and La Fayette crossroads stopping any further movement northward. In addition, Brigadier General Benjamin Helm's infantry supported Wharton's Confederate cavalry. The 4th Indiana attempted to push the cavalry away from the crossroads but had no success. McCook agreed that uniting his cavalry with Crook was a good solution for dealing with the large enemy force. "As their cavalry is here, I think with our forces joined, we may get nearer La Fayette."[57]

At the same time as McCook's last message, Sinclair wrote again to McCook and told him that Crook had already made his reconnaissance to La Fayette that morning and found that Confederate infantry held La Fayette. Sinclair also told McCook that columns of dust suggested another large enemy cavalry force moved in his direction. Sinclair warned: "If you come in contact with this party, fall back slowly and watch their movements, and report to General Stanley." Wharton's cavalry had successfully stymied McCook's advance.[58]

Along the road to the west, Crook's cavalry column began its mission to find the Confederate forces around La Fayette. Crook wanted McCook's two brigades to accompany his advance to La Fayette riding abreast down the parallel road as a show of strength. Because of the positioning of Wheeler's cavalry, McCook could not advance very far. Archibald Campbell's First Brigade of McCook's division joined Long's brigade and the two brigades moved to La Fayette on two parallel roads which converged on the town. Approaching La Fayette, Lieutenant Colonel Elijah Watts' 2nd Kentucky in Long's brigade found only scattered pickets to their front which offered no resistance to the large cavalry force. At 10:00 o'clock, an explosion of cannons and muskets in their front surprised Long's troopers. Watts exclaimed, "The effect was electrical! What could it mean? ... A halt was ordered. Soon after an aide came hurrying from the head of the column looking dreadfully serious, calling out as he passed: 'Face to the rear!'" In the other column, Campbell's brigade had found and charged the enemy line of infantry of John C. Breckinridge's division about three miles south of La Fayette.[59]

Major William H. Sinclair, Assistant Adjutant-General for the Union chief of cavalry, was not just an administrative officer but often rode with the cavalry (Missouri History Museum, St. Louis).

Campbell's brigade left camp at 6:00 a.m. that morning and once his cavalry moved past the initial enemy pickets, they advanced until they found the main line of Brigadier General Daniel Adams' infantry brigade of Breckinridge's division positioned on either side of a wooded area on the road leading to La Fayette. Then, Campbell ordered the column to charge the line in column of fours and Campbell led the charge with the 9th Pennsylvania in the advance followed by the 1st Tennessee, and 2nd Michigan Cavalry. As Campbell's attack pressed ahead, his command received several volleys and then the enemy's artillery opened up on the column. Leading the attack, the 9th Pennsylvania, led by Lieutenant Colonel Roswell Russell, had the most fighting during the day. The 9th Pennsylvania found the Confederate pickets about three miles south of La Fayette and they quickly moved back to the main infantry line. Russell had a line of skirmishers of his own pressing ahead when they received a volley from a line of infantry, killing one of Russell's troopers. Russell pulled his skirmishers back and moved to the top of small hill covered with dense underbrush. Then, Archibald Campbell arrived on the scene and directed Russell to send in more troopers to support the skirmishers. Russell ordered two companies to charge ahead and with a yell the men spurred their horses. However, it was so dusty that the troopers couldn't see ahead as they dashed forward. The troopers rode directly into a deep gully in the road and the first rank of troopers tumbled head long off their mounts. After clearing the road, the companies again charged ahead; but they had ridden no more than two hundred yards when the enemy infantry, now aware of the presence of the Federal cavalry, sent a "a withering enfilading fire, killing 1 man, mortally wounding 2 others, and disabling 8 horses." The remainder of Russell's regiment charged ahead on the heels of the first two companies and they found the first battalion had captured eighteen prisoners. As the cavalry shuttled the prisoners to the rear, the infantry continued their fire and Russell ordered the fences to be torn down in preparation of a full charge by the 9th Pennsylvania. The 2nd Michigan and 1st Tennessee surged ahead and fell into line with Russell's regiment. The prisoners told their captors that the cavalry faced Louisiana infantry supported by artillery.[60]

The 1st Tennessee Cavalry moved to the right flank in support of the 9th Pennsylvania while the 2nd Michigan followed behind. W. R. Carter, 1st Tennessee, recalled that his regiment moved through some trees and came under fire from enemy artillery with one shell exploding directly above the regimental colors. Carter concluded the surprised artillerymen had not had time to lower the guns or they were inexperienced, because none of the shells caused any damage.[61]

Campbell reformed his command and prepared to make a second charge, but Crook arrived on the scene and called off the attack. Crook told Campbell there was more enemy cavalry at the rear of the column and since Crook knew Breckinridge's infantry occupied La Fayette, they had achieved their objective. Wharton's cavalry division was somewhere between Edward McCook's cavalry and Crook's brigades. Crook decided he was too close to large concentrations of the enemy, in the front and rear, with only two brigades and decided he would not be able to make any further progress against the infantry. In front of Crook was Crews' cavalry brigade supporting Adams' Confederate infantry, a force just too large for Crook to move. As the Union cavalry moved away, the 2nd Michigan Cavalry moved into place to cover the withdrawal. Campbell rejoined Edward McCook at Alpine at the end of the day and then, Crook's brigade moved to Dougherty's Gap.[62]

Campbell's attack netted about twenty pickets of the 13th Louisiana Infantry, part of Breckinridge's infantry division. A prisoner, when questioned, revealed much of Bragg's army was concentrated near La Fayette. In the meantime, McCook scouted toward Trion Factory and sent a regiment to scout Summerville without any positive results for his efforts. Stanley, while probably receiving the unofficial version of McCook's report from Crook, wrote to Garfield—"The reconnaissance was very unsatisfactory, and if I can hear anything more definite in regard to it. I will dispatch it to you at once. I will carry out your instructions in regard to the passes, and put myself in closer communication with the right of the army tomorrow. Our marching had been very heavy, and our horses are very much jaded."[63]

Situation on the Northern Flank of the Army and with Washington

As new and more solid intelligence filtered into army headquarters, Rosecrans became more concerned about his position and he ordered Thomas Wood's division to halt at Lee and Gordon's Mill. Then, he sent the remainder of Crittenden's XXI Corps into position on Missionary Ridge. The Reserve Corps still marched ahead and Granger hoped to move into a supporting position the next day. Rosecrans needed Granger's corps to move to Rossville and protect the roads leading to Ringgold and La Fayette, thereby, securing Crittenden's left flank. Garfield's concern was evident as he told Granger: "Hold yourself in readiness...." Crittenden was the furthest away from La Fayette and perhaps felt the least risk, but Rosecrans explained that Bragg's army was concentrating near La Fayette behind the mountains. "Hence the necessity of great caution." Crittenden recognized the increased enemy resistance and explained: "Colonel Wilder has a regiment, from which he has just received word that the enemy is advancing with a strong skirmish line of cavalry on his front. He also states that there is a still stronger force advancing on his left, with a view to turning it."[64]

McIntyre's 4th U.S. Cavalry scouted ahead of Crittenden's corps toward La Fayette going between six and twelve miles and found no concentration of Confederates, only enemy cavalry pickets. Wilder's mounted infantry also pushed to within a mile of Leet's Tanyard and only found a small group of Confederate cavalry, perhaps two hundred men who withdrew before the Union force. Wilder even rode to the top of a large hill which looked toward Ringgold and six miles down the valley and observed no sign of the enemy. Finally, Minty remained on duty with only two regiments and marched to Lee and Gordon's Mills. The 4th Michigan Cavalry pushed as far south as Crawfish Springs where they found Union infantry and returned to Lee and Gordon's Mill.[65]

Washington was not insensitive to Rosecrans' plight and despite the previous day's orders to Burnside, Halleck wrote to Burnside with orders to move south on September 13: "Move down your infantry as rapidly as possible toward Chattanooga to connect with Rosecrans. Bragg may merely hold the passes of the mountains to cover Atlanta, and move his main army through Northern Alabama to reach the Tennessee River, and turn Rosecrans' right and cut off his supplies. In this case he will turn Chattanooga over to you, and move to intercept Bragg." In the meantime, Rosecrans also wrote to Burnside the same day and told him directly that Bragg had not retreated to Rome as originally suspected but he had moved a few miles south of Chattanooga and prepared to battle Rosecrans at La Fayette. Rosecrans told him in no uncertain terms he needed Burnside's cavalry and infantry to assist in dealing with a reinforced Army of Tennessee: "I may say of the utmost importance—that all your cavalry should come to our relief as quickly as possible, and that your infantry force should march in this direction, for there is very little doubt but that they will concentrate every available man in the Southwest against this army." Halleck wrote to Rosecrans regarding Burnside: "He is ordered to move down and connect with you." The message from just two days before told Burnside the Confederates were retreating to Rome and there was no need for his infantry to push south. Now, the urgent message gave contradictory orders; but unfortunately, Burnside now believed he faced a large enemy force converging on his position. Burnside received intelligence that Robert E. Lee had dispatched parts of his army to threaten Knoxville, but the threat Burnside faced was false, except for a brigade of Pickett's infantry. Burnside mistakenly detected the movement of Longstreet's corps which Burnside thought threatened his position, but in fact, Longstreet was moving to join Bragg. Facing such a large enemy, Burnside was reluctant to send any troops to Chattanooga. On September 15, Burnside found his initial intelligence to be incorrect, but new information from deserters assured him Ewell's Corps was heading in his direction. Burnside decided to advance in the direction of the perceived Southern threat, Jonesborough, and planned to send the requested reinforcements to Chattanooga once he dealt in the Confederates in his area.[66]

As the day ended, perhaps the best summary of the situation was by J. C. Van Duzer, head of communications: "[B]y day after tomorrow or Wednesday you may look to hear of Bragg getting hurt. We are in a ticklish place here, but hope to come out with whole skin. Can do nothing but wait."[67]

Cavalry Actions Cause Bragg to Hesitate

While the Federal troops feared an attack, the aggressive action by the Federal cavalry for the second day in a row convinced the Confederate commanders that a Union infantry attack was imminent. The initiative which Bragg had gained only a few days earlier was lost just as quickly. The Confederate generals were not in agreement of what action to take. D. H. Hill recorded that at La Fayette: "The Yankee cavalry had, however, captured the infantry pickets, and upon McCook learning that the men belonged to Breckinridge's division, he became aware that Bragg had been re-enforced, and began a precipitate retreat." Hill made no secret of Bragg's mishandling of the situation and stated that Bragg knew the Union army stretched over sixty miles. Hill wrote that much of Bragg's army was in position and could have attacked either Thomas or McCook which were without support. He bitterly recalled that Bragg hesitated. "The attack, however, was delayed for six days." McCook's and Thomas' efforts to close up on one another, Crittenden's advance from the north, and Union cavalry aggressively pushing from the south caused Bragg to pause. George Brent wrote of the concern of the enemy's advance "from all quarters." Even W. B. Corbitt, 2nd Georgia Cavalry, recorded in his diary: "Yanks all around." After the cavalry actions at La Fayette, D. H. Hill described Bragg as "bewildered by 'the popping out of the rats from so many holes.'" After facing the cavalry advance at La Fayette, Brigadier General Daniel Adams also believed that the infantry must be close behind. Bragg also seemed to agree with Adams. Because Bragg hesitated, he missed the opportunity to strike Rosecrans in detail and allowed Rosecrans the critical time to pull his dispersed army together. Crook's and McCook's cavalry actions are often overlooked as an important, positive aspect of Federal cavalry during the campaign. Fortunately for the Federal forces, the aggressive actions of the Federal cavalry and Bragg's own inability to orchestrate an attack on the Union army, first Negley and secondly Crittenden, coupled with the other command problems caused Bragg to enter a "phase of emotional doldrums." Bragg deemed it unwise to stay in close proximity to any one of Rosecrans' corps and he simply withdrew. His spurt of offensive actions seemed to dissipate as quickly as it began. Rosecrans had been given the gift of time to unite his army while he contemplated Bragg's next move, and Bragg, in turn, contemplated how to defeat Rosecrans with a perceived, disloyal group of commanders who had failed so badly in the two attempts in the past week. Bragg remained paralyzed from September 13 to September 16 as Rosecrans pulled his army together.[68]

Stanley's Illness Persists and the Cavalry Pushes North

September 14 proved to be a day of re-positioning of the two armies as more dust, smoke and sporadic firing occurred throughout the day. Thomas' corps held its position and inched northward establishing a link with Crittenden near Lee and Gordon's Mill without meeting any enemy resistance. General Joseph Reynolds ordered Wilder's brigade to Pond Springs (about a mile west of Catlett's Gap) in search of the enemy. Wilder's horses were so fatigued they could do no more during the day and much of Minty's cavalry remained with Crittenden at his headquarters.[69]

Meanwhile, XX Corps marched toward Thomas' right flank but by a convoluted path due to a misunderstanding from Garfield. The last message from Garfield led McCook to surmise that McLemore's Cove was held by the enemy and that Stanley's cavalry had been ordered to seize Dougherty's Gap with all haste. Because it was impractical for XX Corps to advance northward through McLemore's Cove, he felt he had no choice but to return to Winston's and move down Lookout Valley until he could reach Stevens' Gap as ordered. McCook had his men on a rapid and difficult march as he hastened to Thomas' flank. McCook complained that backtracking was nine miles longer and would take an additional nine hours. However, Garfield interceded with McCook to change his route in a message sent at 11:30 p.m., too late for McCook to change the direction of his march. Garfield explained to McCook that the enemy had evacuated McLemore's Cove and it would more expedient to march directly north. Galling to McCook were the lines; "The general commanding regrets that you are moving back through Winston's Gap.... He directs you to turn back at once to the head of McLemore's Cove, where you can operate this way with infantry at least...." Two points are evident in the miscommunications between headquarters and Alexander. First, the mistake on the part of army headquarters demonstrated the difficulty of long range communications, similar to the situation for which Stanley had been so severely criticized. Secondly, no criticism of poor communication was directed at McCook. Garfield responded to the rebuke of poor communication for a few days before and wrote, "I have not seen the dispatch of Major Bond to General Stanley, complaining that lines of communication were not kept up with department headquarters, but I am assured by the general commanding that he did not intend to censure you in that communication." Apparently, Rosecrans had singled Stanley, alone, for the severe rebuke.[70]

Garfield's message did not reach McCook before he reached Winston's and McCook explained his decision to advance along the route he chose. While army headquarters had been terse with some of the subordinates, McCook replied in a similar manner and justified his decision even though this proved to be a very long march. Rosecrans had placed McCook under command of Thomas "who had discretion to order me up to his support if he deemed it necessary, which he did." McCook declared that he had received two communications from him telling him the only practical route was to backtrack to Winston's and move north. He testily added: "I know as well as anybody that my position was at the head of McLemore's Cove, that being the key of Pigeon Mountain." It was McCook who was required to back track to meet Garfield's orders through a fairly arduous route. McCook also added in a gentlemanly but contrary manner: "I will be pained to take my troops over the route again; they certainly would feel as if I were trifling with them. I beg leave to differ with you in your statement that my troops will not be in co-operation with the rest of the army. Sheridan will be on General

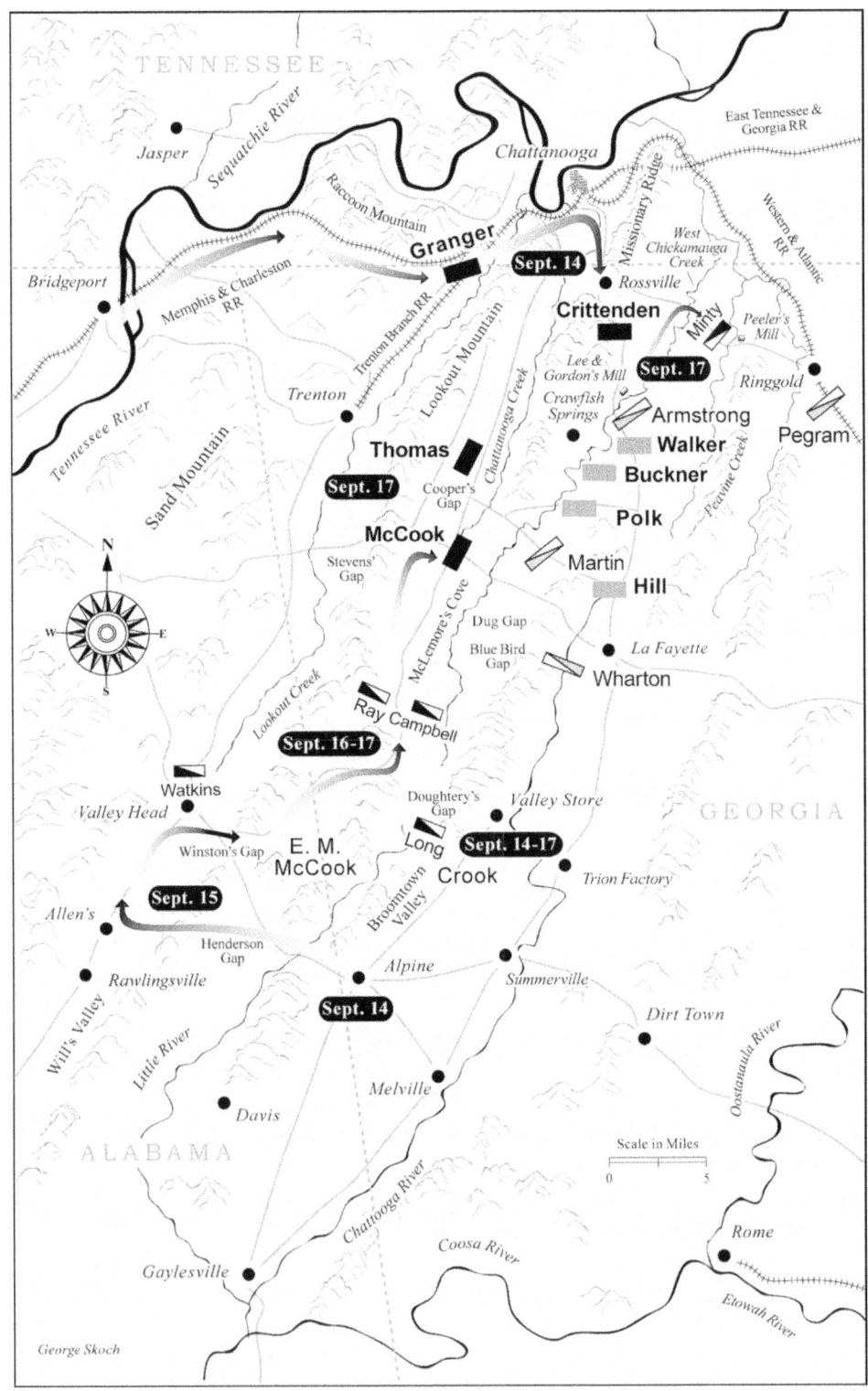

Union cavalry movements: September 14–17.

Thomas' right, should the road be clear at an early hour in the morning." Later that night, Garfield approved McCook's plan and ordered a brigade of cavalry to hold Valley Head. Little did the Federal commander realize the state of confusion of their Confederate adversaries when they lost contact with McCook's entire XX Corps. The Confederate high command again remained in the dark about the location of the various Union commands much in the same way the Federal commanders did not know where Bragg had placed all of his units.[71]

The long, unnecessary march and miscommunications about movement held a heavy toll for those soldiers marching rearward and then northward. A trooper of the 2nd Michigan Cavalry wrote in his diary that the day was a "day of horrors. No water for man or beast after we ascended the mountain. Dust in blinding clouds enveloped us and I to complete the discomforts so afflicted with a boil on my lip that every step of horse pained me. Our canteens had been emptied to make coffee when we met the train.... After a vain effort to reach a little creek to water our animals we laid down with parched lips and covered in dust." The dust proved a plague to all the soldiers. Robert Burns of Minty's cavalry also described the dust as suffocating as the columns of cavalry moved on their daily expeditions. He also noted that sometimes the dust was so bad the horse in front could not be seen. "It gets in our ears, noses, hair and through and under our clothes," lamented Burns.[72]

Granger Arrives at Rossville and the Army Repositions

Good news arrived at Federal army headquarters when the first of Granger's Reserve Corps arrived at Rossville and moved to extend the Union left flank to the Tennessee River. Crittenden, as ordered, maintained his position from Lee and Gordon's Mill to Missionary Ridge. At 12:30 p.m., Crittenden reported finding no concentrations of enemy near him, and the only action near his infantry occurred near Van Cleve's division which came under fire from a section of Confederate artillery. Certainly, Crittenden's over confidence resonated in his message in regard to a Confederate attack: "Indeed, I think I can whip them if they do— all of them. We are, I think, in a position that they can turn, but I also think they dare not pass me." The Union commander encouraged the joining of Thomas' corps to his right flank. Then, Crittenden confirmed that Minty no longer reported to him directly. He encouraged Garfield to leave some cavalry at Rossville and explained his only concern was that Confederate cavalry might temporarily sever his communications. Crittenden also explained that his scouts found no Confederates at Ringgold. Garfield ordered Crittenden to place Minty's cavalry along the roads from Ringgold and La Fayette for security and reconnaissance purposes. In the meantime, Minty had little to say. He only confirmed that he was under orders of Crittenden and that his two regiments moved over Missionary Ridge into Lookout Valley and then into McLemore's Cove. It is ironic that Crittenden suggested that Garfield send orders to Minty and Garfield in return told Crittenden to send orders to Minty. If confusion existed in regard to Minty's commanding officer, Wilder faced the same problem—Garfield, Crittenden or Reynolds.[73]

Stanley, now prostrate from his illness, wrote to Garfield about his movement northward along a trail shared with the infantry. Crook's cavalry moved toward Dougherty's Gap and did not have to backtrack all the way to Winston's, but he reached Little River, an uncommon mountain stream which flowed down the length of Lookout Mountain, overnight and would reach Dougherty's Gap the next morning. Alexander McCook's supply train had to re-ascend Lookout Mountain as XX Corps returned to Winston's in the move northward. Stanley's cavalry train got caught in the congestion of McCook's infantry and supply train and became delayed. The foot soldiers watched the long lines of cavalry move past them throughout the day. At the end of the day, Edward McCook's cavalry stopped at Little River and planned to move to Winston's the next morning. Then, Stanley gave up command of the cavalry—"I am still confined to my bed, and have had to ride in an ambulance to-day coming over the mountain.... General Mitchell is here and will take command of his division in the morning."[74]

Halleck Orders Reinforcements

From Washington, Halleck sent similar messages to both Stephen Hurlbut and Burnside that Rosecrans needed assistance. "There are reasons why you should re-enforce General Rosecrans with all possible dispatch." Halleck, like Rosecrans, now knew that Bragg planned to fight south of Chattanooga and that Bragg had reinforcements. Ironically, Confederate general Sam Jones made another appeal for reinforcements which only emphasized the light resistance Burnside faced at Knoxville: "This part of East Tennessee was left even more defenseless than I had supposed." Any argument on Burnside's behalf that he faced a threat from the enemy which held him Knoxville appeared to be without merit in light of Jones' repeated declaration of having no troops in eastern Tennessee. In fact, after the Battle of Chickamauga, Abraham Lincoln declared in regard to Burnside's attention to the perceived Confederate threat at Jonesborough: "Jonesborough? Jonesborough? Damn Jonesborough," but this exclamation would come too late.[75]

Halleck continued in his efforts on September 15 to obtain reinforcements for Rosecrans. He also requested troops from Ulysses Grant, John Pope in Wisconsin, and John Schofield in Missouri. Schofield declined but troops were ordered to Tuscumbia from the Army of the Tennessee. Halleck confirmed reports of reinforcements from Lee's army in Virginia, believed to be three divisions, and he sent messages to Burnside and the Department of the Ohio to send his troops to Chattanooga with "all possible dispatch." From Cincinnati, Halleck received what appeared to be positive news, but if Halleck observed closely there were no indications that these new troops would be moved to Chattanooga. They were directed to Knoxville. "I have ordered Major General Parke to push forward with the Ninth Corps with all possible dispatch. The First Division is in the vicinity of Cumberland Gap, the Second beyond Nicholasville. I am hurrying forward all the troops I can."[76]

In the meantime, Rosecrans continued to pull his army together. Bragg's hesitation after the actions near La Fayette and his inability to attack Crittenden boded well for the Army of the Cumberland. Crittenden's corps connected with Thomas' corps on the north near Pond Springs and Alexander McCook personally reached Thomas' headquarters and promised his troops would arrive the next day. Granger's Reserve Corps continued its advance and moved into position near Chattanooga. On September 15 Crittenden reported no enemies observed along his front, but Minty reported something different later in the day, "I have strange reports from the citizens. They say positively that Forrest is at Ringgold, Pegram at Leet's, Buckner at Rock Spring, Cleburne and Longstreet at Dalton." Even Granger, newly arrived on the scene at Rossville, supported Minty's intelligence and reported the citizens in the area saw two divisions of infantry near Graysville the day before and these troops marched toward Ringgold. Granger wisely sent a small patrol of mounted infantry in that direction during the day and they returned with intelligence gathered from some citizens that in addition to the infantry, there were four cavalry brigades near Ringgold.[77]

In a serious indictment of Crittenden's dismissiveness of Minty's reconnaissance, Minty's after action report demonstrated the intelligence he gathered was disregarded by the over confident Crittenden—intelligence that could have changed the battle. Minty returned his cavalry to Lee and Gordon's Mill only to be told to move to Peavine Valley and encamp near Leet's Crossroads. Minty dutifully followed his orders and bivouacked near Peeler's Mill on Peavine Creek, a few miles east of Chickamauga Creek. Then, Minty received a message from Crittenden's headquarters expressing disbelief that Confederate infantry was nearby. Minty recalled: "Same night I reported to Major-General Crittenden the information brought in by these parties, and in answer received a letter from Captain Oldershaw, assistant adjutant-general, XXI Army Corps, of which the following is an extract: The major-general commanding directs me to acknowledge the receipt of your report of this date informing him that Forrest is at Ringgold, Longstreet at Dalton, Pegram at Leet's, and Buckner at Rock Spring; all this would indicate infantry, which the major-general commanding cannot believe." Minty felt he could only accomplish his assigned task and report the intelligence he gathered. It was up to Crittenden to responsibly act on this intelligence and it was apparent to Minty that Crittenden chose to ignore it. The next day Minty encamped near Reed's Bridge on the Chickamauga Creek, about four miles west of Ringgold.[78]

Cavalry Moves into the Mountain Passes—Mitchell Assumes Command

In regard to the remainder of the cavalry, Stanley established his headquarters in close proximity of Colonel P. Sidney Post's infantry brigade at Valley Head securing the extreme right flank of Rosecrans' contracting army. Crook occupied Dougherty's Gap that morning but the cavalry horses could not remain at that location long. There was no forage to be had for the horses and they would starve if they could not be moved back into the valley. Edward McCook's horses were in little better condition. Sergeant G. W. Baum, 2nd Indiana recorded in his diary that his regiment was not "used up, but I confess we were considerable worse for the wear." Stanley ordered two brigades of Edward McCook's division to move between Dougherty's and Neal's gaps to close up on Alexander McCook's flank which was relatively easy to accomplish for the cavalry; but the horses needed to be rotated into either Broomtown Valley or McLemore's Cove to be fed.[79]

Stanley finalized the transition of command to Mitchell. He wrote to Garfield: "I am so prostrated that I am not able to sit up, and I will this morning turn the command over to General Mitchell, and go to some place where I can have rest and an opportunity to recover my health. I desire to go to Nashville for treatment." Mitchell reported that David Stanley was "dangerously sick." He continued: "General Stanley will go to the rear to-morrow. He is very sick, and I am fearful that he will have a serious time. Give me specific directions with regard to cavalry movements, and I will endeavor to carry them out. The cavalry are badly used up, both men and horses. We have sent today, and will send tomorrow to Stevenson 300 sick soldiers." Major William H. Sinclair also notified the division commanders of Mitchell's assumption of command during Stanley's illness. Robert Mitchell semi-officially began his command of the cavalry that evening writing to Garfield that Crook was at Dougherty's Gap and he had seen no bodies of enemy near his position. In Mitchell's assessment, more than 2,000 cavalrymen had been lost so far in the campaign due to unserviceable horses and by illness which seemed to be targeting many of the Federal cavalry.[80]

Crook only ran into a group of seventy-five enemy cavalry and chased them down Neal's Gap and secured that gap and Dougherty's Gap as he formed a more determined screen on the southern flank to prevent the enemy from developing the Union army's movements. Crook's cavalry removed the obstructions along the road placed there by enemy cavalry. The Confederate cavalry also watched XX Corps move northward and became bolder along the southern flank. Two brigades of Edward McCook's division (Campbell's and Ray's) would extend the Union line from Dougherty's Gaps to Alexander McCook's corps the next day. Watkins' brigade remained at Valley Head as a reserve.[81]

Minty Watches the Enemy—Bragg Decides to Attack

After the failure to launch two attacks on the Union army on September 10–11 and September 12–13, Bragg decided to launch a full attack on the Army of the Cumberland. He called his corps commanders together and told them that he planned to make the attack north of the main body of the Federal army, cutting it off from Chattanooga. Rosecrans with his most direct supply line severed would have to fight, retake Chattanooga, or retreat. These orders essentially laid the plans for the Confederate attack which would begin the Battle of Chickamauga on September 18. At the close of the meeting, the corps commanders returned to their headquarters to await formal marching orders.[82]

The increased enemy activity detected by Granger and Minty alerted the army commanders about the threat to the left flank of Rosecrans' army. Garfield responded with a message to the corps commanders to prepare for a fight. "There are some indications that the enemy is massing for an attack on our left."[83]

Rosecrans properly continued to pull his army together along the west side of the Chickamauga Creek and urged Halleck to send him reinforcements. He again wrote: "Push Burnside down." Rosecrans established his headquarters at Crawfish Springs and he ordered Thomas to place the bulk of XIV Corps between Gower's and Bird's Mill. Thomas, who had temporarily gained control of Wilder's brigade, found that Wilder had again been ordered for duty on the left flank. McCook's XX Corps would not be fully in place until the next day; but by the end of the day Edward McCook reached Stevens' Gap, a critical location, which effectively secured the flank of XX Corps should Bragg decide to attack him.[84]

With Granger moving to Crittenden's flank, Minty finally received one of his regiments, 4th U.S. Cavalry, which had been appropriated to the infantry a few days before, and Crittenden also agreed to return the 7th Pennsylvania Cavalry, which had been recently appropriated by Crittenden. Minty's cavalry pressed three miles ahead on Ringgold Road the evening before and ran into a line of enemy pickets. Early on the morning of September 16, Minty's pickets again found the enemy pressing ahead and when Minty reinforced his line, the Confederate cavalry, which was suspected to be on a strong reconnaissance, withdrew. After dealing with this body of cavalry, his line was tested by another strong enemy reconnaissance from the direction of Leet's Tanyard, to the south. Minty concluded that Colonel John Scott's Confederate cavalry brigade occupied Ringgold and that Brigadier General Henry B. Davidson's brigade pushed northward from Leet's Tanyard. Then, Minty somewhat prophetically requested assistance from Crittenden which could have greatly assisted in the upcoming battle, still two days hence. "There is a good road running down the valley between Pea Vine Ridge and the Chickamauga, which exposes my rear to attack. Can you post a brigade of infantry at Reed's Bridge? As I am now situated I may be forced to retreat at any moment. I wish, this could be avoided." In the meantime, Minty again expressed his concern about the enemy troops he faced and explained that he did not want to send a scouting force south toward Leet's Tanyard because the Confederate cavalry would probably cut it off and result in the capture of his men. In addition, he explained the difficultly in carrying out orders without having a full brigade of cavalry. Minty felt the presence of the enemy and expected to have to battle them. He needed all his men to do this. "Can you not send me the Seventh Pennsylvania and have the Third Indiana ordered up from Chattanooga? I am not strong enough for the position I am placed in. I think, without doubt, that Longstreet is in this part of the country."[85]

Minty followed with another message at noon from his location near Reed's Bridge, and relayed that immediately after sending his morning message the Confederate cavalry attacked his line on three different roads. In addition, scouts from the 4th U.S. Cavalry observed an infantry column marching south on the La Fayette Road. If infantry gained the road, then Minty would be cut off from direct communications with Crittenden and this forced the Union cavalry to fall back to the west side of Chickamauga Creek at Reed's Bridge. "I still picket the La Fayette road. I have had 1 man killed.... The rebels have been driven on all the roads from 4 to 7 miles."[86]

Minty continued to sound the alert about a large concentration of the enemy nearby, "Strong scouting parties from toward Ringgold and Leet's advanced on me; they were promptly met, driven, and followed. The pickets on the La Fayette and Harrison road, which lies between Pea Vine Ridge and Chickamauga, were attacked from toward La Fayette and my rear threatened." Minty's cavalry withdrew to the west side of the Peavine Ridge to the proximity of Reed's Bridge while guarding the roads in the area. When the enemy stopped their pursuit, the Union cavalry tracked them back toward Leet's Tanyard until they ran into a column of infantry marching toward Ringgold. On receiving the report, General Crittenden answered that the infantry "could be nothing but dismounted cavalry." On September 16 and 17, Minty remained at Reed's Bridge and continued to scout the countryside. The scouts brought back more important information and "reported large bodies of the enemy on our front." Minty was right to be concerned because he was in the path of a major attack by Bragg's infantry. During the day, the 4th U.S. Cavalry clashed with Buckner's infantry near Ringgold while the 9th Pennsylvania encountered some of the infantry in the direction of La Fayette. Both Minty and Wilder would remain critical of Crittenden's over confidence before the battle and his lack of regard of the intelligence both these officers brought to him.[87]

After the war, Minty would record that on September 16 that he found Crittenden at army headquarters with Rosecrans. Minty tried to "convince him that General Bragg was massing on his left; that he had been reinforced by General Longstreet with two corps. He scoffed at the idea, and said: 'Longstreet is in Virginia.' I said: 'Pardon me, General, Longstreet was yesterday at Dalton with two corps from the Army of Northern Virginia.'" Rosecrans appeared to accept Minty's report, but Crittenden "sprang to his feet, and raising his hand above his head, exclaimed: 'General, I will guarantee, with my corps, to whip every rebel within twenty miles of us.'" That exclamation from Crittenden ended the discussion and Minty returned to his duties. It seemed that all in the cavalry brigade knew of the enemy threat. John McLain, 4th Michigan, entered in his diary that night—"the rebs were coming in on us."[88]

Rosecrans wrote to Granger at 5:00 p.m., reminding him that he held a critical position by securing Crittenden's left flank. Next, he optimistically told Granger that he needed to hold this position until Burnside reached the Army of the Cumberland, although there seemed to be little haste on Burnside's part to accomplish this. Rosecrans still believed that Bragg would fight in one of the mountain valleys near La Fayette, but Garfield acknowledged the fighting of Minty near Peeler's Mill as he blocked an attempt by the enemy to swing around his flank.

While the Union cavalry held its assigned positions, Stanley began his return to Nashville by rail. Mitchell now had firm control of the cavalry division. Immediately, William Sinclair sent orders to Edward McCook to move his division to army headquarters at Crawfish Springs while leaving Watkins' brigade at Valley Head. Edward McCook had had a difficult time moving his division from Alpine to Will's Valley and now to McLemore's Cove. His cavalry made three moves over Lookout Mountain since September 9, lamented Sergeant G. W. Baum, 2nd Indiana. When McCook arrived, Crook still held Dougherty's Gap and protected against an attack from the direction of Alpine. McCook's cavalry finished its move forward at two o'clock in the morning. Baum wrote in his diary—"[I]t was the hardest night that I had ever spent in my life." McCook's advance did not go without incident. His men did not reach the location until late that night and the 1st Tennessee Cavalry made an exciting entrance. It was so dark the regiment marched off the trail and W. R. Carter noted: "it was more of a slide than a march. It was a thrilling experience to us, and to this day we cannot understand how we ever reached the base without serious loss." As the campaign continued in the mountainous region, not only was terrain a major component so was fatigue, particularly for the troops marching northward. Julius Thomas, 1st Tennessee Cavalry, described how he slept during the night: "slept by the side of my horse so near that in rolling he struck me in the back with his fore foot did not hurt me much."[89]

On the southern side of the line, Bragg was ready to fight and he sent orders on September 16 about the attack that was planned:

> "VII. Buckner's corps and Walker's reserves will move at daylight tomorrow and take position from Pea Vine Church, north along Pea Vine Creek.
>
> VIII. Polk's corps will move at 8 a.m. tomorrow and take post on Buckner's left, and occupy the ground to near Glass' Mill, so as to command that crossing.
>
> IX. Forrest's cavalry will cover the front and flank of both these movements.
>
> X. Wheeler's cavalry, leaving a small force to observe the road south, will pass through Dug to Catlett's Gap, press the enemy, secure some prisoners if possible, and join our flank near Glass' Mill.
>
> XI. Reed's Bridge, Byram's Ford, Alexander's Bridge, and the fords next above, will be seized and held by our cavalry.
>
> XII. Hill's corps will occupy the gaps across Pigeon Mountain and observe the road to the south, and be ready to move at a moment's notice."[90]

Bragg's plan hinged on the objective of severing Rosecrans from Chattanooga and the capture of two roads would effectively accomplish this task—the main road from La Fayette to Chattanooga which crossed the Chickamauga Creek at Lee and Gordon's Mill and the Dry Valley Road which ran along Missionary Ridge just west of the other road. The attack was planned for 5:00 a.m. the next morning, but Bragg cancelled the attack orders just two hours before it took place.[91]

Minty Protects Reed's Bridge—McCook Moves to McLemore's Cove

Rosecrans continued to shift his army on the west bank of the Chickamauga Creek and communications from Chattanooga to Washington summarized the position of the Army of the Cumberland. J. C. Van Duzer wrote: "General Rosecrans' headquarters at Crawfish Spring, 15 miles from here. Army left, near him; right, 12 or 15 miles farther southwest, at the east foot of Missionary Ridge; Chickamauga Creek in front. Enemy on the other bank, and at the west foot of Pigeon Mountain. Line shorter than ours. Slight skirmishing every day.... No immediate action expected." The apparent threat of attack on the left flank appeared to lessen in Rosecrans' eyes on September 17, but Rosecrans remained cautious. He ordered his corps commanders to provide a solid unbroken line of pickets in front of his full line, and he pulled his infantry even further north. The only action from the Confederates amounted to demonstrations made by the cavalry near Dug Gap.[92]

Signaling that Crittenden did not believe Minty's reports of Confederate infantry near his position, Charles Dana's report to Secretary of War Stanton stated, "We are still without information on Longstreet's arrival." The XIV Corps stretched from Bird's Mill, Owens' Ford, Gower's Ford and Pond Spring with Crittenden on the left flank and McCook on the right flank. Alexander McCook still closed up on the right and as he moved northward he left some troops to guard the gaps across Pigeon Mountain. McCook ended the day in the desired location, but Richard Johnson's division had to march twenty-five miles to be in place. Edward McCook's cavalry held a line in McLemore's cove. Crook's cavalry continued holding Dougherty's Gap, and they watched Blue Bird Gap where columns of dust were observed during the day. All remained quiet along Crook's front except for a minor skirmish in which the 2nd Kentucky Cavalry lost a trooper killed in the exchange.[93]

Crittenden had some "brisk" firing between pickets of his infantry and the 4th Georgia Cavalry, but he believed that only a single cavalry regiment was involved. Crittenden reported his corps in full readiness. Thomas Wood observed clouds of dust moving northward during the day. "The lookout reports the column of dust, when first seen, as moving northward when the firing was heard, and then the column or cloud of dust seemed to cease moving northward." Garfield replied to Wood that the dust resulted in a clash with the 15th Pennsylvania Cavalry and a column of Confederate cavalry near John Palmer's division. All along Crittenden's left flank, a solid screen of Union troops consisted of Wood, Wilder, Minty and finally to the north Granger.[94]

Robert Minty bivouacked his brigade, now with the 7th Pennsylvania Cavalry which returned to his command overnight, at Reed's Bridge and established communications with Granger's Reserve Corps which extended to Rossville and Graysville. He also established communications with Wilder who assumed a defensive position, two miles south at Alexander's Bridge. Minty had some light skirmishing between his scouts and the enemy's pickets throughout the day. His scouting parties rode toward Ringgold and La Fayette and still identified large concentrations of the enemy along his front and even observed columns of dust in the distance. Rosecrans wisely placed Minty and Wilder at two of the most important routes coming from the east. Robert Burns wrote his brother on the evening of September 17 that there had been heavily skirmishing over the past few days. He also knew that Minty faced a large rebel force near his position and wrote: "Our horses are saddled all the time and we sleep booted and spurred."[95]

Rosecrans established his headquarters at Crawfish Springs which W. R. Carter described as: "The Lee Mansion and all out-buildings were used, beside tents. Just a short distance from this old homestead, a large, magnificent spring gushes out from under a ledge of stone. Around this mansion numerous large, stately oaks are found, whose outspreading branches protected our wounded from the hot rays of the sun.... At the celebrated Crawfish Spring a busy water-wheel is to be seen supplying the old mansion with water, the spring not only supplying the water but the power which runs the pump as well." Due to the extremely dry weather, the springs provided a valuable source of fresh water for the Union army. During the upcoming battle, several divisional hospitals set up near the springs and that made this a valuable location to the Union army.[96]

Robert Mitchell temporarily established his headquarters at Pond Spring, a few miles north of Edward McCook's cavalry at Widow Davis' by the end of the day of September 17 and he wrote to Garfield that Edward McCook's orders to move to Crawfish Springs had been cancelled. Instead, McCook was ordered to establish a line at Widow Davis' and Cedar Grove Church in front of Dug Gap while Crook held Dougherty's Gap. McCook's Second Brigade moved down into McLemore's Cove and camped. The concern about his position in front of Dug Gap prompted McCook to order his troopers to keep their horses saddled and prepared to ride even at night. The precautions were justified. Wheeler received orders on the evening of September 17 to replace the infantry which had previously held the various mountain gaps, Blue Bird, Dug, and Catlett's Gaps. D. H. Hill planned to move northward in preparation of the Confederate attack on Rosecrans' army and this left Wheeler the duty of protecting the southern flank and rear of the army.[97]

Captain Robert Burns, 4th Michigan Cavalry, wrote: "Our horses are saddled all the time" (Joseph Vale, *Minty and the Cavalry*, 1886).

George Wagner, commanding the troops at Chattanooga, received communications from Colonel Robert K. Byrd, 1st Tennessee Mounted Infantry, whose furthest southern position of Burnside's troops was still fifteen miles north of Chattanooga. Reportedly, Scott had a few Confederate cavalry active in Cleveland which seemed to occupy Byrd's attention. And Burnside told Halleck, "In my last dispatch I told you of a force I have at Athens, the advance connecting with Rosecrans. That force will be left as it was then there, and the remainder of our force will be concentrated at Greeneville, except such as may be necessary for depot guards." This was Rosecrans last chance of receiving aid from Burnside. Any aid from the Department of the Ohio would have to wait until additional troops were sent from Kentucky, Ohio and Indiana. For Rosecrans, time had run out. The foreboding of the upcoming battle was recorded by Captain Daniel Waite Howe, 79th Indiana Infantry of Van Cleve's division, on the evening of September 17: "I do not hear any satisfactory evidence that Burnside is up yet. The indications seem to point to the greatest battle of the war and that the enemy will attack us and not we them." Captain Joseph Vale, 7th Pennsylvania Cavalry, would bitterly write of Burnside's failure to support Rosecrans—"yet not a regiment or man was sent to Rosecrans from Burnside's Army."[98]

Summary

From September 9–17, the Federal cavalry became more active and skirmishes increased. George Crook and Edward McCook skirmished with Wheeler's cavalry at Alpine and won the exchange. The Union cavalry skirmished again on September 12 and 13 as their commands pressed toward La Fayette, and culminated with Archibald Campbell's clash with Breckinridge's infantry on September 13. In addition, Edward McCook fulfilled Rosecrans' desire to conduct an expedition toward Rome and McCook came away with important intelligence that Bragg had not retreated that far south. During this interval, the cavalry provided good intelligence—Bragg had not retreated to Rome, Wheeler's corps screened a concentration of Bragg's infantry at La Fayette, verified Breckinridge's reinforcements present with Bragg's army, and detected the presence of an ominous number of Confederates concentrating on the northeastern part of Rosecrans' army. In addition, the aggressive probes by Stanley's cavalry from Alpine to La Fayette gave Bragg the impression that Alexander McCook's XX Corps was on the verge of attacking. This, along with the various infantry movements, caused Bragg to shift from an offensive back to a defensive posture and gave Rosecrans valuable time to concentrate his dispersed corps. These actions were of immeasurable value to the Union army.

The terrain continued to be an important variable in this campaign as the two opposing armies lost contact with each other. The cavalries, so used to providing good reconnaissance, struggled to complete its task. It was impractical to expect the two cavalries to accomplish more in this regard. While the cavalries probed each other's lines, the opposing cavalry, supported by such impressive natural obstacles as gaps and mountains, easily screened the main bodies of infantry. The cavalries did not provide significant offensive action, but they did provide as good security and reconnaissance as could be expected. However, during the campaign, neither the Union or Confederate cavalry gave accurate information about the concentrations of the enemy's infantry simply because they could not accomplish this task because of the terrain.

Unfortunately, David Stanley had given up command due to his illness and now the cavalry of the Army of the Cumberland fell under the command of Robert Mitchell who had very little experience with the cavalry. Mitchell began division command in the spring and only a few months later he was granted medical leave. He had been absent through the entire campaign thus far. He had a difficult challenge of facing a dangerous enemy in the mountains south of Chattanooga. Stanley's loss to the cavalry was a severe one. He had demonstrated an ability to lead his troopers with a steady hand and he was a good, professional soldier, at ease in command.

Certainly, Stanley ran contrary to Rosecrans in this campaign and the true reasons for this will remain a mystery because neither Rosecrans nor Stanley ever addressed this issue after the battle. Stanley would later declare that Rosecrans never understood how to use cavalry and he was "given to sending cavalry upon aimless raids, invariably resulting in using up" the cavalry while gaining little in return. This was the case with the Rome raid. The raid shifted from a reconnaissance or demonstration to a full-blown raid. As the day of the raid approached, Stanley felt he did not have enough troops to make the raid. Garfield and Rosecrans insisted on the raid despite the wisdom Jefferson Davis had offered earlier in the campaign to the Confederate generals—"It would be unwise to order its execution by one who foretold failure." The subsequent expedition made by Edward McCook demonstrated the unlikelihood of its success. Soon after, Rosecrans bitterly chastised Stanley about communication without good cause. Stanley was not alone in Rosecrans' criticism. George Thomas had also been taken to task by Rosecrans. Alexander McCook, also being mentioned in the rebuke, explained the cause for poor communications. Ironically, only a few days later poor communications from headquarters sent McCook's XX Corps and Stanley's cavalry on an unnecessarily long movement to reach Thomas' flank.[99]

Finally, Crittenden's disregard of Minty since mid-August robbed him of important intelligence; and as the Battle of Chickamauga approached, he continued to disregard Minty. It was sheer luck that Minty gained three regiments back under his command on September 17, the eve of the battle. Rosecrans and Crittenden both reverted back to a model, of dispersing cavalry regiments under direct control of various infantry commander, proven to be ineffective when Stanley gained command of the cavalry. Rosecrans seemed to have forgotten this, somewhat during the Tullahoma Campaign, and now more severely during the Chickamauga Campaign.

The campaign was becoming interminably long and the cavalry was wearing out.

PART 3—BATTLE OF CHICKAMAUGA

Eight. The Battle Begins— Reed's Bridge (September 18)

...clouds of dust on all the roads in every direction, we knew that they were all coming.—Captain Robert Burns

Robert B. Mitchell Commands the Union Cavalry

Immediately upon returning to the cavalry after a month-long leave of absence, Brigadier General Robert Mitchell commanded the two Union cavalry divisions in the Battle of Chickamauga. Garfield's and Rosecrans' political appointments now yielded their results as a commander with only a few months' experience in the cavalry commanded the Union cavalry in such a complex campaign. Several in the Union army, including George Crook and Brigadier General John Beatty, held Mitchell in low regard. Mitchell had an ability to ingratiate himself with his superiors and was a politician, not dissimilar from many other commanders in the volunteer army. David Stanley was not pleased with Robert Mitchell and later in life he was still adamant of Mitchell's unsuitability for division command. While Mitchell was not apt to make dramatic military moves, he would fight. Mitchell's health (asthma and his wound from an earlier battle) caused him many problems and had prevented him from participating in the advance on Chattanooga. Upon Stanley's departure, Mitchell hurriedly familiarized himself with the geography and developments of the cavalry which had been in the saddle continuously for the past five weeks.[1]

Mitchell had only about three months' experience in the cavalry when the Battle of Chickamauga began on September 18. He had a hefty build, dark hair, and a full beard. Mitchell was an Ohio native and he trained to be a lawyer in Ohio. He served in the Mexican War as a second lieutenant in the 2nd Ohio Volunteers. In the 1850's, he practiced law in Mt. Vernon, Ohio before moving to Linn County, Kansas Territory, in 1856. There, he began his political career. He served in the territorial legislature as a member of the Free-Soil Party from 1857 to 1858. He was appointed territorial treasurer of the Kansas Territory (1859– 1861) and in 1860 he was appointed Adjutant General of Kansas. At the beginning of the Civil War, he recruited a company for the 2nd Kansas Infantry, and was elected captain. He was soon elected colonel when the regiment was organized. During the Battle of Wilson's Creek, he was badly wounded and his regiment earned the nickname, the "Bloody Second." Mitchell, appointed brigadier general in April 1862, later commanded a division at the Battle of Perryville and commanded the Union garrison at Nashville until he was appointed to command the First Cavalry Division in April 1863.[2]

Mitchell made his headquarters at Valley Head as he assumed command of the cavalry. George Crook was firmly in control of Dougherty's Gap after driving away enemy pickets and Edward McCook's First and Second Brigades moved to the right of Alexander McCook's XX Corps while Watkins' Third Brigade remained at headquarters. Watkins had been placed in charge of the sick, wounded, and prisoners until they could be transported back across the Tennessee River. Archibald Campbell's First Brigade and Daniel Ray's Second Brigade held their position near Blue Bird Gap, the next gap on Pigeon Mountain north of Rape's Gap and Dougherty's Gap. McCook also held Bailey's Crossroad in McLemore's Cove, but Wheeler's Confederate cavalry, a real and constant threat, held Blue Bird Gap. McCook's cavalry needed to keep the enemy from crossing the gaps and moving on or past Alexander McCook's flank.[3]

Unfortunately for Mitchell, the day he took command Braxton Bragg decided to resume his offensive against Rosecrans. Bragg primarily focused on the northern part of Rosecrans' army; and Bragg planned to quickly march north and then turn west thereby separating Rosecrans from Chattanooga, hoping the action would result in a retreat by the Federal Army. Bragg's attack would come on Crittenden's flank north of Lee and Gordon's Mill while a strong Confederate infantry column planned to move west as it cut the link to Chattanooga. Then, the remainder of the Confederate forces intended to cross Chickamauga Creek forcing Rosecrans' army back into the wilderness of the mountains to the west. Finally, on the night September 16 he ordered his various commanders to attack, only to hesitate. The Confederate commanders were poised to strike but waited for the orders to advance.[4]

Minty at Reed's Bridge—Wilder at Alexander's Bridge

Without doubt the greatest direct contribution by the Union cavalry during the Battle of Chickamauga was Minty's action at Reed's Bridge. Minty chafed under Crittenden's command and Crittenden had disregarded many of his reports. Along Minty's area, Chickamauga Creek was an important obstacle to troop movements. Despite the drought, Chickamauga Creek was difficult to cross, and Reed's Bridge and Alexander's Bridge were vitally important to the rapid movement of Bragg's infantry and cavalry in the anticipated attack. Two of the Union army's most able colonels drew the duty to hold the bridges. Both Minty and Wilder had detected large concentrations of the enemy over the past few days, and they knew that they faced an imminent attack.[5]

Minty began scouting the area near Reed's Bridge and Leet's Tanyard on September 15. Over the next two days, Minty sent reports of large concentrations of the enemy (infantry and cavalry) to Crittenden, but Crittenden downgraded or disregarded these threats. Although the Union forces temporarily occupied Ringgold, they abandoned the town a few days before when Rosecrans concentrated his army and pulled back to the west side of Chickamauga Creek. As a result of Bragg's orders, a force of Confederate infantry, 10,000 men strong, returned to Ringgold with Forrest's cavalry screening its advance. Robert Minty's lonesome First Cavalry Brigade depleted to only two regiments, 4th Michigan and 4th U.S. cavalries, remained underappreciated, and at the whim of Thomas Crittenden as the sun rose on Sep-

Eight. The Battle Begins—Reed's Bridge (September 18)

Chickamauga Creek, near Reed's Bridge, lazily flowed northward, and it was as deep as ten feet in places with steep, swampy banks (Library of Congress).

tember 17. The day before, Minty believed he faced a serious Confederate threat to his front and again requested his other regiments—the 7th Pennsylvania and the 3rd Indiana.[6]

Minty's brigade camped along the Peavine Ridge near Reed's Bridge after a hard day's skirmishing the day before (September 16th). After the skirmishing, Minty sent his intelligence report to Crittenden reporting, "The force at Ringgold is, I believe, Scott's brigade. Pegram is at Leet's [Tanyard], with an outpost at Pea Vine Church." On September 17, Minty pushed the enemy back along his front collecting twenty-three infantrymen as prisoners and sent Crittenden a report that Longstreet's infantry was in the neighborhood, but Crittenden discounted the threat remarking, "They are only some stragglers you picked up." Crittenden refused to take Minty's concerns seriously, and Minty later criticized Crittenden for disregarding his reports of Confederate infantry when Crittenden exclaimed, "It is nothing but dismounted cavalry." The response from XXI Corps headquarters, Minty recorded, was "all this would indicate infantry, which the major-general commanding cannot believe." A frustrated Minty concluded his report and returned to his command at Reed's Bridge "with heavy heart" over his inability to convince Crittenden and Rosecrans of the threat to the Union left flank. Many in the cavalry knew they had faced a large concentration of enemy troops for a couple of days and Minty was in position to receive a heavy blow if Bragg could ever mount his attack.[7]

Minty was not the only cavalryman to criticize Crittenden's repeated disregard for the cavalry's efforts. Captain Robert Burns, Minty's adjutant general, wrote to his brother after the battle and related that when Minty told Crittenden of a large Confederate force near his position that Crittenden replied: "Pooh, pooh, don't believe it. Keep good watch. Don't get scared." Burns clarified, "Such was the substance of what he said, if not the words." Even Southern general, D. H. Hill, commented that never had there been a general so over confident as Crittenden as he unknowingly faced overwhelming odds.[8]

Minty had initially established his headquarters at Peeler's Mill, but due to the increasingly intense clashes with the Forrest's cavalry, and in particular, heavy skirmishes near Peeler's Mill and along the Harrison and La Fayette Road, he decided to pull back near Reed's Bridge, fearing he could be cut off and isolated from the rest of the Federal army. Even though Minty moved to Reed's Bridge, he still had pickets and scouts active in Peavine Valley, but his cavalry was the only Union force east of Chickamauga Creek, properly named West Chickamauga Creek because East Chickamauga Creek meandered northward from Ringgold. The two branches united a short distance north of the Georgia state line and emptied into the Tennessee River east of Chattanooga. While West Chickamauga Creek lazily flowed northward, it was as deep as ten feet in places and had steep and swampy banks, making it a difficult stream to cross. A series of low hills edged the creek. To the rear of Minty's position was Missionary Ridge about four hundred feet high with a very steep northern slope that formed an arc around the southern side of Chattanooga. The southern slope had a more gradual decline.[9]

Minty and Wilder were right to be concerned about the enemy forces near their positions. For two days Bragg had prepared to attack Crittenden's flank north of Lee and Gordon's Mill. The plan called for Brigadier General Bushrod Johnson's strong Confederate division to move west from Leet's Tanyard as it cut the link to Chattanooga. A second Confederate column, Major General William H. T. Walker's corps, planned to march across Alexander's Bridge a couple of miles south of Reed's Bridge. Bragg also planned to seize Rossville from Granger's Reserve Corps in its push west; but Bragg inexplicably waited two days before ordering the attack.[10]

General Bushrod Johnson led the advance on Minty's cavalry near Reed's Bridge (Alabama Department of Archives and History).

After reaching Rossville, Granger's corps reconnoitered the area around its position and the surrounding territory on September 17, and Brigadier General James Steedman led an advance in the direction of Ringgold. Steedman nearly reached Ringgold where the large concentration of Confederate infantry and cavalry awaited orders to attack. This unwelcome occurrence finally caused Bragg to act. He needed the element of surprise for his plan to work and the unexpected arrival of Steedman prompted immediate action or all could be lost. Bragg ordered John Pegram's cavalry to strengthen the security at Ringgold and Bragg finally issued the orders to attack in the early hours of September 18. Bushrod Johnson's Provisional Division, about 3,700 men strong, would march for Leet's Tanyard, a little south of Minty's position while Walker's corps would move toward Wilder at Alexander's Bridge. Polk's and Buckner's corps planned to attack the Union forces in the vicinity Lee and Gordon's Mill, and Hill would make a flank attack from the south from the direction of McLemore's Cove. Wheeler's cavalry would hold the gaps on Pigeon Mountain while protecting the flank and rear. The remainder of Forrest's cavalry, while not specifically addressed in the orders, would work in conjunction with Johnson's division along the right flank of the Southern Army. In a remarkable stroke of good fortune for the Federal army, the large Confederate cavalry force did not lead the early advance, that could have assured a successful attack, on either Minty's or Wilder's locations. Forrest was in the rear of the infantry column, Scott's brigade was focused on Granger's corps to the north, and Pegram's brigade (commanded by Henry Davidson) remained at Leet's Tanyard with Johnson's two infantry brigades awaiting the arrival of Buckner's corps. Armstrong's cavalry division remained several miles away near Glass Mill.[11]

The otherwise insignificant dust-up with Steedman caused Bragg to adjust his plans one final time. Worried about the lack of security, he ordered Scott's brigade of Pegram's division to go to Ringgold to ensure security along the flank. Then, sometime after midnight on September 18, Bragg ordered Bushrod Johnson's Provisional Division to head for Reed's Bridge instead of Leet's Tanyard where it was previously directed. This meant that Bragg's troops would be positioned even farther north along Rosecrans' flank than originally planned. Unfortunately, Johnson did not receive these new orders until mid-morning on September 18, causing him to back track. Bragg also ordered Forrest to cover Johnson's front and right flank, which proved to be a difficult task given Forrest's lack of available troops for the assigned duty. Thus, on September 18, Bragg sent his army forward with the objective of severing Rosecrans' connection with Chattanooga while attacking Crittenden's left flank. Minty and Wilder stood in his way. The Battle of Chickamauga had begun.[12]

Minty Finds Bushrod Johnson's Columns

Fortunately for Rosecrans, two of his most able colonels were in two of the toughest spots on September 18. John Wilder's mounted infantry (98th Illinois, 123rd Illinois, 17th Indiana, 72nd Indiana, Lilly's 18th Indiana Artillery) held its position at Alexander's Bridge and Robert Minty's cavalry protected Reed's Bridge. The bridges were of paramount importance in Bragg's attack because, even during the drought, the crossing of the creek was so difficult that it could only be easily crossed at fords or bridges. There were three important bridges in the area of Bragg's intended attack—Dyer's Bridge (north of Reed's Bridge), Reed's Bridge, and Alexander's Bridge (south of Reed's bridge). Each of the bridges was about two miles apart, meaning that Bragg intended to advance along a six-mile front that featured three bottlenecks in the form of the bridges. In addition to the bridges, several fords were important to the rapid crossing of the creek by troops. Reed's Bridge and Alexander's Bridge were about ten miles west of Ringgold. To complicate matters for the Union troops, both of Minty's and Wilder's commands were exhausted after a month in the saddle. In regard to Wilder's brigade,

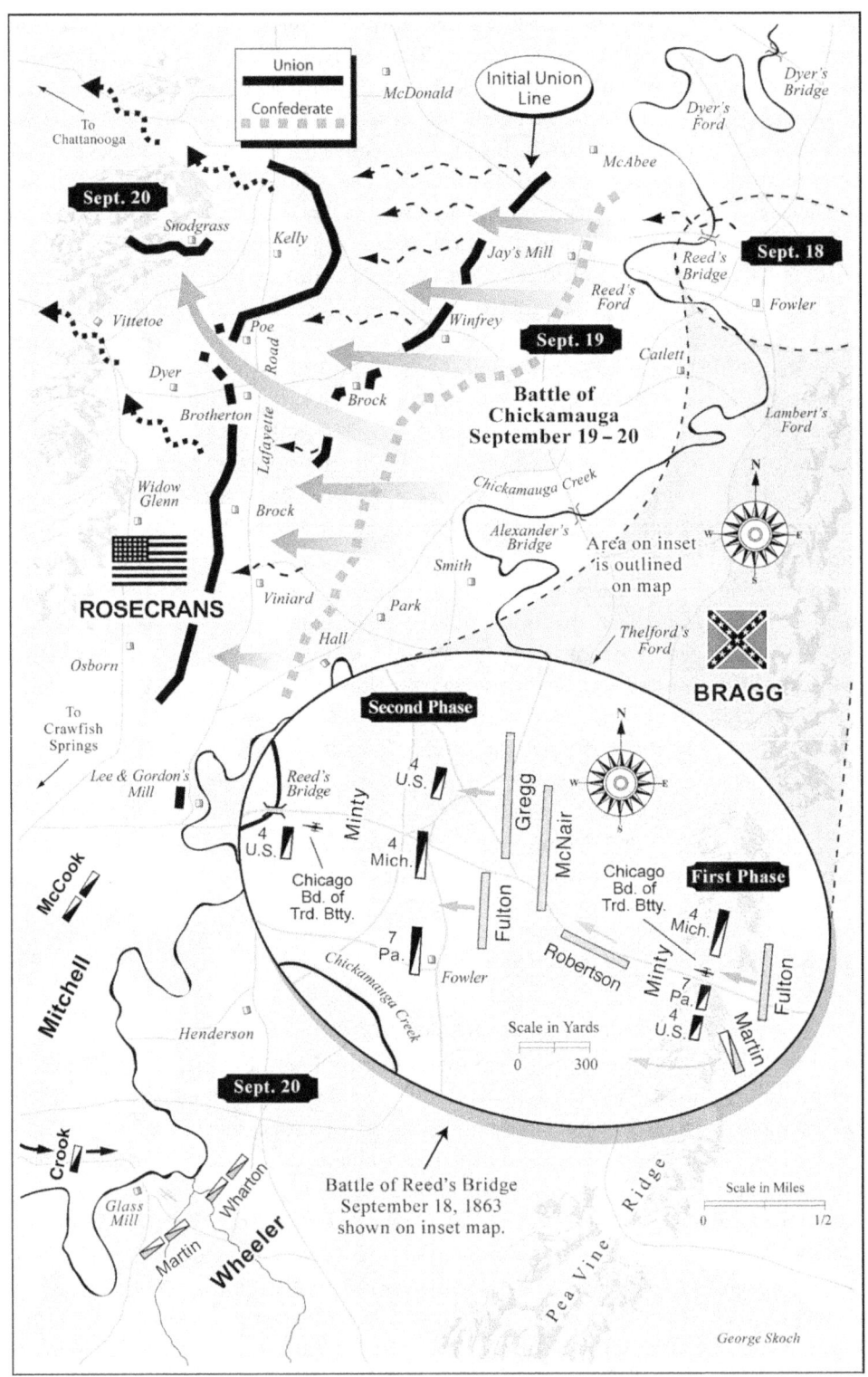

Battle at Reed's Bridge and the general positions on the battlefield.

Eight. *The Battle Begins—Reed's Bridge (September 18)*

it seemed all the infantry commanders had work for Wilder to do while the underappreciated Minty had had his brigade slowly dismantled and its units parceled out. The day before, Minty had command of only the 2nd Michigan and the 4th U.S. Cavalry. Luckily the 7th Pennsylvania returned to his command the previous evening. In all, Minty had less than one thousand officers and men. In addition, Minty's two-gun section of the well-regarded Chicago Board of Trade Horse Artillery was in position along Reed's Bridge Road.[13]

The day would be cloudy and cool and at noon the temperature only reached 62 degrees. Early on September 18, Minty, at his headquarters at James Reed's house just east of Chickamauga Creek, had pickets and patrols out looking for the enemy he believed approached his position. He sent one hundred troopers of the 4th U.S. Cavalry toward Leet's Tanyard (a small tannery owned by a Methodist minister and farmer, The Reverend A. I. Leet), and the same number of 4th Michigan and 7th Pennsylvania rode toward Ringgold looking for the enemy. Captain Heber Thompson commanded the latter patrol. Thompson, a Yale graduate, began his Civil War Service in "The First Defenders," also known as the Washington Artillery of Pottsville, Pennsylvania. Thompson subsequently joined the 7th Pennsylvania Cavalry when it was organized. His command rode to Peavine Ridge in the early morning fog and then he sent out four-man patrols to the east to search for the enemy. One of the patrols, led by Corporal John Williams, reached a house about one hundred yards west of the Peavine Creek and discovered a Confederate patrol advancing to the west. The Union cavalrymen opened fire on the enemy at 7:00 a.m. Thompson then moved ahead with sixteen troopers while keeping the rest of his men in line watching for more of the enemy. In the meantime, Thompson sent a courier who reached Minty at 8:00 a.m. explaining that he saw a large number of infantry marching in his direction. However, he had not observed infantry, but part of John Scott's cavalry brigade. The exchange of gunfire resulted in the killing one of the Union cavalry, John Ward, and in wounding Corporal John Williams. After sending messages to Gordon Granger, John Wilder, Thomas Wood, and Thomas Crittenden about the increased enemy activity, Minty strengthened his pickets along the La Fayette Road and rode forward with the 7th Pennsylvania, 4th Michigan, a battalion of the 4th U.S. and the section of the Chicago Board of Trade Artillery, command by Lieutenant Trumbull D. Griffin. Minty established his defensive line of about 600 troopers along the eastern slope of Peavine Ridge, about two miles east of Reed's Bridge and overlooking the small Peavine Creek, and prepared to the meet Johnson's advancing infantry columns which arrived around 10:00 a. m.[14]

After encountering Scott's cavalry, Captain Thompson had strengthened his defense to a total of twenty men on the east side of the Peavine Creek. Thompson's men saw light action after initially skirmishing with Scott's cavalry in the morning but they soon encountered an even more deadly threat—more soldiers in gray uniforms moving silently through the trees. After firing a few shots at the approaching Confederates, Thompson discovered the strong, advancing skirmish line of the 17th Tennessee Infantry. The advancing infantry drew the immediate attention of Thompson who sent a rider hurrying to Minty with news about the advancing infantry. He then ordered the remainder of his battalion to the west side of the creek and prepared to delay the Confederate advance. Thompson had accomplished what he had hoped when Johnson's main column approached, stopped, and fell into battle line. A daunting sight, the Confederate infantry fell into line three brigades wide, with the fourth brigade in reserve. Robert Burns explained that arriving on the scene, he saw "clouds of dust on all the roads in every direction, we knew that they were all coming." The movement of the Confederate infantry pushed Thompson's men back toward Minty's hastily prepared defensive line. Bushrod Johnson's column included Brigadier General John Gregg's brigade of seven regiments, Brigadier General Evander McNair's five regiments, Colonel John Fulton's four Tennessee regiments, and Brigadier General Jerome Robertson's four regiments of primarily Texas infantry. Johnson, supported by Robertson's brigade, gave him about 5,000 men. Johnson also commanded two additional brigades of Hood's infantry, which were trailing along behind the column. Not having Forrest's cavalry in advance of the column, Johnson did not know the size of the force he faced and he decided on a cautious approach.[15]

Sergeant James Larson, 4th U.S., remarked that the Confederate advance on the morning of September 18 was not a surprise, "we did not expect it to come off so early." The troopers of the 4th U.S. Cavalry were sitting down to their breakfast and had meat and vegetables cooking in a pot over a campfire. Larson had just started making pancakes when "Boots and Saddles" echoed. The men ran for their horses with part of a pancake in their hands as gunfire echoed in the distance. As the regiment moved to the east, it crossed Reed's Bridge and the column slowed because the bridge was only wide enough for two horses to pass side-by-side. This bridge would be the location of the important fighting later in the day.[16]

Fortunately for Minty, Johnson's advance was delayed from the start of the day. Native Ohioan, Bushrod Johnson, graduated from the United States Military Academy in 1840. He began his military career in good fashion, fighting in the Seminole War and in the Mexican War, but in 1847, he was forced to resign, allegedly, because of his involvement in a scheme to sell government property for his own personal gain. He joined the Tennessee militia in 1861 and was immediately transferred to the Confederate Army. He received his commission as brigadier general in 1862 and admirably served in the major battles in the west since Shiloh.[17]

Johnson's began his advance at 4:00 a.m. from Catoosa Platform, a small rail station, a couple of miles southeast of Ringgold. Johnson initially marched to Ringgold and then moved toward Leet's Tanyard. His movement toward Minty's cavalry was delayed by an outdated set of orders directing him to move to Leet's Tanyard instead of Reed's Bridge. After marching three miles, a courier brought Bragg's newly modified orders which directed the infantry column to secure Reed's Bridge and then move southward toward Lee and Gordon's Mill. Once the confusion was sorted out, Johnson's column changed direction and marched toward Robert Minty's position. Nathan Bedford Forrest belatedly caught the column at 10:45 a.m. and he rode with about 350 troopers, including Martin's detachment and a one hundred-man escort of elite cavalry. Martin's detachment was a fragment of the survivors of John Hunt Morgan's ill-fated raid into the north in July.[18]

Thompson's 7th Pennsylvania troopers skirmished with Bushrod Johnson's advancing infantry units near Peeler's Mill with more Southern infantry support following along behind. The 17th Tennessee Infantry of Colonel John Fulton's brigade led the advance and ran into the skirmishers of the 7th Pennsylvania killing three troopers and mortally wounding another; but Minty's cavalry fell into an effective fight-retreat-fight method of delaying the Johnson's advance. When Forrest arrived on the scene, he ordered Martin's small detachment of Southern cavalry to push Thompson's cavalry westward in spite of objections from the infantry about having cavalry in their front. Soon after, Forrest dismounted his cavalry for some reason and had them join the infantry, thereby negating the mobility of his force, because certainly Johnson already had more than enough infantry. Johnson's infantry slowly advanced while contending with Minty's stubborn defense. Trumbull Dorrance Griffin, a native of Clinton, New York, kept a steady hand on his two guns of the Chicago Board of Trade artillery as he assisted Union cavalry troopers to delay the advancing Confederate lines. The size of Bushrod Johnson's division resulted in a "crescent shaped" line of battle converging on Minty's defenders, but the dense woods, hills and streams also aided the Union cavalry by hindering Johnson's advance.[19]

Minty prepared his defensive lines as Thompson's men withdrew but the numbers were on Johnson's side as they pushed the Northern troopers back toward Reed's Bridge, "a narrow, frail structure, which was planked with loose boards and fence-rails." Minty placed the 4th Michigan on the left of the Pennsylvania cavalrymen while the 4th U.S. moved to the right. Lieutenant Jacob Sigmund, 7th Pennsylvania Cavalry, commanded some of Minty's skirmishers, and as Johnson's troops pressed forward, his skirmishers held their position until they were almost overwhelmed. A soldier was killed to the left of Sigmund when Captain May, Company K, rode ahead to order Sigmund to fall back, but May never delivered the order due to the volleys from the enemy. Next, the regimental adjutant yelled to Sigmund, "Sigmund, why don't you fall back? My instructions were to hold this hill," replied the lieutenant, "and I meant to hold it until I was ordered to fall back."[20]

Ominous Dust to the North

Minty's three regimental commanders were good, experienced officers in charge of experienced cavalry and the unfolding action, while difficult, was not new to these officers. A Texan, Captain James McIntyre, commanded the professional 4th U.S. Cavalry. McIntyre graduated from West Point the year after David Stanley and had ten years of experience in the cavalry. The 4th U.S. had two full years of experience during the war, fighting in the important battles in the west.[21]

The fifty-one-year-old, combat veteran Major Horace Gray commanded Minty's own regiment, the 4th Michigan. Gray, a resident of the idyllic Grosse Ile, Michigan, had been a sheriff and hotel proprietor before the war and also served as an agent to the Dakota Indians in the western territories. He served with the 4th Michigan through the Battle of Stones River, Tullahoma Campaign and during the successful defeat of Wheeler and Martin at Shelbyville.[22]

Philadelphian, Lieutenant Colonel James Seibert, commanded the 7th Pennsylvania in September 1863. Seibert began the war as a major and then lieutenant colonel of a three-month regiment. He subsequently joined the 7th Pennsylvania and his battalion had been captured at Murfreesboro in July 1862 by Forrest's cavalry. He was later exchanged and then re-joined the 7th Pennsylvania Cavalry, which had seen plenty of action since its formation in the fall of 1861. Minty's veteran troopers faced a stern task.[23]

Johnson's infantry pushed the Union cavalry steadily back toward Reed's Bridge. The Chicago Board of Trade continued to fire into the advancing Confederate line and Minty's troopers kept steadily firing into the approaching enemy; but Minty noticed another column of dust moving to the north. Fearing he was about to be flanked and already facing more Confederates than he could handle, at 11:00 o'clock he appealed to John Wilder for reinforcements to guard Dyer's Bridge, a few miles north, which Minty believed was the objective of the newly arriving Confederate column. Wilder, who was not engaged at this point, sent two regiments, 123rd Illinois and the 72nd Indiana along with a two-gun section of Lilly's Battery, to Dyer's Bridge. They arrived at noon and deployed to halt any attempt to flank Minty by that route. The remainder of Wilder's brigade held Alexander's Bridge while Minty took on the large Confederate force approaching Reed's Bridge. At the time the two regiments were sent north, there was no indication these would be needed at Alexander's Bridge; however, Walker's Confederate Reserve Corps attacked Wilder at noon after he had dispatched the reinforcements. Fortunately, Minty and Wilder had secured the three key bridges across Chickamauga Creek, thereby preventing a rapid advance of Bushrod Johnson's and William H. T. Walker's Confederates.[24]

While resisting Bushrod Johnson's advance, Minty had deployed a screen of skirmishers. Sergeant James Larson, 4th U.S., one of the first reinforcements to arrive explained that to attempt to hold off the full might of the Confederate infantry was impractical. Instead, several cavalry companies formed a skirmish line, and when the steady advance of the Confederate infantry continued, it faced a fusillade of Union fire, causing the long gray line to pause before resuming it steady advance. The 4th U.S. companies retreated one company at a time in alphabetical order, and then re-deployed in the rear. Minty made good use of the terrain and the fact that the road leading from Ringgold to Reed's Bridge wound through a narrow pass, a "natural choke point," through Peavine Ridge greatly benefited the Union defense. As Johnson's infantry pushed forward, Minty boldly decided to advance his skirmishers to meet the advancing line of Confederates while simultaneously withdrawing his main body back toward Reed's Bridge.[25]

While fighting Confederate infantry to his front, the dust cloud to the north still concerned Minty. Little did he know that Nathan Bedford Forrest had ordered Colonel John Scott's cavalry brigade to guard the Old Federal Road leading to Rossville. As Scott's Confederate cavalry advanced, it ran into Brigadier General Walter Whitaker's First Brigade of James Steedman's Union reserve infantry division at Red House Bridge creating the dust cloud to the north that Minty observed. As a result, Wilder's two regiments which were hastily sent to Dyer's Bridge only saw light action during the day. However, as Bushrod Johnson continued his advance, Minty called on Colonel Abram Miller's 72th Indiana Mounted Infantry, initially positioned at Dyer's Bridge, to cover his left flank because the pressure of the Confederate infantry threatened Minty's flank from the north.[26]

Nathan Bedford Forrest initially joined Johnson's column but subsequently left in search of what he thought was another Union force "upstream." Forrest moved to the location he supposed to be the original encampment of the Federal cavalry. Then, he borrowed the 17th Tennessee Infantry and moved away from the attack to look for an

Colonel John Wilder's mounted infantry brigade held Alexander's Bridge (Library of Congress).

Eight. The Battle Begins—Reed's Bridge (September 18)

opportunity to attack Minty's flank. When Forrest reached this location, he found none of Minty's men there and returned with his force to the fight at Reed's Bridge. Minty held out along Peavine Ridge until 12:30 p.m. before retreating further west. By the time Forrest returned, Minty's cavalry had edged back to the east side of Chickamauga Creek. In the meantime, Bushrod Johnson's infantry secured Peavine Ridge. When Johnson crested the ridge, he observed that he only faced a single brigade of cavalry. The Union troopers watched as the grand advance of fifteen regimental colors fluttered in the wind when Johnson's troops marched over the ridge toward Reed's Bridge. As the bulk of Johnson's men surged past the ridge around 2:00 p.m., the Federal artillery opened on them again. So impressive was the Southern advance, that it appeared the "whole brigade would be captured or annihilated," wrote Captain Joseph Vale, 7th Pennsylvania Cavalry. As the Union cavalry retreated westward, they moved out of the dense forests. Near the bridge, the ground leveled and had been planted with crops earlier in the year. Taking advantage of the more level and cleared terrain, Minty's 4th Michigan and 7th Pennsylvania made a successful mounted charge on the first Confederate troops surging in advance, slowing their advance while the rest of enemy infantry moved along the flanks squeezing the Union cavalry back toward the bridge. Minty realized he could no longer hold his position but he knew that much of his brigade was still on the east side of the creek trying to delay Johnson's advance. Minty began preparing his defenses

The Confederate advance made it appear the "whole brigade would be captured or annihilated," wrote Captain Joseph Vale, 7th Pennsylvania Cavalry (A. R. Waud wartime sketch. From Joseph Brown, *The Mountain Campaign in Georgia, 1886.*).

on the west side of the creek in order to provide covering fire once the remainder of the brigade crossed the bridge. The bridge was so narrow that the Union withdrawal had to be finely tuned. He withdrew Griffin's section of artillery into some bushes about 300 yards on the west side of Chickamauga Creek where a battalion of the 4th U.S. Cavalry was already positioned. As the Union withdrawal began and as the Confederate infantry advanced, the 4th Michigan and 7th Pennsylvania cavalries provided the first line of defense.[27]

Henry Albert Potter, 4th Michigan Cavalry, recorded the intense action as Johnson pushed Minty rearward: "I could see them when they loaded, as soon as the smoke cleared away—order came to fall back—which we did—rejoined the regiment & moved through the woods—our skirmishers soon saw the rebels infantry—we dismounted half of the men and moved upon them—a smart skirmish ensued—but were obliged to fall back by overpowering numbers—formed in line again—again were driven back—passed thro' our camp and past the 'Regulars'—towards the river—which we succeeded in crossing without loss. Formed in a line to cover the retreat of the 4th [Regulars] presently crash! Came the artillery in the midst of us."[28]

Minty Moves Across Reed's Bridge

Minty began his withdrawal across the bridge as the Southern infantry closed in on his position. With Griffin's section of artillery in position on the ridge on the west side of the creek, the 4th Michigan withdrew across the bridge followed by the 7th Pennsylvania. Finally, the remainder of the 4th U.S. Cavalry under the command of Lieutenant Wirt Davis, a Virginian whose family had severed connections with him due to the war, moved across and stopped long enough on the bridge to pull up the planks making a quick crossing difficult for their enemy. But not all of Minty's command had made it across the river. A squadron of the 4th Michigan had been guarding the Harrison Road, southeast of Reed's Bridge, and was cut off due to the rapid advance of the Confederates. Lieutenant John Simpson commanding the detail made a determined stand against the Confederates closing on his position before his troopers finally escaped by swimming Chickamauga Creek.[29]

Minty reassembled his command on the west side of the creek, supported by Griffin's section of artillery, and prepared to delay any movement further westward by Johnson's infantry. With the obstacle of the deep and difficult Chickamauga Creek facing him, Johnson had to decide how best to cross in the face of a thousand Union cavalry, some with repeating rifles, supported by artillery. He had had enough

Virginian, Lieutenant Wirt Davis ordered his 4th U.S. Cavalry to stop and pull up the planks on Reed's Bridge to slow the enemy's attack, postwar photograph (National Archives).

Eight. The Battle Begins—Reed's Bridge (September 18)   191

waiting and he decided to march Fulton's brigade directly toward the bridge. Minty's carbine and artillery fire halted the advance of the Confederate infantry and prevented it from crossing the creek. The men of the 23rd Tennessee Infantry ran to the bridge only to be surprised when they found that the 4th U.S. had stripped its floor planks. At 3:30 p.m., Fulton's infantry again rushed forward. This time the Tennesseans carried planks of their own, torn from James Reed's house and outbuildings, and began to re-floor the bridge under a barrage of grape and carbine fire. Once they repaired the bridge, Forrest arrived and thanked the men for their efforts and then rode ahead. Soon, Fulton's entire brigade followed him, prompting Minty to conclude he could not to resist further at that location and he wisely withdrew his men to a "second rise 700 yards farther west." Shortly, thereafter, General John Bell Hood and his division arrived on the scene amid the cheers of the Southern infantry.[30]

After falling back again, Minty continued to resist the Confederate advance until late afternoon. However, he was being flanked on all sides by ten regiments of Confederate infantry with more in their wake. Also, he received a message from an officer in charge of his supply train informing him that "Colonel Wilder has fallen back from Alexander's Bridge to Gordon's Mills and the enemy are crossing at all points in force." About 4:00 p.m., Minty sent a message to Wilder's troops at Dyer's Bridge to fall back and join him as he retreated about a mile toward Jay's Mill. Even though the Federal cavalry had been engaged throughout the day, the fighting was so intense that Robert Burns wrote, "I never saw a day to pass so quickly."[31]

Early 1900s photograph of the terrain near Jay's Mill (Library of Congress).

Union Cavalry Withdraws to Jay's Mill

Aware of the action on his left flank, Rosecrans ordered Brigadier General James Steedman to send infantry from the Reserve Corps to support Minty's left flank, but Steedman could not get Dan McCook's infantry brigade on the road until 3:30. By that time, the first Confederates along Minty's front were crossing Chickamauga Creek with Hood's division supporting them. About this time, Brigadier General Henry B. Davidson's cavalry brigade of John Pegram's division found and forded Fowler's Ford, about a half mile south of Reed's Bridge. At the same time, John Wilder advised Rosecrans of the situation, "Colonel Minty has fallen back, after being re-enforced by two regiments and two pieces of artillery of mine. A rebel infantry force has crossed Chickamauga between Alexander's Bridge and Reed's Bridge, getting in my rear. I held the rebels at Alexander's Bridge until they outnumbered me on every side. I got off my artillery, and am falling back on General Wood."[32]

Crittenden seemed remarkably nonplussed during the day. Because his headquarters was at the same location as Rosecrans,' he simply waited for Rosecrans to send him instructions instead of being proactive. Brigadier General Thomas Wood, Crittenden's Corps First Division commander, rode to the front after hearing the noise of the battle and smugly discounted the initial reports that Minty and Wilder were under heavy attack. Wood initially thought the fighting was just Confederate cavalry skirmishers. Wood asked where the enemy was located and Wilder told him, "Ride forward, General, ten paces, and you will see for yourself." After observing the scope of the Confederate advance, he exclaimed, "By God, they are here." Then, he ordered his infantry forward to meet the threat. Bushrod Johnson's slow advance combined with Minty's and Wilder's determined defenses thus delayed the Confederate advance for almost a day giving Rosecrans a chance to prepare for Bragg's move.[33]

Minty supported by Wilder's two mounted infantry regiments fell back to Jay's Mill, a steam-powered saw mill about a mile west of Reed's Bridge. Minty held this new position for about an hour until Johnson's and Hood's divisions again overwhelmed his troopers. Hood then marched south in the direction of the Alexander's farm. As Minty and Wilder retired, they combined their commands, forming a single line across the La Fayette Road, and engaged the enemy again. This fight continued for more than an hour and the Union line held. Wood moved his infantry forward and met the advancing Confederate infantry, stalling the enemy's advance; but the day's fighting was not over.[34]

Finally recognizing the threat, Rosecrans rapidly redirected his troops and prepared for battle. Responding to the Confederate attacks on his left flank, Rosecrans hastened to fill the gap between Crittenden and Granger. Also, the action around Reed's Bridge and Alexander's Bridge precipitated a second order for Steedman to send another brigade to bolster the Union left flank. Interestingly, David Stanley's and William Rosecrans's close friend and spiritual advisor, Father Jeremiah Trecy, bore a new message about the movements of Minty and Wilder. Thomas Wood greeted Trecy at 4:40 p.m. and the priest advised him that the two commands had merged into a single line resisting the Confederate advance. The Union line had been shoved back almost to the Chattanooga and Rossville Road, and the Confederates still pushed forward with plenty of infantry, artillery, and cavalry.[35]

Night Attack

Minty's weary troopers fell into line alongside Wilder's brigade at dusk. The two brigades held a line near the Viniard's house about a mile and a half north of Lee and Gordon's Mill facing northeast. Two regiments of infantry, Colonel George Dick's brigade of Van Cleve's division, moved into line south of Minty and Wilder. Minty recorded that the war maps incorrectly placed his regiment in relation to the others. Minty said that Wilder held the northern most position, with his brigade on the right of Wilder and the two infantry regiments deployed to the right of his position.[36]

At dusk, Hood ordered John Gregg's infantry brigade, just south of Minty's position, to attack the 44th Indiana and 59th Ohio infantries of Dick's brigade. The first attack came about an hour after dark. Next, McNair's and Fulton's infantry brigades came up to support Gregg. As the Southern infantry advanced, they met the full firepower of Dick's infantry supported by Minty's carbines and Wilder's Spencer rifles, and the combined firepower effectively halted the attack in its tracks. The Confederate infantry regrouped and thirty minutes later another attack surged ahead only be repulsed again by Dick's infantry and the two mounted commands. When the night attack failed, the fighting ended for the day and the ten-hour battle was over. To the north, Dan McCook's brigade reached the area around Jay's Mill and McCook, unknowingly and precariously, encamped between two Confederate divisions. At 11:00 p.m., Colonel John G. Mitchell's infantry brigade (Reserve Corps) moved into position alongside McCook's.[37]

The aftermath of the last fighting left everyone nervous about the success of the enemy. Robert Burns explained: "We lay that night where we were in a line within 100 yards of the enemy with our horses a quarter mile in our rear. We could hear the rebels talking in the woods. I never passed such a night. It was cold and bleak. We were allowed no fire and not a man slept, every one of us expecting at the dawn to be annihilated." But the situation still did not suit Minty who, with Wilder, held the extreme left flank of Crittenden's corps, as he had for the past month. At 2:00 a.m., he rode to headquarters demanding reinforcements before daylight or else the previous day's fighting would have been for nothing. As a result, Major General John Palmer brought up two infantry brigades to relieve Minty and Wilder. Henry Campbell of the 18th Indiana Artillery of Wilder's brigade recorded in his diary the movement of Thomas' XIV Corps throughout the night to fill the gap between Crittenden and Granger. "They are hurrying to the left, to prevent the Rebels from getting between us & Chattanooga. The night was dreadfully cold.—No fires allowed.—No supper.—No feed for our horses.—The monotonous tramp, tramp, of the passing troops, the rumbling of artillery carriages and the ominous thoughts of the morrow." Thomas' infantry made a difficult march through the night to be in place to face the enemy the next morning.[38]

By midnight on September 18, Rosecrans's army was concentrating around Lee and Gordon's Mill, and readied itself for a day of vicious fighting, the likes of which many of the army had never seen. Robert Minty and John T. Wilder and their commands had performed immeasurable service to the Army of the Cumberland. Luck as well as skill aided Minty's and Wilder's important efforts. Half-way between their positions lay Lambert's Ford. The two Union colonels already faced overwhelming odds, and had the Confederates utilized this crossing, both Minty and Wilder easily could have been flanked. Also, for the most part the Confederate cavalry played little part in the morning's attack allowing Minty and Wilder to focus on the Confederate Infantry. The only other active cavalry engagement was Scott's fight with Whitaker's infantry. Nevertheless, Minty and Wilder held Rosecrans's left flank and gave him time to shift forces to meet what could have been a crushing blow. Bragg faced a critical delay in getting his forces into place and he lost the element of surprise. Because of the action of these two intrepid commanders, George Thomas's XIV Corps marched throughout the night to be in position to face the Confederate attack the next morning. Whatever happened the next day, Minty and Wilder gave Rosecrans what he most needed—time.[39]

While the fighting began on the Union left flank, the bulk of Robert Mitchell's cavalry guarded the Union right flank in inglorious, but important, duty of protecting the gaps and the roads on the southern flank. Notably, Alexander McCook assumed command of Mitchell and the cavalry. McCook commanded the right flank of the Union army and it made sense for him to have full command of the troops on this flank. By 5:00 p.m., Robert Mitchell had moved two brigades of Edward McCook's cavalry to within two miles of Blue Bird Gap and awaited further orders. Those orders came during the evening of September 18 directing his cavalry to close up on the right flank of Alexander McCook's XX Corps, which was also moving northward. Colonel P. Sidney Post's infantry brigade had the task of covering Stevens' Gap after the removal of the cavalry and rest of McCook's infantry. Post protected the corps supply train and had orders to hold the gap at all costs.[40]

By now, there was little doubt in Rosecrans' mind that he had a serious situation on his hands. The intelligence forwarded by Minty and Wilder throughout the day proved beyond a doubt that Bragg intended to cut him off from Chattanooga. Brigadier General George Wagner at Chattanooga confirmed this and reported that "Heavy columns of infantry on Chattanooga road between Chattanooga and Ringgold...." On the other side of the battlefield, the Confederates soldiers were advised "that everything depends upon the issue of this battle."[41]

Summary

Little more needs to be added to the events on September 18. Both Robert Minty and John Wilder's troops provided invaluable service to the Union army throughout the day and that compares favorably to John Buford's cavalry actions at Gettysburg. These commanders held the enemy throughout the late morning, afternoon and evening and gave Rosecrans sufficient time to deploy his army into a solid defensive line. Thanks to the determined stands of Minty and Wilder, Bragg's surprise attack failed. There was no better testament to the success of the actions at these bridges than the frustration of the Confederates in the column in the rear who could not move forward until Minty's and Wilder's troopers were shoved aside.

Many personalities were at work during this campaign, but it would be remiss not to stress the poor relationship between Thomas Crittenden and Robert Minty. The exact nature of their animosity is unknown, but Minty clearly felt disparaged throughout the campaign. While this caused some discomfort, worry and damage to the ego of Minty and his cavalry in the first part of the campaign, it resulted in serious mistakes by Crittenden as the battle approached. Only a few days before, Minty requested that a brigade of infantry be sent to the area around Reed's Bridge, only to have Crittenden dismiss this suggestion. Once the battle began, Minty's reports of the build-up of enemy troops near his position were proven true. In the final summary, Minty professionally and effectively accomplished his duty and along with John Wilder successfully thwarted Bragg's surprise attack.

Nine. September 19–20 and the Battle at Glass Mill

[The] scene was one of a lifetime, terrific, awe inspiring, frightful!—Lt. Col. Elijah Watts

Day 2: The Cavalry Moves to Crawfish Springs

While Minty and Wilder desperately fought two Confederate infantry columns on September 18, Robert Mitchell's three remaining brigades at the front held their positions near McLemore's Cove on the southern flank of the army. Upon receiving orders during the night, the cavalry began to move north to Crawfish Springs to replace Thomas's infantry which held that position on September 18.[1]

George Thomas' XIV Corps, which had marched overnight north of Crittenden, began the morning early and quickly engaged Forrest's cavalry near Jay's Mill. Colonel John Croxton led his infantry brigade near Jay's Mill on the north side of the developing Union line in search of what was thought to be an isolated Confederate infantry brigade. Instead, he found Forrest's dismounted cavalry and the infantry battle began. Throughout the day, Rosecrans and Bragg threw their armies onto the field in a piecemeal fashion and the lines ebbed and flowed. Bragg sent orders for the formidable Confederate cavalry to "develop the enemy" on morning of September 19. For Forrest, the "development" resulted in extensive fighting with the Union infantry throughout the day but no significant involvement from the Union cavalry occurred on the Union left flank. The day before, Wheeler was ordered to move into McLemore's Cove through Dug and Catlett's Gaps and to demonstrate against the enemy. He needed to occupy the attention of the Union command while Bragg implemented his infantry attack. On the morning of September 19, Wheeler moved to Owen's Ford, on Chickamauga Creek, after leaving a substantial force to protect the mountain gaps.[2]

Robert Minty's cavalry which had fought so hard the day before spent a fretful and "bitterly cold" night without any campfires. John Palmer's infantry division held the position previously occupied by Minty and Minty moved his command to a position near Lee and Gordon's Mill until noon and then moved toward Rossville. Along the way, the cavalry stopped to forage the horses and obtain rations for the men. Minty's brigade spent the rest of the day guarding the supply trains coming and going from Chattanooga, and he would end the day near Rossville without participating in the battle. Garfield released Minty from duty with

Crittenden's corps, and he wanted Minty on reconnaissance duty near Rossville to ensure that Bragg made no further attacks which would sever Rosecrans' communications with Chattanooga. After accomplishing his reconnaissance, Minty dispelled any concerns, much to the relief of headquarters, and reported that no large force of Confederate cavalry threatened an attack near Chattanooga on the Rossville Road. Minty kept watch on the Confederate movements and bivouacked near Rossville that evening. At the end of the day, Minty fell under the command of Gordon Granger.[3]

Wheeler Attacks the Cavalry Supply Train

For the bulk of the Union cavalry scattered fifteen miles south along the gaps and valleys, Rosecrans' orders drew them back to the main Union concentration forming along the La Fayette Road. Edward McCook's cavalry awoke on September 19 after a cold night in the mountains and valleys. Henry Hempstead, 2nd Michigan, wrote: "This morning it is still cold, with a high wind and dust flying in blinding clouds." Robert Mitchell's orders sent the three cavalry brigades riding toward Crawfish Springs, Rosecrans's old headquarters and the location of most of the Union army's hospitals. Eli Long's Second Brigade of Crook's Division moved from Rape's Gap into McLemore's Cove during the day and rode toward Crawfish Springs that evening. Only Watkins' brigade had orders to delay until the wounded, sick, and prisoners could be transported to Bridgeport.[4]

During its move to Crawfish Springs, McCook's First Division fought off an opportunistic attack by Wheeler's cavalry on the division's supply train. Colonel Daniel Ray's Second Cavalry Brigade of about 1,300 troopers rode steadily northward and at noon the troopers heard the cannonading from the main body of the army. The 39th Indiana Mounted Infantry commanded by Colonel Thomas J. Harrison trailed the cavalry. Sergeant G. W. Baum upon hearing the cannons knew that "Rosy had got in a hornet's nest." Ray's brigade followed behind Campbell's First Brigade and escorted the division's supply train. At one o'clock, Ray was surprised when Colonel Thomas Harrison's Confederate cavalry brigade attacked the supply train just north of Stevens' Gap and four miles south of Crawfish Springs with four cavalry regiments and a section of artillery. (Ironically, the Confederate brigade commander and the commander of the 39th Indiana Mounted Infantry were both named Thomas Harrison.) Wheeler's cavalry surged ahead at Davis' Ford and tried to seize the supply train; and Major David Briggs, 2nd Indiana Cavalry, and Harrison, 39th Indiana Mounted Infantry, found themselves in a bad position when Wheeler's attack cut off the supply train from the main column. Being at the end of a long cavalry column of two brigades, the only hope for the train and the two regiments was reinforcements. Briggs sent two riders to try to reach the main column while he and Harrison held off Thomas Harrison's Confederate cavalry. Briggs ordered three dismounted companies to defend against the attack from within the train. The remainder of the regiment surrounded the train, still on horseback. Luckily, the riders reached the main column, and the 2nd Indiana and the 39th Indiana held off the Confederate cavalry until help arrived. The Union troops repulsed the first attack on the trains and Harrison tried again to attack the train in a heated engagement. The 1st Wisconsin Cavalry and 4th Indiana Cavalry rode quickly to Brigg's position and the subsequent skirmish lasted about an hour. Colonel Oscar La Grange, 1st Wisconsin, riding to assist those with the train dismounted one half of the regiment and exchanged fire with Harrison's troopers who fell back to a wooded area. La Grange sent the remainder of the regiment to find the Confederate cavalry's flank; and Harrison finally broke off the attack and retired. La Grange lost one man severely wounded and one man missing, the 4th Indiana had two troopers missing, but the train was undamaged. Wheeler's only reference to the action was, "About 2 p.m. I learned the enemy's cavalry were moving up McLemore's Cove. I moved across the river and warmly assailed their flank, dividing the column and driving the enemy in confusion in both directions." Union brigade commander, Daniel Ray, simply referred to this as a "spirited skirmish" and that the supply train continued onward safely. Ray was one regiment short in the skirmish because the 2nd Tennessee Cavalry (U.S.) had been assigned detached duty holding Stevens' Gap. The 2nd Indiana's Sergeant Baum wrote that Wheeler had "caught a tartar, and in 20 minutes fighting let us go." The other two Union commanders, Harrison and Briggs, did not report any casualties during the fight.[5]

Thomas J. Harrison's 39th Indiana Mounted Infantry, armed with Spencer rifles, offered additional firepower during the skirmish. Harrison recorded: "My regiment was delayed in its movements by demonstrations made by the enemy on the La Fayette and Ringgold roads, thereby throwing us in rear of General Mitchell's cavalry. About meridian, the enemy attacked our right flank, and succeeded in cutting off the Second Indiana Cavalry, the cavalry train, and my regiment from the main body of troops. But after considerable fighting, we drove the enemy and rejoined our army; we reached Crawfish Spring at sunset."[6]

Chaplain Robert Bunting, 8th Texas Cavalry, recorded in a letter that scouts spotted the Union cavalry as it moved toward Crawfish Springs and sought to capture the supply

Edward McCook repulsed Wheeler's attack on the supply train of the Union cavalry (from *Frank Leslie's Illustrated Famous Leaders and Battle Scenes of the Civil War*, 1896).

train. In the skirmish along Chickamauga Creek near Davis' Ford, Bunting disparaged the Federal cavalry but concluded his regiment retreated but "not, however, without having several men badly wounded and losing some horses." Colonel William Newton Estes, 3rd Confederate Cavalry, was killed in the exchange with the 39th Indiana a couple of days before and on September 19 Bunting blamed the losses of the brigade on poor planning by Wheeler. Wheeler had overwhelming numbers of cavalry and Bunting felt the entire Confederate division should have been used to attack across the creek. This was another of Wheeler's "languid" actions over the past few days; and historian David Powell wrote that Wheeler was not only offering feeble actions but also "again neglecting his duties."[7]

The remaining ride to Crawfish Springs was difficult for the troopers: "We ... dashed forward at a gallop three or four miles amid such a cloud of dust that the man in advance could not be seen by those in the rear, and the unlucky horse who fell was sure to be run over by those in the rear," record Henry Hempstead.[8]

The Main Battle Intensifies

Shortly after noon, Garfield made an appeal through Alexander McCook, who now had command of the cavalry on the right flank, to hasten Mitchell and the cavalry to Crawfish Springs. Garfield wrote that much of Thomas' corps was engaged with the enemy but the enemy cavalry threatened to sweep into the rear of the infantry. "A considerable cavalry force of the enemy has got in behind us and are threatening some of our trains. The general commanding directs you to hurry Mitchell's cavalry in upon our right, and send a detachment to look out for our rear." This would be one of several important messages to Mitchell about the placement of the cavalry in regard to the battle over the next couple of days. Subsequent to this message, Garfield also notified Alexander McCook that due to his position on the right flank that Mitchell's cavalry fell under his command. "General McCook will take command of the right and the cavalry, and hold himself in readiness to support either flank"—a command that Mitchell would disregard the next day. At 4:00 p.m. Garfield again sent a message to Mitchell to hurry forward: "[B]ring up every available cavalryman, except one battalion, to be left at Stevens' Gap. Do this without a moment's delay. We need all your help to guard our right and rear." Two hours later Mitchell received further orders to guard the hospitals at Crawfish Springs. Negley's infantry which had duty guarding the flank and hospitals began pulling out of Crawfish Springs at 3:00 p.m. to support the Union infantry battle.[9]

At the end of the day, Archibald Campbell had two regiments (4th Indiana and 1st Tennessee) of his brigade protecting ammunition and supply trains in Dry Valley, the 2nd Indiana was positioned on the left of John Wilder's mounted infantry in a reserve position, the 9th Pennsylvania was along the right of Wilder's command a half mile west of Viniard's farm near Widow Glenn's house, Rosecrans' new headquarters. The remainder of Edward McCook's division held positions in the front and right of Crawfish Springs which freed up the infantry which had previously guarded the location. Meanwhile, Crook's cavalry moved from Rape's Gap and Dougherty's Gap and stopped south of Crawfish Springs, having a greater distance to ride during the day. Prior to orders to move from Dougherty's Gap, Crook's cavalry observed the beginnings of the battle from the mountain tops. Lieutenant Colonel Elijah Watts, 2nd Kentucky, recalled that from his position in the mountains to the south—"[W]e heard the sound of guns, we were not entirely sure. The dust indicated the line of march from west to east, and we knew the position of the troops in a general way, and of course that a battle was imminent." Soon orders sent the cavalry forward with the knowledge that a great battle was taking place just to the north. Mitchell initially had a total of 2,500 cavalry in place near Crawfish Springs with Campbell's and Ray's brigades. In addition, a section of the 1st Ohio Artillery and a section of the Chicago Board of Trade Artillery also accompanied Mitchell's cavalry. Upon his arrival, he formed the troopers in battle line and remained in place for the remainder of the day.[10]

Strength of the Federal Cavalry on the Southern Flank[11]

Command	Officers	Men	Commander
First Brigade, First Division	75	1,242	Archibald Campbell
Second Brigade, First Division	81	1,328	Daniel Ray
Third Brigade, First Division	—	650[a]	Louis Watkins
Second Brigade, Second Division	—	900[b]	Eli Long
Total (Officers and Men)	4,276		

[a]—Watkins' approximate strength as reported in the court martial records of the event at Cooper's Gap. [b]—Long's approximate strength was reported in the after-action report regarding the fight at Glass Mill

While the cavalry force was not insignificant, two regiments of Archibald Campbell's brigade, including Campbell himself, were initially dispatched to guard the ammunition and supply trains in Dry Valley, the valley southeast of Missionary Ridge with a road connecting to Widow Glenn's house. The 2nd Indiana Cavalry still remained in reserve for Colonel Wilder's mounted infantry, and the rest of McCook's cavalry division fell into line in the front and left of Crawfish Spring. With Watkins away, this left McCook only seven regiments of Union cavalry to protect the Union hospitals at Crawfish Springs until Crook's brigade and ultimately, Watkins' brigade, could rejoin the command. During the afternoon and evening of September 19, the hospitals and fields around Crawfish Springs began to fill with the wounded from the day's fighting and due to the location of the hospitals the narrow road, which led to Crawfish Springs from the primary battlefield, was often congested with ambulances coming and going to the battle. When the 9th Pennsylvania Cavalry arrived, Captain Thomas McCahan wrote: "I have never seen so many wounded as are coming in...."[12]

Of the skirmishes during the day, Campbell's First Brigade of 1,200 troopers had light duty. Campbell rode from McLemore's Cove through Pond Springs to Crawfish Springs and he had a slight clash with Wheeler's cavalry on his right flank, but he had no casualties. The enemy seemed content with taking pot-shots and then dispersing. Upon approaching Chickamauga Creek, Lieutenant Colonel Roswell Russell, 9th Pennsylvania, recorded: "Left camp at sunrise and moved in line of battle along the left of Crawfish Spring road until reaching Cowan's Ford, a couple of miles south of Glass Mill on the Chickamauga Creek. At this point I was ordered to cross the creek and disperse a squad of rebel cavalry posted in the edge of a corn-field. On the approach of the two companies ... sent in compliance with this order, and to reconnoiter an adjacent wood, the enemy fired a volley and hastily retreated." Once the Union cavalry chased off the enemy, the 9th Pennsylvania moved back to the west side of the creek and moved on to Crawfish Springs. Captain Thomas McCahan's company of 9th Pennsylvania cavalry also skirmished with Confederates on the way to Crawfish Springs. After charging a group of ambushers, McCahan dismounted his company and he took a carbine from one of the troopers who held the horses. As he walked along with his troops, he stepped on a dry twig which cracked very loudly. Then, McCahan humorously noted in his diary: "I jumped, the boys say, 20 feet to the rear and threw the carbine to my face." McCahan brought some needed levity to a serious situation. When the twig cracked, McCahan thought an enemy had fired at him. Fortunately, no further fighting took place and McCahan led his company to Crawfish Springs. At 4:00 p.m., Archibald Campbell sent the regiment to the west side of Chickamauga Creek to hold the fords and he set up a screen of pickets which connected with Wilder's Mounted Infantry to the north. McCook's remaining regiments, the 1st Tennessee Cavalry and 1st Wisconsin Cavalry, moved to Crawfish Springs and remained in battle line into the night. Once the cavalry reached Crawfish Springs, some of the troopers were ordered to carry water from the springs to the parched soldiers along the infantry line.[13]

Only the 2nd Michigan Cavalry had a more heated skirmish but drove the enemy away and claimed the fords near Glass Mill. Major Leonidas Scranton, commanding the 2nd Michigan, initially moved his regiment to Pond Spring and held his position there for two hours before proceeding to Crawfish Springs. Once Campbell's brigade reached Crawfish Springs, Campbell ordered the 2nd Michigan to scout the various fords over Chickamauga Creek. Afterward, the regiment remained in position at the fords during the night. Scranton observed "the enemy in sight more or less all day, and fired some shots at long range, but we wasted no powder." The possession of the fords on Chickamauga Creek by the 2nd Michigan set the stage for a bloody fight the next day. Henry Hempstead of Scranton's regiment explained that he observed that the enemy across from Glass Mill seemed to be stronger than his regiment and as a result those assigned to guard the ford did not confront the enemy across the creek. "We contented ourselves with picketing the road … the roar of battle two or three miles to our left was terrific." Henry Hempstead correctly identified the size of enemy across the creek and by the end of the day his regiment would be opposite the bulk of Wheeler's cavalry corps.[14]

Major Leonidas Scranton's 2nd Michigan Cavalry battled Wheeler's cavalry at Glass Mill (*History of Michigan at Chickamauga*, 1899).

Meanwhile, Rosecrans fought to a draw on September 19, but successfully formed a solid north-south line along La Fayette Road. The day's fighting was hard, but Rosecrans was in a familiar position. His situation was similar to the battles at Iuka, Corinth and Stones River. He fought hard the first day and developed a strong defensive position which had yielded successes in the past. Learning from his near disastrous experience at Stones River, Rosecrans dispatched his supply trains to Chattanooga and his trains near the front consisted only of ammunition wagons and ambulances. Rosecrans met with his top commanders in the evening and decided to contract the Federal line further northward. While this decision would test the command abilities of the cavalry officers on the southern flank, Rosecrans felt confident the next day's battle would end as his previous battles.[15]

Finally, Edward McCook's Third Brigade, commanded by Colonel Louis Watkins, began moving some 400 sick soldiers to the rear. Watkins moved the sick, wounded and prisoners through to rear from Winston's and upon his arrival at Stevens' Gap, he found that he was ordered to Crawfish Springs. This order would to result in a tough fight for Watkins on September 21.[16]

The Final Day: The Engagement at Glass Mill

"The sun arose over the battlefield like a sea of fire," wrote G. W. Baum, 2nd Indiana Cavalry, and a heavy fog draped the landscape. September 20 would be a pivotal day in the life of William Rosecrans and a disastrous day for the Army of the Cumberland. For the Union cavalry, the day held an important engagement between Joseph Wheeler's cavalry corps and George Crook's Second Brigade under command of Colonel Eli Long. So far, Robert Mitchell had successfully moved McCook's division into position along the southern flank of the army. Louis Watkins's brigade, remained separated from the main cavalry column, and Robert Minty's brigade protected the Union left flank. This left three Union brigades, Campbell's, Ray's, and Long's (which would soon arrive), in position around Crawfish Springs. Campbell's and Ray's brigade were part of Edward McCook's First Division, but during the day, McCook split the command responsibilities. McCook would directly command the 9th Pennsylvania (left), 1st Wisconsin (right), and 2nd Indiana (reserve) cavalries which were stationed along the left of the Union defense near Crawfish Springs and loosely connected with John Wilder's mounted infantry. McCook's command held a position on the northern portion of Mitchell's defensive line and his men were stretched because Wilder had moved closer to Widow Glenn's House at the end of the fighting the day before. Mitchell directly commanded the remainder of the cavalry in line "farther to the right." Mitchell placed one of Archibald Campbell's regiments, 2nd Michigan Cavalry, under his command and he also commanded the 2nd Tennessee. Overnight, Archibald Campbell (in command of only two regiments) was released from duty in Dry Valley and rode with the 1st Tennessee and 4th Indiana cavalries to a ridge a mile or so to the south of Crawfish Springs, protecting the southern-most most flank of the Federal army. The 2nd Michigan was placed in front of Crawfish Springs and would be the first Union cavalry regiment involved in a fight later that morning. Crook with Long's brigade had yet to arrive at Crawfish Springs.[17]

During the evening of September 19, John C. Breckinridge's infantry division, which had been on the east side of Chickamauga Creek near Crawfish Springs, moved closer to the main infantry battle and Wheeler replaced him along the Confederate left flank. Wheeler had been given orders to connect with Longstreet's left flank and "to attack the enemy at every opportunity which presented itself." These orders set the stage for a significant cavalry fight near the ford at Glass Mill. Glass Mill was located on Chickamauga Creek about two miles south of Lee and Gordon's Mill at a series of deep bends in the creek. The mill, a multistory building, was used to grind grain for the local farmers. About three-fourths of a mile west of the ford lay the Glenn farm with outbuildings in the middle of several cleared fields. The day before, Negley's division (John Beatty's, Timothy Stanley's and William Sirwell's brigades) held the Union position on the west side of Chickamauga Creek facing D. H. Hill's Corps on the east side of the creek. The Union infantry brigades held position at Glass Mill

Part 3—Battle of Chickamauga

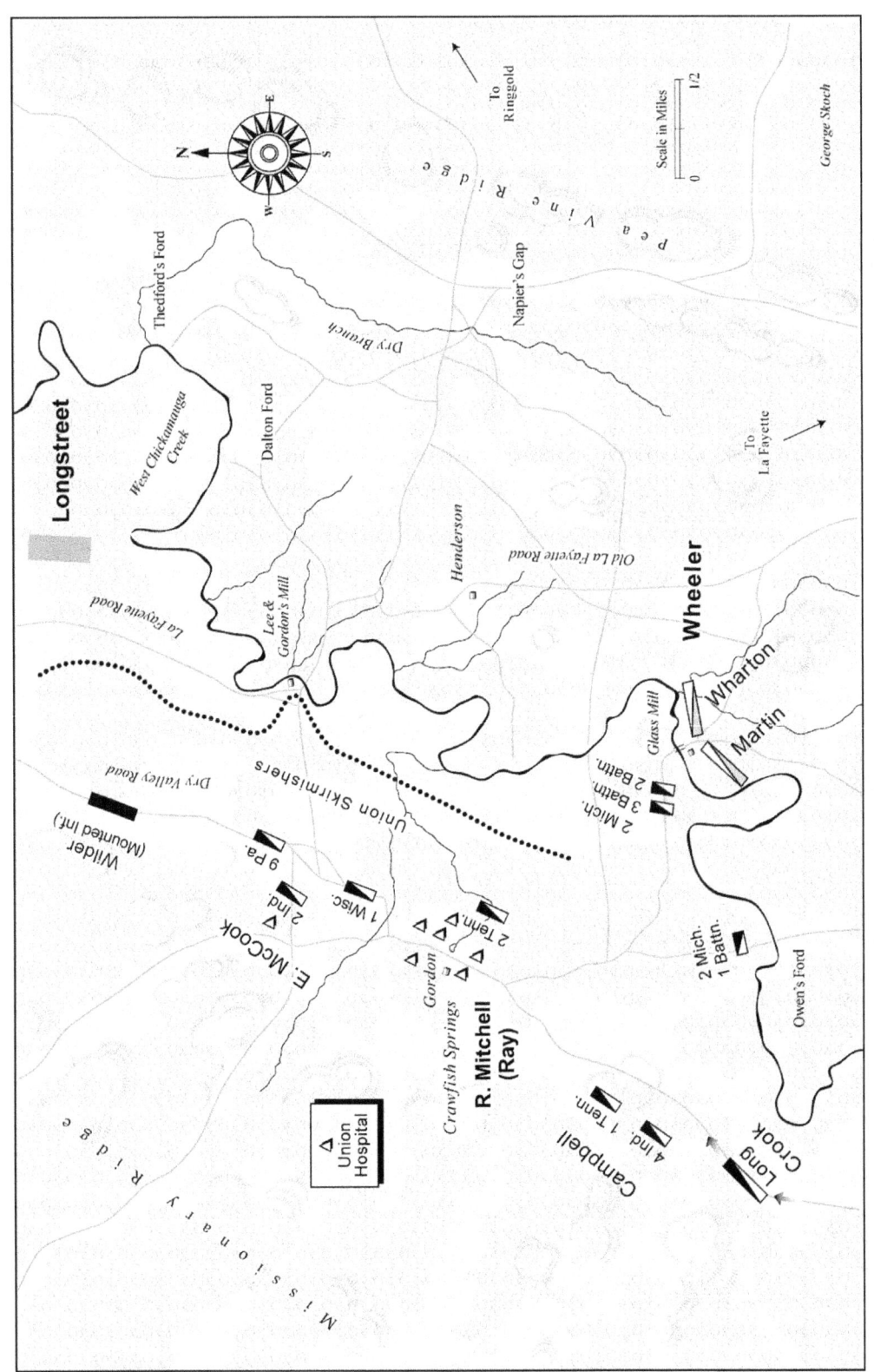

Union cavalry position near Crawfish Springs: Morning September 20 (Archibald Campbell's regiments held the Union right flank and would later move into Dry Valley. Eli Long's brigade arrived at Crawfish Springs around 9:00 a.m.).

and Crawfish Springs until late in the afternoon when they marched northward just as the Southern infantry also moved north. The respective cavalries of Wheeler and Mitchell moved into position opposite the crossing at Glass Mill. The Union cavalry protected the north and west side of Chickamauga Creek where the land jutted forward. Much of McCook's cavalry brigade held a position slightly north and east of Crawfish Springs and was the closest cavalry force to Wilder's mounted infantry which held the southern flank of Sheridan's division.[18]

The location of the hospitals at Crawfish Springs proved to be a problem for Rosecrans. When the hospitals were established, no one expected that the battle would be pulled to the north and this stretched the Union line which was anchored by the hospitals on the south. In addition, there was such a scarcity of clean water due to the drought and Crawfish Springs offered the most valuable supply needed by the surgeons. Historian David A. Rubenstein also noted that, tactically, once the fighting started there was little opportunity to move the hospitals because when the casualties began arriving, the medical staff needed to be prepared to receive them. An important question during the fighting on September 20 for the cavalry commanders was whether their duty centered on protecting the hospitals or joining in the desperate fighting to the north.[19]

The 2nd Michigan Cavalry was in line at daylight on September 20 and skirmished with Colonel Thomas Harrison's Confederate cavalry at the ford near Glass Mill. Amidst the thick fog, the 2nd Michigan had orders to stand "to horse" until after daylight. The Second and Third Battalions claimed the ford from the 8th Texas Cavalry during the early skirmishing and exchanged fire with the enemy throughout the morning. The 2nd Michigan's First Battalion guarded another ford about three-quarters of a mile west, Owen's Ford, but the Second and Third Battalions would have a busy day. The men of the 2nd Michigan thought all was quiet and they were satisfied they had repulsed the Southern attempts at capturing the ford. The Union cavalrymen moved back away from the ford after pushing some of the Confederate pickets away earlier in the morning. The Federal cavalry moved back about a quarter of a mile to the edge of some cleared fields, equal distance between the ford and the Glenn farmstead directly west. The noise from the main battle reached the cavalry at Glass Mill at nine o'clock. Sergeant Henry Mortimer Hempstead, 2nd Michigan Cavalry, was settling down for breakfast when Colonel Thomas Harrison again moved his Southern cavalry toward the Union position across the ford at Glass Mill, but this time the advance was made in force. About 10:00 a.m., the Confederates reappeared intent on joining in the general Confederate attack. Hempstead exclaimed the attack began when artillery shells landed in his midst. Hempstead recorded in his diary, "I got our mess coffee pot filled and nearly boiled when just as the Captain was inquiring if my coffee was done we were diluted with three or four shells in rapid succession from a battery at very short range, being located just back of the mill and evidently aiming at our camp fire.... [We] had retreated a few steps after the company when another shell burst close to or directly in the fire scattering the brands in every direction."[20]

Captain Benjamin White's battery of Southern artillery (two 3-inch Parrott cannons and two 12-pound Howitzers) began firing and the Union cavalry skirmishers were driven back to the main line under a hail of grape and canister. It initially appeared that a single regiment of the enemy attempted to push the Federal pickets away from the river. The 2nd Michigan's Second Battalion retreated back to the center of the farm/plantation and gained some protection by "the house, cabins and corncribs and some trees." Major Leonidas R.

Scranton, 2nd Michigan, observing his Second Battalion being flanked by a group of a hundred Confederates who had crossed the creek, sent forward the Third Battalion, and he was able to drive the Texans back across the creek. The initial Confederate attackers fell back under the protection of their guns, but the Michigan cavalry quickly headed for the rear as "a strong reenforcement again pursued us through the fields and beyond the farm building, but as we got beyond the range of their battery we rallied and held them back until we were reinforced, when we chased them back again." Thomas Colman, 11th Texas, wrote in a letter after the battle that Union cavalry charged like "so many devils." After the initial exchange, Wheeler began his attack with Thomas Harrison's full brigade—3rd Confederate, 3rd Kentucky, 4th Tennessee, 8th Texas, and 11th Texas; and shortly thereafter Wheeler added in entire cavalry corps of 6,800 men into the fight—Martin's and Wharton's cavalry divisions. Colonel Charles C. Crews, a pre-war Georgia physician, moved his brigade to support Harrison's attack. Crews' command included an Alabama regiment, Malone's, and three Georgia regiments, 2nd, 3rd, and 4th, and brought Wharton's total number of men to about 4,400. Will Martin's division, John T. Morgan's and A. A. Russell's brigades, moved in the rear of Wharton's division until there was room to maneuver to the left. Then, the Confederates advanced across a broad front. Hempstead exclaimed, "Again, they came on with augmented force and swept us before them. We made a stand in the open fields.... We looked around and found on our rear and on our flanks a strong force of cavalry had come up and formed along the edge of the woods, and as our battery was making considerable noise we hoped to hold the force in our front." Scranton had just observed the arrival of Eli Long's brigade riding hard to join in the fight.[21]

An 1894 image of the western view of the landscape at Glass Mill. At the time of the battle there was a road running near the woods on the left, and the worn traces of it appear in the picture. The views are taken facing west about 150 yards from Glass Mill. (Louisiana State University, Special Collections: Chickamauga and Chattanooga National Military Park (Ga. and Tenn.) Commission: Louisiana Committee Photographs (Mss. 4504), Louisiana and Lower Mississippi Valley Collections, LSU Libraries, Baton Rouge, Louisiana).

Eli Long's Brigade Joins the Fight

The day began very early for George Crook and Eli Long. William Sinclair sent orders at 2 a.m. directing Crook to hurry his command to Crawfish Springs. When Crook arrived at Crawfish Springs he met with Robert Mitchell, a commander for which he had little respect, but Mitchell "wasn't afraid to fight," exclaimed Crook. Mitchell immediately ordered Crook to Glass Mill about two miles from headquarters at Crawfish Springs to reinforce Scranton's 2nd Michigan. Mitchell, with part of McCook's cavalry, remained at Crawfish Springs in defense of the hospitals and large flank south of the Federal infantry. Crook took a section of the Chicago Board of Trade Artillery over his objections and took the road around a juniper thicket to find the 2nd Michigan hotly engaged and falling back. The troopers of Crook's command did not know the nature of their opponents as they entered the fight. William Crane, 4th Ohio, wrote in his diary: "We knew not how strong, but supposed this force to be the cavalry." Lieutenant Colonel Elijah Watts, 2nd Kentucky, noted the sound of cannonading greeted Long's advancing cavalry as it moved toward Glass Mill.[22]

Elijah Watts explained that along the road to Crawfish Springs the column was peppered by gunfire from "small bodies of rebel cavalry repeatedly attacked along our right, and it became necessary to detach small parties every little while to drive them away." The 4th Ohio Cavalry handled much of this duty as the column hurried to the meeting with Mitchell. Along the way, a bushwhacker had taken aim at the color bearer of the 2nd Kentucky Cavalry and as the column advanced, a shot rang out. "[I]t selected the color bearer in troop 'C' for a target, passed carefully through his hat and buried itself in the flag staff," recalled Watts. Crook's Second Brigade was commanded by Eli Long, and unfortunately, both of these commanders provided woefully inadequate reports of their actions on September 20 in which Wheeler succeeded in sending them to the rear. Equally unfortunate, none of the regimental commanders of this brigade filed after-action reports.[23]

George Crook arrived at Crawfish Springs at 9:00 a.m. with the 1st Ohio, 3rd Ohio, 4th Ohio, 2nd Kentucky and a section of artillery. Elijah Watts recalled he was "rested, hopeful, expectant, with an effort to be buoyant." Upon his arrival at Crawfish Springs, he was surprised to find the cavalry in columns standing "To Horse" and just waiting. "I was astonished that they were not in line of battle," wrote Watts. He wondered "why Gen. Mitchell had not moved forward with a heavy force and drive the rebels back." When Long's brigade was ordered forward, Watts turned to see the remaining cavalry still calmly waiting by their horses. Watts recalled that Stanley was sick and in an ambulance bound for Nashville and wrote, "[I]f he was in command things would have been different." Upon reaching the fields near Glass Mill, the 2nd Kentucky passed some Michigan troopers who remarked they were in for a hot time.[24]

Crook found the 2nd Michigan being pressed as Wheeler brought the weight of his cavalry corps to bear on Scranton's regiment. Scranton's First Battalion hurried from Owen's Ford to join the rest of the regiment as the fight intensified. Scranton told Crook upon his arrival that the woods ahead were full of Confederates. Once Crook arrived the Union troopers began again pushing toward the ford, but first, Long had to interpose his relieving force between the 2nd Michigan and the advancing Confederate cavalry—a tricky maneuver. The 2nd Kentucky Cavalry first took up a position on the right side of the road and after advancing a short distance switched to the left side of the road. The three Ohio regiments dismounted and moved to the right of the 2nd Kentucky which remained mounted. A two-gun section

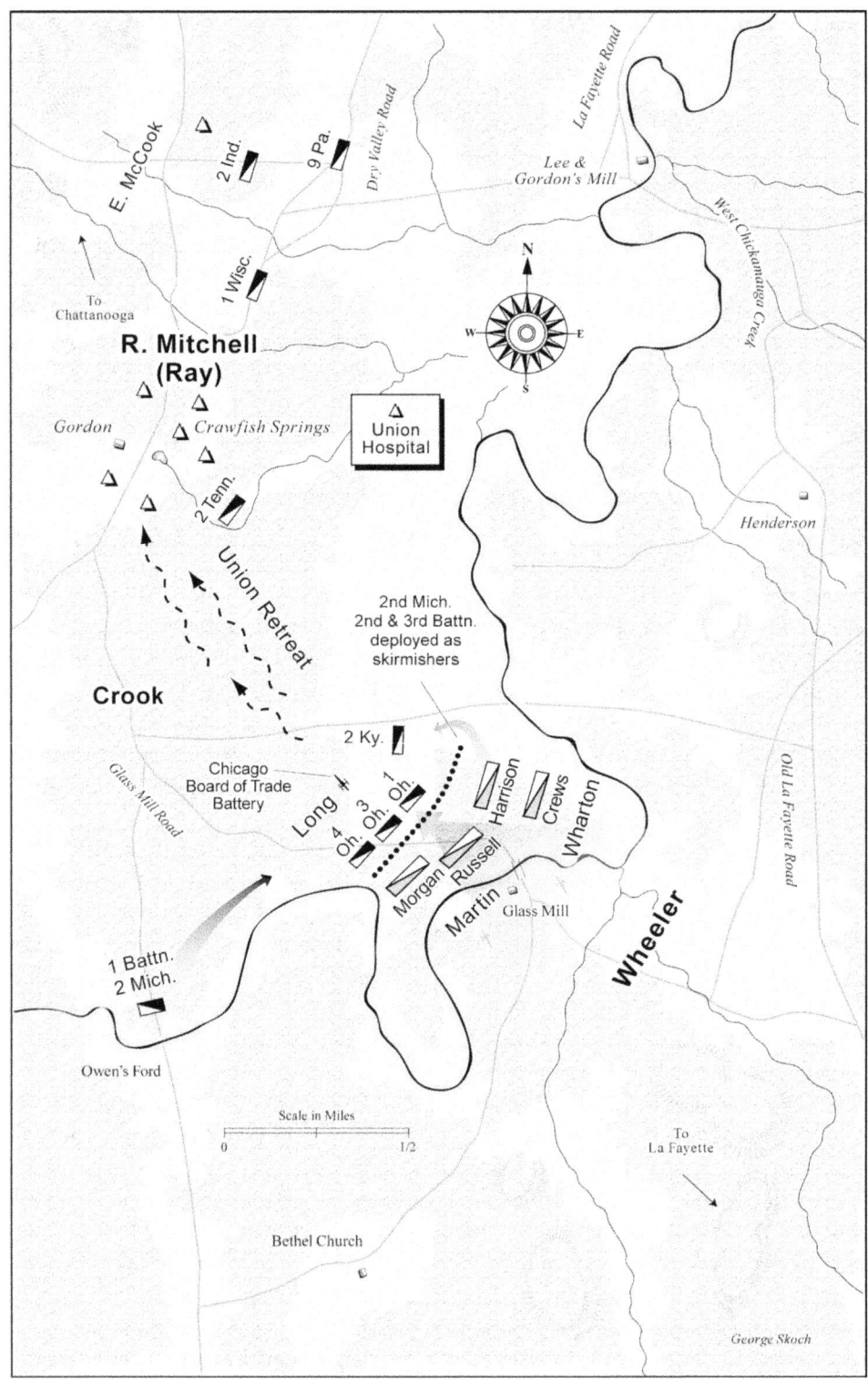

Battle at Glass Mill.

of Chicago Board of Trade horse artillery followed the cavalry and unlimbered and began shelling the advancing enemy. The 2nd Kentucky moved slightly forward of the section of artillery on a hill to the left of the guns with "colors flying, guidons, as well as the regimental colors." Watts exclaimed, "There is an immense panorama spread out before us ... but only God knew what was before us." Indeed, the battle had already begun when Long's cavalry arrived. Franklin Moyer, 3rd Ohio Cavalry, wrote in a letter after the fight: "Before I had seen a rebel and before our regiment had fired a gun, I was struck in the face with a musket ball." The new Union line formed about one-half mile from the Chickamauga Creek and the Confederate battery across the river began firing at the newly arrived Union guns. The fields ahead of Long's cavalry "swarmed with rebel troops." Wheeler noted, "Warm skirmishing commenced." Crook and Long mistook the dismounted cavalry for Hindman's infantry but it was Wheeler's dismounted cavalry that advanced on the Union position. Hindman's infantry had been operating the vicinity the day before and, thus, the Union officers concluded the dismounted cavalry attack came from infantry. Wheeler believed he tricked Long and Crook into thinking the Confederate cavalry was going to attack the flank, but the attack continued across a broad front. Wheeler saw "the enemy wavered. We charged him." The 2nd Michigan ceased its withdrawal upon Crook's arrival and moved to the right of Long's reinforcements extending the flank to meet Wheeler's attack. Scranton observed the reinforcements on his left, Long's brigade, being forced back, leaving him in his original predicament. Next, a company on the left of Henry Hempstead's company "crumbled and broke for the trees" and then Hempstead's company retreated. Scranton's men continued to fall back and he ordered the First Battalion, still firing away, to move back also, but two companies failed to receive the order. Companies A and F unleashed a vicious enfilading volley into the pursuing Confederates who were intent on pushing forward. Soon these two companies hurried to the rear and the entire regiment joined in the retreat to Crawfish Springs.[25]

Captain William Crane, 4th Ohio Cavalry, recorded in his journal that the Ohio cavalry regiments dismounted and advanced to meet the oncoming Confederate attack. The 4th Ohio was greeted with an intense fire from the enemy. The 1st Ohio had the duty of guarding the section of the Chicago Board of Trade Artillery. Vicious volleys were unleashed by both sides and the lines approached. Crane wrote, "It was tough work, the enemy was very strong, and our lines were slowly driven back.... Many were struck dead & large numbers of wounded carried to the rear until all the ambulances were filled." Crane observed that the 4th Ohio and 2nd Kentucky cavalries took the brunt of the attack, and while much criticism resulted from the presence of the Chicago Board of Trade artillery, many of the accounts praised the results of this section during the fight. Benjamin Nourse recorded in his diary that the section of artillery reached the battlefield—"[W]e got into it quickly and in less than 10 minutes lost all the horses belonging to the cannoneers.... Oh, the horror of this day and night."[26]

Much of the result of the fight came from a confusing order. Sergeant John Chapin, 1st Ohio Cavalry, was dismounted and watched as the Confederates charged forward. At about 300 yards, an officer from Crook's staff rode to the 1st Ohio and exclaimed, "Prepare to charge!" Lieutenant Colonel Valentine Cupp, commanding the regiment because Colonel Beroth Eggleston was absent recruiting in Ohio, immediately ordered the 1st Ohio to "sling carbines and draw sabres." The 1st Ohio Cavalry prepared for a suicidal charge into a much superior force. Chapin told a fellow trooper, "If the charge is made not a man can come out alive." Crook saw something was wrong with the 1st Ohio and rode to Cupp and explained the order was to "prepare to *resist* the charge," not to make a charge. Crook remained close to the troops during the fight and at one point he was almost captured by the advancing Confederate soldiers. By the time the correct order reached the Ohioans, the 1st Ohio was some thirty yards in front of the artillery. The regiment was ordered to turn and ride back to the original line, resulting in two turns, during which time the Confederates were constantly firing and charging. The Union artillery fired until the Confederates were 50 yards away and quickly limbered and made its escape. With the artillery safely away, Cupp ordered, "Fours, left about, march!" But before the turn was complete Cupp was shot in the lower abdomen, mortally wounding him. Cupp was gathered off the field and moved to Lee's mansion at Crawfish Springs. As for Chapin, he wrote, just as the about-face was made "a Confederate officer had the impudence to shoot me with a revolver."[27]

Watts' 2nd Kentucky held the Union left flank during the raging battle. He soon found the Rebel battery exploding with "shot and shell" on his position and Confederate soldiers steadily trotting forward in the attack across a harvested cornfield. Wheeler advanced a line of skirmishers followed by a line of dismounted cavalry, and behind them, a second line of dismounted cavalry. Watts declared the "scene was one of a lifetime, terrific, awe inspiring, frightful!" He bitterly recalled that the thin line of Union cavalry faced the enemy while Mitchell's cavalry remained in the rear—"idle troopers waiting orders." The Kentuckians leveled their carbines and the Chicago Board of Trade fired double canister, momentarily staggering the advance which recovered and steadily moved forward. As the Confederate lines moved closer, the Southern artillery shifted its fire away the Union artillery and focused on the line of Union cavalry. The hammering of the Union carbines echoed across the fields "while the enemy,— I see them now! came steadily for our position, with great gallantry." Many of the troops that advanced on the 2nd Kentucky were armed with muzzle loading Enfield carbines and the two lines exchanged fire but the Federal line held. The Confederate line moved closer and the two lines prepared to fight hand-to-hand. Then, Watts noticed Troop B and D were forced back by the 8th Texas Cavalry advancing from the northeast and instead of backing up, these two Kentucky cavalry companies attempted to turn to fall back. When they turned, they found they were more vulnerable to the Confederate attack and were doubled back. The line "folded like a knife." The Texas cavalry pushed forward turning the 2nd Kentucky's flank and this allowed the Confederate attack to surge ahead and the attack reached the left and rear of the Kentuckians. There was nothing left to do but attempt to save as many troopers as possible. Colonel Thomas Nicholas was in front of the regiment

Captain William Crane, 4th Ohio Cavalry, recorded the fight at Glass Mill: "[O]ur lines were slowly driven back" (Lucien Wulsin, *The Story of the Fourth Regiment Ohio Cavalry*, 1912).

maintaining a stable line while waving his sabre over his head when the regiment folded. Watts also recorded he received Crook's order carried by Captain Crane to prepare to charge Wheeler's cavalry just as his regiment was overrun. As the enemy surged ahead, Watts described, "[T]he enemy like an avalanche, sweeping everything from their path." Henry Hempstead, 2nd Michigan, wrote that the 2nd Kentucky Cavalry was sent retreating from the battlefield, "Our 'brave' Kentuckians had after short resistance fled in confusion. I attempted to reach Capt. Johnson again but he had already comprehended the situation and the whole Company were breaking for the woods and liberty." The 2nd Kentucky recorded the greatest losses of the day suffering eleven men killed, another fifty wounded and two missing.[28]

The 2nd Michigan cavalry, armed with Colt revolving rifles, continued to fall back along the right flank of Long's brigade and Henry Hempstead described: "On reaching the wood and finding we were in danger of being immediately enveloped we each took shelter of a large tree and emptied the five chambers of our guns into a swarm of the enemy at a very short range, and the commotion we created satisfied us we had done them some damage. We did not tarry to investigate as the enemy were closing in on all sides but one." Hempstead stopped to aid some wounded Michigan men. Soon, he was greeted with a "clamorous order to surrender. On looking up I was dismayed to see within twenty yards a score or more of the enemy, but as all of them appeared to have no loads in their guns, a few trying to load as they ran, I concluded it best not to go to Andersonville just yet.... I sprang forward ... and soon put a knoll and some bushes between me and the nearest Rebs.... I had been on the run either retreating or pursuing the retreating Enemy almost half the time for the last three hours ... and was glad to reach my trusty horse again."[29]

John A. Wyeth, 4th Alabama Cavalry, described the Confederate side of the fight. The attack by the Confederate cavalry started in earnest when White's artillery opened up on Long's men. The men of 4th Alabama had a good position to watch the fight because they had been ordered to provide security for the battery. "The Federal guns about five hundred yards away soon got the range and threw a lot of shrapnel," wrote Wyeth. Captain D. Coleman, 11th Texas Cavalry, wrote that he though the attack would stall, but the collapse of the right and left flanks of the Union line gave energy to a renewed attack until the entire Federal line retreated. Just as the Union soldiers mistook Wheeler's cavalry for infantry, Colman mistakenly believed the Union cavalry had been supplemented with mounted infantry.[30]

George Guild, 4th Tennessee (CSA) also recalled the battle at Glass Mill. "We moved in column down the road leading to the river and, fording the stream near the mill, formed a line of battle in regular infantry style in the edge of low, level beech woods, and, placing our skirmishers a short distance in front, advanced through the woods. The enemy knew that we were coming and kept up an incessant shelling of the woods, some of our men being injured by limbs of trees torn off by the cannon balls. We had advanced but a short distance when the skirmishers became hotly engaged, which was the signal for a rapid advance, and we swept through the woods, driving the enemy before us. They rallied at a fence at the edge of the woodland, delivered an effective volley, and fell back across a little field to a new line behind a fence and on the edge of another woodland along an eminence where their artillery was planted. As our line emerged from the wood into the open space this battery, shotted with grape, and the line behind the fence, armed with seven-shooting Spencer rifles, opened on us, and a perfect hailstorm of deadly missiles filled the air. Being commanded to lie down, we did so for a few moments, and then arose and charged across the field. Just here we sustained our heaviest loss, and in a few moments the Fourth Tennessee had forty men shot down as we arose from the ground. As we rushed across the field the line sustaining the battery broke; and as they ran off many were killed and wounded, two or three hundred of them surrendering in a body. We were struck here with the gallantry of a Federal officer. He was on horseback and with drawn saber was attempting to hold his men to their position. He was killed, and his body fell into our hands. Papers upon his person indicated that he was colonel of the First Ohio Regiment."

Guild would later discover the fight at Glass Mill resulted from the need for the Union troops to protect the hospitals at Crawfish Springs. Guild recalled the Southern cavalry could not understand why the Federals were making such a determined stand so far from the infantry. He continued: "We have learned since that we were fighting the division of Gen. George Crook. Both sides lost quite a number in killed and wounded. Where a stand had been made they were thick upon the ground. The line of attack for a mile was well defined; but, really, though we gained the fight and drove them from the field, our loss in killed and wounded was as great as theirs."[31]

During the battle, Lieutenant W. L. Curry's, 1st Ohio Cavalry, horse was shot and killed under him and at his side Sergeant C. S. Irwin had been desperately wounded. Irwin was loaded into an ambulance and hurried to the rear. Curry mounted Irwin's horse which he credited for saving him from capture, and he described the gruesome condition of the horse: "I remember that Irwin's saddle was covered with blood, and he had bled so profusely that the blood ran down both his horse's fore legs and down over the hoofs."[32]

Crook was just outmanned as he engaged Martin's and Wharton's divisions. Long's brigade of 900 was no match for two Confederate cavalry divisions. Crook lost 100 of his men in a fifteen-minute interval and he felt many were lost trying to save the guns of the Chicago Board of Trade that Crook had not wanted on the field. He had been overruled by Mitchell who insisted the artillery be moved forward. Eli Long, who was generally not given to discussing his actions on the field, recorded in his autobiography that he was ordered to protect the artillery battery which caused his cavalry to be placed in a position of facing overwhelming odds and that Long's cavalry was unsupported by the remainder of Mitchell's cavalry division. Among the dead was Captain James Hawley, 2nd Michigan Cavalry, who died while trying to rally the Federal cavalry during the attack. Hawley was acting assistant inspector general on Stanley's staff and he had been married for only two months when he was killed. Hawley graduated from college just after the fall of Fort Sumter and joined the army. Only a few weeks earlier, Hawley had located an important crossing on the Tennessee River near Bridgeport. Not only was Hawley active and on the field during the battle, Major William H. Sinclair, Stanley's Assistant Adjutant-General and *de facto* chief of staff, had two horses shot under him in the fight. Robert Mitchell remained at his headquarters at Crawfish Springs as the battle played out at Glass Mill. While many involved in the fight criticized Mitchell for not bringing reinforcements, Mitchell realized he had hospitals, supply trains and a large flank to cover with his cavalry.[33]

Crook rode to the rear with Long's retreating cavalry looking for help, but he got none from Mitchell. Crook found the remainder of the cavalry still standing in a field at Crawfish Springs. Long's brigade fell in line with the rest of the Union cavalry and hastily formed a battle line at the rear of the field providing an excellent field of fire in anticipation of Wheeler's attack which never came. William Crane, 4th Ohio Cavalry, wrote in diary: "When our brig. retired from before Hindman it was supposed that the cav. would follow up. Mitchell formed his lines in a large open field back of the Spring, determined to charge them with sabre—but they did not come." It was unclear what Mitchell intended to do to further delay an attack by Wheeler's division, but George Crook wrote in his memoirs that Mitchell abdicated the arrangement of the Federal cavalry's defense after the fight to Crook. Crook had little respect for Mitchell and in his memoirs Crook explained that after Long's retreat he approached Mitchell. Crook described the scene with Mitchell who asked him to oversee the defenses at Crawfish Springs: "General, you are military man, I wish you would take charge and straighten things out, and make the necessary dispositions." Crook wrote that some of the cavalry were only a few yards from wooded areas which left them vulnerable to a surprise attack from the enemy. Crook re-formed the battle line along a slight ridge facing an open field. Wheeler did not follow up his attack from Glass Mill and Mitchell remained in line throughout the afternoon. On the Southern side of the field, Wheeler had just received conflicting orders—one set from Bragg ordering him to Lee and Gordon's Mill and the other from Longstreet telling him to move up and support his infantry. Wheeler chose the former; and fortunately for the

The Union cavalry moved into position around the hospitals at Crawfish Springs, an important source of water (National Archives).

Union cavalry, Wheeler decided to backtrack to the east side of Chickamauga Creek and move northward on the eastern bank, a more time-consuming route.[34]

While the fight at Glass Mill was taking place, a dramatic turn of events occurred on the main battlefield. The Confederate infantry penetrated Rosecrans's main line near the Brotherton Farm and rolled up the brigades on both sides. Bragg had just won the Battle of Chickamauga. Wheeler's orders to ride to Lee and Gordon's Mill and to attack the enemy, spared Crook and Mitchell from what promised to be a bloody fight. This fight at Glass Mill resulted in a loss in Long's cavalry brigade of 122 men killed, wounded or missing including the death of Lieutenant Colonel Valentine Cupp. In addition, the 2nd Michigan reported—1 killed in action (Hawley of Stanley's staff), six wounded and three captured. The action would become known as the Battle at Glass Mill, but many in the Union cavalry referred to it as the Battle of Crawfish Springs.[35]

The Rest of the Cavalry Division

The fighting was over around noon at Glass Mill. An hour later, Colonel P. Sidney Post's infantry brigade which held the gaps around McLemore's Cove began arriving at Crawfish Springs. Post, in possession of XX Corps' supply train, had been ordered to the join the main body of the army. Post's column did not complete its arrival until 3:00 p.m. when Colonel Michael Gooding's trailing 22nd Indiana Infantry arrived. Once Post's infantry arrived, it moved into the forward position as the cavalry moved to support the tired foot soldiers. Edward McCook's two brigades remained unengaged as Long's brigade and the 2nd Michigan battled two Confederate cavalry divisions. At Crawfish Springs the regiments of Daniel Ray's Second Cavalry Brigade, 2nd Tennessee and 1st Wisconsin, also had a fairly uneventful day. The regiments remained in line of battle throughout the day until the withdrawal of the entire army later in the day. David Briggs, commanding the 2nd Indiana Cavalry, explained in his report that his regiment "was held in reserve for a saber charge on the enemy." Charles Perry Goodrich, 1st Wisconsin, wrote to his wife, revealing the disparity of the action of the Union cavalry: "As usual our cavalry was found in line, in the rear." Robert Merrill, 1st Wisconsin, recorded in his diary: "our Regt was drawn up as skirmishers about 10 or 11 a.m. about a mile from the fight. Were moved about a good deal having filed to the right & we moved up to where we waited." Edward McCook, commanding the cavalry to the north of Crawfish Springs, kept a steady hand on the three regiments he commanded during the day and the 9th Pennsylvania Cavalry maintained a line of communication with Wilder's infantry until about 11:00 a.m. In addition, the 9th Pennsylvania pushed skirmishers ahead as far as Lee and Gordon's Mill and the pickets had orders that if the Confederates attempted to cross at that location to delay them as long as possible before falling back. The skirmishers exchanged shots with the enemy throughout the morning. At noon, the enemy began crossing in front of the Pennsylvanians who held their line until the afternoon, and the men watched the enemy moving on the other side of Chickamauga Creek throughout the day. Mitchell had ordered McCook not to cross the creek and this left McCook's cavalry in a defensive line until mid-afternoon. He reported: "About 3 o'clock in the afternoon General McCook's adjutant-general [Gates Thruston] met me with an order for all the cavalry to come up at once, as the mounted infantry had been compelled to fall back, and the enemy was turning his right." McCook mounted his cavalry and began to ride north when he was overtaken by Mitchell's staff officer, Captain McCormick, who countermanded Thruston's order. McCormick told McCook that Mitchell ordered him to move to Crawfish Springs to reinforce the command there. McCormick told McCook that the enemy had attacked there and "were pressing us hard." However, this last comment appears to be without merit, because Post's infantry held the forward position at this point and he reported no fighting at Crawfish Springs, and neither did the 2nd Tennessee or 1st Wisconsin cavalries, the other cavalry regiments there.[36]

The surgeons in the Union hospitals were having doubts of their own about the positions of the hospitals. At 2:00 p.m., the ranking medical officer at Crawfish Springs, Alonzo Phelps of XXI Corps, sent orders to the medical directors of the six hospitals that the communications had been lost with their respective infantry commanders and Phelps decided to start moving as many wounded toward Chattanooga as possible, either on foot on in wagons. The wounded had stopped arriving at the hospitals at noon after the Confederate breakthrough and this sent an ominous signal to those at Crawfish Springs. Phelps knew that "our situation became very insecure" and he ordered the withdrawal. In addition, Phelps and his other medical directors had to make the painful decision of which medical personnel and wounded to leave behind.[37]

Mitchell pulled his cavalry closer to Crawfish Springs and as a result became more dangerously separated from the main body of the army. Just as Mitchell ordered all of McCook's cavalry to Crawfish Springs, Longstreet was pleading with Bragg for more troops to push into Dry Valley and at 3:00 p.m. Wheeler's cavalry began moving west at Lee and Gordon's Mill

Wheeler's cavalry crossed Chickamauga Creek at Lee and Gordon's Mill at 3:00 p.m. (National Archives).

after moving from Glass Mill along the eastern side of Chickamauga Creek. Fortunately for Mitchell, Bragg denied Longstreet's request and Wheeler's advance only weakly pushed forward. John Allan Wyeth, 4th Alabama Cavalry, explained that the Wheeler's cavalry took an unnecessarily long circuitous route along the east side of the Chickamauga Creek to reach Lee and Gordon's Mill. Wyeth's regiment moved on the extreme left of Wheeler's command and offered very little in regard to offensive action. Wyeth recalled that his regiment marched over ground which showed the effects of a rapid retreat. He declared, "We kept on in vain pursuit for several hours, and then the horse-holders came up, and we mounted and rode to Crawfish Spring, where the enemy had established their headquarters at first. Here we captured their camp and hospitals, and a lot of prisoners, mostly wounded. It was now dark."[38]

While Edward McCook remained with the 9th Pennsylvania, along the southern flank, Colonel Archibald Campbell waited with the 1st Tennessee and 4th Indiana about a mile south of Crawfish Springs. Campbell's other regiment, 2nd Michigan, was commanded directly by Mitchell and had been involved in the Glass Mill fight earlier in the day. Campbell reported that the 9th Pennsylvania had been under McCook's command in front of Lee and Gordon's Mill and had not been "seriously attacked." After 3:00 p.m., Mitchell ordered Campbell's 1st Tennessee and 4th Indiana cavalry into Chattanooga Valley to prevent the enemy from advancing on Chattanooga from the southwest along the Chattanooga Valley Road. When Campbell reached his new position, he observed many of Alexander McCook's retreating solders who told the cavalrymen about the events of the battle. The enemy had broken the main Union line and turned the right flank. Campbell appropriated a regiment of reorganized infantry and a battery of artillery and with his two cavalry regiments he established a solid defensive line. Campbell held this line as all the ambulances and wagon trains from Crawfish Springs and a column of walking wounded marched through on the way to Chattanooga. Campbell continued to establish order to the panicked troops from this position about six miles south of Chattanooga and at dusk, Mitchell sent word to Campbell to have the 2nd Michigan Cavalry, which saw so much action at Glass Mill, escort the wounded and wagon trains to Chattanooga.[39]

Lieutenant Colonel Roswell Russell, 9th Pennsylvania, on the most northern part of the cavalry line had a relatively uneventful time, only occasionally exchanging shots with the enemy. Captain Thomas McCahan's company was on picket duty and skirmished with Confederates until McCahan's pickets were pushed backed to the main line. McCahan rallied the skirmishers and fell back when the enemy advanced in force. McCahan wrote that the Confederates attacked the regiment but "we drove them back." Around 3:00 p.m. the 9th Pennsylvania Cavalry went in search of Sheridan's infantry, but the Pennsylvania cavalry found only enemy troops to the north—Colonel Robert Trigg's 1st Florida Cavalry (Dismounted) and 7th Florida Infantry, supported by artillery near the road. Russell dismounted his men and readied them to attack. Before the attack began, Russell received orders to return to Crawfish Springs. Mitchell would report after the battle that at 3:00 p.m. he was told that the Union right flank had been turned and "to fall back," but this was incorrect. Gates Thruston, Alexander McCook's chief of staff, had ordered him to move north and join in the battle.[40]

As Long's cavalry clashed with Wheeler around 11:00 a.m., other Union mounted troops had fights of their own. While the Federal cavalry held its position on the extreme right flank of the army, at 11:00 a.m. Wilder's mounted infantry, the next brigade to the north, accompanied by the 39th Indiana Mounted Infantry regiment attacked Brigadier General Arthur

Manigault's Alabama and South Carolina infantry brigade which had surged forward when the Union line broke. Wilder initially had good success with a flank attack on the two southern most regiments in the brigade, and Wilder wanted to push his attack forward. Wilder would explain, after the war, why he hesitated. After noon, he was approached by Assistant Secretary of War, Charles Dana, who had become separated from the headquarters staff. Dana described to Wilder that Rosecrans was thought to be dead and the army was in a state of panic. This caused Wilder to hesitate and then Dana demanded that Wilder escort him to Chattanooga. Wilder, unsure of the authority Dana had over him, relented and called off his attack; but, Dana would deny this and he explained that he told Wilder he had no authority over him.[41]

Mitchell's reluctance to move from Crawfish Springs stemmed from orders from Rosecrans and Garfield who told Mitchell to guard the hospitals at Crawfish Springs at all costs. The location had recently been Rosecrans' headquarters and seven of the army's hospitals were located near the springs. Mitchell's actions, or more correctly inaction, would come under severe scrutiny after the battle. About 3:00 p.m. Mitchell still held the cavalry in battle line waiting for another Confederate attack. Colonel Gates Thruston, Alexander McCook's chief of staff, reached Edward McCook and told him that Union "right had been turned," the Federal infantry was falling back. McCook began moving his cavalry join the battle. Another staff officer arrived with orders for Mitchell to move the cavalry north and join in the battle. Mitchell balked: "Not deeming an order of so important a nature as that, coming in such a manner, valid, I did not move, as I had been ordered in the morning to hold Crawfish Spring at all hazards, but sent staff officers to ascertain the position of affairs, and, if possible, communicate with either General McCook or Rosecrans. From them I learned that our right had been driven round and that everything on the right was moving toward Chattanooga up Chattanooga Valley. I therefore, after moving out all trains and loading into ambulances all wounded able to ride from the vicinity of my position." In fact, Mitchell was ordered to move north and join the battle twice during the day—at 11:00 a.m. and 3:00 p.m. Throughout the day along the main battle lines, a vicious battle raged as the Confederates broke the Union line and in the afternoon the battle centered at Snodgrass Farm where George Thomas pulled together a determined defense.[42]

Mitchell's Decisions Regarding the Use of the Cavalry

Mitchell faced many decisions when he learned the right flank had been turned and the entire Union army was retreating to Chattanooga. Once the Union line crumbled in the morning, it was difficult for commanders to get orders because of the confusion on the field. Now, Mitchell made a very difficult decision. He had orders to protect the seven hospitals but he needed to remain connected with army. A more difficult moral, ethical decision is hard to imagine. He was unable to get orders from Rosecrans, and he initially decided to remain in position around the hospitals. Later in the day, he decided to move with the army, abandoning the most severely wounded in the hospitals.

Mitchell had a very complex military problem. He had been given orders by Garfield to guard the hospitals before the battle; however, his immediate commanding officer ordered him twice during the day to join in the battle. He refused. Mitchell would be cited as having disobeyed direct orders during Alexander McCook's court of inquiry regarding McCook's actions during the battle, but no formal charges would ever be made against Mitchell. While Mitchell would state that he did not perceive the orders he received from McCook to be valid, everyone else did. Gates Thruston was the author of the orders and Mitchell had been told by Rosecrans that he was under McCook's command a couple of days before. Gates Thruston was an efficient, responsible officer and rising star in the Union army. Thruston gained prominence during the Battle of Stones River when he saved Alexander McCook's ammunition train by leading a mad dash across the countryside while pursued by John Wharton's cavalry. On the September 18, Thruston told Mitchell that he was ordered to close up on McCook's right and only two days earlier Mitchell was criticized by both McCook and Garfield for his poor communications. "General McCook has been anxious to open communication with you all day, and is now much relieved at receiving your courier. General Rosecrans is very particular that complete and speedy communication should be maintained. Several of your staff are here, not having been able to find you today." More orders followed that day when Thruston wrote: "General McCook directs me to state that it is absolutely necessary for you to dispatch a portion of your force down Chattanooga Valley to dispose of some rebel cavalry reported there."

During the court of inquiry, Thruston was asked: "Did General McCook, so far as you know, give any orders to the cavalry on his right after his own line broke on 20th? Answer. He did; to close up to the left and fill up the gap made by the withdrawal of General Sheridan. I assisted in person in placing the cavalry in position on the right (Wilder's brigade). I then proceeded to the commanding officer of the nearest cavalry division, and gave him an order in General McCook's name to close to the left, and endeavor to support our right. I sent this order in General McCook's name to General Mitchell (commanding the whole cavalry), by a staff officer. General Rosecrans had given General McCook permission to order the cavalry. General Mitchell replied twice that General Rosecrans had ordered him not to leave Crawfish Spring. There was a gap of a mile between the cavalry and Wilder's brigade (mounted infantry, which was immediately on our right). General Rosecrans told General Mitchell subsequently, in my presence, that he should have obeyed General McCook's order, and closed in to the left; that this was in accordance with the general understanding...."

Lieutenant Colonel Gates Thruston ordered Mitchell to move the Union cavalry onto the battlefield twice on September 20 (courtesy Tennessee State Library and Archives).

The findings of the court would clearly show Mitchell disobeyed orders which would have brought the cavalry into the fight. The court ruled: "[T]he senior officers of the cavalry were told they must take orders from him, though attend to their own business.... It is shown, too, that the cavalry did not obey General McCook's orders." Alexander McCook would simply say that the cavalry was not available to him and declined to obey his orders because Mitchell told him he was under orders from headquarters. Mitchell had selectively decided which orders to follow.[43]

The orders to which Mitchell adhered were written by Garfield in the early hours of September 20. The orders stated: "With your entire cavalry force adhere close to General McCook's right, sending patrols with all the wagon trains to the rear. You will defend the hospitals at all hazards. Cover also the closing up of Post's brigade, now on its march to join the main army. The general is dissatisfied that you do not report oftener." Garfield's order presumably came just after midnight because Mitchell hastily sent a return message at 2:00 a.m. about the dispositions of his command. At almost noon, Rosecrans again chastised Mitchell for his lack of communication: "The general commanding directs me to say that more frequent reports from you is a matter of duty. Send at once an intelligent officer with a squad of men to meet Crook, and report his position without delay." Mitchell responded to the last prompt for communication that he had repulsed Wheeler at Glass Mill. "General Crook has arrived and we are warmly engaged at the fords. They are trying to force a passage. We have repulsed them once since I wrote you last in regard to the fight this morning. General Crook says when he left Stevens' Gap Colonel Post had no orders to leave the gap."[44]

In Edward McCook's after-action report, he noted that he attempted to fulfill Thruston's afternoon orders but the order was overridden by Mitchell. Wilder's Brigade had already moved further to the left at 11:00 a.m. as Alexander McCook moved left and therefore Mitchell's command became further isolated. So, instead of moving in the direction of the fighting, Mitchell pulled McCook back to the main body of the cavalry and farther away from the battle. At 3:00 p.m., the body of Wheeler's cavalry had moved northward to Lee and Gordon's Mill and could not have been threatening Mitchell at Crawfish Springs. In addition, having communicated regularly with Thruston and McCook over the past two days, there can be little doubt that Mitchell knew he served under Alexander McCook's command. Certainly, in hindsight, Mitchell chose to stay away from the fighting and protect hospitals which might have been commendable; but he would abandon them in two hours. In addition, Mitchell pulled his cavalry back to Crawfish Springs under the guise to holding off a Confederate attack which did not take place. Wheeler would record that his cavalry gained possession of the Union hospitals "about dark" which would have been well after 6:00 p.m. In contrast, there are Union records which suggest the Confederate cavalry captured the hospitals just after 5:00 p.m. when the Union troops left. In addition, Wheeler reported his position that at 3:00 p.m. to be at Lee and Gordon's Mill and that he "vigorously assailed him. After a short time he commenced retreating in confusion. We followed as rapidly as possible, capturing about 1,000 prisoners, 20 wagons, and a large amount of arms and ordnance stores." This would suggest Wheeler's location was elsewhere and not at Crawfish Springs. Captain D. Coleman of Wheeler's cavalry recorded that his regiments moved to various locations and did not come under any fire for the rest of the day. Likewise, John Allan Wyeth, 4th Alabama Cavalry, would record that Wheeler searched for the enemy in vain in the afternoon, and then at sunset moved to Crawfish Springs and took possession the hospitals. Colonel Post who held the forward position at Crawfish Springs reported no casualties during the day and none of his regimental officers recorded any loses or accounts of skirmishes at the springs. In addition, the 9th Pennsylvania which held the northern most place in the Union cavalry line also reported no casualties in killed or wounded. The 1st Wisconsin and 2nd Tennessee, the next two regiments in line defending Crawfish Springs reported only a total one man killed and four wounded for the entire battle. This again suggests that Wheeler's attention in the afternoon was not directed toward Mitchell, but more likely he followed up the infantry attack gathering up stragglers along the way since no such losses occurred at Crawfish Springs. To make matter worse for Mitchell, he lost contact with the enemy to his front, and really did not know where his enemy was.[45]

On a positive note, Thurston's summary of the fighting on the afternoon of September 20 offered insight in the positive results of the mounted infantry attacks on the flank of the Southern infantry. At 11:00 a.m., Thurston hurried to Crawfish Springs with orders for Mitchell to move cavalry to the north and it was during this first attempt that Rosecrans' lines were penetrated by the Confederate attack. So, the need to close up on the right occurred before the crisis of the battle developed; however, Thurston's need for reinforcements was even more important at the second attempt at 3:00 p.m., after the Federal lines were broken. Thurston was unsuccessful in achieving this objective. The first time Mitchell was ordered to join in the main battle occurred when Wheeler attacked at Glass Mill and this might partially have justified Mitchell's refusal to move northward. However, Mitchell had only committed a third of his force to the Glass Mill engagement, and he kept two brigades unutilized with the fighting to the north or south. Thurston brought the 39th Indiana Mounted Infantry at 11:00 a.m. and in conjunction with Wilder's Mounted Infantry attacked the Confederate infantry pressing forward. Harrison made two attacks and claimed two hundred prisoners. Thurston's account demonstrated that the fighting was not over at this point in the day and the movement of the Federal cavalry could have resulted in some positive results had it moved to the battle.[46]

Neither can Mitchell explain his reluctance to move by waiting for the arrival Colonel Post's brigade, because he wrote a message after the Glass Mill fight that Post had no orders to move forward. To further cast doubt on Mitchell's efforts to stay connected with McCook's XX Corps and the main body of the army, Post reported, "Brigadier-General Mitchell informed me that all communication was cut off with Major-General McCook's corps, and that it was impossible to move to the point indicated in my orders. He therefore assumed command of my brigade and directed me to take a position to repel an attack which he apprehended on his front. After I had placed my men in position, being extremely anxious to rejoin the division, or, if that should be impossible, at least to inform my division and corps commanders of my arrival at Crawfish Spring, I dispatched Capt. Robert Hale, a resolute and discreet officer, to communicate with you, if possible, in which undertaking you are aware he was quite successful. Brigadier-General Mitchell being fully satisfied that direct communication could not be opened with Major-General McCook's corps, directed me to move back upon Chattanooga Creek along with his corps." In this thinly veiled indictment, Post echoes the point that a newly arrived infantryman could find a way to communicate with McCook, but Mitchell, with the most mobile force on the field, could not. It was routine for the cavalry commander to report to headquarters at regular intervals of thirty minutes or less during battles. If Mitchell had been sending regular communications, he should have been aware of the situation at army headquarters.[47]

The important question about Mitchell's decisions echoed from the pages of Marshall Thatcher's history of the 2nd Michigan Cavalry. "To guard the right was important, but they were ready and anxious to do more, and were kept further to the right than they were actually needed. Campbell's discovery in the afternoon proved that, and had Colonel Campbell with his brigade been ordered earlier to the assistance of McCook that general might have been spared the humiliation of so crushing a defeat. There was cavalry enough on the right without Campbell, and that good strong brigade of cavalry thrown into the fight at the proper moment must have had a telling effect."[48]

Finally, Mitchell stated in his after-action report that he was ordered to "fall back" by Thruston at 3:00 p.m. This was untrue and Thruston, instead, endeavored to get Mitchell to bring the cavalry north to engage the enemy, not to "fall back" as Mitchell reported. This was quite a significant difference in terminology.

The Hospitals at Crawfish Springs—The Surgeons' Perspective

On September 19, ten hospitals supported the Union infantry during the battle. Three of the ten hospitals were situated at Dyer's house (1st Div. XIV Corps), Cloud's house (3rd Div., XIV Corps) and the Mullis house (2nd Div. XX Corps) on the northern half of the battlefield. Three hospitals were positioned a mile or so due west from Lee and Gordon's Mill (3rd Div., XX Corps; 2nd and 3rd Div., XXI Corps). The final four hospitals concentrated around Crawfish Springs (1st Div., XX Corps; 2nd and 4th Div., XIV Corps; and 1st Div., XXI Corps). The locations of the hospitals were selected to have a fresh supply of water and to be in close proximity to the respective infantry division; and the necessity to handle the wounded caused the surgeons to halt their movement. During the day and evening of September 19, the three hospitals moved from their locations west of Lee and Gordon's Mill closer to Crawfish Springs. However, Dr. Gustavus Menzies, Medical Director 2nd Division, XXI Corps, decided to return to his original location. Menzies received orders to move closer to the lines and then found the enemy "would turn our left flank and expose us to a cross-fire, and we were ordered back to the first selected spot." This would have placed six hospitals at Crawfish Springs and one hospital about a mile north on the morning of September 20 near Mitchell's cavalry.[49]

Two corps medical directors and five head surgeons of the various other hospitals made reports after the battle. Menzies's hospital near Lee and Gordon's Mill began evacuating at noon because it was the hospital closest to the breakthrough. The remaining surgeons gave less than rousing concern about being directly threatened by the enemy, although the medical staff knew something was wrong as early as noon. Only Surgeon D. J. Griffiths, 3rd Division, XX Corps wrote that at 1:00 p.m., "I was again forced to evacuate." Presumably, Griffiths had moved the hospital to Crawfish Springs and, in light of the recent cavalry battle at Glass Mill, felt insecure in his current position. In addition, Medical Director, Alonzo Phelps, XX Corps wrote that at 2:00 p.m., he observed "that the cavalry was being slowly forced back upon us." Otherwise, all the other reports simply stated that the Union force (medical, cavalry, and Post's arriving infantry) had been separated from the main body of the Union infantry. These reports showed that the wounded stopped arriving at noon and the hospitals began preparing to evacuate from 1:00 to 3:00 p.m. These reports cast a dim light on Mitchell's claims of discovering at 3:00 p.m. that the Union right had been turned. Most of the surgeons reported that they were informed that communications were conclusively cut and that they hospitals were "very insecure" much earlier. The various medical officers hurriedly found as many wagons and ambulances as possible to move the non-ambulatory patients to Chattanooga.[50]

As to the abandonment of the hospitals, the Union cavalrymen understood the orders but didn't like leaving the wounded behind. At 4:00 p.m., the Union cavalry prepared to move out. Initially, the 1st Tennessee troopers let the wounded ride on their horses and the troopers walked beside. Colonel James Brownlow soon put an end to that and he explained the importance of having the troopers in the saddle despite the sadness of the wounded walking. To offer what assistance he could, Brownlow took off his colonel's hat and gave it to one of the wounded soldiers. Bareheaded, Brownlow ordered his men to move out. Julius Thomas, 2nd Tennessee, remarked in diary, "all the regts think a great deal of Col B. he is the right kind of man." Lieutenant John Andes, 2nd Tennessee, wrote in his diary that "I shall never forget the piteous cries of hundreds of our men, as we would ride by." Crook's orderly also recorded: "We shall never forget the sad faces of the wounded, as we left them to the mercy of their enemies." Elbert Squires, an Ohio infantryman, was shot in the arm the day before and went to Crawfish Springs to have his wound attended. Squire would write in a letter that most of the walking wounded were able to move rearward to Chattanooga from the hospitals at Crawfish Springs. As the battle moved forward throughout the day, temporary hospitals were established to the rear of the left wing of the army and many of the wounded were transported directly to Chattanooga when it appeared that Crawfish Springs was cut off. When Mitchell ordered the evacuation, the more severely wounded and the staff assigned to their care remained behind to be captured by Wheeler's cavalry.[51]

At 4:00 p.m. the cavalry started to move away along with Colonel Sidney Post's First Brigade of infantry and Long's cavalry brigade leading the way, escorting as many of the walking wounded as possible. The remainder of the cavalry followed in line. Chesley Mosman of Post's brigade recorded no fighting and wrote that the presence of the cavalry prevented his brigade from being isolated on the southern flank of the Union army. He wrote, "We were certainly in good luck ... to escape without a vicious fight." An hour later the column was gone; and at dusk Wheeler's cavalry followed, capturing the hospitals filled with Union wounded. The 2nd Tennessee Cavalry had the honor of being the last regiment to leave Crawfish Springs, and Lieutenant John Andes recorded that the Tennessee cavalry remained until they were "closely pressed" by the enemy. The Confederate artillery opened up on the position, setting the drought ridden grass on fire as the 2nd Tennessee quickly rode away. Edward McCook's First Division was placed in charge of the rearguard as Mitchell moved west and then northward; and bivouacked between six and nine miles south of Chattanooga. Along the way, the Union cavalry collected two abandoned artillery pieces and also gathered up a regiment-sized group of stragglers. Lieutenant Colonel Roswell Russell, 9th Pennsylvania, manned the rearguard when a regiment of Wheeler's cavalry half-heartedly attacked the rear of Mitchell's column and Russell reported: "Shortly after leaving Crawfish Spring a body of rebel cavalry made a dash on my rear guard ... but was instantly repulsed, and I proceeded without further annoyance ... going into camp at midnight." Edward McCook successfully covered the retreat in close proximity to enemy infantry and cavalry and did not lose a wagon along the way. The column included the ambulances from Crawfish Springs, the cavalry train, and the trains of XX Corps. Later that night, McCook's cavalry fell into a screen in Chattanooga Valley and also held some important mountain gaps including McFarland's Gap. Daniel Ray's brigade fell back to Rocky Ford at the base of Lookout Mountain, just west of Missionary Ridge and along the Chattanooga Road, and held its position over night. Long's brigade stopped at McCulloch's Crossroad that night and also set up a defensive line along the Chattanooga Road.[52]

As the Federal cavalry retreated, a member of Wharton's division cruelly recalled finding Lieutenant Colonel Valentine Cupp who was mortally wounded during the fight at Glass Mill in the Gordon house at Crawfish Springs. "'Well, Colonel, as you will not need your hat or boots any longer, we beg the privilege of exchanging with you,' and as the Colonel could not reply, the boys concluded that silence gives consent." Other accounts reveal the pillaging of Union soldiers despite their cries of pain. In contrast to this event, Private J. K. Womack of the 4th Tennessee (CSA) stood guard over a wounded Union cavalryman at the fight at Glass Mill and protected him from the pillaging by his own comrades with his musket cocked.[53]

At 7:15 p.m., Rosecrans sent Mitchell orders and mild admonishment for his actions during the day but the criticism would turn to a severe rebuke by a court of inquiry after the battle. Rosecrans wrote: "You must watch the movements of Wheeler, lest he goes over the mountains and seize our bridges. If you can spare a cavalry force, pitch into the enemy's left flank. Crook ought to be sufficient to watch Wheeler. I leave to your good judgment what should be done. You will be able to accomplish these two. Hang on the flank of the enemy's infantry, reporting his movements. Let me hear from you often. Had you been on our right today you could have charged the enemy's flank and done much incalculable mischief."[54]

In the end, Mitchell chose to stand by orders issued many hours before the Confederates broke through the Union infantry lines and failed to modify the role of the cavalry as changes occurred on the field. The responsibility for the hospitals was very important and it was commendable that Mitchell recognized this. However, Mitchell failed to grasp that battle plans last only until the first shot is fired and by irresolutely sticking by the first set of orders, he disobeyed orders as the situation changed. The cavalry did provide security for the wounded and the hospital, but the entire right wing was crumbling under the Confederate attack of which Mitchell claimed to be oblivious. Mitchell, like Rosecrans, failed to see the cavalry as an important offensive part of the army.

Minty's Brigade Repulses Scott at Red House

On the left flank of the Army of the Cumberland on September 20 Robert Minty's cavalry brigade remained active in its duty. As usual Minty operated under the command of an infantry commander, this time Gordon Granger in command of the Reserve Corps. In the afternoon, Minty took up Granger's position on the Rossville and Ringgold Road, and he found that Granger had already left this position to support Thomas' defense. With Granger gone, Minty's position was vitally important to prevent the enemy from turning the flank of the Union army. The irascible Granger was making one of his greatest decisions and he committed his Reserve Corps to reinforce George Thomas who was making a desperate defense at Snodgrass Farm and Horseshoe Ridge. After the intense fighting over the past three days, Minty wanted no surprises and sent out reconnaissance patrols in all directions. Minty patrolled the roads leading to Chattanooga which ensured no enemy made an attack to the north. Minty moved his brigade to Missionary Mills and then sent "strong patrols" to Chickamauga Station and Graysville but found no enemy. Later in the afternoon one of the patrols rode to Red House Bridge and found Colonel John Scott's Confederate cavalry brigade on the west side of the Chickamauga Creek. Minty pulled his brigade together and attacked

Scott which resulted in an hour-long fight before Minty successfully pushed Scott's brigade back over the Chickamauga Creek. John McLain, 4th Michigan Cavalry, described in his diary the Confederate cavalry was driven over the creek just before dark and two men in his company were wounded in the fight. Minty concluded in his after-action report: "found Scott's brigade of cavalry and mounted infantry, about 1,500 strong, moving into position on our side of the creek. I immediately attacked them. After a spirited skirmish of about an hour's duration, drove them across the creek with considerable loss." Scott's cavalry had the task of protecting the Confederate flank and at the same time applying pressure to Granger's forces. Minty's cavalry ended the day at McAfee's Church on the Ringgold Road and his men spent a cold night "sitting on the ground bridle in hand."[55]

Captain Richard Robbins, Company F 4th Michigan Cavalry, explained that at the end of the day, the men were exhausted. Robbins wrote: "[H]aving driven Scott's Rebel cavalry across that sluggish and blood stained stream we unsaddled a part of our horses, and lay down to sleep, as well as we could by the side of the Ringgold Road, the most of us having little idea of our whereabouts." Minty wrote to Garfield at 7:35 p.m. that night and complained that his cavalry was being weakened, not through the various fights, but by the various details headquarters demanded. Minty had been lucky, because it was late in the afternoon before he could assemble a sufficient number of troops to fight off Scott's probe on the flank. Minty captured a prisoner who reported that Scott had 1,500 troopers supported with a four-gun battery of artillery. "I had 2 men wounded. I have heard nothing whatever from General Granger or Colonel McCook since they moved from here. I have fallen back to within about half a mile of the crossroads, so as to enable me to cover both roads."[56]

As Minty ended the day, some of Mitchell's cavalry moved into line in the Chattanooga Valley and some moved into McFarland's Gap in Missionary Ridge. The cavalry regiments eased the retreating soldiers' panic and declared "there should be no 'Bull Run' here." The Federal horsemen reorganized many of the infantry into stable companies and returned them to their appropriate commands. Crook, occasionally irascible and with a large ego of his own, made no secret of his dislike for Mitchell and this dislike intensified during the day. He wrote in his autobiography, "I was present when Gen. Mitchell made his verbal report to Gen. Rosecrans and to hear him recount the valorous deeds of his command. How he could have the cheek; after what had passed, surpassed my understanding. It was humiliating to see persons wearing the uniforms of general officers be so contemptible."[57]

Summary

The events of the day offer many questions. If one examines David Stanley's career, one maxim was "march to the sound of the guns." It is difficult to second guess events and with the spotty records which exist from the events of September 20 for the Union cavalry. Among some of the more important questions revolve around Rosecrans' and Mitchell's decisions. On the morning of September 20, Mitchell had three brigades of cavalry around Crawfish Springs, but he only utilized one brigade in the action around Crawfish Springs. It can be argued that events developed so quickly that Mitchell didn't have time to reinforce Crook and Long. This certainly is true with Mitchell two miles in the rear. Hindsight strongly suggests that Mitchell would have been more effective if he had taken the initiative and ridden with Crook to the fighting. However, Mitchell faced a major dilemma. He had been initially ordered to guard the southern flank, the hospitals and the Union supply trains. Throughout the day, he did not make dramatic offensive moves, but he was successful in insuring the hospitals were not overrun, the flank was secure, and all the supply trains were protected. While this was not glorious work, it was an accomplishment worthy of recognition.

Finally, one can question Rosecrans' and Mitchell's vision for the cavalry corps. The Union cavalry on the southern flank had essentially no offensive role during the battle and had lost communications with the main body of the Union infantry until late afternoon. Perhaps, the greater mistake by Mitchell was the loss of contact with Wheeler's cavalry which had threatened his position. While Mitchell remained at Crawfish Springs awaiting an imminent attack, Wheeler had moved away in support of the infantry near Lee and Gordon's Mill. Ultimately, Mitchell chose to stay away from the offensive part of the battle while he guarded hospitals that he, in the end, turned over to the enemy with scarcely a shot. After the war, Rosecrans detailed his account of trying to reorganize the army after the breakthrough, and his third most important priority directed that Mitchell needed to move closer to the battle—"orders must go to Mitchell to extend to extend his cavalry line over the ridge" to connect with Sheridan's infantry.[58]

Michael Fitch, an author of a history of the Chickamauga Campaign, argued that the Federal cavalry did not work in conjunction with the rest of the army and he thought that Forrest needed to be opposed with a relatively equal number of mounted forces. Fitch wrote, "Only one cavalry brigade was needed at Crawfish Springs; the other cavalry brigade together with Wilder's mounted infantry which closed up on the right of McCook, should have given better service at a time when it was most needed.... Mitchell's cavalry was too far away to be effective, when disaster overtook the wing it was supposed to be protecting, but it was farther away from Snodgrass Hill on the right than were the forces of Gordon Granger, at McAfee's church on the left."[59]

The crushing defeat for the Union army and the collapse of the entire line threw everything into confusion. Command and control was lost particularly on the right flank, but Rosecrans long ago discarded his cavalry as an offensive part of his command. Because of this, he left four thousand troops on his right flank to keep guard over his hospitals, but, of course, he never believed he would suffer the blow which struck his line. However, the cavalry was still a powerful fighting force and its primary advantage was mobility. To place your most mobile force in a stationary role seems to remove an important part of the fighting ability of the Army of the Cumberland. But, much of the problem with the cavalry remains with Mitchell who seemed perfectly content to stay in line around Crawfish Springs, neither committing to support the fighting to the south or the north. Once the battle took an unexpected turn, as it did at Chickamauga, then the measure of the commanding officer and his men was determined. Certainly, Mitchell allowed Crook to fight Wheeler at Glass Mill, but then what did he do? He lost contact with the enemy and he lost contact with the rest of the army even though he had the most mobile Union force on the field. As result, much of the Union cavalry remained unengaged throughout the day and had failed to march to the sound of the guns.

Ten. Retreat to Chattanooga (September 21)—Watkins at Cooper's Gap

"You should not be there, Colonel." I replied: "I know that, General; but there I am."—Col. Robert Minty

In the early morning hours of September 21, Robert Mitchell ordered his two division commanders to remain in position in the Chattanooga Valley guarding the Union right flank. Mitchell ordered: "Prevent the enemy from penetrating our line by way of this valley or along Missionary Ridge." Rosecrans had fallen back during the late afternoon the prior day and in the evening, he formed a line resembling a lazy, backward "L." Crittenden's XXI Corps held the left flank on Missionary Ridge, Granger's Reserve Corps had moved to Rossville, Thomas's XIV Corps held the ground near the Rossville Gap and McCook's XX Corps connected with Thomas and formed an east—west line into Chattanooga Valley. Fortunately for Mitchell, Will Martin's cavalry division spent the night at Crawfish Springs and John Wharton's division withdrew to the east side of Chickamauga Creek. This gave Mitchell time to set up his headquarters at Rocky Ford and extend Edward McCook's and George Crook's lines from Missionary Ridge across Chattanooga Valley to Lookout Mountain.[1]

The Cavalry Secures the Flanks

Mitchell kept the cavalry in line of battle throughout the day on September 21 while skirmishing with Wheeler. He received some much-needed help from the detached 15th Pennsylvania Cavalry which moved farther west, ascended Lookout Mountain and defended the signal station there. Early in the morning, Edward McCook opened communications with Alexander McCook and George Thomas, and the 2nd Michigan reached Chattanooga after escorting the ammunition and supply trains which had been in the vicinity of Crawfish Springs. Then, the Michigan cavalry rode east to guard Harrison's Ferry located about ten miles northeast of Chattanooga. With Pegram's Confederate cavalry still active on the northeast part of the battlefield, the Union cavalry needed to guard against a surprise attack. Henry Hempstead, 2nd Michigan Cavalry, was exhausted after the previous day's battle and the subsequent retreat. He wrote in diary, "I was too tired and exhausted to care whether I ever had anything to eat again, so made no effort to stay the pangs of hunger."[2]

On the western flank, Mitchell described: "We have a hell of a front here. We will do the best we can." Mitchell seemed content to command the cavalry for most of the day while sitting astride a rail fence watching the unfolding developments in front of his lines. The Federal cavalry remained in line all day within sight of their Confederate adversaries. McCook placed Campbell's brigade on the right (west) of his line and Daniel Ray's Second Brigade held the left of the line. Ray's regiments connected the cavalry with Alexander McCook's right flank. Then, Edward McCook rode to George Thomas' headquarters to receive orders and he explained the disposition of his cavalry. McCook sent the 2nd Indiana Cavalry to hold a position in Dry Valley near McFarland Gap with instructions to also hold Wood's Gap (along the main road from Crawfish Springs to the Chattanooga Road) on Missionary Ridge that the enemy wanted to control and which would serve as a point to attack the Union forces by a southwesterly route. Daniel Ray fought off an attempt to cut the cavalry from McCook's XX Corps at 10:00 a.m., but the attack on the eastern part of Ray's line failed as the 1st Wisconsin Cavalry joined to stymie two or three assaults. Ray had positioned the 1st Wisconsin on the left flank, the 2nd Indiana in the center, the 2nd East Tennessee on the right (connecting with Campbell's brigade), and the 4th Indiana held a reserve position while supporting Newell's artillery. Edward McCook knew that the enemy wanted to gain possession of the Chattanooga Valley, which if successful, could have finished the Army of the Cumberland. This would have isolated the army along Missionary Ridge. McCook held his line; but he noticed a large cloud dust to his front at 4:00 p.m. when the Confederates again tried to break the lines and he repulsed "a more determined attempt" to breach his line at 5:00 p.m. The 1st Wisconsin Cavalry and the 2nd Tennessee Cavalry (U.S.) "promptly repulsed" the attack

The 2nd Tennessee Cavalry, organized in eastern Tennessee, fought off a Confederate attack on September 21 (courtesy Tennessee State Library and Archives).

which targeted the area in front of McCook's cavalry brigades and to the west of Alexander McCook's infantry line. Again, the Union line held.[3]

Meanwhile, George Crook also spent the day screening the Federal army. Long's brigade spent the night in battle line expecting to fight off a night attack. Early on the morning of September 21, Long ordered his cavalry to ride ahead until the enemy was located, an order sent to most of the cavalry commanders. The 1st Ohio Cavalry rode about two miles and spread out and sent skirmishers ahead. Lieutenant W. L. Curry described what they faced— "[A]ll intensely watching the advancing columns of the enemy that were plainly in view across some open fields with colors flying and bayonets glistening in the bright September sun ... it impressed me as being the grandest scene I had ever looked upon. Now and then a puff of white smoke would rise and a Minnie ball would come zip through the branches over our heads." The opposing forces had a "sharp skirmish" and the cavalry slowly retired, but remained in battle line into the night. Curry recalled that during the night the Federal and Confederate lines were so close the soldiers spoke to one another. He heard one Rebel soldier call out: "When's you all going down to Atlanta?" and shortly after another asked, "Where is old Granny Burnsides now?" Curry bitterly considered that he had no good reply for his adversaries.[4]

The orders to ride directly toward the Confederate line, which would be used to determine the presence of the enemy by the cavalry, were sent to much of the Union cavalry from army headquarters. Garfield ordered this method of reconnaissance—push the cavalry as far ahead of the Federal lines as possible until it ran into opposition or, more practically, a volley from the enemy. This order also went to Robert Minty who fully intended to follow it, but fortunately for Minty, George Thomas became aware to the order and countermanded it. Thomas understanding the callousness of such an order chose not to sacrifice more of Minty's men.[5]

Major Peter Mathews, 4th Ohio Cavalry, also recorded his actions during the day in a letter to his wife: "[We] took a position seven miles south of the town [Chattanooga] and held it all day (all this time [we] are the extreme right of [the] army) with sharp skirmishing, the fighting was heavy on the left and center, the enemy tried desperately to turn [the Union] left and get possession of the town. During ... the night the whole line fell back to the town, except the cavalry."[6]

Mitchell still had Louis Watkins' cavalry brigade detached and he wrote to Garfield on the morning of September 21 that he still had not been able to open communications with Watkins "I ... am at a loss to know what has become of him." Mitchell's last brigade had yet to rejoin his command, but the situation at Crawfish Springs the day before suggested no obvious reason Mitchell could not send a courier to Watkins informing him of the decision to evacuate the town. At 3:30 p.m., Mitchell wrote that he had attempted to make contact with Watkins: "Everything quiet in front except occasional skirmishing. Colonel Campbell just reports a column moving up apparently between him and General Thomas; thinks it is cavalry. I have sent him an additional company. As I said in my previous communication, I have no knowledge of the whereabouts of Colonel Watkins' brigade, nor have I had since I ordered it up from Valley Head. There have been two companies with orders, besides one courier sent to him. I will send another company over the mountain to try and find him." Mitchell seemed confused about his communications to Watkins because the timing of the Mitchell's communications could not have properly informed Watkins of the unfolding sit-

Ten. Retreat to Chattanooga (September 21)—Watkins at Cooper's Gap 227

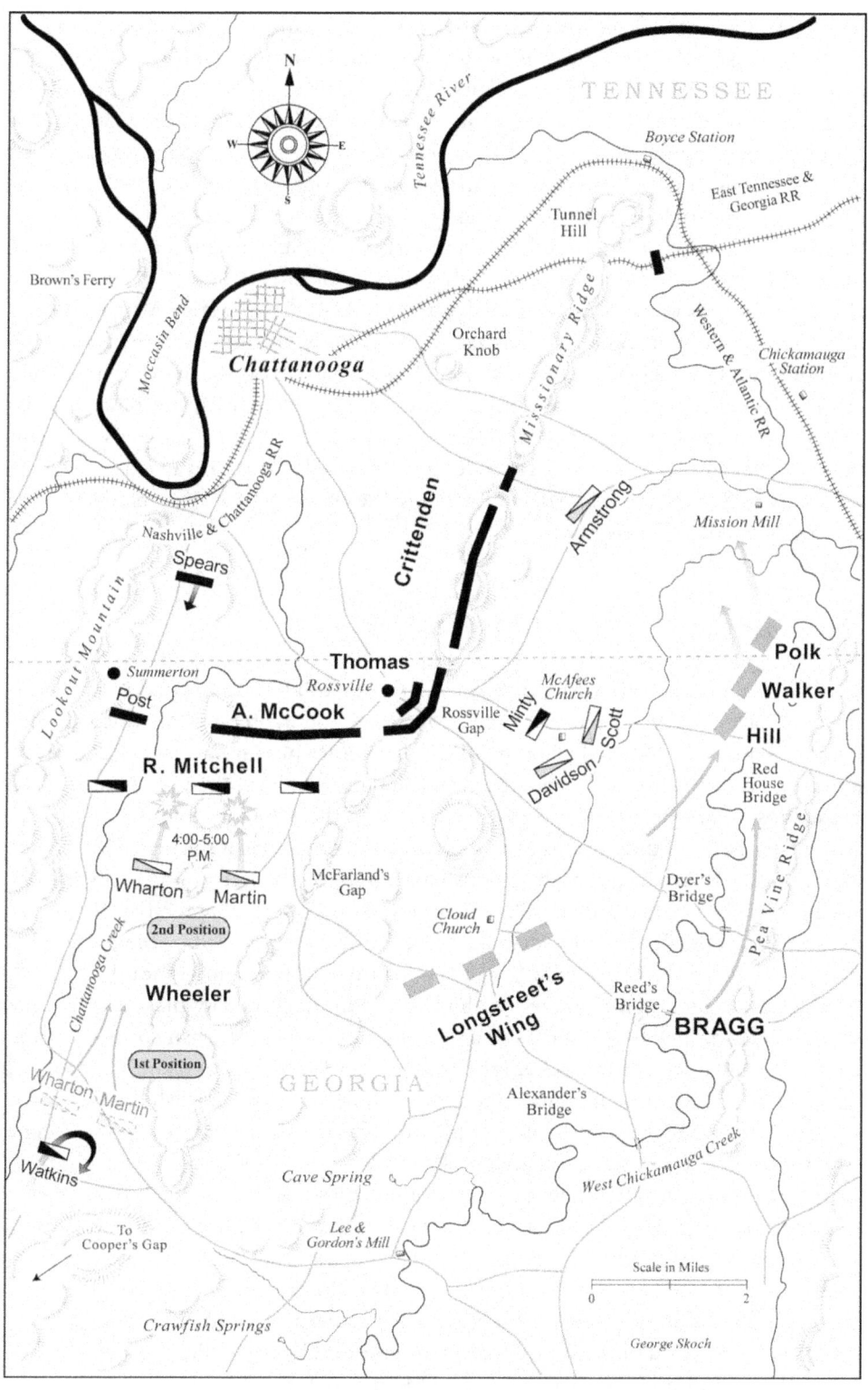

Union cavalry during the retreat to Chattanooga.

uation. As Mitchell said there were two messages sent to hurry Watkins forward. The first was sent sometime before midnight on September 19 and a second company was sent at 2:00 a.m. on September 20 some fourteen hours before Mitchell decided to abandon Crawfish Springs. On September 21 at 10:15 a.m., another set of orders in Mitchell's order book revealed that someone writing under Stanley's signature had been unable to open communications with Watkins. The 3:30 p.m. message similarly reported that Watkins had not been located. This message appeared under Stanley's name and this message indicated a third attempt, a courier, had been dispatched to reach Watkins. (Of course, Stanley could not have authored the orders because he had left the cavalry a few days before.) Unfortunately, by that time, it was too late to help Watkins' Kentucky cavalry brigade. At 4:30 p.m. Major William H. Sinclair penned a fourth set of orders to Watkins asking about his whereabouts. In the final account, all of communications sent prior to September 21 were written before the Union withdrawal from Crawfish Springs and the third message sent on September 21, presumably at 10:15 a.m., was too late to prevent the battle Watkins was destined to fight at Cooper's Gap. Unfortunately, the messages to Watkins were sent either too early before the evacuation of Crawfish Springs, or too late to prevent him from riding into the concentration of Confederate cavalry occupying Mitchell's old position.[7]

Watkins' Brigade Rides for Crawfish Springs

As a result, Louis Watkins' Third Brigade, 4th, 5th, 6th Kentucky cavalries, and cavalry train would have the hardest duty of the Union cavalry on September 21. Watkins was not with the remainder of Mitchell's command the day before because he escorted a variety of men to the rear to be taken by wagon train to Chattanooga. His initial orders directed him to take up position at Stevens' Gap and when he arrived there, he found another set of orders on September 20 directing him to Mitchell's position at Crawfish Springs. Unfortunately, and unknown to Watkins, Crawfish Springs had subsequently fallen into enemy hands. He camped his brigade at the William Shaw farm on the evening of September 20 and Shaw, whose son served in Wheeler's cavalry, had to be somewhat dismayed by the presence of so many Union cavalry. Watkins, who began the next day only ten miles south of Crawfish Springs, followed his original orders but he had encountered enemy pickets since leaving Stevens' Gap. He pushed the pickets aside and proceeded toward Crawfish Springs as ordered. After running into two additional enemy patrols, one at Owen's Ford and another about three miles south of his destination, Watkins rode to within a mile of Crawfish Springs when he encountered more enemy troops. Suspecting the situation was not as he supposed, he sent twenty men under command of Lieutenant Joseph Cowell, 4th Kentucky, to scout forward to Crawfish Springs. Cowell returned within an hour and reported the Confederates had possession of the springs. Then Watkins decided to withdraw his command and he rode about four miles west to the Chattanooga Road. Once gaining the road, Watkins waited for his train to catch up to him. While he waited, his scouts reported Wharton's and Martin's cavalry divisions had discovered his presence and were hurriedly advancing upon his position.[8]

Watkins had only about 550 men in his in force and he determined his closest escape route was through Cooper's Gap over Lookout Mountain. He hastened his train in that direction about 4 miles away. Having left a battalion of the 5th Kentucky at Stevens' Gap, Watkins sent Lieutenant Colonel William T. Hoblitzell with the rest of his 5th Kentucky Cavalry to hurry to the gap to cover the retreat of the train and the other two regiments. The chase was on.

Wheeler's two divisions started the morning several miles apart, but reports from his scouts resulted in a rapid concentration of his cavalry. Watkins, soon, had the unpleasant task of trying to hold off 3,000 experienced Confederate cavalry hot on his heels, with about 400 men of the 4th and 6th Kentucky cavalries; but Watkins hoped to the meet the threat and to give his train a chance to escape. The 6th Kentucky Cavalry, commanded by Major Lewis Gratz, took up position on the left of the Chattanooga Road and the 4th Kentucky, commanded by Colonel Wickliffe Cooper, moved to the right. The regiments sent forth skirmishers as the Confederates rapidly approached. The charging Confederate cavalry simply rode over the skirmishers. Outmanned, the two regiments withdrew after being flanked by superior numbers. The 4th Kentucky took up the first defensive position near Lookout Church while the 6th Kentucky moved further to the rear to establish the next line to cover Cooper's troopers when they withdrew. Watkins wrote, "Being flanked on both sides by overwhelming numbers, the Fourth Kentucky Cavalry was compelled to fall back slowly, fighting with desperation, and rallied on the Sixth Kentucky Cavalry, when the two regiments combined held the enemy in check for fully twenty minutes." Then, the 4th Kentucky and 6th Kentucky retreated and a running battle ensued as the Kentucky cavalry rode for their lives. Finally, the two cavalry regiments reached the base of the mountain only to find the trail blocked in a confusion of wagons attempting to move up the mountain. As a result, the two cavalry regiments had no place to go with the Confederate cavalry on their heels. Thomas Colman, 11th Texas Cavalry, wrote that after a "short stand" the Kentuckians withdrew to the wagon train and after firing five or six volleys at the base of the mountain, Watkins' men broke and tried to escape.[9]

Watkins had expected the 5th Kentucky in line preparing to cover the retreat, but the 5th Kentucky was not to be found. Watkins was enraged at the commander of the 5th Kentucky who had only been released from arrest the day before. If the 5th Kentucky was line, he felt the three regiments could have halted the pursuit long enough to escape up the mountain. Watkins noted in his after-action report that Hoblitzell and his regiment "had retreated through Cooper's Gap at a very rapid rate." The Confederates caught their prey at the base of the mountain. The result of the 4th and 6th Kentucky running into a mountain road tightly packed with supply wagons was disastrous and Watkins noted "after considerable slaughter on both sides the enemy captured a large number of prisoners." Watkins reformed the remainder of his command on the side of the mountain and sent a rider to return Hoblitzell's 5th Kentucky to what was left of the brigade. When Hoblitzell returned, Watkins sent him to ride the rest of the way to Chattanooga at the rear of the train. The remnants of the Union brigade reached Chattanooga about ten o'clock that night. Watkins' command suffered the greatest loss of the Union cavalry during the Battle of Chickamauga in this fight which resulted in 6 officers and 211 enlisted men recorded as missing, presumably captured at the foot of the mountain at Cooper's Gap. The number of casualties amounted to about half of the 4th and 6th Kentucky cavalries' total numbers on that day. In addition, a total of 53 wagons were lost to the Confederate cavalry. C. H. Sowle, 4th Kentucky, recalled that Watkins approached him after the fight and asked him where his company was; but Sowle could only see seven or eight of the men. Sowle wrote in a letter a few days later: "Our brigade was cut to pieces."[10]

To complicate this situation, a feud between Watkins and Hoblitzell, which began in the summer, peaked at Cooper's Gap. Watkins had already brought Hoblitzell up on the charges stemming from misconduct in the summer and the commander of the 5th Kentucky Cavalry had just been released from arrest by Rosecrans the day before. Louis Watkins would again prefer charges against Hoblitzell for cowardice for his actions at Cooper's Gap. The court martial began on July 26, 1864. Louis Watkins testified he had ordered Hoblitzell to take the 5th Kentucky Cavalry and hold the entrance of Cooper's Gap, a narrow and easily defended position. Later, he sent a lieutenant with the same orders to Hoblitzell to make sure there was no confusion. Watkins told the court if the entrance of the gap could have been held for fifteen minutes longer the supply train and the 4th and 6th Kentucky cavalries would have been saved. When Watkins arrived, he found none of the 5th Kentucky Cavalry present. About half way up the mountain, he found part of the regiment—Major James Wharton and 70 troopers, which had been stopped by Watkins' officers. At the top of the mountain, the remaining troopers of the 4th and 6th Kentucky cavalries dismounted, reorganized, and drove off the last of the attacking Confederate cavalry. In addition, the brigade color guard reported that as soon as the troopers of the 5th Kentucky Cavalry present were ordered into line, they moved swiftly and bravely. Watkins dispatched an orderly from the 4th Kentucky Cavalry to bring Hoblitzell back to him. When Hoblitzell was returned to Watkins, Watkins demanded to know where he was. Hoblitzell, who had his saber in his hand, replied: "I could not stop my men, and had to draw my sabre upon them." But Watkins told Hoblitzell that most of his command was on top of Lookout Mountain with the 4th and 6th Kentucky, and demanded to know why he wasn't with his men. Hoblitzell replied that he thought the Union infantry was approaching up the west side of the mountain and he had ridden to speed them along.[11]

There were various accounts of the events. Most serious was the charge of cowardice, and Hoblitzell's defense centered on the confusion of whether the order meant the 5th Kentucky Cavalry should defend the trail at the base of the mountain, or on top of the mountain. Hoblitzell interpreted the order to mean the top of the mountain and Watkins obviously meant the foot of the mountain. By all accounts, Hoblitzell remained at the rear of his command, away from the fighting, and his account stressed he was attempting to rally the troopers and personally seeking assistance from a small group of infantry on the west side of the mountain. The court found Hoblitzell not guilty, but not before Hoblitzell sought to have Watkins dismissed, in retaliation for the first set of charges, by accusing Watkins of returning an ex-slave to his master against his will. The charge was untrue; but Hoblitzell tried to use his political influence and appealed to James Garfield, the War Department, and other politicians for Watkins' dismissal. Early in 1864 Hoblitzell was superseded with Oliver Baldwin as colonel and commanding officer of the 5th Kentucky Cavalry, and Hoblitzell would later be transferred to a position in Missouri.[12]

Immediately after the battle, the 5th Kentucky Cavalry was removed from Watkins' command and an exchange with the 4th Indiana affected the transfer. Robert Mitchell wrote the reason for the transfer resulted from "quarrels and jealousies" within Watkins' brigade, and this seemed to be the quickest and easiest manner of alleviating the immediate conflicts.[13]

The missed communications between Louis Watkins and Robert Mitchell resulted in the loss of about two hundred-fifty men and fifty-three supply and ammunition wagons on September 21. The existing messages detailed the orders to Watkins and his after-action report explained the actions he took in regard to each of the orders. The first two communications ordered Watkins to Crawfish Springs, but subsequent messages were lost or too late to save his command. At best, this sequence of events reflects the difficulty of communicating in the 1860's in difficult terrain. There are no records to suggest that Mitchell tried to communicate with Watkins after his withdrawal from Crawfish Springs at 4:00 p.m. on September 20 until mid-morning the next day. The next message regarding Watkins occurred at 10:15 a.m. on September 21 when presumably another courier was dispatched to Watkins. By that time, it was too late.

The records are incomplete and puzzling in some aspects. For example, did Watkins respond in writing to these orders? If so, why did army headquarters not receive them? Secondly, three of the messages were signed by someone using David Stanley's signature, but Stanley had been transported to Nashville on September 17. He could not have signed the orders. William H. Sinclair signed other messages, and generally the author of messages signed their names and indicated they were by the order of a particular individual in authority. Finally, was Mitchell ever aware that the sequence of orders actually sent Watkins into the ambush? While Watkins did not protest the manner in which he received his orders, he outlined the sequence of events which led him to Crawfish Springs and he even attached the copy of the order sending him there in his after-action report. While it can be argued that Mitchell was involved with the withdrawal of the Union cavalry divisions from Crawfish Springs and that a courier might not have been able to find Watkins' brigade even if one was sent, it remains troubling that no messages were sent for such a long period of time after the evacuation of Crawfish Springs. The headquarters staff seemed equally puzzled by the fact that they had received no reply from Watkins for three days. Ultimately, the delay in sending orders to Watkins until the next morning doomed his command.

Minty Screens for Thomas' Infantry

Meanwhile, on the left flank of the Union line, the ever-vigilant Robert Minty and his brigade of cavalry remained on duty. On the morning of September 21, Minty's brigade held a line, two miles in front of Thomas's XIV Corps, screening the Confederate advance. Captain Richard Robbins, 4th Michigan, recalled that the men of the regiment awakened knowing the previous day had been a bad one for the Federal army, but Thomas' defense at Snodgrass Farm had saved the army. Robbins' first task of the day was to find out where he was after the back and forth fighting of the previous day. He determined his company started the day about a mile in front of Missionary Ridge. Minty sent riders in all directions to determine the location of the enemy and Minty sent riders to the location of Thomas' headquarters on the previous day only to find him gone. None of the cavalry knew where Thomas had moved overnight. Eventually, the couriers found Thomas on Missionary Ridge. Thomas directed Minty to keep his cavalry between Thomas and the enemy as much as possible which would give Thomas time to develop a good defensive position. Minty's cavalry had spent the night just east of Rossville and then moved quickly to a position in front of the infantry on Missionary Ridge where a gap led to Rossville—Rossville Gap. Later, Minty personally rode to Thomas' headquarters and he recalled the conversation with Thomas before being sent to delay the Confederate advance. When Minty reported to Thomas, he said, "'You should not be there, Colonel.' I replied: 'I know that, General; but there I am.' After a moment's thought, he said: 'Well, as you are there, delay the enemy all you can. Give me as much time as possible to prepare to get ready for them.'" Minty returned to his command and positioned his cavalry at a crossroads about one half mile west of McAfee's Church and planned to delay any enemy advance down the roads. Unlike Mitchell who faced a less than energetic pursuit by Wheeler's cavalry, Minty had a single brigade to hold back the much more aggressive Nathan Bedford Forrest. He was soon greeted by Pegram's Division of Scott's and Davidson's Brigades. Minty wrote, "There gave them battle, and, taking advantage of every possible position." The 7th Pennsylvania Cavalry took the greatest loss during this fighting with several men in the regiment being killed or wounded.[14]

Robbins noted the position Minty took left him vulnerable to a "blizzard from both sides"—his front, as the Confederate cavalry and infantry moved forward, and from the rear by nervous Union infantrymen after the fighting from the day before. As the cavalry developed its defensive line, a loud cheer erupted from the Union troops in their rear and cavalrymen believed that Burnside had arrived with his troops. The troopers were soon disappointed, because the cheer merely signaled the arrival of Major General Lovell Rousseau at his division after his recent trip to Washington. Soon, Minty observed the advance of three Confederate columns, Walker, Hill, and Polk, which moved from Missionary Mills, Red House Bridge and Dyer's Ford. Pegram's cavalry division advanced and pushed Minty's cavalry back toward the Union main line. After the fight at Reed's Bridge, Minty was becoming skilled in the "fight, retreat, fight" method of delaying an advance. In addition, the Federal cavalry came under fire from three Confederate batteries, but Barnett's 2nd Illinois Battery counter-fired on the Southern artillery lessening the enemy's affect as the cavalry continued the fighting withdrawal. Also during the morning, Forrest took an expedition with Dibrell's brigade, ascended Missionary Ridge, and observed the Federal positions. He observed all the Federal trains withdrawing to Chattanooga and he hurriedly communicated his findings to Bragg. After this reconnaissance, Dibrell and Forrest joined in the attacks on Minty's cavalry. During the skirmishes, Minty's troopers battled Dibrell's cavalry and even shot Nathan Bedford Forrest's horse through the neck as they withdrew toward Thomas' infantry line under the pressure of the Confederate cavalry and Morton's Confederate artillery.[15]

The first echoes of carbines began around ten o'clock. The Confederates attacked Minty's pickets to his front and right around noon in earnest and by 1:00 p.m. he withdrew to ridge in front of Thomas' command. Minty's believed he faced a double line of infantry which pushed the cavalrymen rearward, but at least, some dismounted Confederate cavalry participated in the fight, including the 6th Georgia Cavalry. Robbins explained that soon thereafter the enemy moved forward "probing their way through the brush." The 4th Michigan, 4th U.S., and 7th Pennsylvania supported by the Chicago Board of Trade artillery settled into another long day of fighting Confederates. "I don't believe many who were there will forget it," wrote Robbins. After a few hours of skirmishing, the Confederates pushed the cavalry back to Missionary Ridge and just as predicted, as Minty's cavalry withdrew near the Union lines, volleys exploded from the line of Federal infantry in the rear which resulted in fatalities in Minty's cavalry ranks. Just south of the gap, the Confederates struck Minty's brigade with a strong force causing the greatest casualties of the day. Minty decided to move his cavalry through the narrow Rossville Gap and finally made it past Thomas' line north of the ridge. The brigade moved past Missionary Ridge and planned to rest for the night. However, the cavalry was not yet safe as some of the shells aimed for the infantry on Missionary Ridge passed over the ridge and landed among the Union troopers.[16]

The day was not over for Minty's cavalry. That evening, George Thomas informed Minty of his intention to move to Chattanooga during the night and asked Minty to deceive the enemy by taking the place of the infantry in line. Thomas said: "Colonel Minty, I am going to fall back to Chattanooga tonight; wagons, ambulances, and tumbrils have already gone; the artillery will follow shortly, and during the night the infantry will be withdrawn. I want you to take possession of our present position, deceive the enemy as long as possible, but as soon as they attack fall back and retire to Chattanooga. Do not endanger your command unnecessarily." Minty's cavalry obediently moved into the passes and along the crest on Missionary Ridge. Thomas received his orders to withdraw at 6:00 p.m. and he sent his orders at nine o'clock to begin pulling the infantry off the ridge. Minty was joined by Rousseau's and John Brannan's divisions with the duty of covering the withdrawal. To avoid congestion along the roads, the other various units of the army began withdrawing overnight at different intervals— Crittenden's corps started withdrawing at 9 p.m., followed by Steedman's division. Negley's division began withdrawing at 10 p.m. followed Reynolds, then McCook's XX Corps, by divisions from left to right. Minty's cavalry, which had accomplished so much during the campaign and during the battle, was again called upon to screen the infantry retreat. Captain Richard Robbins knew that the next morning would bring more fighting: "For the second time in 24 hours we were left 'out in the cold' to receive the first attack of the enemy on awakening."[17]

Mitchell and Cavalry's Withdrawal on the West Flank

On September 21, Edward McCook also worked with George Thomas and Alexander McCook to position his cavalry during the withdrawal. McCook extended the line of his cavalry to the right of Alexander McCook's infantry corps. That evening Brigadier General James Spears' brigade of infantry was expected to arrive and would be used to extend the cavalry line even further on the right flank. The Union commanders were very concerned that the enemy would sweep around the west flank and into the rear of the infantry lines. Spears' brigade, part of the Reserve Corps, had only reached Chattanooga late on September 20 and had been assigned to security duty a few miles south on the Chattanooga Road during the day and had just received orders to march ahead to support the cavalry. Mitchell, a reluctant commander at best, sought the opportunity to shift the command of the defense to Spears as he noted Spears ranked him by a day or two and he suggested the transfer of command to him; but army headquarters left Mitchell in command. Edward McCook was not finished for the day and aggressively sought to find out more about the enemy. On the evening of September 21, he boldly sent out a reconnaissance expedition of a squadron of the 1st Wisconsin and a squadron the 2nd Indiana to move down the Chattanooga Valley as far as the Crawfish Springs road. The Union cavalry patrol slipped through the enemy lines and moved to Crawfish Springs and found that Bragg and his escort had just recently left that location."[18]

As Thomas' infantry moved back to Chattanooga, Edward McCook received his orders to fall back initially behind the infantry lines, in a leap frog maneuver to cover the army's withdrawal during the evening. He sent orders to do this quietly without alerting the enemy and provoking any action on their part. W. R. Carter, 1st Tennessee Cavalry, recalled: "Orders were issued immediately for us to fall back with as little noise as possible. The artillery wheels were muffled by wrapping blankets around them, the cavalry, except the rear-guard, was dismounted, and each man was required to carry his saber in his hand to avoid noise, and in this way, we moved some distance along the foot of Lookout Mountain, leading our horses, not being allowed to speak above a whisper." The cavalry withdrew to the rear away from the close proximity of the enemy and again fell into line. Then, the infantry withdrew, leaving the cavalry to again hold the position facing the enemy.[19]

Eli Long also ordered his cavalry to withdraw toward Chattanooga very early in the morning of September 22 and then fell into line. The troopers of the 4th Ohio awoke after spending a very short night after hearing the movement of troops in front of their position during the night. They were surprised to find, not the enemy in their front, but a regiment of Federal cavalry of McCook's division. Long's brigade, still stinging from the defeat at Crawfish Springs, slowly withdrew to Chattanooga without further action. Major Peter Mathews, 4th Ohio, recorded skirmishing throughout the day but no major engagements resulted near his location.[20]

On the morning of September 22, Mitchell ordered the cavalry to Chattanooga under orders from Garfield. Edward McCook's division continued to cover the retreat of the infantry to Chattanooga and ran into a heated fight as a result. Daniel Ray's Second Brigade of McCook's division screened the withdrawal of James Spears' brigade and the remainder of the cavalry. The thinning of the Union screen and the retreat to Chattanooga resulted in an opportunistic attack by the Confederate cavalry on the morning of September 22. McCook dispatched the 2nd Indiana Cavalry to the Rossville Road to cover the withdrawal of the infantry. When the regiment reached Rossville, the town was abandoned except for a few stragglers. At noon, the 2nd Indiana and the rest of McCook's cavalry ran into a determined Confederate attack which intended to reach the rear of the Union infantry. One of the targets in the attack was Spear's infantry brigade which had also been ordered back to Chattanooga. Spears believed the attack on his brigade included four enemy regiments supported by more cavalry and artillery from John Wharton's Confederate cavalry division. As the fight intensified, Edward McCook ordered Ray's cavalry brigade to advance forward to hold the enemy away from the infantry and then to fall back. As the cavalry moved ahead, they soon found the enemy who opened up with grape and canister and then the troopers moved back out of range. Then, the 2nd Indiana formed a line to stop the advance of the Confederates along the withdrawing Federal line. G. W. Baum wrote: "It was a hot job for a while. The shell come very close to us." The fire was so hot, the 1st Wisconsin Cavalry was yet again ordered to join in a successful defense. The cavalry, which had duty screening the passes and the roads, almost tarried too long and was nearly flanked the advancing Confederate forces. Robert Merrill wrote in his diary: "Came near being cut off in our retreat." Edward McCook described the efforts to hold back Wharton's cavalry which, unimpeded, would have cut off Spears infantry brigade and the rest of the cavalry. The 2nd Indiana held out under "heavy fire of grape and canister" until reinforced by the 1st Wisconsin Cavalry. As the remaining cavalry and infantry moved safely to the rear, the 1st Wisconsin and 2nd Indiana withdrew and fell into a line that Edward McCook had established in their rear. The cavalry held the line long enough for XX Corps to fully develop their defensive lines and then withdrew. McCook complemented the two regiments for their "splendid" action in face of overwhelming odds.[21]

Not noted in Mitchell's report was the much-needed assistance of Colonel P. Sidney Post's infantry brigade. Post received orders from Mitchell after midnight on September 21 to quietly move his brigade and assume a position at a crossroad leading to Rossville. Post fell into line with his right flank touching Missionary Ridge and his left flank extended to a millpond. Post held the line until the Confederate cavalry threatened Mitchell's flank on September 22 and then ordered the infantry brigade across Chattanooga Creek to meet the enemy. He explained: "We soon found the enemy in considerable force with a battery of artillery commanding the road. I formed my line on the side of the mountain, prepared to contest the farther advance of the enemy and to regain the road. Captain Gardner opened with his entire battery with good effect, and soon succeeded in driving away the enemy's battery and clearing the road." The combined efforts of Post, Spears, and McCook repulsed the Southern attack.[22]

Minty Continues to Screen for the Infantry

On the morning of September 22, the 4th U.S. Cavalry held the most advanced position of Minty's brigade and at 7:00 a.m. the Union troopers met the enemy again. Minty's cavalry awoke and began its fight-retreat-fight method of delaying the enemy and inched its way rearward until noon and one of the troopers of the 4th Michigan Cavalry declared Minty's cavalry fired the first, and now, the last shot on the Battle of Chickamauga. The cavalry still contended with nervous infantry in the rear, and August Yenner, 121st Ohio Infantry, wrote in his diary that the "cavalry alarmed us." Minty proudly noted that it took the Confederates six hours to push his small command four miles from Rossville to Chattanooga. Still the day was not over for Minty's cavalry and the 7th Pennsylvania and 4th U.S. cavalry joined the infantry in digging rifle pits near Chattanooga. Next, Robert Mitchell ordered all his cavalry, which desperately needed more forage, to the north of the Tennessee River. At 3:00 a.m. on September 23, Minty's cavalry crossed the Tennessee River to join the rest of Crook's cavalry north of the river for the first time in almost two months. Also of importance, John Wilder's brigade was formally attached to the Union cavalry reporting to Mitchell. Once across the river, many of the Union cavalry unsaddled their horses for the first time since September 18.[23]

While the battle ground to a halt, the Union cavalry fell into its natural role of providing security on the flanks and in some cases, in front, of the infantry. The infantry needed time to organize and the fate of the army depended on the cavalry to prevent a penetration of the line which would unleash the enemy into the rear of the army. For the 5th Iowa Cavalry, its role over past three weeks kept the regiment near McMinnville. Upon hearing of the Federal defeat at Chickamauga, Charles Alley wrote in his diary: "Sorry to hear it, but the sword devours one as well as the other."[24]

Summary

In the end, the Army of the Cumberland reached Chattanooga intact and, behind the defenses in the town, prepared to resist any Confederate advance. Rosecrans settled his defeated army, began improving defenses, and awaited reinforcements as Bragg's army moved onto the ridges south of the town. Perhaps the best summary of the Chickamauga Campaign was made by Sergeant Edwards Summers, 6th Kentucky Cavalry, who wrote in a letter: "And, Oh God, Oh God, the Scenes I have witnessed. I have witnessed Some Dark and horrible Scenes Such as has made my Blood Run Cold. I have Seen men hung Like Dogs in Cold Blood. I have Seen men Shot Down Like Brutes in Cold Blood. I have Seen the flaming innumerable Scenes of Disgust. I have Seen the Rich made poor in a few Short hours. I have Seen Enough of the Horrors of War to Satisfy me." Many in the cavalry had seen enough of the war. Although the casualties were relatively light compared to some of the infantry, the cavalry reported almost five hundred men killed, wounded or captured, in addition, to the many soldiers who had been lost to illness. Eli Long's and Louis Watkins' brigades suffered the greatest losses after their actions at Glass Mill and Cooper's Gap. Robert Minty had remarkably few casualties of less than fifty men even after his extensive fighting during the battle.[25]

Casualties of the Cavalry Corps—Battle of Chickamauga[26]

Command	Killed		Wounded		Captured		Total
	Officers	Men	Officers	Men	Officers	Men	
FIRST DIVISION—Colonel Edward M. McCook							
First Brigade, Colonel Archibald P. Campbell							
2nd Michigan	1	1	0	6	1	2	11
9th Pennsylvania	0	0	0	0	0	3	3
1st Tennessee	0	0	0	0	0	1	1
Total First Brigade	1	1	0	6	1	6	15
Second Brigade, Colonel Daniel M. Ray							
2nd Indiana	0	1	0	4	0	0	5
4th Indiana	0	0	0	2	0	7	9
2nd Tennessee	0	1	0	2	0	0	3
1st Wisconsin	0	0	0	2	0	4	6
Total Second Brig.	0	2	0	10	0	11	23
Third Brigade, Colonel Louis D. Watkins							
4th Kentucky	0	0	0	1	5	90	95
5th Kentucky	0	0	0	0	2	18	20
6th Kentucky	0	2	1	6	2	120	131
Total Third Brigade	0	2	1	7	8	228	246
Total First Division	1	5	1	23	9	245	284
SECOND DIVISION—Brigadier General George Crook							
First Brigade, Colonel Robert H. G. Minty							
3rd Indiana (batt.)	0	0	0	3	0	0	3
4th Michigan	0	1	1	11	0	6	19
7th Pennsylvania	1	4	0	13	0	1	19
4th United States	0	1	0	5	0	1	7
Total First Brigade	1	6	1	32	0	8	48
Second Brigade, Colonel Eli Long							
2nd Kentucky	0	11	5	45	0	2	63
1st Ohio	1	1	0	13	0	7	22
3rd Ohio	0	2	0	7	0	8	17
4th Ohio	1	3	0	9	2	19	34
Total Second Brig.	2	17	5	74	2	36	136
Total Second Div.	3	23	6	103	2	44	184
Total Cavalry Corps	4	28	7	129	11	289	468

Ten. Retreat to Chattanooga (September 21)—Watkins at Cooper's Gap

The Union cavalry performed its duty well during the retreat after the battle. Robert Minty's brigade again provided the most active duty of the all the cavalry, but McCook and Crook also saw important action. Minty, who had performed so well on September 18, again furnished George Thomas with the screen he needed to reform the infantry into an adequate defense. The major blunder regarding Watkins' brigade tainted the performance of cavalry now on the western flank, but the mistake resulted from poor timing, poor communications and confusion at cavalry headquarters. The remainder of Edward McCook's cavalry division performed well on the western front, resisting enemy actions from threatening Chattanooga, while repulsing several attacks on his line. This was important duty, and duty which Rosecrans and George Thomas recognized as valuable to the defeated Union army.

Eleven. Wheeler's Tennessee Raid (September 30–October 9)

*We have been in the saddle every day for two months.
We have wore out our horses running after the rebs.*—Eli Russell

On September 23 the Battle of Chickamauga was over and Rosecrans entrenched his recently defeated army in Chattanooga. In Washington, the War Department immediately began to mobilize reinforcements for the Army of the Cumberland. Over the next month, Henry Slocum's XII Corps and Oliver O. Howard's XI Corps would be dispatched from the east to reinforce the Army of the Cumberland. In addition, part of the Army of the Tennessee under command of William T. Sherman would also join Rosecrans' army at Chattanooga with parts of the XV and XVII Corps.

Immediately after the battle, the Union cavalry moved a couple of miles north of the Tennessee River and began providing reconnaissance and security at the various fords along the river while reconditioning their exhausted mounts. With the army besieged at Chattanooga, supplies immediately became a critical issue. The cavalry had to find any forage possible for the cavalry horses and for the remaining livestock in the town. Henry Albert Potter, 4th Michigan Cavalry, wrote in his diary at the conclusion of the battle: "Boys tired and horses starving."[1]

Fortunately, John Wilder's mounted infantry brigade became part of the Second Cavalry Division after the Battle of Chickamauga and this provided extra firepower to the cavalry. The commanders of Wilder's brigade undoubtedly welcomed the move to the cavalry and away from General Joseph Reynolds' infantry brigade. Due to the increased notoriety of Wilder after the Tullahoma Campaign, jealousies and intrigues abounded and he happily became part of the cavalry. After the recent battle, the Union army seemed to have decided that the mounted infantry should be used as cavalry, rather than infantry. In addition, the benefits to Wilder's brigade included the ability to forage the horses on the north side of the Tennessee River; but the recent campaign had taken its toll on John Wilder who left the army and returned home to recuperate. Brigade command fell to Colonel Abram O. Miller, 72nd Indiana Mounted Infantry, who was a physician before the war. Miller was a native of Madison County Indiana and was raised on a farm at Twelve Mile Prairie in Clinton County, Indiana. He studied medicine at the University of Louisville and graduated in 1856. He helped raise a company for the 10th Indiana Infantry as the war began. Miller was appointed colonel of the 72nd Indiana Infantry in August 1862. He was an experienced commander who had fought at the Battle of Rich Mountain, Battle of Mill Springs, the siege of Corinth and the Tullahoma Campaign. When Wilder departed to recuperate, Miller became an able replacement.[2]

It seemed like a short time since the Army of the Cumberland had retreated back to Chattanooga, but soon reports of large concentrations of Confederate cavalry forming north and west of the town reached army headquarters. It was disturbing to contemplate a large raid by Confederate cavalry in light of the condition of the Union cavalry. The Union cavalry needed time to re-condition the mounts after the recent campaign. Second Brigade Cavalry Inspector, Captain Chris Beck, reported the poor condition of the cavalry: "In consequence of the arduous duties recently performed by the brigade, it is not in a very efficient condition. The horses are very much run down, principally from a want of forage, which, under the circumstances, could not be had. Quite a large number of the men reported for duty are hardly so, but which a little rest and medical attendance will soon remedy.... The command is very much in need of clothing, especially boots." If the Second Brigade was representative of the entire corps, Mitchell had barely 8,000 men ready for duty and in poor overall condition.[3]

Abram O. Miller, colonel of 72nd Indiana Mounted Infantry, was a physician before the war and assumed command of the mounted infantry brigade (Mollus Mass Civil War Collection, United States Army Heritage and Education Center, Military History Institute, Carlisle, Pennsylvania).

The number of troopers in Union cavalry regiments generally varied between 300–400 men present for duty after the recent campaign[4]:

2nd Indiana Cavalry	392
4th Indiana Cavalry	328
4th and 6th Kentucky Cavalry	355
5th Kentucky Cavalry	260
7th Kentucky Cavalry	290
1st Wisconsin Cavalry	406
2nd Tennessee Cavalry	407

The Union cavalry fell into a thin line which stretched from Washington, Tennessee into northern Alabama. On the Union right flank, Colonel William T. Hoblitzell, 5th Kentucky Cavalry, watched across the Tennessee River near Jasper and reported seeing 3,000 Confederate horsemen on the south shore. Crook had the responsibility of the Union left flank and moved his headquarters to Washington and the various regiments in Long's and Minty's brigades guarded numerous fords along the Tennessee River. Most of Edward McCook's division concentrated near Jasper and Bridgeport, but Archibald Campbell's First Brigade patrolled even farther west into Alabama on the extreme right flank.[5]

Mitchell feared the Confederate cavalry planned to breakout into the rear of the Army of the Cumberland. With threats on the right and the left, the Union cavalry was stretched thin across the wide front and this aided Bragg's and Wheeler's next operation.[6]

Union Cavalry Positions September 23, 186[7]

Command	Commander	Station
First Division	**Col. Edward McCook**	**Sevely Springs**[a]
First Brigade	*Colonel A. P. Campbell*	
2nd Michigan Cavalry	Maj. John C. Godley	Dallas
9th Pennsylvania Cavalry	Lt. Colonel Russell	Sevely Springs
1st East Tennessee Cavalry	Lt. Colonel J. P. Brownlow	Sevely Springs
Second Brigade	*Colonel Daniel M. Ray*	
2nd Indiana Cavalry	Maj. J. B. Presdee	Sevely Springs
4th Indiana Cavalry	Lt. Colonel Deweese	Sevely Springs
2nd East Tennessee Cavalry	Lt. Colonel W. R. Cook	Jasper
3rd East Tennessee Cavalry	Colonel W. C. Pickens	Nashville
1st Wisconsin Cavalry	Colonel O. H. La Grange	Sevely Springs
Sect. Batt. D, 1st Ohio Artillery	Lt. N. M. Newell	Sevely Springs
Third Brigade	*Colonel Louis D. Watkins*	
4th Kentucky Cavalry	Colonel Wickliffe Cooper	Sevely Springs
5th Kentucky Cavalry	Lt. Colonel W. T. Hoblitzell	Near Kelley's Ford
6th Kentucky Cavalry	Lt. Colonel Roper	Sevely Springs
7th Kentucky Cavalry	Lt. Colonel J. K. Faulkner	Nashville
Second Division	**Brig. Gen. George Crook**	**Near Island Ferry**
First Brigade	*Colonel Robert H. G. Minty*	
7th Pennsylvania Cavalry	Colonel James J. Seibert	On scout in search of forage
4th Michigan Cavalry	Maj. Horace Gray	On scout in search of forage
4th U.S. Cavalry	Capt. J. B. McIntyre	On scout in search of forage
3rd Indiana Cavalry (detached)	Lt. Colonel Robert Klein	Pikeville, Tennessee
Second Brigade	*Col. Eli Long*	
1st Ohio Volunteer Cavalry	Major Patten	Island Ferry, Tennessee
3rd Ohio Volunteer Cavalry	Lt. Colonel Seidel	Island Ferry, Tennessee
4th Ohio Volunteer Cavalry	Lt. Colonel O. P. Robie	Island Ferry, Tennessee
2nd Kentucky Cavalry	Colonel T. P. Nicholas	Island Ferry, Tennessee
Third Brigade	*Col. William W. Lowe*	
5th Iowa Cavalry	Lt. Colonel Patrick	McMinnville, Tennessee
10h Ohio Volunteer Cavalry	Colonel C. C. Smith	Stevenson, Tennessee
1st Middle Tennessee Cavalry	Lt. Colonel Galbraith	Stevenson, Tennessee
Stokes Battery, Illinois Artillery	Capt. James H Stokes	Island Ferry, Tennessee

([a] a few miles, described by one trooper as five miles, north of Chattanooga)

By September 25, there was little doubt the Confederate cavalry had something planned as Bragg attempted to capitalize on his recent victory. Although some cavalry movement was observed north of Chattanooga, much of the new activity was reported near Bridgeport. Garfield sent orders for McCook's cavalry division to ride immediately to Bridgeport and prepare to repel an attempted crossing. This left Crook to guard the Union left flank over a large geographic area and on September 26, his troopers drew five days' rations in preparation of action with the enemy.[8]

Wheeler's Middle Tennessee Raid

Then Wheeler struck, and he struck where Mitchell was the weakest, on the Union left flank. Wheeler began crossing the Tennessee River during the night of September 29, and George Crook sent a message to Mitchell, "The enemy are endeavoring to cross at Cotton Port Ford, 3 miles from Washington. They are in very heavy force. I am fighting them." Crook later determined from prisoners that Wheeler's success in crossing was cleverly made by selecting a point on the Tennessee River without a known ford, crossing in a location with only a light cavalry guard. A new road had been cut to approach the river and after dark, Davidson's, Wharton's and Martin's divisions crossed at two locations near Cotton Port. Wheeler's men also carried five-seven days' rations and subsequently, a prisoner which had been captured told Crook the raid was to be carried to the west over the mountains.[9]

When Wheeler began his raid through the rear of Rosecrans's defeated army, his move left only one cavalry brigade with Bragg's army around Chattanooga. Three brigades of Forrest's cavalry accompanied Wheeler's force, but Wheeler disparagingly referred to these brigades as mere "skeletons" totaling about 1,500 troopers on worn out horses. Bragg ordered the attack, but Wheeler did not want to initiate the raid because he felt the Confederate cavalry was in too poor condition for such an endeavor. However, Wheeler's total numbers were impressive, as greater than 5,000 Confederate cavalry rode west.[10]

In addition, the assignment of Forrest's cavalry to Wheeler exposed the disregard Bragg and Forrest continued to have for each other and this resulted in an explosive situation. The orders from Bragg simply told Forrest, "The general commanding desires that you will without delay turn over the troops of your command previously ordered to Major General Wheeler." A few days later Frank Armstrong received a message that his division had been dismantled and his regiments reassigned without any input from him. One can imagine how Forrest received these and he simply decided to resign from the army, living up to his vow never to serve under Wheeler. Prior to the beginning of the Chickamauga Campaign, Forrest had offered to move away from Bragg's army to western Tennessee and Mississippi to assume a new command. Now the plan was used to appease Forrest, and he received a new command in western Tennessee and Mississippi; but after his October raid, remarkably Wheeler, who had performed in a less than aggressive manner during the recent battle, retained complete control of his cavalry corps, plus Forrest's cavalry corps.[11]

Crook, with his division scattered at the various locations along the river, was no match for Wheeler's cavalry. He had less than 2,000 cavalry to defend the entire flank. Crook fought with Wheeler for about an hour on September 30 before withdrawing, miraculously saving his supply train. Wheeler made his crossing crashing into Eli Long's brigade which had suffered a defeat at Glass Mill the week before. The brigade lost 136 of the 900 troopers in that fight and again faced the overwhelming numbers of Wheeler's horsemen. The 1st Ohio Cavalry guarded Cotton Port Ford and after the death of Valentine Cupp at Glass Mill, regimental command had fallen to Major Thomas J. Patten, known in the cavalry as "Rough and Ready" Tom. Patton was never so happy as when he was in a mêlée, but on that day, the 1st Ohio was thrown back as Wheeler opened on the Union cavalry with artillery and crossed the river losing only 20 men in the process. In addition, the 4th Ohio Cavalry, north of the Cotton Port Ford crossing, was temporarily cut off but ultimately made its escape. Albert Brant, 4th Ohio Cavalry, exclaimed: "[W]e are in a devil of a fix." Wheeler sent an officer demanding the surrender of the Union cavalry, but Crook declined to surrender. John McLain, 4th Michigan, noted that the soldier carrying the flag of truce remained a prisoner because the Confederates did not stop their attack during the truce. After getting news of the Confederate attack, Minty had his brigade in the saddle and riding toward Long's position at midnight on September 29.[12]

Minty had had a difficult time over the past six weeks dealing with Crittenden and still provided the most valuable cavalry service during the Battle of Chickamauga. Now, he immediately ran afoul of Crook. At the first indication of Wheeler's crossing, Minty sent Thomas McCormick's battalion of the 4th U.S. Cavalry to attempt to delay the movement. The rest of Minty's brigade saddled and prepared to meet the enemy as Wheeler crossed the Tennessee River. Amid a drenching rain, Minty requested permission from Crook to resist the crossing and Crook refused. Instead, Crook told Minty to send two battalions to support McCormick and Minty sent two battalions of the 4th Michigan. Major Horace Gray moved the 4th Michigan to the fight and quickly replied he was outnumbered ten to one. Next, Crook ordered his division south to Sale Creek nearer to Chattanooga, but this meant leaving Gray and McCormick to their fate. Minty insisted he move to their support and again Crook refused. This interaction set the tone for relations between Crook and Minty throughout this campaign. Fortunately, the three battalions extracted themselves from behind Wheeler's line and returned to Minty's brigade. Minty bitterly stated: "Our inactivity was very galling."[13]

Sergeant James Larson, 4th U.S. Cavalry, was part of the encircled Federal cavalry. Larson explained that the enemy thought the Union cavalry had escaped in the darkness but three Union battalions remained quietly surrounded by the enemy. They finally made their escape by passing along a river bottom aided by the heavy rain storm during the night and slipped past the encircling enemy. Larson explained that as they were making their escape the Southern cavalry began to move away and the Union cavalry audaciously moved forward as an apparent part of the enemy column in the darkness. When the main body of a Confederate column stopped, the Union cavalrymen kept moving past the Confederate outposts, and they were challenged about where they were going. In the darkness one brave soul simply replied, "picket," and the Union battalions made their escape unmolested.[14]

William Van Antwerp, 4th Michigan, unhappily wrote in a letter that the Confederate cavalry crossed "directly under our noses." The river was very low due to the drought and Wheeler crossed at a location where Crook "supposed there was no ford." The first reports of the crossing reached Crook at midnight, but due the seriousness of approaching a large number of enemies in the dark, further pursuit was delayed until morning. Van Antwerp noted early the next morning his regiment advanced and found the main body of the enemy about one half mile from the river. The Michiganders ran into carbine fire and soon artillery opened up, forcing them rearward.[15]

Once across the river, Wheeler sent one column south through the Sequatchie Valley with 1,500 troopers and claimed a 32-wagon supply train while a second column, commanded by John Wharton, moved directly west. Wheeler, Martin and Wharton met over a campfire and Wheeler gave his division commanders their orders. Wheeler sent Wharton's division directly to McMinnville despite Wharton's opposition to the idea of splitting the command in enemy territory. The relationship between Wharton and Wheeler had deteriorated so badly over the past year that Wharton willingly accepted this assignment because he wanted away from any further direct contact with Wheeler. The chaplain of the 8th Texas Cavalry wrote in letter that Wharton would prefer resigning than serving further under the command of Wheeler for whom he had "a great contempt." On October 2, Wheeler riding with Martin's division discovered an 800-wagon supply train at Anderson's Crossroads which he handily captured. Anderson's Crossroads was about twenty miles north of Chattanooga and ten miles east of Tracy City. After selecting the supplies he needed, he set fire to the remainder. Robert Mitchell tried to react to the raid and he sent a group of scouts to direct Edward McCook's cavalry, which moved to intercept Wheeler's column, to the site of the attack. Corporal William Fowler, 4th Ohio Cavalry, commanded the detail which carried a message to McCook. When Fowler arrived at Anderson's Crossroad, McCook had not arrived, but the men found themselves surrounded when they heard gunfire to their front and rear. Fowler's detail received some much-needed assistance from a pro–Union citizen who told them where to hide and to observe the fighting around the supply trains. Fowler observed a large body of enemy cavalry overwhelm the 21st Kentucky Infantry and a small detachment of cavalry and then go to work on the supply train. The Union guards held out for about two hours from 9:00 a.m. to 11:00 a.m. until they were defeated; and after pillaging the train, it was set afire. The enemy remained in battle line around the trains until 3:00 p.m. and Fowler worried that McCook would ride into an ambush but he was helpless to prevent this. Fortunately for Fowler and McCook, the enemy cavalry began to withdraw and placed a strong rearguard to prevent a surprise attack. The same citizen who assisted Fowler's detail soon returned after serving as a guide for McCook's cavalry.[16]

The supply train was desperately needed for Rosecrans' defeated army and this was a severe loss. As Wheeler rode through the countryside, the Union cavalry and infantry, in close proximity, were mobilized to stop the raid. When McCook's column reached the location of the wagon trains, Colonel Oscar La Grange's 1st Wisconsin Cavalry and Major David Brigg's 2nd Indiana Cavalry, rode in advance of the column. The two Federal regiments caught Wheeler's rearguard as the main column withdrew after pillaging the train. The 2nd Indiana and 1st Wisconsin had ridden twenty miles from Jasper to reach the Confederate column and they intended to do as much damage as possible to Wheeler's rearguard.[17]

Colonel Oscar La Grange, commander of the 1st Wisconsin Cavalry, "enjoyed nothing more than a headlong cavalry charge" (Mollus Mass Civil War Collection, United States Army Heritage and Education Center, Military History Institute, Carlisle, Pennsylvania).

The reports were vastly different between Wheeler and McCook. As Wheeler left the train, the two Union regiments surged ahead. Wheeler merely reported the skirmish, "Fortunately, the enemy was repulsed." La Grange recorded his pursuit in more detail which resulted in the recapturing a Union surgeon and four other Union prisoners. Edward McCook rode with the 1st Wisconsin and 2nd Indiana and passed the Union wagon train, "Passing the burning train the explosion of ammunition was terrific, and farther on sutlers' goods were strewn." Riding another few miles ahead, La Grange found the rearguard of Brigadier General Will T. Martin's column. La Grange pushed the Confederate rear guard for two miles successfully killing twelve of the enemy and wounding several others. When the chase was delayed by a more concentrated resistance, La Grange dismounted his troops and utilized his repeating rifles to deliver more effective fire than the enemy who remained in their saddles. When confronted with a group of five sharpshooters, La Grange simply charged their position, overwhelming the enemy. The Union regiments caught the rearguard and Edward McCook ordered the 2nd Indiana to the right and the 1st Wisconsin to the left and formed three cavalry lines for each regiment. The first battalion of each regiment formed the first line and the next two battalions formed in the rear. McCook ordered the charge of both regiments and "with such vigor" that the enemy fell back. La Grange's regiment attacked the Southern defenders "a few rods from their column, killed 2 with their sabers and wounded and captured 2 others, whom they brought back to our advance, escaping unharmed a heavy volley from the astonished rebels." Then, the 1st Wisconsin swung further to the left to fire into the flank of the defenders and at the same time the 2nd Indiana swung to the right, dismounted and charged into the right flank. The surprised column swung around preparing to meet the Union cavalry, when a reserve of cavalry charged into the defenders; and La Grange exclaimed he "scattered his wavering ranks in the wildest rout. Thirty-seven of the enemy were killed and wounded, and 42 made prisoners.... The general himself was closely pursued and narrowly escaped." La Grange proudly exclaimed that most of the enemy wounds came from sabers. La Grange and Briggs broke off their pursuit and the Confederate column continued eastward.[18]

Captain Thomas McCahan, 9th Pennsylvania Cavalry, described La Grange in the attack as a "tall heavy man and striking whilst his horse was in the act of jumping, threw him." After sabering two officers, La Grange continued his attack and jumped his horse over a fence in an attempt to strike the opposing cavalry's commanding officer, Will Martin. While La Grange was temporarily and ingloriously unsaddled, he had performed an extraordinary attack on a larger Confederate force. Sergeant G. W. Baum, 2nd Indiana, explained that Federal cavalry chased the enemy about four or five miles in the skirmish. While La Grange had been unceremoniously unhorsed, Baum's horse was killed under him, but he found a mule to replace his mount. Baum noted that the mule had never been ridden and that he had a "gay old time" for a while. La Grange underestimated the number of prisoners captured in his attack. Sixty-one prisoners, including two majors and seven other officers, were moved to the rear after the skirmish. In addition, not all the supply wagons were damaged in the raid, Quartermaster General, M. C. Meigs, estimated that about 360 wagons were destroyed in the raid.[19]

Meanwhile, Crook pulled his Second Division together after he moved southward to prevent being captured and set off in pursuit, but only rode about ten miles before stopping for the first day. This would be the only short day Crook's cavalry would have until October 8 and Crook, in a single-minded, relentless pursuit chased Wheeler at a severe cost to his horses and his men. On October 1, Edward McCook's First Division accompanied by Wilder's mounted infantry mobilized and also began the chase, but McCook lagged behind Crook for much of the pursuit. McCook was delayed because he waited for Campbell's brigade that was unexpectedly late much to the ire of McCook. Wilder's (now Miller's) mounted infantry brigade continued forward and reached Crook's column. By the time the Union cavalry was organized for the pursuit, Wheeler had a twelve to fourteen-hour head start over Crook and even longer for McCook. Robert Mitchell, cavalry corps commander, did not accompany the cavalry in the initial pursuit but he would join McCook's division a few days later. Mitchell, whose health was failing, was to have a difficult ride over the next week.[20]

Much of Crook's personality could be observed in his actions during Wheeler's raid. Crook, born on the family farm near Dayton, Ohio in 1828, was a West Point graduate, class of 1852. He finished near the bottom of his class, 38th of a class of 43. Crook served in the 4th U.S. Infantry in the western United States before the war and returned east at the beginning of the Civil War. He had commanded an infantry brigade in the Battle of South Mountain and Antietam. The tenacity that Crook demonstrated in this pursuit of Wheeler revealed characteristics that would make him one of the best commanders in the western United States after the war. Crook caught the rear of Wheeler's cavalry at Robinson's Trace resulting in a small skirmish on October 2. On October 3, Crook again caught the rear guard of Martin's division, in possession of Hill's Gap near Beersheba, and a heated skirmish resulted. Minty's cavalry began the skirmish, but the advantage of having mounted infantry attached to the cavalry now yielded good results as Crook ordered Miller's mounted infantry to advance and moved Minty into position to support the advance. The 98th Illinois and 17th Indiana led the attack, and 72nd Indiana and 123rd Illinois followed in reserve. A "brisk engagement ensued," recorded Abram Miller. Robert Burns wrote that eleven dead enemy soldiers were found after the enemy retreated and he estimated that twenty-five were killed in total.[21]

The Union mounted infantry charged and broke the Confederate line propelling the defenders back, capturing four guns in the attack. Crook almost surrounded the entire Confederate defense, but darkness fell before he could complete the encirclement and the Confederates slipped away. But, not before Crook was able to draw blood in this heated engagement. He reported, "My loss was 46 killed and wounded. The enemy's loss is not definitely known. We found some 10 of their dead close by the road, and a good many of their wounded scattered along the road in houses." Abram Miller's mounted infantry claimed the 4th Alabama Cavalry's colors during the fight. On the Confederate side of the fight, Wheeler recognized General William T. Martin; Colonel Isaac Avery, 4th Georgia; and Lieutenant Colonel J. C. Griffith, 3rd Kentucky Cavalry (CSA), for their actions in this hard-fought engagement. Darkness ended the fight and Wheeler withdrew. Robert Minty's and Eli Long's men bivouacked for the night "with horses saddled and men under arms." Henry Albert Potter, 4th Michigan Cavalry, simply recorded in his diary "tired-tired-tired."[22]

The hard riding troopers soon exhausted their rations which they received on September 26 as the cavalrymen pressed ahead with little sleep. The entire pursuit tested the endurance of horse and man. "It seems almost incredible that soldiers could have stood such service. At points during the advance the troopers cut down chestnut trees to collect the nuts to eat," wrote Lucien Wilson, historian of the 4th Ohio Cavalry. An officer in the 1st Ohio considered this was the seventh day the cavalry had been in the saddle after drawing five days' rations and the thoughts of fighting Wheeler's men on empty stomachs, riding for hours and all on little sleep was not a "very cheering reflection." The next morning some of the Union troopers breakfasted on a few hard apples.[23]

McMinnville Garrison Destroyed

Still Wheeler rode west, uniting his two columns which had been advancing along different routes, and captured the Union garrison and stores at McMinnville on October 3. The Confederates captured almost 600 men, 200 horses and large amount of supplies. Wheeler's cavalry spent the day destroying the commissary and military stores, a locomotive, rail cars and the Hickory Creek Bridge. But the Union pursuit intensified. McCook pressed ahead to reach the main body of the Confederate cavalry riding toward the heart of Tennessee; but the rest of the Union cavalry lagged behind and Crook still commanded the closest division in hot pursuit.[24]

When Crook reached McMinnville, he found the devastation of Wheeler's actions and Crook found the garrison had surrendered without a fight. "We did not stop," wrote Robert Burns. Crook continued his pursuit, and a few miles outside of McMinnville on the Murfreesboro Road, he encountered Wheeler's rear guard concealed at the edge of some woods. After chasing the Confederate rear guard for some miles, at 6 p.m. the enemy formed a strong defensive line and unlimbered the artillery. In return, Lilly's 18th Indiana Artillery and a section of the Chicago Board of Trade horse artillery unlimbered in an open field and began shelling the enemy. Crook had no time for the delay and he ordered Colonel Eli Long to charge the enemy. Eli Long, with his favorite pipe firmly between his teeth, rode at the head of the 2nd Kentucky Cavalry and "made a most gallant charge of some 5 miles, breaking through his lines ... driving the remainder into the main column, compelling him to turn round and give me fight." During the pursuit, Crook rotated the lead brigade each day. Minty's brigade led the march on October 4 and Long's brigade had moved into the lead position on October 5.[25]

During the day's action Captain William Scott, 1st Ohio Cavalry, paid back some illtreatment of his temporary Confederate hosts. Scott had been captured during Wheeler's breakout over the Tennessee River and had been forced to run beside the Confederate cavalry under threat of death for his unrepentant remarks about the Confederacy. Scott escaped and now rode with Long's cavalry. During the action, the Confederate captain, who had made Scott run, was captured and fell under Scott's control. Scott took charge of the captain and ordered him to dismount. W. L. Curry, 1st Ohio Cavalry, recorded, "It is safe to say that the Texan had to take his turn at hoofing it that day."[26]

Having pushed the skirmishers aside, Crook met a defensive line at the edge of some woods. He called up his mounted infantry, unlimbered his artillery and pushed ahead. The fight lasted about two hours until sunset before pushing the enemy to the rear. Then, Crook's weary cavalrymen lay down for a night's sleep without supper, although the horses were able to graze. Crook recognized the Chicago Board of Trade Battery for another exemplary performance as its fire assisted in knocking out the Confederate artillery during the exchange. Lieutenant Trumbull Griffin, who had performed such good service a few weeks before at Reed's Bridge, commanded the two-gun section during the fight. One of his guns was disabled in the exchange and all the men on that gun were either killed or wounded. Some of the cavalry stopped at the site of an old camp and found poor rations—"some old crackers, blue with mould, and found them to taste delicious."[27]

The destruction of the Union garrison and depot at McMinnville gained the attention of the supporting cavalry in Middle Tennessee. The 5th Iowa Cavalry which was near Decherd learned of the action and immediately mounted and joined in the pursuit on October 5. The momentum of Wheeler's raid seemed to have slowed by October 5. He descended on Woodbury but he was unable to cause destruction at Murfreesboro, settling instead for a "demonstration." The Union cavalry was closing in on Wheeler, who did not have time for any pitched battles. The Federal cavalry began its pursuit at 1:00 a.m. hoping to catch Wheeler and rode about fifty miles during the day. Crook reached Murfreesboro at four o'clock in the afternoon and the officers of Crook's command believed that their pursuit saved Murfreesboro from the fate that McMinnville suffered just days before. When Crook rode through Murfreesboro, he "found every person at Murfreesborough in great consternation, and overjoyed to see us." The citizens of the town feared an attack from Wheeler and the horsemen in blue were a welcome sight. On October 6, Wheeler swung south destroying bridges and railroads on his way to the pro–Union town of Shelbyville, home of Lieutenant Colonel Robert Galbraith, 5th Tennessee Cavalry (U.S.), which he promptly sacked. "All the business houses robbed and the citizens terrorized," wrote Lieutenant W. L. Curry, 1st Ohio. Wheeler also captured a small Union garrison at Wartrace along his route.[28]

Robert Mitchell finally reached Crook's column and he assumed command of the cavalry. Crook sent out scouts while he gave his horsemen a chance to rest. The toll of the pursuit was severe thus far; and approximately five hundred horses were disabled during the pursuit and as result Crook would continue the next day without that number of troopers. While the troopers rested, the blacksmiths went to work re-shoeing the remainder of the horses which was badly needed.[29]

Robert Minty chafed under Crook's command. The expedition began poorly when Crook left Minty's cavalry to its fate as Wheeler crossed the Tennessee River at Cotton Port, and the relationship between Minty and Crook disintegrated over a three-day period starting on October 5. Crook reached McMinnville on October 4 and the next morning Minty came to Crook and asked for thirty minutes for his men to forage their exhausted horses. Minty explained that his men had not had time to forage their horses the evening before and that the mounts would be ruined, or simply "break down," if they were not allowed to feed on grain. Crook had expected Minty to forage his mounts from a large cornfield as the remainder of the division had done the night before. Because Minty had not accomplished this, he denied the request and ordered Minty to advance without forage. Minty was not lax in trying to gather the forage, and he sent two groups of the men to find the grain in the cornfield. Both groups came back saying there were plenty of stalks but no corn. To the frustration of Minty, the men who ground the corn for the remainder of the division told him the other regiments had already found the corn and had fed their horses. Because of Crook's decision, Minty lamented the loss of 256 mounts of a total of 1,000 he had in his brigade at the time. On the next day (October 6), the situation continued to turn sour. Crook sent orders to the division to be ready to move at daylight from Murfreesboro, but it was around 9:00 a.m. before the column began moving out. Minty's brigade did not reach the column at the appointed time because he needed to shoe some of his mounts. Crook would later acknowledge that the condition of the entire division "was bad." Further evidence revealed that Minty had been given permission from headquarters to deal with the horseshoes, but the problem resulted because Crook told Minty's staff there would be rations available for Minty's troops the evening before. Crook sent a message to Minty that headquarters staff would provide the rations for Minty's men; however, the rations weren't ready until 4:00 a.m. the next morning

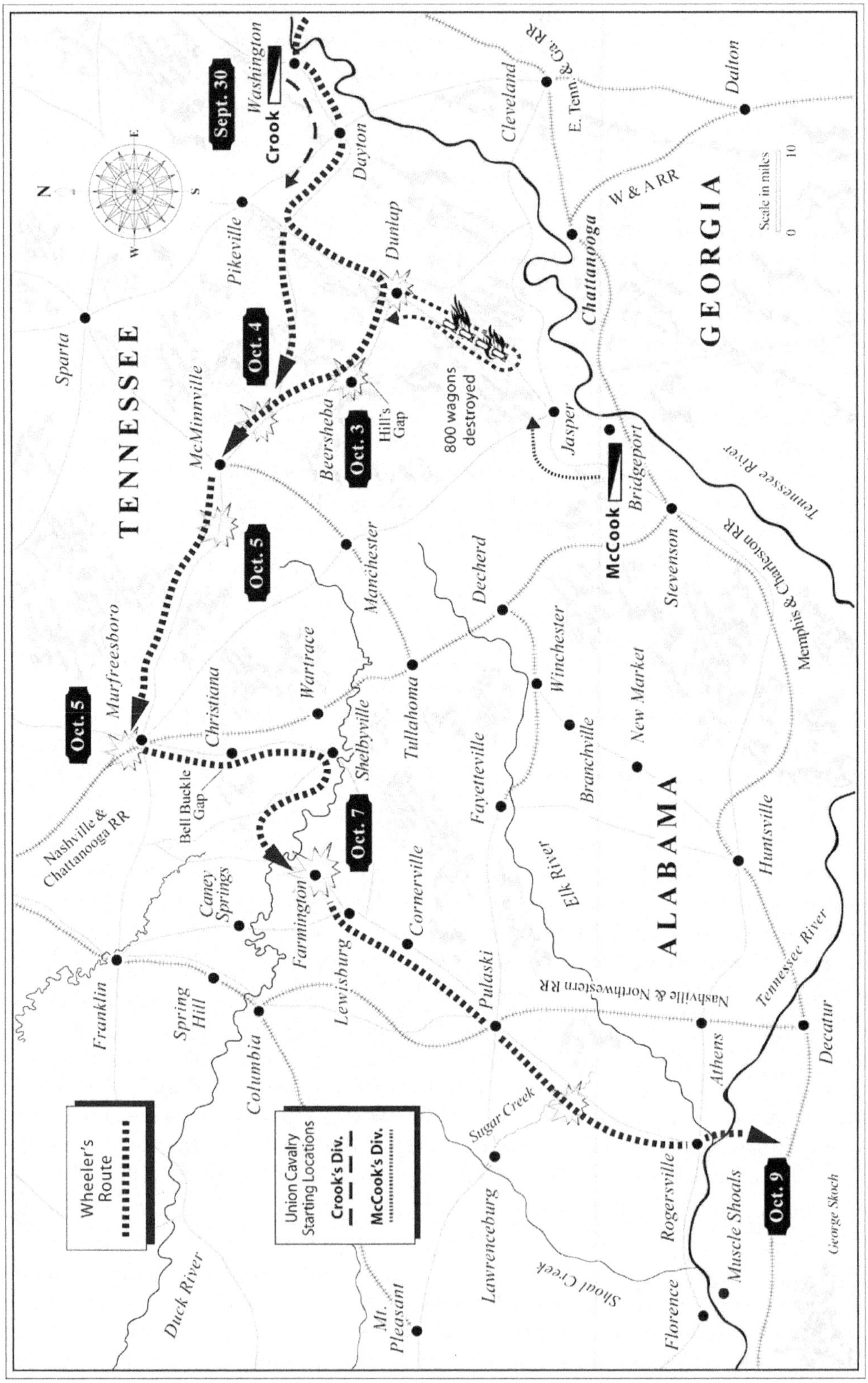

Wheeler's Raid.

Eleven. Wheeler's Tennessee Raid (September 30–October 9) 249

Crook fumed while Minty shoed his mounts, but Captain McIntyre, 4th U.S. Cavalry, exclaimed that the horses were all but "bare-footed" ["Horseshoeing in the Army" (from *Frank Leslie's Illustrated Famous Leaders and Battle Scenes of the Civil War*, 1896, p. 400)].

and this put the shoeing efforts behind schedule. Minty reasoned that his men needed to be fed first and then the horses needed to be shod. He ultimately regained the column, albeit, somewhat late. Captain James McIntyre, 4th U.S. Cavalry, when asked about the importance of shoeing the mounts, declared this was "absolutely necessary." McIntyre exclaimed that the horses were all but "bare-footed" and tired; and he further stated he would have lost, an additional 250–300 horses if they were not shod at that time. The shoeing only delayed Minty about 30–45 minutes, but the delay further angered Crook.[30]

Union Pursuit and the Battle at Farmington

On October 6, the fresh 5th Iowa Cavalry, Lieutenant Colonel Mathewson T. Patrick commanding, which had been serving in Middle Tennessee during the previous Chickamauga Campaign got into action under brigade command of the very capable Colonel William Lowe. The 5th Iowa, stationed near Winchester, received the news about the capture of McMinnville on October 4. Charles Alley of that regiment sarcastically wrote: "Most splendid weather to put men in a condition to kill one another...." Lowe initially moved the regiment from Winchester to Wartrace and as the pursuit continued, the 5th Iowa passed through Tullahoma on the way northward, reaching the Duck River at 3 p.m. The newly arrived Union regiment operated under a distinct disadvantage because all communications to the north had been cut off. Wheeler captured the garrison of Union infantry at Wartrace, but a group of Union infantry, which had avoided capture, reported the enemy cavalry causing destruction to the railroad near Wartrace. Lowe's fresh regiment found the group of raiders, belonging to Martin's Confederate cavalry division, burning a bridge and sent them hurriedly back to the main body of Confederate cavalry. Federal cavalryman George Healy explained that as the 5th Iowa advanced the enemy retreated: "The Rebels showed no fight." The 5th Iowa Cavalry gave chase to the retreating cavalry and caught the rear guard and had "quite a sharp skirmish wounding several and having one man mortally wounded." Eugene Marshall, trooper of the 5th Iowa, explained the skirmish occurred across a small stream and the two enemies fired on each other and the air was permeated with the "singing of bullets." The arrival of the Federal cavalry caused the Confederates to withdraw southward although the Southern reports claimed they repulsed the Union cavalry. Mitchell wrote that the Confederate soldiers say they "whipped the Yankees" but withdrew because they had received orders to move further south. The several reports by the Federal cavalry troopers reported they faced a group of enemy troopers serving as rearguard who emptied their revolvers and then rode toward Shelbyville. During the evening, Federal infantry arrived on the scene and secured the railroad.[31]

On the evening of October 6, Wheeler bivouacked south of the Duck River and he rested his command after sacking the town of Shelbyville. Next, he ordered his division commanders to keep an eye out for the pursuing Union cavalry. According to Wheeler, Brigadier General Henry B. Davidson, commanding Forrest's cavalry, was informed of the Union cavalry position and he was ordered to keep scouts out to watch for any movement. Davidson would be blamed by Wheeler for the results of the fight which would occur the next day near Farmington. Wheeler wrote, "Unfortunately, he failed to comply with this order, and on the following morning was attacked by a superior force of the enemy. I received two consecutive dispatches ... from General Davidson which indicated that he was moving down Duck River, but on questioning his couriers I ascertained that he was moving toward Farmington. I immediately started at a trot toward Farmington with Martin's division, ordering General Wharton and the wagons to follow me. I reached Farmington just in time to place five regiments of Martin's command in position when the enemy appeared. I had ordered General Davidson to form in column by fours on the pike and to charge the enemy when they were repulsed by Martin's division, General Davidson having officially reported to me that only three regiments of the enemy had been seen during the day. The engagement commenced warmly, but the enemy was soon repulsed. General Davidson had failed to form as stated, and instead had moved for some distance. The enemy soon after came up in strong force with a division of infantry and a division of cavalry. We fought them with great warmth for twenty minutes, when we charged the line and drove it back for some distance." Wheeler concluded his report by claiming 188 losses for the Union cavalry in actions at Farmington while he suffered one quarter of these losses. Certainly, military commanders during the Civil War embellished the outcome of various engagements, but perhaps Wheeler took excessive liberties in this report in just about all aspects. Wheeler faced a single brigade of mounted infantry and a brigade of cavalry. A more realistic report can be found in the Union cavalry reports and also in the only other Confederate report of this engagement written by Colonel George B. Hodge which described the action leading up the battle at Farmington.[32]

General Robert Mitchell finally reached Crook's Second Cavalry Division on the evening of October 5 and, with the combined Union cavalry corps, rode in pursuit of Wheeler on the October 6. Mitchell ordered Edward McCook's First Division of cavalry to ride west for Unionville on the north side of the Duck River, and George Crook's Second Division, including Abram Miller's mounted infantry, to advance toward Farmington on the south side of the river on October 7.[33]

Appropriately, it was Crook's column that participated in the heaviest fighting of the day. As the Union cavalry advanced, a local citizen ran to the column and told the troopers the location of the Confederate cavalry. Crook found Henry Davidson's Confederate cavalry in line behind a fence about three miles from Shelbyville and he sent Miller's mounted infantry forward on horseback, pushing the enemy cavalry into a cedar thicket. Next, Eli Long's cavalry brigade charged the Confederate cavalry. Long led "a most gallant saber charge, driving the enemy 3 miles, killing and capturing a great many rebels," exclaimed Crook. The enemy made another attempt to halt the Union attack, and the mounted infantry again rode to the front and drove the enemy to Farmington. Long, who had his horse shot from under him at McMinnville a few days before, was wounded with a Minié ball in his side and his horse was again shot during the attack. During the charge, Colonel Charles Siedel, 3rd Ohio Cavalry, was hurled to the ground when his horse was killed beneath him. When the horse fell, it pinned Siedel to the ground, where he lay until some troopers could lift the horse from him. At this point the Federal cavalry gathered up seventy wounded Confederate troopers and the surgeons went to work on their injuries under some trees near the site of the fight. After retreating, the Confederates again found refuge in a thicket about three quarter of a mile from Farmington and with the mounted infantry in the front and the cavalry on the flank, Crook advanced again. One Union cavalryman referred to the Confederates moving into position for a "last desperate stand." At this point, Will Martin's division moved into position to support Davidson's retreating cavalry. As Wheeler's cavalry concentrated, Crook realized he was vulnerable to an attack on his flank. Then, Crook sent a rider to bring Minty's brigade to the front.[34]

As Crook continued his fight in a misty rain, he assumed Minty had followed his orders, but he soon found Minty was not at the front with the rest of the Crook's troops. This enraged Crook because Minty's absence left him with only 1,500 men. Crook now found himself in a precarious position. He had advanced into Farmington against Wheeler's main body of cavalry with what he thought was his entire division (three brigades) only to find one of his brigades missing. Wheeler moved Martin's dismounted cavalry division into a defensive line in another cedar thicket at Farmington and the battle intensified. Part of Wharton's division, which had moved further south with the supply train and away from the fighting, was ordered to join in the fight. Wheeler's artillery soon opened on the Union column with canister, grape and shell at a distance of about four hundred yards. Crook ordered Chicago Board of Trade Battery forward and along with Lilly's 18th Indiana Battery returned the fire on the Confederate artillery. Captain Stokes ordered the Union artillery to fire and "in three shots he disabled one of their pieces, blowing up a caisson, and throwing their ranks into confusion." In return, the fire of the Confederate battery disabled one of the Chicago Board of Trade's guns, but the cannons from both sides continued to fire. The Confederate cavalry, outnumbering Crook, also moved into position to charge his line, but the Union artillery shifted and began firing on the cavalry which halted its advance.[35]

Crook ordered his mounted infantry forward. Henry Campbell of 18th Indiana Artillery recorded the "brisk engagement" in his diary, "They were formed across the road with 4 pieces of artillery in position on each side. The cedar woods, in which the Rebels had formed their line & through which we had to advance was the thickest I ever seen. The men were obliged to crawl on their hands & knees to move forward. The only clear place was where the road ran. 17th dismounted & formed on the right, & the 123d on the left…. The firing now became terrible—one constant roll—the 7 shooters carrying death & destruction into the Rebel ranks.—The woods were so thick that the lines approached within 30 yards of each other. Rebs stood bravely—holding their position in spite of the dreadful fire." The Union dismounted infantry led the attack and Long's cavalry followed on horseback. Wheeler's and Crook's reports vary on the outcome of the fight. Wheeler claimed he forced Crook to retreat "some distance" while Crook claimed his mounted infantry broke the Confederate line. Alva Griest of Miller's brigade (72nd Indiana Mounted Infantry) recorded in his diary, "they throwing grape and canister into our ranks from their artillery, until we got to within 150 yards, when finding we would surround them and capture their entire force they endeavored to escape, but they had delayed just a little too long to save their artillery and our sharp-shooters shot seven of their horses rendering it impossible to get their guns off the field." While Wheeler claimed victory, other Confederate reports gave a more accurate accounting. Colonel George Hodge recorded that the remnants of his command reached Wheeler's line at four o'clock and that the Confederate division was "broken" at five o'clock and the retreat began again. Wheeler, realizing he had nothing to gain in a prolonged fight behind enemy lines, withdrew; but Wheeler's assessment of the fight at Farmington attempted to show victory instead of defeat.[36]

Colonel Abram Miller, commanding the Union mounted infantry brigade, explained that the 17th and 72nd Indiana Mounted Infantry initiated the attack on Wheeler's cavalry. The 17th Indiana filed into line on the left and 72nd Indiana moved to the right of the road. The 98th Illinois and 123rd Illinois moved in support of these regiments. Miller saw three lines of enemy cavalry before him and overlapping his flanks. Two Union cavalry regiments moved forward on the flanks in support of Miller and the third regiment of Long's cavalry covered the rear. Miller gave the order for his brigade to advance and the colonel of 123rd Illinois Mounted Infantry, James Monroe, was mortally wounded in the attack. As Miller continued the advance the Confederate artillery targeted his lines with grape and canister. "[T]he enemy raking my lines … at a range not exceeding 300 yards, the shell[s] exploding in all directions in the thick cedars above our heads and at our feet. While thus closely engaged the enemy, with terrible energy and loud huzzas, charged my lines, but without effect. At this time Captain Stokes opened fire, which partially drew the attention of the enemy's artillery, and seeing the critical condition of affairs, and believing victory could only be obtained by a successful charge, I at once ordered it, which was promptly executed, the whole line impetuously advancing with a shout, driving back the successive lines of the enemy, and resulting in his complete rout, the capture of three pieces of artillery, and the occupancy of the town, when orders were received from General Crook to halt and await further orders."[37]

R. F. Bunting, Chaplain of the 8th Texas, concluded: "But at Farmington were we well nigh ruined." Bunting gave a good description of the battle at Farmington and the aftermath. He wrote in a letter that John Wharton and Thomas Harrison kept the battle from being a worse disaster for Wheeler than it was. A charge by Wharton's cavalry temporarily halted the Union advance long enough for Wheeler to extract his command. As it was, Bunting wrote:

Eleven. Wheeler's Tennessee Raid (September 30–October 9)

Colonel George B. Hodge, commanding a cavalry brigade, reported: "My gallant brigade was cut to pieces and slaughtered. I had informed the officers and men that the sacrifice of their lives was necessary" ("Cavalry Charge near Culpeper CH" Library of Congress).

"Wheeler's entire force was repulsed and scattered. The attack by Wharton saved Wheeler's cavalry which had been at risk of being a complete and irretrievable route. As it was our loss was severe.... The fight was a disgraceful blunder on the part of Wheeler and demands an investigation." Wharton had his horse killed under him during the fight and Colonel Gustave Cook, 8th Texas Cavalry, was wounded twice in the fight.[38]

Colonel George B. Hodge's Third Confederate Cavalry Brigade after-action report also revealed a significantly different version of the action than Wheeler's report. Hodge had the unenviable task of providing the rearguard action for Davidson's cavalry. Hodge wrote, "For five hours and a half, over 7 miles of country, the unequal contest continued. My gallant brigade was cut to pieces and slaughtered. I had informed the officers and men that the sacrifice of their lives was necessary and they manfully made the sacrifice." The losses claimed by Wheeler and Crook, again, were quite different. Crook reported he lost a total of 111 men for the entire expedition and Abram Miller recorded his loss at 96 for the campaign. Miller also recorded 86 enemy dead and another 270 prisoners during the engagement on October 7 alone. Wheeler claimed a loss of 40–50 men, apparently, for just the engagement at Farmington of his command on October 7 and could not have included Hodge's, and perhaps all of Forrest's detached cavalry. Trooper James Blackburn, 8th Texas Cavalry, also gave the victory to Crook: "The battle of Farmington was now over and the enemy held the field."[39]

Minty's Failure to Join in the Farmington Battle

After the battle, Crook turned his attention to Robert Minty. Crook wrote, "That night after the fighting had ceased, Colonel Minty with his brigade came up, stating that he had no orders to march with me. From this, together with a disposition manifested during the whole expedition to frustrate my designs in a covert manner, I deprived him of his command and sent him to the rear." The animosity which began at the crossing at Cotton Port finally resulted in the arrest of an officer which had performed such positive service to the Federal army only a couple of weeks earlier. This disagreement would result in Minty's court martial which would take place in February 1864. Crook brought Minty up on charges of failure to obey the order to march with the column to Farmington and for two other specifications, much to Minty's surprise, in which Crook alleged resulted in conduct subversive of good order and discipline—Minty's failure to feed his mounts from the cornfield west of McMinnville and his delay caused by shoeing his horses south of Murfreesboro.[40]

The details regarding the miscommunications with Minty came out in the court martial. On the evening of October 6, Crook approached Minty and verbally told him to prepare to march at daylight the next morning in the continuation of the pursuit of Wheeler. Because Minty's brigade led the column during the day, Crook expected him to fall into his normal position at the rear. When asked later if it was his custom to follow verbal orders with written ones, Crook acknowledged that it was but in this case, he did not send Minty any written orders. He did send written orders to Eli Long and Abram Miller. In addition to receiving no orders, additional confusion resulted because Crook mentioned to Minty that part of the command would move to Unionville and part of the command would move to Farmington. This was true, but Crook intended to say that McCook's division would move to Unionville and Crook's entire division would move to Farmington. Upon receiving no orders to march with Crook, Minty expected to receive orders to move to Unionville.[41]

Minty kept about a third of his command saddled during the evening and Minty prepared to continue the advance the next morning. The rest of his brigade was expected to be saddled within two minutes of the notification, and Minty had men ready to ride at daybreak. Still, he remained without orders. As Long's and Miller's brigade rode past Minty's camp, Minty asked a staff member: "I wonder what that is? It looks like Wilder's men." Then he asked his staff member to find Crook and ask him what was going on, but the staff member couldn't find Crook because he rode on the side of the column away from Minty's headquarters. Shortly thereafter, Major William H. Sinclair, Robert Mitchell and Edward McCook all rode into Minty's headquarters and told Minty that McCook would be moving toward Unionville and Mitchell planned to move back to Shelbyville. Sinclair told Minty that Mitchell was trying to ascertain the direction of Wheeler's column and he said it was Mitchell's intention to leave a body of cavalry at Minty's location until Wheeler had been found. This confirmed Minty's expectation to be ordered to Unionville some time later. In the meantime, Minty's brigade surgeon went looking for Crook's divisional surgeon. Dr. George Fish always received orders from division headquarters when the division intended to move but Fish also received no orders from his direct superior, Dr. Myron C. Cuykendall, division surgeon, regarding any advance.[42]

Minty waited, without orders. About mid-day, Mitchell rode back into Minty's camp and told him that Crook expected him with the main column riding toward Farmington.

Minty responded: "He is skirmishing with the enemy? I don't know why he should expect me there. He gave me no orders. Indeed, I thought I had a chance to go to Unionville again." Minty asked Mitchell for permission to ride to Crook and permission was granted. Minty immediately mounted his brigade and rode toward Farmington and Mitchell rode toward Unionville. When asked during the court martial whether he had any evidence to suggest that Minty overtly tried to throw obstacles to thwart the pursuit, Crook acknowledged that he had none—only Minty's failure to ride to Farmington.[43]

The court martial resulted in many of the most important members of the cavalry of the Army of the Cumberland testifying, including, David Stanley, who told the court that Minty was a "most excellent soldier—reliable—always on time and prompt to execute orders." Stanley went on to explain that he always arranged regiments in such a manner that would allow Minty to always be in command. The court found Minty not guilty of all charges.[44]

Union Cavalry Catches Wheeler's Rearguard at Sugar Creek

The morning after the Battle of Farmington, the Union cavalry took up the pursuit of Wheeler as he rode for the Tennessee River. The troopers of the 5th Iowa rode past the previous day's battlefield and one trooper noted that Farmington had only two or three hundred inhabitants and that the town was filled with Wheeler's wounded and dead. Many of the Confederate dead still remained unmoved on the battlefield. Wheeler's retreat to the Tennessee River proved to be an unpleasant task for the cavalry in gray. The Union cavalry had found Wheeler, defeated him at Farmington and garnered fresh troops. Several reports described discarded items along the escaping cavalry's route and the energy of Federal cavalry increased. Some of the Union troopers noticing the Confederate cavalry wore blue clothing declared they "would shoot every man that had our clothes on." Edward Walter, 5th Iowa Cavalry, recorded the action of his regiment as it caught up Wheeler's rearguard the next day, October 8, "No sooner had we reached a creek when Whiz came a volley from a whole brigade ... but you can be assured we soon returned the compliment, and a sharp little fight ensued until the Rebs broke and ran." The fight took place at Sugar Creek where Wheeler ordered a rear guard to the hold the Federal pursuit about ten miles south of Pulaski. George Healy, 5th Iowa, wrote in a letter home: "We drew our sabres and charged on the enemy. They broke and skedaddled. We followed four or five miles as fast as our horses would go. We took over 100 prisoners, and horses and mules." Wheeler sacrificed two or three rearguard regiments as he hurried a valuable supply train across the Tennessee River at Lamb's Ferry.[45]

The fresh 5th Iowa Cavalry led the Union pursuit and trooper Eugene Marshall recorded, "Within fifteen minutes, four horses & three men had been hit, all of them within twenty feet of me ... the bullets fell ... so thick that I could compare them to nothing but a shower of rain." Charles Alley gave the most detailed description of the action. The regiment reached the Confederates along the edge of Sugar Creek, about ten miles south of Pulaski at noon. Two companies of the 5th Iowa acting as skirmishers crossed the creek and then the remainder of the regiment advanced. Two or three regiments of Wheeler's rear guard held a position in line of woods on the top of a steep hill with open fields before them, giving them a good field of fire. The skirmishers moved on foot through a cornfield on the left of the road. Then, the rest of the regiment was ordered to charge directly up the road with sabers drawn. When the 5th Iowa began the assault, they were about six hundred yards from the defenders. Then, the charge was on. The 600 yards fell away and Alley exclaimed: "As we reached the top of the hill the boys replied to the rebel fire with one thundering cheer. The firing of the rebels was very rapid, and bullets flew about us in plenty, but strange not a man or horse was hurt. Another small hollow cleared, up another gentle ascent, and we were upon them, and followed a scene of rout, confusion, and abject terror, I never expected to see. After we dashed through their main line the main body made no resistance of note. All after that came from their dismounted men, who kept up a steady fire from the woods, but only killed one of our horses. The rebels lost in this charge, some 20 killed, about double that number wounded and one hundred and two prisoners. We followed them near 8 miles and here I must thank God for His care for me for to it I attribute my escape from death. For in the heat of the charge I got ahead of the company and dashed into a crowd of not much, if any, of less than a hundred of them, firing my revolver as I came up. An exploded cap caught in the cylinder and I could not get it out at once, so I had to depend on my sabre alone." In the fight, Alley personally captured four of the enemy troopers as the rest of the 5th Iowa arrived on the scene and the Confederates retreated. The Federal cavalry pursuing Wheeler to the Tennessee River found "abundant evidence of a hasty flight, the road being lined with broken-down horses, wagons, artillery, hats and guns," wrote W. R. Carter, 1st Tennessee Cavalry.[46]

Both the 3rd Confederate and 9th Tennessee cavalries participated in the fight at Sugar Creek. John Weatherred, 9th Tennessee Cavalry, recalled the sacrifice Wheeler asked of his men. "We had many fights or skirmishes each day some where. But our battalion had the hardest time at Sugar Creek. Here General Wheeler left us as rear guard for his command. About 10 miles from Tennessee River where he was going to cross over after this raid. We had orders to remain at this place until 12 noon We got to this place about day light (only a creek). Just about 12 noon the enemy advanced and attacked us and the fight began in front of us, but the yanks did not stop, they charged us from the rear: we had to run through them, shoot and run about 1/3 of our battalion was captured, killed and wounded." William W. Lowe, commanding the Union cavalry brigade, reported 85 enemy troopers captured, thirteen killed and some wounded who were able to make an escape. Lowe concluded, "the remnant of his force dispersed in all directions." After the attack of the 5th Iowa, the rest of the cavalry followed and chased the Confederates to the Tennessee River.[47]

Henry Albert Potter, 4th Michigan, watched as the 5th Iowa charged the Confederate rear guard. The 5th Iowa had duty at the rear of the army and now had the opportunity to demonstrate its fighting ability. Potter's regiment started early that morning and the 5th Iowa moved into the forward position in the Union cavalry column and led the charge at Sugar Creek. Potter observed the Iowans pull their sabers as they slammed into the enemy. After driving past the rear guard, the Iowans led the pursuit to Rogersville, Alabama and rode through the town with their sabers held high. Potter wrote, "traveled about 35 miles this day—made the longest charge on our record—six miles—came back & encamped two miles from river—thus endeth Wheeler's great cavalry Raid."[48]

Wheeler wrote that having accomplished his objective he rode for the safety of his lines. For the Union cavalry, it was the case they had finally caught up with Wheeler who rode for his life. Wheeler claimed in his after-action report, "During the trip we captured in action 1,600 prisoners, and killed and wounded as many of their cavalry as would cover our entire loss." Certainly, the destruction of the bridges and railroads, the capture and destruction of the supply depot in McMinnville, and the destruction of the wagon trains all were notable accomplishments for the Confederate cavalry during this raid.[49]

Brigadier General Philip D. Roddey's Confederate cavalry brigade moved across the Tennessee River on October 7 in an attempt to assist Wheeler in his raid. Roddey soon found things were not working well for Wheeler. Roddey wrote from Elk River, "At the same point I met several wounded men and stragglers from General Wheeler's corps.... All agreed in the statement that Wheeler had been severely repulsed at Farmington; that he had a valuable wagon train, and was trying to save it by sending it across the river below Decatur; that he was hard pressed." Roddey attempted to unite his column with Wheeler's at its crossing near Lamb's Ferry and was unsuccessful.[50]

Union Cavalry Casualties—October 1–14, 1863[51]

	Killed	Wounded	Missing	Total
Headquarters cavalry	—	—	1	1
First Division, McCook	—	5	4	9
Second Division, Crook	14	103	—	117
Total	14	108	5	127

With Wheeler crossing back into Alabama, the raid was over. After the Union cavalry's pursuit was complete, Rosecrans ordered Mitchell to keep the cavalry away from Chattanooga. There was little chance of forage for the horses and to keep the cavalry in good shape, it needed to be at another location. One half of the cavalry, Crook's division, moved near Huntsville and McCook's division was posted at Winchester, Tennessee. The past two months of hard duty had taken a severe toll on the cavalry, and Wheeler's raid had severely tested both horses and men. Mitchell wrote, "My command is, of course, very badly used up. Hard marches, scarcity of shoes (although each man carried two at starting), and miserable, worthless saddles that never should have been bought by the Government, or put on a horse's back after they were bought, have ruined many of the horses." McCook's cavalry division had ridden two hundred twenty-five miles in five days and Crook's division had traveled even farther. Eli Russell, 2nd Michigan, wrote to his wife in mid–October explained the situation with his regiment: "We have been in the saddle every day for two months. We have wore out our horses running after the rebs. We have had great fites." Also, Colonel Thomas Jordan, 9th Pennsylvania Cavalry, arrived in Middle Tennessee after recuperating from an illness and found the troopers sleeping without tents. Jordan wisely noted that, "For one who dies by the bullet, another 20 die due to exposure and hard service."[52]

Summary of Wheeler's Raid

The most notable action on the part of the Union cavalry during this raid was by the 1st Wisconsin and 2nd Indiana cavalries at Anderson's Crossroads, the skirmish near McMinnville with the charge of the 2nd Kentucky, the 5th Iowa's attack at Sugar Creek, and Eli Long's and Abram Miller's actions at Farmington. The really hard fighting often fell to the mounted infantry which contribution was immeasurable. Mitchell noted the Union cavalry's efforts outweighed any long-term impact of the raid. He recorded, "We captured six pieces of artillery, and, including killed, wounded, prisoners, and deserters, I think they re-crossed the Tennessee River with between 2,000 and 3,000 less men than they started out with."[53]

At the end of the campaign, Colonel Robert Minty lost command of his brigade for four months and was court martialed for failure to follow orders. Minty pushed for the trial which took place from February 2 through February 16, 1864. In light of the pressure the Union cavalry had been under for the entire year, it is not surprising that tempers flared particularly during the intense pursuit of Wheeler. The crux of the problem revolved around the question of whether or not Minty had orders to move forward. The court martial found Minty not guilty. Ultimately, Crook's decision to place this well-liked, well-respected colonel under arrest made him very unpopular with Minty's brigade. Robert Burns bitterly wrote that Minty and Wilder were the only brigade commanders to gain any "distinction" and others were jealous of their successes. Burns wrote: "Mitchell and Crook are infantry generals, do not understand the management of cavalry, and would do anything to ruin Minty. Gen. C. has seized the opportunity and did his best."[54]

Wheeler's raid, after months of relative inactivity for the Confederate general, provided a great deal of excitement and accomplished the destruction of some important supplies and infrastructure in Middle Tennessee. The destruction of George Thomas's 800 wagon supply train caused a great deal of hardship for the hungry Union soldiers in Chattanooga and Wheeler's raid pulled the entire Union cavalry corps from the Chattanooga area. The 92nd Illinois Mounted infantryman, Albert Woodcock, wrote the hunger of the men at Chattanooga could "not be believed." In addition, the Union cavalry which had labored since mid–August was left in absolute exhaustion at the end of the raid and stationed at Winchester and Huntsville away from Chattanooga. Also notable during the raid, Wheeler's destruction of the railroad bridges delayed the reinforcements bound for Chattanooga until the Confederate cavalry was expelled and the bridges repaired. Finally, until the exact details of Wheeler's raid were known, the initial reports provided a boost in morale for the Confederate infantry at Chattanooga and gave hope the Confederate cavalry could stop communications and supplies reaching Rosecrans' besieged army.[55]

From the Union standpoint, little long-term damage occurred as a result of this raid. At the end, the morale of the Union cavalry was even better than before. They felt they had defeated Wheeler's cavalry, and this was a much-needed boost after the Union army defeat at Chickamauga. Thomas Crofts, 3rd Ohio Cavalry, would write of the campaign: "The campaign had been a remarkable illustration of what men and horses were capable of performing under conditions of deprivation of food and rest ... yet everything was borne cheerfully." Although Mitchell had failed to draw Wheeler into a prolonged cavalry fight, many felt they had severely repulsed Wheeler. The fight at Farmington with only 1,500 Union soldiers was viewed as a Union victory and Wheeler precipitately rode for the friendly confines of the Confederate lines. The pro–Federal press severely criticized Wheeler's raid stating that Wheeler blamed his subordinates for his defeat and that Wheeler's cavalry was more "intent on plundering than military objectives." Even within the Confederate ranks, there were those who felt the raid did more damage than good, including, Colonel George Brent of Bragg's staff and Brigadier General Arthur Manigault. Wheeler continued to need to improve the discipline of his troops and some of the cavalry became intoxicated after capturing the Union wagon train at Anderson's Crossroads. More importantly, the pillaging and crimes against civilians at McMinnville and, particularly, Shelbyville, cost Wheeler the loyalty of many civilians who saw the actions of a rabble and not the impressive cavalry of the South. While the raid through Union-held territory yielded some positive results, the final evaluation showed it to be a failure and it highlighted Wheeler's propensity to claim successes when there were none. "The Confederate cavalry had worn itself out with almost nothing to show for its trouble. Never had Bragg's cavalry been so poorly utilized at such a critical time," wrote historian James Schaefer.[56]

Yet again, Burnside failed to assist the Army of the Cumberland during Wheeler's raid and Rosecrans lashed out at him when Burnside inquired, four days after the event, if Wheeler had broken through at Cotton Port. Rosecrans bitterly replied—"Your dispatch of the 4th received, asking if the rebel cavalry have really crossed the river between us as reported. Having warned you often of the danger for the last ten days, and reported the catastrophe to you on the 1st, and got your promise to send your cavalry to help mine, I am amazed at your dispatch. I now say that your failure to close your troops down to our left has cost 500 wagons loaded with essentials, the post of McMinnville, and Heaven only knows where the mischief will end.... If you don't unite with us soon, you will be responsible for another catastrophe, I fear."[57]

By October 13, bitterness replaced the exultation of the Confederate victory at Chickamauga, as Bragg was unable to capitalize on this victory. The Confederate infantry remained stationary along Missionary Ridge and Lookout Mountain, and Wheeler's raid failed to force the Union armies to the rear. Confederate soldier John W. Harris wrote in a letter in October: "I have been so fearfully disgusted with the way in which our victory had wound up that I have not felt like doing anything at all. Every one here curses Bragg; and he in return blames & arrests Polk & Hindman for our failure to ruin the whole Federal army, there was never such a chance (illegible) before, all we had to do was to pursue and capture them, but instead of doing that, we fooled around nearly an entire day in looking around Yankee hospitals, whilst the Federals were in full retreat and in the greatest confusion. It is the only thing we have had during the war and through Bragg's imbecility we have thrown it away."[58]

Twelve. The Aftermath—Conclusion

[O]ur enemies ... now admit you are dangerous and have left material proof of it upon many a field.—General David Stanley

The Battle of Chickamauga was a Union defeat, but it would prove to be a temporary setback for the Union pursuit of the Army of Tennessee. By the end of November, the Army of Tennessee would be defeated at Missionary Ridge and again retreating southward. Many changes in the Army of the Cumberland would result after the Battle of Chickamauga. The end of Wheeler's raid marked the beginning of a period of transition for the cavalry divisions of the Army of the Cumberland. David Stanley missed the battle of Chickamauga; and during the battle and after the battle, Stanley had been moved to a Union hospital in Nashville. He later returned to his home in Ohio while he recuperated from dysentery. He was transported to Wooster, Ohio, where his wife had been staying with Stanley's old teacher, Dr. Leander Firestone. He was away from the army for about a month where he recuperated on a milk diet. When he returned, he found the Army of the Cumberland vastly different.[1]

On October 9, 1863, Rosecrans relieved both Alexander McCook and Thomas Crittenden of their commands, and the infantry and artillery components of the army were reorganized. The next day, Brigadier General James A. Garfield left the army to serve in Congress; and although Rosecrans praised Garfield, David Stanley detested him as a politician. Unfortunately, the defeat along Chickamauga Creek opened the doors to back biting by the Union generals once they reached Chattanooga. Did Crittenden and Alexander McCook abandon the battlefield? And, for that matter did Rosecrans also abandon the battlefield? Because of Stanley's illness, he did not participate in any of these discussions, but his performance fell under the same scrutiny as the other corps commanders. Only Thomas and Granger appeared to be free of these grumblings while the other top Union commanders became vulnerable to criticisms and finger pointing.[2]

In regard to Ambrose Burnside, he would never reach or even attempt to reach the Army of the Cumberland. Burnside would remain in Knoxville during the winter of 1863 and was subsequently ordered to corps command in the Eastern Theater in 1864. He would be bitterly remembered by those of the Army of the Cumberland who expected him to arrive at Chattanooga. When Burnside was asked to explain his actions, historian Steven Woodworth, wrote, that Burnside replied with "excuses, delays, and questions, conclusively demonstrating his unfitness for independent command...." While those who supported Burnside would argue that Burnside received mixed signals from Halleck and Rosecrans and that he did not have time to reach Chattanooga, there is no evidence that Burnside ever seriously contemplated moving to support Rosecrans during the time he was needed. "There had been time enough, after General Rosecrans' explanations of his proposed plan, to force Burnside, with twenty thousand men, down from East Tennessee, and to have brought all the needed strength for the other flank from the Army of Tennessee on the Mississippi," wrote Brigadier General Henry Boynton. Halleck wrote to Major General J. G. Foster on October 11 that he could not persuade Burnside to go to Rosecrans' aid prior to the Battle of Chickamauga even after, "I telegraphed to him fifteen times to do so, and the President three or four times."[3]

Ulysses Grant assumed command of all the Union forces in the west in October; and upon receiving his promotion, he immediately relieved William Rosecrans of command of the Army of the Cumberland on October 19, 1863, and replaced him with George H. Thomas. In regard to the cavalry, Robert Mitchell's days were also numbered as chief of cavalry. Mitchell wrote on October 14, 1863, "I am out of rations and my horses are breaking down, but will do the best I can. I am as near a dead man on horseback as you ever saw." Four days later, Mitchell appealed to Rosecrans to be relieved of duty, "The severe service devolving on me since having been on duty in this arm of the service has rendered the state of my health much worse than formerly, and the chances of my ultimate recovery more remote, and I feel that in justice to myself I should not expose myself any longer as I have been obliged to do for the last four months." After only a month in command of the cavalry, Mitchell had had enough and sought to give up command; and he left the cavalry corps by the end of the month.[4]

Two days later Brigadier General Washington Lafayette Elliott, who had served in the eastern theater, received orders to report for duty in Chattanooga; and three days after that, Elliott was given command of Mitchell's cavalry division. On November 12, 1863, David Stanley was officially relieved of command of the cavalry and assigned to command the First Division of the IV Corps, serving under Major General Gordon Granger. When he left the cavalry, he brought his trusted staff member, William H. Sinclair with him. Stanley would later write of his demotion, "I did not regret being relieved of the command of the cavalry. It was most unsatisfying and annoying." Stanley's reassignment to the infantry was decided by Major General George Thomas who had been Stanley's instructor at West Point.[5]

The reasons for Stanley's removal as chief of cavalry remains a mystery and certainly suppositions can be made, but the facts are missing. Charles Dana wrote to Washington that Stanley was drinking to excess and to the detriment of his command. These allegations were without substance. Historian David Powell wrote about Dana's efforts to have Rosecrans and other high-ranking Union generals removed: "Dana was sending pure, if vitriolic, nonsense." Perhaps, George Thomas thought the performance of the cavalry during the campaign was such that a change needed to be made. More likely, the close relationship between Stanley and Rosecrans resulted in Stanley's reassignment. While Stanley did not contest this decision, the Union cavalry lost one of its most underrated commanders. Stanley's only comments were preserved in his memoirs. "It is frightful to think what havoc a set of scandal mongers who have access to the ears of the officers, may produce. Had not General Thomas known these men were falsifiers, I should have been left out of the reorganization." Stanley would receive additional commendations for his command abilities during the remainder of the war and would receive the Medal of Honor for his actions at the Battle of Franklin in 1864. Throughout his time with the cavalry, he commanded with a steady hand and the cavalry performed well under his direct leadership. Neither, Robert Mitchell or Washington Lafayette Elliott, subsequent chiefs of cavalry, offered the leadership qualities of Stanley.[6]

On November 20, Stanley sent a message to the troopers of this cavalry corps, "In parting with you, your late commander takes occasion to express his regrets that the changes of services should separate his fortunes from your own. For a year we have served together most pleasantly, and I am happy to congratulate the Cavalry upon their achievements in that time. My poor efforts to render you efficient have been zealously secondly by both officers and men. As to our success, the testimony of our enemies is the more flattering to you, it being forced from them, they now admit you are dangerous and have left material proof of it upon many a field. Though separated from you, I shall serve in the same army with you and shall always watch your course with confident pride.... Your success and glory is assured." Stanley left a strong legacy with the cavalry. He had taken an outnumbered, demoralized group and transformed it into an excellent fighting corps. Brigadier General Washington Lafayette Elliott became the next chief of cavalry for the Army of the Cumberland in November 1863.

Successes of Union Cavalry

It would be incomplete to discuss the role of the Union cavalry in the Chickamauga Campaign without including the four-week advance on Chattanooga. This was an integral and remarkable part of the campaign. During this phase, the Union cavalry was highly successful due, in large part, to the inactivity of their Southern counterparts. The actions of Minty's brigade provided security to Crittenden's flank, and Minty, Wilder and Crittenden successfully provided a feint north of Chattanooga which caused Bragg to focus his attention on the Union forces north of the river. On the southern flank, the Federal cavalry was virtually unopposed by the superior numbers of Confederate cavalry until September 9. In the meantime, both the southern and northern flanks were secured; the Federal infantry had been escorted over the Cumberland Mountains; the Tennessee River was crossed; and Sand Mountain and Lookout Mountain secured. All of this was accomplished virtually without bloodshed. On September 9, the Confederate resistance stiffened, but the Federal cavalry tended to fare well in the exchanges with the opposing cavalry. The Union cavalry won the exchange at Alpine, secured Summerville, and while it was repulsed by infantry, at La Fayette, it succeeded in accomplishing its objective. At La Fayette on September 13, Archibald Campbell's brigade firmly established that the Confederate army had concentrated at that location and that it had been reinforced with troops from other armies. In addition, this clash assisted in successfully shifting the initiative away from Bragg. This bold move caused the Confederate high command to believe that an attack from Alexander McCook' corps was imminent and coupled with Bragg's inability to launch two attacks, shifted Bragg back into a defensive position. This allowed Rosecrans time to pull his dispersed infantry together.

Next, Minty's and Wilder's mounted forces provided the most valuable service for the army by any mounted troops in the entire campaign on September 18. The fights at Reed's Bridge and Alexander's Bridge stymied a potentially devastating attack on Crittenden's division, again gaining time for Rosecrans to re-position his infantry. No better service would be performed by the cavalry during this campaign. Minty's performance is even more notable in light of the apparent disregard of his command by Crittenden during the days and weeks leading up to this attack.

After the battle was fought, the Federal infantry withdrew to Chattanooga and the Union cavalry performed its duty well in providing reconnaissance and security along two vulnerable flanks. Minty's efforts were again particularly noteworthy on September 20–22 and greatly beneficial to Thomas as he assembled a defense after the crushing defeat on the morning of September 20. Edward McCook and George Crook also provided good security on the west side of the battlefield on the evening of September 20 through September 22. These cavalry forces faced heavy skirmishes and prevented a penetration into the rear of the infantry by securing Chattanooga Valley.

The final noteworthy effort by the Federal cavalry occurred during Wheeler's raid from September 30 through October 9. While Wheeler accomplished some destruction in the rear of the Federal army, its impact was temporary and came with a significant price. In the end, Forrest was transferred to the west and Union cavalry's morale increased because they perceived their pursuit to have been more successful than Wheeler's actions during the raid.

Failures of the Union Cavalry

Rosecrans had two objectives for the cavalry moving into the campaign—provide flank security and strike communications at the rear of Bragg's army still in Chattanooga, just as the Confederates seemed to do with ease. In many ways, Rosecrans was a victim of his own successes in relation to his cavalry and infantry. Rosecrans so easily dealt with Bragg during the Tullahoma Campaign that he believed that Bragg's Army of Tennessee would act in the same manner as it had two months earlier. Rosecrans and David Stanley had made such great advances in developing two impressive cavalry divisions over the past year. It was only natural that Rosecrans wanted to put the cavalry to work striking the flank and rear of a demoralized army; but there were flaws in his plans.

Rosecrans insisted that Stanley strike the Confederates on September 8 to force the Confederate army out of Chattanooga. Rosecrans failed to hear Stanley's objection that he did not have enough men to successfully do this. He also seemed to discount the fact that Stanley faced two Confederate divisions; and he failed to consider that the Confederates had already contemplated a Union attack at this location and had prepared for this contingency. Finally, he failed to take into consideration the time it would take to accomplish such an expedition. In the Atlanta Campaign in 1864, the cavalry of the Army of the Cumberland would be assigned the tasks of destroying railroads around Atlanta and it typically took at least a half day to make a significant impact on the railroad. These raids were usually not successful, even though the Union cavalry had a greater advantage in regard to numbers than they did during the Chickamauga Campaign. Rosecrans' planned raid in September 1863 also failed to consider the terrain the cavalry needed to cross. There were mountains and rivers to cross which could be easily defended. Historically, the raid was poorly planned and failed to consider that if Stanley had successfully penetrated to the rail line at Rome, how he was expected to return to the Union lines. One historian wrote that Rosecrans' aggressive pursuit on "the retreating Confederates bordered on recklessness." The records show that Wheeler's cavalry kept a close eye on Stanley for this very contingency and prepared to move in defense of the railroad at Rome if needed. In addition, Forrest had moved a division of his own within striking distance on the very day the raid was planned. Despite all these problems, it appears from the records that Stanley fully intended on carrying out the raid, albeit, a day late. Stanley told Garfield that he delayed because of the need to shoe the horses and because he received an additional 600 troopers by a single day's delay. In the meantime, Bragg evacuated from Chattanooga and the raid became unimportant because of the new need for the cavalry to locate Bragg's retreating army. Stanley's greatest fault in this enterprise seems to have been that Rosecrans found out the cavalry raid did not take place before Stanley's message reached him.[7]

Meanwhile, on the northern flank Minty provided good flank security for Crittenden's division; but once Bragg evacuated Chattanooga, Rosecrans appeared to ignore Minty's brigade. Minty's cavalry was one of the last units to cross the Tennessee River, rather than one of the first. Then, Crittenden and Rosecrans parceled the cavalry for various smaller tasks with little coordination or direction. Finally, the intelligence provided by the mounted forces on the north was not taken seriously by corps or army headquarters.

Stanley suffered a second rebuke from Rosecrans for poor communications and this was an unfair and bitter response by army headquarters. This criticism reflects more the pressure on those at army headquarters than Stanley's communications. Nor was Stanley the only high-level commander to come under Rosecrans' criticism during the campaign. Importantly, Rosecrans discounted any further contributions from the cavalry in the campaign and just assigned it to reconnaissance, guarding mountain passes and army hospitals.

The next major consideration centers on Robert Mitchell's command, particularly on the actions of September 20. Clearly, Rosecrans' and Garfield's decision to appoint a man who had limited experience in the cavalry to such a position yielded the results as might be expected. The decision to appoint high level commanders, unsuited for the position, and generally from outside the cavalry corps plagued the cavalry for two years—1863–1864. Edward McCook, George Crook, Robert Minty, and Eli Long are good examples of capable commanders with years of experience who could have assumed the role of chief of cavalry in Stanley's absence. Instead, Robert Mitchell was unfamiliar with his command, in terms of overall experience or recent events, due to his medical furlough. Negative results were many, especially on September 20—Long's defeat at Glass Mill, failure to stay in contact with Wheeler after the fight at Glass Mill, the lost connection with Wilder's mounted infantry on September 20, failure to follow orders to close up on Alexander McCook's right flank, and ill-timed communications with Louis Watkins' brigade. Mitchell's reports reflected equally disingenuous accounts of the action. He failed to adequately communicate with McCook's and Rosecrans' headquarters. He overrode orders from Gate Thruston for the cavalry to join in the infantry battle at 11:00 a.m. and 3:00 p.m. on September 20. His report stated that at 3:00 p.m., he was ordered to "fall back" when in fact he was ordered to advance. He told headquarters that he had attempted to communicate with Louis Watkins, but he didn't tell headquarters all of his communications were made prior to the decision to withdraw from Crawfish Springs, or made too late to save Watkins from riding into the rear of two divisions of Confederate cavalry. At best, these were just poorly timed messages sent to Watkins. Mitchell would also suffer under the pen of P. Sidney Post when he told Post he could not get communications to the main body of the army and Post sent a rider of his own with complete success. In addition, a rider from headquarters was able to deliver orders to Mitchell at 3:00 p.m. but Mitchell would claim he could not establish communications in return. Further, the cavalry and medical staff knew they had been cut off from the rest of the army by noon. Mitchell's decision to remain at Crawfish Springs remains controversial, but not without merit. Certainly, it was commendable to defend the sick and wounded, but Mitchell received direct orders from his commanding officer to join in the battle. Instead, he clung to outdated orders issued before the many unexpected events occurred during the day.[8]

Conclusions

Terrain, Terrain, Terrain. Terrain proved to be the important variable in this campaign that ensured both armies would remain blind to the location of each other through much of the month of September. This was particularly true for both opposing cavalries which had the duty of being the eyes and ears of the army. In addition, the terrain also caused important communication problems. Rosecrans criticized most of his top commanders at some point in the campaign and this was especially true with Stanley. The extreme distances and the inability of Stanley and Rosecrans to agree upon objectives adversely impacted the cavalry's actions. It generally took many hours for messages to reach their final destinations and situations frequently changed during that time period. Any objections to orders had to be resolved by return messages which often delayed the implementation of the original orders resulting in added stress on the top commanders.

Secondly, many of the important lessons about the effective use of the cavalry seemed to have been discarded during this campaign. Stanley established early in his tenure as chief of cavalry that the most effective use of cavalry resulted when brigade size cavalry units were commanded by cavalry officers which reported to the chief of cavalry. The ineffective use of cavalry, broken into regiments and battalions under the command of infantry commanders, had been shown to be ineffective; but Rosecrans reverted to this command style with Minty's brigade and nearly paid a severe price for this. Rosecrans also removed from his chief of cavalry the design, implementation, and timing of actions by the cavalry. Cavalry brigades often worked directly from army headquarters, not Stanley or Mitchell, many miles away from the front lines. Army headquarters often directly commanded the cavalry even to the brigade level after assigning command to others. This became evident with Robert Minty's brigade which served under brigade, division, corps, and army headquarters commanders outside the cavalry chain of the command. Despite Mitchell's overall performance on September 19 and 20, he was somewhat justified in his confusion of whether he should follow Alexander McCook's orders or Garfield's order regarding his action on the afternoon of September 20. In the end, the Federal cavalry was most effective when it worked in close support of the infantry to screen the opposing infantry and when offering flank security. On a positive note, Rosecrans and Stanley worked diligently to increase the number of Union cavalry regiments over the past ten months and these efforts paid off during the campaign. While the Union cavalry still remained out-manned, it provided a formidable challenge for its Confederate counterparts.[9]

Finally, the selection of top cavalry commanders for reasons other than those of merit would plague the cavalry of the Army of the Cumberland throughout its existence. Too often top cavalry officers were appointed for political reasons and too often officers from outside the ranks of the cavalry corps itself resulted in poor quality officers commanding the cavalry. This would continue into 1864. Fortunately, the brigade commanders tended to be very capable cavalry officers.

There were many lessons to be learned during this campaign, but unfortunately, many would go unheeded in the future.

1. The chief of cavalry needed to be included in the design and planning of missions involving the cavalry;
2. The past errors of fragmenting the cavalry to serve in the direct control of individual infantry commanders had been discarded, but reinstituted during this campaign, particularly in regard to Minty's brigade;
3. The selection of top cavalry commanders needed to be based on experience, performance and leadership, not politically based appointments;
4. The lure of the glory of cavalry raids often led to unrealistic expectations by top infantry commanders;
5. The cavalry should have been an effective offensive weapon as well as a defensive one;
6. The Union cavalry was most effective working closely to screen the infantry, providing security and blocking the Confederate cavalry; and finally,[10]
7. The tradition of naming a commander based solely on the date of his appointed rank was dangerous and took good decisions away from the top commanders.

The cavalry of the Army of the Cumberland would have a proud history which would include many successes. While the Union cavalry is often disregarded by historians as insignificant during the Battle of Chickamauga, this force provided many positive results. However, the cavalry was underutilized due to errors made by the top commanders. Once the Battle of Chickamauga was over, Stanley, Mitchell and Crook would all soon be gone and new top commanders would be appointed—Washington L. Elliott, Kenner Garrard, Alvan Gillem, Hugh Judson Kilpatrick and Edward McCook. The cavalry of the Army of the Cumberland would swell to four divisions when the Atlanta Campaign began in 1864. Finally, during the Atlanta Campaign, the Union cavalry would meet and exceed the numbers of their formidable opponents. The cavalry of the Army of the Cumberland would continue until October 1864 when it lost its designation and attachment to that army. The Union cavalry would continue to fight in the numerous battles through the end of the war and offer important contributions to its outcome. However, many of the lessons learned in the Chickamauga Campaign would go unheeded and destined the cavalry to re-learn these again in the next long, hot Georgia summer.[11]

Dulce bellum inexpertis
—Pindar

Appendix I: Organization of the Army of the Cumberland—September 19–20

Major General William Rosecrans
General Headquarters

1st Battalion Ohio Sharpshooters. Capt. Gershom M. Barber
10th Ohio Infantry, Lieut. Col. William M. Ward
15th Pennsylvania Cavalry, Col. William J. Palmer

Fourteenth Army Corps
Maj. Gen. George H. Thomas
General Headquarters

Provost guard—9th Michigan Infantry, Col. John G. Parkhurst
Escort—1st Ohio Cavalry, Company L, Capt. John D. Barker

1st Division—
Brig. Gen. Absalom Baird

First Brigade
Col. Benjamin F. Scribner
Second Brigade
Brig. Gen. John C. Starkweather

Third Brigade
Brig. Gen. John H. King
Artillery

3rd Division—
Brig. Gen. John Brannan

First Brigade
Col. John M. Connell
Second Brigade
Col. John T. Croxton
Col. William H. Hays
Third Brigade
Col. Ferdinand Van Derveer
Artillery

2nd Division—
Maj. Gen. James Negley

First Brigade
Brig. Gen. John Beatty
Second Brigade
Col. Timothy R. Stanley
Col. William L. Stoughton

Third Brigade
Col. William Sirwell
Artillery

4th Division—
Maj. Gen. Joseph Reynolds

First Brigade
Col. John T. Wilder
Second Brigade
Col. Edward A. King
Col. Milton S. Robinson
Third Brigade
Brig. Gen. John B. Turchin
Artillery

Twentieth Army Corps
Maj. Gen. Alexander McCook
General Headquarters

Provost guard—81st Indiana Infantry, Company H, Capt. William J. Richards
Escort—2d Kentucky Cavalry. Company I, Lieut. George W. L. Batman

1st Division—
Brig. Gen. Jefferson C. Davis

First Brigade
Col. P. Sidney Post
Second Brigade
Brig. Gen. William P. Carlin
Third Brigade
Col. Hans C. Heg
Col. John A. Martin

2nd Division—
Brig. Gen. Richard Johnson

First Brigade
Brig. Gen. August Willich
Second Brigade
Col. Joseph B. Dodge
Third Brigade
Col. Philemon P. Baldwin
Col. William W. Berry

3rd Division—*Maj. Gen. Philip Sheridan*

First Brigade
Brig. Gen. William H. Lytle
Col. Silas Miller
Second Brigade
Col. Bernard Laboldt
Third Brigade
Col. Luther P. Bradley
Col. Nathan H. Walworth
Artillery

Twenty-First Army Corps
Maj. Gen. Thomas L. Crittenden
General Headquarters

Escort—15th Illinois Cavalry, Company K, Capt. Samuel B. Sherer

1st Division—
Brig. Gen. Thomas Wood

First Brigade
Col. George P. Buell
Second Brigade
Brig. Gen. George D. Wagner
Third Brigade
Col. Charles G. Harker
Artillery

2nd Division—
Maj. Gen. John M. Palmer

First Brigade
Brig. Gen. Charles Cruft
Second Brigade
Brig. Gen. William B. Hazen
Third Brigade
Col. William Grose
Artillery

3rd Division—*Brig. Gen. Horatio P. Van Cleve*

First Brigade
Brig. Gen. Samuel Beatty
Second Brigade
Col. George F. Dick
Third Brigade
Col. Sidney M. Barnes
Artillery

Appendix I: Organization of the Army of the Cumberland—September 19–20

Reserve Corps
Maj. Gen. Gordon Granger

1st Division—
Brig. Gen. James B. Steedman

First Brigade
Brig. Gen. Walter C. Whitaker
Second Brigade
Col. John G. Mitchell

2nd Division

Second Brigade
Col. Daniel McCook

Cavalry Corps (See Chapter 1 and Chapter 4)

Appendix II: Organization of the Army of Tennessee—September 19–20

General Braxton Bragg
General Headquarters

Escort—Capt. Guy Dreux
Dreux's Company Louisiana Cavalry, Lieut. O. De Buis
Holloway's Company Alabama Cavalry, Capt. E. M. Holloway

Right Wing
Lieut. Gen. Leonidas Polk

CHEATHAM'S DIVISION—*Maj. Gen. Benjamin F. Cheatham*

Jackson's Brigade	*Maney's Brigade*
Brig. Gen. John K. Jackson	Brig. Gen. George Maney
Smith's Brigade	*Wright's Brigade*
Brig. Gen. Preston Smith	Brig. Gen. Marcus J. Wright
Col. Alfred J. Vaughan, Jr.	*Strahl's Brigade*
Artillery	Brig. Gen. Otho F. Strahl

Hill's Corps
Lieut. Gen. Daniel H. Hill

CLEBURNE'S DIV.—	BRECKINRIDGE'S DIV.—
Maj. Gen. Pat. Cleburne	*Maj. Gen. John Breckinridge*
Wood's Brigade	*Helm's Brigade*
Brig. Gen. S. A. M. Wood	Brig. Gen. Benjamin H. Helm
Polk's Brigade	Col. Joseph H. Lewis
Brig. Gen. Lucius E. Polk	*Adams' Brigade*
Deshler's Brigade	Brig. Gen. Daniel W. Adams
Brig. Gen. James Deshler	Col. Randall L. Gibson
Col. Roger Q. Mills	*Stovall's Brigade*
Artillery	Brig. Gen. Marcellus A. Stovall
	Artillery

Appendix I: Organization of the Army of Tennessee—September 19-20

Reserve Corps
Maj. Gen. William H. T. Walker

WALKER'S DIV.—
Brig. Gen. States R. Gist

Gist's Brigade
Brig. Gen. States R. Gist
Col. Peyton H. Colquitt
Lieut. Col. Leroy Napier
Ector's Brigade
Brig. Gen. Matthew D. Ector
Wilson's Brigade
Col. Claudius C. Wilson
Artillery

LIDDELL'S DIV.—
Brig. Gen. St. John Liddell

Liddell's Brigade
Col. Daniel C. Govan
Walthall's Brigade
Brig. Gen. Edward C. Walthall
Artillery

Left Wing
Lieut. Gen. James Longstreet

HINDMAN'S DIVISION—
Maj. Gen. Thomas C. Hindman/Brig. Gen. Patton Anderson

Anderson's Brigade
Brig. Gen. Patton Anderson
Col. J. H. Sharp
Deas' Brigade
Brig. Gen. Zach. C. Deas

Manigault's Brigade
Brig. Gen. Arthur M. Manigault

Buckner's Corps
Maj. Gen. Simon B. Buckner

STEWART'S DIV.—
Maj. Gen. Alexander

Johnson's Brigade
Brig. Gen. Bushrod R. Johnson
Col. John S. Fulton
Bate's Brigade
Brig. Gen. William B. Bate
Brown's Brigade.
Brig. Gen. John C. Brown
Col. Edmund C. Cook
Clayton's Brigade
Brig. Gen. Henry D. Clayton
Artillery

PRESTON'S DIV.—
Brig. Gen. Wm. Preston Stewart

Gracie's Brigade
Brig. Gen. Archibald Gracie, Jr.

Third Brigade
Col. John H. Kelly
Trigg's Brigade
Col. Robert C. Trigg
Artillery

JOHNSON'S DIV.—Brig. Gen. Bushrod R. Johnson

Gregg's Brigade
Brig. Gen. John Gregg
Col. Cyrus A. Sugg
McNair's Brigade
Brig. Gen. Evander McNair
Col. David Coleman

Reserve Corps Artillery—Maj. Samuel C. Williams

Appendix II: Organization of the Army of Tennessee—September 19–20

Longstreet's Corps
Maj. Gen. John B. Hood

McLaws' Div.—
  Brig. Gen. Joseph B. Kershaw
  Maj. Gen. Lafayette McLaws

Kershaw's Brigade
Brig. Gen. Joseph B. Kershaw
Humphreys' Brigade
Brig. Gen. Benjamin G. Humphreys
Wofford's Brigade
Brig. Gen. William T. Wofford
Bryan's Brigade
Brig. Gen. Goode Bryan

Hood's Div.—
  Maj. Gen. John Hood
  Brig. Gen. E. McIver Law

Jenkins' Brigade
Brig. Gen. Micah Jenkins
Robertson's Brigade
Brig. Gen. Jerome S. Robertson
Col. Van H. Manning
Law's Brigade
Brig. Gen. E. McIver Law
Col. James L. Sheffield
Anderson's Brigade
Brig. Gen. George T. Anderson
Benning's Brigade
Brig. Gen. Henry L. Benning

CORPS ARTILLERY—*Col. E. Porter Alexander*

RESERVE ARTILLERY—*Maj. Felix H. Robertson*

Cavalry Corps (See Chapter 3)

Chapter Notes

Chapter One

1. Gregg Biggs, "The Battle of Shelbyville: Turning Point for the Union Cavalry in the West," *Blue & Gray*, Vol. XXVII (2010), Number 1, 45; Michael R. Bradley, *The Raiding Winter* (Gretna, LA: Pelican Publishing Co., 2013), 19–22; William Rosecrans, *The War of the Rebellion. A Compilation of the Official Records of the Union and Confederate Armies*, Series 1, Vol. 16, Part 2 (Washington, D.C.: U.S. Government Printing Office, 1880–1901), 655. [Hereafter designated as *Official Records*]; David Stanley, *An American General: The Memoirs of David Sloan Stanley*, Samuel W. Fordyce IV, ed. (Santa Barbara, CA: The Narrative Press, 2004), 150.
2. John Londa, "The Role of Union Cavalry during the Chickamauga Campaign," Master's Thesis, Command and General Staff College, Fort Leavenworth, Kansas, 1991, 28.
3. W. L. Elliott, Letters February 29, 1864 and March 1, 1864, Correspondence of the Chief of Cavalry, NARA RG 39, Letters Sent, NARA; Berkley Lewis, *Notes on Cavalry Weapons of the Civil War, 1861–1865* (Washington, D.C.: American Ordnance Association, 1961), 5–30; James Arthur Schaefer, "The Tactical and Strategic Evolution of Cavalry During the American Civil War," Ph. D. Dissertation, The University of Toledo, 1982, 20–24; Gervase Phillips, "Warhorses of the U.S. Civil War," *History Today*, Vol. 55 (Dec. 2005) Issue 12:13.
4. William Sinclair, General Order No. 3, December 2, 1862, Letters and Orders, First Cavalry Division, Record Group 393, Part 2, Number 2468, NARA; Chelsea A. Medlock, "Delayed Obsolescence: The Horse in European and American Warfare from the Crimean War to the Second World War," Master's Thesis, Oklahoma State University, 2009, 18–19.
5. Lloyd Lewis, *Sherman: Fighting Prophet* (Lincoln: University of Nebraska Press, 1960), 337; Charles W. Ramsdell, "General Robert E. Lee's Horse Supply, 1862–1865," *The American Historical Review*, 35 (July 1930), 758; Chelsea A. Medlock, "Delayed Obsolescence," 17–27; John Lee Yaryan, "Stone River," In *War Papers Read before the Indiana Commandery* (Indianapolis: MOLLUS, 1898), 161; James Arthur Schaefer, "The Tactical And Strategic Evolution Of Cavalry During The American Civil War," 28; W. R. Friend, "Rout of Rosecrans," In *New Annals of the Civil War*, edited by Peter Cozzens and Robert Girardi (Mechanicsburg, PA: Stackpole Books, 2004), 212; W. L. Curry, *Four Years in the Saddle:* *History of First Regiment Ohio Volunteer Cavalry* (Columbus: Champlin Printing Co., 1898), 307.
6. Joseph Wheeler, *A Revised System of Cavalry Tactics, for the Use of the Cavalry and Mounted Infantry, C. S. A.* (Mobile: S. H. Goetzel & Co., 1863), 1–478.
7. Laurence D. Schiller, "Of Sabers and Carbines: The Emergence of the Federal Dragoon," *The Papers of the Blue & Gay Education Society*, Monograph Number 11, August 1, 2001, 9.
8. David Stanley, *An American General*, 150.
9. Berkley Lewis, *Notes on Cavalry Weapons of the Civil War*, 33–34; Willard Glazier, *Three Years in the Federal Cavalry* (New York: R.H. Ferguson, 1870), 22; Lawyn C. Edwards, "Confederate Cavalry at Chickamauga: What Went Wrong," Master's Thesis, U.S. Army Command and General Staff College, Fort Leavenworth, Kansas, 1990, 33.
10. Lawyn C. Edwards, "Confederate Cavalry at Chickamauga," 10–18, 31–32; Jonathan J. Boniface, *The Cavalry Horse and His Pack* (Kansas City: Hudson-Kimberly Publishing Co., 1908), 24.
11. James Arthur Schaefer, "The Tactical and Strategic Evolution of Cavalry During the American Civil War," 5–30; Brent Nosworthy, *The Bloody Crucible of Courage: Fighting Methods and Combat Experience of the Civil War* (New York: Carroll & Graf Publishers, 2003), 488–490.
12. *Official Register of the Officers and Cadets of the U.S. Military Academy* (West Point, NY: U.S. Military Academy, 1852), 7; David Stanley, *An American General*, 49–50.
13. William D. Bickham, *Rosecrans' Campaign with the Fourteenth Army Corps of the Army of the Cumberland* (Cincinnati: Moore, Wilstach, Keys & Co., 1863), 81; David Stanley, *An American General*, 150.
14. W. L. Curry, *Four Years in the Saddle*, 82; Martin Buck, "From Capt. Buck's Co.," *Highland Weekly News*, December 25, 1862, 3.
15. David Stanley, *An American General*, 98; Eli Long, Diary, July 29, 1857, Eli Long Papers 1855–1892, United States Army Heritage and Education Center (USAHEC), Carlisle, Pennsylvania; David S. Stanley, "David Stanley Diary, United States 2nd Dragoons of a March from Fort Smith, Arkansas, to San Diego, California, made in 1853," Crimmins (Martin Lalor) Papers, Briscoe Center for American History, University of Texas at Austin, Austin.
16. David Stanley, *An American General*, 150; Stephen Z. Starr, "Cold Steel: The Sabre and Union Cav-

alry," *In Battles Lost and Won: Essays from Civil War History*, John T. Hubbell, ed. (Westport, Conn.: Greenwood Press, 1975), 116; Brent Nosworthy, *The Bloody Crucible of Courage*, 482–484.

17. David Power Conyngham Papers (CON), "Soldiers of the Cross," University of Notre Dame Archives (UNDA), Notre Dame, IN., 26–29; Also see Dennis W. Belcher, *General David S. Stanley, USA: A Civil War Biography* (Jefferson, NC: McFarland, 2014), 74.

18. William S. Rosecrans, Letter Undated, William S. Rosecrans Papers, Box 59, Folder 54, University of California–Los Angeles; Thomas M. Vincent, "David Sloane Stanley," *The Thirty-fourth Annual Reunion of the Association Graduates of the United States Military Academy at West Point*, New York (Saginaw, MI: Seeman and Peters Printers and Binders, 1903), 62.

19. William S. Rosecrans, *Official Records*, Series I, Vol. 23, Part 1, 418.

20. *Harper's Weekly*, "Brigadier General Robert B. Mitchell," April 4, 1863; Also see Dennis W. Belcher, *Cavalry of the Army of the Cumberland* (Jefferson, NC: McFarland and Co., 2016), 72.

21. James Edwin Love, Letter to Wife May 20, 1863, James Edwin Love Papers (1859–1865) ARC A0940, Missouri Historical Society, St. Louis.

22. Marshall P. Thatcher, *A Hundred Battles in the West: The Second Michigan Cavalry* (Detroit: L. F. Kilroy, Printer, 1884), 124.

23. Thomas Speed, *Union Regiments of Kentucky*, Vol. I (Louisville: The Courier Journal Job Printing, Co., 1897), 185.

24. H. Levin, editor, *Lawyers and Lawmakers of Kentucky* (Chicago: Lewis Publishing Co., 1897), 530.

25. *The Union Army, A History of Military Affairs in the Loyal States 1861–65*, Vol. 8 (Madison, WI: Federal Publishing Co., 1908), 292.

26. Frederick H. Dyer, *A Compendium of The War of the Rebellion* (Des Moines, IA: The Dyer Publishing Co., 1908), 1269–1270.

27. Joseph Vale, *Minty and the Cavalry: A History of Cavalry Campaigns in the Western Armies* (Harrisburg, PA: Edwin K. Myers, Printer and Binder, 1886), 475; *Commemorative Biographical Encyclopedia of Dauphin County, Pennsylvania* (Chambersburg, PA: J. M. Runk & Co., 1896), 1194–1195.

28. W. R. Carter, *History of the First Regiment of Tennessee Volunteer Cavalry* (Knoxville: Gaut-Ogden Co., Printers and Binders, 1902), 19–62; Myers E. Brown, *Tennessee's Union Cavalrymen* (Charleston, Portsmouth, San Francisco: Arcadia Publishing Co., 2008), 27.

29. Leroy Graf and Ralph Haskins, editors, "Telegram from Rosecrans April 12, 1863," In *Papers of Andrew Johnson*, Vol. 6 (Knoxville: University of Tennessee Press, 1983), 211; Julius Thomas Diary June 4, 1863, Julius E. Thomas Diary, 1863–1864, Julius E. Thomas Collection, MS.2720, University of Tennessee, Knoxville; W. R. Carter, *History of the First Regiment of Tennessee Volunteer Cavalry*, Ibid.

30. *National Cyclopedia of American Biography*, Vol. VI (New York: James T. White Co., 1896), 448.

31. George Hazzard, *Hazzard's History of Henry County, Indiana, 1822–1906*, Vol. 1 (New Castle, IN: George Hazzard, 1906), 187; *The Daily Wabash Express* (Terre Haute, Indiana), "Cavalry," November 16, 1861, 3.

32. Robert Stevens, *The Bracken Rangers: Company K, 28th Regiment, 1st Indiana Cavalry* (Miami: Three Stars Press, 2011), 103.

33. Frederick H. Dyer, *A Compendium of the War of the Rebellion*, 1106; Roger Hunt, *Colonels in Blue: Indiana, Kentucky and Tennessee* (Jefferson, NC: McFarland & Co., 2013), 102.

34. Thomas Speed, *Union Regiments of Kentucky*, Vol. I (Louisville: The Courier Journal Job Printing, Co., 1897), 161–163; William T. Hoblitzell Court Martial, June, 1864, Record Group (RG) 153, Adjutant General's Office, Court Martial Case Files, 1809–1854, case number NN-3269, NARA, Washington, D.C.

35. L. Wallace Duncan and Charles F. Scott, editors, *History of Allen and Woodson Counties, Kansas: Embellished with Portraits of Well-Known People of These Counties, With Biographies of Our Representative Citizens, Cuts of Public Buildings and a Map of Each County* (Iola, KS: Iola Registers, Printers and Binders, 1901), 880–884; John Andes and Will McTeer, *Loyal Mountain Troopers: The Second and Third Tennessee Volunteer Cavalry in the Civil War* (Maryville, TN: Blount County Genealogical and Historical Society, 1992), 38, 41–42; Second Tennessee Regimental Papers, Letter, January 29, 1863, Record Group 94, Box 4661, Second Tennessee Cavalry Papers, NARA, Washington, D.C.; *Knoxville News Sentinel*, "Readers' Civil War Stories," November 5, 2011.

36. Edwin B. Quiner, "1st Cavalry," In *E. B Quiner's Military History of Wisconsin* (Chicago: Clark and Co., 1866), 884.

37. Edwin B. Quiner, "Biographical Sketches," In *E. B Quiner's Military History of Wisconsin* (Chicago: Clark and Co., 1866), 1002.

38. Earnest East, "Lincoln's Russian General," *Journal of the Illinois State Historical Society*, Vol. 52 (1959), No. 1, 106–122; Don Carlos Buell, *Official Records*, Series 1, Vol. 16, Part 2, 71.

39. David Stanley, *Official Records*, Series 1, Vol. 23, Part 1, 334–335; Stanley, *An American General*, 158–159.

40. William Henry Powell, editor, *Officers of the Army and Navy (volunteer) Who Served in the Civil War* (Philadelphia: L. R. Hamersly, 1893), 313.

41. *The Vevay Reveille*, "Necrology Col. Robert Klein," Vol. 85, number 13, Thursday, 27 March 1902, page 5, columns 3 and 4; W. N. Pickerill, *History of the Third Indiana Cavalry* (Indianapolis: Aetna Printing Co., 1906), 40–46; Frederick H. Dyer, *A Compendium of the War of the Rebellion*, 1105–1106.

42. Frederick H. Dyer, *A Compendium of the War of the Rebellion*, 1161–1162; Charles C. Nott, *Sketches of the War: A Series of Letters to the North Moore Street School of New York* (New York: Anson D. F. Randolph, 1865), 43–44; Kurt D. Bergmann, *Brackett's Battalion: Minnesota Cavalry in the Civil War and Dakota War* (St. Paul, MN: Borealis Books, 2004), 56.

43. *Twenty-Ninth Annual Reunion of the Association of Graduates of the United States Military Academy at West Point* (Saginaw: Seemann & Peters, Printers and Binders, 1898), 83–83.

44. Mark Hoffman, *My Brave Mechanics: The First Michigan Engineers and Their Civil War* (Detroit: Wayne State University Press, 2007), 132; James W. Sligh papers, 1842–1865 (Box 1), Bentley Historical Library, University of Michigan, Ann Arbor; Frank Mix, *Official*

Records, Series 1, Vol. 20, Part 1, 629–630; Frederick H. Dyer, *A Compendium of the War of the Rebellion*, 1271.

45. William Sipes, *History and Roster of the 7th Pennsylvania Veteran Volunteers* (Pottsville: Miners' Journal Print, 1905), 1–3; Chester Bailey, *The Mansfield Men in the Seventh Pennsylvania Cavalry, Eighth Regiment* (Mansfield, PA: Published by Author, 1986), 1–6; Gerould Otis Gibson, Diary November 19, 1862, Pennsylvania Regimental Files, Stones River National Park, Technical Information Center, Murfreesboro, TN.; T. F. Dornblaser, *My Life Story for Young and Old* (USA: Privately printed, 1930), 55.

46. George C. Wynkoop, Biography, MS 076: George C. Wynkoop Papers, Gettysburg College, Musselman Library, Special Collections & College Archives, Gettysburg; Francis W. Reed, Letter December 19, 1862, *Civil War Times Illustrated* Collection, USAHEC.

47. James Alex Baggett, *Homegrown Yankees: Tennessee's Union Cavalry in the Civil War* (Baton Rouge: Louisiana State University, 2009), 30, 46–47.

48. Francis Bernard Heitman, *Historical Register and Dictionary of the United States Army 1789–1903* (Washington, DC: U.S. Government Printing Office, 1903), 669; George W. Cullum, *Biographical Register of the Officers and Graduates of the U.S. Military Academy*, Vol. 2 (New York: D. Van Nostrand, 1868–79), 559–560; Joseph Vale, *Minty and the Cavalry*, 146–147.

49. *A Military Record of Battery D, First Ohio Veteran Volunteers, Light Artillery* (Oil City, PA: The Derrick Publishing Co., 1908), 9, 39, 57–58.

50. David Stanley, *Official Records*, Series 1, Vol. 20, Part 1, 619; Marshall Thatcher, *A Hundred Battles in the West: The Second Michigan Cavalry*, 124.

51. Thomas Speed, *Union Regiments of Kentucky* Vol. I (Louisville: The Courier Journal Job Printing, Co., 1897), 120.

52. W. L. Curry, *Four Years in the Saddle: History of First Regiment Ohio Volunteer Cavalry*, 1–52; *Portrait and Biographical Album of Sedgwick County, Kan.* (Chicago: Chapman Brothers, 1888), 469–471.

53. Thomas Crofts, *History of the Service of the Third Ohio Veteran Volunteer Cavalry* (Toledo: Stoneman Press, 1910), 12–13, 103–104, 239; Nancy Pape-Findley, *The Invincibles: The Story of Fourth Ohio Veteran Volunteer Cavalry* (Tecumseh, MI: Blood Road Publishing, 2002), 146; Noel V. Bourasaw, "Arthur C. Seidel, Civil War Veteran and Builder in Old Woolley," *Skagit River Journal of History & Folklore*, 2000; Charles S. Brown, *Military Biography of Col. Charles B. Seidel, Third Ohio Vol. Cav. U.S.A. Born at Berlin, Germany, April 1, at Lyndon, Ky., March 14, 1916, Together with Funeral Oration by of Chicago, Ill.* (Chicago: Germantown Printing. Company, 1916), 1–12.

54. W. L. Curry, *Four Years in the Saddle*, 9–12; Nancy Pape-Findley, *The Invincibles*, 112, 360; United States Census, 1860; C. S. Williams, *Williams' Cincinnati Directory* (Cincinnati: C. S. Williams, 1860), 254.

55. "Letter to Governor David Tod" June 3, 1862, In *Correspondence to the Governor and Adjutant General, 1861–1866*, Vol. 34, Series 147–39: 90, Ohio Historical Society, Columbus, Ohio.

56. *Historical Sketch of the Chicago Board of Trade Battery* (Chicago: The Henneberry Co. Publishers, 1902), 42–44.

57. *Twenty-Second Annual Reunion of the Association of the Graduates of the United States Military Academy: June 12th, 1891* (Saginaw: Seemann & Peters, Printers and Binders, 1891), 40–41.

58. Stephen Z. Starr, *The Union Cavalry in the Civil War: The War in the West*, Vol. III (Baton Rouge: Louisiana State University, 2007), 225.

59. David Stanley, *An American General*, 150; James Arthur Schaefer, "The Tactical and Strategic Evolution of Cavalry During the American Civil War," 132–133.

60. David Stanley, *Personal Memoirs of Major-General D. S. Stanley USA* (Cambridge, MA: Harvard University Press, 1917), 136–137; David Stanley, *Official Records*, Series 1, Vol. 23, Part 1, 334–335; Stanley, *An American General*, 158–159.

61. David Stanley, *Personal Memoirs of Major-General D. S. Stanley*, 136–137; Brandon Beck, *Streight's Foiled Raid on the Western & Atlantic Railroad* (Charleston, SC: The History Press, 2016), 41–41.

Chapter Two

1. William S. Rosecrans, *Official Records*, Series 1, Vol. 23, Part 1, 424; Robert S. Brandt, "Lighting and Rain in Middle Tennessee: The Tullahoma Campaign of June-July 1863," In *the Battle of Stones River and the Fight for Middle Tennessee*, Timothy D. Johnson, editor (Nashville: The Tennessee Historical Society, 2012), 133–134.

2. Edwin Stanton, *Official Records*, Series 1, Vol. 23, Part 2, 518; William Rosecrans, *Official Records*, Series 1, Vol. 23, Part 2, 518; William Lamers, *The Edge of Glory: A Biography of General William S. Rosecrans, U.S.A.* (New York: Harcourt, Brace & World, Inc., 1961), 295.

3. Don Carlos Buell, *Official Records*, Series 1, Vol. 16, Part 2, 563–564; George Cullum, *Biographical Register of the Officers and Graduates of the U.S. Military Academy, 1841–1867*, Vol. II (New York: D. Van Nostrand, 1868), 396; Horatio Wright, *Official Records*, Series 1, Vol. 16, Part 2, 523; Horatio Wright, *Official Records*, Series 1, Vol. 16, Part 2, 908–909.

4. Minor Millikin, *Official Records*, Series 1, Vol. 16, Part 2, 648–649; Joseph Wheeler, "Bragg's Invasion of Kentucky," In *Battles and Leaders of the Civil War*, Vol. III (New York: The Century Company, 1888), 4; John S. Scott, *Official Records*, Series 1, Vol. 16, Part 1, 938–939; Kenneth Hafendorfer, *They Died by Twos and Tens: The Confederate Cavalry in the Kentucky Campaign of 1862* (Louisville, KY: KH Press, 1995), 739, 742; Leonidas Polk, *Official Records*, Series 1, Vol. 16, Part 1, 1110; Braxton Bragg, *Official Records*, Series 1, Vol. 16, Part 1, 1094.

5. J. P. Garesché, *Official Records*, Series 1, Vol. 20, Part 2, 94; David Stanley, *An American General: The Memoirs of David Sloan Stanley*, Samuel W. Fordyce IV, ed. (Santa Barbara, CA: The Narrative Press, 2004), 149; William Rosecrans, *Official Records*, Series 1, Vol. 20, Part 1, 182.

6. Christopher S. Dwyer, "Raiding Strategy: As Applied by the Western Confederate Cavalry in the American Civil War," *The Journal of Military History*, 63 (April 1999): 266–272; Michael R. Bradley, *The Raiding Winter* (Gretna, LA: Pelican Publishing Co., 2013), 11–16.

7. William Rosecrans, *Official Records*, Series 1, Vol.

20, Part 2, 182, 189; Thomas Jordan and J. P. Pryor, *The Campaigns Lieut.-Gen. N. B. Forrest, and of Forrest's Cavalry* (New Orleans, Memphis, and New York: Blelock and Company, 1868), 193–194; Julius P. Garesché, *Official Records*, Series 1, Vol. 20, Part 2, 241.

8. Fifth Tennessee Cavalry Papers, Letters, December 14, 24, 1862, Record Group 94, Box 4667, Fifth Tennessee Cavalry Papers, NARA, Washington, D.C.; William Rosecrans, *Official Records*, Series 1, Vol. 20, Part 1, 182; R. H. G. Minty, "The Saber Brigade," *National Tribune*, August 11, 1892; John Andes and Will McTeer, *Loyal Mountain Troopers: The Second and Third Tennessee Volunteer Cavalry in the Civil War* (Maryville, TN: Blount County Genealogical and Historical Society, 1992), 38, 41–42; Second Tennessee Regimental Papers, Letter, January 29, 1863, Record Group 94, Box 4661, Second Tennessee Cavalry Papers, NARA, Washington, D.C.; Paul Hersch, Letter October 12, 1862, Hersh, Paul Papers (Civil War Misc. Collection), Sergeant's Transcribed Letters, Oct. 12, 1862-May 25, 1865, USAHEC, Carlisle, PA; James Weir Diary, William Palmer Papers, Colorado Springs Pioneers Museum; George Fobes, "An Account of the Mutiny in the Anderson Cavalry, at Nashville, Tenn., December 1862," In *Leaves of a Trooper's Dairy*, by John Williams (Philadelphia: Published by Author, 1869), 78–103.

9. William Rosecrans, *Official Records*, Series 1, Vol. 20, Part 1, 184, 189–190; C. Goddard, *Official Records*, Series 1, Vol. 20, Part 2, 242; Jefferson C. Davis, *Official Records*, Series 1, Vol. 20, Part 1, 262.

10. Lewis Zahm, *Official Records*, Series 1, Vol. 20, Part 1, 633–635; William E. Crane, "William E. Crane's Daily Journal of Life in the Field during the War of the Rebellion," December 26–27, 1862 entries, Mss. 980, Cincinnati Historical Society, Cincinnati Museum Center; Baxter Smith, "8th Tennessee Cavalry Regiment, Confederate, History of Regiment and Biographical information," Box 107, Folder 10, undated, USAHEC; Isaac Skillman, Diary December 26, 1862, MMS1083, Bowling Green State University, Bowling Green Ohio; Lucien Wulsin, *The Fourth Regiment Ohio Veteran Volunteer Cavalry* (Cincinnati: Fourth Ohio Volunteer Cavalry Association, 1912), 34.

11. Robert Minty, *Official Records*, Series 1, Vol. 20, Part 1, 623; Frank Mix, *Official Records*, Series 1, Vol. 20, Part 1, 629–630; Frank Mix, Letter from Frank Mix, January 9, 1863, Elisha Mix Papers, 1818–1898, Bentley Historical Library, University of Michigan, Ann Arbor.

12. Julius Garesché, *Official Records*, Series 1, Vol. 20, Part 2, 255; Alexander McCook, *Official Records*, Series 1, Vol. 20, Part 2, 256–257.

13. Larry Daniel, *Days of Glory, The Army of the Cumberland 1861–1865* (Baton Rouge: Louisiana State University Press, 2006), 211; Lanny Smith, *The Stone's River Campaign: 26 December 1862-5 January 1863, Army of Tennessee* (n.p.: Lanny Smith, 2010), 450–454.

14. David Stanley, January 9, 1863, Report, Stanley, Wright, West Papers, USAHEC, Carlisle, Pennsylvania; William D. Bickham, *Rosecrans' Campaign with the Fourteenth Army Corps, of the Army of the Cumberland* (Cincinnati: Moore, Wilstach, Keys & Co., 1863), 246; Robert Minty, Letter to Backus November 11, 1906, Robert Minty Papers, Civil War Collection, USAHEC, Carlisle, Pennsylvania.

15. Lewis Zahm, *Official Records*, Series 1, Vol. 20, Part 1, 637–638; Abraham Buford, *Official Records*, Series 1, Vol. 20, Part 1, 971; Joseph Wheeler, *Official Records*, Series 1, Vol. 20, Part 1, 959.

16. Edwin Stanton, *Official Records*, Series 1, Vol. 20, Part 2, 306; William Rosecrans, *Official Records*, Series 1, Vol. 20, Part 2, 328; Ephraim Otis, "The Murfreesboro Campaign," In *Campaigns in Kentucky and Tennessee include the Battle of Chickamauga, 1862–1864, Papers of the Military Historical Society of Massachusetts*, Vol. VII (Boston: Military Historical Society of Massachusetts, 1908), 296–297; Basil Duke, *Morgan's Cavalry* (New York: The Neale Publishing Co., 1909), 193–194; Larry Daniel, *Battle of Stones River* (Baton Rouge: Louisiana State University Press, 2012), 10–11; Michael Bradley, "Tullahoma: The Wrongly Forgotten Campaign," *Blue & Gray*, Vol. XXVII (2010), Number 1, 49.

17. James Alex Baggett, *Homegrown Yankees: Tennessee's Union Cavalry in the Civil War* (Baton Rouge: Louisiana State University, 2009), 87.

18. George Brent, *Official Records*, Series I, Vol. 23, Number 2, 701; Robert Lanier, *Photographic History of the Civil War* (New York: The Review of Reviews Co., 1911), 270; Robert George Hartje, *Van Dorn: The Life and Times of a Confederate General* (Nashville: Vanderbilt University Press, 1967), 316–319.

19. Stephen Z. Starr, *The Union Cavalry in the Civil War: The War in the West*, Vol. III (Baton Rouge: Louisiana State University, 2007), 225.

20. Dennis W. Belcher, *Cavalry of the Army of the Cumberland* (Jefferson, NC: McFarland & Co., 2016), 289.

21. Ulysses Simpson Grant, *Personal Memoirs of U.S. Grant* (New York: Charles L. Webster & Co., 1894), 249; Henry Halleck, *Official Records*, Series 1, Vol. 20, Part 2, 123–124; Abraham Lincoln, *Official Records*, Series 1, Vol. 23, Part 2, 369; Henry Halleck, *Official Records*, Series 1, Vol. 23, Part 2, 383.

22. Henry Halleck, *Official Records*, Series 1, Vol. 23, Part 2, 376–377, 383.

23. David Stanley, *An American General*, 162.

24. Theodore Clarke Smith, *The Life and Letters of James A. Garfield* (New Haven: Yale University Press, 1925), 309–310.

25. Frederick H. Dyer, *A Compendium of the War of the Rebellion* (Des Moines: The Dyer Publishing Co., 1908), 1189–1667.

26. Michael Bradley, "Varying Results of Cavalry Fighting: Western Flank vs. Eastern Flank," *Blue and Grey*, Vol. XXVII (2010), Number 1: 21.

27. Ibid.; W. L. Curry, *Four Years in the Saddle: History of First Regiment Ohio Volunteer Cavalry* (Columbus: Champlin Printing Co., 1898), 22, 99.

28. Michael Bradley, "Tullahoma: The Wrongly Forgotten Campaign," *Blue & Gray*, Vol. XXVII (2010), Number 1:22; William Lamers, *The Edge of Glory*, 275.

29. Larry J. Daniel, *Days of Glory: The Army of the Cumberland*, 267; William Rosecrans, *Official Records*, Series 1, Vol. 23, Part 1, 404–405.

30. Henry Mortimer Hempstead, "Diary, June 23, 1863," Hempstead, Henry Mortimer Papers, Bentley Historical Library, University of Michigan, Ann Arbor; Michael Bradley, *Tullahoma: The 1863 Campaign for the Control of Middle Tennessee* (Shippensburg, PA: White Mane Publishing Co., 1999), 51–52; Thomas McCahan, Diary, June 24, 1863, Thomas McCahan Papers Histor-

ical Society of Pennsylvania, Philadelphia; *National Tribune*, "Tullahoma Campaign," May 6, 1882; John Randolph Poole, *Cracker Cavaliers: The 2nd Georgia Cavalry Under Wheeler and Forrest* (Macon, GA: Mercer University Press, 2000), 78.

31. David Stanley, *Official Records*, Series 1, Vol. 23, Part 1, 538; Thomas Jordan, Letter to Wife June 26, 1863, Thomas J. Jordan Civil War Letters Box Number: 1, Folder 12, Historical Society of Pennsylvania, Philadelphia, Pennsylvania; Edward G. Longacre, *A Soldier to the Last: Maj. Gen. Joseph Wheeler in Blue and Gray* (Washington: Potomac Books Inc., 2007), 103.

32. David Stanley, *Official Records*, Series 1, Vol. 23, Part 1, 538–540; David A. Powell, *Failure in the Saddle* (New York and California: Savas Beatie, 2010), 5–6.

33. Robert Brandt, "Lightning and Rain in Middle Tennessee," 130.

34. Joseph Vale, *Minty and the Cavalry: A History of Cavalry Campaigns in the Western Armies* (Harrisburg, PA: Edwin K. Myers, Printer and Binder, 1886), 174–175; David Stanley, *Official Records*, Series 1, Vol. 23, Part 1, 539.

35. Michael Bradley, *Tullahoma: The 1863 Campaign*, 76; David Stanley, *Official Records*, Series 1, Vol. 23, Part 1, 539; George Steahlin, "Stanley's Cavalry: Minty's Sabre Brigade at Guy's Gap," *National Tribune*, May 27, 1882, 1, col. 5.

36. Michael Bradley, "Tullahoma: The Wrongly Forgotten Campaign," 44; David Stanley, *Official Records*, Series 1, Vol. 23, Part 1, 540–541.

37. Michael Bradley, "Tullahoma: The Wrongly Forgotten Campaign," 44.

38. Stephen Z. Starr, *The Union Cavalry in the Civil War, Vol. 3: The War in the West, 1861–1865* (Baton Rouge: Louisiana State University Press, 1985), 245–246; John Allan Wyeth, *With Sabre and Scalpel: The Autobiography of a Soldier and Surgeon* (New York and London: Harper Brothers Publishers, 1914), 214; William B. Sipes, *Official Records*, Series 1, Vol. 23, Part 1, 565.

39. George Steahlin, "Stanley's Cavalry," *National Tribune*, May 27, 1882, pp. 1–2.

40. Edward G. Longacre, *A Soldier to the Last*, 105; Michael Bradley, "Tullahoma: The Wrongly Forgotten Campaign," 47; Stephen Starr, *The Union Cavalry in the Civil War*, 246–247.

41. David Stanley, *Official Records*, Series 1, Vol. 23, Part 1, 540; C. Goddard, *Official Records*, Series 1, Vol. 23, Part 2, 472.

42. David Stanley, *An American General*, 166.

43. Richard J. Brewer, "The Tullahoma Campaign: Operational Insights," Master's Thesis, U.S. Army Command and General Staff College, Leavenworth, KS., 1978, 142; David Stanley, *Official Records*, Series 1, Vol. 23, Part 1, 540–541; John Allan Wyeth, *With Sabre and Scalpel*, 232.

44. John Turchin, *Official Records*, Series 1, Vol. 23, Part 1, 554.

45. T. F. Dornblaser, *Sabre Strokes of the Pennsylvania Dragoons* (Philadelphia: Lutheran Publication Society, 1884), 118–119; Thomas Crofts, *History of the Service of the Third Ohio Veteran Volunteer Cavalry* (Toledo: Stoneman Press, 1910), 108.

46. Stephen Starr, *The Union Cavalry in the Civil War*, 237; James A. Garfield, *Official Records*, Series 1 Vol. 23, Number 2, 465; Richard J. Brewer, "The Tullahoma Campaign," 73.

Chapter Three

1. Braxton Bragg, *Official Records*, Series 1, Vol. 23, Part 1, 585.

2. W. W. Mackall, *Official Records*, Series 1, Vol. 23, Part 1, 620; W. B. Richmond, *Official Records*, Series 1, Vol. 23, Part 1, 626.

3. H. W. Walter, *Official Records*, Series 1, Vol. 23, Part 2, 902.

4. David A. Powell, *Failure in the Saddle* (New York and California: Savas and Beatie, 2010), 242–243; William Rosecrans, *Official Records*, Series 1, Vol. 23, Part 2, 573–574.

5. Clement A. Evans, editor, *Confederate Military History*, Vol. I (Atlanta: Confederate Publishing Co., 1899), 699–702.

6. John W. DuBose, *General Joseph Wheeler and the Army of Tennessee* (New York: The Neale Publishing Co., 1912), 91; John Watson Morton, *The Artillery of Nathan Bedford Forrest's Cavalry* (Nashville, TN and Dallas, TX: Publishing House of the M. E. Church, 1909), 45–46; Edward Longacre, *A Soldier to the Last: Maj. Gen. Joseph Wheeler in Blue and Gray* (Washington, D.C.: Potomac Books, Inc., 2007), 11, 61.

7. Thomas Jordan and J. P. Pryor, *The Campaigns Lieut.-Gen. N. B. Forrest, and of Forrest's Cavalry* (New Orleans, Memphis, and New York: Blelock and Company, 1868), 225–231, 283–284; Michael Bower Cavender, *The First Georgia Cavalry in the Civil War: A History and Roster* (Jefferson, NC: McFarland Publishing, 2016), 129.

8. Jonathan Withers, *Official Records*, Series 1, Vol. 30, Part 4, 562; V. Sheliha, *Official Records*, Series 1, Vol. 30, Part 4, 562, 591.

9. Carolyn Thomas Foreman, "The Armstrongs of Indian Territory: General Frank Crawford Armstrong, Part III," *Chronicles of Oklahoma*, Vol. 31, No. 1 (1953): 56–65.

10. Clement Evans, ed. *Confederate Military History*, Vol. VIII (Atlanta: Confederate Publishing Co., 1899), 288–292; David Powell, *Failure in the Saddle*, xxiii–xxiv.

11. Janey Dudney, "Cumberland Tales: General George Gibbs Dibrell and the 8th Cavalry," *Herald Citizen* (Cookeville, TN), January 6, 2013; Bruce S. Allardice, *Confederate Colonels: A Biographical Register* (Columbia: University of Missouri Press, 2008), 391.

12. Ezra J. Warner, *Generals in Gray: Lives of the Confederate Commanders* (Baton Rouge: Louisiana State University Press, 1959), 231–232; Clement A., Evans, ed., *Confederate Military History: A Library of Confederate States History*. Vol. 3 (Atlanta: Confederate Publishing Co., 1899), 19–22; Peter Carmichael, *Lee's Young Artillerist: William R. J. Pegram* (Charlottesville: University of Virginia Press, 1995), 12–13, 32; *The Daily Dispatch* (Richmond), "Col. John Pegram," July 24, 1861; Walter Griggs, Jr., *Hidden History of Richmond* (Charleston, S. C.: Arcadia Publishing Co., 2012), 62–63; David Powell, *The Chickamauga Campaign: A Mad Irregular Battle* (El Dorado Hills, CA: Savas Beatie, 2014), 61–62.

13. Tucker Randolph, "Letter November 12, 1862 and December 8, 1862," Sgt. Tucker St. Joseph Ran-

dolph, Co. F, 21st Virginia Infantry and staff of Gen. John Pegram, May 1861–May 1864, American Civil War Museum, Richmond, VA; Howell Carter, *A Cavalryman's Reminiscences of the Civil War* (New Orleans: American Printing Co., n.d.), 65–70.

14. George Cullum, *Biographical Register of the Officers and Graduates of the U.S. Military Academy, 1841–1867*, Vol. II (New York: D. Van Nostrand, 1868), 550; David A. Powell, *Failure in the Saddle*, xxxiv–xxxv; Howell Carter, *A Cavalryman's Reminiscences of the Civil War* (Port Hudson, LA: Old South Books, 1979), 26–30, 65–70, 92.

15. *Ibid.*, Carter.

16. Howell Carter, *A Cavalryman's Reminiscences of the Civil War*, 13–15; David Powell, *Failure in the Saddle*, xxxv.

17. Edward Longacre, *Soldier to the Last*, 103; David Stanley, *An American General*, 166; Robert J. Dalessandro, "Morale In The Army Of The Cumberland During The Tullahoma And Chickamauga Campaigns," Master's Thesis, U.S. Army Command and General Staff College, Leavenworth, KS., 1980, 74; Michael Bradley, "Varying Results of Cavalry Fighting: Western Flank vs. Eastern Flank," *Blue and Grey*, Vol. XXVII (2010), Number 1, 21. [Also see Dennis W. Belcher, *General David S. Stanley, USA: A Civil War Biography* (Jefferson, NC: McFarland, 2014), 138–139.]

18. Edward Longacre, *A Soldier to the Last*, 7–11; J. P. Dyer, "The Civil War Career of General Joseph Wheeler," *Georgia Historical Quarterly*, Vol. 19 No. 1 (Mar. 1935), 17–46; Lawyn C. Edwards, "Confederate Cavalry at Chickamauga: What Went Wrong," Master's Thesis, U.S. Army Command and General Staff College, Fort Leavenworth, Kansas, 1990, 49.

19. Edward Longacre, *Soldier to the Last*, 14–15; J. P. Dyer, *Ibid.*

20. Edward Longacre, *Soldier to the Last*, 16–17.

21. J. P. Dyer, "The Civil War Career of General Joseph Wheeler," 17–46.

22. Edward Longacre, *A Soldier to the Last*, 55–60; Baxter Smith, "8th Tennessee Cavalry Regiment, Confederate, History of Regiment and Biographical information," Box 107, Folder 10, undated, USAHEC; J. P. Dyer, "The Civil War Career of General Joseph Wheeler," 17–46; John Randolph Poole, *Cracker Cavaliers: The 2nd Georgia Cavalry Under Wheeler and Forrest* (Macon, GA: Mercer University Press, 2000), 54; Arthur Fremantle, *Three Months in the Southern States, 1864* (New York: John Bradburn Co., 1864), 158; William Brooksher and David Snider, "The War Child Rides: Joe Wheeler at Stones River," *Civil War Times Illustrated* 14: (1976): 4–10.

23. William Wharton Groce, "Major General John A. Wharton," *The Southwestern Historical Quarterly*, Vol. 19, No. 3 (Jan., 1916), 271–278; C. C. Jeffries, *Terry's Rangers* (New York: Vantage Press, 1961), 17–29.

24. William Wharton Groce, *ibid.*; David Powell, *Failure in the Saddle*, xxx.

25. C. C. Jeffries, *Terry's Rangers*, 17–29, 59; Lucian L. Knight, *Standard History of Georgia and Georgians*, Vol. 4 (Chicago and New York: The Lewis Publishing Co., 1917), 2281; David Powell, *ibid.*

26. Spencer C. Tucker, editor, *American Civil War: The Definitive Encyclopedia and Document Collection*, Vol. I (Santa Barbara, Denver, Oxford: ABC-CLIO, 2013), 1204.

27. Braxton Bragg, *Official Records*, Series 1, Vol. 23, Part 2, 944.

28. Willis Brewer, *Alabama, Her History, Resources, War Record, and Public Men* (Montgomery: Barrett & Brown, Steam Printers and Book Binders, 1872), 225; David Powell, *Failure in the Saddle*, xxxii–xxxiii.

29. Clement Evans, editor, *Confederate Military History, Alabama*, Vol. VII (Cartersville, GA: Eastern Digital Resources, 2014), 440–441.

30. Nathan B. Forrest, *Official Records*, Series 1, Vol. 23, Part 2, 955–956; Jefferson Davis, *Official Records*, Series 1, Vol. 30, Part 4, 507.

31. Christopher S. Dwyer, "Raiding Strategy: As Applied by the Western Confederate Cavalry in the American Civil War," *The Journal of Military History*, 63 (April 1999): 263–281, 266–272.

Chapter Four

1. John L. Mitchell, *John L. Mitchell's Tennessee State Gazetteer and Business Directory for 1860–1861* (Nashville: John L. Mitchell, 1860), 26–31; Larry Daniel, *Days of Glory, The Army of the Cumberland 1861–1865* (Baton Rouge: Louisiana State University Press, 2006), 287; John H. Eicher and David Eicher, *Civil War High Commands* (Stanford: Stanford University Press, 2001), 6.

2. Jack Welsh, *Medical Histories of Confederate Generals* (Kent, OH: Kent State University Press, 1995), 23; Peter Cozzens, *This Terrible Sound: The Battle of Chickamauga* (Urbana and Chicago: University of Illinois Press, 1992), 27–28.

3. Patton Anderson, *Official Records*, Series 1, Vol. 23, Part 2, 912.

4. Peter Cozzens, *This Terrible Sound: The Battle of Chickamauga*, 29; S. B. Buckner, *Official Records*, Series 1, Vol. 23, Part 2, 903.

5. George B. Pickett, *Official Records*, Series 1, Vol. 23, Part 2, 900; H. W. Walter, *Official Records*, Series 1, Vol. 23, Part 2, 914, 925; Joseph Wheeler, *Official Records*, Series 1, Vol. 23, Part 2, 916; John W. DuBose, *General Joseph Wheeler and the Army of Tennessee* (New York: The Neale Publishing Co., 1912), 184; John Newton Smith, Letter July 27, 1863, Wiggins Artillery Regimental File, Stones River National Military Park, Technical Information Center, Murfreesboro.

6. Patton Anderson, *Official Records*, Series 1, Vol. 23, Part 2, 916; G. P. Thruston, *Official Records*, Series 1, Vol. 23, Part 2, 519; Alexander McCook, *Official Records*, Series 1, Vol. 23, Part 2, 519.

7. Robert S. Brandt, "Lightning and Rain in Middle Tennessee," In *The Battle of Stones River and The Fight for Middle Tennessee*, Timothy Johnson, ed. (Nashville: Tennessee Historical Society, 2012), 133; Phil Sheridan, *Official Records*, Series 1, Vol. 23, Part 2, 519.

8. William Lamers, *The Edge of Glory: A Biography of General William S. Rosecrans, U.S.A.* (New York: Harcourt, Brace & World, Inc., 1961), 295.

9. Henry Halleck, *Official Records*, Series 1, Vol. 23, Part 2, 531.

10. Henry Halleck, *Official Records*, Series 1, Vol. 23, Part 2, 552; John W. DuBose, *General Joseph Wheeler and the Army of Tennessee*, 188.

11. William Rosecrans, *Official Records*, Series 1, Vol. 23, Part 2, 555; Henry Halleck, *Official Records*, Series 1,

Vol. 23, Part 2, 556; John W. Taylor, *Official Records*, Series 1, Vol. 23, Part 2, 601; David Stanley, *Official Records*, Series 1, Vol. 23, Part 2, 548.

12. Patton Anderson, *Official Records*, Series 1, Vol. 23, Part 2, 932, 934–935; John Andes and Will McTeer, *Loyal Mountain Troops, The Second and Third Tennessee Volunteer Cavalry* (Maryville, TN: Blount County Genealogical and Historical Society, 1992), 63.

13. George Thomas, *Official Records*, Series 1, Vol. 23, Part 2, 551; Kinloch Falconer, *Official Records*, Series 1, Vol. 23, Part 2, 938; Edward G. Longacre, *A Soldier to the Last: Maj. Gen. Joseph Wheeler in Blue and Gray* (Washington: Potomac Books Inc., 2007), 109; James A. Garfield, *Official Records*, Series 1, Vol. 23, Part 2, 527; David Stanley, *Official Records*, Series 1, Vol. 23, Part 2, 548.

14. David S. Stanley, Special Orders No. 8, July 7, 1863, RG 94, 7th Kentucky Cavalry Regimental Order Book, NARA; Eugene Bronson, Letter July 26, 1863, Eugene Bronson Collection, Kalamazoo College, Kalamazoo; Paul H. Bergeron, *The Papers of Andrew Johnson: Vol. 15, September 1883 to April 1869* (Knoxville: University of Tennessee Press, 1999), 383.

15. Braxton Bragg, *Official Records*, Series 1, Vol. 23, Part 1, 584; David Stanley, *Official Records*, Series 1, Vol. 23, Part 1, 538, 541.

16. William Sinclair, August 4 letter to E. M. McCook, Letters sent by Chief of Cavalry, RG 393, entry 2460, NARA.

17. James A. Garfield, *Official Records*, Series 1, Vol. 23, Part 2, 527; David Stanley, *Official Records*, Series 1, Vol. 23, Part 2, 548; *Nashville Daily Press*, "Court-Martialed," July 16, 1863; Court Martial Record, August 14, 1863, RG 94, 4th Kentucky Cavalry, Orders and Correspondence books, NARA; 4th U.S. Cavalry, Correspondence July 16, 1863 and September 4, 1863, RG 391, Entry 731, 4th U.S. Cavalry regimental books, NARA.

18. *Chicago Times*, "An Expedition into the Enemy's Country," July 22, 1863; Julius E. Thomas, Diary July 5. 1863, Julius E. Thomas Collection, MS.2720, University of Tennessee, Knoxville, Tennessee; Thomas Vincent, Special Orders No. 9, July 13, 1863, RG 94, 7th Kentucky Regimental Orders Book, NARA.

19. George Kryder, Diary June 8, 1863, MS 163 George Kryder (1834–1925), William T. Jerome Library, Bowling Green State University, Bowling Green, Ohio; John McLain, Diary Entry February 13, 1863, John McLain, Papers (c.00111), Michigan State University Archives & Historical Collections, East Lansing, Michigan; W. R. Carter, *History of the First Regiment of Tennessee Volunteer Cavalry* (Knoxville: Gaut-Ogden Co., Printers and Binders, 1902), 80; Charles Perry Goodrich, July 16, 1863, letter, *Letters from Home from the First Wisconsin Cavalry*, Richard N. Larson, editor (Madison: State Historical Society of Wisconsin, not published); Stephen Z. Starr, "The Third Ohio Volunteer Cavalry: A View from the Inside," *Ohio History*, Vol. 85, Autumn 1976, Number 4: 306–318, 315–317.

20. David Stanley, *An American General: The Memoirs of David Sloan Stanley*, Samuel W. Fordyce IV, ed. (Santa Barbara, CA: The Narrative Press, 2004), 167–168; John Beatty, *The Citizen Soldier: The Memoirs of a Civil War Volunteer* (Lincoln and London: Bison Books University of Nebraska Press, 1998), 303; Mary Jane Chadwick, *Incidents of the War: The Civil War Journal of Mary Jane Chadwick*, Nancy Rohr, ed. (Huntsville: Silver Thread Publishing, 2005), 110; James Garfield, *Official Records*, Series 1, Vol. 23, Part 2, 527; W. S. Rosecrans, *Official Records*, Series 1, Vol. 23, Part 2, 529; W. L. Curry, *Four Years in the Saddle: History of First Regiment Ohio Volunteer Cavalry* (Columbus: Champlin Printing Co., 1898), 106; Robert D. Richardson, "Rosecrans' Staff at Chickamauga: The Significance of Major General William S. Rosecrans' Staff on the Outcome of the Chickamauga Campaign." Master's Thesis, Command and General Staff College, Fort Leavenworth, Kansas, 1989, 62.

21. Charles Perry Goodrich, July 18, 1863, *Letters from Home from the First Wisconsin Cavalry*; Julius Thomas, July 17, 1863, diary entry; John McLain, Diary entries July 20–30, 1863; Robert Merrill, "July 7, 1863," *Robert Sidney Merrill, Co. K. 1st Wis. Cav.* (Cedarsburg, WI.: MSG Publishing, 1995); W. R. Carter, *History of the First Regiment of Tennessee Volunteer Cavalry*, 79; Charles Perry Goodrich, "July 16, 1863," *Letters from Home from the First Wisconsin Cavalry*; 4th Ohio Morning Reports: Company E, July 15–17, 1863, RG 94, E 112–115, NARA, Washington, D.C.; 3rd Ohio Cavalry, Morning Reports: Company C, July 15–17, 1863, RG 94, E 112–115, NARA, Washington, D.C.

22. *Staunton Spectator*, "Huntsville, Ala." July 28, 1863, 2; *Alexandria Gazette*, "From the Army of the Cumberland," July 25, 1863, 3; *Washington City Evening Star*, "The Taking of Huntsville," July 25, 1863, 4; Thomas Speed, "Cavalry Operations in the West Under Rosecrans and Sherman," In *Battle and Leaders of the Civil War*, Vol. 4 (New York: The Century Company, 1884, 1888), 415.

23. *The Abingdon Virginian*, "Interesting Letter," August 7, 1863, 2.

24. George D. Wood, Letter July 23, 1863, Slayton Family Papers, Bentley Historical Library, University of Michigan, Ann Arbor; James Perry, Letter July 14, 1863, MMS 1457, James H. M. Perry Papers, 1863, William T. Jerome Library, Bowling Green State University, Bowling Green, Ohio; Alexander McCook, *Official Records*, Series 1, Vol. 23, Part 2, 544.

25. W. S. Merrill, *The Middle Tennessee and Chattanooga Campaigns of June, July, August, and September 1863* (New York : Julius Bien & Co. Lith., 1891), 1–10; W. C. Whitaker, *Official Records*, Series 1, Vol. 52, Part 1, 428; F. W. Weatherbee, Jr., *The 5th (1st Middle) Tennessee Cavalry Regiment, U.S.A.* (Carrollton, MS: Pioneer Publishing Co., 1992), 28; John Brandon, Letter to father September 30, 1863, Brandon Collection of Civil War Letters, Civil War Collection, Box 14, folder 8, USAHEC, Carlisle, PA.

26. David Stanley, *Official Records*, Series 1, Vol. 23, Part 2, 548–549.

27. Jefferson Davis, *Official Records*, Series 1, Vol. 20, Part 2, 449- 450; Jefferson Davis, "Letter to Varina Howell Davis," December 15, 1862, *Papers of Jefferson Davis*, Vol. 8, Linda Lasswell Crist, Mary Seaton Dix, and Kenneth H. Williams, eds. (Baton Rouge and London: Louisiana State University Press, 1995), 5; Patton Anderson, *Official Records*, Series 1, Vol. 23, Part 2, 930; Kinloch Falconer, *Official Records*, Series 1, Vol. 23, Part 2, 938; W. S. Merrill, *The Middle Tennessee and Chattanooga Campaigns*, 1–10; George Wm. Brent, *Official Records*, Series 1, Vol. 23, Part 2, 936; Lawyn C. Edwards, "Confederate Cavalry At Chickamauga: What Went

Wrong," Master's Thesis, U.S. Army Command and General Staff College, Fort Leavenworth, Kansas, 1990, 107; West Walker, Letter to family July 19, 1863, West Walker Letters, 4th Tennessee Cavalry, Confederate Collection, Box 11, Folder 35, Tennessee State Library and Archives, Nashville.

28. Henry Albert Potter, Letter July 23, 1863, Henry Albert Potter Collection. MS 91–480, Accession Box 461 Folder 2, Michigan Historical Society, Lansing, Michigan; Charles Perry Goodrich, July 25, 1863, letter, *Letters from Home from the First Wisconsin Cavalry*; Robert Minty, 4th Michigan Cavalry Orders and Correspondence, July 23 and 26, September 7, 1863, RG 94, 4th Michigan Cavalry Regimental Records, NARA, Washington, D.C.; Horace Gray, 4th Michigan Cavalry Orders and Correspondence, July 28, 1863, RG 94, 4th Michigan Cavalry Regimental Records, NARA.

29. David Stanley, *Official Records*, Series 1, Vol. 23, Part 2, 548–549; William Sinclair, *Official Records*, Series 1, Vol. 23, Part 2, 568; Joseph Vale, *Minty and the Cavalry: A History of Cavalry Campaigns in the Western Armies* (Harrisburg, PA.: Edwin K. Myers, Printer and Binder, 1886), 196; Isaac Skillman, Diary August 9, 1863, MMS1083, Bowling Green State University, Bowling Green, Ohio.

30. John Beatty, *The Citizen Soldier*, 306–307; I. R. Conwell, Diary entry August 2, 1863, Conwell Diary, S2753, F3, Indiana Historical Society, Indianapolis.

31. W. L. Curry, *Four Years in the Saddle: History of First Regiment Ohio Volunteer Cavalry*, 106–107; William H. Sinclair, *Official Records*, Series 1, Vol. 23, Part 2, 565.

32. William Sinclair, *Official Records*, Series 1, Vol. 23, Part 2, 567–568; G. P. Thruston, *Official Records*, Series 1, Vol. 23, Part 2, 568.

33. Henry Halleck, *Official Records*, Series 1, Vol. 23, Part 2, 552–553; W. S. Rosecrans, *Official Records*, Series 1, Vol. 23, Part 2, 551; William Sinclair, *Official Records*, Series 1, Vol. 23, Part 2, 565.

34. Leonidas Polk, *Official Records*, Series 1, Vol. 23, Part 2, 937–938.

35. Braxton Bragg, *Official Records*, Series 1, Vol. 23, Part 2, 948, 952–953; Joseph Johnston, *Official Records*, Series 1, Vol. 23, Part 2, 950; Jefferson Davis, *Official Records*, Series 1, Vol. 23, Part 2, 953; S. C. Cooper, *Official Records*, Series 1, Vol. 23, Part 2, 948; Thomas Connelly, *Autumn of Glory: The Army of Tennessee 1862–1865* (Baton Rouge: Louisiana State University Press, 1971), 148; George Wm. Brent, *Official Records*, Series 1, Vol. 23, Part 2, 953.

36. George D. Wood, Letter July 25, 1863, Slayton Family Papers, Bentley Historical Library, University of Michigan; John Lynch, Letter August 21, 1863, Morris Fitch Papers, Bentley Historical Library, University of Michigan.

37. William Rosecrans, *Official Records*, Series 1, Vol. 23, Part 2, 585–586; John W. Taylor, *Official Records*, Series 1, Vol. 23, Part 2, 601.

38. Henry Halleck, *Official Records*, Series 1, Vol. 23, Part 2, 592–593; William Rosecrans, *Official Records*, Series 1, Vol. 23, Part 2, 590; Ambrose Burnside; *Official Records*, Series 1, Vol. 23, Part 2, 592.

39. William Rosecrans, *Official Records*, Series 1, Vol. 23, Part 2, 594, 598.

40. David Stanley, Letter to Stoneman, August 24, 1863, Letter sent by Chief of Cavalry, RG 393, Entry 2460, NARA.

41. *Ibid.*

42. *Ibid.*

43. *Ibid.*

44. Thomas Jordan and J. P. Pryor, *The Campaigns of Lieut.-Gen. Nathan B. Forrest of Forrest's Cavalry* (New Orleans, Memphis, NY: Blelock & Co., 1868), 293–295.

45. Simon Buckner, *Official Records*, Series 1, Vol. 23, Part 1, 842; John Scott, *Official Records*, Series 1, Vol. 23, Part 1, 840–842; George Hartsuff, *Official Records*, Series 1, Vol. 23, Part 1, 829–831.

46. Robert Minty, *Official Records*, Series 1, Vol. 23, Part 1, 845–846; David A. Powell "A Legend in the Making: Nathan Bedford Forrest at Chickamauga" In *Gateway to the Confederacy: New Perspectives on the Chickamauga and Chattanooga Campaigns, 1862–1863*, edited by Evans C. Jones and Wiley Sword (Baton Rouge: Louisiana State University Press, 2014), 65.

47. Horatio Van Cleve, *Official Records*, Series 1, Vol. 23, Part 2, 595.

48. John B. Rodgers, *Official Records*, Series 1, Vol. 30, Part 3, 7.

49. George Dibrell, *Official Records*, Series 1, Vol. 23, Part 1, 847–848; Kent Dollar, "Spirited Engagement in White County During Civil War," *Herald Citizen*, October 12, 2014, Cookeville, TN.

50. Robert Minty, *Official Records*, Series 1, Vol. 23, Part 1, 846–847; Joseph Vale, *Minty and the Cavalry*, 201; Robert Minty, "Minty's Sabre Brigade: Minty's Close Call," *National Tribune*, February 25, 1892.

51. George Dibrell, *Official Records*, Series 1, Vol. 23, Part 1, 847–848.

52. George Dibrell, *Ibid.*; Robert Minty, *Official Records*, Series 1, Vol. 23, Part 1, 846–847; Horatio Van Cleve, *Official Records*, Series 1, Vol. 30, Part 3, 21.

53. William Rosecrans, *Official Records*, Series 1, Vol. 30, Part 3, 4.

54. Edward McCook, *Official Records*, Series 1, Vol. 23, Part 2, 595.

55. William Rosecrans, *Official Records*, Series 1, Vol. 30, Part 3, 274–275.

56. William Rosecrans, *Official Records*, Series 1, Vol. 23, Part 2, 598, 601–602; Ambrose Burnside, *Official Records*, Series 1, Vol. 23, Part 2, 603: Henry Halleck, *Official Records*, Series 1, Vol. 23, Part 2, 602.

57. William Rosecrans, *Official Records*, Series 1, Vol. 23, Part 2, 607; Braxton Bragg, *Official Records*, Series 1, Vol. 23, Part 2, 957.

58. Braxton Bragg, *Official Records*, Series 1, Vol. 23, Part 2, 954; Simon Buckner, *Official Records*, Series 1, Vol. 23, Part 2, 946, 962.

59. William Rosecrans, *Official Records*, Series 1, Vol. 30, Part 3, 11.

60. Edward McCook, *Official Records*, Series 1, Vol. 30, Part 3, 43.

61. S. A. Hurlbut, *Official Records*, Series 1, Vol. 30, Part 3, 19; W. H. Lytle, *Official Records*, Series 1, Vol. 30, Part 3, 20; Ambrose Burnside, *Official Records*, Series 1, Vol. 30, Part 3, 22.

62. C. Goddard, *Official Records*, Series 1, Vol. 30, Part 3, 28; P. O'Connell, *Official Records*, Series 1, Vol. 30, Part 3, 28; George Thomas, *Official Records*, Series 1, Vol. 30, Part 3, 28; Alexander McCook, *Official Records*, Series 1, Vol. 30, Part 3, 28–29; John M. Palmer,

Official Records, Series 1, Vol. 30, Part 3, 29; William Rosecrans, *Official Records*, Series 1, Vol. 30, Part 3, 33.

Chapter Five

1. William Rosecrans, *Official Records*, Series 1, Vol. 30, Part 3, 32–34; D. S. Stanley, *Official Records*, Series 1, Vol. 30, Part 3, 42; C. Goddard, *Official Records*, Series 1, Vol. 30, Part 3, 34.
2. C. Goddard, *Official Records*, Series 1, Vol. 30, Part 3, 35–36.
3. C. Goddard, *Official Records*, Series 1, Vol. 30, Part 3, 36–37.
4. C. Goddard, *Official Records*, Series 1, Vol. 30, Part 3, 37.
5. Ibid.
6. Ibid.
7. Ibid.; Gordon Granger, *Official Records*, Series 1, Vol. 30, Part 3, 309; 5th Tennessee Cavalry, Order Book, June 3–August 14, 1863, RG 94, E 112–115, NARA, Washington, D.C.; John Londa, "The Role of Union Cavalry during the Chickamauga Campaign," Master's Thesis, Command and General Staff College, Fort Leavenworth, Kansas, 1991, 9.
8. Alexander McCook, *Official Records*, Series 1, Vol. 30, Part 3, 38; W.H. Lytle, *Official Records*, Series 1, Vol. 30, Part 3, 39.
9. Edward McCook, *Official Records*, Series 1, Vol. 30, Part 3, 106; I. R. Conwell, Diary entry August 14, 1863, Conwell Diary, August 14, 1863, S 2753, F. 3, Indiana Historical Society, Indianapolis; Robert Merrill, "August 14, 1863," *Robert Sidney Merrill, Co. K. 1st Wis. Cav.* (Cedarsburg, WI.: MSG Publishing, 1995).
10. Edward M. McCook, *Official Records*, Series 1, Vol. 30, Part 3, 43; George Baum, Diary entry August 13, 1863, Book 10, M 674 B1 F3, Baum Diaries, Indiana Historical Society.
11. John Platter, *Official Records*, Series 1, Vol. 30, Part 3, 44; W. H. Lytle, *Official Records*, Series 1, Vol. 30, Part 3, 52; Peter Williamson, Letter to Wife, August 23, 1863, Williamson, Peter J. 1823–1907, Special Collections Division of the Nashville Public Library, 615 Church Street, Nashville.
12. Edward McCook *Official Records*, Series 1, Vol. 30, Part 3, 60–62; W. H. Lytle, *Official Records*, Series 1, Vol. 30, Part 3, 69; Letter from Rollin to sister, August 15, 1863, In I. R. Conway Correspondence, S 2753, F. 4, Indiana Historical Society; Joseph Frederick Shelly, "The Shelly Papers", Fanny Anderson, ed., *Indiana Magazine of History*, 44, no. 2 (June 1948): 181–198, 195; John Large, Letter to father July 7, 1863, John Large Letters, VFM 455, Ohio Historical Society, Columbus, Ohio.
13. Louis Watkins, *Official Records*, Series 1, Vol. 30, Part 3, 53; Edward McCook, *Official Records*, Series 1, Vol. 30, Part 3, 105: C. H. Sowle, Military Record of C. H. Sowle, unpublished, Manuscript C. S., undated, Filson Historical Society, Louisville, Kentucky; Charles Sowle, Letter August 20, 1863, Sowle, Charles H. Papers, Sec. A Box 123, Rubenstein Library, Duke University.
14. Frank H. Hamilton, *Official Records*, Series 1, Vol. 30, Part 3, 246–248.
15. Archibald Campbell, *Official Records*, Series 1, Vol. 30, Part 3, 71.
16. George Wm. Brent, *Official Records*, Series 1, Vol. 30, Part 4, 502; P. D. Roddey, *Official Records*, Series 1, Vol. 30, Part 4, 505.
17. Frank Bond, *Official Records*, Series 1, Vol. 30, Part 3, 42; Robert Minty, *Official Records*, Series 1, Vol. 30, Part 3, 44; J. J. Reynolds, *Official Records*, Series 1, Vol. 30, Part 3, 51.
18. Charles R. Thompson, *Official Records*, Series 1, Vol. 30, Part 3, 53; Horatio Van Cleve, *Official Records*, Series 1, Vol. 30, Part 3, 53, 70.
19. Charles Eugene Belknap, ed., *History of the Michigan Organizations at Chickamauga, Chattanooga, and Missionary Ridge* (Lansing: Robert Smith Printing Co., 1899), 88; Robert Minty, *Official Records*, Series 1, Vol. 30, Part 1, 920–921.
20. G. G. Dibrell, *Official Records*, Series 1, Vol. 30, Part 2, 527; Robert Minty, *Official Records*, Series 1, Vol. 30, Part 1, 920–921; William Sipes, *History and Roster of the 7th Pennsylvania Veteran Volunteers* (Pottsville: Miners' Journal Print, 1905), 10.
21. John McLain, Diary Entry, August 17, 1863, John McLain, Papers (c.00111), Michigan State University Archives & Historical Collections, East Lansing, Michigan; William Antwerp, Letters August 28, 1863, Van Antwerp, William W., 1833–1887, Bentley Historical Library, University of Michigan; Othniel Gooding, Letter August 29, 1863, Othniel Gooding Collection (c.00275), Kalamazoo College.
22. G. G. Dibrell, *Official Records*, Series 1, Vol. 30, Part 2, 527; George Dibrell, "Eight Tennessee Cavalry," In John Berrien Lindsley, *The Military Annals of Tennessee, Confederate* (Nashville: J. M. Lindsley & Co., Publishers, 1886), 658; James B. Jones, Jr., "Fevers Ran High," In *Rural Life and Culture in the Upper Cumberland*, Michael E. Birdwell and W. Calvin Dickinson, eds. (Lexington: University of Kentucky Press, 2004), 86–87.
23. Robert Minty, *Official Records*, Series 1, Vol. 30, Part 1, 920–921; Robert Burns, Letter, August 25, 1863, Robert Burns Letterbook, MSS M642, Minnesota Historical Society, St. Paul, MN.; Joseph Vale, *Minty and the Cavalry: A History of Cavalry Campaigns in the Western Armies* (Harrisburg, PA: Edwin K. Myers, Printer and Binder, 1886), 208.
24. Robert Minty, *Official Records*, Series 1, Vol. 30, Part 1, 921; Joseph Vale, *Minty and the Cavalry*, 206–207.
25. William Rosecrans, *Official Records*, Series 1, Vol. 30, Part 3, 55; Frank S. Bond, *Official Records*, Series 1, Vol. 30, Part 3, 56; Ambrose Burnside, *Official Records*, Series 1, Vol. 30, Part 3, 72; Nathan Finegan, Letter August 8, 1863, Nathan Finegan Papers, Ohio Historical Society, Columbus; W. L. Curry, Diary entry August 20, 1863, In *Four Years in the Saddle: History of First Regiment Ohio Volunteer Cavalry, by W. L. Curry* (Columbus: Champlin Printing Co., 1898), 107; Franklin F. Moyer, Letter August 21, 1863, *Journal and Letters of Franklin F. Moyer*, Robert H. Wieser, editor (Dayton: Robert Wieser, 2008).
26. J. T. Wilder, *Official Records*, Series 1, Vol. 30, Part 3, 78; Henry Campbell, *Three Years in the Saddle: A Diary of the Civil War*, Unpublished (n.d.), Wabash College, Crawfordsville, Indiana, 72. (Poe's Tavern is called Soddey-Daisy today.)
27. V. Sheliha, *Official Records*, Series 1, Vol. 30, Part 4, 527; S. B. Buckner, *Official Records*, Series 1, Vol. 30, Part 4, 521, 526.

28. Horatio Van Cleve, *Official Records*, Series 1, Vol. 30, Part 3, 79; William Rosecrans, *Official Records*, Series 1, Vol. 30, Part 3, 79–81; Larry Daniel, *Days of Glory: The Army of the Cumberland 1861–1865* (Baton Rouge: Louisiana State University Press, 2004), 289.

29. William Antwerp, Letter August 28, 1863.

30. Joseph Vale, *Minty and the Cavalry*, 211–212.

31. R. H. G. Minty, *Official Records*, Series 1, Vol. 30, Part 3, 191; George Clark, Letter August 28, 1863, George Clark Collection, GLC06167.08, Gilder Lehrman Institute of American History, New York; W. Todd Groce, *Mountain Rebels: East Tennessee Confederates and the Civil War, 1860–1870* (Knoxville, University of Tennessee Press, 1999), 122.

32. Horatio Van Cleve, *Official Records*, Series 1, Vol. 30, Part 3, 91–92.

33. William Rosecrans, *Official Records*, Series 1, Vol. 30, Part 3, 98–99; George Burroughs, *Official Records*, Series 1, Vol. 30, Part 3, 99; R. S. Thoms, *Official Records*, Series 1, Vol. 30, Part 3, 101.

34. John Wilder, *Official Records*, Series 1, Vol. 30, Part 3, 100–101, 122–123; Alva Griest, Diary entry August 23, 1863, *Three Years in Dixie: Personal Adventures, Scenes and Incidents of the March: The Journal of Alva C. Griest*, Journal Entry, Alva Griest Collection, William Henry Smith Memorial Library, Indiana Historical Society, Indianapolis, Indiana; William Allen Clark, "Please Send Stamps: The Civil War Letters of William Allen Clark," Part IV, edited by Margaret Black Taturn, *Indiana Magazine Of History*, XCI (December, 1995: 288–319), 298; Henry Campbell, Diary Entry, September 21, 1863, *Three Years in the Saddle: A Diary of the Civil War, Unpublished* (n.d.), Wabash College, Crawfordsville, Indiana.

35. Thomas Wood, *Official Records*, Series 1, Vol. 30, Part 3, 103; William Rosecrans, *Official Records*, Series 1, Vol. 30, Part 3, 112; John Wilder, *Official Records*, Series 1, Vol. 30, Part 3, 123–124; T. M. Jack, *Official Records*, Series 1, Vol. 30, Part 4, 524; Thomas Hindman, *Official Records*, Series 1, Vol. 30, Part 4, 524; Patton Anderson, *Official Records*, Series 1, Vol. 30, Part 4, 525; W. H. Lytle, *Official Records*, Series 1, Vol. 30, Part 3, 102.

36. Braxton Bragg, *Official Records*, Series 1, Vol. 30, Part 4, 529; Joseph Johnston, *Official Records*, Series 1, Vol. 30, Part 4, 529; W. W. Mackall, *Official Records*, Series 1, Vol. 30, Part 4, 531; Samuel L. Adams, *Official Records*, Series 1, Vol. 30, Part 4, 531.

37. H. D. Clayton, *Official Records*, Series 1, Vol. 30, Part 4, 533–534; A. P. Stewart, *Official Records*, Series 1, Vol. 30, Part 4, 535; Simon B. Buckner, *Official Records*, Series 1, Vol. 30, Part 4, 537, 540; V. Sheliha, *Official Records*, Series 1, Vol. 30, Part 4, 554; Journal of the 4th Michigan Cavalry, August 21, 1863, RG 94, 4th Michigan Cavalry Regiment, NARA, Washington. (Smith's Crossroads is currently named Dayton.)

38. E. A. Otis, *Official Records*, Series 1, Vol. 30, Part 3, 107.

39. Thomas L. Crittenden, *Official Records*, Series 1, Vol. 30, Part 3, 117; Robert Minty, *Official Records*, Series 1, Vol. 30, Part 3, 125; Horatio Van Cleve, *Official Records*, Series 1, Vol. 30, Part 3, 125; Robert Burns, Letter, August 25, 1863; John McLain, Diary Entry, August 21, 1863.

40. Thomas Crittenden, *Official Records*, Series 1, Vol. 30, Part 3, 137; William B. Hazen, *Official Records*, Series 1, Vol. 30, Part 3, 138; Robert Minty, *Official Records*, Series 1, Vol. 30, Part 3, 139; Horatio Van Cleve, *Official Records*, Series 1, Vol. 30, Part 3, 139.

41. Thomas Crittenden, *Official Records*, Series 1, Vol. 30, Part 3, 153; Horatio Van Cleve, *Official Records*, Series 1, Vol. 30, Part 3, 140, 190; Robert Minty, *Official Records*, Series 1, Vol. 30, Part 3, 139; P. P. Oldershaw, *Official Records*, Series 1, Vol. 30, Part 3, 140; Alva Griest, Diary Entry, August 22, 1863.

42. Horatio Van Cleve, *Official Records*, Series 1, Vol. 30, Part 3, 157; J. P. Drouillard, *Official Records*, Series 1, Vol. 30, Part 3, 153; Robert Minty, *Official Records*, Series 1, Vol. 30, Part 3, 155.

43. A. E. Burnside, *Official Records*, Series 1, Vol. 30, Part 3, 107.

44. W. S. Rosecrans, *Official Records*, Series 1, Vol. 30, Part 3, 111, 113; W. H. Lytle, *Official Records*, Series 1, Vol. 30, Part 3, 116; George Thomas, *Official Records*, Series 1, Vol. 30, Part 3, 132; Joseph Reynolds, *Official Records*, Series 1, Vol. 30, Part 3, 132–133.

45. William. G. Anderson, *Official Records*, Series 1, Vol. 30, Part 1, 910–911; Daniel Ray, *Official Records*, Series 1, Vol. 30, Part 3, 142–143; William Sinclair, *Official Records*, Series 1, Vol. 30, Part 3, 142; 4th Ohio Morning Reports: Company E, August 21–23, 1863, RG 94, E 112–115, NARA, Washington, D.C.; 1st Ohio Morning Reports: Company E, August 15–22, 1863, RG 94, E 112–115, NARA, Washington, D.C.; Richard Reid, *Fourth Indiana Cavalry Regiment: A History* (Fordsville, KY: Sandefur Offset Printing, undated), 89; Philip J. Baker Jr., "Command and Control Mechanisms in the Chickamauga Campaign: The Union Experience," U.S. Army Command and General Staff College, Fort Leavenworth, Kansas, 1989, 74.

46. 10th Ohio Cavalry, Order Book, Companies A-I, August 21, 1863, RG 94, E 112–115, NARA, Washington, D.C.

47. Julius Thomas Diary August 21, 27, 1863, Julius E. Thomas Collection, MS.2720, University of Tennessee, Knoxville.

48. William Rosecrans, *Official Records*, Series 1, Vol. 30, Part 3, 147; Gates Thruston, *Official Records*, Series 1, Vol. 30, Part 3, 152.

49. E. S. Burford, *Official Records*, Series 1, Vol. 30, Part 3, 545; W. S. Merrill, *The Middle Tennessee and Chattanooga Campaigns of June, July, August, and September 1863* (New York: Julius Bien & Co. Lith., 1891), 1–10; H. B. Clayton, *Official Records*, Series 1, Vol. 30, Part 4, 544; Simon Buckner, *Official Records*, Series 1, Vol. 30, Part 4, 546; J. K. P. Blackburn, *Reminiscences of the Terry Rangers* (n. p.: University of Texas, 1919), 40.

50. William Rosecrans, *Official Records*, Series 1, Vol. 30, Part 3, 171; William B. Hazen, *Official Records*, Series 1, Vol. 30, Part 3, 176; John J. Funkhouser, *Official Records*, Series 1, Vol. 30, Part 3, 177; George Hartsuff, *Official Records*, Series 1, Vol. 30, Part 3, 180; Ambrose Burnside, *Official Records*, Series 1, Vol. 30, Part 3, 169.

51. E. A. Otis, *Official Records*, Series 1, Vol. 30, Part 3, 190; Robert Minty, *Official Records*, Series 1, Vol. 30, Part 3, 190–191.

52. Edward Ferrero, *Official Records*, Series 1, Vol. 30, Part 3, 196; V. Sheliha, *Official Records*, Series 1, Vol. 30, Part 4, 562; James Wiswell, Letter August 24, 1863, James Wiswell Letters, RUB Bay 0035:06. Rubenstein Library, Duke University.

53. William Marvel, *Burnside* (Chapel Hill & London: University of North Carolina Press, 1991), 242.

54. William Marvel, *Burnside*, 244–245; Charles D. Mitchell, "The Sanders Raid into East Tennessee, June, 1863" In *Sketches of War History 1861–1865* (Cincinnati: Monfort & Company, 1908), 238–251.

55. William Marvel, *Burnside*, 265–276; Henry Halleck, *Official Records*, Series 1, Vol. 23, Part 2, 593.

56. Edwin Stanton, *Official Records*, Series 1, Vol. 30, Part 3, 229–230; *Milwaukee Journal*, "Eccentric Brother of Famous Editor," November 27, 1897, 11.

57. Horatio Van Cleve, *Official Records*, Series 1, Vol. 30, Part 3, 178; Robert Minty, *Official Records*, Series 1, Vol. 30, Part 3, 178; Edward McCook, *Official Records*, Series 1, Vol. 30, Part 3, 168, 179; Edward McCook, *Official Records*, Series 1, Vol. 30, Part 3, 194; Louis Watkins, *Official Records*, Series 1, Vol. 30, Part 3, 194; David Stanley, Telegram to E. M. McCook, August 20, 1863, Telegrams sent by Chief of Cavalry RG 393, Entry 2463, NARA.

58. James Hawley, *Official Records*, Series 1, Vol. 30, Part 3, 193; G. W. Baum, Diary entry August 28, 1863, Book 10, M 674 B1 F3, Baum diaries, Indiana Historical Society; Benjamin Nourse, "Diary" Entry August 28, 1863, Duke University, David M. Rubenstein Rare Book & Manuscript Library, Durham, North Carolina.

59. William Rosecrans, *Official Records*, Series 1, Vol. 30, Part 3, 199; W. S. Merrill, *The Middle Tennessee and Chattanooga Campaigns*, 1–10; J.P. Drouillard, *Official Records*, Series 1, Vol. 30, Part 3, 204; William Sinclair, Letter to Campbell, August 28, 1863, Letters sent by Chief of Cavalry, RG 393, Entry 2460, NARA.

60. George Thomas, *Official Records*, Series 1, Vol. 30, Part 3, 214; John Brannan, *Official Records*, Series 1, Vol. 30, Part 3, 216; Joseph Reynolds, *Official Records*, Series 1, Vol. 30, Part 3, 217; William Rosecrans, *Official Records*, Series 1, Vol. 30, Part 3, 213; Philip Sheridan, *Official Records*, Series 1, Vol. 30, Part 3, 220.

61. Henry Mortimer Hempstead, Diary entry August 29 and September 1, 1863, Henry Mortimer Hempstead Diaries and Letters, Bentley Historical Library, University of Michigan; Daniel Prickitt, Diary, August 29, 1863 entry, ed. Edwin Stoltz, Bowling Green State University.

62. John W. Harris, Letter August 30, 1863 to Ma, Confederate Collection, Box 9, Folder 22, Civil War Collection, Tennessee State Library; Horatio Van Cleve, *Official Records*, Series 1, Vol. 30, Part 3, 222; George Wagner, *Official Records*, Series 1, Vol. 30, Part 3, 220–221.

63. W. N. Estes, *Official Records*, Series 1, Vol. 30, Part 4, 564; Alexander McCook, *Official Records*, Series 1, Vol. 30, Part 3, 344–345; John Brown Gordon, *Reminiscences of the Civil War* (New York: Charles Scribner's Sons, 1903), 196.

64. William Mackall, *Official Records*, Series 1, Vol. 30, Part 4, 561, 564; E. S. Burford, *Official Records*, Series 1, Vol. 30, Part 4, 567; W. N. Estes, *Official Records*, Series 1, Vol. 30, Part 4, 564; Alexander McCook, *Official Records*, Series 1, Vol. 30, Part 3, 344–345; Thomas Connelly, *Autumn of Glory: The Army of Tennessee 1862–1865* (Baton Rouge: Louisiana State University Press, 1971), 168–169; Lawyn C. Edwards, "Confederate Cavalry At Chickamauga: What Went Wrong," Master's Thesis, U.S. Army Command and General Staff College, Fort Leavenworth, Kansas, 1990, 120; David Powell, *The Chickamauga Campaign: A Mad Irregular Battle* (El Dorado Hills, CA: Savas Beatie, 2014), 88; Joseph Wheeler, *Official Records*, Series 1, Vol. 30, Part 2, 520.

65. David A. Powell, *Failure in the Saddle* (New York and California: Savas Beatie, 2010), 14–15; Edward G. Longacre, *A Soldier to the Last: Maj. Gen. Joseph Wheeler in Blue and Gray* (Washington: Potomac Books Inc., 2007), 109; Grady McWhiney, *Braxton Bragg and the Confederate Defeat*, Vol. I (New York and London: Columbia University Press, 1969), 35, 45; George Guild, *Brief Narrative of the Fourth Tennessee Cavalry Regiment* (Nashville: n.p., 1913), 21–22; Braxton Bragg, *Official Records*, Series 1, Vol. 30, Part 2, 26; George Knox Miller, *An Uncompromising Secessionist The Civil War of George Knox Miller, Eighth (Wade's) Confederate Cavalry*, edited by Richard M. McMurry (Tuscaloosa: University of Alabama Press, 2007), 142; Benjamin Franklin Batchelor and George Batchelor, *Batchelor-Turner Letters, 1861–1864: Written by Two of Terry's Texas Rangers*, H. J. H. Rugeley, editor (Austin: The Streck Company, 1961), 66; Benjamin Burke, Letter August 6, 1863, In *A Terry's Ranger Write Home: Letters of Pvt. Benjamin F. Burke*, Jessie Burke Head, ed., compiled 1965, Missouri History Museum, St. Louis.

66. Eli Long, *Official Records*, Series 1, Vol. 30, Part 1, 926-927; Thomas Crofts, *History of the Service of the Third Ohio Veteran Volunteer Cavalry* (Toledo: Stoneman Press, 1910), 111; George Kryder, Diary August 30, 1863, MS 163 George Kryder (1834–1925), William T. Jerome Library, Bowling Green State University, Bowling Green, Ohio.

67. Valentine Cupp, *Official Records*, Series 1, Vol. 30, Part 1, 927–928; Daniel Prickitt, Diary Sept 3, 1863.

68. George E. Flynt, *Official Records*, Series 1, Vol. 30, Part 3, 234; James Garfield, *Official Records*, Series 1, Vol. 30, Part 3, 236.

69. William Rosecrans, *Official Records*, Series 1, Vol. 30, Part 3, 242; Edward McCook, *Official Records*, Series 1, Vol. 30, Part 3, 240–241.

70. Gordon Granger, *Official Records*, Series 1, Vol. 30, Part 3, 178, 192; William C. Russell, *Official Records*, Series 1, Vol. 30, Part 3, 179; 5th Tennessee Cavalry, Order Book, August 22, 1863, RG 94, E 112–115, NARA, Washington, D.C.; 10th Ohio Cavalry, Morning Reports, August 1–31, 1863, RG 94, E 112–115, NARA, Washington, D.C.; William W. Lowe, Orders and Correspondence Books, July 31 and August 3, 1863, RG 94, 5th Iowa Regimental Books, NARA; F. W. Weatherbee, Jr., *The 5th (1st Middle) Tennessee Cavalry Regiment, U.S.A.* (Carrollton, MS: Pioneer Publishing Co., 1992), 29; David Stanley, Letter to Andrew Johnson, September 1, 1863, Letters sent by Chief of Cavalry, RG 393, Entry 2460, NARA.

71. William Rosecrans, *Official Records*, Series 1, Vol. 30, Part 3, 244–245; T. F. Dornblaser, *Sabre Strokes of the Pennsylvania Dragoons* (Philadelphia: Lutheran Publication Society, 1884), 124.

72. Edward King, *Official Records*, Series 1, Vol. 30, Part 1, 468–469.

73. J. J. Reynolds, *Official Records*, Series 1, Vol. 30, Part 3, 250–251.

74. S. B. Buckner, *Official Records*, Series 1, Vol. 30, Part 4, 568; Leonidas Polk, *Official Records*, Series 1, Vol. 30, Part 4, 566–567; D. H. Hill, "Chickamauga: The Great Battle of the West," In *Battles and Leaders in the Civil War, Vol. III* (New York: The Century Co., 1888), 640.

75. W. W. Mackall, *Official Records*, Series 1, Vol. 30, Part 4, 579: J. L. Abernathy, *Official Records*, Series 1, Vol. 30, Part 3, 254–255; T. H. Mauldin, *Official Records*, Series 1, Vol. 30, Part 4, 574; David Powell, *The Chickamauga Campaign: A Mad Irregular Battle* (El Dorado Hills, CA: Savas Beatie, 2014), 105.

76. T. H. Mauldin, *Official Records*, Series 1, Vol. 30, Part 4, 574; W. B. Corbitt, August 31, 1863, Subseries 1.1 Civil War-era documents, 1860–1865, Box 2, Folder 37 Corbitt, W.B., diary from September 13, 1862-October 31, 1864, Manuscript, Archives, and Rare Book Library, Emory University. Atlanta.

77. Peter Cozzens, *This Terrible Sound: The Battle of Chickamauga* (Urbana and Chicago: University of Illinois Press, 1992), 45.

Chapter Six

1. William Rosecrans, *Official Records*, Series 1, Vol. 30, Part 3, 279; George Thomas, *Official Records*, Series 1, Vol. 30, Part 3, 282; George Burroughs, *Official Records*, Series 1, Vol. 30, Part 3, 285; Jonathan Pratt, *Official Records*, Series 1, Vol. 30, Part 3, 315; Edward McCook, *Official Records*, Series 1, Vol. 30, Part 1, 894; George Baum, Diary entry September 2, 1863, Book 10, M 674 B1 F3, Baum Diaries, Indiana Historical Society; "The First Wisconsin Cavalry," Quiner Scrapbooks: Correspondence of the Wisconsin Volunteers, 1861–1865, Vol. 10, Wisconsin Historical Society, Madison; Benjamin Nourse, "Diary" Entry September 1, 1863, Duke University, David M. Rubenstein Rare Book & Manuscript Library, Durham, North Carolina; Peter Williamson, Letter to Wife, September 7, 1863, Williamson, Peter J. 1823–1907, Special Collections Division of the Nashville Public Library, 615 Church Street, Nashville; Marshall P. Thatcher, *A Hundred Battles in the West: The Second Michigan Cavalry* (Detroit: L. F. Kilroy, Printer, 1884), 138.

2. George Wm. Brent, *Official Records*, Series 1, Vol. 30, Part 4, 579; Kinloch Falconer, *Official Records*, Series 1, Vol. 30, Part 3, 580; Braxton Bragg, *Official Records*, Series 1, Vol. 30, Part 4, 583–584; William W. Mackall, *Official Records*, Series 1, Vol. 30, Part 4, 584; Peter Cozzens, *This Terrible Sound: The Battle of Chickamauga* (Urbana and Chicago: University of Illinois Press, 1992), 45; Doyle D. Broome, "Intelligence Operations Of The Army Of The Cumberland During The Tullahoma And Chickamauga Campaigns," Master's Thesis, U.S. Army Command and General Staff College, Leavenworth, KS., 1989, 73.

3. E. S. Burford, *Official Records*, Series 1, Vol. 30, Part 4, 584–586; W. E. Wailes, *Official Records*, Series 1, Vol. 30, Part 4, 585; W. W. Mackall, *Official Records*, Series 1, Vol. 30, Part 4, 584; Thomas Connelly, *Autumn of Glory: The Army of Tennessee 1862–1865* (Baton Rouge: Louisiana State University Press, 1971), 171; John Fleming, Letter August 28, 1863, Midwest MS John Fleming Box 1 Folder 49, Newberry Independent Research Library, Chicago, Il.; Lawyn C. Edwards, "Confederate Cavalry At Chickamauga: What Went Wrong," Master's Thesis, U.S. Army Command and General Staff College, Fort Leavenworth, Kansas, 1990, 124–125.

4. Thomas Crittenden, *Official Records*, Series 1, Vol. 30, Part 3, 286–287, 305; William B. Hazen, *Official Records*, Series 1, Vol. 30, Part 3, 288; H. P. Van Cleve, *Official Records*, Series 1, Vol. 30, Part 3, 289.

5. George L. Hartsuff, *Official Records*, Series 1, Vol. 30, Part 3, 319; Robert Minty, *Official Records*, Series 1, Vol. 30, Part 3, 306–307, 316–317; *Rome Tri-Weekly Courier*, "Summary of the Latest News," September 3, 1863, 2; *Alexandria Gazette*, "Gen. Burnside Telegraphs," September 5, 1863, 4. Col. 2.

6. George Flynt, *Official Records*, Series 1, Vol. 30, Part 3, 300–301; Jefferson C. Davis, *Official Records*, Series 1, Vol. 30, Part 3, 302; Frank S. Bond, *Official Records*, Series 1, Vol. 30, Part 3, 303; E. A. Otis, *Official Records*, Series 1, Vol. 30, Part 3, 328.

7. Gordon Granger, *Official Records*, Series 1, Vol. 30, Part 3, 328, 373; C. Goddard, *Official Records*, Series 1, Vol. 30, Part 3, 309; Joseph Cooper, et. al. *Official Records*, Series 1, Vol. 30, Part 3, 330–331; 5th Tennessee Cavalry, Morning Reports: Company G, September 2, 1863, RG 94, E 112–115, NARA, Washington, D.C.; Matthewson Patrick, Orders and Correspondence Books, September 11, 1863, RG 94, 5th Iowa Cavalry regimental books, NARA; George Healy Papers, September 5, 1863, State Historical Society of Iowa, Des Moines (1F 006: F22; N14/3/4-B/HU); Charles Alley, Diary September 6, 1863, Charles Alley Diary 1861–1865, Western History Collection, University of Oklahoma.

8. James D. Morgan, *Official Records*, Series 1, Vol. 30, Part 3, 311–312; 10th Ohio Cavalry, Morning Reports: Company C, August 30, 1863, RG 94, E 112–115, NARA, Washington, D.C.; Edward McCook, Orders September 2, 1863, RG 393, Number 2527, Letters Sent First Cavalry Division, NARA; Thomas Speed, *Union Regiments of Kentucky*, Vol. I (Louisville: The Courier Journal Job Printing, Co., 1897), 186; Eugene Marshall, Diary entry August 21, 1863, Eugene Marshall Papers, RL.00850, David M. Rubenstein Rare Book & Manuscript Library, Duke University.

9. Alexander McCook, *Official Records*, Series 1, Vol. 30, Part 3, 326.

10. J. A. Garfield, *Official Records*, Series 1, Vol. 30, Part 3, 322–323.

11. *Ibid.*

12. D. S. Stanley, *Official Records*, Series 1, Vol. 30, Part 3, 331; William Garrett, *Reminiscences of Public Men in Alabama* (Atlanta: Plantation Publishing Co.'s Press, 1872), 230.

13. G. W. Baum, Diary entry September 3, 1863, Book 10, M 674 B1 F3, Baum diaries, Indiana Historical Society; I. R. Conwell, Diary entry September 3, Conwell Diary, S 2753, F. 3, Indiana Historical Society; Marshall P. Thatcher, *A Hundred Battles in the West: The Second Michigan Cavalry* (Detroit: L. F. Kilroy, Printer, 1884), 140; Edward McCook, Orders September 2, 1863, RG 393, Number 2527, Letters Sent First Cavalry Division, NARA; W. R. Carter, *History of the First Regiment of Tennessee Volunteer Cavalry* (Knoxville: Gaut-Ogden Co., Printers and Binders, 1902), 83; Benjamin Nourse, "Diary" Entry September 4, 1863; Elisha Peterson, Letter to parents September 29, 1863, Elisha Peterson Manuscript, Sec. A Box 104, Rubenstein Library, Duke University.

14. R. B. Mitchell, *Official Records*, Series 1, Vol. 30, Part 3, 331–332; O. F. Strahl, *Official Records*, Series 1, Vol. 30, Part 4, 588; Peter Cozzens, *This Terrible Sound*, 49–50; Ephraim Dodd, *Diary of Ephraim Shelby Dodd* (Austin: Press of E. L. Steck, 1914), 22–23.

15. Alexander McCook, *Official Records*, Series 1, Vol. 30, Part 3, 332.
16. E. M. McCook, *Official Records*, Series 1, Vol. 30, Part 3, 332; Robert Mitchell, *Official Records*, Series 1, Vol. 30, Part 1, 891.
17. Alexander McCook, *Official Records*, Series 1, Vol. 30, Part 3, 343–345; W. S. Rosecrans, *Official Records*, Series 1, Vol. 30, Part 3, 339.
18. Alexander McCook, *Official Records*, Series 1, Vol. 30, Part 3, 344.
19. Alexander McCook, *Official Records*, Series 1, Vol. 30, Part 3, 345–346.
20. David Stanley, *Official Records*, Series 1, Vol. 30, Part 3, 353–354; G. W. Baum, Diary entry September 4, 1863.
21. James A. Garfield, *Official Records*, Series 1, Vol. 30, Part 3, 500; Douglas H. Galuszka, "Logistics in Warfare: The Significance Of Logistics In The Army Of The Cumberland During The Tullahoma And Chickamauga Campaigns," U.S. Army Command and General Staff College, Fort Leavenworth, KS, 2005, 140–142; William H. Sinclair, *Official Records*, Series 1, Vol. 30, Part 3, 355; Edward McCook, *Official Records*, Series 1, Vol. 30, Part 3, 354–355; Henry Mortimer Hempstead, Diary entry August 29 and September 4, 1863, Henry Mortimer Hempstead Diaries and Letters, Bentley Historical Library, University of Michigan September 4, 1863.
22. Braxton Bragg, *Official Records*, Series 1, Vol. 30, Part 4, 594; D. H. Hill, *Official Records*, Series 1, Vol. 30, Part 4, 588; Peter Cozzens, *This Terrible Sound*, 54.
23. Braxton Bragg, *Official Records*, Series 1, Vol. 30, Part 2, 21.
24. William Rosecrans, *Official Records*, Series 1, Vol. 30, Part 3, 357–358, 360–362.
25. P. P. Oldershaw, *Official Records*, Series 1, Vol. 30, Part 3, 370; John Wilder, *Official Records*, Series 1, Vol. 30, Part 3, 365–367; William Rosecrans, *Official Records*, Series 1, Vol. 30, Part 3, 357–358, 360–362.
26. Robert Minty, *Official Records*, Series 1, Vol. 30, Part 3, 355–356, 372; P. P. Oldershaw, *Official Records*, Series 1, Vol. 30, Part 3, 370; William Hazen, *Official Records*, Series 1, Vol. 30, Part 3, 356, 371, 392.
27. John McLain, Diary Entry, September 4, 1863, John McLain, Papers (c.00111), Michigan State University Archives & Historical Collections, East Lansing, Michigan; William Van Antwerp, Letters September 4, 1863, Van Antwerp, William W., 1833–1887, Bentley Historical Library, University of Michigan.
28. William Sinclair, *Official Records*, Series 1, Vol. 30, Part 3, 375; David Stanley, *Official Records*, Series 1, Vol. 30, Part 3, 374.
29. Edward McCook, *Official Records*, Series 1, Vol. 30, Part 3, 375.
30. Edward McCook, *Official Records*, Series 1, Vol. 30, Part 1, 894; Archibald Campbell, *Official Records*, Series 1, Vol. 30, Part 1, 899; James P. Brownlow *Official Records*, Series 1, Vol. 30, Part 1, 906; Daniel Ray, *Official Records*, Series 1, Vol. 30, Part 1, 907; G. W. Baum, Diary entry September 5, 1863; Jesse Leeper, Diary Sept. 6, 1863, *The Civil War Diary of Private Jesse Leeper*, Richard Reid, ed., Stones River National Park, Technical Information Center, Murfreesboro, TN.
31. Edward McCook, *Official Records*, Series 1, Vol. 30, Part 3, 376; D. S. Stanley, *Official Records*, Series 1, Vol. 30, Part 1, 887.

32. George Crook, *Official Records*, Series 1, Vol. 30, Part 1, 917–918; W. L. Curry, *Four Years in the Saddle: History of First Regiment Ohio Volunteer Cavalry* (Columbus: Champlin Printing Co., 1898), 108–109.
33. W. L. Curry, *Ibid.*
34. Braxton Bragg, *Official Records*, Series 1, Vol. 30, Part 4, 600; George Brent, *Official Records*, Series 1, Vol. 30, Part 4, 603–605.
35. William Rosecrans, *Official Records*, Series 1, Vol. 30, Part 3, 381; Henry Halleck, *Official Records*, Series 1, Vol. 30, Part 3, 381; William Hazen, *Official Records*, Series 1, Vol. 30, Part 3, 386, 398; John Wilder, *Official Records*, Series 1, Vol. 30, Part 3, 386; P. H. Watson, *Official Records*, Series 1, Vol. 30, Part 3, 399–400.
36. James Garfield, *Official Records*, Series 1, Vol. 30, Part 3, 397–398.
37. David S. Stanley, *Official Records*, Series 1, Vol. 30, Part 1, 887; James Love, *My Dear Molly: The Civil War Letters of Captain James Love*, M. W. Kodner, ed. (St. Louis: Missouri History Museum, 2015), 344.
38. William J. Hardee, *Official Records*, Series 1, Vol. 30, Part 4, 608; Braxton Bragg, *Official Records*, Series 1, Vol. 30, Part 4, 621; Peter Cozzens, *This Terrible Sound*, 59.
39. George W. Brent, *Official Records*, Series 1, Vol. 30, Part 4, 610–611, 621; Peter Cozzens, *This Terrible Sound*, 55.
40. Joseph Wheeler, *Official Records*, Series 1, Vol. 30, Part 4, 614–615.
41. Joseph Wheeler, *Official Records*, Series 1, Vol. 30, Part 4, 614–615; David A. Powell, *Failure in the Saddle* (New York and California: Savas Beatie, 2010), 69.
42. N. B. Forrest, *Official Records*, Series 1, Vol. 30, Part 4, 615.
43. W. S. Rosecrans, *Official Records*, Series 1, Vol. 30, Part 3, 406–407; Ambrose E. Burnside, *Official Records*, Series 1, Vol. 30, Part 3, 433–434.
44. Thomas Wood, *Official Records*, Series 1, Vol. 30, Part 3, 416.
45. James Garfield, *Official Records*, Series 1, Vol. 30, Part 3, 417; Thomas Wood, *Official Records*, Series 1, Vol. 30, Part 3, 419–425; Thomas Crittenden, *Official Records*, Series 1, Vol. 30, Part 3, 424–425; Peter Cozzens, *This Terrible Sound*, 51–52.
46. Thomas Wood, *Official Records*, Series 1, Vol. 30, Part 3, 455–457; James Garfield, *Official Records*, Series 1, Vol. 30, Part 3, 458.
47. James Garfield, *Official Records*, Series 1, Vol. 30, Part 3, 432; David Stanley, *Official Records*, Series 1, Vol. 30, Part 3, 431–432.
48. Edward McCook, Orders—September 7, 1863, RG 393, Number 2527, Letters Sent First Cavalry Division, NARA; David Briggs, *Official Records*, Series 1, Vol. 30, Part 1, 909; I. R. Conwell, Diary entry September 9, Conwell Diary, S 2753, F. 3, Indiana Historical Society; Henry Mortimer Hempstead, Diary entry September 6, 1863; George Kryder, Diary September 7, 1863, MS 163 George Kryder (1834–1925), William T. Jerome Library, Bowling Green State University, Bowling Green, Ohio; Marshall P. Thatcher, *A Hundred Battles in the West*, 138; George Healy Letter, August 24, 1863; Edward Amsden, Letter September 8, 1863, Edward Amsden Letters, GLC02156.14, Gilder-Lehrman Institute of American History, New York.
49. Edward McCook, Orders September 7, 1863,

RG 393, Number 2527, Letters Sent First Cavalry Division, NARA; Peter Williamson, Letter to Wife, September 7, 1863, Williamson, Peter J. 1823–1907, Special Collections Division of the Nashville Public Library, 615 Church Street, Nashville.

50. George E. Flynt, *Official Records*, Series 1, Vol. 30, Part 3, 410; H. C. Jones, *Official Records*, Series 1, Vol. 30, Part 3, 418.

51. Thomas Connelly, *Autumn of Glory: The Army of Tennessee 1862–1865* (Baton Rouge: Louisiana State University Press, 1971), 173.

52. Robert Minty, *Official Records*, Series 1, Vol. 30, Part 3, 427; William Hazen, *Official Records*, Series 1, Vol. 30, Part 3, 433; John McLain, Diary entry September 6, 1863.

53. Frank S. Bond, *Official Records*, Series 1, Vol. 30, Part 3, 444; W. S. Rosecrans, *Official Records*, Series 1, Vol. 30, Part 3, 442; Edward Summers, Letter to Arthur Johnson, November 2, 1863, Edward Summers Letter, MS 2714, Special Collections, University of Tennessee, Knoxville.

54. David Stanley, *Official Records*, Series 1, Vol. 30, Part 3, 468; William Rosecrans, *Official Records*, Series 1, Vol. 30, Part 3, 467–468; David Stanley, Telegrams sent August 28–31, Telegrams Sent by Chief of Cavalry, RG 393, Entry 2463, NARA.

55. G. W. Baum, Diary entry, September 8, 1863, 52; David Stanley, *Official Records*, Series 1, Vol. 30, Part 3, 468; Edward McCook, NARA, Letter September 7, 1863, Record Group 393, Part 2, Number 2527, Correspondence, First Cavalry Division, NARA, Washington, D.C.; I. R. Conwell, Diary entry September 8, 1863; Henry Mortimer Hempstead, Diary entries September 7–8, 1863; Daniel Prickitt diary, September 8, 1863, ed. Edwin Stoltz, Bowling Green State University; Julius Thomas Diary September 8, 1863, Julius E. Thomas Diary, 1863–1864, Julius E. Thomas Collection, MS.2720, University of Tennessee, Knoxville; Edward McCook, Orders September 7, 1863, RG 393, Number 2527, Letters Sent First Cavalry Division, NARA; Peter Williamson, Letter to Wife, September 7, 1863, Williamson, Peter J. 1823–1907, Special Collections Division of the Nashville Public Library, 615 Church Street, Nashville.

56. Peter Williamson, *Ibid.*; David Stanley, *Ibid.*

57. John Allan Wyeth, *Life of General Nathan Bedford Forrest* (New York and London: Harper & Brothers Publishers, 1899), 238–239; W. B. Corbitt, September 8, 1863, Subseries 1.1 Civil War-era documents, 1860–1865, Box 2, Folder 37, Corbitt, W.B.; diary from September 13, 1862–October 31, 1864, Manuscript, Archives, and Rare Book Library, Emory University, Atlanta; David A. Powell, *Failure in the Saddle* (New York and California: Savas Beatie, 2010), 54; David Powell, *The Chickamauga Campaign: A Mad Irregular Battle* (El Dorado Hills, CA: Savas Beatie, 2014), 108, 131; Walter Brian Cisco, *States Rights Gist: A South Carolina General of the Civil War* (Gretna, LA: Pelican Publishing, 2008), 96.

58. James Garfield, *Official Records*, Series 1, Vol. 30, Part 3, 468–469.

59. James Garfield, *Official Records*, Series 1, Vol. 30, Part 3, 451; William H. Sinclair, *Official Records*, Series 1, Vol. 30, Part 3, 469–470; Edward McCook, *Official Records*, Series 1, Vol. 30, Part 3, 469; G. P. Thruston, *Official Records*, Series 1, Vol. 30, Part 3, 452.

60. Robert Mitchell, *Official Records*, Series 1, Vol. 30, Part 1, 891.

61. James Negley, *Official Records*, Series 1, Vol. 30, Part 3, 446, 447–449.

62. George Wagner, *Official Records*, Series 1, Vol. 30, Part 3, 459–460; C. Goddard, *Official Records*, Series 1, Vol. 30, Part 3, 459.

63. W. B. Hazen, *Official Records*, Series 1, Vol. 30, Part 3, 446; Robert Minty, *Official Records*, Series 1, Vol. 30, Part 3, 461; Simon B. Buckner, *Official Records*, Series 1, Vol. 30, Part 4, 622–623; George Wagner, *Official Records*, Series 1, Vol. 30, Part 3, 464; John McLain, Diary entry September 8, 1863.

64. George Crook, *General George Crook: His Biography* (Norman & London: University of Oklahoma Press, 1960), 104.

65. "Summary of the Latest News," *Rome Tri-Weekly Courier*, September 12, 1863, 2.

Chapter Seven

1. E. S. Burford, *Official Records*, Series 1, Vol. 30, Part 4, 627; Archer Anderson, *Official Records*, Series 1, Vol. 30, Part 4, 627; George Brent, *Official Records*, Series 1, Vol. 30, Part 3, 627; Joseph Freeman, Letter, Freeman to his sister, September 16, 1863, MS.0806, Special Collections, University of Tennessee, Knoxville; Thomas B. Wilson, "Reminiscences," 1904, Collection Number: 01736-z, The Southern Historical Collection at the Louis Round Wilson Special Collections Library, University of North Carolina, 57.

2. N. B. Forrest, *Official Records*, Series 1, Vol. 30, Part 4, 628.

3. W.S. Rosecrans, *Official Records*, Series 1, Vol. 30, Part 3, 479; James Garfield, *Official Records*, Series 1, Vol. 30, Part 3, 482.

4. Alexander McCook, *Official Records*, Series 1, Vol. 30, Part 3, 483.

5. James Garfield, *Official Records*, Series 1, Vol. 30, Part 3, 469, 500; William Sinclair, *Official Records*, Series 1, Vol. 30, Part 3, 500; John Wilder, *Official Records*, Series 1, Vol. 30, Part 3, 495; H. Thrall, *Official Records*, Series 1, Vol. 30, Part 3, 493–494; Edward McCook, Orders September 8, 1863, RG 393, Number 2527, Letters Sent First Cavalry Division, NARA.

6. George Thomas, *Official Records*, Series 1, Vol. 30, Part 3, 484; James Garfield, *Official Records*, Series 1, Vol. 30, Part 3, 488; Kinloch Falconer, *Official Records*, Series 1, Vol. 30, Part 4, 629; George Brent, *Official Records*, Series 1, Vol. 30, Part 4, 629–630; James. A. Garfield, *Official Records*, Series 1, Vol. 30, Part 3, 483; Peter Cozzens, *This Terrible Sound*, 63; Will T. Martin, "A Defence of Bragg's Conduct at Chickamauga," *Southern Historical Society Papers*, Vol 11, January–December, 1883, 203–204.

7. Ambrose Burnside, *Official Records*, Series 1, Vol. 30, Part 3, 501; William Rosecrans, *Official Records*, Series 1, Vol. 30, Part 3, 479–507.

8. George Crook, *Official Records*, Series 1, Vol. 30, Part 1, 917–918; Robert Mitchell, *Official Records*, Series 1, Vol. 30, Part 1, 891–892; G. W. Baum, Diary entry, September 9, 1863; Elijah Watts, "Chickamauga Campaign" (hand written account, undated), Watts, Elijah S., Papers. 1861–1907, Mss./A/W349; John W. Rowell,

Yankee Cavalrymen (Knoxville: University of Tennessee Press, 1971), 143; Thomas Crofts, *History of the Service of the Third Ohio Veteran Volunteer Cavalry* (Toledo: Stoneman Press, 1910), 112; Nancy Pape-Findley, *The Invincibles: The Story of Fourth Ohio Veteran Volunteer Cavalry* (Tecumseh, Michigan; Blood Road Publishing: 2002), 158; Robert Merrill, Diary September 9, 1863, *Robert Sidney Merrill, Co. K. 1st Wis. Cav.* (Cedarsburg, WI.: MSG Publishing, 1995).

9. Elijah Watts, "Chickamauga Campaign."

10. W. L. Curry, *Four Years in the Saddle: History of First Regiment Ohio Volunteer Cavalry* (Columbus: Champlin Printing Co., 1898), 110; Benjamin Nourse, "Diary" Entry September 9, 1863; David S. Stanley, *Official Records*, Series 1, Vol. 30, Part 1, 888.

11. David Powell, *Failure in the Saddle*, 71; Thomas W. Cutrer, *Our Trust is in the God of Battles: The Civil War Letters of Robert Franklin Bunting, Chaplain, Terry's Texas Rangers* (Knoxville: University of Tennessee Press, 2006), 196; Benjamin Nourse, "Diary" Entry September 9, 1863.

12. David S. Stanley, *Official Records*, Series 1, Vol. 30, Part 1, 887–888; Julius Thomas, Diary September 9, 1863; D. G. Reed, *Official Records*, Series 1, Vol. 30, Part 1, 889; David Powell, *The Chickamauga Campaign: A Mad Irregular Battle*, 138–139.

13. John Palmer, *Official Records*, Series 1, Vol. 30, Part 1, 711; John Palmer, *Official Records*, Series 1, Vol. 30, Part 3, 518.

14. John Wilder, *Official Records*, Series 1, Vol. 30, Part 3, 512–513; P. P. Oldershaw, *Official Records*, Series 1, Vol. 30, Part 3, 515, 519; W. Grose, *Official Records*, Series 1, Vol. 30, Part 3, 520.

15. James Negley, *Official Records*, Series 1, Vol. 30, Part 3, 509–510.

16. Peter Cozzens, *This Terrible Sound*, 69–70; J.P. Drouillard, *Official Records*, Series 1, Vol. 30, Part 3, 511.

17. Louis Watkins, *Official Records*, Series 1, Vol. 30, Part 1, 913–914; John Randolph Poole, *Cracker Cavaliers: The 2nd Georgia Cavalry Under Wheeler and Forrest* (Macon, GA: Mercer University Press, 2000), 86.

18. Archibald Campbell, *Official Records*, Series 1, Vol. 30, Part 1, 899–900; Robert Mitchell, *Official Records*, Series 1, Vol. 30, Part 1, 891–893; Edward McCook, *Official Records*, Series 1, Vol. 30, Part 1, 895; Henry Mortimer Hempstead, Diary entry September 10, 1863.

19. David Stanley, *Official Records*, Series 1, Vol. 30, Part 1, 889; W. B. Corbitt, Diary September 10–11, 1863, Subseries 1.1 Civil War-era documents, 1860–1865, Box 2, Folder 37, Corbitt, W.B. September 13, 1862-October 31, 1864, Manuscript, Archives, and Rare Book Library, Emory University, Atlanta; Frank Vogel, "Dairy of Frank Vogel," Frank L. Vogel Collection, MS 67-111: Accession Box 12 Folder 6, Michigan Historical Center, Lansing, Michigan, 5.

20. Henry Halleck, *Official Records*, Series 1, Vol. 30, Part 3, 555; William Marvel, *Burnside* (Chapel Hill & London: University of North Carolina Press, 1991), 280; John Fitch, *Chickamauga: The Price of Chattanooga* (Philadelphia, J. B. Lippincott & Co., 1864), 26.

21. Peter Cozzens, *This Terrible Sound*, 66–67; William Palmer, *Official Records*, Series 1, Vol. 30, Part 3, 533; Henry Halleck, *Official Records*, Series 1, Vol. 30, Part 3, 530.

22. Will T. Martin, "A Defence of Bragg's Conduct at Chickamauga," *Southern Historical Society Papers*, Vol. 11, January–December, 1883: 203–204.

23. George H. Thomas, *Official Records*, Series 1, Vol. 30, Part 3, 534.

24. William Palmer, *Official Records*, Series 1, Vol. 30, Part 3, 532–33; Smith Atkins, *Official Records*, Series 1, Vol. 30, Part 3, 538; James Garfield, *Official Records*, Series 1, Vol. 30, Part 3, 539–540; George Thomas, *Official Records*, Series 1, Vol. 30, Part 3, 538–539; Alexander McCook, *Official Records*, Series 1, Vol. 30, Part 3, 539; James Garfield, *Official Records*, Series 1, Vol. 30, Part 3, 541; Thomas Crittenden, *Official Records*, Series 1, Vol. 30, Part 3, 545; Robert E. Harbison, "Wilder's Brigade in the Tullahoma and Chattanooga Campaigns of the American Civil War," Master's Thesis, U.S. Army Command and General Staff College, Fort Leavenworth, Kansas, 2002, 60.

25. Alexander McCook, *Official Records*, Series 1, Vol. 30, Part 3, 539–542, 551.

26. Louis Watkins, *Official Records*, Series 1, Vol. 30, Part 1, 914.

27. Joseph Wheeler, *Official Records*, Series 1, Vol. 30, Part 4, 636.

28. James Brownlow, *Official Records*, Series 1, Vol. 30, Part 1, 906; Robert Mitchell, *Official Records*, Series 1, Vol. 30, Part 1, 892; Edward McCook, *Official Records*, Series 1, Vol. 30, Part 1, 895–896; Archibald Campbell, *Official Records*, Series 1, Vol. 30, Part 1, 899–900; Leonidas S. Scranton, *Official Records*, Series 1, Vol. 30, Part 1, 901–902; Roswell Russell, *Official Records*, Series 1, Vol. 30, Part 1, 903–904.

29. Thomas McCahan, Diary September 10, 1863, Thomas McCahan Papers (Am. 6092) Historical Society of Pennsylvania, Philadelphia; Samuel Wiley and W. Scott Garner, ed., *Biographical and Portrait Cyclopedia of Blair County, Pennsylvania* (Philadelphia: Gresham Publishing Co., 1892), 192.

30. W. R. Carter, *History of the First Regiment of Tennessee Volunteer Cavalry*, 87–88.

31. James Garfield, *Official Records*, Series 1, Vol. 30, Part 3, 551; Alexander McCook, *Official Records*, Series 1, Vol. 30, Part 3, 551.

32. George Crook, *Official Records*, Series 1, Vol. 30, Part 3, 552–553; Edward McCook, *Official Records*, Series 1, Vol. 30, Part 3, 552.

33. William Rosecrans, *Official Records*, Series 1, Vol. 30, Part 3, 561; Sam Jones, *Official Records*, Series 1, Vol. 30, Part 4, 644–645; Edward L. Anderson, "The Truth about Chickamauga," *The Journal of the United States Cavalry Association*, Vol. 13, Number 92, 1912: 185–206; Doyle D. Broome, "Intelligence Operations of the Army of the Cumberland During the Tullahoma and Chickamauga Campaigns," 50.

34. James Seddon, *Official Records*, Series 1, Vol. 30, Part 4, 639–640; Jefferson Davis, *Official Records*, Series 1, Vol. 30, Part 4, 639.

35. George Thomas, *Official Records*, Series 1, Vol. 30, Part 3, 563–564.

36. C. Goddard, *Official Records*, Series 1, Vol. 30, Part 3, 564–565.

37. George Thomas, *Official Records*, Series 1, Vol. 30, Part 3, 566–567.

38. George Thomas, *Official Records*, Series 1, Vol. 30, Part 3, 565–566, 568; James. S. Negley, *Official Records*, Series 1, Vol. 30, Part 3, 567.

39. Edward McCook, *Official Records*, Series 1, Vol. 30, Part 3, 569; *Rome Tri-Weekly Courier*, "From the Front," September 12, 1863, 2.

40. Alexander McCook, *Official Records*, Series 1, Vol. 30, Part 3, 569–570; David Powell, *The Chickamauga Campaign: A Mad Irregular Battle* (El Dorado Hills, CA: Savas Beatie, 2014), 189.

41. Frank Bond, *Official Records*, Series 1, Vol. 30, Part 3, 588.

42. David Stanley, *Official Records*, Series 1, Vol. 30, Part 3, 589.

43. Peter Cozzens, *This Terrible Sound*, 87, 114; W. R. Carter, *History of the First Regiment of Tennessee Volunteer Cavalry*, 90; David Powell, *Failure in the Saddle*, 72; A. D. Frankenberry, "Carrying Dispatches from General Rosecrans To General Stanley," In *History of the Fifteenth Pennsylvania Volunteer Cavalry*, Reiff, J. C., ed. (Philadelphia, PA: Society of the Fifteenth Pennsylvania Cavalry, 1906), 222–224; Philip J. Baker Jr., "Command and Control Mechanisms in the Chickamauga Campaign: The Union Experience," U.S. Army Command and General Staff College, Fort Leavenworth, Kansas, 1989, 95; [The full description of the difficulty in communications between all the corps is covered in detail in Baker's thesis and includes descriptions of George Thomas relying on infantry to serve as couriers. Baker also describes Rosecrans constantly badgering all his senior officers into providing more communications.]

44. C. Goddard, *Official Records*, Series 1, Vol. 30, Part 3, 574; John Wilder, *Official Records*, Series 1, Vol. 30, Part 3, 575; Thomas L. Crittenden, *Official Records*, Series 1, Vol. 30, Part 3, 575.

45. Thomas Crittenden, *Official Records*, Series 1, Vol. 30, Part 3, 575–577.

46. James Garfield, *Official Records*, Series 1, Vol. 30, Part 3, 577.

47. Thomas Crittenden, *Official Records*, Series 1, Vol. 30, Part 3, 577–578; Robert E. Harbison, "Wilder's Brigade in the Tullahoma and Chattanooga Campaigns of the American Civil War," 60–61; William Sylvester Dillon, diary September 12–13, 1863, Dillon Diary, Small Manuscripts, Archives and Special Collections, J.D. Williams Library, The University of Mississippi; Thomas W. Davis, "The Civil War Diary of Thomas W. Davis," Chattanooga Hamilton County Bicentennial Library, Chattanooga.

48. Peter Cozzens, *This Terrible Sound*, 82–85; George Brent, *Official Records*, Series 1, Vol. 30, Part 2, 50; Steven E. Woodworth, *Six Armies in Tennessee: The Chickamauga and Chattanooga Campaigns* (Lincoln and London: University of Nebraska Press, 1998), 75–76; David Powell, *The Chickamauga Campaign: A Mad Irregular Battle*, 200–201.

49. C. Goddard, *Official Records*, Series 1, Vol. 30, Part 3, 590; Robert Minty, *Official Records*, Series 1, Vol. 30, Part 3, 590.

50. Robert Mitchell, *Official Records*, Series 1, Vol. 30, Part 1, 892; Edward McCook, *Official Records*, Series 1, Vol. 30, Part 1, 895–896.

51. David Stanley, *Official Records*, Series 1, Vol. 30, Part 3, 589; Robert Mitchell, *Official Records*, Series 1, Vol. 30, Part 1, 892; Edward McCook, *Official Records*, Series 1, Vol. 30, Part 1, 895–896; Archibald Campbell, *Official Records*, Series 1, Vol. 30, Part 1, 899–900; Leonidas S. Scranton, *Official Records*, Series 1, Vol. 30, Part 1, 901–902; Roswell Russell, *Official Records*, Series 1, Vol. 30, Part 1, 903–904; David Briggs, *Official Records*, Series 1, Vol. 30, Part 1, 908–909; G. W. Baum, Diary entry, September 12, 1863.

52. J. R. Fitch, *Official Records*, Series 1, Vol. 30, Part 3, 598; George Thomas, *Official Records*, Series 1, Vol. 30, Part 3, 598.

53. George Thomas, *Official Records*, Series 1, Vol. 30, Part 3, 598, 600–601.

54. Alexander McCook, *Official Records*, Series 1, Vol. 30, Part 3, 598–600, 603.

55. Alexander McCook, *Official Records*, Series 1, Vol. 30, Part 3, 603–604.

56. William Sinclair, *Official Records*, Series 1, Vol. 30, Part 3, 615–616.

57. Edward McCook, *Official Records*, Series 1, Vol. 30, Part 3, 616; Edward McCook, *Official Records*, Series 1, Vol. 30, Part 1, 895; G. W. Baum, Diary entry, September 13, Book 10, M 674 B1 F3, Baum diaries, Indiana Historical Society; David Powell, *Failure in the Saddle*, 79–80; David Powell, *The Chickamauga Campaign: A Mad Irregular Battle*, 207.

58. Edward McCook, *Official Records*, Series 1, Vol. 30, Part 3, 616–617; William H. Sinclair, *Official Records*, Series 1, Vol. 30, Part 3, 616–617; David Briggs, *Official Records*, Series 1, Vol. 30, Part 1, 908–909.

59. George Crook, *Official Records*, Series 1, Vol. 30, Part 1, 918; Robert Mitchell, *Official Records*, Series 1, Vol. 30, Part 1, 892; Elijah Watts, "Chickamauga Campaign"; Thomas Crofts, *History of the Service of the Third Ohio Veteran Volunteer Cavalry*, 112; Benjamin Nourse, "Diary" Entry September 13, 1863; James Thompson, Diary entry, James Thomson Papers. 1861–1865 (VFM 2167) Ohio Historical Society, Columbus, Ohio.

60. Roswell Russell, *Official Records*, Series 1, Vol. 30, Part 1, 904–904; John W. Rowell, *Yankee Cavalrymen* (Knoxville: University of Tennessee Press, 1971), 144; Thomas McCahan, Diary, September 13, 1863, Thomas McCahan Papers (Am. 6092) Historical Society of Pennsylvania, Philadelphia.

61. W. R. Carter, *History of the First Regiment of Tennessee Volunteer Cavalry*, 89.

62. George Crook, *Official Records*, Series 1, Vol. 30, Part 1, 918; Leonidas Scranton, *Official Records*, Series 1, Vol. 30, Part 1, 901–902; Archibald Campbell, *Official Records*, Series 1, Vol. 30, Part 1, 899–900; David Powell, *The Chickamauga Campaign: A Mad Irregular Battle*, 208.

63. David Stanley, *Official Records*, Series 1, Vol. 30, Part 1, 890.

64. P. P. Oldershaw, *Official Records*, Series 1, Vol. 30, Part 3, 608; C. Goddard, *Official Records*, Series 1, Vol. 30, Part 3, 607; James A. Garfield, *Official Records*, Series 1, Vol. 30, Part 3, 613.

65. John Wilder, *Official Records*, Series 1, Vol. 30, Part 3, 609; Thomas L. Crittenden, *Official Records*, Series 1, Vol. 30, Part 3, 609; John McLain, Diary September 13, 1863.

66. Henry Halleck, *Official Records*, Series 1, Vol. 30, Part 3, 596, 617; William Rosecrans, *Official Records*, Series 1, Vol. 30, Part 3, 617–618; William Marvel, *Burnside*, 278–280; David Powell, *The Chickamauga Campaign: A Mad Irregular Battle*, 230.

67. J. C. Van Duzer, *Official Records*, Series 1, Vol. 30, Part 3, 596.

68. George W. Brent, Journal September 15, 1863, William Palmer Collection of Braxton Bragg Papers, Western Reserve Historical Society, Cleveland; Peter Cozzens, *This Terrible Sound*, 86; Thomas Connelly, *Autumn of Glory*, 189; D. H. Hill, *Official Records*, Series 1, Vol. 30, Part 2, 139; John Randolph Poole, *Cracker Cavaliers*, 86; W. B. Corbitt, September 14, 1863 diary entry; D. H. Hill, "Chickamauga-The Great Battle of the West," *Century*, Vol 33, No. 6 (April, 1887): 937–962, 944–945; W. L. Curry, *Four Years in the Saddle*, 110; W. M. Polk, "General Bragg and the Chickamauga Campaign," *Southern Historical Society Papers*, Vol. 12, January–December 1884, 378–390, 381–383; Steven E. Woodworth, *Six Armies in Tennessee: The Chickamauga and Chattanooga* Campaigns, 77.

69. George Flynt, *Official Records*, Series 1, Vol. 30, Part 3, 625; J. J. Reynolds, *Official Records*, Series 1, Vol. 30, Part 3, 625; George Thomas, *Official Records*, Series 1, Vol. 30, Part 3, 624; J. M. Connell, *Official Records*, Series 1, Vol. 30, Part 3, 625–626; Samuel Bachtell, *Official Records*, Series 1, Vol. 30, Part 3, 623; George Brent, *Official Records*, Series 1, Vol. 30, Part 3, 624.

70. James Garfield, *Official Records*, Series 1, Vol. 30, Part 3, 628–629; Alexander McCook, *Official Records*, Series 1, Vol. 30, Part 3, 627–628; Thomas Speed, *Union Regiments of Kentucky*, Vol. I (Louisville: The Courier Journal Job Printing, Co., 1897), 122–123.

71. James A. Garfield, *Official Records*, Series 1, Vol. 30, Part 3, 630; Alexander McCook, *Official Records*, Series 1, Vol. 30, Part 3, 629–630; Thomas Connelly, *Autumn of Glory*, 191; D. H. Hill, "Chickamauga: The Great Battle of the West," In *Battles and Leaders in the Civil War*, Vol. III (New York: The Century Co., 1888), 645.

72. Henry Mortimer Hempstead, Diary entry September 15, 1863; Elijah Watts, "The Chickamauga Campaign"; Roberts Burns, Letter September 17, 1863, Robert Burns Letterbook, MSS M642, Minnesota Historical Society, St. Paul, MN.

73. James Garfield, *Official Records*, Series 1, Vol. 30, Part 3, 633; Gordon Granger, *Official Records*, Series 1, Vol. 30, Part 3, 631; Thomas Crittenden, *Official Records*, Series 1, Vol. 30, Part 3, 631–632; Robert Minty, *Official Records*, Series 1, Vol. 30, Part 1, 922; Robert E. Harbison, "Wilder's Brigade in the Tullahoma and Chattanooga Campaigns of the American Civil War," 64–65.

74. David Stanley, *Official Records*, Series 1, Vol. 30, Part 3, 637; Edward McCook, *Official Records*, Series 1, Vol. 30, Part 3, 637; Robert Mitchell, *Official Records*, Series 1, Vol. 30, Part 1, 890; Edward McCook, *Official Records*, Series 1, Vol. 30, Part 1, 895–896; Archibald Campbell, *Official Records*, Series 1, Vol. 30, Part 1, 899; Jonathan Pratt, *Official Records*, Series 1, Vol. 30, Part 3, 637–638; William E. Crane, "William E. Crane's Daily Journal of Life in the Field during the War of the Rebellion," September 15, 1863, Mss. 980, Cincinnati Historical Society, Cincinnati Museum Center; Chesley Mosman, *The Rough Side of War: The Civil War Journal of Chesley A. Mosman*, Arnold Gates, ed. (Garden City, NY: The Basin Publishing Co., 1987), 80.

75. Sam Jones, *Official Records*, Series 1, Vol. 30, Part 4, 650; Henry Halleck, *Official Records*, Series 1, Vol. 30, Part 1, 36; Paul M. Fink, *Jonesborough: The First Century of Tennessee's First Town, 1776–1876* (Johnson City, TN: The Overmountain Press, 2002), 90.

76. Henry Halleck, *Official Records*, Series 1, Vol. 30, Part 3, 642–644, 655; W. P. Anderson, *Official Records*, Series 1, Vol. 30, Part 3, 655; John M. Schofield, *Official Records*, Series 1, Vol. 30, Part 3, 643.

77. Gordon Granger, *Official Records*, Series 1, Vol. 30, Part 3, 651; George Wagner, *Official Records*, Series 1, Vol. 30, Part 3, 652; J. J. Reynolds, *Official Records*, Series 1, Vol. 30, Part 3, 647; George Flynt, *Official Records*, Series 1, Vol. 30, Part 3, 647; Thomas L. Crittenden, *Official Records*, Series 1, Vol. 30, Part 3, 650; Robert Minty, *Official Records*, Series 1, Vol. 30, Part 3, 650–651; W. N. Pickerill, *History of the Third Indiana Cavalry* (Indianapolis, Aetna Printing Co., 1906), 60–62.

78. Robert Minty, *Official Records*, Series 1, Vol. 30, Part 1, 922; Joseph Vale, *Minty and the Cavalry*, 217.

79. David Stanley, *Official Records*, Series 1, Vol. 30, Part 3, 652–653; P. Sidney Post, *Official Records*, Series 1, Vol. 30, Part 3, 648; G. W. Baum, Diary entry, September 15, 1863.

80. Robert Mitchell, *Official Records*, Series 1, Vol. 30, Part 3, 653; David S. Stanley, *Official Records*, Series 1, Vol. 30, Part 3, 653; George Crook, *Official Records*, Series 1, Vol. 30, Part 3, 654–655; William H. Sinclair, *Official Records*, Series 1, Vol. 30, Part 3, 654–655; William Rosecrans, *Official Records*, Series 1, Vol. 30, Part 1, 106; William Crane, Diary September 15, 1863.

81. Robert B. Mitchell, *Official Records*, Series 1, Vol. 30, Part 3, 654; William Sinclair, *Official Records*, Series 1, Vol. 30, Part 3, 654–655; David S. Stanley, *Official Records*, Series 1, Vol. 30, Part 3, 653; Edward McCook, September 15, 1863, Letter and Orders Received by Chief of Cavalry, RG 393, Entry 2469, NARA.

82. Peter Cozzens, "This Terrible Sound: The Battle of Chickamauga," 101–103.

83. James Garfield, *Official Records*, Series 1, Vol. 30, Part 3, 668.

84. Frank S. Bond, *Official Records*, Series 1, Vol. 30, Part 3, 668; George Thomas, *Official Records*, Series 1, Vol. 30, Part 3, 670; William Rosecrans, *Official Records*, Series 1, Vol. 30, Part 3, 666; Brent, *Official Records*, Series 1, Vol. 30, Part 3, 667; James A. Garfield, *Official Records*, Series 1, Vol. 30, Part 3, 670; George Thomas, *Official Records*, Series 1, Vol. 30, Part 3, 670; James Garfield, *Official Records*, Series 1, Vol. 30, Part 3, 669.

85. Robert Minty, *Official Records*, Series 1, Vol. 30, Part 3, 679; Thomas Crittenden, *Official Records*, Series 1, Vol. 30, Part 3, 679.

86. Robert Minty, *Official Records*, Series 1, Vol. 30, Part 3, 680; Journal of the 4th Michigan Cavalry, September 16, 1863, RG 94, 4th Michigan Cavalry Regimental Books, NARA.

87. Robert Minty, *Official Records*, Series 1, Vol. 30, Part 1, 922; Joseph Vale, "Address of Captain Joseph Vale," In *Pennsylvania at Chickamauga and Chattanooga*, George W. Skinner, editor (Harrisburg, PA: William Stanley Ray, State Printer of Pennsylvania, 1897), 302–303; Joseph Vale, *Minty and the Cavalry*, 220.

88. George W. Skinner, editor, *Pennsylvania at Chickamauga and Chattanooga* (Harrisburg, PA: William Stanley Ray, State Printer of Pennsylvania, 1897), 90; John McLain, Diary September 16, 1863.

89. James A. Garfield, *Official Records*, Series 1, Vol. 30, Part 3, 689–590; C. Goddard, *Official Records*, Series

1, Vol. 30, Part 3, 689; William Sinclair, *Official Records*, Series 1, Vol. 30, Part 3, 689; G. W. Baum, Diary September 16, 1863; Julius Thomas, Diary September 16, 1863; W. R. Carter, *History of the First Regiment of Tennessee Volunteer Cavalry*, 91.

90. George William Brent, *Official Records*, Series 1, Vol. 30, Part 4, 656–657.

91. Kinloch Falconer, *Official Records*, Series 1, Vol. 30, Part 4, 660; W. F. Mastin, *Official Records*, Series 1, Vol. 30, Part 4, 658; Thomas Connelly, *Autumn of Glory*, 193.

92. William Fuller, *Official Records*, Series 1, Vol. 30, Part 3, 701; J.C. Van Duzer, *Official Records*, Series 1, Vol. 30, Part 3, 701.

93. James Garfield, *Official Records*, Series 1, Vol. 30, Part 3, 707; James Garfield *Official Records*, Series 1, Vol. 30, Part 3, 708; George Thomas, *Official Records*, Series 1, Vol. 30, Part 3, 703; Alexander McCook, *Official Records*, Series 1, Vol. 30, Part 3, 705–706; William E. Crane, Diary September 17, 1863; Charles Dana, *Official Records*, Series 1, Vol. 30, Part 1, 189; Wayne Fanebust, *Major General Alexander M. McCook, USA: A Civil War Biography* (Jefferson, NC: McFarland & Co., 2013), 178.

94. Thomas Crittenden, *Official Records*, Series 1, Vol. 30, Part 3, 708–709; Thomas Wood, *Official Records*, Series 1, Vol. 30, Part 3, 710–711.

95. Thomas Wood, *Official Records*, Series 1, Vol. 30, Part 3, 712; Robert Minty's, *Official Records*, Series 1, Vol. 30, Part 1, 922; Robert Minty, *Official Records*, Series 1, Vol. 30, Part 3, 709–710; Journal of the 4th Michigan Cavalry, September 16, 1863, RG 94, 4th Michigan Cavalry Regimental Books, NARA; Robert Burns, September 17, 1863.

96. W. R. Carter, *History of the First Regiment of Tennessee Volunteer Cavalry*, 96.

97. George H. Purdy, *Official Records*, Series 1, Vol. 30, Part 1, 910; Robert Mitchell, *Official Records*, Series 1, Vol. 30, Part 3, 716; *Official Records*, Series 1, Vol. 30, Part 1, 892–893; Edward McCook, *Official Records*, Series 1, Vol. 30, Part 1, 895, 898; Edward McCook, *Official Records*, Series 1, Vol. 30, Part 3, 716–717; Archibald Campbell, *Official Records*, Series 1, Vol. 30, Part 1, 899; George Brent, *Official Records*, Series 1, Vol. 30, Part 4, 662.

98. George D. Wagner, *Official Records*, Series 1, Vol. 30, Part 3, 714–715; Ambrose Burnside, *Official Records*, Series 1, Vol. 30, Part 3, 717–718; Daniel Waite Howe, Diary entry September 17, 1863, Ms. 148, Box 1, Folder 17, Indiana Historical Society, Indianapolis; Joseph Vale, *Minty and the Cavalry*, 218; Thomas William Humes, *The Loyal Mountaineers of Tennessee* (Knoxville: Ogden Brothers & Co., 1888), 221–222.

99. Jefferson Davis, *Official Records*, Series 1, Vol. 23, Part 2, 953; David Stanley, *An American General: The Memoirs of David Sloan Stanley*, Samuel W. Fordyce IV, ed. (Santa Barbara, CA: The Narrative Press, 2004), 156.

Chapter Eight

1. David Stanley, *Personal Memoirs of Major-General D. S. Stanley USA* (Cambridge, MA: Harvard University Press, 1917), 136–137; Jack Welsh, *Medical Histories of Union Generals* (Kent, OH: Kent State University Press, 1996), 233 [Also see: Dennis W. Belcher, *The Cavalry of the Army of the Cumberland* (Jefferson, NC: McFarland, 2016), 143.]

2. *Harper's Weekly*, "Brigadier General Robert B. Mitchell," April 4, 1863; Philip J. Baker Jr., "Command and Control Mechanisms in the Chickamauga Campaign: The Union Experience," U.S. Army Command and General Staff College, Fort Leavenworth, Kansas, 1989, 44.

3. Edward McCook, *Official Records*, Series 1, Vol. 30, Part 1, 898; Archibald Campbell, *Official Records*, Series 1, Vol. 30, Part 1, 899–900; Leonidas Scranton, *Official Records*, Series 1, Vol. 30, Part 1, 901–902.

4. Peter Cozzens, *This Terrible Sound* (Urbana and Chicago: University of Illinois Press, 1992), 97.

5. William G. Robertson, et. al, *The Staff Ride Handbook for the Battle of Chickamauga: 18–20 September 1863* (U. S. Army Command and General Staff College, Command Studies Institute, Fort Leavenworth, KS, 1992), 173.

6. Eric Wittenberg, *The First Day at Chickamauga: September 18, 1863* (El Dorado Hills, CA: Savas Beatie, 2017), manuscript in preparation.

7. Robert Minty, *Minty's Sabre Brigade: The Part They Took in the Chattanooga Campaign* (Wyandotte, MI: The Herald Steam Presses, 1892), 9; D. L. Haines, "Record of the Fourth Michigan Cavalry," Bentley Historical Library, University of Michigan.

8. Robert Burns, Letter, October 30, 1863, Robert Burns Letterbook, MSS M642, Minnesota Historical Society, St. Paul, MN; D. H. Hill, "Chickamauga: The Great Battle of the West," In *Battles and Leaders in the Civil War*, Vol. III (New York: The Century Co., 1888), 643.

9. Eric Wittenberg, *The First Day at Chickamauga: September 18, 1863* (El Dorado Hills, CA: Savas Beatie, 2017), manuscript in preparation.

10. Peter Cozzens, *This Terrible Sound*, 89.

11. David Powell, *The Chickamauga Campaign: A Mad Irregular Battle* (El Dorado Hills, CA: Savas Beatie, 2014), 250–254; Newton Cannon, *The Reminiscences of Newton Cannon: First Sergeant, CSA*, Campbell Brown, editor (Franklin, TN: Carter House Association, 1963), 31–33.

12. Braxton Bragg, *Official Records*, Series 1, Vol. 30, Part 2, 31.

13. Charles Eugene Belknap, ed., *History of the Michigan Organizations at Chickamauga, Chattanooga, and Missionary Ridge* (Lansing: Robert Smith Printing Co., 1899), 276–277.

14. Eric Wittenberg, *The First Day at Chickamauga: September 18, 1863* (El Dorado Hills, CA: Savas Beatie, 2017), manuscript in preparation; Robert Minty, *Official Records*, Series 1, Vol. 30, Part 1, 923; David Powell, *Failure in the Saddle* (New York and California; Savas Beatie, 2010), 104; *Obituary Record of the Graduates of Yale University, Deceased from June 1910, to July 1915* (New Haven: Yale University Press, 1915), 40–43; William G. Robertson, et. al., *The Staff Ride Handbook for the Battle of Chickamauga*, 173.

15. Eric Wittenberg, *The First Day at Chickamauga: September 18, 1863* (El Dorado Hills, CA: Savas Beatie, 2017), manuscript in preparation; Robert Burns, Letter October 30, 1863; John McLain, Diary Entry September 18, 1863, John McLain, Papers (c.00111),

Michigan State University Archives & Historical Collections, East Lansing, Michigan; Robert Minty, *Official Records*, Series 1, Vol. 30, Part 1, 923; David Powell, *Failure in the Saddle* (New York and California; Savas Beatie, 2010), 104; *Obituary Record of the Graduates of Yale University, Deceased from June 1910, to July 1915* (New Haven: Yale University Press, 1915), 40–43; William G. Robertson, et. al., *The Staff Ride Handbook for the Battle of Chickamauga*, 173; David Powell, *The Chickamauga Campaign: A Mad Irregular Battle*, 253, 257–258.

16. James Larson, *Sergeant Larson, 4th Cavalry* (San Antonio: Southern Literary Institute, 1935), 174–176.

17. Mike West, "Like the Army of Tennessee, Bushrod Johnson Faced Both Glory, Despair," *Murfreesboro Post*, November 9, 2008; James W. Rabb, *Confederate General Lloyd Tilghman: A Biography* (Jefferson, N.C.: McFarland, Publishers, 2004), 68.

18. Eric Wittenberg, *The First Day at Chickamauga: September 18, 1863* (El Dorado Hills, CA: Savas Beatie, 2017), manuscript in preparation; Thomas Franklin Berry, *Four Years with Morgan and Forrest* (Oklahoma City: Harlow-Ratliff Company, 1914), 235; David Powell, *Failure in the Saddle*, 100–104; Mike West, "Like the Army of Tennessee, Bushrod Johnson Faced Both Glory, Despair"; James W. Rabb, *Confederate General Lloyd Tilghman*, 68.

19. Eric Wittenberg, *The First Day at Chickamauga: September 18, 1863* (El Dorado Hills, CA: Savas Beatie, 2017), manuscript in preparation; Robert Minty, *Official Records*, Series 1, Vol. 30, Part 1, 923; T. F. Dornblaser, *Sabre Strokes of the Pennsylvania Dragoons* (Philadelphia: Lutheran Publication Society, 1884), 131–132; David Powell, *Failure in the Saddle*, 104–105; Trumbull D. Griffin, Typeset document, B241: Papers of Trumbull Dorrance Griffin (ca. 1836–1912), 1862–1911, Missouri Historical Museum, St. Louis, MO.

20. Eric Wittenberg, *The First Day at Chickamauga: September 18, 1863* (El Dorado Hills, CA: Savas Beatie, 2017), manuscript in preparation; Robert Minty, *Official Records*, Series 1, Vol. 30, Part 1, 923; T. F. Dornblaser, *Sabre Strokes of the Pennsylvania Dragoons* (Philadelphia: Lutheran Publication Society, 1884), 131–132; David Powell, Failure *in the Saddle*, 104–105.

21. Francis Bernard Heitman, *Historical Register and Dictionary of the United States Army 1789–1903* (Washington, DC: U.S. Government Printing Office, 1903), 669; George W. Cullum, *Biographical Register of the Officers and Graduates of the U.S. Military Academy*, Vol. 2 (New York: D. Van Nostrand, 1868–79), 559–560.

22. Grosse Ile Historical Society, *Images of American: Grosse Ile* (Charleston, Chicago, Portsmouth, San Francisco: Arcadia Publishing Co., 2007), 33–49.

23. William Sipes, *History and Roster of the 7th Pennsylvania Veteran Volunteers* (Pottsville: Miners' Journal Print, 1905), 3–13; Christopher Cox, *History of Pennsylvania Civil War Regiments* (Raleigh: Lulu Publishing Co., 2013), 93.

24. Robert Minty, "The Fourth Michigan Cavalry," In *History of the Michigan Organizations at Chickamauga, Chattanooga, and Missionary Ridge*, Charles Eugene Belknap, ed. (Lansing: Robert Smith Printing Co., 1899), 91; Robert Minty, "Minty's Saber Brigade: Chickamauga," *National Tribune*, March 3, 1892; Robert E. Harbison, "Wilder's Brigade in the Tullahoma and Chattanooga Campaigns of the American Civil War," Master's Thesis, U.S. Army Command and General Staff College, Fort Leavenworth, Kansas, 2002, 70–71; Peter Cozzens, *This Terrible Sound*, 104; Robert Minty, *Official Records*, Series 1, Vol. 30, Part 1, 923; Henry Campbell, Diary Entry, September 18, 1863, *Three Years in the Saddle: A Diary of the Civil War*, Unpublished (n.d.), Wabash College, Crawfordsville, Indiana.

25. James Larson, *Sergeant Larson, 4th Cavalry*, 177–178.

26. David Powell, *Failure in the Saddle*, 105–107; Robert Minty, *Official Records*, Series 1, Vol. 30, Part 1, 922–923; Abram O. Miller, *Official Records*, Series 1, Vol. 30, Part 1, 451–452.

27. Robert Minty, "The Fourth Michigan Cavalry," 91; Robert Minty, *Official Records*, Series 1, Vol. 30, Part 1, 923; David Powell, *The Chickamauga Campaign: A Mad Irregular Battle*, 262–265; Joseph Vale, *Minty and the Cavalry: A History of Cavalry Campaigns in the Western Armies* (Harrisburg, PA: Edwin K. Myers, Printer and Binder, 1886), 227.

28. Henry Albert Potter, September 18, 1863, Diary Entry, MS 91–480 Henry Albert Potter Collection, Accession Box 461 Folder 2, Archives of Michigan. Historical Society of Michigan, Lansing.

29. Robert Minty, "The Fourth Michigan Cavalry," 91; Joseph Vale, *Minty and the Cavalry*, 227; Robert Minty, *Official Records*, Series 1, Vol. 30, Part 1, 923; David Powell, *Failure in the Saddle*, 107; Charles Gatewood, *Lt. Charles Gatewood and His Apache Wars Memoir*, Louis Kraft, ed. (Lincoln: University of Nebraska Press, 2005), 214.

30. Eric Wittenberg, *The First Day at Chickamauga: September 18, 1863* (El Dorado Hills, CA: Savas Beatie, 2017), manuscript in preparation; John McLain, Diary September 18, 1863; David Powell, *Failure in the Saddle*, 109; David Powell, *The Chickamauga Campaign: A Mad Irregular Battle*, 264.

31. Robert Burns, Letter, letter October 30, 1863; Joseph Vale, "Address of Captain Joseph Vale," In *Pennsylvania at Chickamauga and Chattanooga*, George W. Skinner, editor (Harrisburg, PA: William Stanley Ray, State Printer of Pennsylvania, 1897), 304; Robert Minty, *Official Records*, Series 1, Vol. 30, Part 1, 923.

32. John Wilder, *Official Records*, Series 1, Vol. 30, Part 3, 724–725; Charles Eugene Belknap, *History of the Michigan Organizations at Chickamauga*, 278; Robert Minty, "Minty's Saber Brigade, The Part They Took in the Chattanooga Campaign," *National Tribune*, March 3, 1892.

33. Robert Burns, Letter October 30, 1863; Joseph Vale, *Minty and the Cavalry* 229–230; Charles Eugene Belknap, *History of the Michigan Organizations at Chickamauga*, 278; Robert Minty, "Minty's Saber Brigade, The Part They Took in the Chattanooga Campaign," *National Tribune*, March 3, 1892; Ethan Rafuse, "In the Shadow of the Rock: Thomas L. Crittenden, Alexander M. McCook, and the 1863 Campaigns for Middle and East Tennessee," In *The Chickamauga Campaign*, Steven E. Woodworth, ed. (Carbondale and Edwardsville: Southern Illinois University Press, 2010), 21.

34. Joseph Vale, *Minty and the Cavalry*, 230; Abram Miller, *Official Records*, Series 1, Vol. 30, Part 1, 464–465; Bushrod Johnson, *Official Records*, Series 1, Vol. 30, Part 1, 452–453.

35. Thomas Wood, *Official Records*, Series 1, Vol. 30,

Part 3, 728; David Powell, *The Chickamauga Campaign: A Mad Irregular Battle* (El Dorado Hills, CA: Savas Beatie, 2014), 297.

36. Robert Minty, "The Fourth Michigan Cavalry," 92.

37. Eric Wittenberg, *The First Day at Chickamauga: September 18, 1863* (El Dorado Hills, CA: Savas Beatie, 2017), manuscript in preparation; George F. Steahlin, "Address and Historical Sketch," 310; Robert Burns, Letter October 30, 1863; George Dick, *Official Records*, Series 1, Vol. 30, Part 1, 822–823.

38. Eric Wittenberg, *The First Day at Chickamauga: September 18, 1863* (El Dorado Hills, CA: Savas Beatie, 2017), manuscript in preparation; George F. Steahlin, "Address and Historical Sketch," 310; Robert Burns, Letter October 30, 1863; James R Carnahan, "Personal Recollections of Chickamauga" In *Sketches of War History: 1861–1865*, Vol. I Ohio, MOLLUS (Cincinnati, Robert Clarke & Co. 1888), 407; Henry Campbell, Diary Entry, September 18, 1863, *Three Years in the Saddle: A Diary of the Civil War*; Israel Webster, "Chickamauga: Going into Action with Hands Full of Bacon and Coffee," *National Tribune*, July 2, 1891.

39. Clement Evans, *Confederate Military History*, Vol. IV (Atlanta: Confederate Publishing Co., 1899), 247–248.

40. Robert Mitchell, *Official Records*, Series 1, Vol. 30, Part 3, 730; James A. Garfield, *Official Records*, Series 1, Vol. 30, Part 1, 75; William F. Colton, "The Chickamauga Campaign," In *History of the Fifteenth Pennsylvania Volunteer Cavalry*, J. C. Reiff, ed. (Philadelphia, PA: Society of the Fifteenth Pennsylvania Cavalry, 1906), 233; Chesley Mosman, *The Rough Side of War: The Civil War Journal of Chesley A. Mosman*, Arnold Gates, ed. (Garden City, NY: The Basin Publishing Co., 1987), 81–82.

41. George Wagner, *Official Records*, Series 1, Vol. 30, Part 1, 730.

Chapter Nine

1. Benjamin T. Smith, *Private Smith's Journal: Recollections of the Late War*, Clyde C. Walton ed. (Chicago: R. R. Donnelley & Sons Company, 1963), 89–90.

2. John W. DuBose, *General Joseph Wheeler and the Army of Tennessee* (New York: The Neale Publishing Co., 1912), 199; Nathan Forrest, *Official Records*, Series 1, Vol. 30, Part 2, 524.

3. James Garfield, *Official Records*, Series 1, Vol. 30, Part 1, 73; C. Goodard, *Official Records*, Series 1, Vol. 30, Part 1, 76; Charles Eugene Belknap, ed., *History of the Michigan Organizations at Chickamauga, Chattanooga, and Missionary Ridge* (Lansing, Robert Smith Printing Co., 1899), 94; C. Goddard, Sept. 19 Orders, Letter and Orders Received by Chief of Cavalry, RG 393, Entry 2469, NARA; Robert Mitchell, *Official Records*, Series 1, Vol. 30, Part 3, 744–745; James Garfield, *Official Records*, Series 1, Vol. 30, Part 3, 741.

4. John W. Rowell, *Yankee Cavalrymen* (Knoxville: University of Tennessee Press, 1971), 145; Henry Mortimer Hempstead, "Diary September 19, 1863," Hempstead, Henry Mortimer, 1832–1916, Papers, Bentley Historical Library, University of Michigan, Ann Arbor.

5. Daniel Ray, *Official Records*, Series 1, Vol. 30, Part 1, 907; Louis Watkins *Official Records*, Series 1, Vol. 30, Part 1, 915; G. W. Baum, diary September 19, Book 10, M 674 B1 F3, Baum diaries, Indiana Historical Society; Henry Mortimer Hempstead, "Diary September 19, 1863," Robert Merrill, "September 19, 1863,"*Robert Sidney Merrill, Co. K. 1st Wis. Cav.* (Cedarsburg, WI.: MSG Publishing, 1995); Archibald Campbell, Oscar La Grange David Briggs, G. H. Purdy, *Official Records*, Series 1, Vol. 30, Part 1, 899–909.

6. Julius E. Thomas Diary September 19, 1863, 1863–1864, Julius E. Thomas Collection, MS.2720, University of Tennessee, Knoxville; Thomas Harrison, *Official Records*, Series 1, Vol. 30, Part 1, 548.

7. Thomas W. Cutrer, *Our Trust is in the God of Battles: The Civil War Letters of Robert Franklin Bunting, Chaplain, Terry's Texas Rangers* (Knoxville: University of Tennessee Press, 2006), 197; David Powell, *The Chickamauga Campaign: A Mad Irregular Battle* (El Dorado Hills, CA: Savas Beatie, 2014), 661; D. Coleman, Diary entry September 17, 1863, D. Coleman Diary, 1863–1864, Collection Number: 03317-z, The Southern Historical Collection at the Louis Round Wilson Special Collections Library, University of North Carolina.

8. Henry Hempstead, Diary September 19, 1863; Julius Thomas Diary September 19, 1863; Thomas Harrison, *Official Records*, Series 1, Vol. 30, Part 1, 548.

9. James A. Garfield, *Official Records*, Series 1, Vol. 30, Part 1, 68, 76, 963; J. R. Hayden, *Official Records*, Series 1, Vol. 30, Part 1, 344.

10. Elijah Watts, "Chickamauga Campaign" (hand written account, undated), Watts, Elijah S., Papers. 1861–1907, Mss./A/W349, Filson Historical Society; John W. Rowell, *Yankee Cavalrymen*, 145; Archibald Campbell, *Official Records*, Series 1, Vol. 30, Part 1, 899–900; Edward McCook, *Official Records*, Series 1, Vol. 30, Part 1, 895–896; Frank S. Bond, *Official Records*, Series 1, Vol. 30, Part 3, 743; Eli Long, *Official Records*, Series 1, Vol. 30, Part 1, 927; Robert Minty, *Official Records*, Series 1, Vol. 30, Part 3, 744.

11. Robert Mitchell, *Official Records*, Series 1, Vol. 30, Part 3, 743; Robert Mitchell, *Official Records*, Series 1, Vol. 30, Part 1, 893; George Crook, *Official Records*, Series 1, Vol. 30, Part 1, 919; William T. Hoblitzell Court Martial, July 1864, Record Group (RG) 153, Adjutant General's Office, Court Martial Case Files, 1809–1854, Case Number NN-2774, NARA, Washington, D.C.

12. John Andes and Will McTeer, *Loyal Mountain Troopers: The Second and Third Tennessee Volunteer Cavalry in the Civil War* (Maryville, TN: Blount County Genealogical and Historical Society, 1992), 65; Benjamin T. Smith, *Private Smith's Journal: Recollections of the Late War*, 90–91; Edward McCook, *Official Records*, Series 1, Vol. 30, Part 1, 894; Thomas McCahan, Diary, September 19, 1863, Thomas McCahan Papers (Am. 6092) Historical Society of Pennsylvania, Philadelphia.

13. Daniel Ray, *Official Records*, Series 1, Vol. 30, Part 1, 907; Roswell Russell, *Official Records*, Series 1, Vol. 30, Part 1, 904; Archibald Campbell; *Official Records*, Series 1, Vol. 30, Part 1, 900; James P. Brownlow, *Official Records*, Series 1, Vol. 30, Part 1, 906; Thomas McCahan, Diary, September 19, 1863.

14. Henry Hempstead, Diary September 19, 1863; Leonidas Scranton, *Official Records*, Series 1, Vol. 30, Part 1, 901–902; Joseph Wheeler, *Official Records*, Series 1, Vol. 30, Part 2, 520; Archibald Campbell; *Official Records*, Series 1, Vol. 30, Part 1, 900; David A. Powell,

The Chickamauga Campaign: Glory or the Grave: The Breakthrough, the Union Retreat to Chattanooga (Eldorado Hills, CA: Savas Beatie, 2015), 26.

15. David A. Powell, *The Chickamauga Campaign: Glory or the Grave: The Breakthrough, the Union Retreat to Chattanooga*, 27, 35.

16. L. M. Hosea, *Official Records*, Series 1, Vol. 30, Part 1, 917; Louis Watkins, *Official Records*, Series 1, Vol. 30, Part 1, 916.

17. Edward McCook, *Official Records*, Series 1, Vol. 30, Part 1, 896; G. W. Baum, Diary September 20, 1863; Edward McCook, Archibald Campbell, Daniel Ray, Louis Watkins, George Crook, Eli Long Reports, *Official Records*, Series 1, Vol. 30, Part 1, 895–926; Archibald Campbell, *Official Records*, Series 1, Vol. 30, Part 1, 900; William G. Robertson, et. al, *The Staff Ride Handbook for the Battle of Chickamauga: 18–20 September 1863* (U. S. Army Command and General Staff College, Command Studies Institute, Fort Leavenworth, KS, 1992), 176.

18. Ed Porter Thompson, *History of the Orphan Brigade* (Louisville, KY.: Lewis N. Thompson, 1898), 212; Joseph Wheeler, *Official Records*, Series 1, Vol. 30, Part 2, 520; Edward McCook, Archibald Campbell, Daniel Ray, Louis Watkins, George Crook, Eli Long Reports, *Official Records*, Series 1, Vol. 30, Part 1, 895–926.

19. David Rubenstein, "A Study of the Medical Support to the Union and Confederate Armies During the Battle of Chickamauga: Lessons and Implications for Today's U.S. Army Medical Department Leaders," Master's Thesis, U.S. Army Command and General Staff College, Fort Leavenworth, KS, 1990.

20. Henry Mortimer Hempstead, "Diary, September 20, 1863"; Thomas Colman, Letter October 5, 1863, Colman-Hayter Family Papers, C-84, Folder 6, Missouri Historical Society.

21. Henry Mortimer Hempstead, "Diary, September 20, 1863"; James Hagan, "3rd Alabama Cavalry," SG024911, Alabama Department of History and Archives, Montgomery; L. S. Scranton, *Official Records*, Series 1, Vol. 30, Part 1, 902; Peter Cozzens, *This Terrible Sound*, 464; David Powell, *Failure in the Saddle*, 160; David A. Powell, *The Chickamauga Campaign: Glory or the Grave*, 465–469; Thomas Colman, *ibid.*

22. William E. Crane, "William E. Crane's Daily Journal of Life in the Field during the War of the Rebellion," September 20, 1863 entry, Mss. 980, Cincinnati Historical Society, Cincinnati Museum Center; Elijah Watts, "Chickamauga Campaign"; George Crook, *General George Crook: His Biography* (Norman & London: University of Oklahoma Press, 1960), 105.

23. Elijah Watts, "Chickamauga Campaign"; Thomas Crofts, *History of the Service of the Third Ohio Veteran Volunteer Cavalry* (Toledo: Stoneman Press, 1910), 113; William Sinclair, Letters September 1863, Letters Sent, Chief of Cavalry, RG 393, Number 151 (2460) NARA, Washington, D.C.

24. Robert B. Mitchell, Letter September 20, Letters Sent, Chief of Cavalry, RG 393, Number 151 (2460) NARA, Washington, D.C.; Elijah S. Watts, "Chickamauga Campaign."

25. Charles Eugene Belknap, ed., *History of the Michigan Organizations at Chickamauga, Chattanooga, and Missionary Ridge* (Lansing: Robert Smith Printing Co., 1899), 78; George Crook, *General George Crook: His Biography*, 105–107; Joseph Wheeler, *Official Records*, Series 1, Vol. 30, Part 2, 521; L. S. Scranton, *Official Records*, Series 1, Vol. 30, Part 1, 902; Eli Long, *Official Records*, Series 1, Vol. 30, Part 1, 927; Franklin F. Moyer, Letter September 29, 1863, *Journal and Letters of Franklin F. Moyer*, Robert H. Wieser, editor (Dayton: Robert Wieser, 2008); Elijah Watts, "Chickamauga Campaign."

26. Eli Long, "Autobiography," Eli Long Papers, Civil War Collection, Box 1, USAHEC, Carlisle, Pennsylvania; Nancy Pape-Findley, *The Invincibles: The Story of Fourth Ohio Veteran Volunteer Cavalry* (Tecumseh, Michigan; Blood Road Publishing, 2002), 162; William E. Crane, Diary September 20, 1863; Benjamin Nourse, "Diary" Entry September 20, 1863.

27. W. L. Curry, *Four Years in the Saddle: History of First Regiment Ohio Volunteer Cavalry* (Columbus: Champlin Printing Co., 1898), 111; Whitelaw Reid, *Ohio in the War: Her Statesmen, Her Generals, and Soldiers*, Vol. I (New York: Moore, Wilstach & Baldwin: 1868), 751; John Chapin, "At Chickamauga," In *Reunions of the First Ohio Volunteer Cavalry* (Columbus, OH: Landon Printing, Co., 1891), 15–17.

28. Henry Mortimer Hempstead, "Diary, September 20, 1863"; Elijah S. Watts, "Chickamauga Campaign"; David Powell, *Failure in the Saddle*, 165.

29. Henry Mortimer Hempstead, "Diary, September 20, 1863."

30. John Allan Wyeth, *The Life General Nathan Bedford Forrest* (New York and London: Harper and Brothers, 1899), 247; D. Coleman, Diary entry September 20, 1863, D. Coleman Diary, 1863–1864, Collection Number: 03317-z, The Southern Historical Collection at the Louis Round Wilson Special Collections Library, University of North Carolina.

31. George Guild, *A Brief Narrative of the Fourth Tennessee Cavalry Regiment* (n. p.: Nashville, 1913), 27–28.

32. W. L. Curry, *Four Years in the Saddle*, 111. [It is worthy to note that there are various accounts of where Lt. Col. Cupp's body was taken and the time of his death.]

33. Robert Mitchell, *Official Records*, Series 1, Vol. 30, Part 1, 893–894; George Kryder, Diary September 25, 1863, MS 163 George Kryder (1834–1925), William T. Jerome Library, Bowling Green State University, Bowling Green, Ohio; David A. Powell, *Failure in the Saddle*, 160; Eli Long, "Autobiography" and "Synopsis of the Military Career of Brevet Major-General Eli Long," Eli Long Papers, Civil War Collection, Box 1, USAHEC, Carlisle, Pennsylvania; Elisha Peterson, Letter to parents September 29, 1863, Elisha Peterson manuscript, Sec. A Box 104, Rubenstein Library, Duke University.

34. George Crook, *General George Crook: His Biography*, 106–107; David Power, *Failure in the Saddle*, 168–169; 1st Ohio Cavalry, Morning reports. Company G, September 20, 1863, RG 94, E 112–115, NARA, Washington, D.C.; William Crane, September 20; Leonidas S. Scranton, *Official Records*, Series 1, Vol. 30, Part 1, 901–902.

35. 1st Ohio Cavalry, Morning reports. Company G, September 20, 1863, RG 94, E 112–115, NARA, Washington, D.C.; William Crane, September 20; George Crook, General *George Crook: His Biography*, 106; Joseph Wheeler, *Official Records*, Series 1, Vol. 30, Part 2, 521; Leonidas S. Scranton, *Official Records*, Series 1,

Vol. 30, Part 1, 901–902: Eli Long, *Official Records*, Series 1, Vol. 30, Part 1, 927.

36. Edward McCook, *Official Records*, Series 1, Vol. 30, Part 1, 896; Roswell Russell, *Official Records*, Series 1, Vol. 30, Part 1, 904; David Briggs, *Official Records*, Series 1, Vol. 30, Part 1, 909; Robert Merrill, Diary September 20, 1863; John W. Rowell, *Yankee Cavalrymen*, 147; Jesse Leeper, Diary Sept. 6, 1863, *The Civil War Diary of Private Jesse Leeper*, Richard Reid, ed., Stones River National Park, Technical Information Center, Murfreesboro, TN., 9; Charles Perry Goodrich, September 24, 1863, letter, *Letters from Home from the First Wisconsin Cavalry*, Richard N. Larson, editor (Madison: State Historical Society of Wisconsin, not published); Thomas McCahan, Diary, September 20, 1863, Thomas McCahan Papers (Am. 6092) Historical Society of Pennsylvania, Philadelphia; P. Sidney Post, *Official Records*, Series 1, Vol. 30, Part 1, 507; Michael Gooding, *Official Records*, Series 1, Vol. 30, Part 1, 513. [The records do not indicate which McCormick brought the message from Robert Mitchell. There were two officers named McCormick serving in the 7th Pennsylvania—Robert and Charles.]

37. Alonso Phelps, *Medical and Surgical History of the War of the Rebellion*, Vol. 1, Appendix, 277–278; D. J. Griffiths, *Medical and Surgical History of the War of the Rebellion*, Vol. 1, Appendix, 277; W. W. Blair, *Medical and Surgical History of the War of the Rebellion*, Vol. 1, Appendix, 278–279.

38. Peter Cozzens, *This Terrible Sound*, 456; John Allan Wyeth, *With Sabre and Scalpel: The Autobiography of a Soldier and Surgeon* (New York and London: Harper Brothers Publishers, 1914), 252–253.

39. Archibald Campbell, *Official Records*, Series 1, Vol. 30, Part 1, 900; James P. Brownlow, *Official Records*, Series 1, Vol. 30, Part 1, 906.

40. Roswell Russell, *Official Records*, Series 1, Vol. 30, Part 1, 904–905; David Powell, *The Chickamauga Campaign—Glory or the Grave: The Breakthrough, the Union Retreat to Chattanooga* (Eldorado Hills, CA: Savas Beatie, 2015), 741; Thomas McCahan, Diary September 20, 1863; Gates Thruston, *Official Records*, Series 1, Vol. 30, Part 1, 118, 129, 955–956; Robert Mitchell, *Official Records*, Series 1, Vol. 30, Part 1, 893.

41. David Powell, *The Chickamauga Campaign—Glory or the Grave*, 309–310; Peter Cozzens, *This Terrible Sound*, 395–396.

42. Robert Mitchell, *Official Records*, Series 1, Vol. 30, Part 1, 893; John W. Rowell, *Yankee Cavalrymen*,147; Robert E. Harbison, "Wilder's Brigade in the Tullahoma and Chattanooga Campaigns of the American Civil War," Master's Thesis, U.S. Army Command and General Staff College, Fort Leavenworth, Kansas, 2002, 82–83; David Powell, *Failure in the Saddle*, 170–171; John Bowers, *Chickamauga and Chattanooga: The Battles That Doomed the Confederacy* (New York: Harper-Collins Publishers, 1994), 117.

43. James Garfield, *Official Records*, Series 1, Vol. 30, Part 1, 963; Gates Thruston, *Official Records*, Series 1, Vol. 30, Part 1, 118, 129, 955–956; James Garfield, *Official Records*, Series 1, Vol. 30, Part 1, 955–956; Alexander McCook, *Official Records*, Series 1, Vol. 30, Part 1, 967.

44. Robert Mitchell, *Official Records*, Series 1, Vol. 30, Part 1, 137, 140–141; James Garfield, *Official Records*, Series 1, Vol. 30, Part 1, 137; J. P. Drouillard, *Official Records*, Series 1, Vol. 30, Part 1, 140.

45. John Wilder, *Official Records*, Series 1, Vol. 30, Part 1, 448; Edward McCook, *Official Records*, Series 1, Vol. 30, Part 1, 895; William Rosecrans, *Official Records*, Series 1, Vol. 30, Part 1, 178; Thomas Jordan and J. P. Pryor, *The Campaigns of Lieut.-Gen. Nathan B. Forrest of Forrest's Cavalry* (New Orleans, Memphis, NY: Blelock & Co., 1868), 345; Edward G. Longacre, *A Soldier to the Last: Maj. Gen. Joseph Wheeler in Blue and Gray* (Washington: Potomac Books Inc., 2007), 113; Joseph Wheeler, *Official Records*, Series 1, Vol. 30, Part 2, 521; David Powell, *The Chickamauga Campaign—Glory or the Grave: The Breakthrough, the Union Retreat to Chattanooga*, 743; John Andes and Will McTeer, *Loyal Mountain Troopers: The Second and Third Tennessee Volunteer Cavalry in the Civil War* (Maryville, TN: Blount County Genealogical and Historical Society, 1992), 65; John Allan Wyeth, *With Sabre and Scalpel*, 252–253; D. Coleman, Diary September 20, 1863, D. Coleman Diary, 1863–1864, Collection Number: 03317-z, The Southern Historical Collection at the Louis Round Wilson Special Collections Library, University of North Carolina.

46. Gates Thruston, "Crisis at Chickamauga," In *Battles and Leaders in the Civil War*, Vol. 3 (New York: The Century Co., 1888), 664–665; John E. Brown, "At Headquarters During the Battle of Chickamauga," In *History of the Fifteenth Pennsylvania Volunteer Cavalry*, J. C. Reiff, ed. (Philadelphia, PA: Society of the Fifteenth Pennsylvania Cavalry, 1906), 247–248.

47. P. Sidney Post, *Official Records*, Series 1, Vol. 30, Part 1, 507–508.

48. Marshall P. Thatcher, *A Hundred Battles in the West: The Second Michigan Cavalry* (Detroit: L. F. Kilroy, Printer, 1884), 152.

49. Gustavus Menzies, *Medical and Surgical History of the War of the Rebellion*, Vol. 1, Appendix, 280; David Rubenstein, "A Study of the Medical Support to the Union and Confederate Armies During the Battle of Chickamauga," 76; Samuel Turney, *Medical and Surgical History of the War of the Rebellion*, Vol. 1, Appendix, 280; D. J. Griffiths, *Medical and Surgical History of the War of the Rebellion*, Vol. 1, Appendix, 277.

50. L. D. Waterman, *Medical and Surgical History of the War of the Rebellion*, Vol. 1, Appendix, 275; R. C. Bogue, *Medical and Surgical History of the War of the Rebellion*, Vol. 1, Appendix, 272; W. W. Blair, *Medical and Surgical History of the War of the Rebellion*, Vol. 1, Appendix, 277.

51. T. F. Dornblaser, *Sabre Strokes of the Pennsylvania Dragoons* (Philadelphia: Lutheran Publication Society, 1884), 131; Julius Thomas, Diary September 20, 1863; Elbert Squires, Letter September 28, 1863, Stones River National Park, Technical Information Center, Murfreesboro, TN.; W. R. Carter, *History of the First Regiment of Tennessee Volunteer Cavalry* (Knoxville: Gaut-Ogden Co., Printers and Binders, 1902), 97; John Andes and Will McTeer, *Loyal Mountain Troops, The Second and Third Tennessee Volunteer Cavalry* (Maryville, TN: Blount County Genealogical and Historical Society, 1992), 65; Glover Perin, *Official Records*, Series 1, Vol. 30, Part 1, 227; David Powell, *The Chickamauga Campaign—Glory or the Grave: The Breakthrough, the Union Retreat to Chattanooga*, 743.

52. Robert Mitchell, *Official Records*, Series 1, Vol.

30, Part 1, 893; Edward McCook, *Official Records*, Series 1, Vol. 30, Part 1, 896; Roswell Russell, *Official Records*, Series 1, Vol. 30, Part 1, 905; Daniel Ray, *Official Records*, Series 1, Vol. 30, Part 1, 908; Michael Hendrick Fitch, *The Chattanooga Campaign*, Wisconsin History Commission (n.p.: Democrat Printing Co., State Printer March 1911), 124; John W. Rowell, *Yankee Cavalrymen*, 148; David Powell, *Failure in the Saddle*, 171; Roswell Russell, *Official Records*, Series 1, Vol. 30, Part 1, 905; John Andes and Will McTeer, *Loyal Mountain Troops, The Second and Third Tennessee Volunteer Cavalry*, 65; Chesley Mosman, *The Rough Side of War: The Civil War Journal of Chesley A. Mosman*, Arnold Gates, ed. (Garden City, NY: The Basin Publishing Co., 1987), 84–85; Leroy S. Mayfield, "Letters and Diaries of Leroy S. Mayfield," *Indiana Magazine of History*, Vol. 39, no. 2 (June 1943): 144–91, 161.

53. J. K. P. Blackburn, *Reminiscences of the Terry Rangers* (n. p.: University of Texas, 1919), 41; Peter Cozzens, *This Terrible Sound*, 465–466; J. K. Womack, "Chickamauga As I Saw It," *Confederate Veteran*, Vol. XXV, No. 2 (February 1917): 74.

54. William Rosecrans, *Official Records*, Series 1, Vol. 30, Part 1, 71.

55. Joseph Vale, "Address of Captain Joseph Vale," In *Pennsylvania at Chickamauga and Chattanooga*, George W. Skinner, editor (Harrisburg, PA: William Stanley Ray, State Printer of Pennsylvania, 1897), 307; George F. Steahlin, "Address and Historical Sketch," In *Pennsylvania at Chickamauga and Chattanooga*, George W. Skinner, editor (Harrisburg, PA: William Stanley Ray, State Printer of Pennsylvania, 1897), 310; Joseph Vale, *Minty and the Cavalry: A History of Cavalry Campaigns in the Western Armies* (Harrisburg, PA: Edwin K. Myers, Printer and Binder, 1886), 235; Henry Albert Potter, Diary September 20, 1863, Henry Albert Potter Collection. MS 91–480, Michigan Historical Society, Lansing, Michigan; Stirling D. Popejoy, "The Second Tennessee Cavalry in the American Civil War," Master's Thesis, 2014, U.S. Army Command and General Staff College, Fort Leavenworth, KS, 61; Robert Minty, *Official Records*, Series 1, Vol. 30, Part 1, 923–924; John McLain, Diary entry September 20, 1863, McLain Papers (c.00111), Michigan State University Archives & Historical Collections, East Lansing.

56. Robert Minty, *Official Records*, Series 1, Vol. 30, Part 1, 144; Richard Robbins, "Reminiscences," Richard Robbins Papers, Bentley Historical Library, University of Michigan; McLain Diary, September 20, 1863.

57. Marshall P. Thatcher, *A Hundred Battles in the West*, 147; Archibald Campbell, *Official Records*, Series 1, Vol. 30, Part 3, 754; Charles Eugene Belknap, ed., *History of the Michigan Organizations at Chickamauga* 79; George Crook, *General George Crook: His Biography*, 107.

58. W. S. Rosecrans, "The Campaign for Chattanooga," *The Century Illustrated Monthly Magazine* (1887) Vol. 34:129–135, 143.

59. Michael Hendrick Fitch, *The Chattanooga Campaign*, 153–154; William Rosecrans, *Official Records*, Series 1, Vol. 30, Part 1, 71.

Chapter Ten

1. William Sinclair, *Official Records*, Series 1, Vol. 30, Part 3, 768; David A. Powell, *The Chickamauga Campaign—Barren Victory: The Retreat into Chattanooga* (New York and California: Savas Beatie, 2016), 8.

2. Robert Mitchell, *Official Records*, Series 1, Vol. 30, Part 1, 896; John Williams, *Leaves of a Trooper's Diary* (Philadelphia: Published by Author, 1869), 69–70; Henry Mortimer Hempstead, Diary, September 21, 1863, Hempstead, Henry Mortimer, 1832–1916, Papers, Bentley Historical Library, University of Michigan, Ann Arbor; Smith Cozens, "Company L on Lookout Mountain," In *History of the Fifteenth Pennsylvania Volunteer Cavalry*, J. C. Reiff, ed. (Philadelphia, PA: Society of the Fifteenth Pennsylvania Cavalry, 1906), 287–291.

3. Robert Mitchell, *Official Records*, Series 1, Vol. 30, Part 1, 155, 893; Edward McCook, *Official Records*, Series 1, Vol. 30, Part 1, 896; Daniel Ray, *Official Records*, Series 1, Vol. 30, Part 1, 907; G. W. Baum September 21, 1863, Book 10, M 674 B1 F3, Baum diaries, Indiana Historical Society, Indianapolis; George Hazzard, *Hazzard's History of Henry County, Indiana, 1822–1906*, Vol. 1 (New Castle, IN: George Hazzard, 1906), 118; Edward McCook, *Official Records*, Series 1, Vol. 30, Part 1, 896; Chesley Mosman, *The Rough Side of War: The Civil War Journal of Chesley A. Mosman*, Arnold Gates, ed. (Garden City, NY: The Basin Publishing Co., 1987), 86.

4. W. L. Curry, *Four Years in the Saddle: History of First Regiment Ohio Volunteer Cavalry* (Columbus: Champlin Printing Co., 1898), 112–113.

5. Charles Greeno, "Address of Lieut.-Col. Charles L. Greeno," In *Pennsylvania at Chickamauga and Chattanooga*, George W. Skinner, editor (William Stanley Ray, State Printer of Pennsylvania, 1897), 312–313; Robert Mitchell, *Official Records*, Series 1, Vol. 30, Part 3, 766–767.

6. Nancy Pape-Findley, *The Invincibles: The Story of Fourth Ohio Veteran Volunteer Cavalry* (Tecumseh, MI: Blood Road Publishing, 202), 164.

7. David Stanley, Letter to Garfield Sept. 20, 1863, 2 a.m., Sept. 21 at 10:30 a.m., Letters sent by Chief of Cavalry, RG 393, Entry 2460, NARA [Please note that the author of this letter is David Stanley, but this cannot be correct because Stanley was no longer at headquarters. Instead, Robert Mitchell or a member of his staff was probably the author of this message. The message was not signed]; Robert Mitchell, *Official Records*, Series 1, Vol. 30, Part 1, 151, 155.

8. Louis Watkins, *Official Records*, Series 1, Vol. 30, Part 1, 915; Charles Sowle, Letter September 26, 1863, Sowle, Charles H. Papers, Sec. A Box 123, Rubenstein Library, Duke University; Steven L. Wright, "Louisville Daily Journal October 9, 1863," In *Kentucky Soldiers and Their Regiments in the Civil War*, Vol. III (Utica, KY: McDowell Publications, 2009); David A. Powell, *The Chickamauga Campaign—Barren Victory*, 140–142.

9. Louis Watkins, *Official Records*, Series 1, Vol. 30, Part 1, 915; Steven L. Wright, "Louisville Daily Journal October 9, 1863"; David A. Powell, *The Chickamauga Campaign—Barren Victory*, 145; Thomas Colman, Letter October 5, 1863, Colman-Hayter Family Papers, C-84, Folder 6, Missouri Historical Society.

10. Louis Watkins, *Official Records*, Series 1, Vol. 30, Part 1, 915; C. H. Sowle, "Military Record of C. H. Sowle," unpublished, Manuscript C. S., undated, Filson Historical Society, Louisville, Kentucky; Charles Sowle, Letter September 26, 1863, Sowle, Charles H. Papers, Sec. A Box 123, Rubenstein Library, Duke University.

11. William T. Hoblitzell Court Martial, July 1864, Record Group (RG) 153, Adjutant General's Office, Court Martial Case Files, 1809–1854, Case Number NN-2774, NARA, Washington, D.C.; William T. Hoblitzell Court Martial, June, 1864, Record Group (RG) 153, Adjutant General's Office, Court Martial Case Files, 1809–1854, case number NN-3269.

12. William T. Hoblitzell Court Martial, July 1864.

13. Robert Mitchell, Letter to C. Goddard, September 28, 1863, Letters sent by the chief of cavalry, RG 393, Entry 2460, NARA.

14. Joseph Vale, *Minty and the Cavalry* 240; Robert Minty, "The Fourth Michigan Cavalry," Charles Eugene Belknap, ed., In *History of the Michigan Organizations at Chickamauga, Chattanooga, and Missionary Ridge* (Lansing: Robert Smith Printing Co., 1899), 95; David A. Powell, *The Chickamauga Campaign—Barren Victory*, 10.

15. Minty, *Ibid.*; Vale, *Ibid.*, Richard Robbins, "Reminiscences," Richard Robbins Papers, Bentley Historical Library, University of Michigan; Michael Bower Cavender, *The First Georgia Cavalry in the Civil War: A History and Roster* (Jefferson, NC: McFarland Publishing, 2016), 77; Eddy W. Davison and Daniel Foxx, *Nathan Bedford Forest: In Search of the Enigma* (Gretna, LA: Pelican Publishing Co., 2007), 172.

16. Robert Minty, *Official Records*, Series 1, Vol. 30, Part 1, 151–152, 924; Richard Robbins, "Reminiscences"; George Thomas, *Official Records*, Series 1, Vol. 30, Part 1, 254; Joseph Vale, "Address of Captain Joseph Vale," In *Pennsylvania at Chickamauga and Chattanooga*, George W. Skinner, editor (Harrisburg, PA: William Stanley Ray, State Printer of Pennsylvania, 1897), 308; George F. Steahlin, "Address and Historical Sketch," In *Pennsylvania at Chickamauga and Chattanooga*, George W. Skinner, editor (Harrisburg, PA: William Stanley Ray, State Printer of Pennsylvania, 1897), 311; Robert Burns, Letter, October 30, 1863, Robert Burns Letterbook, MSS M642, Minnesota Historical Society, St. Paul, MN.; Joseph Vale, *Minty and the Cavalry: A History of Cavalry Campaigns in the Western Armies* (Harrisburg, PA: Edwin K. Myers, Printer and Binder, 1886), 235; John Watson Morton, *The Artillery of Nathan Bedford Forrest's Cavalry* (Nashville, Tennessee and Dallas, TX: Publishing House of the M. E. Church, 1909), 126; David A. Powell, *The Chickamauga Campaign—Barren Victory*, 14–15; Mamie Yeary, *Reminiscences of the Boys in Gray* (Smith and Lamar Publishing House: Dallas, 1912), 547.

17. Robert Minty, "The Fourth Michigan Cavalry," 95; Robert Minty, *Official Records*, Series 1, Vol. 30, Part 1, 924; Richard Robbins, "Reminiscences"; George Thomas, *Official Records*, Series 1, Vol. 30, Part 1, 255; Terry H. Cahal, Letters, September 30, 1863, Confederate Collection, Box 8, Folder 17, Tennessee State Library and Archives; Robert Burns, Letter October 30, 1863; Glenn Tucker, *Chickamauga: Bloody Battle in the West* (Dayton, OH: Press of Morningside Bookshop, 1984), 374–375.

18. Edward McCook, *Official Records*, Series 1, Vol. 30, Part 1, 896; Charles Greeno, "Address of Lieut.-Col. Charles L. Greeno," In *Pennsylvania at Chickamauga and Chattanooga*, George W. Skinner, editor (William Stanley Ray, State Printer of Pennsylvania, 1897), 312–313; Robert Mitchell, *Official Records*, Series 1, Vol. Part 3, 767; James Spears, *Official Records*, Series 1, Vol. 30, Part 1, 884.

19. W. R. Carter, *History of the First Regiment of Tennessee Volunteer Cavalry*. (Knoxville: Gaut-Ogden Co., Printers and Binders, 1902), 9; Edward McCook Report September 30, 1863, RG 393, Number 2527, Letters Sent First Cavalry Division, NARA.

20. Nancy Pape-Findley, *The Invincibles*, 164–165.

21. G W. Baum, Diary September 22, 1863; Robert Merrill, "September 22, 1863," *Robert Sidney Merrill, Co. K. 1st Wis. Cav.* (Cedarsburg, WI.: MSG Publishing, 1995); "Bridgeport, Tenn. October 2, 1863," by "Will," Quiner Scrapbooks: Correspondence of the Wisconsin Volunteers, 1861–1865, Vol. 10, Wisconsin Historical Society, Madison; Edward McCook, Report September 30, 1863, RG 393, NARA, Washington; James Garfield, *Official Records*, Series 1, Vol. 30, Part 3, 783; Daniel Ray, *Official Records*, Series 1, Vol. 30, Part 1, 907; James Spears, *Official Records*, Series 1, Vol. 30, Part 1, 885.

22. P. Sidney Post, *Official Records*, Series 1, Vol. 30, Part 1, 508–509.

23. Richard Robbins, "Reminiscences"; Robert Burns, Letter October 30, 1863; Robert Merrill Diary, September 23, 1863; August Yenner, Diary Entry September 27, 1863, Augustus L. Yenner, 1837–1924, Papers, Western Michigan University, Kalamazoo, Michigan; C. Goddard, *Official Records*, Series 1, Vol. 30, Part 1, 166–167; John L. Herberich, *Masters of the Field: The Fourth United States Cavalry in the Civil War* (Atglen, PA; Schiffer Publishing Co., 2015), 128.

24. Charles Alley, Diary October 4, 1863, Charles Alley Diary 1861–1865, Western History Collection, University of Oklahoma; Eugene Marshall, Diary entry September 15–25, 1863, Eugene Marshall Papers, RL.00850, David M. Rubenstein Rare Book & Manuscript Library, Duke University.

25. Edward Summers, Letter November, 1863, Edward Summers Papers, MS.2714, University of Tennessee Knoxville; Letter September 26, 1863, Isaac Barton Ulmer papers, 1838–1929, Collection Number: 01834, The Southern Historical Collection at the Louis Round Wilson Special Collections Library, University of North Carolina; Braxton Bragg letter to wife September 28, 1863, Braxton Bragg Papers, Collection: A0164, Missouri History Museum, St. Louis.

26. William Rosecrans, *Official Records*, Series 1, Vol. 30, Part 1, 178–179.

Chapter Eleven

1. Henry Albert Potter, September 24, 1863, Diary Entry, MS 91–480 Henry Albert Potter Collection, Accession Box 461 Folder 2, Archives of Michigan. Historical Society of Michigan, Lansing; Robert Mitchell, Abram O. Miller, *Official Records*, Series 1, Vol. 30, Part 3, 804.

2. Robert E. Harbison, "Wilder's Brigade in the Tullahoma and Chattanooga Campaigns of the American Civil War," Master's Thesis, U.S. Army Command and General Staff College, Fort Leavenworth, Kansas, 2002, pp. 49–50, 91–93; Samuel Harden and John Spahr, *Early Life and Times in Boone County, Indiana* (Indianapolis: Carlon and Hollenbeck, 1887), 453–454.

3. Chris Beck, *Official Records*, Series 1, Vol. 30, Part 3, 833–834.

4. Daniel Ray, *Official Records*, Series 1, Vol. 30, Part 3, 952; Louis Watkins, *Official Records*, Series 1, Vol. 30, Part 3, 900.

5. W. T. Hoblitzell, *Official Records*, Series 1, Vol. 30, Part 3, 920.

6. Robert Mitchell, *Official Records*, Series 1, Vol. 30, Part 3, 856–867.

7. Robert Mitchell, *Official Records*, Series 1, Vol. 30, Part 3, 836.

8. William H. Sinclair, *Official Records*, Series 1, Vol. 30, Part 3, 857, 880.

9. *New York Times*, "Wheeler's Raid Into Tennessee," December 27, 1863; George Crook, *Official Records*, Series 1, Vol. 30, Part 3, 952; Stephen Z. Starr, *The Union Cavalry in the Civil War: The War in the West*, Vol. III (Baton Rouge: Louisiana State University, 2007), 292; Thomas W. Cutrer, *Our Trust is in the God of Battles: The Civil War Letters of Robert Franklin Bunting, Chaplain, Terry's Texas Rangers* (Knoxville: University of Tennessee Press, 2006), 202; William Gibbs Allen, "Memoirs," Civil War Collection (Confederate), Box 12, Folder, 3, Tennessee State Library and Archives, Nashville.

10. Joseph Wheeler, *Official Records*, Series 1, Vol. 30, Part 2, 723; Edward G. Longacre, *A Soldier to the Last: Maj. Gen. Joseph Wheeler in Blue and Gray* (Washington: Potomac Books Inc., 2007), 123.

11. Henry B. Davidson, Letter to Frank Armstrong, October 5, 1863 American Civil War Museum, Richmond, Virginia; Edward G. Longacre, *A Soldier to the Last*, 118–119; Thomas Jordan and J. P. Pryor, *The Campaigns of Lieut.-Gen. Nathan B. Forrest of Forrest's Cavalry* (New Orleans, Memphis, NY: Blelock & Co., 1868), 358–359; George W. Brent, *Official Records*, Series 1, Vol. 30, Part 4, 710; Jack Hurst, *Nathan Bedford Forrest: A Biography* (New York: Vintage Books, 1994), 139–140.

12. Lucien Wulsin, *The Fourth Regiment Ohio Veteran Volunteer Cavalry* (Cincinnati: Fourth Ohio Volunteer Cavalry Association, 1912), 38; Nancy Pape-Findley, *The Invincibles: The Story of Fourth Ohio Veteran Volunteer Cavalry* (Tecumseh, MI: Blood Road Publishing, 202), 171; James Pike, *Scout And Ranger: Personal Adventures Corporal Pike* (Cincinnati and New York: J. R. Hawley & Co., 1865), 317; John McLain, Diary Entry September 30, 1863, John McLain, Papers (c.00111), Michigan State University Archives & Historical Collections, East Lansing, Michigan; W. L. Curry, *The Raid of the Confederate Cavalry through Central Tennessee, October 1863* (Columbus: The Ohio Commandery of the Loyal Legion, MOLLUS, 1908), 4–6; Thomas W. Davis, "The Civil War Diary of Thomas W. Davis, Chattanooga Hamilton Country Bicentennial Library.

13. Robert Minty, "Picketing and Scouting," August 31, 1893, *National Tribune*; "An Incident after Chickamauga," *National Tribune*, March 9, 1893; W. L. Curry, *The Raid of the Confederate Cavalry through Central Tennessee*, 6.

14. James Larson, *Sergeant Larson, 4th Cavalry* (San Antonio: Southern Literary Institute, 1935), 200–201.

15. William Van Antwerp, Letters October 28, 1863, Van Antwerp, William W., 1833–1887, Bentley Historical Library, University of Michigan; Frank L. Klement, editor, "I Whipped Six Texans: A Civil War Letter of an Ohio Soldier," *Ohio History*, Vol. 73 (Summer. 1964: 180–182), 182; James Wiswell, Letter October 8, 1863, James Wiswell Letters, RUB Bay 0035:06. Rubenstein Library, Duke University.

16. Robert Mitchell, Letter to James Garfield, October 3, 1863, Letters sent by chief of cavalry, RG 393, Entry 2460, NARA; John W. DuBose, *General Joseph Wheeler and the Army of Tennessee* (New York: The Neale Publishing Co., 1912), 208–209; Thomas W. Cutrer, *Our Trust is in the God of Battles*, 203; Wilbur F. Mims, *War History of the Prattville Dragoons* (Prattville, Alabama: n.p., n.d.), 10–11; Jesse Hyde, Diary entry October 2, 1863, Kentucky Historical Society, Jesse Hyde Diary, SC 1274, Frankfort; Aaron Aster, *Civil War along Tennessee's Cumberland Plateau* (Charleston: History Press, 2015), 107.

17. G. W. Baum, Diary October 2, 1863, Book 10, M 674 B1 F3, Baum diaries, Indiana Historical Society, Indianapolis; John T. Young, Letter November 20, 1863, Walter King Hoover Papers, Civil War Collection Box 2, folder 11, Tennessee State Library and Archives, Nashville.

18. E. B. Quiner, "Regimental History, First Cavalry," In *The Military History of Wisconsin* (Chicago, Clarke & Co., Publishers, 1866), 889; Robert Merrill, "October 2, 1863," *Robert Sidney Merrill, Co. K. 1st Wis. Cav.* (Cedarsburg, WI.: MSG Publishing, 1995); Edward McCook Report October 23, 1863, RG 393, Number 2527, Letters Sent First Cavalry Division, NARA.

19. G. W. Baum, Diary October 2, 1863; Edward McCook, Letter October 3, 1863, RG 393, Number 2527, Letters Sent First Cavalry Division, NARA; Jonathan Pratt, Letter October 3, 1863, RG 393, Number 2527, Letters Sent First Cavalry Division, NARA; M. C. Meigs, *Official Records*, Series 1, Vol. 30, Part 4, 58–59; Thomas McCahan, Diary, October 3, 1863, Thomas McCahan Papers (Am. 6092) Historical Society of Pennsylvania, Philadelphia; Wesley M. Pirkle, "Major General George Crook's Use Of Counterinsurgency Compound Warfare During the Great Sioux War 1876–77," Master's thesis, U.S. Army Command and General Staff College, Fort Leavenworth, KS, 2008, 9–11.

20. George Crook, *Official Records*, Series 1, Vol. 30, Part 2, 684–685.

21. Henry Albert Potter, Entry Diary October 3, 1863. Henry Albert Potter papers, 1862–1908, Bentley Historical Library, University of Michigan, Ann Arbor, Michigan; Robert Burns, Letter, October 30, 1863, Robert Burns Letterbook, MSS M642, Minnesota Historical Society, St. Paul, MN.; Abram Miller, *Official Records*, Series 1, Vol. 30, Part 2, 693.

22. Alva Griest, Diary entry October 4, 1863, *Three Years in Dixie: Personal Adventures, Scenes and Incidents of the March—The Journal of Alva C. Griest*, Journal Entry, Alva Greist Collection, William Henry Smith Memorial Library, Indiana Historical Society, Indianapolis, Indiana; Henry Albert Potter, Entry Diary October 3, 1863. Henry Albert Potter papers, 1862–1908, Bentley Historical Library, University of Michigan, Ann Arbor, Michigan; George Crook, *Official Records*, Series 1, Vol. 30, Part 2, 685; Joseph Wheeler, *Official Records*, Series 1, Vol. 30, Part 2, 723.

23. W. L. Curry, *Four Years in the Saddle: History of First Regiment Ohio Volunteer Cavalry* (Columbus:

Champlin Printing Co., 1898), 136; Lucien Wulsin, *The Fourth Regiment Ohio Veteran Volunteer Cavalry* (Cincinnati: Fourth Ohio Volunteer Cavalry Association, 1912), 40.

24. G. W. Baum, Diary October 4, 1863; Joseph Wheeler, *Official Records*, Series 1, Vol. 30, Part 2, 724.

25. Robert Burns, Letter October 30, 1863; Eli Long, Autobiography, Eli Long Papers, United States Army Heritage and Education Center, Carlisle, PA; "Military Synopsis of the Military Career," pamphlet, no author, no date, Eli Long Papers, United States Army Heritage and Education Center, Carlisle, PA; W. L. Curry, *Four Years in the Saddle*, 137; George Crook, *Official Records*, Series 1, Vol. 30, Part 2, 685–686; W. C. Dodson, *Campaigns of Wheeler and his Cavalry, 1862–1865* (Atlanta: Hudgins Publishing Co., 1899), 124; Henry Campbell, Diary Entry, October 4, 1863, *Three Years in the Saddle: A Diary of the Civil War* (Unpublished, n.d.), Wabash College, Crawfordsville, Indiana; Robert H. G. Minty Court Martial Case File, 1864, Case Number NN-1210, NARA, Washington.

26. W. L. Curry, "The Raid of the Confederate Cavalry through Central Tennessee, October 1863," 9–10.

27. Robert Burns, Letter October 30, 1863; W. L. Curry, *Four Years in the Saddle*, 137; W. L. Curry, "The Raid of the Confederate Cavalry through Central Tennessee, October 1863," 9–10; W. L. Curry, "The Raid of the Confederate Cavalry through Central Tennessee," *Journal of the United States Cavalry Association*, Vol. 19 (1908/1909), 823; Trumbull D. Griffin, Typeset document, B241: Papers of Trumbull Dorrance Griffin (ca. 1836–1912), 1862–1911, Missouri Historical Museum, St. Louis, MO.

28. G. W. Baum, Diary October 5, 1863; W. L. Curry, *Four Years in the Saddle*, 137; James Hagan, "3rd Alabama Cavalry," SG024911, Alabama Department of History and Archives, Montgomery; Joseph Wheeler, *Official Records*, Series 1, Vol. 30, Part 2, 724; George Crook, *Official Records*, Series 1, Vol. 30, Part 2, 686.

29. W. L. Curry, "The Raid of the Confederate Cavalry through Central Tennessee," 12.

30. Robert H. G. Minty Court Martial Case File, 1864, Case Number NN-1210, NARA, Washington.

31. George Healy, Letter October 15, 1863, George Healy Papers (Box 006, Folder 22), State Historical Society of Iowa, Des Moines; Charles Alley, Diary October 6, 1863, Charles Alley Diary 1861–1865, Western History Collection, University of Oklahoma, Norman; William H. Hardie, *Brothers in Arms: The Hardie Family in the Civil War* (Mobile, Alabama: Thornhill Foundation, 1994, 1998), n.p.; Edward Walter Letter, November 19, 1863, McEwen Family Papers A 269, Missouri Historical Museum. Special Collections, St. Louis, Missouri; Robert Mitchell letter to Garfield October 7, 1863, Letters sent by Chief of Cavalry, RG 393, Entry 2460, NARA; Eugene Marshall, Diary entry October 6, 1863, Eugene Marshall Papers, RL.00850, David M. Rubenstein Rare Book & Manuscript Library, Duke University.

32. Joseph Wheeler, *Official Records*, Series 1, Vol. 30, Part 2, 724.

33. John W. Rowell, *Yankee Cavalrymen* (Knoxville: University of Tennessee Press, 1971), 153; Michael Brown, McCook Report, October 23, 1863, Michael Brown Letters, Civil War Collection, United States Army Heritage and Education Center; Robert Mitchell, *Official Records*, Series 1, Vol. 30, Part 2, 670.

34. George Crook, *Official Records*, Series 1, Vol. 30, Part 2, 686; Thomas Crofts, *History of the Service of the Third Ohio Veteran Volunteer Cavalry* (Toledo: Stoneman Press, 1910), 114; Whitelaw Reid, *Ohio in the War: Her Statesmen, Her Generals, and Soldiers*, Vol. I (New York: Moore, Wilstach & Baldwin: 1868), 861; John Stutsman, Letter November 10, 1863, Civil War Times Illustrated Collection, USAHEC, Carlisle, Pennsylvania.

35. George Crook, *Official Records*, Series 1, Vol. 30, Part 2, 686–687; *Historical Sketch of the Chicago Board of Trade Battery: Horse Artillery Illinois Volunteers* (Chicago: The Henneberry Company Printers, 1902), 26; *Sacramento Daily Union*, "Wheeler's Raid Through Tennessee," November 16, 1863, 5.

36. R. F. Bunting, Undated (1863–1865) biography of John A. Wharton, Wharton, John Austin Papers, 1862–1866, Accession Number, 25–0567, Galveston and Texas History Center, Rosenberg Library, Galveston, TX, 10; Alva Griest, Diary October, 1863; Henry Campbell, Diary Entry, October 7, 1863, *Three Years in the Saddle: A Diary of the Civil War*, Unpublished (n.d.), Wabash College, Crawfordsville, Indiana; George Hodge, *Official Records*, Series 1, Vol. 30, Part 2, 726.

37. Abram Miller, *Official Records*, Series 1, Vol. 30, Part 2, 694; George Crook, *Official Records*, Series 1, Vol. 30, Part 2, 686–687.

38. Thomas W. Cutrer, *Our Trust is in the God of Battles*, 212; Benjamin Franklin Batchelor and George Batchelor, *Batchelor-Turner Letters, 1861–1864: Written by Two of Terry's Texas Rangers*, H. J. H. Rugeley, editor (Austin: The Streck Company, 1961), 71; R. F. Bunting, "John A. Wharton," 11.

39. J. K. P. Blackburn, *Reminiscences of the Terry Rangers* (n. p.: University of Texas, 1919), 46; George Hodge, *Official Records*, Series 1, Vol. 30, Part 2, 726; George Crook, *Official Records*, Series 1, Vol. 30, Part 2, 686–687; Samuel J. Martin, *General Braxton Bragg, CSA* (Jefferson, NC: McFarland, 2011), 341.

40. Robert Burns, Letter October 30, 1863; George Crook, *Official Records*, Series 1, Vol. 30, Part 2, 686–687.

41. Robert H. G. Minty Court Martial Case File, 1864, Case Number NN-1210, NARA, Washington.

42. *Ibid.*

43. *Ibid.*

44. *Ibid.*

45. Robert Burns, Letter October 30, 1863; George Crook, Report Nov. 5, 1863, Second Cavalry Brigade Letters sent, RG 393, Number 2500, NARA, Washington; Thomas Stutsman, Letter to friend, Nov. 10, 1863, Civil War Times Illustrated Collection, United States Army and Heritage Center; George Kryder, Letter to Wife November 2, 1863, George Kryder Papers MS 163, Bowling Green State University, Special Collections, Bowling Green Ohio; Edward Walter Letter, November 19, 1863, McEwen Family Papers A 269, Missouri Historical Museum. Special Collections, St. Louis, Missouri; A. A. Stuart, "Colonel William W. Lowe," In *Iowa Colonels and Regiments Being a History of Iowa Regiments* (Des Moines: Mills & Company, 1865), 621–630; Eugene Marshall, Diary entry October 8, 1863, Eugene Marshall Papers, RL.00850, David M. Rubenstein

Rare Book & Manuscript Library, Duke University; George Healy, October 15, 1863 letter.

46. Charles Alley, Diary October 9, 1863, Charles Alley Diary 1861–1865, Western History Collection, University of Oklahoma; Thomas Crofts, *History of the Service of the Third Ohio Veteran Volunteer Cavalry*, 115; W. R. Carter, *History of the First Regiment of Tennessee Volunteer Cavalry* (Knoxville: Gaut-Ogden Co., Printers and Binders, 1902), 103; Clark G. Reynolds, "The Civil and Indian War Diaries of Eugene Marshall, Minnesota Volunteer," Master's Thesis, Duke University, Durham, NC., 1963.

47. John Weatherred, "The Wartime Diary of John Weatherred," private collection of Jack Masters, Gallatin, TN.; William W. Lowe, *Official Records*, Series 1, Vol. 30, Part 2, 690.

48. George Healy, October 15, 1863 letter; Henry Albert Potter, Entry Diary October 9, 1863; Isaac Botsford, "Narrative of Brackett's Battalion of Cavalry," In *Minnesota in the Civil and Indian Wars, 1861–1865*, Minnesota Legislature, eds. (St. Paul: Pioneer Press Company, 1890), 579.

49. Joseph Wheeler, *Official Records*, Series 1, Vol. 30, Part 2, 725.

50. Phillip D. Roddey, *Official Records*, Series 1, Vol. 30, Part 2, 729.

51. Robert Mitchell, *Official Records*, Series 1, Vol. 30, Part 2, 673.

52. G. W. Baum, Diary October 9, 1863; Robert Mitchell, *Official Records*, Series 1, Vol. 30, Part 2, 673; Thomas Jordan, Letter to Wife October 25, 1863, Thomas J. Jordan Civil War Letters [2066] Box Number: 1, Folder 13, Historical Society of Pennsylvania, Philadelphia, Pennsylvania; Charles Alley, Diary October 9, 1863, Tennessee State Library and Archives, Nashville, Tennessee; Edwin Stuart, "The Federal Cavalry with the Armies in the West: 1861–1865," *Journal of the United States Cavalry Association*, Vol. XVII (October 1906), No. 62: 195–259.

53. W. L. Curry, *Fours in the Saddle*, 141; Robert Mitchell, *Official Records*, Series 1, Vol. 30, Part 2, 673.

54. Robert Burns, Letter October 30, 1863; Paul Magid, *George Crook: From the Redwoods to Appomattox* (Norman: University of Oklahoma Press, 2011), 167–171; James Larson, *Sergeant Larson, 4th Cavalry* (San Antonio: Southern Literary Institute, 1935), 206.

55. Horace McLean, Letter October 20, 1863, McLean, Horace letters (1862–1864), Auburn University, Auburn; Dan Butterfield, *Official Records*, Series 1, Vol. 30, Part 2, 714; Albert Woodcock, Letter October 11, 1863, Woodcock (Albert) Papers, 1863–1865 1994.043, Pearce Civil War Collection, Navarro College, Corsicana; John Henry Hammond, Letter to McClellan December 13, 1863, Hammond (John Henry) Papers, 1863 1996.029, Pearce Civil War Collection, Navarro College, Corsicana.

56. Thomas Crofts, *History of the Service of the Third Ohio Veteran Volunteer Cavalry*, 115; Peter Cozzens, *The Shipwreck of Their Hopes: The Battle for Chattanooga* (Urbana and Chicago University of Illinois Press, 1994), 19, 34–35; James Arthur Schaefer, "The Tactical And Strategic Evolution Of Cavalry During The American Civil War," Ph. D. Dissertation, The University of Toledo, 1982, 173; Henry Campbell, *The Years in the Saddle*, news clipping, 124; Edward Longacre, *A Soldier to the Last*, 123; George Walsh, *Those Damn Horse Soldiers* (New York: A Tom Doherty Associates Book, 2006), 235.

57. William Rosecrans, *Official Records*, Series 1, Vol. 30, Part 4, 114.

58. John W. Harris, Letter October 13, 1863 to George, Confederate Collection, Box 9, Folder 22, Civil War Collection, Tennessee State Library.

Chapter Twelve

1. David Stanley, *An American General: The Memoirs of David Sloan Stanley*, Samuel W. Fordyce IV, ed. (Santa Barbara, CA: The Narrative Press, 2004), 171; James Lee McDonough, *Chattanooga: A Death Grip on the Confederacy* (Knoxville: University of Tennessee Press, 1984), 48–49.

2. Allan Peskin, *Garfield: A Biography* (Kent, OH: Kent State University Press, 1999), 212.

3. Henry Boynton, *Chattanooga and Chickamauga. Reprint of Gen. H. V. Boynton's Letters to the Cincinnati Commercial Gazette, August, 1888* (Washington, D.C.: G.R. Gray, Printer, 1891), 21; Steven E. Woodworth, *Six Armies in Tennessee: The Chickamauga and Chattanooga Campaigns* (Lincoln and London: University of Nebraska Press, 1998), 136; Henry Haymond, Letter to Pa September 24, 1863, Haymond (Henry) Papers, 1863, 2001.241, Pearce Civil War Collection, Navarro College, Corsicana; Henry Halleck, *Official Records*, Series 1, Vol. 29, Part 2, 277.

4. Robert Mitchell, *Official Records*, Series 1, Vol. 30, Part 4, 371, 462.

5. William McMichael, *Official Records*, Series 1, Vol. 31, Part 3, 126; David Stanley, *An American General*, 171; Benson Bobrick, *Master of War: The Life of George H. Thomas* (New York: Simon and Schuster, 2009), 38; William H. Sinclair, Letter to General, December 1, 1864, Record Group 94, General Records of the Adjutant General's Office, Records relating to Wars, Civil War, 1861–1865, Staff Papers, NARA, Washington, D.C.

6. David Stanley, *An American General*, 172; David A. Powell, *The Chickamauga Campaign—Barren Victory: The Retreat into Chattanooga* (New York and California: Savas Beatie, 2016), 155.

7. Philip J. Baker Jr., "Command and Control Mechanisms in the Chickamauga Campaign: The Union Experience," U.S. Army Command and General Staff College, Fort Leavenworth, Kansas, 1989, 117.

8. John Londa, "The Role of Union Cavalry during the Chickamauga Campaign," Master's Thesis, Command and General Staff College, Fort Leavenworth, Kansas, 1991, 103.

9. William Lamers, *The Edge of Glory: A Biography of General William S. Rosecrans, U.S.A.* (New York: Harcourt, Brace & World, Inc., 1961), 309.

10. D. H. Hill, "Chickamauga: The Great Battle of the West," In *Battles and Leaders in the Civil War, Vol. III* (New York: The Century Co., 1888), 644.

11. Jerry Morelock, "Ride to the River of Death: Cavalry Operations in the Chickamauga Campaign," *Military Review*, Vol. LXIV (October 1984), No. 10: 2–21, 18.

Bibliography

Primary Sources—Published

Batchelor, Benjamin Franklin, and George Batchelor. *Batchelor-Turner Letters, 1861–1864: Written by Two of Terry's Texas Rangers*, H. J. H. Rugeley, editor. Austin: The Streck Company, 1961.

Beatty, John. *The Citizen Soldier: The Memoirs of a Civil War Volunteer*. Lincoln and London: Bison Books University of Nebraska Press, 1998.

Chadwick, Mary Jane. *Incidents of the War: The Civil War Journal of Mary Jane Chadwick*, Nancy Rohr, ed. Huntsville: SilverThread Publishing, 2005.

Curry, W. L. Diary, In W. L. Curry. *Four Years in the Saddle: History of First Regiment Ohio Volunteer Cavalry*. Columbus: Champlin Printing Co., 1898.

Cutrer, Thomas W. *Our Trust is in the God of Battles: The Civil War Letters of Robert Franklin Bunting, Chaplain, Terry's Texas Rangers*. Knoxville: University of Tennessee Press, 2006.

Davis, Jefferson. *Papers of Jefferson Davis*, Volume 8, Linda Lasswell Crist, Mary Seaton Dix, and Kenneth H. Williams, eds. Baton Rouge and London: Louisiana State University Press, 1995.

Dodd, Ephraim. *Diary of Ephraim Shelby Dodd*. Austin: Press of E. L. Steck, 1914.

Fremantle, Arthur. *Three Months in the Southern States, April-June, 1863*. New York: John Bradburn Co., 1864.

Graf, Leroy and Ralph Haskins, editors, "Telegram from Rosecrans," In *Papers of Andrew Johnson*, Vol. 6. Knoxville: University of Tennessee Press, 1983.

Love, James. *My Dear Molly: The Civil War Letters of Captain James Love*, M. W. Kodner, ed. St. Louis: Missouri History Museum, 2015.

Mayfield, Leroy S. "Letters and Diaries of Leroy S. Mayfield," *Indiana Magazine of History*, Vol. 39, no. 2 (June 1943): 144–191.

Merrill, Robert. *Robert Sidney Merrill, Co. K. 1st Wis. Cav.* Cedarsburg, WI.: MSG Publishing, 1995.

Miller, George Knox. *An Uncompromising Secessionist: The Civil War of George Knox Miller, Eighth (Wade's) Confederate Cavalry*, edited by Richard M. McMurry. Tuscaloosa: University of Alabama Press, 2007.

Mosman, Chesley A. *The Rough Side of War: The Civil War Journal of Chesley A. Mosman*, Arnold Gates, ed. Garden City, NY: The Basin Publishing Co., 1987.

Moyer, Franklin F. *Journal and Letters of Franklin F. Moyer*, Robert H. Wieser, editor. Dayton: Robert Wieser Publisher, 2008.

Williams, Thomas. Diary, In John W. Rowell. *Yankee Cavalrymen*. Knoxville: University of Tennessee Press, 1971.

Smith, Benjamin T. *Private Smith's Journal: Recollections of the Late War*. Chicago, R. R. Donnelley & Sons, Co., 1963.

Williams, John. *Leaves of a Trooper's Dairy*. Philadelphia: Published by Author, 1869.

Primary Sources—Unpublished

Alabama Department of Archives and History, Montgomery
James Hagan Papers

American Civil War Museum, Richmond, Va.
Sgt. Tucker St. Joseph Randolph, Letters, Co. F, 21st Virginia Infantry and staff of Gen. John Pegram, May 1861–May 1864

Auburn University—Special Collections and Archives
McLean, Horace letters (1862–1864)

Bowling Green State University, William T. Jerome Library
Daniel Prickitt, Diary
George Kryder Letters
James H. M. Perry Papers
Isaac Skillman, Diary

Chattanooga—Hamilton Bicentennial Library
Thomas W. Davis, Diary

Cincinnati Historical Society, Cincinnati Museum Center
William E. Crane, "William E. Crane's Daily Journal of Life in the Field during the War of the Rebellion"

Colorado Springs Pioneers Museum
James Weir Diary, in William Palmer Papers

Duke University, David M. Rubenstein Rare Book & Manuscript Library
Eugene Marshall, Diary
Benjamin Nourse, Diary
Elisha Peterson, Letters
Charles Sowle, Letters
James Wiswell, Letters

Emory University, Manuscript, Archives, and Rare Book Library
W. B. Corbitt, Civil War-era documents (1860–1865)

Filson Historical Society, Louisville, Kentucky
C. H. Sowle, unpublished, Manuscript C. S.
Elijah Watts, "Biographical Note" and "Chickamauga Campaign" (hand written account, undated), Watts, Elijah S., Papers. 1861–1907, Mss./A/W349

Galveston and Texas History Center, Rosenberg Library
John Austin Wharton Papers, 1862–1866, Accession Number, 25-0567

Gettysburg College, Musselman Library
George C. Wynkoop Papers, MS—076

The Gilder Lehrman Institute of American History, New York City
Collection of Edward W. Amsden
George Clark Collection

Historical Society of Pennsylvania, Philadelphia
Thomas J. Jordan Civil War Letters
Thomas McCahan Papers

Indiana Historical Society, Indianapolis
George Baum Diaries, M 674 B1 F3
Homer C. Carpenter, Collection M 694 OM 369
I. R. Conwell, Diary, S2753, F3
Alva Griest, *The Journal of Alva C. Griest*
Daniel Waite Howe, MS 148

Kalamazoo College, Kalamazoo
Eugene Bronson Collection

Kentucky Historical Society
Jesse Hyde Diary, SC 1274

Masters, Jack—Personal Collection
John Weatherred, "The Wartime Diary of John Weatherred," (private collection of Jack Masters, Gallatin, TN.)

Michigan Historical Society, Lansing, Michigan
Henry Albert Potter Collection, Diary and Letters. MS 91–480, Accession Box 461 Folder 2
Frank L. Vogel Collection, Diary, MS 67-111, Accession Box 12 Folder 6

Michigan State University Archives & Historical Collections, Michigan State University
Othniel Gooding Letters (c.00275)
John McLain Diary and Papers (c.00111)

Minnesota Historical Society, St. Paul, Minnesota
Robert Burns Letters (Mss. M642)

Missouri History Museum, St. Louis
Braxton Bragg Papers, Collection: A0164
Benjamin Burke, *A Terry's Ranger Write Home: Letters of Pvt. Benjamin F. Burke*
Trumbull D. Griffin Papers, B241
James Edwin Love Papers (1859–1865) ARC A0940
McEwen Family Papers A 269

Missouri Historical Society, Columbia, Missouri
Colman-Hayter Family Papers, C-84, Folder 6, Missouri Historical Society

Nashville, Tennessee Public Library, Special Collections
Peter J. Williamson, Letters

National Archives Records Administration, Washington, D. C. (Nara)
RG 94—Regimental Books—Orders and correspondence, and morning reports:
2nd Indiana Cavalry
3rd Indiana Cavalry
4th Indiana Cavalry
5th Iowa Cavalry
2nd Kentucky Cavalry
4th Kentucky Cavalry
5th Kentucky Cavalry
6th Kentucky Cavalry
7th Kentucky Cavalry
2nd Michigan Cavalry; (Journal of the 2nd Michigan Cavalry)
4th Michigan Cavalry
1st Ohio Cavalry
3rd Ohio Cavalry
4th Ohio Cavalry
10th Ohio Cavalry
7th Pennsylvania Cavalry
9th Pennsylvania Cavalry
2nd Tennessee Cavalry
5th Tennessee Cavalry
General Records of the Adjutant General's Office, Staff Papers—William Sinclair
RG 153:
Adjutant General's Office, Court Martial Case Files, 1809–1854:
William T. Hoblitzell Court Martial Case Files, 1864, Case Number NN-2774
William T. Hoblitzell Court Martial, 1864, Case Number NN-3269
Robert H. G. Minty Court Martial Case File, 1864, Case Number NN-1210
RG 391—Regimental Books:
Orders and correspondence, and morning reports 4th U. S. Cavalry
RG 393 Part 1, E960, Volume 230 dc, Army of the Cumberland—Chickamauga Reports:
J. P. Brownlow Reports
Campbell Reports
George Crook Reports
Edward McCook Reports
Robert Mitchell Reports
D. Ray Reports
R. M. Russell Reports
L. Scranton Reports

Cavalry Communications
General Orders, First Cavalry Division, RG 393, Number 2533
Letters and Telegrams Received, Cavalry Corps, RG 393, Number 2468
Letters Sent, First Cavalry Division, RG 393, Number 2527
Letters Sent, Second Cavalry Division, RG 393, Number 2500
Letters Sent by Chief of Cavalry, RG 393, entry 2460
Special Orders, Chief of Cavalry, RG 393, entry 2473
Telegrams sent by Chief of Cavalry, RG 393, Entry 2463

Navarro College, Pearce Civil War Collection
Hammond (John Henry) Papers
Haymond (John) Papers
Woodcock (Albert) Papers

Newberry Independent Research Library, Chicago
John Fleming Letters, Manuscript Midwest

Ohio Historical Society
Correspondence to the Governor and Adjutant General, 1861–1866
Nathan Finegan Papers, 1858–1911

John Large Letters, VFM 455
James Thomson Papers, 1861–1865

State Historical Society of Iowa, Des Moines
George Healy Papers (Box 006, Folder 22)

State Historical Society of Wisconsin, Madison
Charles Perry Goodrich, "Letters from Home from the First Wisconsin Cavalry," Richard N. Larson editor (Madison: State Historical Society of Wisconsin, not published)
Quiner's Scrapbook, Volume 10, Correspondence, Mss. 600; WIHVQ500-A, Quiner Scrapbooks: Correspondence of the Wisconsin Volunteers, 1861–1865.

Stones River National Park, Technical Information Center, Murfreesboro, Tn.
Gerould, Otis Gibson, Diary
Civil War Diary of Pvt. Jesse Leeper
Elbert Squires Letters
John Newton Smith Letters

Tennessee State Library And Archives, Nashville, Tennessee
William Gibbs Allen, Confederate Collection, Box 12, Folder 1
Charles Alley, Diary, E601.A4
John W. Harris, Confederate Collection, Box 9, Folder 22
Walter King Hoover, Union Collection, Box 2, Folder 11
Terry H. Cahal, Confederate Collection, Box 8, Folder 17
William E. Sloan, Diary, Confederate Collection, Box 7, Folder 7
West Walker Letters, Confederate Collection, Box 11, Folder 35

United States Army Heritage and Education Center (USAHEC)
Brandon Collection of Civil War Letters, Civil War Collection
Michael Brown Letters, Civil War Collection
Eli Long, Diary and Papers 1855–1892, Civil War Collection
Paul Hersh Papers, Civil War Collection
Robert Minty Papers, Civil War Collection
Frances W. Reed Papers, Civil War Times Illustrated Collection
Baxter Smith, "8th Tennessee Cavalry Regiment," Civil War Collection
Stanley, Wright, West Papers
John Stutsman, Letters, Civil War Times Illustrated Collection

University of California, Los Angeles, Department of Special Collections
William S. Rosecrans Papers: 1810–1920, Collection 663

University of Georgia, Hargett Rare Book and Manuscript Library
William Joseph and Nancy Wallis Short Family Papers, MS 3863

University of Michigan, Bentley Historical Library
William W. Van Antwerp papers
Morris Fitch Papers
D. L. Haines, *Record of the Fourth Michigan Cavalry*
Henry Mortimer Hempstead Papers

Elisha Mix Papers
Richard Robbins Papers
Slayton Family Papers
James W. Sligh Papers

University of Mississippi, Archives and Special Collections, J. D. Williams Library
William Sylvester Dillon, Diary

University of North Carolina, Louis Round Wilson Special Collections Library
D. Coleman Diary, 1863–1864, Collection Number: 03317-z
Isaac Barton Ulmer papers, 1838–1929, Collection Number: 01834
Thomas B. Wilson reminiscences, 1904, Collection Number: 01736-z

University of Notre Dame Archives (Unda), Notre Dame
Conyngham, David Power, Papers (CON)

University of Oklahoma, Norman
Charles Alley, Diary 1861–1865, Western History Collection

University of Tennessee, Knoxville
Joseph Oliver Freeman Letter, MS 0806
Edward Summers Letter, MS 2714
Julius E. Thomas Collection, MS 2720

University of Texas at Austin, Briscoe Center for American History
Crimmins (Martin Lalor) Papers, David S. Stanley, "David Stanley Diary, United States 2nd Dragoons of a March from Fort Smith, Arkansas, to San Diego, California, made in 1853," Accession No.:1936; 1950.

Wabash College, Crawsfordsville, In
Henry Campbell, Diary, "Three Years in the Saddle"

Western Michigan University, Kalamazoo, Michigan
Augustus L. Yenner, Papers and Diary (1837–1924)

Western Reserve Historical Society
George Brent, Journal, Braxton Bragg Papers, Ms 2000

Regimental Histories

Andes, John and Will McTeer. *Loyal Mountain Troops, The Second and Third Tennessee Volunteer Cavalry.* Maryville, Tennessee: Blount County Genealogical and Historical Society, 1992.
Bailey, Chester. *The Mansfield Men in the Seventh Pennsylvania Cavalry, Eighth Regiment.* Mansfield, Pennsylvania: Published by Author, 1986.
Carter, W. R. *History of the First Regiment of Tennessee Volunteer Cavalry.* Knoxville: Gaut-Ogden Co., Printers and Binders, 1902.
Cavender, Michael Bower. *The First Georgia Cavalry in the Civil War: A History and Roster.* Jefferson, NC: McFarland Publishing, 2016.
Crofts, Thomas. *History of the Service of the Third Ohio Veteran Volunteer Cavalry.* Toledo: Stoneman Press, 1910.
Curry, W. L. *Four Years in the Saddle: History of the First Regiment Ohio Volunteer Cavalry.* Columbus, Ohio: Champlin Printing Company, 1898.
Dornblaser, T. F. *Sabre Strokes of the Pennsylvania Dragoons in the War of 1861–1865; Interspersed with Per-*

sonal Reminiscences. Philadelphia: Lutheran Publication Society, 1884.
Guild, George. *Brief Narrative of the Fourth Tennessee Cavalry Regiment.* Nashville: n.p., 1913.
Herberich, John L. *Masters of the Field: The Fourth United States Cavalry in the Civil War.* Atglen, PA; Schiffer Publishing Co., 2015.
Historical Sketch of the Chicago Board of Trade Battery. Chicago: The Henneberry Co. Publishers, 1902.
Hoffman, Mark. *My Brave Mechanics: The First Michigan Engineers and their Civil War.* Detroit: Wayne State University Press, 2007.
Jeffries, C. C. *Terry's Rangers.* New York: Vantage Press, 1961.
A Military Record of Battery D, First Ohio Veteran Volunteers, Light Artillery. Oil City, Pennsylvania: The Derrick Publishing Co., 1908.
Pape-Findley, Nancy. *The Invincibles: The Story of Fourth Ohio Veteran Volunteer Cavalry.* Tecumseh, Michigan: Blood Road Publishing: 2002.
Pickerill, W. N. *History of the Third Indiana Cavalry.* Indianapolis: Aetna Printing Co., 1906.
Poole, John Randolph. *Cracker Cavaliers: The 2nd Georgia Cavalry under Wheeler and Forrest.* Macon, Georgia: Mercer University Press, 2000.
Reid, Richard. *Fourth Indiana Cavalry Regiment: A History.* Fordsville, Kentucky: Sandefur Offset Printing, undated.
Reiff, J. C., ed. *History of the Fifteenth Pennsylvania Volunteer Cavalry.* Philadelphia, Pennsylvania: Society of the Fifteenth Pennsylvania Cavalry, 1906.
Rowell, John W. *Yankee Cavalrymen.* Knoxville: University of Tennessee Press, 1971.
Sipes, William. *History and Roster of the 7th Pennsylvania Veteran Volunteers.* Pottsville: Miners' Journal Print, 1905.
Stevens, Robert. *The Bracken Rangers: Company K, 28th Regiment, 1st Indiana Cavalry.* Miami: Three Stars Press, 2011.
Tarrant, Sergeant E. *Wild Riders of the First Kentucky Cavalry: A History of the Regiment, in the Great War of the Rebellion 1861–1865.* Louisville: R. H. Carothers Press, 1894.
Thatcher, Marshall P. *A Hundred Battles in the West: The Second Michigan Cavalry.* Detroit: L. F. Kilroy, Printer, 1884.
Vale, Joseph. *Minty and the Cavalry: A History of Cavalry Campaigns in the Western Armies.* Harrisburg, Pennsylvania: Edwin K. Myers, Printer and Binder, 1886.
Weatherbee, F. W. *The 5th (1st Middle) Tennessee Cavalry Regiment, USA.* Carrollton, Mississippi: Pioneer Publishing Co., 1992.
Wulsin, Lucien. *The Fourth Regiment Ohio Veteran Volunteer Cavalry.* Cincinnati: Fourth Ohio Volunteer Cavalry Association, 1912.

Journal Articles

Anderson, Edward L. "The Truth about Chickamauga," *The Journal of the United States Cavalry Association,* Vol. 13 (1912), Number 92: 185–206.
Biggs, Gregg. "The Battle of Shelbyville: Turning Point for the Union Cavalry in the West." *Blue & Gray,* Volume XXVII (2010), Number 1: 45.
Bourasaw, Noel V. "Arthur C. Seidell, Civil War Veteran and Builder in Old Woolley." *Skagit River Journal of History & Folklore,* 2000.
Bradley, Michael. "Tullahoma: The Wrongly Forgotten Campaign," *Blue & Gray,* Volume XXVII (2010), Number 1: 49.
Bradley, Michael. "Varying Results of Cavalry Fighting: Western Flank vs. Eastern Flank," *Blue and Grey,* Volume XXVII (2010), Number 1: 21.
Brooksher, William and David Snider. "The War Child Rides: Joe Wheeler at Stones River," *Civil War Times Illustrated,* Vol. 14 (1976): 4–10.
Clark, William Allen. "Please Send Stamps: The Civil War Letters of William Allen Clark," Part IV, Edited by Margaret Black Taturn, *Indiana Magazine of History,* XCI (December, 1995): 288–319.
Curry, W. L. "The Raid of the Confederate Cavalry through Central Tennessee," *Journal of the United States Cavalry Association,* Volume 19 (1908/1909): 815–835.
Dwyer, Christopher S. "Raiding Strategy: As Applied by the Western Confederate Cavalry in the American Civil War," *The Journal of Military History,* 63 (April 1999): 263–281.
Dyer, J. P. "The Civil War Career of General Joseph Wheeler," *The Georgia Historical Quarterly,* Vol. 19 (Mar. 1935), No. 1: 17–46.
East, Earnest. "Lincoln's Russian General," *Journal of the Illinois State Historical Society,* Vol. 52 (1959), No. 1: 106–122.
Foreman, Carolyn Thomas. "The Armstrongs Of Indian Territory: General Frank Crawford Armstrong, Part III," *Chronicles of Oklahoma,* Vol. 31 (1953), No. 1: 56–65.
Groce, William Wharton. "Major General John A. Wharton," *The Southwestern Historical Quarterly,* Vol. 19 (Jan., 1916), No. 3: 271–278.
Hill, D. H. "Chickamauga-The Great Battle of the West," *The Century Illustrated Monthly Magazine,* Vol. 33 (April, 1887) No. 6: 937–962.
Martin, Will T. "A Defence of Bragg's Conduct at Chickamauga," *Southern Historical Society Papers,* Vol. 11 (January—December, 1883): 203–204.
Morelock, Jerry. "Ride to the River of Death: Cavalry Operations in the Chickamauga Campaign," *Military Review,* Volume LXIV (October 1984), No. 10: 2–21.
Phillips, Gervase, "Warhorses of the U. S. Civil War," *History Today,* Vol. 55 (Dec. 2005), Issue 12: 10–17.
Polk, W. M. "General Bragg and the Chickamauga Campaign," *Southern Historical Society Papers,* Vol. 12 (January—December 1884): 378–390.
Ramsdell, Charles W. "General Robert E. Lee's Horse Supply, 1862–1865." *The American Historical Review,* 35 (July 1930): 758–777.
Rosecrans, W. S. "The Campaign for Chattanooga," *The Century Illustrated Monthly Magazine,* Volume 34 (1887):129–135.
Schiller, Laurence D. "Of Sabers and Carbines: The Emergence of the Federal Dragoon." *The Papers of the Blue & Gay Education Society,* Monograph Number 11, August 1, 2001.
Shelly, Joseph Frederick. "The Shelly Papers," Fanny Anderson, ed. *Indiana Magazine of History,* 44 (June 1948), No. 2: 181–198.
Starr, Stephen Z. "The Third Ohio Volunteer Cavalry:

A View from the Inside," *Ohio History*, Volume 85 (Autumn 1976), Number 4: 306–318.

Stuart, Edwin. "The Federal Cavalry with the Armies in the West: 1861–1865," *Journal of the United States Cavalry Association*, Volume XVII (October 1906), No. 62: 195–259.

Womack, J. K. "Chickamauga As I Saw It," *Confederate Veteran*, Volume XXV (February 1917), No. 2: 74.

Government Documents

United States Census, 1860

Medical and Surgical History of the War of the Rebellion, Washington, 1870.

The War of the Rebellion: A Compilation of the Official Records of the Union and Confederate Armies, Washington, 1880–1901.

Newspapers

Abingdon Virginian
Alexandria Gazette (VA)
Chicago Times
Daily Dispatch (Richmond, VA)
Daily Wabash Express (Terra Haute)
Harper's Weekly
Herald Citizen (Cookeville, TN)
Highland Weekly News (OH)
Knoxville News Sentinel
Milwaukee Journal
Murfreesboro Post
Nashville Daily Press
National Tribune (Washington)
Rome Tri-Weekly Courier (GA)
Sacramento Daily Union
Staunton Spectator (VA)
Vevay Reveille (Vevay, IN)
Washington City Evening Star

Other Sources

Allardice, Bruce S. *Confederate Colonels: A Biographical Register.* Columbia: University of Missouri Press, 2008.

Aster, Aaron. *Civil War along Tennessee's Cumberland Plateau.* Charleston: History Press, 2015.

Baggett, James Alex. *Homegrown Yankees: Tennessee's Union Cavalry in the Civil War.* Baton Rouge: Louisiana State University, 2009.

Baker, Philip J., Jr. "Command and Control Mechanisms in the Chickamauga Campaign: The Union Experience," U.S. Army Command and General Staff College, Fort Leavenworth, Kansas, 1989.

Beck, Brandon. *Streight's Foiled Raid on the Western & Atlantic Railroad.* Charleston, SC: The History Press, 2016.

Belcher, Dennis W. *Cavalry of the Army of the Cumberland.* Jefferson, NC: McFarland, 2016.

Belcher, Dennis W. *General David S. Stanley, USA: A Civil War Biography.* Jefferson, NC: McFarland, 2014.

Belknap, Charles Eugene ed. *History of the Michigan Organizations at Chickamauga, Chattanooga, and Missionary Ridge.* Lansing: Robert Smith Printing Co., 1899.

Bergeron, Paul H. *The Papers of Andrew Johnson: September 1868 to April 1869*, Volume 15. Knoxville: University of Tennessee Press, 1999.

Bergmann, Kurt D. *Brackett's Battalion: Minnesota Cavalry in the Civil War and Dakota War.* St. Paul, Minnesota: Borealis Books, 2004.

Berry, Thomas Franklin. *Four Years with Morgan and Forrest.* Oklahoma City: Harlow-Ratliff Company, 1914.

Bickham, William D. *Rosecrans' Campaign with the Fourteenth Army Corps, of the Army of the Cumberland.* Cincinnati: Moore, Wilstach, Keys & Co., 1863.

Blackburn, J. K. P. *Reminiscences of the Terry Rangers.* n. p.: University of Texas, 1919.

Bobrick, Benson. *Master of War: The Life of George H. Thomas.* New York: Simon & Schuster, 2009.

Boniface, Jonathan J. *The Cavalry Horse and His Pack.* Kansas City: Hudson-Kimberly Publishing Co., 1908.

Botsford, Isaac. "Narrative of Brackett's Battalion of Cavalry," In *Minnesota in the Civil and Indian Wars, 1861–1865*, Minnesota Legislature, editors. St. Paul: Pioneer Press Company, 1890.

Bowers, John. *Chickamauga and Chattanooga: The Battles That Doomed the Confederacy.* New York: HarperCollins Publishers, 1994.

Boynton, Henry B. *Chattanooga and Chickamauga. Reprint of Gen. H. V. Boynton's letters to the Cincinnati Commercial Gazette, August, 1888.* Washington, D.C.: G. R. Gray, Printer, 1891.

Bradley, Michael. *Tullahoma: The 1863 Campaign for the Control of Middle Tennessee.* Shippensburg, Pennsylvania: White Mane Publishing Co., 1999.

Bradley, Michael R. *The Raiding Winter.* Gretna, Louisiana: Pelican Publishing Co., 2013.

Brandt, Robert S. "Lighting and Rain in Middle Tennessee: the Tullahoma Campaign of June-July 1863," In *The Battle of Stones River and the Fight for Middle Tennessee*, Timothy D. Johnson, editor. Nashville: The Tennessee Historical Society, 2012.

Brewer, Richard J. "The Tullahoma Campaign: Operational Insights," Master's Thesis, U.S. Army Command and General Staff College, Leavenworth, KS, 1978.

Brewer, Willis. *Alabama, Her History, Resources, War Record, and Public Men.* Montgomery: Barrett & Brown, Steam Printers and Book Binders, 1872.

Broome, Doyle D. "Intelligence Operations of the Army of the Cumberland During the Tullahoma and Chickamauga Campaigns," Master's Thesis, U.S. Army Command and General Staff College, Leavenworth, KS, 1989.

Brown, John E. "At Headquarters during the Battle of Chickamauga," In *History of the Fifteenth Pennsylvania Volunteer Cavalry*, J. C. Reiff, ed. Philadelphia, Pennsylvania: Society of the Fifteenth Pennsylvania Cavalry, 1906.

Brown, Myers E. *Tennessee's Union Cavalrymen.* Charleston, Portsmouth, San Francisco: Arcadia Publishing Co., 2008.

Cannon, Newton. *The Reminiscences of Newton Cannon: First Sergeant, CSA*, Campbell Brown, editor. Franklin, TN: Carter House Association, 1963.

Carmichael, Peter. *Lee's Young Artillerist: William R. J. Pegram.* Charlottesville: University of Virginia Press, 1995.

Carnahan, James R. "Personal Recollections of Chickamauga" In *Sketches of War History: 1861–1865* Vol. I, Ohio, MOLLUS. Cincinnati, Robert Clarke & Co. 1888.

Carter, Howell. *A Cavalryman's Reminiscences of the Civil War.* New Orleans: American Printing Co., n.d.

Carter, Howell. *A Cavalryman's Reminiscences of the Civil War.* Port Hudson, LA: Old South Books, 1979.

Cisco, Walter Brian. *States Rights Gist: A South Carolina General of the Civil War.* Gretna, LA: Pelican Publishing, 2008.

Colton, William F. "The Chickamauga Campaign," In *History of the Fifteenth Pennsylvania Volunteer Cavalry,* J. C. Reiff, ed. Philadelphia, Pennsylvania: Society of the Fifteenth Pennsylvania Cavalry, 1906.

Commemorative Biographical Encyclopedia of Dauphin County, Pennsylvania. Chambersburg, PA: J. M. Runk & Co., 1896.

Connelly, Thomas L. *Autumn of Glory: The Army of Tennessee 1862–1865.* Baton Rouge: Louisiana State University Press, 1971.

Cox, Christopher. *History of Pennsylvania Civil War Regiments.* Raleigh: Lulu Publishing Co., 2013.

Cozzens, Peter. *The Shipwreck of Their Hopes: The Battle for Chattanooga.* Urbana and Chicago: University of Illinois Press, 1994.

Cozzens, Peter. *This Terrible Sound: The Battle of Chickamauga.* Urbana and Chicago: University of Illinois Press, 1992.

Cozzens, Smith. "Company L on Lookout Mountain," In *History of the Fifteenth Pennsylvania Volunteer Cavalry,* J. C. Reiff, ed. Philadelphia, Pennsylvania: Society of the Fifteenth Pennsylvania Cavalry, 1906.

Cullum, George W. *Biographical Register of the Officers and Graduates of the US Military Academy,* Vol. 2. New York: D. Van Nostrand, 1868–79.

Cullum, George. *Biographical Register of the Officers and Graduates of the U. S. Military Academy, 1841–1867,* Vol. II. New York: D. Van Nostrand, 1868.

Dalessandro, Robert J. "Morale in the Army of the Cumberland During the Tullahoma and Chickamauga Campaigns," Master's Thesis, U.S. Army Command and General Staff College, Leavenworth, KS, 1980.

Daniel, Larry. *Battle of Stones River.* Baton Rouge: Louisiana State University Press, 2012.

Daniel, Larry. *Days of Glory, The Army of the Cumberland 1861–1865.* Baton Rouge: Louisiana State University Press, 2006.

Davison, Eddy W., and Daniel Foxx. *Nathan Bedford Forest: In Search of the Enigma.* Gretna, LA: Pelican Publishing Co., 2007.

Dodson, W. C. *Campaigns of Wheeler and his Cavalry, 1862–1865.* Atlanta: Hudgins Publishing Co., 1899.

Dornblaser, T. F. *My Life Story for Young and Old.* USA: Privately printed, 1930.

DuBose, John W. *General Joseph Wheeler and the Army of Tennessee.* New York: The Neale Publishing Co., 1912.

Duke, Basil. *Morgan's Cavalry.* New York: The Neale Publishing Co., 1909.

Duncan, L. Wallace, and Charles F. Scott, editors. *History of Allen and Woodson Counties, Kansas: Embellished with Portraits of Well-Known People of These Counties, With Biographies of Our Representative Citizens, Cuts of Public Buildings and a Map of Each County.* Iola, Kansas: Iola Registers, Printers and Binders, 1901.

Dyer, Frederick H. *A Compendium of the War of the Rebellion.* Des Moines: The Dyer Publishing Co., 1908.

Edwards, Lawyn C. "Confederate Cavalry at Chickamauga: What Went Wrong." Master's Thesis, U.S. Army Command and General Staff College, Fort Leavenworth, Kansas, 1990.

Eicher, John H., and David Eicher. *Civil War High Commands.* Stanford: Stanford University Press, 2001.

Evans, Clement A., editor. *Confederate Military History,* Volume I, III, VII and VIII. Atlanta: Confederate Publishing Co., 1899.

Fanebust, Wayne. *Major General Alexander M. McCook, USA: A Civil War Biography.* Jefferson, NC: McFarland, 2013.

Fink, Paul M. *Jonesborough: The First Century of Tennessee's First Town, 1776–1876.* Johnson City, TN: The Overmountain Press, 2002.

Fitch, John. *Chickamauga: The Price of Chattanooga.* Philadelphia: J. B. Lippincott & Co., 1864.

Fitch, Michael Hendrick. *The Chattanooga Campaign, Wisconsin History Commission.* n.p.: Democrat Printing Co., State Printer, 1911.

Fobes, George. "An Account of the Mutiny in the Anderson Cavalry, at Nashville, Tenn., December 1862," In *Leaves of a Trooper's Dairy,* by John Williams. Philadelphia: Published by Author, 1869.

Frankenberry, A. D. "Carrying Dispatches from General Rosecrans To General Stanley," In *History of the Fifteenth Pennsylvania Volunteer Cavalry,* Reiff, J. C., ed. Philadelphia, Pennsylvania: Society of the Fifteenth Pennsylvania Cavalry, 1906.

Friend, W. R. "Rout of Rosecrans," In *New Annals of the Civil War,* Peter Cozzens and Robert Girardi, eds. Mechanicsburg, PA: Stackpole Books, 2004.

Galuszka, Douglas H. "Logistics in Warfare: The Significance of Logistics in the Army of the Cumberland During the Tullahoma and Chickamauga Campaigns," U.S. Army Command and General Staff College, Fort Leavenworth, KS, 2005.

Garrett, William. *Reminiscences of Public Men in Alabama.* Atlanta: Plantation Publishing Co.'s Press, 1872.

Gatewood, Charles. *Lt. Charles Gatewood and His Apache Wars Memoir,* Louis Kraft, ed. Lincoln: University of Nebraska Press, 2005.

Glazier, Willard. *Three Years in the Federal Cavalry.* New York: R.H. Ferguson, 1870.

Gordon, John Brown. *Reminiscences of the Civil War.* New York: Charles Scribner's Sons, 1903.

Grant, Ulysses Simpson. *Personal Memoirs of U. S. Grant.* New York: Charles L. Webster & Co., 1894.

Greeno, Charles. "Address of Lieut.-Col. Charles L. Greeno," In *Pennsylvania at Chickamauga and Chattanooga,* George W. Skinner, ed. Harrisburg, Pennsylvania: William Stanley Ray, State Printer of Pennsylvania, 1897.

Griggs, Walter, Jr. *Hidden History of Richmond.* Charleston, S. C.: Arcadia Publishing Co., 2012.

Groce, W. Todd. *Mountain Rebels: East Tennessee Confederates and the Civil War, 1860–1870.* Knoxville, University of Tennessee Press, 1999.

Grosse Ile Historical Society. *Images of American: Grosse Ile.* Charleston, Chicago, Portsmouth, San Francisco: Arcadia Publishing Co., 2007.

Hafendorfer, Kenneth. *They Died by Twos and Tens: The Confederate Cavalry in the Kentucky Campaign of 1862.* Louisville, KY: KH Press, 1995.

Harbison, Robert E. "Wilder's Brigade in the Tullahoma and Chattanooga Campaigns of the American Civil

War." Master's Thesis, U.S. Army Command and General Staff College, Fort Leavenworth, Kansas, 2002.

Hartje, Robert George. *Van Dorn: The Life and Times of a Confederate General.* Nashville: Vanderbilt University Press, 1967.

Hazzard, George. *Hazzard's History of Henry County, Indiana, 1822–1906*, Vol. 1. New Castle, Indiana: George Hazzard Publisher, 1906.

Heitman, Francis Bernard. *Historical Register and Dictionary of the United States Army 1789–1903.* Washington, D.C.: U.S. Government Printing Office, 1903.

Hill, D. H. "Chickamauga: The Great Battle of the West," In *Battles and Leaders in the Civil War*, Vol. III. New York: The Century Co., 1888.

Humes, Thomas William. *The Loyal Mountaineers of Tennessee.* Knoxville: Ogden Brothers & Co., 1888.

Hunt, Roger. *Colonels in Blue—Indiana, Kentucky and Tennessee.* Jefferson, NC: McFarland, 2013.

Hurst, Jack. *Nathan Bedford Forrest: A Biography.* New York: Vintage Books, 1994.

Jones, James B., Jr. "Fevers Ran High," In *Rural Life and Culture in the Upper Cumberland*, Michael E. Birdwell and W. Calvin Dickinson, eds. Lexington: University of Kentucky Press, 2004.

Jordan, Thomas and J. P. Pryor. *The Campaigns Lieut.-Gen. N. B. Forrest, and of Forrest's Cavalry.* New Orleans, Memphis, and New York: Blelock and Company, 1868.

Knight, Lucian L. *Standard History of Georgia and Georgians*, Volume 4. Chicago and New York: The Lewis Publishing Co., 1917.

Lamers, William. *The Edge of Glory: A Biography of General William S. Rosecrans, U. S. A.* New York: Harcourt, Brace & World, Inc., 1961.

Lanier, Robert. *Photographic History of the Civil War.* New York: The Review of Reviews Co., 1911.

Levin, H., editor. *Lawyers and Lawmakers of Kentucky.* Chicago: Lewis Publishing Co., 1897.

Lewis, Berkley. *Notes on Cavalry Weapons of the Civil War, 1861–1865.* Washington, D. C.: American Ordnance Association, 1961.

Lewis, Lloyd. *Sherman: Fighting Prophet.* Lincoln: University of Nebraska Press, 1960.

Lindsley, John Berrien, editor. *The Military Annals of Tennessee. Confederate.* Nashville: J. M. Lindsley & Co., Publishers, 1886.

Londa, John. "The Role of Union Cavalry during the Chickamauga Campaign," Master's Thesis, Command and General Staff College, Fort Leavenworth, Kansas, 1991.

Longacre, Edward G. *A Soldier to the Last: Maj. Gen. Joseph Wheeler in Blue and Gray.* Washington: Potomac Books Inc., 2007.

Magid, Paul. *George Crook: From the Redwoods to Appomattox.* Norman: University of Oklahoma Press, 2011.

Martin, Samuel J. *General Braxton Bragg, CSA.* Jefferson, NC: McFarland, 2011.

Marvel, William. *Burnside.* Chapel Hill & London: University of North Carolina Press, 1991.

McDonough, James Lee. *Chattanooga: A Death Grip on the Confederacy.* Knoxville: University of Tennessee Press, 1984.

Medlock, Chelsea A. "Delayed Obsolescence: The Horse in European and American Warfare from the Crimean War to the Second World War." Master's Thesis, Oklahoma State University, 2009.

Merrill, W. S. *The Middle Tennessee and Chattanooga Campaigns of June, July, August, and September 1863.* New York: Julius Bien & Co. Lith., 1891.

Mims, Wilbur F. *War History of the Prattville Dragoons.* Prattville, Alabama: n.p., n.d.

Minty, Robert. *Minty's Sabre Brigade: The Part They Took in the Chattanooga Campaign.* Wyandotte, MI: The Herald Steam Presses, 1892.

Mitchell, Charles D. "The Sanders Raid into East Tennessee, June, 1863" In *Sketches of War History 1861–1865.* Cincinnati: Monfort & Company, 1908.

Mitchell, John L. *John L. Mitchell's Tennessee State Gazetteer and Business Directory for 1860–1861.* Nashville: John L. Mitchell Publisher, 1860.

Morton, John Watson. *The Artillery of Nathan Bedford Forrest's Cavalry.* Nashville, Tennessee and Dallas, Texas: Publishing House of the M. E. Church, 1909.

National Cyclopedia of American Biography, Vol. VI. New York: James T. White Co., 1896.

Nosworthy, Brent. *The Bloody Crucible of Courage: Fighting Methods and Combat Experience of the Civil War.* New York: Carroll & Graf Publishers, 2003.

Nott, Charles C. *Sketches of the War: A Series of Letters to the North Moore Street School of New York.* New York: Anson D. F. Randolph, 1865.

Official Register of the Officers and Cadets of the U. S. Military Academy. West Point, NY: U. S. Military Academy, 1852.

Otis, Ephraim. "The Murfreesboro Campaign," In *Campaigns in Kentucky and Tennessee include the Battle of Chickamauga, 1862–1864, Papers of the Military Historical Society of Massachusetts* Vol. VII. Boston: Military Historical Society of Massachusetts, 1908.

Peskin, Allan. *Garfield: A Biography.* Kent, Ohio: Kent State University Press, 1999.

Pirkle, Wesley M. "Major General George Crook's Use of Counterinsurgency Compound Warfare During the Great Sioux War 1876–77," Master's Thesis, U.S. Army Command and General Staff College, Fort Leavenworth, KS, 2008.

Popejoy, Stirling D. "The Second Tennessee Cavalry in the American Civil War," Master's Thesis, U.S. Army Command and General Staff College, Fort Leavenworth, KS, 2014.

Portrait and Biographical Album of Sedgwick County, Kan. Chicago: Chapman Brothers, 1888.

Powell, David. *The Chickamauga Campaign—Barren Victory: The Retreat into Chattanooga, the Confederate Pursuit, and the Aftermath of the Battle, September 21 to October 20, 1863.* Eldorado Hills, CA: Savas Beatie, 2016.

Powell, David. *The Chickamauga Campaign—Glory or the Grave: The Breakthrough, the Union Retreat to Chattanooga.* Eldorado Hills, CA: Savas Beatie, 2015.

Powell, David. *The Chickamauga Campaign: A Mad Irregular Battle.* El Dorado Hills, CA: Savas Beatie, 2014.

Powell, David. *Failure in the Saddle.* New York and California: Savas Beatie, 2010.

Powell, David. "A Legend in the Making: Nathan Bedford Forrest at Chickamauga" In *Gateway to the Confederacy: New Perspectives on the Chickamauga and Chattanooga Campaigns, 1862–1863*, Evans C. Jones and Wiley Sword, ed. Baton Rouge: Louisiana State University Press, 2014.

Powell, William Henry, editor. *Officers of the Army and Navy (volunteer) Who Served in the Civil War.* Philadelphia: L. R. Hamersly, 1893.

Quiner, Edwin B. "1st Cavalry," In *E. B. Quiner's Military History of Wisconsin*. Chicago: Clark and Co., 1866.

Quiner, Edwin B. "Biographical Sketches," In *E. B Quiner's Military History of Wisconsin*. Chicago: Clark and Co., 1866.

Rabb, James W. *Confederate General Lloyd Tilghman: A Biography*. Jefferson, N.C.: McFarland, 2004.

Rafuse, Ethan. "In the Shadow of the Rock: Thomas L. Crittenden, Alexander M. McCook, and the 1863 Campaigns for Middle and East Tennessee," In *The Chickamauga Campaign*, Steven E. Woodworth, ed. Carbondale and Edwardsville: Southern Illinois University Press, 2010.

Reynolds, Clark G. "The Civil and Indian War Diaries of Eugene Marshall, Minnesota Volunteer," Master's Thesis, Duke University, Durham, NC., 1963.

Richardson, Robert D. "Rosecrans' Staff at Chickamauga: The Significance of Major General William S. Rosecrans' Staff on the Outcome of the Chickamauga Campaign." Master's Thesis, Command and General Staff College, Fort Leavenworth, Kansas, 1989.

Robertson, William G., Edward Shanahan, John Boxberger, and George Knapp, *The Staff Ride Handbook for the Battle of Chickamauga: 18-20 September 1863*, U. S. Army Command and General Staff College, Command Studies Institute, Fort Leavenworth, KS, 1992.

Rubenstein, David. "A Study of the Medical Support to the Union and Confederate Armies During the Battle of Chickamauga: Lessons and Implications for Today's US Army Medical Department Leaders," Master's Thesis, U.S. Army Command and General Staff College, Fort Leavenworth, KS, 1990.

Schaefer, James Arthur. "The Tactical and Strategic Evolution of Cavalry during the American Civil War," Ph. D. Dissertation, The University of Toledo, 1982.

Skinner, George W., editor. *Pennsylvania at Chickamauga and Chattanooga*. Harrisburg, Pennsylvania: William Stanley Ray, State Printer of Pennsylvania, 1897.

Smith, Lanny. *The Stone's River Campaign: 26 December 1862-5 January 1863, Army of Tennessee*. n.p.: Lanny Smith, 2010.

Smith, Theodore Clarke. *The Life and Letters of James A. Garfield*. New Haven: Yale University Press, 1925.

Speed, Thomas. "Cavalry Operations in the West under Rosecrans and Sherman," In *Battle and Leaders of the Civil War*, Vol. 4. New York: The Century Company, 1884, 1888.

Speed, Thomas. *Union Regiments of Kentucky*, Vol. I. Louisville: The Courier Journal Job Printing, Co., 1897.

Stanley, David. *An American General—The Memoirs of David Sloan Stanley*, Samuel W. Fordyce IV, ed. Santa Barbara, California: The Narrative Press, 2004.

Stanley, David. *Personal Memoirs of Major-General D. S. Stanley USA*. Cambridge, Massachusetts: Harvard, University Press, 1917.

Starr, Stephen Z. "Cold Steel: The Sabre and Union Cavalry," In *Battles Lost and Won: Essays from Civil War History*, John T. Hubbell, ed. Westport, Conn.: Greenwood Press, 1975.

Starr, Stephen Z. *The Union Cavalry in the Civil War: The War in the West*, Volume III. Baton Rouge: Louisiana State University, 2007.

Steahlin, George F. "Address and Historical Sketch," In *Pennsylvania at Chickamauga and Chattanooga*, George W. Skinner, editor. Harrisburg, Pennsylvania: William Stanley Ray, State Printer of Pennsylvania, 1897.

Stuart, A. A. "Colonel William W. Lowe," In *Iowa Colonels and Regiments Being a History of Iowa Regiments*. Des Moines: Mills & Company, 1865.

Thompson, Ed Porter. *History of the Orphan Brigade*. Louisville, KY: Lewis N. Thompson, 1898.

Thruston, Gates. "Crisis at Chickamauga," In *Battles and Leaders in the Civil War*, Vol. 3. New York: The Century Co., 1888.

Tucker, Glenn. *Chickamauga: Bloody Battle in the West*. Dayton, OH: Press of Morningside Bookshop, 1984.

Tucker, Spencer C., editor. *American Civil War: The Definitive Encyclopedia and Document Collection*, Volume I. Santa Barbara, Denver, Oxford: ABC-CLIO, 2013.

Twenty-Ninth Annual Reunion of the Association of Graduates of the United States Military Academy at West Point. Saginaw: Seemann & Peters, Printers and Binders, 1898.

Twenty-Second Annual Reunion of the Association of the Graduates of the United States Military Academy: June 12th, 1891. Saginaw: Seemann & Peters, Printers and Binders, 1891.

The Union Army, A History of Military Affairs in the Loyal States 1861-65, Vol. 8. Madison, WI: Federal Publishing Co., 1908.

Vale, Joseph. "Address of Captain Joseph Vale," In *Pennsylvania at Chickamauga and Chattanooga*, George W. Skinner, editor. Harrisburg, Pennsylvania: William Stanley Ray, State Printer of Pennsylvania, 1897.

Vincent, Thomas M. "David Sloane Stanley," *The Thirty-fourth Annual Reunion of the Association Graduates of the United States Military Academy at West Point, New York*. Saginaw, Michigan: Seeman and Peters Printers and Binders, 1903.

Walsh, George. *Those Damn Horse Soldiers*. New York: A Tom Doherty Associates Book, 2006.

Warner, Ezra J. *Generals in Gray: Lives of the Confederate Commanders*. Baton Rouge: Louisiana State University Press, 1959.

Welsh, Jack. *Medical Histories of Confederate Generals*. Kent, Ohio: Kent State University Press, 1995.

Welsh, Jack. *Medical Histories of Union Generals*. Kent, Ohio: Kent State University Press, 1996.

Wheeler, Joseph. "Bragg's Invasion of Kentucky," In *Battles and Leaders of the Civil War*, Volume III. New York: The Century Company, 1888.

Wheeler, Joseph. *A Revised System of Cavalry Tactics, for the Use of the Cavalry and Mounted Infantry, C. S. A.* Mobile: S. H. Goetzel & Co., 1863.

Wiley, Samuel and W. Scott Garner, ed. *Biographical and Portrait Cyclopedia of Blair County, Pennsylvania*. Philadelphia: Gresham Publishing Co., 1892.

Williams, C. S. *Williams' Cincinnati Directory*. Cincinnati: C. S. Williams Publisher, 1860.

Woodworth, Steven E. *Six Armies in Tennessee: The Chickamauga and Chattanooga Campaigns*. Lincoln and London: University of Nebraska Press, 1998.

Wittenberg, Eric. *The First Day at Chickamauga: September 18, 1863*. El Dorado Hills, CA: Savas Beatie, 2017 (manuscript in preparation).

Wright, Steven L. *Kentucky Soldiers and Their Regiments in the Civil War*, Volume III. Utica, Kentucky: McDowell Publications, 2009.

Wyeth, John Allan. *The Life General Nathan Bedford Forrest*. New York and London: Harper and Brothers Publisher, 1899.

Wyeth, John Allan. *With Sabre and Scalpel: The Autobiography of a Soldier and Surgeon*. New York and London: Harper Brothers Publishers, 1914.

Yaryan, John Lee. "Stone River," In *War Papers Read before the Indiana Commandery*. Indianapolis: MOLLUS, 1898.

Yeary, Mamie. *Reminiscences of the Boys in Gray*. Smith and Lamar Publishing House: Dallas, 1912.

Index

Numbers in ***bold italics*** indicate pages with illustrations

Abingdon Virginian 71
Adams, Brig. Gen. Daniel 163–164, 166, 270
Alabama troops: 1st Cavalry 59, 120, 129; 3rd Cavalry 56, 59, 114, 116, 120, 139; 4th Cavalry 47, 59–60, 120, 139, 209, 213, 217, 245; 5th Cavalry 60; 5th Infantry 59; 7th Cavalry 58; 7th Infantry 60; 14th Battalion 35; 19th Infantry 56; 51st Cavalry 43, 47, 59, 110, 120, 124, 139; 53rd Cavalry 60; Roddey's Regiment 60
Alexander's Bridge 1, 174, 180, 182–183, 188, 191–192, 262
Alexandria Gazette 71
Allen's House 115, 119, 146
Alley, Charles 235, 249, 255–256
Alpine skirmish 4–5, 144–148, 177, 262
Anderson, Brig. Gen. George T. 272
Anderson, Brig. Gen. Patton 63, 66, 85, 88, 100, 103, 271
Anderson, Lt. Col. Paul F. 58
Anderson Cavalry *see* 15th Pennsylvania Cavalry
Anderson's Crossroads 243, 257–258
Andes, Lt. John 66, 220
Antietam, Battle of 25, 74, 245
Arkansas troops: 2nd Cavalry 56; 3rd Cavalry 53; Wiggins' Artillery 44, 59
Armstrong, Brig. Gen. Frank 4, 50–***52***, 117, 131, 137, 148, 150, 152, 160, 183, 241
Army Corps: IX 74, 106; XI 238; XII 238; XIV 4, 41, 66, 74, 77, 84, 86–87, 98, 142, 156, 159, 161, 172, 175, 193–195, 219–220, 223; XV 238; XVI 21, 85; XVII 238; XX 4, 66, 77, 113, 115–116, 125, 142, 157, 167, 169–170, 172, 177–178, 180, 194, 212, 218–220, 223, 225, 233–234; XXI 41, 67, 77, 84, 87, 98, 115–116, 143, 148, 159, 161, 165, 171, 181, 213, 219, 223

Army of Kentucky 32
Army of Mississippi 32, 34, 50
Army of Tennessee 4, 32, 34, 36–37, 40, 49–51, 53, 57, 61–65, 75, 84, 88, 129, 132, 141, 151, 160, 165, 260–261, 263, 270–272
Army of the Cumberland 1–4, 6, 9–10, 14, 16–17, 19, 23–25, 27–29, 31–34, 36–38, 41, 48, 61, 63, 65–66, 77–80, 83, 85, 88, 94–95, 103, 105, 107, 109, 114–115, 117–118, 120, 125, 132, 140, 143, 150–151, 154, 157, 170, 172, 174–175, 177, 193, 201, 221, 223, 225, 235, 238–239, 255, 259–263, 266; composition of the cavalry 83; dates of arrival of cavalry units 39
Army of the Mississippi 12, 38
Army of the Ohio 32–33, 51, 63, 65, 79, 95, 106, 117, 154
Ashby, Col. Henry 33, 54
Avery, Col. Isaac 245
Avery, Col. L W. 58

Bailey, Lt. Benjamin F. 104
Barnett, Col. James 26
Baum, Sgt. G.W. 120, 136, 146, 171, 174, 196–197, 201, 234, 244
Bayles, Col. Jesse 18
Beatty, Brig. Gen. John 70, 74, 179, 201, 267
Beck, Capt. Chris 239
Bickham, William D. 14
Biffle, Col. Jacob B. 52
Blackburn, James 254
Blake, Lt. A.A. 59
"blind adherence" of orders 133
Blue Bird Gap 57, 175–176, 180, 194
Blythe's Ferry 85, 87, 100–102, 104–105, 116, 126, 139
Bond, Maj. Frank 157–158, 161, 167
Bounds, Lt. Col. J.M. 58
Boynton, Brig. Gen. Henry 261
Brackett, Maj. Alfred B. 83
Bradley, Michael 40, 44

Bragg, Gen. Braxton 3–4, 9, 19, 48–51, 53–56, 70, 73, 75–77, 84–88, 91, 95, 97–98, 100, 105–107, 110–117, 119, 121, 123, 135, 137–144, 164–166, 169–170, 172–173, 177, 180–183, 186, 192, 194–196, 211–214, 232–233, 235, 240–241, 258–259, 262–264, 270; attack at McLemore's Cove 148–152; contemplates Rosecrans' advance 125–127; gains initiative 154, 156–162; issues battle orders 174–175; Kentucky Campaign 32; orders evacuation 129–132; Stones Rivers Campaign 34–40; Tullahoma Campaign 41, 43, 47; withdraws to Chattanooga 60–67
Brandon, John 72
Brannan, Maj. Gen. John 43, 87, 109, 113, 233, 267
Brant, Albert 241
Breckinridge, Gen. John C. 63, 100, 130, 158, 162–164, 166, 177, 201, 270
Brent, George 166, 258
Bridgeport 63–64, 66–69, 72–73, 77, 84–89, 91, 95, 98, 100, 103, 108–110, 112–113, 115–119, 125, 140, 143, 196, 210, 239–240
Briggs, Maj. David 196–197, 212, 243
Broomtown Valley 123–124, 128, 135, 138, 143–144, 171
Brownlow, Lt. Col. James P. 16, 19, 83, ***104***, 128, 153–154, 157, 200, 240
Brownlow, Col. John Bell 20
Brownlow, "Parson" William G. 20
Buckner, Maj. Gen. Simon B. 51, 62–63, 65, 75, 79, 84, 95, 100, 104–106, 115, 130–132, 135, 139, 149, 156, 170–171, 173–174, 183, 271
Buell, Maj. Gen. Don Carlos 20, 22, 24, 32–33, 38, 65, 75
Buford, Brig. Gen. Abraham 35

Bull Run, Battle of 24, 28, 51, 74, 222
Bunting, Chaplain Robert F. 148, 197–198, 252
Burdsall, Lt. Col. Henry W. 28
Burns, Capt. Robert 86, 93–94, 101, 169, **176**, 179, 182, 185, 191, 193, 245–246, 258
Burnside, Maj. Gen. Ambrose 51, 63, 65, 75, 77–80, 83, 85, 87, **95**, 97, 101–107, 110, 115–117, 125–126, 129, 132, 139–141, 144, 151, 154, 156, 165–166, 170, 172, 174, 176–177, 226, 232, 259–261
Bushwhackers 72, 89, 107, 205
Butler, Col. J.R. 58
Byrd, Col. Robert K. 176

Campbell, Col. Archibald P. 16–**18**, 19, 38, 45, 83–85, 89, 91, 104, 108, 127, 134, 150, 153, 172, 175, 180, 196, 198–202, 214, 219, 225–226, 236, 239–240, 244, 262; fight at La Fayette 162–164
Campbell, Henry 191, 251–252
Caperton's Ferry 66, 91, 98, 109, 112, 116, 123, 125
Carlisle Barracks 14, 56
Carrick, Dr. Anthony 68
Carter, Brig. Gen. Samuel 19, 34
Carter, W.R. 69, 71, 120, 153, 159, 164, 174, 176, 233, 256
"Carthage brigade" 88
Casey, Thomas 13
cavalry: organization (Confederate) 52, 54, 58–60, (Union) 14, 83; tactics 10–13, 15; training manuals 10–13
Cavalry Bureau 78
Chadwick, Mary Jane 70
Chapin, Sgt. John 207–208
Chase, Sec. of Treasury Salmon 39
Cheatham, Maj. Gen. Benjamin 63, 160, 273
Cheek, Maj. Christopher 150
Chicago Times 106, 129
Chickamauga Creek 5, 100, 148, 171–173, 175, 180–**181**, 182, 185, 188–190, 192, 195–196, 199–201, 203, 207, 212–214, 221–222, 258
Chilton, William P. 59
Christmas Raid (Morgan's) 19, 21
Cincinnati Commercial 14
Cist, Brig. Gen. States Rights 135, 141
civilians 68, 70, 73, 97, 108, 128, 130, 258
Clark, George 95
Clayton, Brig. Gen. Henry D. 100, 271
Cleburne, Maj. Gen. Patrick 104, 149, 151, 170, 270

Coleman, Capt. D. 209, 217, 271
Colman, Thomas 204, 209, 227
Colt revolving rifle 10, 12–**13**, 44, 78, 209
Confederate troops: 3rd Cavalry 73, 108–111, 114, 198, 204, 256; 8th Cavalry 56, 59, 73, 139; 10th Cavalry 54; Jefferson Davis Legion 56
Conner, Capt. C.H. 59
Conwell, Lt. I.R. 74, 89, 120, 134, 136
Cook, Lt. Col. Gustave 58, 253
Cooke, Gen. Philip St. George 10
Cooper, Col. Robert Wickliffe 16, 18, 83, 229, 240
Cooper, Gen. Samuel 61, 76
Cooper's Gap 6–7, 139, 156, 199, 224, 228–230, 236
Corbitt, W.B. 164
Corinth, Battle of 14, 38, 52, 200
Corinth, Siege of 14–15, 19, 24, 26–27, 239
Cotton Port ford 241, 247, 254, 259
Cowell, Lt. Joseph 228
Cox, Col. Nicholas 50, 52
Cozzens, Peter 4, 114, 149, 158, 160
Crane, Captain William 144, 205, 207–**208**, 209, 211
Crawfish Springs 6, 165, 172, 174–176, 195–203, 205, 208, 210–**211**, 212–226, 228, 231, 233–234, 262
Crews, Col. Charles C. 51, 58–59, 89, 127–**128**, 130, 162, 204
Crittenden, Maj. Gen Thomas 4–5, 35–36, 41, 43, 69, 77, 84, 86–**87**, 92, 94–95, 97–98, 101–102, 105, 109–110, 112, 114–117, 119, 125–126, 132–133, 135, 139–140, 142–144, 148–149, 151–152, 156, 159–161, 165–167, 169–175, 178, 180, 182–183, 185, 192–196, 224, 235, 242, 258, 262, 264, 268
Crofts, Thomas 258
Crook, Brig. Gen. George 4–5, 14, 49, 67, **74**, 77, 79, 83–84, 86, 89, 103, 119, 128, 135–136, 140, 150, 154, 166, 169, 171–172, 174–177, 179–180, 196, 199, 217, 220–224, 239–242, 263–264, 266; advances to Alpine 138; Alpine battle 143–144, 146–148; battle at Glass Mill 201, 205, 207–212; charges against Minty 254–255; covers the retreat 226, 235–237; fight at La Fayette 161–164; moves to Broomtown Valley 123; Wheeler's Raid 241, 244–247, 249–255, 257–258
Cumberland Mountain Tunnel 64

Cupp, Lt. Col. Valentine 83, 111, 207–208, 212, 221, 239
Curry, Lt. W.L. 40, 74, 94, 128–129, 147, 210, 226, 246–247
"Curtis Horse" 24
Cuykendall, Dr. Myron C. 255

Dana, Charles A. (assistant secretary of war) **107**, 175; on the battlefield with Wilder 215; the removal of Stanley 261
Davidson, Brig. Gen. Henry B. 4, 51, 54, 173, 183, 192, 232, 241, 250–251, 253
Davis, Pres. Jefferson 73, 75–76, 128, 156, 178
Davis, Gen. Jefferson C. 87, 117, 120, 125, 148, 258
Davis, Lt. Wirt 188, **190**
deserters 69, 89, 98, 100, 105, 110–111, 114, 117, 123, 138–139, 166, 258
Deweese, Lt. Col. John 240
Dibrell, Col. George 51–52, 62, **81**, 86–87, 98, 105, 131, 140, 232; fights at Sparta 79–82, 91–94
Dick, Col. George 193
Dickinson, Lt. Col. William 25
discipline 22, 68–69, 72, 78, 89, 104, 110–111, 113, 117, 254, 258
diseases *see* illness
Dodge, Brig. Gen. Grenville 60
Dornblaser, T.F. 48
Dougherty's Gap 121, 161, 163, 167, 169–172, 174–176, 180, 198
Dover, battle at 50, 58
Dry Valley Road 175, 198–199, 201–202, 213, 225
DuBose, John W. 50
Dug Gap 144, 149, 151, 156–157, 175–176
Dyer's Bridge 183, 187–188, 191

Edwards, Lawyn 12
Eggleston, Col. Beroth B. 16, 27, 207
Elliott, Brig. Gen. Washington Lafayette 261–262, 266
Estes, Col. William Newton 58, 110–111, 198
Ewell's Corps 166

Farmington, battle at 7, 249–258
Faulkner, Col. John K. 16, 20, 240
Ferguson, Champ 82
Ferrell, Capt. C.B. 60
fever *see* illness
Field, Capt. J.H. 59
Firestone, Dr. Leander 13, 260
Fish, Dr. George 254
Fitch, John 151
flag of truce 127, 240

Index

Florida troops: 1st Cavalry (Dismounted) 214; 7th Infantry 214
Folk, Col. George N. 54
Forrest, Nathan Bedford 4, 9, 24–26, 31, 33–34, 37, *39*–41, 45, 47–53, 55, 57, 61, 66, 72, 75, 79–80, 84, 86–87, 95, 97–98, 100, 104–106, 110, 117, 120, 131–131, 134, 137, 140–143, 148, 152–153, 162, 170–171, 174, 180, 182–183, 186–189, 191, 195, 223, 232, 241, 250, 253, 263
Foster, Maj. Gen. J.G. 261
Fowler, William 243
Fowler's Ford 192
Frankenberry, A.D. 158
Freeman, Capt. Samuel 26
Fremantle, Sir Arthur 50
Frémont, Maj. Gen. John C. 24
Frémont's Hussars 24
Friend, W.R. 11
Fulton, Col. John 186, 191, 193, 271

Galbraith, Lt. Col. Robert 25, 44, 72, 91, 113, 240, 247
Garfield, Brig. Gen. James A. 22–23, 29, 31, 39, 85, 102, 119–121, 123–124, 127, 129–130, 133–134, 137–138, 141, 143–148, 154, 158–159, 161–162, 164–165, 167, 169, 171–172, 174–176, 178–179, 195, 198, 215–217, 222, 226, 230, 234, 240, 260, 264–265
Garnett, Brig. Gen. Robert 53
Garrard, Brig. Gen. Kenner 103, 266
Gay, Capt. Ebenezer 33–34
Georgia troops: 1st Cavalry 52; 2nd Cavalry 58, 150, 166; 3rd Cavalry 20, 58, 150; 4th Cavalry 58, 148, 175; 6th Cavalry 148, 232; Ferrell's Artillery 60
Gillem, Brig. Gen. Alvan 266
Glass Mill 4–5, 174, 183, 193, 199–201, 203–*204*, 205–212, 214, 217–219, 221, 223, 236, 239, 264
Goddard, Lt. Col. Charles 47, 160
Godley, Maj. John C. 16, 83, 240
Goode, Col. C.T. 54
Gooding, Col. Michael 212
Gooding, Othiel 93
Goodrich, Charles 69, 71, 73, 212
Granger, Maj. Gen. Gordon 18, 21, 41, 43–45, 47–48, 68, 87–88, 94, 97, 112–113, 117–118, 135, 143, 165, 169–172, 174–175, 182–183, 185, 193, 196, 221–224, 260–261, 269
Grant, Maj. Gen. Ulysses 12, 32, 38–39, 104, 106–107, 170, 261
Gratz, Maj. Louis A. 83, 229

Gray, Maj. Horace 83, 187, 240, 242
Graysville 130, 149, 171, 175, 221
Gregg, Brig. Gen. John 130, 186, 193, 271
Griest, Alva 272
Griffin, Lt. Trumbull D. 185, 187, 190, 244
Griffith, Lt. Col. J.C. 245
Griffiths, Dr. D.J. 217
Grose, Col. William 149, 268
Guild, George 209–210

Hagan, Col. James 51, 56, **59**
Haggard, Col. David R. 21
Hale, Capt. Robert 218
Halleck, Gen.-in-Chief Henry 32–*33*, 38–39, 65–66, 75–78, 83, 106, 108, 115, 129, 132, 135, 144, 150–151, 154, 165, 170, 172, 176, 260–261
Hambrick, Lt. Col. J.M. 59
Hamilton, Medical Inspector Frank H. 91
Hardee, Lt. Gen. William 35–36, 41, 43, 63, 75, 130
Harmon, Col. M.W. 60
Harris, John W. 259
Harrison, Col. Thomas (CSA) 51, 58, 132, 149, 152, 162, 196–197, 203–204, 252
Harrison, Col. Thomas J. (U.S.) 6, 16, 119, 152–153, 156, 196–197, 218
Harrison's Ferry/Landing 86, 95, 99, 102, 135, 224
Hart, Col. John R. 54
Hartsuff, Brig. Gen. George 14
Hartsville, raid 21
Hawley, Capt. James 108, 210, 212
Haynes, Lt. Col. William E. 83
Hazen, Brig. Gen. William B. 101, 112, 116, 126, 135, 139–140, 268
Healy, George 134, 250, 255
Heg, Col. Hans 109, 268
Helm, Brig. Gen. Benjamin 163, 270
Hempstead, Henry Mortimer 109, 134, 136, 198, 200, 202–204, 207, 209, 224
Henderson's Gap 144
Hill, Lt. Gen. Daniel Harvey 63, 100, 113, 125–128, 135, 142, 151, 156, 162, 166, 174, 176, 182, 232, 270
Hindman, Maj. Gen. Thomas 99, 105, 115, 149, 151, 160, 207, 211, 259, 271
Hoblitzell, Lt. Col. William T. 7, 16, 21, 83, 229–230, 237, 240
Hobson, Col. A.W. 52
Hodge, Col. George 162, 250, 252–253
Holman, Col. Daniel Wilson 52
horse holder 13, 214

horseshoeing 136–*137*, 247, **249**
horses 10–*11*, 68, 71, 74, 78–81, 89, 110, 134, 137, 164, 171, 176, 222, 233, 238–239, 245, 247, 257, 261
hospitals 125, 134; at Crawfish Springs 176, 196, 198–199, 203, 205, 210–211, 213–215, 217, 219–221, 223, 259–260, 264
Howard, Maj. Gen. Oliver O. 238
Howe, Capt. Daniel Waite 177
Huggins, Capt. A.L. 52
Huntsville, expedition 69–*70*, 71–72
Hurlbut, Maj. Gen. Stephen A. 69, 85, 170
Huwald, Capt. Gustave 54

Illinois troops: 2nd Artillery 232; 15th Cavalry 268; 92nd Infantry 258; 98th Mounted Infantry 183, 245, 252; 123rd Mounted Infantry 183, 188, 245, 252; Chicago Board of Trade Battery 16, 28, 37, 40, 83, 120, 147, 185, 199, 205, 207–208, 210, 232, 238, 246, 249
illness 89, 91, 134
Indiana troops: 1st Cavalry 21; 2nd Cavalry 16, 20–21, 34, 74, 83, 89, 115, 120, 127–128, 134, 136, 146, 171, 174, 196–199, 201, 212, 225, 233–234, 236, 239–240, 243–244, 257; 3rd Cavalry 16, 24, 35–36, 44–45, 80–81, 83, 87–88, 92, 95–96, 102, 105, 116, 160, 181, 198, 214, 225, 230, 236, 240; 4th Cavalry 16, 39, 73, 83, 89, 103, 107, 128, 162–163, 196, 201, 236, 239–240; 16th Infantry 21; 17th Mounted Infantry 183, 245, 252; 18th Artillery (Lilly's) 99, 183, 188, 193, 246, 251; 22nd 212; 39th Mounted Infantry 6, 14, 37, 39, 110, 119, 152, 158, 196–198, 214, 218; 44th 193; 72nd Mounted Infantry 181, 188, 238–239, 245, 252
Iowa troops: 5th Cavalry 16, 24, 39, 67, 72, 83, 113, 118, 134, 235, 240, 244, 249–250, 255–257
Ireland, Chaplain John 16
Irwin, Sergeant C.S. 210
Ison, Lt. Col. F.M. 58

Jackson, Brig. Gen. James S. 26
Jackson, Col. William "Red" 37, 56, 63
James, Lt. Col. Thomas C. 19
Jay's Mill *191*–193, 195
Jennings, Maj. William H. 25
Johnson, Maj. A.H. 59

Johnson, Brig. Gen. Bushrod *182*-183, 185-190, 192, 271
Johnson, Penelope 57
Johnson, Col. Robert 19-20
Johnson, Lt. Col. W.A. 60
Johnston, Gen. Joseph 39, 65, 75-77, 85, 100, 104, 123, 126, 130, 132
Jones, Maj. Gen. Sam 154, 170
Jonesborough 142, 166, 170
Jordan, Col. Thomas J. 14, 19, 255
Julian, Capt. W.R. 60

Kansas troops: 2nd Infantry 17, 179; 8th Infantry 17, 130
Keim, Maj. Gen. William 19
Kelly's Ford 49, 99, 134
Kennett, Col. John 28, 33-34
Kentucky Military Institute 26
Kentucky troops: (**CSA**) 1st/3rd Cavalry 60, 204, 245; 2nd Cavalry 52; (**U.S.**) 1st Infantry 18, 148-149; 2nd Cavalry 16, 26-27, 39, 83, 111, 146-147, 163, 175, 197-198, 205, 207-208, 236, 240, 246, 257, 268; 3rd Cavalry 34, 36; 4th Cavalry 16, 18, 39, 68, 127, 228-230, 236, 239-240; 5th Cavalry 16, 21, 39, 83, 150, 228-230, 236, 239-240; 6th Cavalry 16, 18-19, 39, 83, 107, 150, 228-230, 235-236, 239-249; 7th Cavalry 16, 18, 39, 67, 115, 118, 239-240; 20th Infantry 18; 21st Infantry 243
Kilpatrick, Brig. Gen. Hugh Judson 266
King, Col. Edward 113
Kirkpatrick, Capt. M.L. 59
Klein, Lt. Col. Robert 16, 24, 80, 83, 240
Knoxville, military actions 63, 75, 79, 87, 95, 105-106, 116, 129, 170, 260
Kryder, George 69

La Fayette, cavalry charge at 6-7, 162-164, 177
La Grange, Col. Oscar H. 16, 22, 83, 196-197, 240, *243*-244
Lambert's Ford 193
L'Anguille Ferry skirmish 22
Large, John 89
Larson, Sgt. James 186, 188, 242
Lee and Gordon's Mill 152, 159, 161, 165, 167, 171, 175, 180, 182-183, 186, 193, 195, 201, 211-*213*, 214, 217, 219, 223
Leet, Reverend A.I. 185
Leet's Tanyard 160, 165, 170-171, 173, 180-183, 185-186
Lesslie, Maj. Joseph 103
Lewis, Lt. Col. James H. 52
Libby Prison 21

Lincoln, Pres. Abraham 22, 28, 106, 142, 170
Lochiel Cavalry *see* 9th Pennsylvania Cavalry
Long, Col. Eli 6, 12, 16, 22, 26-*27*, 28, 31, 41, 43, 47, 74, 83, 87, 89, 103, 108, 119, 123, 140, 150, 162, 196, 234, 236, 240-241, 245-246, 251, 254, 257, 264; Alpine battle 146; battle at Glass Mill 199, 201-202, 204-205, 210; Trenton expedition 111-112
Longstreet, Lt. Gen. James 123, 130, 165-166, 170-171, 173-175, 181, 201, 211, 214, 271
Lookout Mountain 110, 113-114, 116-117, 119-*121*, 123, 126, 128-133, 135-136, 138-139, 143-144, 146, 157, 169-170, 174, 220, 224, 228-230, 234, 259, 262
Louisiana troops: 1st Cavalry 54; 3rd Infantry 52; 13th Infantry 164; Robinson's Artillery 54
Love, Capt. James 17, 130
Lowe, Col. William 24, *67*, 83, 86-87, 103, 110, 113, 117-119, 240, 248-250, 256
"Lowe's Hell Hounds" 24
Lowrey, Brig. Gen. Mark 101
Lynch, John 76
Lytle, Brig. Gen. William 89, 100, 103, 268

Mackall, Brig. Gen. William W. 49, 110, 116
Maddin, Dr. Thomas 91
Malone, Jr., Col. J.C. 58, 202
Manigault, Brig. Gen. Arthur 215, 258, 271
Marshall, Eugene 250-255
Martin, Lt. Col. R.M. 54
Martin, Brig. Gen. William "Will" Thomas 6, 41, 44-45, 48-49, 51, 55, 58-60, 62, 88, 105, 110, 116-117, 120, 124, 134, 138-*139*, 144, 149, 156-157, 187, 204, 210, 224, 228, 241-245, 250-251; attack at McLemore's Cove 151
Mathews, Maj. Peter 226, 234
Mauldin, Lt. Col. T.H. 59, 114
McAfee's Church 222-223, 232
McCahan, Capt. Thomas 153, 199-200, 214, 242
McClellan, Maj. Gen. William 53, 58
McCook, Maj. Gen. Alexander 14, 21, 35-36, 41, 43, *66*, 77, 87, 98, 109, 112-113, 116-117, 119, 121, 123, 125, 130, 134-135, 142-144, 152, 154, 156-159, 161-162, 166-167, 169-172, 175, 177-178, 180, 194, 198, 212, 214-219, 223-226, 233, 260, 264-265
McCook, Col. Dan 192-193, 222, 269
McCook, Col. Edward 6, 16, *20*-21, 31, 33-34, 38, 66, 68, 74, 77, 82-84, 86-89, 103, 127-128, 130, 135-137, 140-141, 143, 157, 166, 170-172, 174-178, 180, 194, 205, 210, 217, 220, 239-240, 263-264, 266, 268; advances on La Fayette 160-164; advances to Alpine 138; Alpine battle 146-148; attempts to join the battle 212-215; covers the retreat 224-226, 233-237; issues orders for raid 134; moves across the Tennessee River 107, *112*, 115; moves to Crawfish Springs 196-201, 203; Rome expedition completed 152-154; scouts Wills Valley 118-120, 123-124; Wheeler's Raid 243-246, 251, 254, 257
McCormick, Thomas 242
McCulloch, Brig. Gen. Ben 51
McDonald, Maj. Charles 52
McGinnis, Capt. Hamilton 52, 81
McIntosh, Col. James 51
McIntyre, Capt. James B. 16, 25, 81, 83, 165, 187, 240, 249
McKenzie, Col. George W. 56
McLain, John 69, 93, 101, 174, 222, 242
McLemore, Col. William S. 52, 92-93
McLemore's Cove, battle at 138-139, 144, 149-152
McNair, Brig. Gen. Evander 130, 186, 193, 271
Meigs, Quartermaster Gen. M.C. 242
Memphis and Charleston Railroad 64
Menzies, Dr. Gustavus 219
Mercer, Corp. George W. 68
Merrill, Robert S. 136, 212, 234
Metcalfe, Col. Leonidas 18
Mexican War 18, 21, 52, 179, 186
Michigan troops: 1st Michigan Engineers and Mechanics 25, 57; 2nd Cavalry 16-19, 23, 40, 43, 72, 76, 78, 83, 89, 91, 104, 108-1090, 115, 120, 124, 127, 134, 136, 153, 163-164, 169, 185, 194, 200-201, 203-205, 207, 209-210, 212, 214, 218, 224, 236, 240, 257; 3rd Cavalry 23; 4th Cavalry 16, 23, 25, 34-35, 44-45, 69, 73, 78, 81-83, 92-95, 99, 126, 148-149, 165, 174, 180, 185, 187, 189-190, 222, 231-232, 235-236, 238, 240, 242, 245, 256

Middleton, Tennessee expedition 20–21
Miller, Col. Abram 188, 238–**239**, 244–245, 251–254, 257
Millikin, Col. Minor 27, 33, 36
Minty, Col. Robert H.G. 6–7, 12, 15–16, 22–**24**, 25–26, 31, 34–36, 38, 43–45, 47, 49, 55, 58, 61, 73, 88, 97–98, 107, 112, 114, 119, 129, 133, 134–137, 139–140, 143–144, 148, 154, 159–160, 165, 167, 178, 201, 239–240, 262–266; battle at Reed's Bridge 180–183, 185, 187–196; conflicts with Crittenden 104–105, 125–127; court martial charges 254–255; covers the retreat 226, 231–233, 235–237; fights at Sparta 75, 77, 79, 91–95; joined by Burnside's cavalry 116–117; moves to Reed's Bridge 176–176; repulses Scott at Red House 221–222, 224; at Smith's Crossroads 100–102, 104–105; warns of enemy troops 169–176; Wheeler's Raid 242, 245–247, 249, 251, 254–255, 258
Missionary Ridge 138, 165, 169, 175, 182, 199, 220, 224–225, 231–234, 259–260
Mississippi troops: 1st Cavalry 56; 2nd Cavalry Battalion 58; Darden's Artillery 47
Mitchell, Col. John G. 193, 269
Mitchell, Brig. Gen. Robert B. 6–7, 16–**17**, 18, 20, 22, 31, 41, 45–49, 67–69, 71, 74, 79, 82–84, 136, 140, 146, 154, 156, 161, 176–177, 179–180, 193–194, 205–206, 239, 241, 243, 245, 247, 250–251, 254–255, 257–258, 261, 264–265; assumes command 170–172, 174; communications with Watkins 226–231; covers the retreat 225, 230–235; decisions at Crawfish Springs 210–226; evacuates Crawfish Springs 213–214; moves to Crawfish Springs 9, 201, 203
Mix, Maj. Frank W. 16, 25, 36, 45
morale 29, 55, 63, 73, 117, 258, 263
Morgan, Brig. Gen. John H. 9, 19, 21, 25, 28, 33–34, 37, **40**–41, 48, 51, 54, 75, 79, 84, 106, 186
Morgan, Brig. Gen. John T. **59**, 139, 204
Morrison, Col. James J. 54
Morton, Capt. J.W., Jr. 52, 232
Mosman, Chesley 220
mounted infantry 6, 11–13, 31, 37, 56, 156, 171, 183, 188, 192, 196–203, 209, 214–215, 218, 223, 238, 244–246, 250,252, 257–258, 264
Mounted Riflemen 56
mounts *see* horses
Murray, Lt. Col. Douglas A. 27–28

Nashville and Chattanooga Railroad 64, 66
National Rifles 19
Naughton's Irish Dragoons 24
Negley, Maj. Gen. James 35, 135, 138–139, 142, 144, 149, 151, 156, 160, 166, 198, 201, 233, 267
New York Times 129
Newell, Lt. Nathaniel M. 16, 23, 26, 83, 152, 225, 240
Nicholas, Judge Samuel Smith 27
Nicholas, Col. Thomas P. 16, 27, 83, 146, 208, 240
Nixon, Lt. Col. James O. 54
North Carolina troops: 6th Cavalry 54; 64th Infantry 21
Nourse, Benjamin 120, 147, 207

oath of allegiance 72, 74–75
Ohio troops, artillery: 1st Artillery 16, 24, 26, 83, 199, 240; 2nd Infantry 179; 1st Cavalry 11, 16, 29, 33, 35, 40, 68, 78, 83, 94, 111, 128, 146–147, 205, 207–208, 210, 226, 236, 240–241, 245–247; 3rd Cavalry 16, 27, 35–36, 48, 69, 78, 83, 89, 109, 111, 128, 146, 205, 209, 236, 240, 251, 258; 4th Cavalry 16, 26, 28, 35, 40, 78, 83, 111, 146, 205, 207–208, 211, 226, 234, 236, 240–241, 243, 245; 10th Cavalry 16, 28, 67, 83, 113, 118, 240; 18th 44; 59th Infantry 192; 121st Infantry 235
"Old Wristbreaker" saber 10
Osage Rifles 24
Owen's Ford 195, 203, 205, 228

Palmer, Maj. Gen. John 43, 148–149, 152, 160, 175, 193, 195
Palmer, Col. William 152, 267
Paramore, Col. James 27
Patrick, Lt. Col. Matthewson T. 16, 24, 240, 247
Patten, Maj. Thomas J. 240–241
Patterson, Col. Josiah 60
Pea Ridge, Battle of 20
Peavine Valley 171, 173, 181–182, 185, 188–189
Peeler's Mill 171, 174, 182, 186
Pegram, Brig. Gen. John 6, 51–**53**, 54–55, 84, 95, 100, 105, 135, 139, 149, 152, 160, 162, 170–171, 181, 183, 192, 224, 232
Pemberton, Gen. John C. 39
Pennsylvania troops: 7th Cavalry 16, 25, 35, 43–45, 48, 73, 81, 83, 92–94, 172–173, 175, 179, 181, 185, 187, 189–190, 232, 235–236, 240; 9th Cavalry 16, 19, 40, 43, 83, 91, 153, 163–164, 173, 198–199, 201, 212, 214, 217, 220, 236, 240, 244, 257; 15th Cavalry 6, 35, 84, 152, 158, 162, 175, 224, 265
Perryville, Battle of 17–20, 24–27, 32–33, 56–57, 63, 180
Phelps, Dr. Alonzo 213, 219
Pickens, Col. W.C. 240
Pigeon Mountain 144, 151, 157, 161, 167, 174–175, 180, 183
Pinson, Col. R.A. 56
Platter, Col. John A. 16, 21, 83, 134
Polk, Lt. Gen. Leonidas 35, 41, 43, 49, 63, 99, 130–131, 135, 149, 154, 160, 162, 174, 183, 232, 259, 270; plans an offensive 75–**76**; September 12–13 attack orders 160; warns army headquarters 113
Pomeroy, Lt. Col. Henry 83
pontoon bridge 67, 95, 97–98, 103, 105, **108**–109, 113, 115, 126
Pope, Maj. Gen. John 170
Post, Col. P. Sidney 171, 194, 212, 220, 234, 264, 268
Potter, Henry Albert 73, 190, 238, 245, 256
Powell, David 6, 131, 158, 198, 261
Presdee, Maj. Joseph B. 83, 240
Preston, Brig. Gen. William C. 57, 63, 162
Price, Maj. Gen. Sterling 52
Prickitt, Sgt. Daniel 109, 111
Pugh, Maj. John 28

"raiding strategy" 34, 61
Randolph, Sgt. Tucker St. Joseph 53
"Rape of Athens" 22, 68
Rape's Gap 180, 196, 198
Ray, Col. Daniel M. 84, 89, 113, 127, 153, 182, 196, 199, 201, 212, 220, 227, 234
Red House skirmish 221–222
Reed, James 185, 191
Reed's Bridge 5–6, 142, 171, 173–175, 179–**189**, 190, 192, 194, 232, 246, 262
Reynolds, Maj. Gen. Joseph 84, 86, 98, 103, 109, 113, 156, 167, 233, 238, 267
Rich Mountain, Battle of 38, 53, 239
Richmond, Lt. W.B. 49
Richmond (Kentucky), Battle of 18
Ringgold 62, 130–131, 144, 148–

149, 152, 162, 165, 169–173, 176, 180–183, 185–186, 188
"Ripon Rifles" 22
river boats 66, 82, 98, 103, 105, 117
Robbins, Capt. Richard 222, 231–233
Robie, Lt. Col. Oliver P. 16, 28, 83, 240
Robinson, Lt. Winslow 54
Roddey, Brig. Gen. Philip Dale 60, 63, 73, 86, 257
Rome (Wharton's cavalry brigade) 109–111
Rome expedition 135–137, 140–141, 153–154
Rome Tri-Weekly Courier 141
Rosecrans, Maj. Gen. William S. 5–9, 12, 14–**15**, 16, 20, 22–23, 25–26, 29, 31–39, 41, 43, 47–48, 51, 53, 61–67, 75–77, 79–80, 91–92, 100–106, 121, 129–135, 138–141, 143–144, 149, 151–152, 154, 165–167, 170–181, 183, 192–196, 200–203, 212, 215–218, 221–224, 230, 235, 237–238, 241, 243, 257–265, 265; anger at Stanley 136, 156–162; orders infantry to move across the Tennessee 109–119; orders Rome expedition 125–127; plans a feint to the north 94–95, 97–98; plans movement on Chattanooga 82–88
Rossville gap/road 130, 144, 165, 169–170, 175, 182, 188, 192, 195–196, 221, 231–232, 234–235
Rousseau, Maj. Gen. Lovell 35, 67, 232, 235
Rubenstein, Dr. David A. 203
Rucker, Col. E.W. 54
Russell, Col. A.A. 51, 59–60, 204
Russell, Eli 238, 257
Russell, Lt. Col. Roswell M. 83, 163–164, 199 214, 220, 240

"Sabre Brigade" 23
saddles 10, 37, 78, 109
Sand Mountain 111, 113–114, 116–120, 123–124, 127, 140, 262
Sanders, Col. William 106
Sanderson, Col. J.P. 65
Schaefer, James 259
Schofield, Maj. Gen. John 170
Scott, Col. John 33, 51, 53–**54**, 55–56, 79, 84, 105, 139, 149, 152, 162, 173, 176, 181, 183, 185, 188, 193, 221–222, 232
Scott, Capt. William 246
Scranton, Maj. Leonidas R. 108, **200**, 204–205, 207
Seddon, Sec. of War James 115, 154, 156

Seibert, Maj. James J. 83, 187, 240
Seidel, Lt. Col. Charles B. 16, 28, 83, 240
Sequatchie Valley 86–87, 95, 98, 105, 112, 242
Shaw, Maj. Joseph 52
Shaw, William (farm) 228
Shelbyville, Battle of 43–47, 49, 55, 58, 61
Shelly, Joseph 89
Sheridan, Maj. Gen. Phil 14, 18–19, 64, 66, 68, 72, 85, 87, 89, 108–109, 127, 162, 167, 203, 214, 216, 223, 268
Sherman, Maj. Gen. William T. 21, 238
Shiloh, Battle of 26–27, 50, 56–58, 60, 186
Siege of New Madrid and Island Number 10 14, 19, 75
Sigmund, Lt. Jacob 187
Simpson, Lt. John 190
Sinclair, Maj. William 68, 127, 162–**163**, 172, 205, 210, 228, 231, 254, 261
Sipes, Lt. Col. William B. 16, 25, 45
Sirwell, Col. William 201, 267
slaves/ex-slaves 22, 70–71, 230
Slocum, Maj. Gen. Henry 16, 238
Smith, Maj. Gen. A.J. 21
Smith, Col. Baxter 35, 49, 56
Smith, Col. Charles C. 16, 28, 240
Smith, Maj. Gen. E. Kirby 32, 35, 53–54
Smith, Brig. Gen. Green Clay 18
Smith, Gen. Persifor 51
Smith's Crossroads 94, 100–102, 114, 125, 132, 135, 144
Snodgrass Hill 215, 221, 223, 231
Sowle, C.H. 229
Sparta skirmishes 79–82, 87, 91–94
Spears, Brig. Gen. James 118, 233–235
Spencer repeating carbine 10, 12, 81, 92, 193, 197, 209
Stanley, Maj. Gen. David S. 6–**14**,15–17, 22–29, 31, 34–41, 43–45, 47–48, 61, 64, 75, 82–83, 85–86, 91–92, 98, 103–104, 107–108, 112, 114, 116, 119–121, 123–125, 127, 138, 140–1, 147–150, 152, 154, 177–179, 187, 192, 201, 205, 210, 222, 228, 231, 255, 260–266; clashes with Rosecrans 136, 156–162; condition of the cavalry 68, 77–79; conversion to Roman Catholicism 15; dysentery 123, 158, 260; fails to implement raid 134–137; gets authority for operations 142–144; Huntsville Expedition illness 66–73;

leaves due to illness 169–170, 172; plans Rome Raid 129–130; relieved of command 261; requests delay of raid 133
Stanley, Col. Timothy 199, 267
Stanton, Sec. of War Edwin 32, 37, 54, 65, 83, 107, 175
Starnes, Col. James 92, 139
Starr, Stephen 45, 48
Staunton Spectator 71
Steedman, Brig. Gen. James 182–183, 188, 192, 233, 269
Stevens' Gap 119, 121, 135, 139, 143, 167, 170, 194, 196–197, 201, 217, 228
Stewart, Maj. Gen. A.P. 100
Stewart, Lt. Col. Robert R. 16, 23
Stokes, Capt. James H. 16, 28–29, 40, 83, 240, 251–252
Stokes, Col. William B. 16, 25, 72, 83, 90
Stoneman, Maj. Gen. George 78, 81
Stones River, Battle of 9–11, 15, 20–21, 24, 25–29, 34, 36–38, 40, 53, 55, 57–61, 65, 73, 187, 200, 216
Strahl, Brig. Gen. Otho F. 160, 270
Streight, Col. Abel 31, 50, 60
Stuart, Gen. J.E.B. 15, 57–58
Sugar Creek skirmish 255–257
Summers, Sgt. Edwards 235
Summerville 116, 123, 128, 130, 137–138, 143–144, 146, 148, 150, 152–153, 160–161, 164, 262
Tennessee River 49, 51, 60, 63–64, 66, 69, 72–73, 75, 77, 79, 82, 84–89, 91, 93, 95, 97–**99**, 100–101, 103–105, 107–111, 113–118, 125–126, 135, 139–140, 165, 169, 180, 210, 235, 238–239, 241–242, 244–245, 255–258, 262, 264
Tennessee troops - (**CSA**) 1st/6th Cavalry 52; 2nd Cavalry 54; 3rd Cavalry 256; 4th Cavalry 52, 56, 92, 204, 209–210, 221; 5th Cavalry 54, 56; 8th Cavalry 52, 79–81, 92–93; 9th Cavalry 52, 256; 10th Cavalry 52; 11th Cavalry 52; 12th Cavalry Battalion 54; 16th Cavalry Battalion 54; 17th Infantry 185–186, 188; 18th Cavalry Battalion; 23rd Infantry 191; 25th Infantry 52; 26th Infantry 47; Freeman's Artillery 26, 50; Huggins' Artillery 52; Huwald's Artillery 54; Morton's Artillery 52, 232; O.P. Hamilton's Cavalry Battalion 52; R.D. Allison's Cavalry Squadron 52; Rucker's Cavalry Regiment 54; Shaw's Cavalry

Battalion 52; White's Artillery 52, 203, 209; (**Union**) 1st Cavalry 16, 19–20, 40, 68–69, 71, 83, 88–89, 104, 120, 128, 153, 157, 159, 163–164, 174, 196, 200, 214, 220, 233, 236, 240; 1st Mounted Infantry 176; 2nd Cavalry 16, 21, 35–36, 66, 68, 72, 78, 83, 100, 103, 113, 124, 197, 201, 212–213, 217, 220, **225**, 236–237, 240; 3rd Cavalry 78, 113, 240; 4th 35, 78; 3rd Infantry 19, 118; 4th Infantry 16; 5th Cavalry 16, 25, 35, 44, 67, 72, 78, 83, 85, 88–89, 91, 103, 113, 118, 240, 247; 6th Infantry, 16; 9th Cavalry 20
Terry, Col. B.F. 57
Texas troops: 8th Cavalry 11, 57–58, 105, 111, 148, 197, 203–204, 208, 240, 252–253; 11th Cavalry 58, 204, 209, 229
Thatcher, Capt. Marshall 18, 115, 120, 134, 218
Thomas, Maj. Gen. George 35, 41, 43, 48, 66–68, 77, 84, 86–**87**, 98–99, 105, 109, 112–113, 115–116, 119–121, 123, 130–132, 135, 142–144, 149–154, 156–162, 165–167, 169–170, 172, 178, 193, 195, 198, 221, 224–226, 231–232, 237, 258, 261, 263, 267
Thomas, Julius 20, 68, 104, 174, 220
Thompson, Capt. Heber 185–187
Thompson, Lt. Col. R. 58
Thruston, Col. Gates 212–**216**, 217–219, 264
Trecy, Father Jeremiah 15, 192
Trenton, expedition 111–112
Trigg, Col. Robert 214, 271
Trion Factory 153–154, 157, 160–162, 164
Tullahoma Campaign 5, 9, 12, 15, 17, 19, 24, 26–27, 29, 32, 36–37, 40–41, 43, 45–49, 51–52, 55, 58, 60–68, 73–74, 77–78, 82, 105–106, 110, 178, 187, 238–239
Turchin, Brig. Gen. John B. 16, 22–**23**, 29, 31, 41, 43, 47–48, 68–69, 71, 73–74, 103; court martial 22

United States Military Academy 13, 24, 53, 56, 74, 186
United States troops: 1st Cavalry 25–26; 1st Dragoons 53–54, 56; 2nd Cavalry 19, 24, 27; 4th Cavalry 22, 25–26, 36, 44–45, 81, 92–94, 97, 159–160, 165, 172–173, 180, 185–188, 190–191, 232, 235, 240, 242, 245, 249; 5th Cavalry 19; 7th Infantry 25

Vale, Capt. Joseph 43, 93–94, 97, 177, 189
Valley Head 119, 144, 169, 172, 174, 180, 226
Van Antwerp, William 93, 97, 126, 242
Van Cleve, Maj. Gen. Horatio 79–80, 87, 97–98, 100–102, 105, 126, 140, 148, 169, 177, 193
Van Dorn, Maj. Gen. Earl 9, 26, 34, 37, 40, 51, 55
Van Duzer, J.C. 166, 175
Vimont, Lt. Col. Thomas T. 83
Viniard's field 193, 198
Virginia troops: 20th Infantry 53

Wade, Lt. Col. William B. 56
Wagner, Brig. Gen. George 112, 126, 139, 160, 176, 194
wagon trains (supply) 36, 94, 98, 103, 119–120, 125, 157, 200, 213–214, 219–220, 226, 229–230, 233, 242–244, 250, 257–259
Walker, Maj. Gen. William H.T. 100, 125, 129–131, 135, 142, 149–150, 160, 174, 182–183, 188, 232
Walter, Edward 255
Warner, Capt. Philip H. 83
Washington Artillery of Pottsville 185
Washington City Evening Star 71
Watkins, Col. Louis D. 6, 16, 19, **67**, 77, 82–85, 89, 107, 112, 118, 134, 150, 152–53, 172, 174, 180, 196, 199, 201, 226, 236–237, 240, 264; at Cooper's Gap 228–231
Watson, Asst. Sec. of War Peter H. 129
Watts, Lt. Col. Elijah 144; at Alpine 146–147; at Glass Mill 163
weapons: carbines **10**, 12–13, 15, 35, 78, 208 (*see also* Colt revolving rifles; Spencer rifles); revolvers **10**, 13, 78; sabers **10**–11, 13, 15, 23, 45, 92, 123, 212, 232, 244, 251, 256
Weatherred, John 256
Wharton, Maj. James 230
Wharton, Brig. Gen. John 6, 26, 33, 36, 41, 49–51, 56–**57**, 58, 64, 105, 110, 116, 120, 124, 130–131, 134, 136–138, 146–148, 150, 152–154, 157, 162–164, 204, 210, 216, 221, 224, 228, 232, 241–243, 250–253
Wheeler, Col. John T. 51–52
Wheeler, Maj. Gen. Joseph 6–7, 9, 11, 33–34, 36–37, 40–**41**, 43–45, 47–51, 55–61, 63–64, 66, 73, 75, 79, 84, 86, 88, 91, 105, 107, 114–117, 120, 123, 125–127, 134–137, 139–144, 148, 152–154, 157, 160, 162–163, 174, 176–177, 180, 183, 187, 195–200, 217–218, 220–221, 223–224, 228–230, 238; battle at Glass Mill 201, 203–205, 207–209, 211–214; condition of the cavalry 109–111; "point" 55; rejects Bragg's orders 130–131; Tennessee Raid 240–243, 245–247, 250–260, 263–264
Whitaker, Brig. Gen. Walter 72, 188, 194
White, Capt. B.F., Jr. 58
Widow Glenn's House 198–199, 201
Wilder, John 6–7, 12–13, 37, 86–87, 92, 103, 112, 119, 125–126, 134, 140, 149, 152, 156, 159–160, 165–167, 172–173, 175–176, 180, 198–201, 203, 212, 214–218, 223, 235, 238–239, 244, 252, 258, 262, 264; advances to the north Chattanooga 95, 97–100; battle at Alexander's Bridge 182–183, 185, 187–**188**, 191–195
Williams, Col. Edward C. 19
Williamson, Lt. Peter 134, 136
Wills Valley 115–117, 119–120, 124–125, 127–129, 131, 161, 174
Wilson, Lucien 245
Wilson's Creek, Battle of 179
Wilson's Creek Campaign 16–17
Winston, Col. William O. 119, 123
Wisconsin troops: 1st Cavalry 16, 21–22, 40, 69, 71, 73, 83, 115, 134, 136, 196, 200–201, 212–213, 217, 225, 233–234, 236, 239–240, 243–244, 257; 4th Infantry 22
Wiswell, James 97
Wofford, Col. Frank 117
Womack, Pvt J.K. 221
Wood, George 72
Wood, Brig. Gen. Thomas 99, 116, 132–133, 135, 148, 165, 175, 185, 192
Woodward, Lt. Col. Thomas G. 52
Wyeth, John Allan 47, 137, 209, 214, 217
Wynkoop, Col. George 25
Wynkoop, Maj. John E. 25
Wynkoop, Lt. Nicholas 25

Yenner, August 235

Zahm, Col. Lewis 27, 33–36

www.ingramcontent.com/pod-product-compliance
Lightning Source LLC
Chambersburg PA
CBHW081539300426
44116CB00015B/2687